D1073717

The United Nations and Cambodia, 1991-1995

The United Nations
Blue Books Series, Volume II

The United Nations and
Cambodia

1991-1995

**With an introduction by
Boutros Boutros-Ghali,
Secretary-General of the United Nations**

Department of Public Information
United Nations, New York

Published by the United Nations
Department of Public Information
New York, NY 10017

Editor's note:

Each of the United Nations documents and other materials reproduced in this book ("Texts of documents", pages 87-346) has been assigned a number (e.g. Document 1, Document 2, etc.). This number is used throughout the Introduction and other parts of this book to guide readers to the document texts. For other documents mentioned in the book but not reproduced, the United Nations document symbol (e.g. S/1994/645, A/47/285-S/24183) is provided. With this symbol, such documents can be consulted at the Dag Hammarskjöld Library at United Nations Headquarters in New York, at other libraries in the United Nations system or at libraries around the world which have been designated as depository libraries for United Nations documents.

Copyright © 1995 United Nations

The United Nations and Cambodia, 1991-1995
The United Nations Blue Books Series
Volume II
ISBN 92-1-100548-5

United Nations Publication
Sales No. E. 95.I.9 (Soft)

Printed by the United Nations Reproduction Section
New York, NY

X
977.2
K3
54
995

Contents

Section One:
Introduction by Boutros Boutros-Ghali,
Secretary-General of the United Nations

Section Two:
Chronology and Documents

Section One
Introduction

I   Overview

1   The United Nations' involvement in seeking a resolution to Cambodia's long-standing political conflict represents an unparalleled international diplomatic effort. Massive in size, comprehensive in scope and precise in its mandate, the United Nations Transitional Authority in Cambodia (UNTAC) set a new standard for peace-keeping operations undertaken by the international community. As with any unprecedented endeavour, UNTAC, and the Paris Peace Agreements which articulated its mandate, contained certain risks and experiments within its framework and implementation. It is for this reason that the outcomes of such an operation deserve careful scrutiny.

2   The international community negotiated a vision of peace for Cambodia in Paris that hinged on the conflicting parties' willingness to submit to the world Organization and allow the Cambodian people to choose their fate democratically on a level playing-field. When the plan was put into action, complications arose immediately as the warring factions relinquished their authority only grudgingly and in some cases not at all, and as unforeseen diplomatic and logistical hurdles presented almost daily challenges to UNTAC's operational mandate. The degree of success achieved by the UNTAC mission in the end attests to the importance of a unified decision-making apparatus in New York, competent and dedicated personnel in the field and a local context in which there is room for conciliation and momentum for change. UNTAC's outcomes also suggest the need for a realistic understanding of the conditions—social, political and infrastructural—on the ground *before* a plan is made operational; better institutional procedures for equipping and maintaining large overseas operations; and a command structure in the field that can coordinate diverse groups of professionals while remaining flexible enough to meet changing needs.

3   The narrative which follows elaborates the situation leading up to the United Nations presence in Cambodia, and the events which defined the UNTAC period. In it a picture emerges of certain tensions inherent in the process of translating diplomatic decision-making into practical action. Part II provides background information on the Cambodian conflict, including the history of the United Nations diplomatic efforts there, which culminated in UNTAC. Part III traces the peace process from the signing of the Paris Agreements through the deployment of an intermediary United Nations force—the United Nations Advance Mission in Cambodia (UNAMIC)—to the actual formation of UNTAC. In part IV, some of the early and enduring challenges to the peace plan

are outlined, and the repatriation of Cambodian refugees is described. Part V continues the analysis of the significant obstacle to peace posed by the Khmer Rouge and describes the efforts undertaken by the Security Council to resolve this issue. The election process is the focus of parts VI and VII. The difficult and ultimately successful events surrounding this aspect of UNTAC's work are examined with an eye to explaining how the election succeeded despite those groups and conditions which threatened it. Part VIII chronicles the post-election period, including the formation of the new Cambodian Government, the withdrawal of UNTAC and the final six-month period of operation ending in May 1994. Part IX offers some concluding remarks concerning the United Nations' implementation of the Paris Agreements in Cambodia, and the important, positive changes it brought about in the country's social, political, and economic circumstances.

4   The collection of United Nations documents reproduced on pages 87-346 includes resolutions of the General Assembly and Security Council, reports of Secretaries-General to both bodies, communications from Member States, selected correspondence between myself and some of the parties involved, and other materials, and provides a comprehensive record of the Organization's efforts in Cambodia. These documents are referenced throughout the introduction and listed chronologically on pages 73-82, along with a brief description of their content. It is my hope that making such materials available together in one volume will facilitate public understanding of the work of the United Nations.

II   Background to UN involvement

5   The Paris Agreements served as a necessary guideline for the development and implementation of UNTAC's unprecedented peace-keeping operation. The process by which these Agreements were negotiated and signed is therefore of great significance to an understanding of UNTAC, and may offer valuable insights for the development of future UN peace-keeping operations.

Civil war, cold war and diplomacy

6   Before the implementation of the United Nations–brokered Paris Agreements, Cambodia was in a state of deep internal conflict and relative isolation from much of the world. Since its emergence from French colonialism in the 1950s, the country had suffered not only the effects of the spillover of the war in Viet Nam of the 1960s and 1970s, including massive bombardment by United States forces, but also devastating civil conflicts and the vastly destructive totalitarian regime of Pol Pot. That regime—known to the world as the "Khmer Rouge"—controlled Cambodia from 1975 to 1979, a period during which approximately 1 million Cambodians perished, leaving the remaining 7 million permanently scarred in ways not yet fully comprehended. (Estimates of both population and death tolls for this period vary.) The intervention of Vietnamese troops brought the Pol Pot regime to an end and inaugurated a period in which several hundred thousand Cambodians fled their country. An even greater number became internally displaced as the forces of the newly installed Government and those of an opposition coalition, which included Pol Pot's forces and was led by Prince Norodom Sihanouk, battled for control of the country, keeping Cambodia in a state of war for most of the 1980s.

7   The United Nations became involved in the Cambodian situation many years before the Paris Peace Agreements were signed on 23 October 1991. The Security Council first considered the issue in 1979, following Viet Nam's intervention in Cambodia in late 1978, but lack of unanimity among its five permanent members—China, France, the Union of Soviet Socialist Republics (USSR), the United Kingdom of Great Britain and Northern Ireland and the United States of America—prevented it from taking any action in response. In 1982, the three groups which opposed the Phnom Penh Government (the People's Republic of Kampuchea), including the United National Front for an Independent,

Neutral, Peaceful and Cooperative Cambodia (FUNCINPEC), the Khmer People's National Liberation Front (KPNLF) and the Party of Democratic Kampuchea (PDK, also known as the Khmer Rouge), formed a coalition party led by Prince Sihanouk. This party, known first as the Coalition Government of Democratic Kampuchea and later as the National Government of Cambodia, occupied the seat reserved for Cambodia at the United Nations (under the designation Democratic Kampuchea) from 1982 until the signing of the Paris Agreements.

8   International support for one or the other opposing camps reflected the ideological divide of the cold-war era. The Phnom Penh Government was backed by the USSR and fielded approximately 50,000 troops. The coalition led by Prince Sihanouk received support from, among others, the United States, China and the Association of South-East Asian Nations (ASEAN)—Brunei Darussalam, Indonesia, Malaysia, the Philippines, Singapore and Thailand. The coalition's combined armed forces, estimated to number between 50,000 and 60,000, operated from Thailand and north-western Cambodia and reportedly controlled between 10 and 20 per cent of Cambodia's territory.

9   Long and difficult diplomatic efforts were undertaken to find a solution to the Cambodian conflict. In July 1981, the United Nations General Assembly convened the International Conference on Kampuchea in New York, which was attended by 93 Member States. Viet Nam declined to take part (as did several other States from the Eastern bloc), but nevertheless indicated its readiness to accept the good offices of the Secretary-General. Accordingly, the Secretary-General's Special Representative for Humanitarian Affairs in South-East Asia, Mr. Rafeeuddin Ahmed (Pakistan), visited the region many times in subsequent years, and in early 1985 my predecessor, Secretary-General Javier Pérez de Cuéllar, did so himself. In his report to the General Assembly that year, he outlined for the first time the main elements of a comprehensive political settlement. The General Assembly, for its part, adopted a series of resolutions over the years reiterating its call for a peaceful settlement.

10   In December 1987, Prince Sihanouk and Mr. Hun Sen, who had become Prime Minister of the Phnom Penh Government in 1985, met for the first time in France. They held a second round of talks one month later. Following the initiation of this dialogue, the Secretary-General put forward proposals that elaborated the objectives he had identified in 1985 and suggested that the various elements be integrated into a comprehensive scheme leading to an independent, neutral and non-aligned Cambodian State. The process of dialogue and negotiation began to gather momentum when the four Cambodian factions had their first face-to-face talks in July 1988 at the Jakarta Informal Meeting. Indonesia hosted a second Informal Meeting in February 1989.

The Paris Conference

11   At the initiative of the French Government, the Paris Conference on Cambodia was convened from 30 July to 30 August 1989. Nineteen countries and the four Cambodian factions attended, with France and Indonesia serving as Co-Chairmen and the Secretary-General of the United Nations participating in his official capacity. The Conference succeeded in mapping out a broad strategy for peace but was suspended without achieving a comprehensive settlement. The two primary stumbling-blocks were the formula for power-sharing among the four factions during a transitional period in which elections would be held and a new constitution drafted, and the future participation of the Party of Democratic Kampuchea. Some Member States were against including the PDK in an interim government, given the group's responsibility for extreme and grave human rights violations in the late 1970s. As a result of this stalemate, no international verification mechanism was in place when Viet Nam announced its troop withdrawal from Cambodia between 21 and 26 September 1989.

12   Among the countries attending the 1989 Paris Conference on Cambodia were the five permanent members of the Security Council ("the Five"). Their presence marked a shared interest in achieving a negotiated solution, following the post-cold-war *rapprochement* between the United States and the Soviet Union and an improvement in relations among China, ASEAN and Viet Nam. In January 1990, the Five began a series of unprecedented high-level consultations in New York and Paris to discuss the situation.[1] The basis for their discussions was a proposal put forward by Australia in October 1989, which called for enhancing the role of the United Nations in the settlement process by placing the civil administration in Cambodia under the supervision and control of the United Nations until the establishment of an elected government.

1/Document 1
See page 87

13   In the course of their deliberations, the Five also took account of the discussions among the four Cambodian factions held at Jakarta in February 1990 and at Tokyo in June 1990. They also maintained regular contact with the Secretary-General's office and supported my predecessor's decision to establish a task force to facilitate contingency planning for an eventual United Nations operation in Cambodia. United Nations fact-finding missions were sent to Cambodia to study, among other things, the communications and transportation infrastructure, water supply, sanitation, housing, modalities for the repatriation and reintegration of refugees and displaced persons and the country's existing administrative structures.

14   At their sixth meeting, on 27 and 28 August 1990, the Five announced a breakthrough: agreement on a settlement framework which

2/Document 2
See page 88

3/Document 3
See page 93

4/Document 4
See page 95

included a principal role for the United Nations in supervising and controlling the activities of Cambodia's existing administrative structures during a transitional period.[2] The four Cambodian factions accepted the framework in September 1990 and agreed to form the Supreme National Council (SNC) as the unique legitimate body in which, throughout the transitional period, the independence, national sovereignty and unity of Cambodia would be enshrined.[3] On 20 September 1990, in resolution 668 (1990), the Security Council endorsed the framework.[4] The Five then called upon France and Indonesia, the co-Chairmen of the Paris Conference, to negotiate the framework into a full-fledged peace agreement.

The peace agreements

5/Document 5
See page 95;
Document 6
See page 96

6/Document 8
See page 113

15   By 26 November 1990, subsequent to consultations with the Secretary-General and his Special Representative, the Co-Chairmen and the Five were able to agree on a text for the peace agreement.[5] Following the SNC's concurrence on most of the fundamental points, the draft agreements were presented to Thailand and Viet Nam in February 1991. On 22 April 1991, the Secretary-General issued a joint appeal with France and Indonesia for a temporary cessation of hostilities between the Cambodian factions as a gesture of good faith.[6] The factions said they would voluntarily comply with this initiative, and the first cease-fire in 12 years went into effect in Cambodia. Compromise solutions to the main outstanding issues—the degree of demobilization by the armed forces and the nature of the electoral system—were reached in a series of meetings over the next several months.[7] A result of more than a decade of diplomacy, the accords were signed at the second session of the Paris Conference on Cambodia, from 21 to 23 October 1991. The United Nations signed the accords as a witness, and there were 19 signatory States: Cambodia (represented by the Supreme National Council), the five permanent members of the United Nations Security Council, the six members of ASEAN, Cambodia's other neighbours (the Lao People's Democratic Republic and Viet Nam), Australia, Canada, India, Japan and the Socialist Federal Republic of Yugoslavia (in its capacity as Chairman of the Movement of Non-Aligned Countries; at the time of the first session of the Paris Conference on Cambodia, Zimbabwe had been Chairman of the Movement).

7/Document 7
See page 112;
Document 9
See page 113;
Document 10
See page 115;
Document 11
See page 116;
Document 12
See page 117;
Document 14
See page 120;
Document 15
See page 122;
Document 16
See page 124

16   The peace plan consisted of a Final Act and three instruments: the Agreement on a Comprehensive Political Settlement of the Cambodia Conflict; the Agreement concerning the Sovereignty, Independence, Territorial Integrity and Inviolability, Neutrality and National Unity of Cambodia; and the Declaration on the Rehabilitation and Reconstruc-

tion of Cambodia.[8] To ensure implementation of the accords, "all powers necessary" were to be delegated by the SNC to the United Nations for a transitional period lasting from the signing of the Agreements through the creation of a new government following the elections. The Agreements invited the Security Council to establish the United Nations Transitional Authority in Cambodia and to provide it with a far-reaching mandate.

8/Document 18
See page 131;
Document 20
See page 149

17   Under the Agreements, the United Nations was to organize and conduct free and fair elections; coordinate the repatriation of Cambodian refugees and displaced persons; coordinate a major programme of economic and financial support for rehabilitation and reconstruction; supervise or control the existing administrative structures in Cambodia; supervise, monitor and verify the withdrawal of foreign forces, the cease-fire, the cessation of outside military assistance to all Cambodian factions and the demobilization of at least 70 per cent of the military forces of the factions; coordinate, with the International Committee of the Red Cross, the release of all prisoners of war and civilian internees; and foster an environment of peace and stability in which all Cambodians could enjoy the rights and freedoms embodied in the Universal Declaration of Human Rights and other relevant international human rights instruments.

18   On 31 October 1991, in resolution 718 (1991), the Security Council expressed its full support for the Paris peace plan, called on all Cambodian factions to comply with the cease-fire and called on the SNC and all Cambodians to cooperate fully with the United Nations.[9] The General Assembly followed suit with its support on 20 November 1991, in resolution 46/18, calling on all parties concerned to respect the rights and freedoms of the Cambodian people.[10]

9/Document 21
See page 149

10/Document 23
See page 150

III   From UNAMIC to UNTAC

19   The four Cambodian factions—FUNCINPEC, the KPNLF, the PDK and the Government of the State of Cambodia (SOC)—showed great political will in signing the Paris Peace Agreements, but implementation of the peace plan would prove to be an even greater challenge. The international community's support of the peace process in Cambodia was strong, and my predecessor pledged that the United Nations would continue to assist all parties to the Cambodian conflict in resolving the situation in a peaceful and democratic manner. This meant the rapid establishment of an advance mission, followed by careful development of the transitional authority itself.

Deployment of UNAMIC

11/Document 15
See page 122

20   On 26 August 1991, during the final negotiations leading to the Paris Agreements, Prince Norodom Sihanouk, President of the Supreme National Council (SNC), requested that the United Nations send observers to Cambodia as quickly as possible in order to sustain the impetus of the peace process and monitor the fragile cease-fire.[11] The Secretary-General therefore recommended that the Security Council establish the United Nations Advance Mission in Cambodia (UNAMIC). The Security Council agreed on 16 October 1991, resolving in resolution 717 (1991) that UNAMIC should be sent to Cambodia immediately after the signing of the Paris Agreements.[12]

12/Document 13
See page 119;
Document 17
See page 125;
Document 18
See page 131

21   The chief goal of UNAMIC was to assist in maintaining the cease-fire. The plan called for a team of 50 military liaison officers who would, in a good-offices role, aim to facilitate communications between the military headquarters of the four Cambodian factions by, for example, passing messages between the factions and arranging meetings between them. UNAMIC was also to serve as liaison with the SNC on preparations for the deployment of UNTAC and on other matters related to the role of the United Nations in the implementation of the Paris Agreements. In addition, a 20-person mine-awareness unit would train civilians in how to avoid land-mines and booby-traps. The entire Advance Mission would be absorbed into UNTAC as soon as the latter was deployed.

13/Document 22
See page 150

22   The first UNAMIC personnel arrived in Cambodia on 9 November 1991.[13] UNAMIC's mandate was expanded soon thereafter amid a growing awareness in the international community that

Cambodia

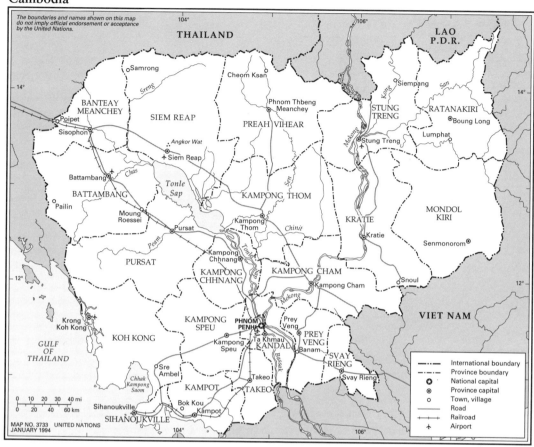

Among the initial challenges facing both UNAMIC and UNTAC was the debilitated state of Cambodia's physical infrastructure. Operations were also impeded by the presence of approximately 4 million land mines scattered throughout the countryside.

mine clearance was an urgent priority. On 30 December 1991, the Secretary-General recommended that UNAMIC train Cambodians in mine clearance and initiate a mine-clearing programme using a specialized international military unit.[14] The new work would be carried out in conjunction with the Office of the United Nations High Commissioner for Refugees (UNHCR) and a mine-clearance commission established by the SNC and would focus on repatriation routes, reception centres and resettlement areas. UNAMIC would also now undertake road and bridge repair to prepare for the expected increase in traffic volume owing to the anticipated influx of approximately 8,000 United Nations vehicles. On 8 January 1992, by its resolution 728 (1992), the Security Council approved the plan, which called for some 1,100 additional personnel, including a 700-person field engineering battalion.[15]

14/Document 25
See page 152

15/Document 26
See page 155

Structuring UNTAC

16/Document 30
See page 158

23 On 19 February 1992, I submitted my proposed operational plan for UNTAC to the Security Council.[16] At an estimated cost of US$1.9 billion—the repatriation and rehabilitation efforts were to be funded separately through voluntary contributions—I recommended that some 15,900 troops, 3,600 civilian police monitors and 1,000 international staff be sent to Cambodia. Additionally, 1,400 international election monitors and 56,000 Cambodians recruited locally to work with polling teams would join UNTAC at election time, which was scheduled to occur no later than May 1993. Just prior to submitting my plan, the General Assembly approved, on 14 February, my request for an early appropriation of $200 million for the first phase of UNTAC's deployment, specifically to enable such vital preliminary actions as equipment procurement and delivery, establishment of advance parties and commissioning and installation of equipment and stores.[17] During this period, Prince Sihanouk had reiterated his wish to see the deployment of UNTAC accelerated as much as possible to prevent any erosion of the peace process.[18]

17/Document 27
See page 155

18/Document 28
See page 156;

Document 29
See page 157

24 Seven distinct components of UNTAC were outlined in the plan: human rights, electoral, military, civil administration, police, repatriation and rehabilitation. A short description of the intended purpose of each component is given below.

25 **Human rights.** The Paris Agreements made UNTAC responsible for fostering an environment in which respect for basic human rights was ensured. According to the UNTAC framework, the activities of the human rights component would concentrate on several broad areas: encouraging the SNC to ratify the relevant international human rights instruments, conducting an extensive campaign of human rights education, investigating allegations of human rights abuses and exercising general oversight of human rights aspects of every component of UNTAC.

26 **Electoral.** Free and fair general elections for a national constituent assembly were the focal point of the Paris Peace Agreements. The electoral component of UNTAC was to be responsible for designing and implementing a system for every phase of the electoral process, including a legal framework consisting of an electoral law and code of conduct; civic education on the purposes and importance of the elections and, particularly, the secrecy and integrity of the ballot; training for electoral staff; registration of voters and political parties; and the polling itself.

27 **Military.** The objectives of the military component during the transitional period were to stabilize the security situation and to build confidence among the four Cambodian factions. The military contingents included observers, infantry, engineers, an air support group, a signals unit, a medical unit, military police, a logistics battalion and a naval element. This component of UNTAC, headed by a Force Commander, was charged with several main functions: verifying the withdrawal and non-return of all categories of foreign forces, their arms, ammunition and equipment; supervising the cease-fire and the cantonment, disarming and demobilization of the forces of the four Cambodian factions; weapons control, including monitoring the cessation of outside military assistance and locating and confiscating caches of weapons and military supplies throughout Cambodia; and assisting with mine clearance. According to information provided by the four Cambodian factions, their regular military forces numbered more than 200,000 soldiers, deployed at some 650 locations. In addition, militias totalling some 250,000 personnel operated throughout the country; these were armed with over 300,000 weapons of all types and some 80 million rounds of ammunition. UNTAC's military component was also to be responsible for investigating alleged non-compliance with military provisions of the Agreements, assisting with the release of prisoners of war and helping with the repatriation effort by, among other things, escorting refugee convoys or providing security at reception centres.

28   **Civil administration.** The civil administration functions envisioned in the Paris Agreements were to give the United Nations an unprecedented level of involvement in a country's official activities during a peace-keeping operation. In order to ensure a neutral political environment conducive to free and fair elections, the United Nations was to exercise direct supervision or control over those of the SOC's administrative agencies, bodies and offices which could directly influence the outcome of the elections, especially in the ministries dealing with foreign affairs, national defence, finance, public security and information. A lesser degree of scrutiny was to be extended to other administrative structures, such as those concerned with public health, education, agriculture, fishing, transport, energy, tourism and historic monuments. The Special Representative of the Secretary-General was to have the right of unrestricted access to all administrative operations and information, as well as the right to reassign or dismiss officials should the need arise.

29   **Police.** UNTAC's police component was to ensure that law and order among the civilian population were maintained effectively and impartially, and that human rights and fundamental freedoms were fully protected. Although responsibility for the management of Cambodia's police forces would continue to rest with the Cambodian factions, they were to operate under UNTAC supervision or control during the transitional period. The strength of the police component would give it an

estimated ratio of 1 per 15 local civil police, or one for every 3,000 Cambodians.

30   **Repatriation.** UNHCR was designated as the lead agency in fulfilling the functions of the repatriation component. The Paris Agreements provided that all Cambodian refugees and displaced persons would have the right to return to Cambodia and to live in safety, security and dignity, free from intimidation or coercion of any kind. Towards this end, an inter-agency effort was to be mounted involving UNHCR, the United Nations Development Programme (UNDP), the United Nations Children's Fund (UNICEF), the World Food Programme (WFP), the World Health Organization (WHO), the United Nations Educational, Scientific and Cultural Organization (UNESCO) and the International Labour Organization (ILO).

31   **Rehabilitation.** According to the Paris peace plan, the most urgent needs to be met by the rehabilitation component were: humanitarian needs, such as food security, health, housing, education and other essentials, particularly for women, children, handicapped persons and the disadvantaged; resettlement needs, including agricultural inputs, potable water and vocational training; and the restoration, maintenance and support of basic infrastructure, institutions, utilities and other services, such as major roadways, railways, ports, airports, telecommunications and banks.

32   An **information/education** division of UNTAC was also to be formed to help educate Cambodians about the Paris Agreements, United Nations peace-keeping, UNTAC and the public's own rights and responsibilities.

33   The proposed operational plan set out four essential conditions that would have to be met for UNTAC to discharge its responsibilities effectively and with complete impartiality: UNTAC would have to have the full support of the Security Council, the full cooperation of the four Cambodian factions and all other concerned parties, full freedom of movement and communications and the necessary financial resources provided by Member States in full and on time.

34   On 28 February 1992, in resolution 745 (1992), the Security Council approved the plan, authorizing the establishment of UNTAC for a period not to exceed 18 months.[19] The Council also welcomed the appointment, effective 9 January 1992, of Mr. Yasushi Akashi (Japan) as the Special Representative of the Secretary-General for Cambodia. In a letter to me, Prince Sihanouk expressed his gratitude for the creation of UNTAC and pledged his support, as well as that of the Cambodian people, to the mission.[20]

19/Document 31
See page 184

20/Document 32
See page 185

IV   Establishing UNTAC

35   The situation "on the ground" shaped the outcome of UNTAC as significantly as did the architecture of the Paris Agreements. UNTAC faced immense practical challenges from the very moment of its creation. The first was simply to establish a presence in Cambodia. By the time UNTAC was created, four months had elapsed since the signing of the Paris Agreements, during which time numerous cease-fire violations had taken place, including an attack on a UNAMIC helicopter. In addition, public demonstrations had been mounted against the return to Phnom Penh of PDK officials as well as against the Phnom Penh authorities, prompting an appeal for calm from the five permanent members of the Security Council.[21] And although the SNC had issued several pleas for the quickest possible deployment of UNTAC, the rainy season, which could be expected to slow the mision's deployment and operations, was due to begin in May. These obstacles, combined with intransigence on the part of the PDK and unforeseen problems in the repatriation of refugees, represent three of the largest hurdles UNTAC had to overcome. This section will review the establishment of UNTAC, with emphasis on those challenges and on the search for their resolution.

21/Document 24
See page 190

UNTAC *struggles to establish a presence*

36   My Special Representative and the UNTAC Force Commander, Lieutenant-General John M. Sanderson (Australia), arrived in Phnom Penh on 15 March 1992, and UNTAC began to establish itself politically and militarily. On 1 April 1992, the draft Electoral Law drawn up by UNTAC was presented to the SNC for review. The repatriation effort was started on 30 March 1992, and by the end of April 5,763 persons had returned to Cambodia. By that time, more than 3,600 UNTAC troops had been deployed, and progress had been made in gaining the cooperation of the Cambodian factions. The members of the SNC also decided, during my visit to Cambodia in April, that Cambodia should accede to two of the major legal instruments in the body of international human rights law, the International Covenant on Civil and Political Rights and the International Covenant on Economic, Social and Cultural Rights—an important sign of their willingness to overcome the serious mistakes of the past. I launched during my visit an international appeal to provide $593 million to meet the costs of rehabilitation and repatriation.

37 Despite such steady progress, unfortunate delays did occur. The necessary vehicles, prefabricated housing, office and communication equipment and other items were slow to arrive in Cambodia. Several factors were to blame, foremost among them the sheer size of the UNTAC operation. Also contributing to the hold-ups were the cumbersome procedures for procurement and budget authorization within the United Nations and the difficulty of recruiting highly specialized personnel to fulfil UNTAC's various civilian functions. This resulted in late deployment of some military and civilian personnel. In addition, the Security Council had decided, just one week prior to the creation of UNTAC, to establish the United Nations Protection Force (UNPROFOR) in response to the conflict in the former Yugoslavia. By agreeing to undertake two large and complicated peace-keeping operations at the same time, Member States had placed exceptional demands on the United Nations, and the Organization's ability to respond was stretched to the limit.

22/Document 33
See page 185

38 In my progress report on the Cambodia operation dated 1 May 1992, I stated that the delays could "have an adverse impact on UNTAC's ability to maintain its tight schedule".[22] I suggested that Member States might wish "to re-examine the manner in which existing financial and administrative rules and regulations of the Organization" were applied to operations as large and complex as UNTAC. (These and related issues—and, more generally, the need to improve the capacity of the United Nations in preventive diplomacy, peacemaking, peace-keeping, and post-conflict peace-building—have been the subject of considerable discussion within the international community. See, for example, "An Agenda for Peace" (A/47/277-S/24111), the annual "Report on the Work of the Organization" (A/47/1, A/48/1, A/49/1), and "Financing an Effective United Nations: A report of the Independent Advisory Group on United Nations Financing" (A/48/565).)

PDK non-compliance

39 The PDK's unwillingness to comply with the cease-fire and demobilization proved to be a second major challenge. Under the Paris Agreements, the four Cambodian factions had agreed to undertake a phased and balanced process of demobilizing at least 70 per cent of their military forces, a process to be completed prior to the end of the voter registration exercise. On 9 May 1992, the UNTAC Force Commander announced that phase I of the official cease-fire, in effect since the signing of the Paris Agreements, would be followed by phase II—the regroupment, cantonment, disarming and demobilization of forces—beginning

on 13 June. The Force Commander took this step after obtaining assurances from the four Cambodian factions that each would, among other things, grant freedom of movement to UNTAC personnel, vehicles and aircraft; mark minefields in the areas under its control; provide UNTAC with information on its troops, arms, ammunition and equipment; and adhere to the Paris Agreements.

40   The Party of Democratic Kampuchea, however, chose not to follow through on these commitments. The PDK refused to allow UNTAC troops to proceed with their deployment in the areas under the PDK's control, failed to provide information on the number of its soldiers and *matériel*, did not mark minefields and was responsible, UNTAC believed, for many cease-fire violations. In addition, on one occasion the armed forces of the PDK prevented senior UNTAC personnel, including my Special Representative and the Force Commander, from proceeding through PDK-controlled territory to the Thai border. A personal appeal from me to Mr. Khieu Samphan, President of the PDK and a member of the SNC, seeking the PDK's compliance with the Paris Agreements, went unheeded. UNTAC had been in existence only for a short time, yet the operation had already reached a critical stage. The PDK's lack of cooperation challenged the very foundations of the Paris accords and gravely compromised UNTAC's ability to adhere to its timetable.

41   Explaining their position, PDK representatives asserted that Vietnamese military personnel remained in Cambodia and that, until their withdrawal and non-return had been verified by UNTAC, the faction's security considerations required that it defer any moves to disarm. While firmly rejecting this view, UNTAC attempted to address the PDK's concerns. Under the Paris Agreements, any foreign forces, advisers and military personnel remaining in Cambodia were to have been withdrawn from Cambodia as of the entry into force of the Agreements on 23 October 1991. To verify the non-presence and non-return of such forces, UNTAC had established checkpoints on Cambodia's borders with Viet Nam, Thailand and the Lao People's Democratic Republic and posted observers at the airports, at the port of Kompong Som and on major routes within the country. Responding specifically to the PDK's most recent allegations, UNTAC established 10 checkpoints on the border with Viet Nam, one more than originally envisaged, and at an earlier time than had been specified in the peace plan. UNTAC also invited representatives of the four factions to participate in manning the checkpoints. Viet Nam, for its part, reaffirmed on 10 June 1992 that it had withdrawn all of its troops, weapons and equipment from Cambodia by September 1989.[23]

23/Document 34
See page 190

42   The Security Council faced a difficult decision concerning the PDK's lack of cooperation with UNTAC. Some members of the international community favoured strong measures that would force the PDK to

UNTAC Sectors of Cantonment and Demobilization

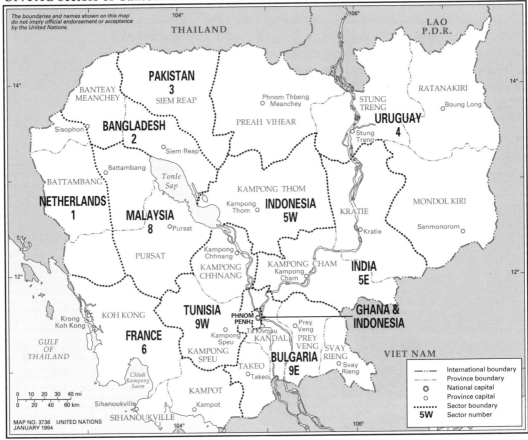

UNTAC's initial deployment was designed for phase II of the cease-fire, in which the armed forces of the four parties were to gather separately in cantonment areas, relinquish their weapons to UNTAC and begin their reintegration into civil society. (Names of UN Member States indicate which troop-contributing country was in command of a given sector.)

adhere to the provisions of the Paris Agreements. Others wanted to rely on the power of persuasion, the increasingly substantial UNTAC military presence in Cambodia and the ongoing work of the mission's components. That debate—over whether peace-keeping should at some point become something more assertive—was joined at several points during the course of the operation. The Paris Agreements did not specifically provide for enforcement or any kind of sanction in the event of non-compliance except for article 29, under which the two Co-Chairmen of the Paris Conference could, in the event of a violation or threat of violation, undertake consultations "with a view to taking appropriate steps to ensure respect" for commitments made under the Agreements. Rather, the Agreements were premised on the "good faith" of the factions to carry out their obligations.

43   The PDK's refusal notwithstanding, FUNCINPEC, the KPNLF and the SOC expressed their readiness to begin the regroupment and cantonment process, as long as it was done in a manner which minimized any military disadvantage they would suffer *vis-à-vis* the PDK. After careful consideration, I concluded that phase II had to begin on 13 June 1992 regardless of the PDK's refusal to cooperate.[24] Any significant delay would jeopardize the elections and undermine all that had been so carefully accomplished since UNTAC's arrival in March. On 12 June 1992, the Security Council supported my position, urged that the full deployment of UNTAC be accelerated and called on the factions to cooperate fully.[25]

24/Document 35
See page 191

25/Document 36
See page 194

Refugee repatriation

44   The repatriation component also had to surmount early difficulties. Two thirds of the more than 360,000 refugees living in camps along the Thai border had been engaged in agriculture prior to their flight from Cambodia in the late 1970s. Under the original plan for the voluntary return of refugees and displaced persons, each returning family would be given approximately two hectares of agricultural land. The plan was to be implemented in three stages:

- Transport to the final destination in Cambodia of their choice;
- Immediate assistance (housing materials and household kits) and food for an average period of 12 months;
- Reintegration programmes, including "quick-impact projects" (QIPs) and medium- to long-term development projects managed jointly with UNDP.

45   More than half of the refugee population in the camps registered to return to north-western Cambodia, even though many did not originate from that area. Press reports said that this reflected the refugees' fears of renewed fighting and their desire to be able to flee swiftly across the Thai border. As the north-western provinces of Cambodia were heavily mined and short of good agricultural land, UNHCR had to shift its policy quickly to provide more repatriation options and to avoid jeopardizing the election schedule. One of the major goals of the Paris Agreements was to complete the repatriation process so that the returnees could register to vote and participate fully in the electoral campaign.

46   On 20 May 1992, UNHCR decided to broaden the range of options open to the returnees to include:

- Option A(Agriculture): a plot of land (up to two hectares per family) and wood for the construction of a house;

- Option B(Building): an extended plot of land for a house, wood for the construction of a house and sufficient space to engage in vegetable farming and poultry raising;
- Option C(Cash): $50 per adult and $25 per child under 12 with no additional material aid but not excluding the eventual allocation of agricultural land;
- Option E(Employment): employment (with UNTAC or another organization) and reintegration money as per option C;
- Option F(Family reunion): transportation to the distribution point closest to where immediate relatives were located, and reintegration money as per option C.

47   Initially, the returnees favoured option B, but wood shortages resulted, and subsequent waves of returnees selected option C. This did not mean that the so-called "land option" was no longer viable; rather, UNTAC continued to exert its best efforts to identify mine-free land in areas free of malaria. But with repatriation no longer hinging on the availability of land, UNHCR was able to accelerate the overall process of return. In April 1992, 4,777 persons were repatriated. In July, August and September 1992, the monthly average surpassed 30,000. By the end of September, more than 130,000 refugees and displaced persons had returned to Cambodia.

V Challenges to the peace plan

48   The period from June to November 1992 saw what were perhaps the most critical challenges to the implementation of the Paris Agreements, most of them the result of the PDK's continued lack of cooperation. The Khmer Rouge's consistent refusals to assist UNTAC in the disarming and cantonment of its soldiers seemed a blatant attempt to derail the peace process, and at times came dangerously close to doing just that. However, continued cooperation by the other factions, combined with the international community's constant diplomatic efforts to balance negotiation with a unanimous determination to proceed, allowed UNTAC to work around the obstacles presented by the PDK and continue with the work of peace-building in Cambodia.

49   An attempt to resolve the impasse with the PDK was made at the 22 June 1992 Ministerial Conference on the Rehabilitation and Reconstruction of Cambodia held in Tokyo. At this Conference, 33 nations pledged $880 million in recovery aid for Cambodia, substantially in excess of the $593 million which I had called for in April. It was also decided to create the International Committee on the Reconstruction of Cambodia. "We are hopeful", these nations affirmed in the Tokyo Declaration, "that Cambodia can expand and diversify its external trade and investment relationships, so that it can be integrated into the dynamic economic development of the Asia-Pacific region and of the world."[26] Japan was the leading contributor, offering $200 million; the United States pledged $135 million. Pledges also came from several intergovernmental organizations; for example, UNDP committed $54 million.

26/Document 37
See page 194

50   In addition to pledges for aid, an informal "proposal for discussion" was presented to the Cambodian factions, setting out a number of measures designed to respond to the concerns expressed by the PDK. The suggestions included having the Supreme National Council (which included PDK representatives) assume a more active role in advising my Special Representative, accelerating UNTAC's deployment of its civil administration staff and having observers from each of the four factions work with UNTAC in investigating allegations concerning foreign forces and other military matters.

51   At an emergency meeting of the SNC convened in Tokyo that same day, three of the Cambodian factions accepted the proposal. The PDK promised to respond in time, but subsequent meetings of the SNC in Cambodia, as well as meetings between my Special Representative and Mr. Khieu Samphan, failed to secure the PDK's compliance. In a

27/Document 38
See page 198;

Document 40
See page 201

number of proposals, the PDK maintained that the SNC was not exercising its legitimate powers and that the SOC continued to exert too much control over the country's administrative structures.[27] Furthermore, Mr. Khieu Samphan called for the dissolution of the main structures and institutions established by the SOC. The United Nations position was that the Paris Agreements stated clearly that UNTAC oversight should be exercised through existing administrative structures, and that therefore these structures could not be abolished or dismantled. In a letter to Mr. Khieu Samphan, I stressed that UNTAC would continue its efforts to carry out, with full impartiality, the provisions of the Paris Agreements.[28]

28/Document 39
See page 199

UNTAC moves forward

52   Despite these stumbling blocks, UNTAC continued to move towards full strength. Military deployment had reached 14,300 troops by mid-July, with the rest en route. Initial priority in their placement was given to areas where refugees and displaced persons were being resettled and to border checkpoints where the UNTAC military component sought to verify the non-presence and non-return of foreign forces. As the civilian police component of UNTAC extended its presence, increasing emphasis was placed on the growing problem of banditry and on training the local police in such areas as criminal investigation, crime prevention and riot control. By late September 1992, UNTAC was close to full deployment throughout almost all of Cambodia, and its activities were becoming increasingly familiar to all Cambodians. The civil administration component had established offices in all 21 provinces by 15 July 1992. On a day-to-day basis, control was being exercised in various ways, including the physical presence of civil administration personnel alongside their highest-ranking counterparts in the existing administrative structures, weekly meetings between UNTAC staff and these officials and the attempt to establish clear lines of decision-making. The component's Foreign Affairs Service supervised policies regarding passports and visas, controlled border functions such as immigration and customs and assumed control over the receipt and distribution of foreign aid. In the area of finance, full deployment was established in early September, with financial controllers present in each of the ministries, in the National Bank of Cambodia and in all the SOC's provincial administrations.

53   Even though its presence in Cambodia was expanding, UNTAC's ability to adhere to its timetable remained seriously compromised by the PDK's failure to allow disarmament and demobilization to proceed in a meaningful manner. Once phase II of the cease-fire began

UN Member States contributing uniformed personnel
(number of personnel at peak strength, June 1993)

Military Component		Civilian Police Component	
Algeria	16	Algeria	157
Argentina	2	Australia	11
Australia	685	Austria	19
Austria	17	Bangladesh	220
Bangladesh	942	Brunei Darussalam	12
Belgium	5	Bulgaria	74
Brunei Darussalam	3	Cameroon	73
Bulgaria	748	Colombia	144
Cameroon	14	Egypt	100
Canada	218	Fiji	50
Chile	52	France	141
China	444	Germany	74
France	1,350	Ghana	218
Germany	137	Hungary	97
Ghana	912	India	421
India	1,336	Indonesia	224
Indonesia	1,779	Ireland	40
Ireland	11	Italy	75
Japan	605	Japan	66
Malaysia	1,090	Jordan	83
Namibia	43	Kenya	100
Netherlands	809	Malaysia	224
New Zealand	67	Morocco	98
Pakistan	1,106	Nepal	85
Philippines	127	Netherlands	2
Poland	666	Nigeria	150
Russian Federation	52	Norway	20
Senegal	2	Pakistan	197
Singapore	35	Philippines	224
Thailand	716	Singapore	75
Tunisia	883	Sweden	36
United Kingdom	130	Tunisia	29
United States	49		
Uruguay	940		
Total	**15,991**	**Total**	**3,359**

on 13 June 1992, UNTAC was to complete the regroupment and cantonment process within four weeks, or by 11 July 1992. Instead, by 10 July 1992 only 13,500 troops had been cantoned, less than 7 per cent of the estimated total of 200,000 soldiers in the country. With the PDK refusing to take part, the three other Cambodian factions had become increasingly hesitant to disarm. The Security Council again found itself at a crossroads.

54   I presented two possible courses of action: to suspend the operation until all four factions complied with the Paris Agreements, or to pursue the process, thereby demonstrating the firmness of the international community's commitment to the Cambodian people.[29] I recommended the second option, and suggested that the cantonment be pursued in such a way as would not place the cooperating factions at a military disadvantage, for example, by concentrating on areas where there was no military confrontation. This was still a temporary solution; full implementation of the Paris Agreements was impossible under the existing conditions. On 21 July 1992, by its resolution 766 (1992), the Security Council again approved the continued implementation of the accords, despite the difficulties being encountered.[30] The Council also requested that international assistance for the rehabilitation and reconstruction of Cambodia from that point on benefit only the factions fulfilling their obligations under the Agreements and cooperating fully with UNTAC. A troubling question remained unanswered: whether the PDK could be persuaded to participate in the cantonment phase, cooperate with UNTAC and adhere to the commitments it had agreed to in Paris.

Ongoing diplomatic efforts

55   The month of September saw additional efforts to break the deadlock with the PDK. Australia issued a paper setting out a number of suggestions designed to demonstrate the resolve of the international community to carry on with implementation of the peace process.[31] Australia proposed, among other things, that the Co-Chairmen of the Paris Conference on Cambodia should undertake consultations in an attempt to break the deadlock, that the Security Council should set a date for the imposition of sanctions against the PDK and that, should these steps fail to elicit a positive response from the PDK, the peace process, including elections, should proceed without the PDK. In a letter to me, Mr. Khieu Samphan stated that the steps outlined in Australia's paper would "jeopardize the integrity" of the Paris Agreements.[32] In an earlier letter addressed to me, my Special Representative suggested that strong action by the Security Council, with particular emphasis on economic pressures against the PDK, might be necessary.[33]

29/Document 41
See page 201

30/Document 42
See page 205

31/Document 44
See page 208

32/Document 47
See page 222

33/Document 43
See page 206

56   Another contribution to the search for a solution to the impasse came from Mr. Son Sann, President of the KPNLF and a member of the SNC, who outlined a number of conditions which, in his view, once met would leave the PDK with no more acceptable reasons to continue its non-compliance with the Paris Agreements.[34] Additional backing for UNTAC's efforts came from the five permanent members of the Security Council when, following my meeting with their representatives on 25 September 1992, they assured me of their firm determination not to allow the difficulties to undermine the principles of the Paris Agreements or delay their implementation.[35]

34/Document 48
See page 224

35/Document 46
See page 219

57   Amidst this ongoing diplomatic activity, I assured the Security Council that UNTAC would press forward with all the provisions of the Paris Agreements.[36] On 13 October 1992 the Security Council confirmed in resolution 783 (1992) that the electoral process should proceed according to schedule and again demanded that the PDK cooperate with UNTAC.[37] The Council also invited the Governments of Japan and Thailand, which had been actively involved in trying to find solutions to the various problems, to continue their diplomatic efforts and report to the Co-Chairmen of the Paris Conference by 31 October 1992, and requested that I report to the Council no later than 15 November 1992. The Council would then decide how to proceed.

36/Document 45
See page 211

37/Document 49
See page 225

58   On 31 October 1992, the Governments of Thailand and Japan reported that they had been unable to resolve the difficulties.[38] I subsequently requested the Co-Chairmen of the Paris Conference (France and Indonesia) to undertake appropriate consultations, as provided for in article 29 of the Paris Agreements as well as under paragraph 12 of Security Council resolution 783 (1992).[39] I also informed Prince Sihanouk that such recourse had been taken, and welcomed his proposal to meet in Beijing on 7 and 8 November 1992 with the co-Chairmen of the Paris Conference and with members of the SNC.[40]

38/Document 54
See page 229

39/Document 50
See page 227;
Document 51
See page 227

40/Document 52
See page 228

59   Unfortunately, despite these intensive efforts—and despite the presence at the Beijing consultations of members of the SNC and representatives of Australia, Germany, Japan, Thailand and the five permanent members of the Security Council—I was forced to report to the Council on 15 November 1992 that the PDK remained unwilling to carry out the provisions of the Paris accords.[41] As a result, the cantonment, disarmament and demobilization process had been effectively suspended. In fact, the PDK had stiffened its position in Beijing, saying that it would not take part in the electoral process or the elections as long as it felt that a neutral political environment had not been created. In a letter to me, Prince Sihanouk communicated his concern at this turn of events and reiterated his support for UNTAC's mission.[42]

41/Document 54
See page 229

42/Document 53
See page 229

60   The PDK's new stance on its participation in the electoral process represented an ominous development, in the light of recent events in Angola. There, the demobilization of troops and storage of weapons had not taken place to the extent envisioned in the peace accords, and a dispute over the election results had led to renewed fighting which had plunged the country into depths of killing and destruction not seen even during the country's long civil war. It was not unreasonable to think that a similar outbreak of hostilities was possible in a still fractious and heavily armed Cambodia. Already, artillery exchanges and other cease-fire violations in central and northern Cambodia were prompting fears of another round of dry-season combat starting in November between the forces of the PDK and the SOC. Attacks on Vietnamese-speaking villagers and fishermen by PDK forces appeared aimed at exacerbating Cambodians' concerns over the issue of foreign residents and immigrants, and raised the spectre of ethnically motivated violence and new displacements of people.

61   In another disturbing turn of events, UNTAC personnel and helicopters were coming under attack in areas where PDK forces were known to be present. This tense situation left the Security Council facing two difficult decisions. The first was the question of what further action should be taken to persuade the PDK to end its non-compliance with the Paris Agreements. Diplomatic efforts had not succeeded thus far. Press reports indicated that the SOC, for its part, wanted to conduct a military campaign against the PDK and have it expelled from the SNC. But noting the steady progress being made by UNTAC, I informed the Council that I continued to believe that "patient diplomacy" remained the best means of getting the peace process back on track.

62   The Council also had to determine yet again whether UNTAC should press on with implementing the Paris Agreements notwithstanding the non-cooperation of the PDK. Withdrawal was an unacceptable option, given all that had been achieved in the areas of repatriation, human rights and preparations for the election. Suspending the project until the PDK's cooperation was secured was also unfeasible; neither the political nor the economic situation in Cambodia would sustain a prolonged transitional period. Moreover, a holding operation would require the international community to maintain indefinitely a large operation costing almost $100 million per month. I therefore concurred with the Co-Chairmen of the Paris Conference that the peace process had to continue, and that the elections should be held as scheduled, even with a substantial part of the Cambodian forces remaining under arms. I also proposed that the full deployment of UNTAC's military component be maintained until the elections and adjusted to enhance the protection of voters, candidates and electoral officials, and to foster a general sense of security in Cambodia, especially in remote or insecure areas. My implemen-

tation plan had envisaged a reduction in troop strength by this time, but given the PDK's continuing failure to enter phase II of the cease-fire, this was no longer feasible.

63   On 30 November 1992 the Security Council adopted resolution 792 (1992), confirming that the elections for a constituent assembly would be held no later than May 1993 and instructing UNTAC to proceed with preparations for elections in all areas of the country to which it had full and free access as of 31 January 1993.[43] The Council also condemned the PDK's failure to comply with its obligations and demanded that it not impede voter registration or the activities of other political parties.

43/Document 55
See page 243

64   In a statement following the vote (S/PV.3143), the permanent representative of the United Kingdom laid out the rationale behind the resolution: "This Council has been very patient, and it will remain so. But it also has to be determined . . . We are not saying that the Khmer Rouge can no longer be a part of the settlement process. On the contrary, we make it clear that we want it to join in that process. If it decides after all to honour its commitments, it will be able to take part in the elections for a constituent assembly leading to the formation of a new government. But if it decides to exclude itself, that is the Khmer Rouge's responsibility. What must not happen, and what will not happen, is the postponement of the elections . . . The Cambodian people have waited long enough for the opportunity to frame their own constitution and to choose their own government . . ."

65   The Security Council also moved at this time to tighten economic pressure on the PDK. First, it called for measures to prevent the supply of petroleum products from reaching areas occupied by any Cambodian faction not complying with the military provisions of the Paris Agreements. The Council also undertook to consider other measures, such as freezing PDK assets held outside Cambodia, should the PDK continue to obstruct implementation of the peace plan. The Council also addressed for the first time the need to protect Cambodia's natural resources. A report by the United Nations Development Programme and evidence gathered by UNTAC had documented the heavy toll being taken on the environment as a result of the exploitation, by Cambodian nationals and by nationals of Cambodia's neighbours (particularly Thailand), of the country's natural resources, primarily timber, minerals and gems, but also fisheries and rubber. The Council supported the September 1992 adoption by the SNC of a country-wide moratorium on the export of logs, an action taken by the SNC over the objections of the PDK. It also requested the SNC to consider adopting a similar moratorium on the export of minerals and gems.

VI   Preparing for elections

66   The pre-election phase of the United Nations' mission in Cambodia proved to be a complicated and delicate balancing act among the various components of UNTAC and between the Cambodian political parties themselves. A population unaccustomed to democracy had to be convinced that their votes would matter; an atmosphere of security and neutrality had to be created in the midst of ethnic violence, political intimidation, and cease-fire violations; and each of UNTAC's components had to choreograph its activities carefully to reinforce the aims and mandates of every other component at this crucial stage. Hindered by inter-factional violence and various kinds of non-compliance by all the major parties, UNTAC's mandate to put the democratic process in action was gradually realized through the efforts of United Nations personnel both within and outside Cambodia, and especially by the Cambodian people themselves.

Electoral process

67   The Electoral Law was adopted by the SNC on 5 August 1992 and promulgated one week later. Two important amendments to the Electoral Law were made in the four months between its initial submission to the SNC and its promulgation. First, it was decided that, in order to meet the concern expressed by the parties that the franchise be restricted to "Cambodian persons" (i.e., non-Vietnamese), the text of the Paris Agreements should be interpreted as giving the right to register to "every Cambodian person" who had reached the age of 18 at the time of application to register, or who would turn 18 during the registration period, and who met either of the following definitions: (a) a person born in Cambodia, at least one of whose parents had been born in Cambodia; or (b) a person, wherever born, at least one of whose parents was or had been a Cambodian person within the meaning of (a). Secondly, the Electoral Law was amended to permit overseas Cambodians to vote at one polling station in Europe, one in North America and one in Australia. Several members of the SNC had sought to amend the law so that Cambodians living overseas could register outside Cambodia. However, because such a change would likely create logistical delays that would make it practically impossible to hold the elections in May 1993, I decided that, unless the Security Council decided otherwise, such a change should not be approved.[44]

44/Document 63
See page 252

68   The voter registration process reflected the Cambodian people's strong desire for a chance to express their opinions on the question of Cambodia's future. From 5 October 1992, when the exercise began, to 31 January 1993, some 4.6 million Cambodians registered to vote, representing nearly all of the estimated eligible voters to which UNTAC had territorial access. The registration period was extended from its original closing date of 31 December 1992 to ensure the registration of the maximum number of voters. Special arrangements were made for refugees and displaced persons who could not register before the 31 January 1993 deadline. To help manage the registration process, UNTAC established a computer system designed to store as many as 5.2 million voter registration records.

69   Uncertainty over the PDK's intentions made it unclear whether voter education, training and registration would be able to proceed in the zones under PDK control. In close cooperation with the UNTAC civilian and military components, UNTAC electoral staff were able to move into some zones where the PDK was operating or present. They reported high levels of interest on the part of locals and had moderate success in registering some of them as voters. For the most part, though, UNTAC was denied access to PDK-controlled areas, which were generally considered to be populated by about 5 per cent of the total population of Cambodia.

70   Information played a key role in preparing Cambodians for the elections and informing them about UNTAC, the Paris Agreements and the public's rights and responsibilities. UNTAC's information and education division faced special challenges in Cambodia. After two decades of fighting and isolation resulting from an international embargo on all trade and diplomatic contact, many Cambodians had little awareness of the changes that had occurred in the outside world, or of the international community's concern for their country. Many were also sceptical about the applicability in Cambodia of basic concepts of human rights, including free and fair elections and multi-party political campaigning. These doubts proved to be well founded as all the major Cambodian factions engaged in a certain degree of misleading propaganda and political coercion during the registration/campaign period. Ironically, this may have contributed to the large percentage of eligible Cambodians registering to vote. Reports indicate that several of the factions coerced the local populations under their control to register as party members and also with UNTAC, assuming, incorrectly, that people would be too intimidated to ultimately vote their conscience rather than for the party to which they "belonged".

71   In addition to the challenges of a doubtful population and partisan propaganda, UNTAC also faced physical obstacles in disseminating information. The impact of any written materials was hindered by

low literacy rates throughout the country, and the country's radio and television facilities were old, in bad repair and had limited range. One of UNTAC's most effective measures in getting its message out was the creation of its own radio station. On 9 November 1992, Radio UNTAC began broadcasting from a Phnom Penh–based transmitter, offering programmes concentrating primarily on the electoral process but also featuring other aspects of the UNTAC mandate such as mine awareness and human rights. UNTAC information officers also produced videos, posters, information leaflets, flyers and large banners and advertisements for public display. All materials were produced in the Khmer language, and UNTAC made strenuous efforts to recruit qualified translators. An UNTAC Information Centre was opened in Phnom Penh in November 1992 for Cambodians to read UNTAC materials or watch UNTAC video productions. The Centre also served as a venue for meetings of Cambodian journalists and for media-related seminars.

72   The UNTAC human rights component also mounted an extensive public education campaign. Training programmes brought important human rights concepts to diverse audiences, including judges, police, defence lawyers, monks, teachers, public defenders, electoral supervisors, women's associations, health professionals and representatives of the Cambodian political parties. Mobile information units equipped with loudspeakers and video monitors were set up in each province to show films on basic human rights concepts. Together with UNESCO, UNTAC enlisted a team of traditional singers to tour the provinces with a performance featuring human rights messages. Posters, leaflets and stickers were produced and distributed, formal human rights training was introduced into the Cambodian education system and curricular materials were distributed to instructors in primary and secondary schools as well as at Phnom Penh University. An International Symposium on Human Rights in Cambodia was convened from 30 November to 2 December 1992 in Phnom Penh—the first such gathering to be held in the country.

73   Other human rights activities included the formation of a Prisons Control Commission, established at UNTAC's recommendation, which conducted a review that led to the release of more than 250 prisoners who had been detained without trial. In September 1992, the SNC decided that Cambodia should accede to the Convention on the Rights of the Child, the Convention and Protocol relating to the Status of Refugees, the Convention on the Elimination of All Forms of Discrimination against Women and the Convention against Torture and Other Cruel, Inhuman or Degrading Treatment or Punishment. In a separate development, the United Nations Commission on Human Rights adopted, on 19 February 1993, a resolution in which it requested me to ensure a continued United Nations human rights presence in Cambodia

after the expiration of UNTACs mandate.[45] The Commission's resolution was unprecedented in that it authorized, for the first time, a field presence of the United Nations Centre for Human Rights.

45/Document 70
See page 277

74   The provisional registration of political parties began on 17 August 1992. Under the Paris Agreements, the election of 120 members to the Constituent Assembly was to be held on a provincial basis in accordance with a system of proportional representation. The Agreements provided for a multi-party electoral system in which people voted for political parties, not for individuals. The list of party candidates for each province was to be published before the elections. On 27 January 1993, 20 of the 22 provisionally registered political parties applied for official registration, in accordance with the Electoral Law, by submitting a list of at least 5,000 registered voters who were members of the party. Upon successful completion of the registration procedure, these became the 20 parties that contested the election. The PDK had announced in November 1992 the formation of a political party, the National Unity of Cambodia Party, but it allowed the January 1993 deadline to pass without filing to take part in the elections.

75   On 28 January 1993, the SNC decided that the election would be held from 23 to 25 May 1993. Voting during this period was to take place at fixed polling stations; I subsequently recommended that three additional voting days be added to allow mobile polling units to reach remote areas. The election campaign would run from 7 April through 19 May 1993, followed by a four-day cooling-off period. The electoral component had been examining a proposal put forth by Prince Sihanouk to hold a presidential election simultaneously with the elections for a constituent assembly. This idea had been advanced by Prince Sihanouk as offering a stabilizing effect during the period following elections when the Constituent Assembly was to draft a new constitution. However, such an election was not provided for in the Paris Agreements and needed Security Council authorization as well as additional resources if it were to take place. Preparations for the presidential election were put on hold when Prince Sihanouk informed the SNC at its 28 January meeting of his decision that such an election should be held after the adoption of the new Cambodian Constitution by the Constituent Assembly.[46]

46/Document 57
See page 246;
Document 68
See page 269

76   In the area of national defence, the leaders of the armed forces of the three factions complying with the Paris Agreements signed, in late January 1993, a directive prepared by UNTAC which placed limits on the political activity of their military personnel. In the area of public security, a set of "interim penal provisions" relating to the judiciary and criminal law and procedures was adopted by the SNC at UNTAC's initiative. In implementing this measure, UNTAC established a programme of training for magistrates and police officials. Working with the

International Committee of the Red Cross, UNTAC achieved marked improvements in water and sanitation services at prisons in Phnom Penh and the provinces. UNTAC also established controls over Cambodia's central bank functions, sources of revenue such as taxes, and customs and expenditures. The SNC adopted a financial control directive prepared by UNTAC on the transfer of public assets in order to introduce orderly and transparent procedures into the process of privatization of property owned by the existing administrative structures. UNTAC also sought to stabilize the country's economy in order to reduce possible causes of unrest that might have adverse effects on the electoral environment; efforts in this respect focused on financial assistance programmes undertaken by donors such as the World Bank, the International Monetary Fund and the Asian Development Bank, as well as bilateral donors.

77   One area where UNTAC did not play a role in the electoral process was in developing democratic political structures for the contending parties. In a country such as Cambodia, where the United Nations was seeking to oversee the first free vote in decades, it was not enough to register voters and provide ballot boxes; there had to be training for parties and candidates in how to formulate their positions, communicate with the public and engage in political debate that was both meaningful and fair. In the United Nations–sponsored election in Cambodia, the task of training parties in the art of politics fell primarily to two United States–based organizations—the National Democratic Institute and the International Republican Institute. While this type of activity falls outside the mandate of the United Nations, future missions involving democratization efforts must somehow include political party training as an essential ingredient in the holding of free and fair elections.

78   In the repatriation component, nearly 310,000 refugees and displaced persons had returned to Cambodia without incident by the end of February 1993, and it appeared likely that the repatriation process would be completed in time to enable all eligible returnees to take part in the elections. By December 1992, four of the nine border camps had closed. Of more than $9 million earmarked for quick- impact projects in the UNHCR programme, some $3.4 million had been distributed by the end of January 1993. However, the shortage of safe, available land continued to limit the reintegration of returnees into Cambodia, and recurrent fighting forced some returnees to become internally displaced persons. Thirty-five other rehabilitation projects, representing more than $340 million, had also been approved by the SNC since the Tokyo Ministerial Conference of June 1992.

Cambodia refugees: repatriation and relief

Returnees: monthly and cumulative flows

(From start of repatriation in March 1992 through conclusion of operation in April 1993)

		Number of convoys	Number of returnees	Number of returnees (cumulative totals)
1992	March	2	928	928
	April	11	4,777	5,705
	May	23	13,068	18,773
	June	35	19,830	38,603
	July	42	31,021	69,624
	August	44	30,935	100,559
	September	46	31,865	132,424
	October	41	28,992	161,416
	November	44	34,010	195,426
	December	42	34,454	229,880
1993	January	45	39,776	269,656
	February	32	39,890	309,546
	March	31	32,038	341,584
	April	18	20,625	362,209

Source: UNHCR

Repatriation: assistance options chosen by returnees

Option	persons	families
Agricultural land	10,261 (2.8%)	2,435 (3.0%)
Building with housing plot	24,147 (6.7%)	9,177 (11.1%)
Cash	317,442 (87.6%)	69,080 (83.9%)
Employment with UNTAC/others	4,214 (1.2%)	937 (1.2%)
Family reunion (transport plus cash)	462 (0.1%)	112 (0.1%)
No information	5,683 (1.6%)	575 (0.7%)
Total	362,209 (100.0%)	82,316 (100.0%)

Source: UNHCR

Cease-fire violations

79 For all the gathering momentum towards elections, the political environment called for in the Paris Agreements did not yet exist and the sense of insecurity among Cambodians was heightened by a spate of violent incidents in the period leading up to the elections.[47]

80 Cease-fire violations continued. One sustained period of shelling in the Bavel area of Battambang Province in December 1992 forced about 15,000 people to flee their homes. Also that month, PDK forces illegally detained UNTAC personnel on several occasions, prompting strong condemnation by the Security Council. The PDK responded that such incidents had been provoked by UNTAC's having entered PDK-controlled territory without informing the PDK beforehand, and stated further that such acts were part of a "smear campaign . . . designed to mislead the United Nations Security Council into enforcing sanctions" against the PDK.[48] In early February 1993, in response to moves taken by the armed forces of the PDK to consolidate its influence over areas in north-west Cambodia, forces of the State of Cambodia launched attacks on the armed forces of the PDK in a number of districts, sparking the worst fighting since the signing of the Paris Agreements. UNTAC pointed out that the SOC's moves exceeded the bounds of its rights of self-defense against hostile action by PDK forces.

81 Killings of Vietnamese civilians, attributed mainly to the PDK, prompted thousands of ethnic Vietnamese, mostly fishermen and their families living along Cambodia's Tonle Sap (Great Lake), to uproot themselves and move down-river towards Viet Nam in search of safety. On 30 December 1992, Viet Nam's Minister for Foreign Affairs strongly condemned what he described as "barbarous acts of terrorism" committed by the PDK against persons of Vietnamese descent.[49] Viet Nam registered another protest following an incident on 10 March 1993 in which 33 ethnic Vietnamese, including 12 children, were massacred.[50] UNTAC investigations concluded that the attackers were PDK soldiers.

82 Politically motivated murders, abductions, bombings, threats and other forms of intimidation also increased, most of them carried out by soldiers, police or supporters of the SOC against FUNCINPEC, the Buddhist Liberal Democratic Party (BLDP, the political wing of the KPNLF) and other political parties engaged in lawful political activity. In response, UNTAC's civilian police and military components instituted intensive patrols and guard duty to improve the security of political party offices considered to be most at risk.

83 There also seemed to be a growing reluctance on the part of the existing administrative structures of the three parties in compliance

47/Document 65
See page 254;
Document 69
See page 269

48/Document 57
See page 246;
Document 58
See page 246;
Document 59
See page 248

49/Document 60
See page 248

50/Document 72
See page 280

with the peace plan to accept the various control and supervision functions entrusted to UNTAC, particularly in the SOC ministries responsible for foreign affairs, public security, defence and information. This hindered, among other things, the ability of the civilian police and human rights components of UNTAC to investigate reports of human rights abuses and violations. Some of this new resistance appeared to have come in response to the PDK's ongoing obstruction and non-compliance. In this connection, I reiterated that non-compliance by one party should not be invoked by any other party as a pretext for failing to honour its obligations under the Paris Agreements.[51]

84   The moratorium on logging was also being breached. UNTAC border control teams detected numerous and large-scale violations by the SOC, the PDK and FUNCINPEC, but their attempts to monitor the trade were incomplete because UNTAC had not been able to establish checkpoints in PDK-controlled zones along the border with Thailand. The Thai Government, concerned about infringement of its sovereignty, had insisted that such posts be within Cambodian territory,[52] and the PDK refused to allow UNTAC into the area. While the Thai Government cooperated with UNTAC, there were press reports that elements of the Thai military and some Thai companies were taking part in the logging and gem-mining trades in PDK-controlled areas. In December 1992, UNTAC had clear evidence of significant PDK logging and mining activity, and feared that revenue from these industries was facilitating continued PDK military strength and political non-cooperation. On 10 February 1993, over the PDK's objections, the SNC adopted a moratorium on the export of minerals and gems from Cambodia.[53]

85   The deteriorating security situation and the continuing refusal of the PDK to participate in the demobilization of forces made it necessary to redeploy UNTAC's military component. The original deployment pattern had been based on the requirements of regroupment and cantonment. The new alignment, completed on 31 December 1992, corresponded with the borders of the Cambodian provinces and with the planned deployment of electoral teams for the campaign and polling, thereby shortening the time needed to respond to potential threats to these locations (see map, page 36).

86   Confronting yet again the question of whether to proceed despite the less-than-full compliance with the Paris Agreements, I remained convinced that the existing framework still offered the best hope for a solution to the problems of Cambodia, and that maintaining the momentum achieved towards holding an election was crucial to attaining this goal.

87   I was aware, however, that some of the Cambodian parties favoured other measures, including official action against the PDK for cease-fire and disarmament violations. Prince Sihanouk informed my

51/Document 65
See page 254

52/Document 56
See page 245

53/Document 65
See page 254;
Document 69
See page 269

UNTAC Military Deployment for Electoral Support

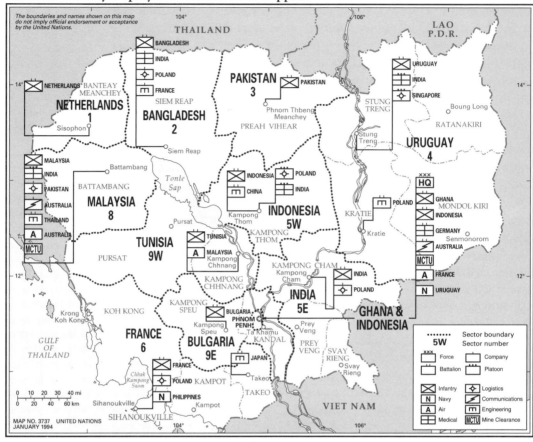

UNTAC realigned its military contingents to correspond with Cambodia's provincial borders in order to assist UNTAC electoral teams during the voter registration exercise and to ensure security during the election itself.

Special Representative on 4 January 1993 that the persistent violent attacks on FUNCINPEC offices and staff had obliged him to cease cooperation with UNTAC. The following day, his son, Prince Norodom Ranariddh, the President of FUNCINPEC, stated that he would suspend working relations with UNTAC until effective measures were taken to put an end to the climate of violence.[54] Mr. Hun Sen, for his part, wrote in a letter to me that the exceptional gravity of the situation warranted the "appropriate measures" set out in article 29 of the Paris Agreements and, perhaps, enforcement measures under Chapter VII of the Charter of the United Nations.[55] I assured Prince Ranariddh that I shared his concerns and that UNTAC would do its utmost to improve public security and work towards the creation of a neutral political environment for elections.[56] In my reply to Mr. Hun Sen I sought his cooperation in putting an end to acts of intimidation and violence in the areas controlled

54/Document 62
See page 251

55/Document 61
See page 249

56/Document 66
See page 268

by the SOC.[57] Both Prince Sihanouk and Prince Ranariddh subsequently expressed their continued support for UNTAC's efforts.

57/Document 67
See page 268

88   On 8 March 1993, in resolution 810 (1993), the Security Council maintained its united position on the question of Cambodia, endorsing the proposed election dates and expressing its readiness to support fully the Constituent Assembly and the process of drawing up a constitution and establishing a new government.[58] The stage was thus set for the next phase of the peace process. As the permanent representative of France noted in his statement to the Council (S/PV.3181): "The election campaign will begin in a few weeks. We remain gravely concerned by the acts of violence and intimidation in the country. We therefore appeal for tolerance, moderation and political maturity on the part of the people and the leaders of the Cambodian parties, so the elections can take place in the neutral political climate specified and required by the Paris Agreements . . . The Cambodians themselves bear the primary responsibility to restore peace and stability in Cambodia. That is no less true today than it will be tomorrow. The United Nations intervened at the request of the Cambodians themselves and it can in no case replace them if their political will should flag."

58/Document 71
See page 278

VII Elections

89   As Cambodia stood poised to begin the process of choosing its first democratically elected government since the 1960s, UNTAC could already be credited with some major achievements. Hundreds of thousands of Cambodian refugees had peacefully returned home from the Thai camps, and a freer exchange of ideas was occurring nationally in print, broadcasts and word of mouth than was permissible even months before. "Human rights" had become a household term for most Cambodians, and an effective buffer had been erected between the Phnom Penh Administration and its opponents by UNTAC. Although ideal circumstances for sending Cambodians to the polls did not exist, it seemed that the situation on the ground could be significantly improved without jeopardizing these precious gains. With or without the cooperation of the PDK, the election of a constituent assembly—the centre-piece of the Paris Agreements—was to take place as planned. The run-up to the vote, the week of polling and election results all presented UNTAC with certain challenges.

The electoral campaign

90   I visited Cambodia to mark the start of the electoral campaign on 7 April 1993 and met with members of the Supreme National Council and with representatives of the 20 political parties. In the course of these serious and businesslike discussions, I announced that despite the set-backs with which UNTAC had struggled in preparing the country for elections, the essential conditions for the electoral campaign, in my view, were present. Moreover, in an important development, Prince Sihanouk agreed during my visit to stay on as head of the SNC during the immediate post-election period in order to provide leadership and stability until the formation of the elected constituent assembly and government. Prince Sihanouk had previously indicated his intention to resign by 28 May. Just prior to my visit, however, the PDK had announced that it would not participate in the elections, asserting that "Vietnamese forces of aggression" continued to occupy the country. On 13 April 1993, the PDK closed its offices in Phnom Penh and withdrew, citing fears about security. UNTAC offered to ensure the PDK's security should the faction decide to return to Phnom Penh.[59] This offer was declined.

59/Document 75
See page 282

91   The electoral campaign began as scheduled on 7 April 1993. During the six-week period, scores of political meetings and rallies attended by tens of thousands of people took place without major incident throughout the country. UNTAC civilian police monitored these rallies, and also provided protection for political party offices considered to be most at risk. By mid-May, all the necessary electoral equipment and supplies, including the ballot papers and boxes, had been delivered to Cambodia under heavy guard. Training was under way for some 900 International Polling Station Officers from 44 countries and the Inter-Parliamentary Union, 130 more from the United Nations Secretariat and 370 from within UNTAC, as well as for more than 50,000 Cambodian electoral staff. As provided for in the Electoral Law, polling stations were established in New York, Paris and Sydney. The SOC, through its political party—the Cambodian People's Party (CPP)—raised questions about some of the technical preparations but pledged its confidence in UNTAC's electoral work.[60]

60/Document 80
See page 302

92   Radio UNTAC intensified its efforts to reach as many Cambodians as possible. Programming was increased to 15 hours a day; radio relay stations were established to widen the broadcast radius; and hundreds of thousands of radios were distributed to people across the country through a donation by the Japanese Government and Japanese non-governmental organizations. The main emphasis of UNTAC's electoral education messages at this point was the secrecy of the ballot. PDK radio broadcasts were attempting to frighten the Cambodian people in this regard, saying that their votes would not be private and could later be used against them, a threat that had familiar resonances with certain control tactics of the previous Pol Pot regime.

93   To ensure fair access to the media during the campaign, Radio UNTAC offered weekly segments to each political party for the broadcast of political material and allowed a "right of response" whenever a political party or its candidate or official believed it had been unfairly attacked or its public statements misrepresented. UNTAC took particular issue with the SOC for its efforts to limit or deny other political parties access to SOC-controlled media and their right to freedom of movement. As a result of strong intervention by UNTAC, FUNCINPEC was able to obtain the release from the SOC of the television broadcasting equipment it had imported for campaign purposes. All political parties had access to UNTAC information media, and three political parties were granted assistance from UNTAC with air transport for campaign purposes. UNTAC information videos, including round-table discussions involving representatives of the 20 political parties contesting the election, were shown on Phnom Penh television and distributed throughout the country. UNTAC erected billboards to accommodate the posters of all the political parties and prepared special banners and posters.

94   UNTAC also vigorously raised the issue of the separation of party and State in several public and private meetings with the Phnom Penh authorities, in response to indications that the SOC was mobilizing State employees—police, armed forces and civil servants—sometimes against their will, to conduct political campaign activities on behalf of the CPP. UNTAC "control teams", established by the civil administration component, sought to verify that provincial, district and village administration was being conducted in a politically neutral manner.

95   Looking to the post-election period, UNTAC also sought to prepare the Cambodian political parties for the central task to be faced by the newly elected Constituent Assembly: drafting a constitution. The question of constitutional principles had been a regular agenda item at meetings of the SNC since September 1992, and UNTAC sponsored a number of special seminars on the subject. A seminar held from 29 March to 3 April 1993 concentrated on four main features: constitutions and conflicts, Cambodia's constitutional history, crucial issues facing the Constituent Assembly and developing procedures for debate.

96   A fundamental goal of UNTAC was achieved with the official closing of Site 2, the last and largest of nine refugee camps on the Thai-Cambodian border, by UNHCR on 30 March 1993, exactly one year after the repatriation operation had begun. By the end of April 1993, the movement phase of the repatriation was completed. The final tally of individuals moved by UNHCR from Thailand into Cambodia was 362,209. UNHCR also repatriated 1,129 Cambodians from Indonesia, 633 from Viet Nam, 214 from Malaysia and 1 each from Singapore and Hong Kong. Nearly 23,000 additional Cambodians returned "spontaneously" or under the auspices of Thai authorities.

97   All four Cambodian factions scrupulously respected the freedom of choice of the returnees. Most people chose to settle in areas controlled by the Phnom Penh authorities, and more than half of the returnees settled in the northern provinces of Banteay Meanchey and Battambang. With the help of some 60 international and local nongovernmental organizations and United Nations agencies, more than 60 quick-impact projects were implemented through a successful UNHCR-UNDP reintegration programme. Examples of these projects included literacy training for demobilized soldiers, rehabilitation of schools and hospitals, provision of wells and latrines, small credit schemes, provision of draught and farm animals and improvement of roads and bridges. Rapid reintegration was further facilitated by the distribution of food assistance to all returnee families for a 400-day period by the World Food Programme, working through the Cambodian Red Cross.

Cambodia Repatriation: final destination of returnees by province

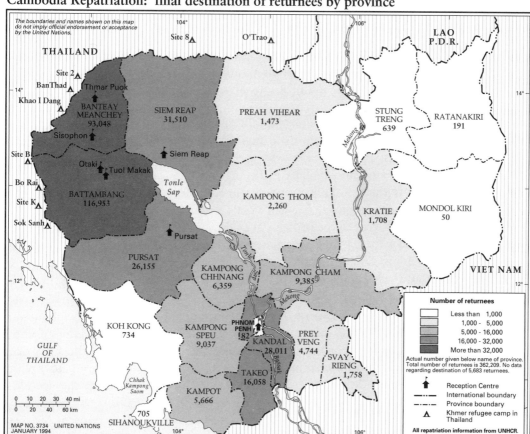

The boundaries and names shown on this map do not imply official endorsement or acceptance by the United Nations.

THAILAND

LAO P.D.R.

Site 8

O'Trao

Site 2

Ban Thad

Khao I Dang

Thmar Puok

BANTEAY MEANCHEY
93,048

SIEM REAP
31,510

PREAH VIHEAR
1,473

STUNG TRENG
639

RATANAKIRI
191

Sisophon

Site B

Bo Rai

Otaki

Tuol Makak

Siem Reap

Tonle Sap

KAMPONG THOM
2,260

KRATIE
1,708

MONDOL KIRI
50

BATTAMBANG
116,953

Site K

Sok Sanh

Pursat

PURSAT
26,155

KAMPONG CHHNANG
6,359

KAMPONG CHAM
9,385

VIET NAM

GULF OF THAILAND

KOH KONG
734

KAMPONG SPEU
9,037

PHNOM PENH
182

KANDAL
28,011

PREY VENG
4,744

SVAY RIENG
1,758

Chhak Kampong Saom

TAKEO
16,058

KAMPOT
5,666

705
SIHANOUKVILLE

0 10 20 30 40 mi
0 20 40 60 km

Number of returnees

	Less than 1,000
	1,000 - 5,000
	5,000 - 16,000
	16,000 - 32,000
	More than 32,000

Actual number given below name of province. Total number of returnees is 362,209. No data regarding destination of 5,683 returnees.

↑ Reception Centre
--- International boundary
-·-·- Province boundary
▲ Khmer refugee camp in Thailand

All repatriation information from UNHCR.

MAP NO. 3734   UNITED NATIONS
JANUARY 1994

More than half of the 362,209 Cambodian returnees from Thailand chose to settle in north-western Cambodia despite the presence of land mines and a shortage of arable land, owing in part to lingering concerns about the durability of the peace process.

Pre-election violence

98   The pre-election period saw an unfortunate amount of violence and intimidation. Cease-fire violations included small-scale clashes or exchanges of fire between PDK forces and the SOC army in the central and western parts of the country. Banditry increased, often committed by former soldiers or serving soldiers who were inadequately paid. According to UNTAC investigations, between the beginning of April and the middle of May, 100 Cambodians were killed as a result of violence and a further 179 injured. The victims included members of all four Cambodian factions—although some of the killings had no identifiable motivation—as well as members of UNTAC itself.[61]

99   Many of the dead were ethnic Vietnamese. By the end of April 1993, more than 21,000 ethnic Vietnamese, many of them second- or

61/Document 73
See page 281;

Document 74
See page 281;

Document 76
See page 282;

Document 77
See page 283;

Document 78
See page 284

third-generation residents of Cambodia, had fled their homes in search of safety. The issue of the status of ethnic Vietnamese resident in Cambodia had not been provided for in the Paris accords, and some within UNTAC's leadership were inclined to think of the situation as an internal security issue for Cambodian authorities to resolve. There was also the consideration of the PDK's perspective on the situation; their participation in the elections was still not ruled out, and UNTAC would only jeopardize the chances of the PDK's joining the process by appearing to make exceptions to their mandate on behalf of ethnic Vietnamese. UNTAC's compromise was to have its naval units and civilian police monitor the movements of fleeing Vietnamese in Cambodia and try to ensure that local authorities assumed their responsibility to protect these displaced persons. SOC officials only reluctantly committed civilian police forces to the protection of the ethnic Vietnamese refugees camped out on their boats near the banks of the Tonle Sap and Tonle Bassac rivers in Phnom Penh; the other factions, for their part, stated publicly that these people had no claim on Cambodian citizenship and should be deported to Viet Nam.

100 Harassment of political opponents continued, including verbal threats and petty vandalism of political posters. Many of these incidents were attributed to supporters of the SOC. In the final days before the elections, there were press reports of Cambodians stockpiling food and other supplies in fear of increasing violence during the elections. In an effort to halt some of the violence, an UNTAC directive was issued on 17 March 1993 prohibiting the possession and carrying of firearms and explosives by unauthorized persons. The resulting confiscation of firearms led to a significant decrease in reported serious crimes in Phnom Penh.

101 Less controllable was the violence and intimidation sponsored by the PDK with the intention of disrupting the polling. Not only did the PDK intensify its propaganda in the countryside to discourage people from voting, there were also reports of large-scale troop movements by PDK forces around the perimeters of Phnom Penh and intelligence reports about strategic locations being targeted during the weeks preceding the scheduled vote. There was an air of tense expectation on all sides in the final days before the polling started.

102 It was clear that the elections would not be taking place in an environment as stable and neutral as had been envisaged under the Paris accords. This was attributed largely to the impossibility of fulfilling all of the United Nations' mandate in Cambodia because of the PDK's refusal to cooperate with UNTAC. The question of whether to proceed with the elections still lingered, even at this late date. Important questions regarding the legitimacy of the results of an election carried out in such an atmosphere were seriously considered as I made my last two pre-election reports to the Security Council.[62] In those reports, I stated that despite the continuation of violent acts in Cambodia, the United Nations was obligated to carry out the election as planned. I argued that to do otherwise would be, in effect, to give a veto over peace to one armed faction in Cambodia, and to let down the Cambodian people and the international community who entrusted the United Nations with the task of peace-building in Cambodia. I also suggested that perhaps the international community had maintained unreasonable standards for a neutral election environment in Cambodia, given the country's internal divisions and traumatized population. The fact that ideal conditions did not exist in Cambodia was not sufficient reason to prevent elections from taking place; after all, I stated, this was only the beginning of Cambodia's renewal, not its end.

62/Document 79
See page 285;
Document 81
See page 303

103   Acknowledging that continued violence and attacks were likely, I recommended that elections be held as scheduled. I pledged that UNTAC would conduct the most impartial election possible under imperfect circumstances, and that all steps would be taken to ensure maximum security. To this end, security for all polling stations and their vicinity was to be provided exclusively by UNTAC. The armed forces of FUNCINPEC, the KPNLF and the SOC were to assist UNTAC by conveying information on possible or actual threats to the election and ensuring internal security in zones under their control.

104   No polling would be conducted in the areas controlled by the PDK to which UNTAC had not been permitted access, or in some remote, thinly populated areas in which PDK forces were operating. Other parts of the country were designed as high-, medium- and low-risk zones, with each to receive different levels of security measures. In high-risk zones, armed UNTAC military personnel were to be stationed at and around polling stations, physical fortifications were strengthened and electoral staff were issued protective gear. UNTAC civilian personnel were withdrawn from some locations and, in response to the heightened threat in Kompong Thom Province, the number of polling sites there was reduced from 102 to 51.[63] Since the Cambodian parties had primary responsibility for maintaining the security of the zones they controlled, UNTAC agreed to the request by the SOC, FUNCINPEC and the KPNLF that some of the weapons cantoned by UNTAC under phase II of the cease-fire be returned to the factions.

63/Document 86
See page 309

105   On 20 May 1993, in resolution 820 (1993), the Security Council expressed its satisfaction with the arrangements made for the conduct of the elections, deplored all acts of non-cooperation with the Paris Agreements and condemned all acts of violence committed on political and ethnic grounds, as well as intimidation of and attacks on UNTAC personnel. It expressed full support for the measures taken by UNTAC to protect the polls and reminded all Cambodian parties of their

64/Document 83
See page 306

65/Document 82
See page 306

66/Document 84
See page 307

obligation to comply fully with the election results.[64] Coming just three days before the central event of the process established by the Paris Agreements, the resolution was a clear expression of the Council's determination to go forward with the elections as scheduled. The Foreign Ministers of the Association of South-East Asian Nations issued a statement of support on 18 May.[65] On 22 May, the Security Council again called on the Cambodian people to exercise their right to vote.[66] Also on 22 May, in an important act of support for the elections, Prince Sihanouk returned to Phnom Penh from Beijing, where he had been undergoing medical treatment, and urged Cambodians to vote for the parties of their choice. After many months of work and exhortations, still no one knew what the voters—or the PDK—would do.

Elections

106   Predictions of the mass media and others to the contrary, the Cambodian election was carried out in a generally peaceful and jubilant atmosphere. The voters showed uncommon bravery and fortitude, sometimes walking several miles to cast their ballots, apparently undaunted by threats of violence or banditry, rough terrain or the heavy rain that swept much of the country. More than 4.2 million votes were cast, representing nearly 90 per cent of the registered voters. About 200 PDK soldiers and several hundred members of their families in Poipet, Banteay Meanchey Province, took part in the voting, as did soldiers and civilians in certain areas under PDK control in Battambang Province. News of this travelled quickly via Radio UNTAC, further emboldening Cambodians to turn out at the polls.

107   Except for a few scattered incidents of violence and the killing of one Cambodian civilian when several mortar rounds were fired in Kampong Cham Province, Cambodian voters exercised their right to cast their ballots without fear in an atmosphere of calm that was almost completely free of violence and intimidation. There are several theories attempting to explain the PDK's failure to disrupt the election, from the suggestion of some kind of eleventh-hour intervention to reports by deserters from PDK forces of a general unwillingness or inability to attack the polling sites. Whatever the reason, the PDK's boycott of the elections and subsequent plans to sabotage it were unsuccessful. About 46 per cent of the registered voters, or 2.2 million people, voted on the first day, the largest voter turnout on any single day. Polling took place from 0800 to 1600 hours each day, but provision was made to extend the hours on the final day to accommodate any remaining voters. Some slight technical difficulties arose, including the rupture of several plastic and padlock seals on the ballot boxes in transit owing to rough roads. The process was observed in its entirety by international

observers, by Cambodian political party agents, representatives of Cambodian human rights groups and members of the local and international media.

108   Addressing the Supreme National Council on 29 May 1993 as the counting of the ballots was proceeding, my Special Representative declared, on my behalf, that the conduct of the election had been free and fair.[67] The Security Council endorsed this declaration on 2 June 1993 in resolution 835 (1993).[68] In a letter to Prince Sihanouk, I stated my view that his return to Phnom Penh had contributed greatly to the ability of UNTAC to hold free and fair elections, and I congratulated the Cambodian people for their massive participation in the balloting.[69] In his response, Prince Sihanouk declared his satisfaction with the electoral process and thanked my Special Representative, UNTAC and all the international observers for their efforts.[70]

67/Document 88
See page 310

68/Document 89
See page 311

69/Document 85
See page 308

70/Document 87
See page 310

109   The success of the elections cannot be understood without mentioning the efforts of the UNTAC electoral team, which was staffed largely by young volunteers from all over the world who risked their personal safety in many cases to reach potential voters in remote and contested districts of Cambodia. These individuals were regarded by UNTAC personnel and local Cambodians alike as unparalleled in their commitment, integrity and enthusiasm for the democratic process. Not only were they effective in convincing people of the importance of each vote and the secrecy of each ballot, but also they served as consistent and highly visible examples of UNTAC's non-partisan role in the election. This group of United Nations volunteers deserves special credit for helping create an image of UNTAC as fair and neutral among the Cambodian population.

110   In order to ensure that the ballot counting was as accurate and transparent as possible, the counting proceeded rather more slowly than anticipated. UNTAC started releasing interim results twice daily, but as the early count showed FUNCINPEC ahead in the vote, this procedure brought protests from the Cambodian People's Party (CPP). It was noted in this connection, however, that the information on the vote count, being known to the Cambodian political party agents and human rights groups present while UNTAC electoral officials performed the tally, was already in the public domain.

111   The CPP subsequently asserted that the elections had been tainted by irregularities and fraud. The allegations were based on the claims that CPP agents were unable to inspect the "safe havens" where ballot boxes were stored overnight, the rupture of some plastic seals used to seal the boxes overnight, the inefficacy of the indelible ink, the alleged partiality of some locally recruited Cambodian polling staff and alleged discrepancies in the numbers of ballot papers in the boxes. The CPP also requested UNTAC to hold new elections in seven provinces, including

Distribution of Seats in the Constituent Assembly

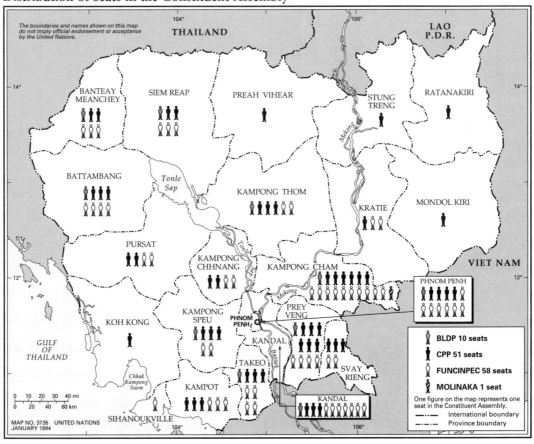

Four parties divided the 120 seats in the new Constituent Assembly:
FUNCINPEC, the CPP, the BLDP (the political party of the KPNLF) and
MOLINAKA (Molinaka and Naktaorsou Khmere for Freedom).

the capital, Phnom Penh. In cases where specific complaints had been made and details provided, UNTAC conducted investigations on the spot, to the complete satisfaction of party agents.

71/Document 92

See page 313

112   The final tally was released on 10 June 1993.[71] Of 4,011,631 valid ballots, FUNCINPEC won 1,824,188 votes, or 45.47 per cent. The CPP came in second with 1,533,471 votes, or 38.23 per cent. The BLDP (the KPNLF's political party) won 152,764 votes, or 3.81 per cent, and the remainder of the vote was shared among the 17 other political parties. That same day, I authorized my Special Representative to declare that the results "fairly and accurately reflect the will of the Cambodian people and must be respected". He also stated that the alleged irregularities cited by the CPP did not amount to fraud and that "none of the CPP's allegations, even if true, would affect the outcome".[72]

72/Document 92

See page 313

113   Momentous events followed in quick succession. On 10 June 1993, the leaders of the armed forces of FUNCINPEC, the KPNLF and the SOC agreed to work together to set up a single army—to be known as the Cambodian Armed Forces—that would be loyal to the work of the Constituent Assembly. On 14 June, the new Assembly was sworn in to begin drafting a new Constitution. At its inaugural meeting it proclaimed Prince Sihanouk head of State with "full and special powers".

114   The Constituent Assembly faced an immediate crisis: a "secession" movement in the eastern part of the country. On 12 June 1993, an "autonomous zone" of seven eastern provinces was proclaimed by Prince Norodom Chakrapong, a son of Prince Sihanouk, half-brother of Prince Ranariddh, and Deputy Prime Minister of the SOC. Other SOC figures were also reported to have been involved in the secessionist move. Prince Chakrapong rejected the results of the elections and asked UNTAC to withdraw from the seven provinces, saying that he could not guarantee the safety of UNTAC personnel. Following attacks on UNTAC offices and vehicles and threats to some civilian peace-keepers, UNTAC ordered a temporary withdrawal from three provinces and Prince Ranariddh prepared his troops for battle against those allied with Prince Chakrapong. The motives for the secessionist move were unclear, and there were press reports that additional members of the CPP had been involved. On 15 June, the short-lived effort collapsed and Prince Chakrapong fled to Viet Nam.

115   The Security Council endorsed the election results by its resolution 840 (1993) of 15 June 1993, fully supporting the new Constituent Assembly.[73] On 7 June, the Council had condemned additional attacks against UNTAC and warned that it would take "appropriate measures" against those trying to "overturn the democratic process in Cambodia through violence".[74] The European Community, on 10 June, and the Association of South-East Asian Nations (ASEAN), on 18 June, called on all Cambodian parties to respect the results of the elections.[75] Viet Nam, on 3 June, pledged its continued support for the Paris Agreements.[76] On 16 June, Prince Sihanouk announced the formation of an Interim Joint Administration with Prince Ranariddh and Mr. Hun Sen as the Co-Chairmen of a Council of Ministers. Though this arrangement had not been foreseen under the Paris Agreements, it appeared to provide a cooperative framework that would contribute to the country's stability and reconciliation.

116   On 21 June 1993, with many elected CPP representatives already participating in the work of the new Constituent Assembly, the SOC formally recognized the election results. On 22 July 1993, ASEAN welcomed the formation of the Interim Joint Administration and reiterated its support for the process of Cambodia's national reconciliation.[77] And on 13 July 1993, Mr. Khieu Samphan returned to Phnom Penh,

73/Document 94
See page 318

74/Document 91
See page 313;
Document 96
See page 319

75/Document 93
See page 312;
Document 95
See page 319

76/Document 90
See page 312

77/Document 99
See page 326

ending the PDK's three-month absence from the capital. At a meeting of the SNC on the same day, he spoke of the need for national reconciliation and said that the PDK might be willing to merge its forces into a national army and end its resistance. These overtures towards reconciliation subsequently proved shallow.

117   Notwithstanding the many difficulties that still lay ahead, the Cambodian people, with help from the United Nations and the international community, had just registered a significant triumph for the principles of democracy and self-determination. In doing so Cambodia had also become, especially for other shattered or disaster-stricken countries, the world's newest symbol of hope and possibility.

VIII   Towards a new government

118   It was in a triumphant atmosphere, but one not free from worry about the future, that UNTAC was to declare its mandate complete, withdraw its personnel and assess future United Nations involvement in rehabilitation, reconstruction and human rights work in Cambodia.

Post-election period

119   Cease-fire violations continued after the elections, as did banditry and attacks on ethnic Vietnamese and UNTAC personnel. In mid-August 1993, following attacks by PDK forces on civilians and on part of the ancient Angkor Wat complex in Siem Riep Province, the Cambodian Armed Forces launched an offensive against the PDK. This internal military conflict with the Khmer Rouge continues to this day and is the single greatest threat to all the achievements of the UNTAC period.

120   There were other, more encouraging developments in the months following the election, foremost among them the existence of a Constituent Assembly concentrating on the main task of the interim period: drafting and adopting a new Cambodian Constitution. Under the Paris Agreements, the work was to be completed within three months from the date of the election, at which point the Assembly would transform itself into a legislative assembly, forming the basis of a new Cambodian Government. At the request of the Interim Joint Administration, UNTAC provided technical comments on the draft Constitution, placing particular emphasis on strengthening the human rights–related provisions.

121   An important move aimed at reducing banditry, improving stability and promoting a smooth and orderly transfer to the new Government was effected in mid-July 1993, when the Security Council agreed that UNTAC should provide $20 million in emergency financial assistance to Cambodia.[78] The funds were to be used to pay the salaries of civil servants, police and members of the armed forces, many of whom had gone months if not longer without being paid, and to provide budgetary support for the administrative, police and military structures of the provisional government. It was hoped that such assistance would also encourage Cambodians to begin redirecting their allegiance from the factions of the past to their future government.

78/Document 98
See page 325

UNTAC *withdraws*

79/Document 97
See page 320;
Document 100
See page 326

122   UNTAC troops began withdrawing from Cambodia on 2 August 1993.[79] By this time, the repatriation component and most of the electoral staff had already left the country. Civil administration staff continued performing their functions, seeking to ensure a smooth transition. The remaining members of the information/education division shifted their focus to post-UNTAC concerns, such as producing radio programmes on human rights, reconstruction and long-term development. Human rights officers were preparing for the opening of a Centre for Human Rights office in Cambodia (the office was established on 1 October).[80] Several local human rights non-governmental organizations had been established in Cambodia, and UNTAC provided these groups with materials, training, small grants for basic office expenses and a resource centre and library for all to use collectively. By the time of the elections, membership in Cambodian human rights non-governmental organizations, including Buddhist, student and women's groups, amounted to some 150,000 persons.

80/Document 109
See page 340

123   On 27 August, in resolution 860 (1993), the Security Council, while confirming that UNTAC's mandate would end upon the creation of a new Cambodian Government, took note of the request by the Interim Joint Administration to maintain UNTAC's mandate until the Constituent Assembly had completed its work on the Constitution and a new Government was established.[81]

81/Document 101
See page 330

124   Cambodia's historic achievement was consolidated at a ceremony in Phnom Penh on 24 September 1993. First, the new Constitution was formally promulgated by Prince Sihanouk. The document established a constitutional monarchy, "The Kingdom of Cambodia", an independent, sovereign, peaceful, neutral and non-aligned State. Accordingly, Prince Sihanouk was then elected King by the Royal Council of the Throne. By article 7 of the new Constitution, the Monarch holds the throne but shall not hold power. In his first act, King Sihanouk named Prince Ranariddh and Mr. Hun Sen as First and Second Prime Ministers in Cambodia's new Government. The Constituent Assembly then transformed itself into a legislative assembly. Speaking to the press following the ceremony, King Sihanouk said, "From now on, the Cambodian people are masters of their own destiny."

82/Document 102
See page 331;
Document 103
See page 339;
Document 104
See page 334

Continued United Nations presence

125   With these events, UNTAC's mandate came to an end.[82] However, this did not mean the end of United Nations involvement in Cambodia in either the short or long term. Indeed, much of the United

Nations system was expected to be involved in the ongoing venture of Cambodia's reconstruction and development. Most immediately, though, the country faced ongoing security concerns. This led the two Prime Ministers, in early October 1993, to ask the United Nations to consider dispatching a limited number of unarmed military observers to Cambodia as a confidence-building measure and thus contribute to the stability of the country and its new Government.

126   On 4 November 1993, the Security Council by its resolution 880 (1993) extended the period of withdrawal of the mine clearance and training unit until 30 November and, for elements of the military police and medical components of UNTAC, until 31 December.[83] The Council also established a team of 20 military liaison officers for a single six-month period to report on matters affecting security in Cambodia, maintain liaison with the Government and assist the Government in dealing with residual military matters relating to the Paris Agreements. During its time in Cambodia, the liaison team followed the integration of factional forces into the Government Army and, at the Government's request, conducted observation missions to Pailin, to the Officer Training Academy in Kompong Speu Province, to the Military Police Training School in Phnom Penh and to other areas.[84]

127   Even after the conclusion of UNTAC and the end of the mandate of the military liaison team, the Paris Agreements remained in force, with a shift in focus from peace-keeping to post-conflict peace-building. "There is a danger", said my predecessor, Javier Pérez de Cuéllar, at the 23 October 1991 ceremony at which the Paris Agreements were signed, "that peace will remain ephemeral if the Cambodian people and some of its immediate neighbours continue to live in destitution and poverty. Peace on the battlefield should be enriched and consolidated by a concerted effort for the reconstruction and development of Cambodia . . ."

128   The Declaration on the Rehabilitation and Reconstruction of Cambodia, one of the three main instruments of the Paris Agreements, gives the United Nations and its specialized agencies an important role in supporting Cambodia's reconstruction and advancement. The activities to be carried out following the departure of UNTAC were to emphasize rehabilitation, mine clearance, human rights, public administration reform, reintegration of returnees and displaced persons, humanitarian and technical work in the fields of agriculture, health care, education, public utilities and other social services. In the light of a request by the new Government, and as an indication of the Organization's continuing commitment to Cambodia, in April 1994 I appointed Mr. Benny Widyono (Indonesia) as my Representative in Cambodia to coordinate the United Nations presence there.

129   As the Cambodian people contemplated their nation's long-

83/Document 105
See page 335;
Document 106
See page 336;
Document 107
See page 338;
Document 108
See page 339

84/Document 110
See page 341;
Document 112
See page 343;
Document 115
See page 344

term prospects following the elections and the phased withdrawal of UNTAC, they were filled with both high expectations and lingering uncertainties. On the one hand, they and their leaders had made a good start in creating a new society based on justice, freedom, mutual tolerance and a better life for all. But two important questions remained unanswered.

130   First, would the PDK choose to stay outside the peace process? By early February 1994, approximately 3,000 PDK soldiers had defected to the government side, but the PDK retained a substantial force and was still a threat to the peace. During a joint visit by the First and Second Prime Ministers to United Nations Headquarters in New York on 4 and 5 October 1993, Prince Ranariddh told the General Assembly and the Security Council that the new Government was "prepared to welcome the Khmer Rouge into the Royal Armed Forces of Cambodia" and as advisers to the Government, provided that it recognized the Government and dismantled its army and administration. At the time, there were signs that the PDK was in fact seeking to rejoin the Cambodian political community, but the subsequent resumption of armed confrontations between the PDK and Government forces has cast doubt over the immediate chances for real peace. Amid ongoing fighting in the north and north-western parts of the country, the internal security situation in Cambodia grew increasingly precarious. King Sihanouk wrote to me expressing his concern. I assured King Sihanouk that I shared his concern, supported his efforts aimed at convening talks on national reconciliation and would do my utmost to help the people of

85/Document 113
See page 344;
Document 114
See page 344

Cambodia to achieve peace and rebuild their country.[85] On 13 May 1994, the Security Council decided not to extend the mandate of the 20-person Military Liaison Team but rather agreed that I should appoint three military advisers to assist my Representative in Cambodia following the end of the Team's mandate. These advisers, from Belgium, France and Malaysia, took up their posts the same month, continuing a United Nations presence in Cambodia which, in the Government's view,

86/Document 115
See page 345

contributed to a sense of security among the Cambodian people.[86]

131   Secondly, would Cambodia's fate sustain the outside world's interest during an era of limited resources and "donor fatigue"? Actual funding for UNTAC's rehabilitation efforts had been delayed considerably by donors' pre-election fears about the durability of the peace process. But donor response following the elections was relatively positive, and as of 31 October 1993, $290 million in pledges had been disbursed, covering food security and village development. Although extensive rebuilding efforts had been undertaken by UNTAC, massive reconstruction was still required throughout the country.

132   Following the end of UNTAC's mandate, reconstruction was to be coordinated and monitored by the International Committee on the

Reconstruction of Cambodia—a consultative body envisaged under the Paris Agreements whose membership was open to all countries and international organizations contributing to the long-term reconstruction of Cambodia. At a September 1993 meeting of the Committee, new pledges of $120 million were made. I reiterated at that time that the future of Cambodia's freedom and democracy remained a matter of great importance to the international community. At the Committee's second meeting, held in Tokyo in March 1994, I renewed my call for a speedy and effective international response in support of Cambodia's efforts at the monumental task of nation-building.[87] While taking full account of the sovereign wishes of the new Cambodian Government, the United Nations will continue to offer its full support to the Government and people of Cambodia.

87/Document 111
See page 342

133   UNTAC's mandate ended on 24 September 1993 with the establishment of the new Cambodian Government. The military component of UNTAC completed its withdrawal in mid-November, and the small number of remaining administrative and other personnel left Cambodia at the end of May 1994.

134   I met with Foreign Minister Prince Norodom Sirivudh on 1 October 1994 when he was in New York for the 49th session of the General Assembly. In response to a request from the Cambodian Government, I wrote to the Security Council on 10 October 1994 to inform it of my decision to extend Mr. Widyono's term for a further six months to April 1995 and that he should continue to be assisted by three military advisers for the same duration.[88] The Security Council welcomed this decision on 19 October 1994.[89] As the United Nations continues its cooperation with the Government of Cambodia in 1995, I remain ready to assist as Cambodians pursue national reconciliation and the reconstruction of their country.

88/Document 116
See page 346

89/Document 117
See page 346

IX   Conclusion

135   The United Nations was drawn into the situation in Cambodia long before UNTAC was conceived. The rise of communism in Indo-China, the spillover from the war in Viet Nam and the multiple violent changes in the Cambodian power structure over the past 25 years all elicited comment from the international community. The East-West split of the cold war years was reflected in the involvement of foreign interests on all sides of the Cambodian battlefield, and peace seemed to elude the country even as its neighbours began to rebuild. The United Nations articulated its position on the Cambodian situation consistently through the late 1970s and into the 1980s, but not until an embryonic vision of peace began to form among the Cambodian factions in 1988, and finally took shape in Paris in 1989, did the scope of the United Nations' role in the peace process fully emerge. Not only would international peace-keepers monitor a cease-fire in the Cambodian civil war, but the United Nations would oversee the disarming of the warring factions, provide transportation home for more than 360,000 refugees, organize and carry out a free and fair election and provide financial and logistical support to rehabilitate the country's infrastructure. For the first time in the history of the United Nations, this comprehensive approach to international assistance went well beyond either conflict resolution or the provision of humanitarian aid; rather, UNTAC sought actively to support Cambodia's social, political and economic institutions as part of the transition to peace.

136   UNTAC brought 15,500 troops and 6,000 civilians to Cambodia to staff a $1.7 billion effort that reached out to nearly every district in every province of the country. One of the four Cambodian factions—the Khmer Rouge—decided early on that it was not willing to honour its commitment to the peace plan or to cooperate with the UN forces. This defiance and refusal to work towards reconciliation disrupted the work of UNTAC at nearly every turn, and forced the abandonment of a major component of the peace plan: demobilization of the four Cambodian armies. Beyond this stumbling block, though, the momentum for peace, democracy and economic stability throughout the country was sufficient for UNTAC to carry out the rest of its mandate with a significant degree of success. The fact that a huge number of people, some of whom had been living in refugee camps for up to 15 years, were able to return peacefully and willingly to their country in time to participate in its democratic renewal represents a major achievement. UNTAC also boosted Cambodia's economy by raising funds internation-

ally for economic rehabilitation and expansion throughout the country. The most striking achievement of the UNTAC period in Cambodia was the democratic election that brought the Cambodian people and the international community together in a tense and poignant moment of shared triumph. After a remarkably peaceful election, a new coalition Government was formed, and the country seemed to embrace the spirit of political resolve and courage embodied in its new leadership. Certain problems remain in post-UNTAC Cambodia, the most significant being the continued aggression of the Khmer Rouge forces, but UNTAC showed the potential for addressing political reconciliation and socio-economic rehabilitation on multiple fronts simultaneously as a viable intervention strategy.

137 Another notable feature of UNTAC was the way in which United Nations personnel translated diplomatic policy into consequential actions. The Paris Agreements provided a road-map for implementing peace in Cambodia, but much of the detail was left to decision makers "on the ground", and to individual UNTAC personnel, to work out. The difficulties faced by UNTAC civilian administrators attempting to exert control over local government bodies is just one example. The provision in the Paris Agreements allowing for UNTAC's direct supervision of certain State of Cambodia functions was initially criticized as being unfairly restrictive of the Phnom Penh Government, but this provision turned out to be nearly impossible to achieve because of language problems, lack of enforcement measures and inadequate experience on the part of UNTAC personnel with the kind of bureaucratic structures and procedures employed by the SOC.

138 The international community can take satisfaction from the peace-keeping operation it mounted and supported in Cambodia. As the new Government seeks to maintain the gains made during the UNTAC period, it is safe to say that UNTAC's 18-month presence in Cambodia left encouraging legacies: confidence in the democratic process, the will to engage and compete on the international stage and an inclination to find political rather than military solutions to internal conflicts. It is also clear that the country's situation will continue to reveal lessons for the evolving role of effective United Nations peace-building.

BOUTROS BOUTROS-GHALI

Index

[The numbers following the entries refer to paragraph numbers in the text.]

Section Two
Chronology and Documents

I Chronology of events

18 March 1970
While on a visit to the Soviet Union, Prince Norodom Sihanouk is removed as head of State in a *coup d'état* led by his Prime Minister, General Lon Nol. Prince Sihanouk sets up a government-in-exile (the Royal Government of National Union of Cambodia). The Khmer Republic established by General Lon Nol becomes involved in the Viet Nam war.

17 April 1975
The forces of the Khmer Rouge, under Pol Pot, overrun the Government of General Lon Nol.

1975-1978
The Khmer Rouge regime (also known as Democratic Kampuchea) institutes policies of forced agrarian labour. An estimated 1 million Cambodians die from disease, starvation, torture and execution.

25 December 1978
Vietnamese forces enter Cambodia. The People's Revolutionary Party of Kampuchea, backed by Viet Nam, takes control of Phnom Penh and establishes the People's Republic of Kampuchea.

14 November 1979
The General Assembly adopts the first of its series of resolutions calling for the withdrawal of all foreign forces and for self-determination for the Cambodian people. The resolutions also request the Secretary-General to exercise his good offices in order to contribute to a peaceful solution of the problem.

22 June 1982
Three opposition factions — the United National Front for an Independent, Neutral, Peaceful and Cooperative Cambodia (FUNCINPEC), the Khmer People's Liberation Front (KPNLF) and the Khmer Rouge (also known as the Party of Democratic Kampuchea, or PDK) — form a coalition government-in-exile led by Prince Sihanouk. The coalition occupies the seat reserved for Cambodia at the United Nations under the name Democratic Kampuchea.

4-5 December 1987
Prince Sihanouk and Mr. Hun Sen, Prime Minister of the Phnom Penh Government, hold talks in France.

June-July 1988
The Secretary-General, Javier Pérez de Cuéllar, sends his Special Representative for Humanitarian Affairs in South-East Asia, Mr. Rafeeuddin Ahmed, to the region to relay to concerned Governments and the four Cambodian parties — the three opposition factions and the Phnom Penh authorities — a set of proposals for a comprehensive settlement plan.

25-28 July 1989
The three opposition factions and the Phnom Penh Government hold direct talks in Indonesia.

30 July–30 August 1989
The Paris Conference on Cambodia, attended by the four Cambodian parties, 19 countries (including France and Indonesia as Co-Chairmen), the United Nations Secretary-General and his Special Representative for Humanitarian Affairs in South-East Asia, maps out a broad strategy for peace but is suspended without achieving agreement on a comprehensive political settlement.

October 1989
Australia puts forward a proposal for a solution based on a United Nations role in the administration of Cambodia during a transitional period.

15-16 January 1990
The five permanent members of the Security Council begin talks on the situation in Cambodia.
See Document 1, page 87

27-28 August 1990
At talks in New York, the five permanent members of the Security Council reach a breakthrough agreement on a framework for a comprehensive political settlement involving, among other things, a principal role for the United Nations.
See Document 2, page 88

9-10 September 1990
At talks in Jakarta, the four Cambodian parties accept the framework and agree to form the Supreme National Council (SNC).
See Document 3, page 93

20 September 1990
The Security Council endorses the framework.
See Document 4, page 94

26 November 1990
At deliberations in Paris in which the Secretary-General's representative participates actively, the Co-Chairmen of the Paris Conference (France and Indonesia) and the five permanent members of the Security Council agree on the text of the draft Agreements on a Comprehensive Political Settlement of the Cambodia Conflict.
See Document 5, page 95; and Document 6, page 96

21-23 December 1990
At talks in Paris, the Co-Chairmen of the Paris Conference formally present to the SNC the 26 November text of the draft settlement agreements. The SNC concurs on most of the fundamental points.
See Document 6, page 96

1-2 February 1991
The Co-Chairmen of the Paris Conference visit Thailand and Viet Nam to formally present the draft agreements.
See Document 7, page 112

22 April 1991
The Secretary-General and the Co-Chairmen of the Paris Conference issue a joint appeal for a voluntary cease-fire as a gesture of good faith for the success of the peace process. The Cambodian parties inform the Secretary-General that they intend to respect the appeal.
See Document 8, page 113

1 May 1991
A cease-fire goes into effect.

24-26 June 1991
At talks in Pattaya, Thailand, the SNC decides to call for an immediate and unconditional voluntary cease-fire and a halt to outside military assistance.
See Document 9, page 113

16-17 July 1991
At talks in Beijing, the SNC elects Prince Sihanouk as its President and requests the Secretary-General to send a survey mission to Cambodia to begin the process of preparing for the military aspects of a peace-keeping operation.
See Document 10, page 115

17-18 July 1991
In Beijing, the five permanent members of the Security Council and the representative of Indonesia, in his capacity as Co-Chairman of the Paris Conference,

meet with Prince Sihanouk to exchange views on the situation and on the direction the ongoing negotiations could be expected to take.
See Document 12, page 117

19 July 1991
The Foreign Ministers of the Association of South-East Asian Nations (ASEAN) reiterate their support for the peace process.
See Document 11, page 116

8 August 1991
The Secretary-General informs the Security Council that he intends to dispatch a survey mission to Cambodia as soon as possible.
See Document 13, page 119

26-29 August 1991
At talks in Pattaya, the SNC achieves significant progress in finding compromise solutions to most of the outstanding difficulties.
See Document 15, page 122

29-30 August 1991
In Pattaya, the five permanent members of the Security Council, the co-Chairmen of the Paris Conference and the SNC hold their first joint meeting and express their satisfaction with the progress towards a settlement.
See Document 14, page 120

20-21 September 1991
In New York, the five permanent members of the Security Council and the representative of the Indonesian Co-Chairman hold a second joint meeting with members of the SNC and note that the process of creating a settlement agreement seems to have entered its final phase.
See Document 16, page 124

30 September 1991
The Secretary-General submits to the Security Council his proposals for a United Nations Advance Mission in Cambodia.
See Document 17, page 125

16 October 1991
The Security Council establishes the United Nations Advance Mission in Cambodia (UNAMIC) and calls for its deployment immediately after the signature of the settlement agreements.
See Document 18, page 131

23 October 1991
In Paris, the Agreements on a Comprehensive Political Settlement of the Cambodia Conflict are

signed at the final meeting of the Paris Conference on Cambodia, marking the beginning of the transitional period in Cambodia.
See Document 19, page 132; and Document 20, page 149

31 October 1991
The Security Council expresses its full support for the Paris Agreements and requests the preparation of a detailed plan of implementation.
See Document 21, page 149

9 November 1991
The first UNAMIC personnel arrive in Cambodia. On **14 November**, the Secretary-General informs the Security Council that UNAMIC is operational and that deployment will proceed rapidly.
See Document 22, page 150

20 November 1991
The General Assembly expresses its full support for the Paris Agreements.
See Document 23, page 150

28 December 1991
The five permanent members of the Security Council appeal to all Cambodian parties to respect the Paris Agreements.
See Document 24, page 151

30 December 1991
The Secretary-General recommends that the mandate of UNAMIC be expanded to include training in mine clearance and the initiation of a mine-clearance programme.
See Document 25, page 152

8 January 1992
The Security Council approves the Secretary-General's recommendations and expands UNAMIC's mandate accordingly.
See Document 26, page 155

9 January 1992
The newly elected Secretary-General, Boutros Boutros-Ghali, names Mr. Yasushi Akashi (Japan) as his Special Representative for Cambodia.

18 January 1992
To prepare for the first phase of the deployment of the United Nations Transitional Authority in Cambodia (UNTAC) and prevent any erosion of the peace process, the Secretary-General seeks early approval by the General Assembly of an initial appropriation of $200 million. The Assembly approves the Secretary-General's request on **14 February**.
See Document 27, page 155

20 January 1992
In a letter to Prince Sihanouk, the Secretary-General states that he will continue to do all he can to accelerate the deployment of UNTAC. In a reply dated **23 January**, Prince Sihanouk pledges his continued support as well as that of the SNC.
See Document 28, page 156; and Document 29, page 157

19 February 1992
The Secretary-General submits to the Security Council his proposed implementation plan for UNTAC.
See Document 30, page 158

28 February 1992
The Security Council establishes UNTAC.
See Document 31, page 184

8 March 1992
In a letter to the Secretary-General, Prince Sihanouk expresses his thanks for the creation of UNTAC and pledges his support for the mission.
See Document 32, page 185

15 March 1992
The Special Representative of the Secretary-General and the UNTAC Force Commander, Lieutenant-General John M. Sanderson (Australia), arrive in Cambodia.
See Document 33, page 185

30 March 1992
The Office of the United Nations High Commissioner for Refugees (UNHCR) begins the repatriation of more than 360,000 Cambodian refugees and displaced persons from camps in Thailand and along the Thai-Cambodian border.
See Document 33, page 185

1 April 1992
A draft Electoral Law drawn up by UNTAC is presented to the SNC for review.
See Document 33, page 185

20 April 1992
The Secretary-General launches an international humanitarian appeal for $593 million to meet the costs of the repatriation and rehabilitation efforts.
See Document 33, page 185

1 May 1992
In his first progress report on UNTAC, the Secretary-General reports that the mission has begun to establish itself both politically and militarily.
See Document 33, page 185

9 May 1992
The UNTAC Force Commander announces that, subsequent to the cease-fire in effect since 1 May 1991, phase II of the cease-fire — the regroupment, cantonment, disarming and demobilization of forces — will begin on 13 June 1992.
See Document 35, page 191

30 May 1992
Viet Nam states that it has no military forces, weapons or equipment on Cambodian territory and that there are no military forces, weapons, ammunition or military equipment of any Cambodian parties on Vietnamese territory.
See Document 34, page 190

12 June 1992
In a special report to the Security Council, the Secretary-General states that he has concluded that phase II of the cease-fire must proceed as scheduled despite the declared intention of the PDK not to participate in the process. In a Presidential Statement, the Security Council endorses the Secretary-General's position.
See Document 35, page 191; and Document 36, page 194

13 June 1992
Phase II of the cease-fire begins.

22 June 1992
At the Ministerial Conference on the Rehabilitation and Reconstruction of Cambodia held in Tokyo, donors pledge $880 million and agree to establish the International Committee on the Reconstruction of Cambodia. In separate talks, the PDK does not accept an informal "proposal for discussion" designed to facilitate its participation in implementation of the Paris Agreements.
See Document 37, page 194

27 June 1992
In a letter to the Secretary-General, Mr. Khieu Samphan of the PDK forwards a set of proposals concerning cooperation between UNTAC and the SNC. In a reply dated 7 July, the Secretary-General states that UNTAC will continue its efforts to implement the Paris Agreements and seeks the faction's compliance with phase II of the cease-fire
See Document 38, page 198; and Document 39, page 199

12 July 1992
The PDK puts forth a proposal linking its regroupment and cantonment with a dismantling of the Phnom Penh Government.
See Document 40, page 200

14 July 1992
The Secretary-General reports to the Security Council on the continuing non-compliance of the PDK and on efforts to persuade it to comply with its obligations under the Paris Agreements.
See Document 41, page 201

21 July 1992
The Security Council approves the efforts of the Secretary-General and UNTAC to continue to implement the Paris Agreements, and states that international assistance for the rehabilitation and reconstruction of Cambodia should now benefit only those factions fulfilling their obligations under the accords.
See Document 42, page 205

27 July 1992
In a letter to the Secretary-General, the Special Representative reviews the situation in Cambodia, stating that he will continue his efforts to gain the PDK's cooperation and implement the Paris Agreements.
See Document 43, page 206

12 August 1992
The Electoral Law is promulgated.
See Document 45, page 211

17 August 1992
The registration of political parties begins.
See Document 45, page 211

16 September 1992
Australia spells out a series of ideas for the coming months of the peace process in Cambodia, stating, among other things, that UNTAC should press on with implementation as fully as possible with or without the PDK, that the Co-Chairmen of the Paris Conference on Cambodia should undertake consultations in an attempt to break the deadlock and that the Security Council should set a date for the imposition of sanctions against the PDK.
See Document 44, page 208

21 September 1992
In his second progress report on UNTAC, the Secretary-General states that the electoral process should be carried out in accordance with the implementation timetable.
See Document 45, page 211

22 September 1992
The SNC sets a moratorium on the export of logs in order to protect Cambodia's natural resources; this action is taken over the objections of the PDK.
See Document 65, page 254

25 September 1992
Following a meeting with the Secretary-General, the five permanent members of the Security Council assure him of their determination to support his efforts to overcome the difficulties being experienced in securing full implementation of the Paris Agreements.
See Document 46, page 219

29 September 1992
In a letter to the Secretary-General, Mr. Khieu Samphan states that several steps outlined in Australia's paper of 16 September 1992 would "jeopardize the integrity" of the Paris Agreements.
See Document 47, page 222

30 September 1992
With a view to finding a solution to the deadlock in the peace process, Mr. Son Sann of the KPNLF sets out his views on a variety of issues.
See Document 48, page 224

5 October 1992
Voter registration begins.

13 October 1992
The Security Council confirms that the electoral process shall proceed according to the timetable.
See Document 49, page 225

31 October 1992
The Governments of Thailand and Japan report to the Secretary-General that their talks with the PDK failed to resolve certain of its objections to implementation of the Agreement.
See Document 54, page 229

2 November 1992
The Secretary-General requests the Co-Chairmen of the Paris Conference (France and Indonesia) to undertake consultations with a view to fully implementing the peace process, informs Prince Sihanouk that this step has been taken and welcomes Prince Sihanouk's intention to meet in Beijing on 7 and 8 November 1992 with the Co-Chairmen of the Paris Conference and with members of the SNC.
See Document 50, page 227; Document 51, page 227; and Document 52, page 228

7-8 November 1992
Consultations in Beijing fail to break the impasse with the PDK, which says it will not take part in the electoral process or the elections as long as it feels that the "neutral political environment" called for in the Paris Agreements has not been created.
See Document 54, page 229

9 November 1992
Radio UNTAC begins broadcasting from Phnom Penh.

12 November 1992
In a letter to the Secretary-General, Prince Sihanouk expresses his regret at the lack of progress in Beijing.
See Document 53, page 229

15 November 1992
The Secretary-General reports that, despite the efforts of the Co-Chairmen of the Paris Conference, the PDK is not prepared to comply with its obligations under the Paris Agreements, and that the process of cantonment, disarmament and demobilization has been effectively suspended. Acknowledging concern about increased military tensions in the country, the Secretary-General nevertheless advises that "patient diplomacy" remains the best means of getting the peace process back on track.
See Document 54, page 229

30 November 1992
The Security Council confirms that the elections will be held no later than May 1993 and calls for measures to prevent the supply of petroleum products from reaching areas occupied by any party not complying with the military provisions of the Paris Agreements.
See Document 55, page 243

30 November 1992
Thailand states that border checkpoints referred to in paragraph 12 of Security Council resolution 792 (1992) should be established according to the Paris Agreements, on the Cambodian side of the border and inside Cambodia.
See Document 56, page 245

2 December 1992
In a Presidential statement, the Security Council condemns attacks against United Nations personnel serving with UNTAC and with other United Nations peacekeeping operations.
See Document 57, page 246

20 December 1992
The PDK claims that recent incidents in which UNTAC personnel were detained by the PDK were provoked by UNTAC and are part of a "smear campaign . . . designed to mislead the United Nations Security Council into enforcing sanctions" against the PDK.
See Document 58, page 246

22 December 1992
In a Presidential statement, the Security Council strongly condemns the illegal detention of UNTAC personnel in Cambodia by elements of the PDK.
See Document 59, page 248

30 December 1992
In a letter to the Secretary-General, the Minister for Foreign Affairs of Viet Nam expresses his deep concern at killings by PDK forces of people of Vietnamese descent.
See Document 60, page 248

31 December 1992
UNTAC military personnel complete their redeployment so that their positions correspond with Cambodia's provincial borders and the planned deployment of electoral teams for the campaign and polling; the original military deployment pattern had been based on the requirements of the regroupment and cantonment process.
See Document 65, page 254

5 January 1993
In separate letters to the Secretary-General, Mr. Hun Sen and Prince Norodom Ranariddh, son of Prince Sihanouk and President of FUNCINPEC, express their concern at the continuing difficulties, particularly those posed by the PDK, being encountered in implementing the Paris Agreements.
See Document 61, page 249; and Document 62, page 251

15 January 1993
ASEAN Foreign Ministers express their deep concern over the impasse in the Cambodian peace process.
See Document 64, page 253

19 January 1993
In a letter to the Secretary-General, several members of the SNC express their view that Cambodians living overseas should be permitted to register to vote overseas.
See Document 63, page 252

25 January 1993
In his third progress report on UNTAC, the Secretary-General notes the "remarkable success" of the voter registration process but states that UNTAC's efforts to create and maintain a neutral political environment needed for elections are being hampered by a number of negative developments.
See Document 65, page 254

28 January 1993
The SNC decides that the elections will take place from 23 to 25 May 1993; for logistical reasons, three days

of voting are added, so that the elections are scheduled to run from 23 to 28 May 1993.

28-29 January 1993
Replying to the 5 January 1993 letters from Mr. Hun Sen and Prince Ranariddh, the Secretary-General reaffirms UNTAC's commitment to improving public security, creating a neutral political environment for elections and fully implementing the Paris Agreements.
See Document 66, page 268; and Document 67, page 268

31 January 1993
The voter registration period ends.

1 February 1993
The Secretary-General informs the Security Council of Prince Sihanouk's decision that the presidential election should take place after the constituent assembly adopts the new constitution of Cambodia; Prince Sihanouk had suggested that such an election might be held concurrently with the elections for the constituent assembly.
See Document 68, page 269

10 February 1993
The SNC sets a moratorium on the export of minerals and gems; this action is taken over the objections of the PDK.
See Document 69, page 269

13 February 1993
In a report to the Security Council, the Secretary-General discusses progress made and difficulties encountered as UNTAC proceeds with preparations for the elections.
See Document 69, page 269

19 February 1993
The United Nations Commission on Human Rights adopts a resolution requesting the Secretary-General to ensure a continued United Nations human rights presence in Cambodia after the end of the UNTAC mandate, including through the operational presence of the United Nations Centre for Human Rights.
See Document 70, page 277

8 March 1993
The Security Council endorses the proposed election dates and expresses its readiness to support the constituent assembly to be elected.
See Document 71, page 278

11 March 1993
Viet Nam denounces attacks committed on 10 March by the forces of Democratic Kampuchea against Vietnamese residents of the village of Chong Kneas, Cambodia.
See Document 72, page 280

30 March 1993
UNHCR closes Site 2, the last and largest of nine refugee camps along the Thai-Cambodian border.

5 April 1993
In a Presidential statement, the Security Council strongly condemns attacks on UNTAC, which had resulted in the death of two Bangladeshi and three Bulgarian members of UNTAC.
See Document 73, page 281

7 April 1993
The electoral campaign begins.
See Document 79, page 285

7 April 1993
The European Community expresses its strong support for the implementation of the Paris Agreements and its concern at the continued cease-fire violations, in particular attacks on UNTAC military and civilian personnel and on people of Vietnamese origin.
See Document 74, page 281

13 April 1993
The PDK declares that it will not participate in the elections, closes its office in Phnom Penh and withdraws from the capital. UNTAC offers to provide security should the PDK decide to return to the city.
See Document 75, page 282

22 April 1993
In a Presidential statement, the Security Council condemns the killings of United Nations peace-keeping personnel, including members of UNTAC.
See Document 76, page 282

23 April 1993
The States signatory to the Paris Agreements condemn all acts of violence, declare their firm determination to support the electoral process and call upon all Cambodian parties to abide by their commitments under the Agreements.
See Document 77, page 283

26 April 1993
The Secretary-General reports to the Security Council on the results of UNTAC investigations into recent incidents resulting in the deaths of UNTAC personnel.
See Document 78, page 284

3 May 1993
In his fourth progress report on UNTAC, the Secretary-General states that, despite the likelihood of further violence, the United Nations must do its utmost to proceed with the best possible elections under imperfect conditions.
See Document 79, page 285

7 May 1993
In a letter to the Secretary-General, Mr. Hun Sen makes various requests concerning the electoral process.
See Document 80, page 302

15 May 1993
In his final pre-election report to the Security Council, the Secretary-General outlines the security measures that have been taken to protect the polling.
See Document 81, page 303

18 May 1993
The ASEAN Foreign Ministers express their concern about attempts to disrupt the elections, state that the elections should proceed as scheduled and call on all Cambodian parties to respect the election results.
See Document 82, page 306

19 May 1993
The electoral campaign ends.

20 May 1993
The Security Council expresses its satisfaction with the arrangements made by the United Nations for the conduct of the elections and fully supports the decision of the Secretary-General that the elections should be held as scheduled.
See Document 83, page 306

22 May 1992
In a Presidential statement, the Security Council condemns shelling attacks on UNTAC on 21 May in which two persons were killed, and calls upon the Cambodian people to exercise their right to vote.
See Document 84, page 307

23-28 May 1993
Voting takes place peacefully and without major incident.
See Document 88, page 310; and Document 92, page 313

28 May 1993
In a letter to Prince Sihanouk, the Secretary-General congratulates the Cambodian people for their massive participation in the elections and welcomes Prince Sihanouk's pledge of support for the next stages of the peace process. In his reply of 31 May, Prince Sihanouk thanks UNTAC for the work it has done.
See Document 85, page 308; and Document 87, page 309

28 May 1993
The Secretary-General reports to the Security Council on UNTACs investigation of the 21 May shelling incident.
See Document 86, page 309

29 May 1993
The Special Representative of the Secretary-General declares the conduct of the elections to have been free and fair.
See Document 88, page 310

2 June 1993
The Security Council endorses the conduct of the elections.
See Document 89, page 311

4 June 1993
Viet Nam reaffirms its commitment to observe the Paris Agreements and expresses its willingness to recognize a new government in Cambodia.
See Document 90, page 312

8 June 1993
In a Presidential statement, the Security Council strongly condemns an armed attack carried out on 7 June against Pakistani and Malaysian platoons of UNTAC.
See Document 91, page 313

10 June 1993
The final vote tally is released. FUNCINPEC wins 45 per cent of the vote, the Cambodian People's Party — CPP, the political party of the Government of the State of Cambodia (SOC) — wins 38 per cent and the rest of the vote is shared among 18 other political parties. The Special Representative of the Secretary-General declares that the results fairly and accurately reflect the will of the Cambodian people and must be respected. FUNCINPEC, the SOC and the KPNLF agree to set up a single national army.
See Document 92, page 313

10 June 1993
The European Community congratulates the people of Cambodia on the successful elections, calls on all Cambodian parties to respect the results and pledges continued support for the peace process.
See Document 93, page 317

12 June 1993
A secessionist movement proclaims an "autonomous zone" in the eastern part of the country.

14 June 1993
The newly elected Constituent Assembly is sworn in.
See Document 97, page 320

15 June 1993
The secessionist threat collapses.

15 June 1993
The Security Council endorses the results of the election and fully supports the newly elected Constituent Assembly.
See Document 94, page 318

16 June 1993
Prince Sihanouk announces the formation of an Interim Joint Administration with Prince Ranariddh, the leader of FUNCINPEC, and Mr. Hun Sen, the leader of the CPP, as Co-Chairmen of a Council of Ministers.
See Document 97, page 320

18 June 1993
ASEAN Foreign Ministers call on all Cambodian parties to respect the results of the elections and urge the international community to support the Constituent Assembly and the new Cambodian Government.
See Document 95, page 319

22 June 1993
The Secretary-General reports to the Security Council on UNTAC's investigation into the 7 June armed attacks against Pakistani and Malaysian contingents.
See Document 96, page 320

14 July 1993
The Secretary-General recommends $20 million in emergency financial assistance to support the Interim Joint Administration's administrative, police and military structures. The Security Council approves this recommendation on **16 July.**
See Document 98, page 325

16 July 1993
The Secretary-General reports to the Security Council on developments since the election, outlines UNTAC's withdrawal plan and discusses preparations for the post-UNTAC period.
See Document 97, page 320

22 July 1993
The ASEAN Foreign Ministers welcome the formation of the Interim Joint Administration and call on the international community to continue to assist Cambodia with reconstruction and post-conflict peace-building.
See Document 99, page 326

2 August 1993
UNTAC troops begin to withdraw.
See Document 100, page 326

26 August 1993
The Secretary-General reports to the Security Council on further details concerning UNTAC's withdrawal and preparations for the post-UNTAC period.
See Document 100, page 326

27 August 1993
The Security Council approves the UNTAC withdrawal plan and decides that withdrawal would be completed by 15 November 1993.
See Document 101, page 330

24 September 1993
A new Cambodian Constitution is promulgated. Prince Sihanouk is elected King and names Prince Ranariddh and Mr. Hun Sen First and Second Prime Minister, respectively, in a new Government. The Constituent Assembly transforms itself into a legislative assembly. UNTAC's mandate ends.
See Document 103, page 333

30 September 1993
Following a meeting with the Secretary-General, the five permanent members of the Security Council note the successful fulfilment by UNTAC of its mandate and agree to consider, at the request of the Cambodian Government, how a future United Nations presence in Cambodia would contribute further to peace and stability after the departure of UNTAC.
See Document 102, page 331

1 October 1993
The United Nations Centre for Human Rights establishes a Cambodia field office in Phnom Penh to carry out a wide-ranging human rights programme in cooperation with the Cambodian Government and Cambodian non-governmental organizations.

5 October 1993
The Secretary-General reports to the Security Council on the end of UNTAC's mandate and the withdrawal of its personnel.
See Document 103, page 333

5 October 1993
In a Presidential statement, the Security Council stresses the importance of the continued support of the international community to the consolidation of peace and democracy and the promotion of development in Cambodia.
See Document 104, page 334

7 October 1993
The Secretary-General reports to the Security Council on a request by the Government of Cambodia for the dispatch of 20 to 30 unarmed United Nations military observers to Cambodia for six months following the end of UNTAC's mandate.
See Document 105, page 335

27 October 1993
The Secretary-General reports to the Security Council, setting out the proposed objectives and terms of reference for a team of 20 military liaison officers to be established in Phnom Penh for a single period of six months.
See Document 106, page 336

28 October 1993
The Secretary-General reports to the Security Council that limited extensions are required in the UNTAC withdrawal plan.
See Document 107, page 338

4 November 1993
The Security Council extends the period of UNTAC withdrawal and establishes a team of 20 military liaison officers for a single six-month period to report on matters affecting security in Cambodia and to assist the Government in dealing with residual matters relating to the Paris Agreements.
See Document 108, page 339

20 December 1993
The General Assembly adopts a resolution on the situation of human rights in Cambodia, welcoming the establishment in Cambodia of an operational presence of the Centre for Human Rights and outlining its tasks.
See Document 109, page 340

31 December 1993
UNTAC troops complete their withdrawal from Cambodia.

14 February 1994
The Secretary-General reports to the Security Council on the United Nations Military Liaison Team in Cambodia.
See Document 110, page 341

10-11 March 1994
At a meeting of the International Committee on the Reconstruction of Cambodia, the Secretary-General stresses the need for a continuing commitment by the international community and the United Nations to assist the Cambodian people in the task of nation-building.
See Document 111, page 342

29 March 1994
The Secretary-General appoints Mr. Benny Widyono (Indonesia) as representative in Cambodia to co-ordinate the post-UNTAC United Nations presence.

6 May 1994
The Secretary-General informs the Security Council that, should the mandate of the Military Liaison Team not be extended beyond 15 May 1994, he would appoint three military personnel as advisers to his Special Representative for Cambodia.
See Document 112, page 343

7 May 1994
In a letter to the Secretary-General, King Sihanouk expresses his concern at the deterioration in the situation in Cambodia. In his reply of **19 May**, the Secretary-General states that the United Nations is resolved to help the people of Cambodia to achieve peace and rebuild their country.
See Document 113, page 344; and Document 114, page 344

15 May 1994
The mandate of the Military Liaison Team expires and the team ceases operations.
See Document 115, page 345

31 May 1994
The Secretary-General reports to the Security Council on the activities of the Military Liaison Team and informs the Council that three military advisers have been retained in Cambodia to assist his representative in Cambodia.
See Document 115, page 345

10 October 1994
The Secretary-General extends the appointment of his representative in Cambodia for a further six months, assisted by three military advisers.
See Document 116, page 346

14 October 1994
The Security Council welcomes the Secretary-General's decision to extend the appointment of his representative in Cambodia.
See Document 117, page 346

II List of reproduced documents

The documents reproduced on pages 87-346 include resolutions of the General Assembly and Security Council, statements by the President of the Security Council and the reports of the Secretary-General, letters to and from the Secretary-General, statements and other communications from United Nations Member States and regional groups, and other communications.

1990

Document 1
Letter dated 16 January 1990 from China, France, the Union of Soviet Socialist Republics (USSR), the United Kingdom of Great Britain and Northern Ireland and the United States of America transmitting summary of conclusions following a meeting of the five permanent members of the Security Council on the Cambodian problem.
S/21087, 18 January 1990
See page 87

Document 2
Letter dated 30 August 1990 from China, France, the USSR, the United Kingdom and the United States transmitting statement and framework document adopted by their representatives at a meeting in New York, 27-28 August 1990.
A/45/472-S/21689, 31 August 1990
See page 88

Document 3
Letter dated 11 September 1990 from France and Indonesia, as Co-Chairmen of the Paris Conference on Cambodia, transmitting joint statement on Cambodia issued at the end of talks held in Jakarta, 9-10 September 1990.
A/45/490-S/21732, 17 September 1990
See page 93

Document 4
Security Council resolution on settlement of the Cambodia situation.
S/RES/668, 20 September 1990
See page 94

Document 5
Letter dated 29 November 1990 from France and Indonesia transmitting communiqué of the five permanent members of the Security Council concerning settlement of the Cambodia situation issued at the end of talks held in Paris, 23-26 November 1990.
A/45/829-S/21985, 6 December 1990
See page 95

1991

Document 6
Letter dated 8 January 1991 from France and Indonesia transmitting statement issued at the end of a meeting between the Co-Chairmen of the Paris Conference on Cambodia and the Supreme National Council of Cambodia in Paris, 21-23 December 1990.
A/46/61-S/22059, 11 January 1991
See page 96

Document 7
Letter dated 21 February 1991 from France and Indonesia transmitting joint statement issued at the end of talks held at Hanoi, 1-2 February 1991, between representatives of the Paris Conference on Cambodia and Vietnamese leaders.
A/46/112-S/22344, 8 March 1991
See page 112

Document 8
Letter dated 22 April 1991 from France and Indonesia transmitting appeal for a voluntary cease-fire in Cambodia issued on 22 April 1991 by the Co-Chairmen of the Paris Conference on Cambodia and the United Nations Secretary-General.
A/46/161-S/22552, 29 April 1991
See page 113

Document 9
Letter dated 26 June 1991 from Cambodia transmitting communiqué of the Supreme National Council meeting in Pattaya, Thailand, 24-26 June 1991.
A/46/271-S/22740, 26 June 1991
See page 113

Document 37
Letter dated 24 June 1992 from Japan transmitting Tokyo Declaration on the Cambodia Peace Process and the Tokyo Declaration on the Rehabilitation and Reconstruction of Cambodia, issued at the conclusion of the Ministerial Conference on the Rehabilitation and Reconstruction of Cambodia, 22 June 1992.
A/47/285-S/24183, 25 June 1992
See page 194

Document 38
Letter dated 27 June 1992 from Mr. Khieu Samphan, member of the Supreme National Council, transmitting proposal of the Party of Democratic Kampuchea (PDK) on cooperation between UNTAC and the Supreme National Council.
Not issued as a United Nations document.
See page 198

Document 39
Letter dated 7 July 1992 from the Secretary-General to Mr. Khieu Samphan, member of the Supreme National Council, referring to letter of 27 June and concerning implementation by UNTAC of the provisions of the Paris Agreements.
Not issued as a United Nations document.
See page 199

Document 40
Proposal dated 12 July 1992 of the Party of Democratic Kampuchea on the implementation of phase II of the cease-fire and the regroupment and cantonment of the forces of the PDK.
Not issued as a United Nations document.
See page 200

Document 41
Second special report of the Secretary-General on UNTAC and phase II of the cease-fire.
S/24286, 14 July 1992
See page 201

Document 42
Security Council resolution on implementation of the Paris Agreements.
S/RES/766, 21 July 1992
See page 205

Document 43
Letter dated 27 July 1992 from the Special Representative of the Secretary-General for Cambodia to the Secretary-General concerning the situation in Cambodia.
Not issued as a United Nations document.
See page 206

Document 44
"Cambodia: next steps", Australian paper dated 16 September 1992.
Not issued as a United Nations document.
See page 208

Document 45
Second progress report of the Secretary-General on UNTAC.
S/24578, 21 September 1992
See page 211

Document 46
Statement by the Foreign Ministers of the five permanent members of the Security Council following a meeting with the Secretary-General, 25 September 1992.
S/24587, 25 September 1992
See page 219

Document 47
Letter dated 29 September 1992 from Mr. Khieu Samphan, member of the Supreme National Council, to the Secretary-General referring to "Cambodia: next steps", Australian paper.
Not issued as a United Nations document.
See page 222

Document 48
Contribution dated 30 September 1992 by Mr. Son Sann, member of the Supreme National Council, to the search for a solution to the deadlock in the implementation of the Paris Agreements.
Not issued as a United Nations document.
See page 224

Document 49
Security Council resolution on implementation of the Cambodia peace process.
S/RES/783, 13 October 1992
See page 225

Document 50
Letter dated 2 November 1992 from the Secretary-General to Mr. Roland Dumas, Minister for Foreign Affairs of France and Co-Chairman of the Paris Conference on Cambodia, referring to Security Council resolution 783 (1992) and requesting that the Co-Chairmen undertake consultations with a view to implementing the peace process.
Not issued as a United Nations document.
See page 227

Document 51
Letter dated 2 November 1992 from the Secretary-General to Mr. Ali Alatas, Minister for Foreign Affairs of Indonesia and Co-Chairman of the Paris Conference on Cambodia, referring to Security Council resolution 783 (1992) and requesting that the Co-Chairmen undertake consultations with a view to implementing the peace process.
Not issued as a United Nations document.
See page 227

Document 52
Letter dated 2 November 1992 from the Secretary-General to Prince Norodom Sihanouk transmitting report by Governments of Japan and Thailand in accordance with paragraph 12 of Security Council resolution 783 (1992).
Not issued as a United Nations document.
See page 228

Document 53
Letter dated 12 November 1992 from Prince Norodom Sihanouk to the Secretary-General concerning consultations in Beijing, 7-8 November 1992.
Not issued as a United Nations document.
See page 229

Document 54
Report of the Secretary-General on the implementation of Security Council resolution 783 (1992) on the Cambodia peace process. Also contains a brief overview of the main developments in Cambodia since second progress report dated 21 September 1992; a report dated 31 October 1992 by Japan and Thailand to the Secretary-General and the Co-Chairmen of the Paris Conference; and a report and statement by the Co-Chairmen.
S/24800, 15 November 1992
See page 229

Document 55
Security Council resolution on implementation of Cambodia peace process.
S/RES/792, 30 November 1992
See page 243

Document 56
Letter dated 30 November 1992 from Thailand outlining the position of the Royal Thai Government with regard to Security Council resolution 792 (1992).
S/24873, 30 November 1992
See page 245

Document 57
Statement by the President of the Security Council on the increasing number of attacks against United Nations personnel serving in peace-keeping operations.
S/24884, 2 December 1992
See page 246

Document 58
Letter dated 20 December 1992 from Mr. Khieu Samphan, member of the Supreme National Council, to the Secretary-General transmitting statement by the PDK on alleged violations by UNTAC of PDK-controlled zones.
Not issued as a United Nations document.
See page 246

Document 59
Statement by the President of the Security Council concerning illegal detention of UNTAC personnel in Cambodia by elements of the PDK.
S/25003, 22 December 1992
See page 248

Document 60
Letter dated 30 December 1992 from Mr. Nguyen Manh Cam, Minister for Foreign Affairs of Viet Nam, to the Secretary-General concerning violence against Vietnamese residents in Cambodia.
S/25053, 5 January 1993
See page 248

1993

Document 61
Letter dated 5 January 1993 from Mr. Hun Sen, member of the Supreme National Council, to the Secretary-General transmitting declaration by the State of Cambodia.
Not issued as a United Nations document.
See page 249

Document 62
Letter dated 5 January 1993 from Prince Norodom Ranariddh, member of the Supreme National Council, to the Secretary-General concerning the political situation in Cambodia.
Not issued as a United Nations document.
See page 251

Document 63
Letter dated 19 January 1993 from Prince Norodom Ranariddh, Mr. Ieng Mouly, Mr. Sam Rainsy and Mr. Son Sann, members of the Supreme National Council, to the Secretary-General concerning the electoral registration of Cambodians residing abroad.
Not issued as a United Nations document.
See page 252

Document 78

Letter dated 26 April 1993 from the Secretary-General to the President of the Security Council transmitting information relating to recent incidents which resulted in the deaths of members of UNTAC.
S/25669, 27 April 1993
See page 284

Document 79

Fourth progress report of the Secretary-General on UNTAC.
S/25719, 3 May 1993
See page 285

Document 80

Letter dated 7 May 1993 from Mr. Hun Sen, member of the Supreme National Council, to the Special Representative of the Secretary-General for Cambodia, concerning the electoral process.
Not issued as a United Nations document.
See page 302

Document 81

Report of the Secretary-General in pursuance of paragraph 6 of Security Council resolution 810 (1993) on preparations for the election for the constituent assembly in Cambodia.
S/25784, 15 May 1993
See page 303

Document 82

Letter dated 18 May 1993 from Singapore transmitting statement by the ASEAN Foreign Ministers on the election in Cambodia.
S/25794, 18 May 1993
See page 306

Document 83

Security Council resolution on the election for the constituent assembly in Cambodia.
S/RES/826, 20 May 1993
See page 306

Document 84

Statement by the President of the Security Council concerning the act of violence against UNTAC on 21 May 1993.
S/25822, 22 May 1993
See page 307

Document 85

Letter dated 28 May 1993 from the Secretary-General to Prince Norodom Sihanouk on the conduct of the election in Cambodia.
Not issued as a United Nations document.
See page 308

Document 86

Letter dated 28 May 1993 from the Secretary-General to the President of the Security Council reporting further on the shelling in Kompong Cham Province, Cambodia, 21 May 1993.
S/25871, 1 June 1993
See page 309

Document 87

Letter dated 31 May 1993 from Prince Norodom Sihanouk to the Secretary-General concerning the election in Cambodia and paying tribute to UNTAC.
Not issued as a United Nations document.
See page 309

Document 88

Letter dated 2 June 1993 from the Secretary-General transmitting statement made by the Special Representative of the Secretary-General for Cambodia at the Supreme National Council meeting on 29 May 1993; endorses the statement of the Special Representative that the conduct of the election was free and fair.
S/25879, 2 June 1993.
See page 310

Document 89

Security Council resolution on the completion of the election in Cambodia.
S/RES/835, 2 June 1993
See page 311

Document 90

Letter dated 4 June 1993 from Viet Nam transmitting statement from the Ministry of Foreign Affairs concerning the general elections in Cambodia.
S/25886, 5 June 1993
See page 312

Document 91

Statement by the President of the Security Council concerning armed attacks against Pakistani and Malaysian platoons of UNTAC.
S/25896, 8 June 1993
See page 313

Document 92

Report of the Secretary-General on the conduct and results of the election in Cambodia.
S/25913, 10 June 1993
See page 313

The following is a breakdown, by category, of documents reproduced in this book.

Document 76 (SC/5597/Rev.2)
Document 84 (S/25822)
Document 91 (S/25896)
Document 104 (S/26531)

Resolution of the Commission on Human Rights
Document 70 (E/CN.4/RES/1993/6)

Communications from Member States
Document 1 (S/21087)
Document 2 (A/45/472-S/21689)
Document 3 (A/45/490-S/21732)
Document 5 (A/45/829-S/21985)
Document 6 (A/46/61-S/22059)
Document 7 (A/46/112-S/22344)
Document 8 (A/46/161-S/22552)
Document 9 (A/46/271-S/22740)
Document 10 (A/46/310-S/22808)
Document 11 (A/46/328-S/22850)
Document 12 (A/46/340-S/22889)
Document 14 (A/46/418-S/23011)
Document 15 (A/46/494-S/23066)
Document 16 (A/46/508-S/23087)
Document 19 (A/46/608-S/23177)
Document 24 (A/47/63-S/23335)
Document 34 (S/24082)
Document 37 (A/47/285-S/24183)
Document 46 (S/24587)
Document 56 (S/24873)
Document 60 (S/25053)
Document 64 (S/25133)
Document 72 (S/25409)
Document 74 (S/25563)
Document 77 (S/25658)
Document 82 (S/25794)
Document 90 (S/25886)
Document 93 (S/25940)
Document 95 (S/25971)
Document 99 (S/26138)
Document 102 (S/26517)

Reports and letters of the Secretary-General to the Security Council
Document 13 (S/22945)
Document 17 (S/23097 and Add.1)
Document 20 (S/23179)
Document 22 (S/23218)
Document 25 (S/23331 and Add.1)
Document 27 (S/23458)
Document 30 (S/23613 and Add.1)
Document 33 (S/23870)
Document 35 (S/24090)
Document 41 (S/24286)
Document 45 (S/24578)
Document 54 (S/24800)

Document 65 (S/25124)
Document 68 (S/25273)
Document 69 (S/25289)
Document 78 (S/25669)
Document 79 (S/25719)
Document 81 (S/25784)
Document 86 (S/25871)
Document 88 (S/25879)
Document 92 (S/25913)
Document 96 (S/25988)
Document 97 (S/26090)
Document 98 (S/26095)
Document 100 (S/26360)
Document 103 (S/26529)
Document 105 (S/26546)
Document 106 (S/26649 and Add.1)
Document 107 (S/26675)
Document 110 (S/1994/169)
Document 112 (S/1994/572)
Document 115 (S/1994/645)
Document 116 (S/1994/1182)

Correspondence of the Secretary-General
Document 28*
Document 29*
Document 32*
Document 38*
Docu.nent 39*
Document 43*
Document 47*
Document 50*
Document 51*
Document 52*
Document 53*
Document 58*
Document 61*
Document 62*
Document 63*
Document 66*
Document 67*
Document 85*
Document 87*
Document 113 (A/49/160-S/1994/570)
Document 114*

Other materials
Document 40*
Document 44*
Document 48*
Document 75*
Document 80*
Document 111*
Document 117 (S/1994/1183)

*Not issued as a United Nations document.

III Other documents of interest

Readers seeking additional information about the United Nations Transitional Authority in Cambodia (UNTAC) and the situation in Cambodia might wish to consult the following documents, which are available in the Dag Hammarskjöld Library at United Nations Headquarters in New York City, at other libraries in the United Nations system or at libraries around the world which have been designated as depository libraries for United Nations documents

Resolutions of the General Assembly

The General Assembly appeals for humanitarian relief for Kampuchean civilians and refugees and requests the Secretary-General to explore the possibility of holding an international conference on Kampuchea.
A/RES/34/22, 14 November 1979

The General Assembly decides to convene, early in 1981, an international conference on Kampuchea, outlines seven issues for negotiation and foresees a role for the United Nations should the conflict be settled.
A/RES/35/6, 22 October 1980

The General Assembly approves the report of the International Conference on Kampuchea and adopts: (a) Declaration on Kampuchea; (b) Resolution 1 (I) on the establishment of the Ad Hoc Committee of the International Conference on Kampuchea.
A/RES/36/5, 21 October 1981

The General Assembly outlines four components for resolving the Kampuchean problem, acknowledges the report of the Ad Hoc Committee (A/CONF.109/6) and requests that it continue its work, pending the reconvening of the Conference.
A/RES/37/6, 29 October 1982

The General Assembly outlines four components for resolving the Kampuchean problem, acknowledges the report of the Ad Hoc Committee (A/CONF.109/7) and requests that it continue its work, pending the reconvening of the Conference.
A/RES/38/3, 27 October 1983

The General Assembly outlines four components for resolving the Kampuchean problem, acknowledges the report of the Ad Hoc Committee (A/CONF.109/8) and requests that it continue its work, pending the reconvening of the Conference.
A/RES/39/5, 30 October 1984

The General Assembly outlines four components for resolving the Kampuchean problem, acknowledges the report of the Ad Hoc Committee (A/CONF.109/9) and requests that it continue its work, pending the reconvening of the Conference.
A/RES/40/7, 5 November 1985

The General Assembly outlines four components for resolving the Kampuchean problem, acknowledges the report of the Ad Hoc Committee (A/CONF.109/11 and Corr.1) and requests that it continue its work, pending the reconvening of the Conference.
A/RES/41/6, 21 October 1986

The General Assembly outlines four components for resolving the Kampuchean problem, acknowledges the report of the Ad Hoc Committee (A/CONF.109/12) and requests that it continue its work, pending the reconvening of the Conference.
A/RES/42/3, 14 October 1987

The General Assembly outlines six components for resolving the Kampuchean problem, including national reconciliation under the leadership of Prince Norodom Sihanouk. Acknowledges the report of the Ad Hoc Committee (A/CONF.109/13) and requests that it continue its work, pending the reconvening of the Conference.
A/RES/43/19, 3 November 1988

The General Assembly outlines six components for resolving the Kampuchean problem, including national reconciliation under the leadership of Prince Norodom Sihanouk. Acknowledges the report of the Ad Hoc Committee (A/CONF.109/15) and calls for an intensification of efforts to reach a political settlement.
A/RES/44/22, 16 November 1989

The General Assembly welcomes the agreement reached by the Cambodian factions in Jakarta in forming a Su-

preme National Council and calls for consultations to reconvene the Paris Conference. The role of the United Nations in free and fair elections is stressed.
A/RES/45/3, 15 October 1990

The General Assembly expresses its full support for the agreements on a comprehensive political settlement of the Cambodia conflict and supports efforts to set up a United Nations Transitional Authority.
A/RES/46/18, 20 November 1991

Reports of the Secretary-General to the General Assembly

Pursuant to General Assembly resolution 34/22, the Secretary-General discusses the situation in Kampuchea, United Nations humanitarian assistance activities and efforts towards a political settlement.
A/35/501, 30 September 1980

Pursuant to General Assembly resolution 35/6, the Secretary-General discusses the situation in Kampuchea, the International Conference on Kampuchea and ongoing efforts to find a peaceful resolution of the problem.
A/36/583, 12 October 1981

Pursuant to General Assembly resolution 36/5, the Secretary-General discusses the situation in Kampuchea and implementation of the Programme of Humanitarian Assistance to the People of Kampuchea.
A/37/496, 8 October 1982

Pursuant to General Assembly resolution 37/6, the Secretary-General discusses the situation in Kampuchea and continuing efforts to seek a peaceful resolution of the problem.
A/38/513, 18 October 1983

Pursuant to General Assembly resolution 38/3, the Secretary-General discusses the situation in Kampuchea and continuing efforts to seek a peaceful resolution of the problem.
A/39/576, 12 October 1984

Pursuant to General Assembly resolution 39/5, the Secretary-General discusses his trip to South-East Asia and reports that a reasonable degree of convergence has emerged on the main elements of a comprehensive political settlement.
A/40/759, 17 October 1985

Pursuant to General Assembly resolution 40/7, the Secretary-General discusses the situation in Kampuchea, humanitarian assistance programmes and the refugee situation along the Thai-Kampuchean border.
A/41/707, 14 October 1986

Pursuant to General Assembly resolution 41/6, the Secretary-General discusses the situation in Kampuchea, humanitarian assistance programmes and the refugee situation along the Thai-Kampuchean border.
A/42/608, 6 October 1987

Pursuant to General Assembly resolution 42/3, the Secretary-General discusses the situation in Kampuchea, security and protection for the border population and ongoing efforts to elaborate a framework for a comprehensive political settlement.
A/43/730, 21 October 1988

Pursuant to General Assembly resolution 43/19, the Secretary-General discusses the situation in Kampuchea, provision of humanitarian assistance, the situation of refugees and displaced persons, the Paris Conference on Cambodia and various initiatives and diplomatic exchanges.
A/44/670, 24 October 1989

Pursuant to General Assembly resolution 44/22, the Secretary-General discusses the situation in Cambodia, provision of humanitarian assistance, the situation of refugees and displaced persons and the acceptance by the Cambodian parties and other countries concerned of the framework for a comprehensive political settlement.
A/45/605, 10 October 1990

Pursuant to General Assembly resolution 45/3, the Secretary-General reports on humanitarian relief assistance to the Cambodian people and on the negotiations leading to the signing in Paris on 23 October 1991 of the Agreements on a Comprehensive Political Settlement of the Cambodia Conflict.
A/46/617, 7 November 1991

Other statements and communications

Letter dated 2 August 1989 from the Secretary-General to the President of the Security Council containing excerpts from a statement delivered at the Paris Conference on Cambodia, 30 July 1989.
S/20768, 3 August 1989

Letter dated 9 November 1989 from France and Indonesia transmitting press release by the Co-Chairmen of the International Conference on Cambodia.
A/44/719-S/20958, 10 November 1989

Letter dated 9 November 1989 from France and Indonesia transmitting statement of 30 August 1989 issued at the conclusion of the International Conference on Cambodia, Paris, 30 July-30 August 1989.
A/44/720-S/20959, 10 November 1989

Letter dated 13 February 1990 from China, France, the Union of Soviet Socialist Republics (USSR), the United Kingdom of Great Britain and Northern Ireland and the United States of America transmitting text of press statement following consultations of the five permanent members of the Security Council on Cambodia.

A/45/127-S/21149, 15 February 1990
Letter dated 15 March 1990 from China, France, the USSR, the United Kingdom and the United States concerning modalities of a comprehensive political settlement of the Cambodia conflict.
A/45/167-S/21196, 16 March 1990

Letter dated 29 May 1990 from China, France, the USSR, the United Kingdom and the United States concerning modalities of a comprehensive political settlement of the Cambodia conflict.
A/45/293-S/21318, 29 May 1990

Letter dated 19 July 1990 from China, France, the USSR, the United Kingdom and the United States transmitting summary of conclusions reached at the fifth meeting of the five permanent members of the Security Council on Cambodia, Paris, 16-17 July 1990.
A/45/353-S/21404, 23 July 1990

Letter dated 24 July 1990 from Indonesia transmitting joint statement by the Foreign Ministers of the Association of South-East Asian Nations (ASEAN) concerning the Cambodia situation, issued in Jakarta, 23 July 1990.
A/45/355-S/21408, 25 July 1990

Letter dated 1 August 1990 from Malaysia transmitting joint communiqué of the Twenty-third ASEAN Ministerial Meeting, held in Jakarta, 24-25 July 1990.
A/45/389-S/21455, 7 August 1990

Letter dated 1 October 1990 from China, France, the USSR, the United Kingdom and the United States transmitting statement issued by the Ministers for Foreign Affairs of the five permanent members of the Security Council following a meeting with the Secretary-General, 28 September 1990.
S/21835, 2 October 1990

Letter dated 18 October 1990 from China, France, the USSR, the United Kingdom and the United States transmitting statement concerning political settlement of the Cambodian situation.
A/45/671-S/21908, 25 October 1990

Letter dated 12 November 1990 from France and Indonesia transmitting press statement issued at the conclusion of the Working Group Meeting of the Paris Conference on Cambodia, held in Jakarta, 9-10 November 1990.
A/45/719-S/21940, 13 November 1990

Financing of UNAMIC, UNTAC and the United Nations Military Liaison Team in Cambodia: resolutions and decisions of the General Assembly and reports of the Secretary-General to the General Assembly

UNAMIC
A/46/723, 3 December 1991
A/46/763, 10 December 1991
A/46/823, 20 December 1991
A/RES/46/198 A, 20 December 1991
A/46/855, 31 January 1992
A/46/873, 11 February 1992
A/46/823/Add.1, 13 February 1992
A/RES/46/198 B, 14 February 1992
ST/ADM/SER.B/369, 21 April 1992

A/46/903, 7 May 1992
A/46/916, 15 May 1992
A/46/879/Add.1, 21 May 1992

UNTAC
A/46/235/Add.1, 31 January 1992
A/46/874, 11 February 1992
A/46/879, 13 February 1992
A/RES/46/222 A, 14 February 1992
ST/ADM/SER.B/372, 29 April 1992

A/46/903, 7 May 1992
A/46/916, 15 May 1992
A/46/879/Add.1, 21 May 1992
A/RES/46/222 B, 22 May 1992
ST/ADM/SER.B/382, 25 June 1992
A/47/733, 3 December 1992
A/47/763, 10 December 1992
A/47/824, 21 December 1992
A/RES/47/209 A, 22 December 1992
A/47/733/Add.1, 27 July 1993
A/47/982, 27 July 1993
A/47/824/Add.1, 9 September 1993
A/RES/47/209 B, 14 September 1993
A/48/701, 8 December 1993
A/48/775, 17 December 1993
A/48/818, 23 December 1993
A/DEC/48/469, 23 December 1993
A/48/701/Add.1, 17 January 1994
A/48/701/Corr.1, 19 January 1994
A/48/701/Corr.2, 22 March 1994
A/48/917, 30 March 1994
A/48/917/Corr.1, 7 April 1994
A/48/818/Add.1, 10 May 1994
A/RES/48/255, 26 May 1994

Military Liaison Team
A/48/786, 17 December 1993
A/48/800, 21 December 1993

A/48/829, 23 December 1993
A/DEC/48/480, 23 December 1993
A/48/800/Corr.1, 19 January 1994
ST/ADM/SER.B/429, 15 March 1994
A/48/919, 30 March 1994
A/48/829/Add.1, 10 May 1994
A/RES/48/257, 26 May 1994
A/49/521, 14 October 1994
ST/ADM/SER.B/440, 13 July 1994

Continued United Nations human rights presence in Cambodia

Report of the Special Representative for human rights in Cambodia to the Commission on Human Rights.
E/CN.4/1994/73, 24 February 1994; and addendum, E/CN.4/1994/73/Add.1, 21 February 1994

Report of the Secretary-General to the General Assembly concerning the situation of human rights in Cambodia and on the activities of the Centre for Human Rights in Cambodia; contains report and recommendations of the Special Representative for human rights in Cambodia.
A/49/635, 3 November 1994; and addendum, A/49/635/Add.1, 3 November 1994

IV Texts of documents

The texts of the 117 documents listed on pages 73-82 are reproduced below. A subject index to the documents appears on pages 347-352.

Document 1

Letter dated 16 January 1990 from China, France, the Union of Soviet Socialist Republics (USSR), the United Kingdom of Great Britain and Northern Ireland and the United States of America transmitting summary of conclusions following a meeting of the five permanent members of the Security Council on the Cambodian problem

S/21087, 18 January 1990

Representatives of our Governments met in Paris on 15 and 16 January to discuss the situation in Cambodia.

We have the honour to enclose the text of the statement agreed to at the meeting, and should be grateful if you would arrange for it to be circulated as a document of the Security Council.

(*signed*) LI Luye
Permanent Representative of China
to the United Nations

(*signed*) Jean-Marc ROCHEREAU de LA SABLIÈRE
Chargé d'affaires a.i. and
Deputy Permanent Representative of France
to the United Nations

(*signed*) Aleksandr BELONOGOV
Permanent Representative of
the Union of Soviet Socialist Republics
to the United Nations

(*signed*) Sir Crispin TICKELL
Permanent Representative of
the United Kingdom
of Great Britain
and Northern Ireland
to the United Nations

(*signed*) Thomas R. PICKERING
Permanent Representative
of the United States of America
to the United Nations

Annex
Summary of Conclusions of the Meeting of the Five Permanent Members of the Security Council on the Cambodian Problem

Paris, 15-16 January 1990

The Five Permanent Members of the United Nations Security Council meeting in Paris on 15-16 January 1990, agreed that they would be guided by the following principles in working for a resolution of the Cambodian problem:

-No acceptable solution can be achieved by force of arms.

-An enduring peace can only be achieved through a comprehensive political settlement, including the verified withdrawal of foreign forces, a cease-fire, and cessation of outside military assistance.

-The goal should be self-determination for the Cambodian people through free, fair and democratic elections.

-All accept an enhanced United Nations role in the resolution of the Cambodian problem.

-There is an urgent need to speed up diplomatic efforts to achieve a settlement.

-The complete withdrawal of foreign forces must be verified by the United Nations.

-The Five would welcome an early resumption of a constructive dialogue among the Cambodian factions which is essential to facilitating the transition process, which should not be dominated by any one of them.

-An effective United Nations presence will be required during the transition period in order to assure internal security.

-A special representative of the United Nations Secretary-General is needed in Cambodia to supervise United Nations activities during a transition period culminating in the inauguration of a democratically elected government.

-The scale of the United Nations operation should

be consistent with the successful implementation of a Cambodian settlement, and its planning and execution should take account of the heavy financial burden that may be placed on member States.

-Free and fair elections must be conducted under direct United Nations administration.

-The elections must be conducted in a neutral political environment in which no party would be advantaged.

-The Five Permanent Members commit themselves to honouring the results of free and fair elections.

-All Cambodians should enjoy the same rights, freedoms, and opportunities to participate in the election process.

-A Supreme National Council might be the repository of Cambodian sovereignty during the transition process.

-Questions involving Cambodian sovereignty should be resolved with the agreement of the Cambodian parties.

-The Five support all responsible efforts by regional parties to achieve a comprehensive political settlement, and will remain in close touch with them with a view to reconvening the Paris Conference at an appropriate time.

Document 2

Letter dated 30 August 1990 from China, France, the USSR, the United Kingdom and the United States transmitting statement and framework document adopted by their representatives at a meeting in New York, 27-28 August 1990

A/45/472-S/21689, 31 August 1990

Representatives of our Governments met in New York on 27 and 28 August 1990 for a sixth exchange of views on the terms of a comprehensive political settlement of the Cambodia conflict.

We have the honour of transmitting to you, herewith, the Statement which, together with the appended framework document, was adopted at that meeting, and we should be grateful if you would be so kind as to have these texts and this letter circulated as a document of the General Assembly, under items 32 and 38 of the provisional agenda, and of the Security Council.

(signed) Pierre-Louis BLANC
Permanent Representative of France
to the United Nations

(signed) LI Daoyu
Permanent Representative of the People's
Republic of China to the United Nations

(*signed*) Thomas R. PICKERING
Permanent Representative of the United States
of America to the United Nations

(*signed*) Yuli M. VOLONTSOV
Permanent Representative of the Union of Soviet
Socialist Republics to the United Nations

(*signed*) Crispin TICKELL
Permanent Representative of the United Kingdom
of Great Britain and Northern Ireland
to the United Nations

Annex
Statement of the Five Permanent Members of the Security Council of the United Nations on Cambodia

The Five Permanent Members of the UN Security Council have held in Paris and New York six meetings in 1990 at the Vice Ministerial level in order to define the key elements of a comprehensive political settlement of the Cambodia conflict based on an enhanced UN role.

At the end of their sixth meeting, held in New York on August 27-28, 1990, the Five reached final agreement on a framework for a settlement. The framework document is composed of five sections comprising the indispensable requirements for such a settlement:

I. - Transitional arrangements regarding the administration of Cambodia during the pre-election period;

II. - Military arrangements during the transitional period;

III. - Elections under United Nations auspices;

IV. - Human rights protection;

V. - International guarantees.

This document will be made public after it has been communicated to the interested parties.

The Five also recalled the two documents elaborated by the 1989 Paris Conference on Cambodia on repatriation of refugees and displaced persons and on reconstruction.

Taken together, these documents outline a settlement process based on national reconciliation and involving an enhanced United Nations role which would ensure a just and lasting political solution to the conflict.

The basic principle behind the Five's approach is to

enable the Cambodian people to determine their own political future through free and fair elections organized and conducted by the United Nations in a neutral political environment with full respect for the national sovereignty of Cambodia.

Implementation of this approach requires the full support of all parties to the Cambodia conflict. The Five therefore urge the acceptance of this framework document in its entirety as the basis for settling the Cambodia conflict.

The Five thus now call on the Cambodian parties to the conflict to commit themselves to this process and to form the Supreme National Council as soon as possible on the basis outlined in the framework document.

To this end, the Five support Indonesia's efforts to convene in Jakarta a meeting with the Cambodian parties. They urge the two Co-Chairmen of the Paris Conference to commend the framework to the Cambodian parties and to persuade them to form the Supreme National Council accordingly.

The early formation of a Supreme National Council would permit that body to designate its representative to occupy the Cambodian seat in the United Nations and other international organizations.

Once the Cambodian parties have accepted this framework and the SNC has been formed, the Paris Conference, which includes all interested parties and the Secretary-General of the UN, should be reconvened. Its task should be to adopt the elements of the comprehensive political settlement and draw up a detailed plan of implementation in accord with this framework.

The Paris Conference would then invite the Secretary-General of the UN to report to the Security Council and to transmit to it the Conference's recommendation that the Council adopt a resolution endorsing the final agreement on the comprehensive political settlement and enabling the Secretary-General to implement it.

As a first step, the Five call on all parties to the conflict to exercise maximum self-restraint so as to create the peaceful climate required to facilitate the achievement and the implementation of a comprehensive political settlement.

During the course of their meeting, the five Heads of delegation met with the United Nations Secretary-General and with Under-Secretary-General Rafeeuddin AHMED to inform them of the results of their work. They also met representatives of a number of countries participating in the Paris Conference, notably the Co-Chairmen of the Committees and the three neighbouring countries, to exchange views about the next steps in the peace process.

To sustain the momentum of this process, the Five will continue to work with all those concerned with the Cambodia conflict and the UN Secretary-General. To this end, they have agreed to convene another meeting in Paris at an appropriate time before mid-October.

NYC, 28 August 1990

Appendix
Framework for a Comprehensive Political Settlement of the Cambodia Conflict

Sections:

I. - Transitional arrangements regarding the administration of Cambodia during the pre-electoral period (paragraphs 1 to 12)

II. - Military arrangements during the transitional period (paragraphs 13 to 19)

III. - Elections under United Nations auspices (paragraphs 20 to 23)

IV. - Human rights protection (paragraphs 24 to 30)

V. - International guarantees (paragraphs 31 to 36)

Section 1
Transitional arrangements regarding the administration of Cambodia during the pre-electoral period

1. In order to restore and maintain peace in Cambodia, prevent the continuation of the conflict, promote national reconciliation and ensure the realization of national self-determination through free and fair general elections, it is essential to establish a unique legitimate body and source of authority in which, throughout the transitional period, national sovereignty and unity would be enshrined.

2. In the light of their discussions during their first five meetings and taking account of the wishes of parties concerned, the Five believe it is appropriate to establish at an early date a Supreme National Council (SNC) of Cambodia.

3. The composition of the SNC, including the selection and number of its members, should be decided by the Cambodian parties through consultations. No party should be dominant in this process.

4. The SNC should be composed of representative individuals with authority among the Cambodian people. They should be acceptable to each other. They may include representative individuals of all shades of opinion among the people of Cambodia. The members of the SNC should be committed to the holding of free and fair elections as the basis for forming a new and legitimate government.

5. Should Prince Norodom SIHANOUK be elected by the SNC as its President, the Five would welcome this decision.

6. All countries should respect an agreement on this matter reached among the Cambodian parties.

7. The SNC should be the embodiment of the independence, sovereignty and unity of Cambodia. It

should represent Cambodia externally and occupy the seat of Cambodia at the United Nations, in the UN specialised agencies, and in other international institutions and international conferences.

8. Being the unique legitimate body and source of authority in Cambodia during the transitional period, the SNC, at the time the comprehensive political settlement is signed, will delegate to the United Nations Transitional Authority in Cambodia (UNTAC) all powers necessary to ensure the implementation of the comprehensive agreement, including those relating to the conduct of free and fair elections and the relevant aspects of the administration of Cambodia.

9. The SNC should offer advice to the UNTAC which will comply with this advice provided there is a consensus among the members of the SNC, and provided this advice is consistent with the objectives of the comprehensive political settlement. The Special Representative of the UN Secretary-General will determine whether such advice is consistent with the comprehensive political settlement. He should attend the meetings of the SNC and give its members all necessary information on the decisions taken by UNTAC.

10. In order to ensure a neutral political environment conducive to free and fair general elections, administrative agencies, bodies and offices which could directly influence the outcome of elections should be placed under direct UN supervision or control. In that context special attention will be given to foreign affairs, national defence, finance, public security and information. To reflect the importance of these subjects, UNTAC needs to exercise such control as is necessary to ensure the strict neutrality of the bodies responsible for them. The UN in consultation with the SNC would identify which agencies, bodies and offices could continue to operate in order to ensure normal day-to-day life in the country.

11. Adequate provision must be made within the terms of the comprehensive political settlement for the exercise of routine law enforcement functions under UNTAC supervision.

12. The Special Representative of the Secretary-General should investigate complaints and allegations regarding actions by the existing administrative structures in Cambodia that are inconsistent with or work against the objectives of a comprehensive political settlement.

Section 2
Military arrangements during the transitional period

13. The enhanced United Nations role requires the establishment of a United Nations Transitional Authority in Cambodia (UNTAC) with a military as well as a civilian component.

14. The function of the military component should be to carry out the peace-keeping aspects of the comprehensive political settlement.

15. Once a ceasefire takes effect, UNTAC will supervise, monitor and verify the ceasefire and related measures, including:

a) Verification of the withdrawal from Cambodia of all categories of foreign forces, advisers and military personnel and their weapons, ammunition and equipment, and their non-return to the country.

b) Liaison with neighbouring governments over any developments in or near their territory which could endanger the implementation of the comprehensive political settlement.

c) Monitoring the cessation of outside military assistance to all Cambodian parties.

d) Locating and confiscating caches of weapons and military supplies throughout the country.

e) Undertaking training programmes in mine clearance and a mine awareness programme among the Cambodian people.

16. The military component should be composed of a certain number of contingents provided by member States at the request of the UN Secretary-General. These contingents will be chosen in consultation with parties concerned and with the approval of the Security Council.

17. The Five consider that a ceasefire is an indispensable element of a comprehensive agreement. As a first step, they call on all parties to the conflict to exercise maximum self restraint. To facilitate the UN deployment necessary for the agreement to come into effect, a peaceful situation should prevail in Cambodia. At the time of the signing of the agreement, all forces should immediately disengage and refrain from any deployment, movement or action which would extend the territory they control or which might lead to the resumption of fighting. The formal ceasefire envisaged should enter into force at the time the comprehensive political settlement agreement takes effect.

18. In accordance with an operational timetable to be agreed upon, all forces will begin regrouping and relocating to specifically designated cantonment areas under the supervision of UNTAC. While the forces are in the cantonments, their arms will be stored on site under UNTAC supervision.

19. UNTAC will then initiate a phased process of arms control and reduction in such a way as to stabilize the security situation and build confidence among the parties to the conflict. The ultimate disposition of the factional forces and their weapons will be dealt with so as to reinforce the objectives of a comprehensive political settlement and minimize the risks of a return to warfare.

Section 3
Elections under United Nations auspices

20. The United Nations should be responsible for the organization and conduct of free and fair elections on the basis of genuine and verified voter registration lists of Cambodian citizens. Eligibility to vote, including provisions regarding the conditions of residence in Cambodia, will be established in the electoral regulations. Principles covering voting and candidate eligibility criteria will also be set out within the comprehensive political settlement. Special electoral arrangements should be agreed to guarantee the right to vote of Cambodian refugees and displaced persons.

21. The electoral process should be guided by the following principles:

a) The system and procedures adopted should be, and be seen to be, absolutely impartial while the arrangements should be as administratively simple and efficient as possible;

b) All Cambodian participants in the elections should have the same rights, freedoms and opportunities to take part in the election process;

c) All parties should commit themselves to honouring the results.

22. The provisions for the holding of free and fair elections under United Nations auspices, as part of a comprehensive political settlement, must include inter alia:

a) The establishment of a system of laws, procedures and administrative measures necessary for free and fair elections required by the electoral process:

b) The design and implementation of a voter education programme (ballot secrecy, voting procedures, etc.) to support the election process and a voter registration process to guard against fraud and to ensure that eligible voters have the opportunity to register;

c) Measures to monitor and facilitate the participation of Cambodians in the elections, the political campaign, and the balloting procedures;

d) Coordinated arrangements by the United Nations in consultation with the Supreme National Council to facilitate the presence of foreign observers wishing to observe the campaign and voting;

e) Identification and investigation of complaints of electoral irregularities and appropriate corrective action;

f) Fair access to the media, including press, TV and radio, for all candidates;

g) Overall direction of polling and the vote count;

h) Certification by the United Nations whether or not the elections were free and fair and the list of persons duly elected;

i) Adoption of a Code of Conduct regulating participation in the elections in a manner consistent with respect for human rights, including the prohibition of coercion or financial inducement in order to influence voter preference.

23. A comprehensive political settlement must include a specified period within which elections will take place. The duration of the electoral process should be consistent with the above and as short as possible. It should lead to a single election of a constituent assembly which would draft and approve a Constitution and transform itself into a legislative assembly, which will create the new Government. The principles on which the new Cambodian Constitution should be based will be an integral part of a comprehensive political settlement.

Section 4
Human rights protection

24. Cambodia's tragic recent history requires special measures to assure protection of human rights. Therefore, the comprehensive political settlement should commit Cambodia to comply with the obligations of the relevant international human rights instruments as well as with relevant resolutions of the UN General Assembly. Necessary measures should be taken in order to observe human rights and ensure the non-return to the policies and practices of the past.

25. Articles 55 and 56 of the UN Charter pledge all member States to take joint and separate action to promote universal respect for, and observance of, human rights and fundamental freedoms for all without distinction as to race, sex, language or religion.

26. All Cambodian people and others in Cambodia and all Cambodian refugees and displaced persons should enjoy the rights enshrined in the Universal Declaration of Human Rights and other relevant international human rights instruments. Fundamental rights and freedoms should form part of the constitutional principles within the comprehensive political settlement.

27. In recognition of the need to promote respect for human rights in Cambodia and for all Cambodians, the comprehensive political settlement should include provisions under UN auspices to guarantee the following during the transitional period:

a) Development and implementation of a programme of human rights education to promote respect for and understanding of human rights;

b) General human rights oversight of all aspects of the transitional administration; and

c) Investigation of human rights complaints, and, where appropriate, corrective action.

28. Following the elections, the UN Human Rights Commission should continue to monitor closely the human rights situation in Cambodia, including if necessary

by the appointment of a Special Rapporteur who would report his findings annually to the Commission and to the General Assembly.

29. As part of the comprehensive political settlement the other participating States should undertake to promote and encourage respect for and observance of human rights and fundamental freedoms in Cambodia as embodied in relevant international instruments so as to prevent the recurrence of human rights abuses.

30. In the event of future serious violations of human rights in Cambodia, other States should, consistent with the provisions of the section on international guarantees, call upon the competent organs of the UN to take appropriate action in accordance with relevant international instruments.

Section 5
International guarantees

31. The aim of the provisions of this section should be to: safeguard the independent and neutral status of Cambodia; prevent foreign aggression against Cambodia or interference in the affairs of that country; safeguard human rights in Cambodia and prevent a return to the policies and practices of the past; facilitate a comprehensive and durable political settlement based on self-determination of the Cambodian people, and ensure that the settlement agreed upon is implemented in its entirety.

32. Cambodia will solemnly undertake to maintain, preserve and defend its independence, sovereignty, territorial integrity and inviolability, and national unity, with perpetual neutrality proclaimed and enshrined in the Cambodian Constitution to be adopted after free and fair elections.

33. As part of a comprehensive political settlement, the states participating in the Paris Conference will conclude a multilateral agreement to recognize and respect the independence, sovereignty, territorial integrity and inviolability, neutrality, national unity of Cambodia. This agreement will be open to adherence by all member States of the United Nations.

34. The details of the respective obligations of Cambodia and the other participating States will be based upon the consensus achieved in the Second Committee of the Paris Conference on Cambodia, including in particular undertakings with respect to:

a) Refraining from entering into military alliances or other military agreements between Cambodia and other States that would be inconsistent with Cambodia's neutrality without prejudice to its right to receive or acquire the necessary military equipment, arms, munitions and assistance to enable it to exercise its legitimate right of self-defence and to maintain law and order;

b) Refraining from interference in any form in the internal affairs of Cambodia;

c) Terminating the treaties and agreements which are incompatible with Cambodia's independence, sovereignty, territorial integrity and inviolability, neutrality and national unity;

d) Settling all disputes between Cambodia and other States through peaceful means;

e) Consistent with the United Nations Charter, refraining from the use or threat of use of force, or the use of their territories or the territories of other States to impair the independence, sovereignty, territorial integrity and inviolability, neutrality and national unity of Cambodia;

f) Refraining from the use of Cambodian territory to impair the independence, sovereignty and territorial integrity of other States;

g) Refraining from the introduction or stationing of foreign forces or the establishment of foreign military bases or facilities in Cambodia, except pursuant to United Nations authorisation for the implementation of the comprehensive political settlement;

h) Respect for human rights in Cambodia, including observance of relevant international instruments.

35. The participating States will call upon all other States to recognize and respect in every way the independence, sovereignty, territorial integrity and inviolability, neutrality and national unity of Cambodia and to refrain from any action inconsistent with these principles.

36. In the event of a violation or threat of violation of the independence, sovereignty, territorial integrity, neutrality and national unity of Cambodia, or of any of the other commitments herein, including those relating to human rights, the participating States will immediately undertake appropriate consultations with a view to adopting all appropriate measures to ensure respect for these commitments. Such measures may include, inter alia, reference to the Security Council of the United Nations or recourse to the means for the peaceful settlement of disputes referred to in Article 33 of the Charter of the United Nations. The participating States may also seek the good offices of the Co-Chairmen of the Paris Conference on Cambodia.

Document 3

Letter dated 11 September 1990 from France and Indonesia, as Co-Chairmen of the Paris Conference on Cambodia, transmitting joint statement on Cambodia issued at the end of talks held in Jakarta, 9-10 September 1990

A/45/490-S/21732, 17 September 1990

As Co-Chairmen of the Paris International Conference on Cambodia, we have the honour to transmit herewith the joint statement, issued at Jakarta on 10 September 1990, of the Informal Meeting on Cambodia, which was recently held from 9 to 10 September 1990 (see annex).

We would be grateful if you could have the present letter and its annex circulated as a document of the General Assembly, under item 32 of the provisional agenda, and of the Security Council.

(*signed*) Pierre-Louis BLANC
Ambassador
Permanent Representative of France
to the United Nations

(*signed*) Nana S. SUTRESNA
Ambassador
Permanent Representative of Indonesia
to the United Nations

Annex
Joint statement of the Informal Meeting on Cambodia, issued at Jakarta on 10 September 1990

In the exercise of the mandate conferred upon them by the International Conference on Cambodia held in Paris from 30 July to 30 August 1989, the two Co-Chairmen convened an Informal Meeting of the Cambodian parties at Jakarta on 9 and 10 September 1990. The objective of the Meeting was to ascertain the views of the Cambodian parties on their support and acceptance of the framework of a comprehensive settlement as agreed upon by the five permanent members of the United Nations Security Council in New York on 28 August 1990, as well as to finalize the formation of the Supreme National Council (SNC).

The Cambodian parties accepted the framework document formulated by the five permanent members of the Security Council in its entirety as the basis for settling the Cambodia conflict, and committed themselves, in full co-operation with all other participants of the Paris International Conference on Cambodia (PICC), to elaborating this framework into a comprehensive political settlement through the processes of the PICC.

In this context, the Cambodian parties addressed the question of a Supreme National Council of Cambodia, and agreed on the Nature and Functions of the SNC as stipulated in the P-5 document. They specifically agreed as follows:

(a) The SNC is the unique legitimate body and source of authority in which, throughout the transitional period, the independence, sovereignty and unity of Cambodia is embodied;

(b) The SNC is composed of representative individuals with authority among the Cambodian people and reflecting all shades of opinion among them;

(c) The SNC will represent Cambodia externally and occupy the seat of Cambodia at the United Nations, in the United Nations specialized agencies, and in other international institutions and international conferences;

(d) The SNC at the time of signature of the comprehensive settlement will delegate to the United Nations all powers necessary to ensure the implementation of the comprehensive agreement, including those relating to the conduct of free and fair elections and the relevant aspects of the administration of Cambodia;

(e) All decisions of the SNC will be made by consensus among its members.

Accordingly, the Cambodian parties agreed to form the SNC with the following composition:*

1. H.E. Mr. Chau Sen Coosal
2. H.E. Mr. Chem Snguon
3. H.E. Mr. Hor Namhong
4. H.E. Mr. Hun Sen
5. H.E. Mr. Ieng Mouly
6. H.E. Mr. Khieu Samphan
7. H.E. Mr. Kong Som Ol
8. H.E. Mr. Prince Norodom Ranariddh
9. H.E. Mr. Sin Song
10. H.E. Mr. Son Sann
11. H.E. Mr. Son Sen
12. H.E. Mr. Tea Banh

The Cambodian parties further agreed to accept H.R.H. Prince Norodom Sihanouk's proposal, as contained in his statement of 8 September 1990, that if the 12 members of the SNC so desire, they could elect a Chairman

*By decision of the two Co-Chairmen and for practical reasons, this list is arranged in alphabetical order instead of in order of age seniority, as in the PICC.

for the SNC, who would, in such case, be the "13th member" of the SNC.

The SNC is to hold its first session as soon as possible.

The two Co-Chairmen agreed to consult with all the other participating countries of the PICC with a view to reconvening the PICC at the earliest possible date.

Document 4

Security Council resolution on settlement of the Cambodia situation

S/RES/668 (1990), 20 September 1990

The Security Council,

Convinced of the need to find an early, just and lasting peaceful solution of the Cambodia conflict,

Noting that the Paris Conference on Cambodia, which met from 30 July to 30 August 1989, made progress in elaborating a wide variety of elements necessary for reaching a comprehensive political settlement,

Taking note with appreciation of the continuing efforts of China, France, the Union of Soviet Socialist Republics, the United Kingdom of Great Britain and Northern Ireland and the United States of America, which have resulted in the framework for a comprehensive political settlement of the Cambodia conflict, 1/

Also taking note with appreciation of the efforts of the countries of the Association of South-East Asian Nations and other countries involved in promoting the search for a comprehensive political settlement,

Further taking note with appreciation of the efforts of Indonesia and France as Co-Presidents of the Paris Conference on Cambodia and of all participants in the Conference to facilitate the restoration of peace to Cambodia,

Noting that these efforts are aimed at enabling the Cambodian people to exercise their inalienable right to self-determination through free and fair elections organized and conducted by the United Nations in a neutral political environment with full respect for the national sovereignty of Cambodia,

1. *Endorses* the framework for a comprehensive political settlement of the Cambodia conflict 1/ and encourages the continuing efforts of China, France, the Union of Soviet Socialist Republics, the United Kingdom of Great Britain and Northern Ireland and the United States of America in this regard;

2. *Welcomes* the acceptance of this framework in its entirety by all the Cambodian parties, as the basis for settling the Cambodia conflict, at the informal meeting of the Cambodian parties at Jakarta on 10 September 1990 and their commitment to it;

3. *Also welcomes* the commitment of the Cambodian parties, in full co-operation with all other participants in the Paris Conference on Cambodia, to elaborating this framework into a comprehensive political settlement through the processes of the Conference;

4. *Welcomes*, in particular, the agreement reached by all Cambodian parties at Jakarta 2/ to form a Supreme National Council as the unique legitimate body and source of authority in which, throughout the transitional period, the independence, national sovereignty and unity of Cambodia is embodied;

5. *Urges* the members of the Supreme National Council, in full accord with the framework document, to elect the Chairman of the Council as soon as possible, so as to implement the agreement referred to in paragraph 4 above;

6. *Notes* that the Supreme National Council will therefore represent Cambodia externally and it is to designate its representatives to occupy the seat of Cambodia at the United Nations, in the United Nations specialized agencies and in other international institutions and international conferences;

7. *Urges* all parties to the conflict to exercise maximum self-restraint so as to create the peaceful climate required to facilitate the achievement and the implementation of a comprehensive political settlement;

8. *Calls upon* the Co-Presidents of the Paris Conference to intensify their consultations with a view to reconvening the Conference, whose task will be to elaborate and adopt the comprehensive political settlement and to draw up a detailed plan of implementation in accord with the above-mentioned framework;

9. *Urges* the Supreme National Council, all Cambodians and all parties to the conflict to co-operate fully in this process;

10. *Encourages* the Secretary-General to continue, within the context of preparations for reconvening the Paris Conference and on the basis of the present resolution, preparatory studies to assess the resource implications, timing and other considerations relevant to the United Nations role;

11. *Calls upon* all States to support the achievement of a comprehensive political settlement as outlined in the above-mentioned framework.

1/ S/21689 [Document 2]
2/ S/21732 [Document 3]

Document 5

Letter dated 29 November 1990 from France and Indonesia transmitting communiqué of the five permanent members of the Security Council concerning settlement of the Cambodia situation issued at the end of talks held in Paris, 23-26 November 1990

A/45/829-S/21985, 6 December 1990

Upon the instructions of our Governments, who are Co-Chairmen of the Paris Conference on Cambodia, we have the honour to transmit herewith the text of the communiqué of the five permanent members of the United Nations Security Council, issued in Paris on 26 November 1990 (see annex).

We should be grateful if you could have the text of the present letter and its annex circulated as a document of the General Assembly, under agenda item 32, and of the Security Council.

(*signed*) M. Pierre-Louis BLANC
Ambassador
Permanent Representative of France
to the United Nations

(*signed*) Nana S. SUTRESNA
Ambassador
Permanent Representative of Indonesia
to the United Nations

Annex
Communiqué

1. The Five Permanent Members of the United Nations Security Council met in Paris on November 23-26, 1990 to assist the efforts of the Co-Chairmen of the Paris Conference on Cambodia to bring about a comprehensive political settlement of the Cambodia conflict. Joining them were Indonesian Foreign Minister Ali Alatas, Co-Chairman of the Paris Conference on Cambodia, and UN Under-Secretary-General Rafeeuddin Ahmed.

2. The meeting reviewed the positive results of the November 9-10 Working Group Meeting in Jakarta under the Co-Chairmanship of the two Co-Chairmen of the Paris Conference. Building on the work of the Jakarta consultations and reflecting written contributions by a number of countries participating in the Working Group Meeting, the two Co-Chairmen and the Five reached consensus on a draft comprehensive political settlement developed directly from the framework agreement of August 28, 1990 which was endorsed by the UN Security Coucil in Resolution 668 and by acclamation of the General Assembly on October 15.

This document contains a draft agreement covering the major aspects of the settlement with annexes dealing respectively with: the proposed mandate for UNTAC; withdrawal, cease-fire and related measures; elections; repatriation of Cambodian refugees and displaced persons; and principles for a new constitution for Cambodia. A draft agreement concerning the sovereignty, independence, territorial integrity and inviolability, neutrality and national unity of Cambodia and a draft declaration on rehabilitation and reconstruction of Cambodia were also elaborated.

3. The two Co-Chairmen and the Five have thus fulfilled the first necessary condition for the successful reconveneing of the PCC.

The two Co-Chairmen are now in a position to present to the Coordinating Committee of the PPC a draft Agreement which could, after consideration by the Committee, be submitted for adoption by the Conference meeting at the ministerial level.

4. In the light of the positive results achieved at the present meeting, it is now urgent that the Cambodians themselves make their contribution to this process through the SNC. The Co-Chairmen and the Five therefore strongly urge the Cambodians to ensure that the SNC is fully functioning so that the Conference can be reconvened.

5. The two Co-Chairmen and the Five took note of the presence in Paris of Prince Sihanouk and expressed their strong hope that the members of the SNC would speedily resolve with him the outstanding issues which have so far prevented the SNC from playing its proper role in the settlement process. The Five welcomed the readiness of the two Co-Chairmen to meet with a functioning SNC in Paris in order to explain the contents of the draft Agreement and seek their support for it and its implementation.

6. The two Co-Chairmen and the Five believe that it is now urgent to resolve the problem of the leadership of the SNC. The Five reaffirmed their view that should Prince Sihanouk be elected Chairman, they would welcome this decision. They consider that related questions including the possible expansion of the SNC and the vice-chairmanship should be decided by the Cambodians themselves through consultations, flexibly and in a spirit

of national reconciliation. They would expect that should Prince Sihanouk be elected Chairman, he and the other members of the SNC would approach these matters in such a spirit.

7. The Co-Chairmen, the Five and the Repre-

sentative of the Secretary General of the United Nations call upon all the parties to the conflict to exercise maximum self-restraint so that the Paris Conference on Cambodia can be reconvened in a peaceful environment.

Paris, 26 November 1990

Document 6

Letter dated 8 January 1991 from France and Indonesia transmitting statement issued at the end of a meeting between the Co-Chairmen of the Paris Conference on Cambodia and the Supreme National Council of Cambodia in Paris, 21-23 December 1990

A/46/61-S/22059, 11 January 1991

As you know, Mr. Roland Dumas and Mr. Ali Alatas, Co-Chairmen of the Paris Conference on Cambodia, held in Paris, from 21 to 23 December 1990, a meeting with the 12 members of the Supreme National Council of Cambodia (SNC); your representative, Mr. Rafeeuddin Ahmed, also attended the meeting.

As representatives of the two Co-Chairmen, we have the honour to transmit to you herewith the final statement that was issued at the end of the meeting (see annex I). We also enclose the draft agreements on a comprehensive political settlement prepared by the two Co-Chairmen and the permanent members of the Security Council, which have been formally presented to the members of the SNC during the above-mentioned meeting of 21 to 23 December (see annex II). These drafts will be considered by the Co-ordinating Committee of the Paris Conference on Cambodia, which should be reconvened as soon as the conditions necessary to ensure a successful meeting are met.

Finally, we are transmitting an informal explanatory note concerning certain provisions of the drafts, which was provided in the course of the meeting in December (see annex III).

We should be grateful if you could have the text of the present letter and its annexes circulated as a document of the General Assembly, under the item entitled "The situation in Cambodia", and of the Security Council.

(signed) Pierre-Louis BLANC
Ambassador
Permanent Representative of France
to the United Nations

(signed) Nana S. SUTRESNA
Ambassador
Permanent Representative of the Republic
of Indonesia to the United Nations

Annex I
Final statement

The two Co-Chairmen of the Paris Conference on Cambodia (PCC), Mr. Roland Dumas and Mr. Ali Alatas, convened a meeting in Paris, from 21 to 23 December 1990, for the purpose of consultations with the 12 members of the Supreme National Council (SNC).* The representative of the Secretary-General of the United Nations, Mr. Rafeeuddin Ahmed, was also present. The Co-Chairmen formally presented to the members of the Supreme National Council the draft agreements on a comprehensive political settlement as prepared by the two Co-Chairmen of the PCC and the permanent members of the Security Council on 26 November 1990. The members of the Supreme National Council then expressed their views on them.

Upon the request from members of the Supreme National Council, an informal explanatory note concerning certain provisions in the texts was provided.

In the course of the discussions, the members of the SNC reiterated their acceptance of the Framework document formulated by the five permanent members of the Security Council in its entirety as the basis for settling the Cambodia conflict.

As regards the draft agreements of 26 November, there was concurrence on most of the fundamental points.

*Composition of the SNC (in alphabetical order)
  Mr. CHAU SEN COOSAL
  Mr. CHEM SNGUON
  Mr. HOR NAM HONG
  Mr. HUN SEN
  Mr. IENG MOULY
  Mr. KHIEU SAMPHAN
  Mr. KONG SOM OL
  Prince NORODOM RANARIDDH
  Mr. SIN SONG
  Mr. SON SANN
  Mr. SON SEN

The remaining questions will be further discussed at the Co-ordinating Committee and among the members of the SNC, taking into account the views expressed by the SNC members. It was agreed that the draft agreements be transmitted, together with the explanatory note, to the Co-ordinating Committee of the PCC, which should be reconvened at an early date.

The two Co-Chairmen, the 12 members of the Supreme National Council and the representative of the United Nations Secretary-General agreed that for the Paris Conference to be reconvened in an atmosphere propitious to national reconciliation, one important condition would be for all parties to the conflict to exercise genuine restraint on the battlefield.

Annex II
Proposed structure for the agreements on a comprehensive political settlement of the Cambodia conflict

I. FINAL ACT

II. AGREEMENT ON A COMPREHENSIVE POLITICAL SETTLEMENT OF THE CAMBODIA CONFLICT
ANNEXES

  1. Proposed mandate for UNTAC

    (a) Civil administration
    (b) Military functions
    (c) Elections
    (d) Human rights

  2. Withdrawal, cease-fire and related measures

  3. Elections

  4. Repatriation of Cambodian refugees and displaced persons

  5. Principles for a new constitution for Cambodia

III. AGREEMENT CONCERNING THE SOVEREIGNTY, INDEPENDENCE, TERRITORIAL INTEGRITY AND INVIOLABILITY, NEUTRALITY AND NATIONAL UNITY OF CAMBODIA

IV. DECLARATION ON REHABILITATION AND RECONSTRUCTION OF CAMBODIA

II. AGREEMENT ON A COMPREHENSIVE POLITICAL SETTLEMENT OF THE CAMBODIA CONFLICT

The States participating in the Paris Conference on Cambodia, namely Australia, Brunei Darussalam, Cambodia, Canada, the People's Republic of China, the French Republic, the Republic of India, the Republic of Indonesia, Japan, the Lao People's Democratic Republic, Malaysia, the Republic of the Philippines, the Republic of Singapore, the Kingdom of Thailand, the Union of Soviet Socialist Republics, the United Kingdom of Great Britain and Northern Ireland, the United States of America, the Socialist Republic of Viet Nam and the Socialist Federal Republic of Yugoslavia,

In the presence of the Secretary-General of the United Nations,

In order to maintain, preserve and defend the sovereignty, independence, territorial integrity and inviolability, neutrality and national unity of Cambodia,

Desiring to restore and maintain peace in Cambodia, to promote national reconciliation and to ensure the exercise of the right to self-determination of the Cambodian people through free and fair elections,

Convinced that only a comprehensive political settlement to the Cambodia conflict will be just and durable and will contribute to regional and international peace and security,

Noting the formation of the Supreme National Council of Cambodia as the unique legitimate body and source of authority in Cambodia in which, throughout the transitional period, national sovereignty and unity are enshrined, and which represents Cambodia externally,

Recognizing that an enhanced United Nations role requires the establishment of a United Nations Transitional Authority in Cambodia (UNTAC) with civilian and military components, which will act with full respect for the national sovereignty of Cambodia,

Welcoming the statement made at the conclusion of the meeting held at Jakarta on 10 September 1990,

Welcoming United Nations Security Council resolution 668 (1990) of 20 September 1990 and General Assembly resolution 45/3 of 15 October 1990 on Cambodia,

Recognizing that Cambodia's tragic recent history requires special measures to assure protection of human rights, and the non-return to the policies and practices of the past,

Have agreed as follows:

PART I
Arrangements during the transitional period

Section I
Transitional period

Article 1
For the purposes of this Agreement, the transitional period shall commence with the entry into force of this Agreement and terminate when the constituent assembly elected through free and fair elections, organized and certified by the United Nations, has approved the constitution and transformed itself into a legislative assembly, and thereafter a new government has been created.

Section II
United Nations Transitional Authority in Cambodia

Article 2

(1) The Signatories invite the United Nations Security Council to establish a United Nations Transitional Authority in Cambodia (hereinafter referred to as "UNTAC") with civilian and military components under the direct responsibility of the Secretary-General of the United Nations. For this purpose the Secretary-General will designate a special representative to act on his behalf.

(2) The Signatories further invite the United Nations Security Council to provide UNTAC with the mandate set forth in annex 1 and to keep its implementation under continuing review through periodic reports submitted by the Secretary-General.

Section III
Supreme National Council

Article 3

The Supreme National Council (hereinafter referred to as "the SNC") is the unique legitimate body and source of authority in which, throughout the transitional period, the sovereignty, independence and unity of Cambodia are enshrined.

Article 4

The members of the SNC shall be committed to the holding of free and fair elections organized and conducted by the United Nations as the basis for forming a new and legitimate Government.

Article 5

The SNC shall, throughout the transitional period, represent Cambodia externally and occupy the seat of Cambodia at the United Nations, in the United Nations specialized agencies, and in other international institutions and international conferences.

Article 6

The SNC hereby delegates to the United Nations all powers necessary to ensure the implementation of this Agreement, as described in annex 1.

In order to ensure a neutral political environment conducive to free and fair general elections, administrative agencies, bodies and offices which could directly influence the outcome of elections will be placed under direct United Nations supervision or control. In that context, special attention will be given to foreign affairs, national defence, finance, public security and information. To reflect the importance of these subjects, UNTAC needs to exercise such control as is necessary to ensure the strict neutrality of the bodies responsible for them. The United Nations, in consultation with the SNC, will identify which agencies, bodies and offices could continue to operate in order to ensure normal day-to-day life in the country.

Article 7

The relationship between the SNC, UNTAC and existing administrative structures is set forth in annex 1.

Section IV
Withdrawal of foreign forces and its verification

Article 8

Immediately upon entry into force of this Agreement, any foreign forces, advisers, and military personnel remaining in Cambodia, together with their weapons, ammunition, and equipment, shall be withdrawn from Cambodia and not be returned. Such withdrawal and non-return will be subject to UNTAC verification in accordance with annex 2.

Section V
Cease-fire and cessation of arms supply

Article 9

The cease-fire shall take effect at the time this Agreement enters into force. All forces shall immediately disengage and refrain from all hostilities and from any deployment, movement or action that would extend the territory they control or that might lead to renewed fighting.

The Signatories hereby invite the Security Council of the United Nations to request the Secretary-General to provide good offices to assist in this process until such time as the military component of UNTAC is in position to supervise, monitor and verify it.

Article 10

Upon entry into force of this Agreement, there shall be an immediate cessation of all outside military assistance to all Cambodian parties.

Article 11

The objectives of military arrangements during the transitional period shall be to stabilize the security situation and build confidence among the parties to the conflict, so as to reinforce the purposes of this Agreement and to prevent the risks of a return to warfare.

Detailed provisions regarding UNTAC's supervision, monitoring, and verification of the cease-fire and related measures, including verification of the withdrawal of foreign forces and the regrouping, cantonment and ultimate disposition of all Cambodian forces and their weapons during the transitional period, are set forth in annex 1, section B, and annex 2.

PART II
Elections

Article 12

The Cambodian people shall have the right to determine their own political future through the free and fair election of a constituent assembly, which will draft and approve a new Cambodian Constitution in accordance with article 23 and transform itself into a legislative assembly, which will create the new Cambodian Government. This election will be held under United Nations auspices in a neutral political environment with full respect for the national sovereignty of Cambodia.

Article 13

UNTAC shall be responsible for the organization and conduct of these elections based on the provisions of annex 1, section C, and annex 3.

Article 14

All Signatories commit themselves to respect the results of these elections once certified as free and fair by the United Nations.

PART III
Human rights

Article 15

(1) All persons in Cambodia and all Cambodian refugees and displaced persons shall enjoy the rights and freedoms embodied in the Universal Declaration of Human Rights and other relevant international human rights instruments.

(2) To this end,

(a) Cambodia undertakes:

-To ensure respect for and observance of human rights and fundamental freedoms in Cambodia;

-To support the right of all Cambodian citizens to undertake activities which would promote and protect human rights and fundamental freedoms;

-To take effective measures to ensure that the policies and practices of the past shall never be allowed to return;

-To adhere to relevant international human rights instruments;

(b) The other Signatories to this Agreement undertake to promote and encourage respect for and observance of human rights and fundamental freedoms in Cambodia as embodied in the relevant international instruments in order, in particular, to prevent the recurrence of human rights abuses.

Article 16

UNTAC shall be responsible during the transitional period for fostering an environment in which respect for human rights shall be ensured, based on the provisions of annex 1, section D.

Article 17

After the end of the transitional period, the United Nations Commission on Human Rights should continue to monitor closely the human rights situation in Cambodia, including, if necessary, by the appointment of a Special Rapporteur who would report his findings annually to the Commission and to the General Assembly.

PART IV
International guarantees

Article 18

Cambodia undertakes to maintain, preserve and defend, and the other Signatories undertake to recognize and respect, the sovereignty, independence, territorial integrity and inviolability, neutrality and national unity of Cambodia, as set forth in a separate Agreement.

PART V
Refugees and displaced persons

Article 19

Upon entry into force of this Agreement, every effort will be made to create in Cambodia political, economic and social conditions conducive to the voluntary return and harmonious integration of Cambodian refugees and displaced persons.

Article 20

(1) Cambodian refugees and displaced persons, located outside Cambodia, shall have the right to return to Cambodia and to live in safety, security and dignity, free from intimidation or coercion of any kind.

(2) The Signatories request the Secretary-General of the United Nations to facilitate the repatriation in safety and dignity of Cambodian refugees and displaced persons, as an integral part of the comprehensive political settlement and under the overall authority of the Special Representative of the Secretary-General, in accordance with the guidelines and principles on the repatriation of refugees and displaced persons as set forth in annex 4.

PART VI
Release of prisoners of war
and civilian internees

Article 21

The release of all prisoners of war and civilian internees shall be accomplished at the earliest possible date under the direction of the International Committee of the Red Cross (ICRC) in co-ordination with UNTAC, with the assistance, as necessary, of other appropriate international humanitarian organizations and the Signatories.

Article 22

The expression "civilian internees" refers to all persons who are not prisoners of war and who, having contributed in any way whatsoever to the armed or political struggle, have been arrested or detained by any of the parties by virtue of their contribution thereto.

PART VII
Principles for a new Constitution for Cambodia

Article 23

Basic principles, including those regarding human rights and fundamental freedoms as well as regarding Cambodia's status of neutrality, which the new Cambodian Constitution will incorporate, are set forth in annex 5.

PART VIII
Rehabilitation and reconstruction

Article 24

The Signatories urge the international community to provide economic and financial support for the rehabilitation and reconstruction of Cambodia as provided for in a separate declaration.

PART IX
Final provisions

Article 25

The Signatories shall, in good faith and in a spirit of co-operation, resolve through peaceful means any disputes with respect to the implementation of this Agreement.

Article 26

The Signatories request other States, international organizations and other bodies to co-operate and assist in the implementation of this Agreement and in the fulfilment by UNTAC of its mandate.

Article 27

The Signatories shall provide their full co-operation to the United Nations to ensure the implementation of its mandate, including by the provision of privileges and immunities, and by ensuring and facilitating freedom of movement and communication within and through their respective territories.

Article 28

(1) The Signatories shall comply in good faith with all obligations undertaken in this Agreement and shall extend full co-operation, including the provision of the information which UNTAC requires in the fulfilment of its mandate.

(2) The signature on behalf of Cambodia by the members of the SNC shall commit all Cambodian parties and armed forces to the provisions of this Agreement.

Article 29

Without prejudice to the prerogatives of the Security Council of the United Nations, and upon the request of the Secretary-General, the two Co-Chairmen of the Paris Conference on Cambodia, in the event of a violation or threat of violation of this Agreement, will immediately undertake appropriate consultations with a view to taking appropriate steps to ensure respect for these commitments.

Article 30

This Agreement shall enter into force upon signature.

Article 31

This Agreement shall remain open for accession by all States. The instruments of accession shall be deposited with the Governments of the French Republic and Republic of Indonesia. For each State acceding to the Agreement it shall enter into force on the date of deposit of its instruments of accession. Acceding States shall be bound by the same obligations as the Signatories.

Article 32

The originals of this Agreement, of which the Chinese, English, French, Khmer and Russian texts are equally authentic, shall be deposited with the Governments of the French Republic and Republic of Indonesia, which shall transmit certified true copies to the Governments of the other States participating in the Paris Conference on Cambodia, as well as the Secretary-General of the United Nations.

IN WITNESS WHEREOF the undersigned Plenipotentiaries, being duly authorized thereto, have signed this Agreement.

DONE AT ... this ... of ..., one thousand nine hundred and ... .

Annex 1
Proposed mandate for UNTAC

Section (a) *Civil administration*

1. In accordance with article 6 of the Agreement, UNTAC will exercise the powers necessary to ensure the implementation of this Agreement, including those relating to the organization and conduct of free and fair elections and the relevant aspects of the administration of Cambodia.

2. The Supreme National Council (SNC) will offer advice to UNTAC, which will comply with this advice provided there is a consensus among the members of the SNC and provided this advice is consistent with the objectives of the present Agreement. The Secretary-General's Special Representative will determine whether such advice is consistent with this Agreement.

If there is no consensus on any given matter among the members of the SNC, the Secretary-General's Special Representative should make every endeavour to reach a consensus on such a matter. In case it is unattainable, the Secretary-General's Special Representative is entitled to make the final decision, taking fully into account views expressed in the SNC.

This mechanism will be used to resolve all issues relating to the implementation of this Agreement which may arise between the Secretary-General's Representative and the SNC.

3. The Secretary-General's Special Representative or his delegate will attend the meetings of the SNC and of any subsidiary body which might be established by it and give its members all necessary information on the decisions taken by UNTAC.

4. In accordance with article 6 of the Agreement, all administrative agencies, bodies and offices acting in the field of foreign affairs, national defence, finance, public security and information will be placed under the direct control of UNTAC, which will exercise it as necessary to ensure strict neutrality. In this respect, the Secretary-General's Special Representative will determine what is necessary and may issue directives to the above-mentioned administrative agencies, bodies and offices. Such directives may be issued to and will bind all Cambodian Parties.

5. In accordance with article 6 of the Agreement, the Secretary-General's Special Representative, in consultation with the SNC, will determine which other administrative agencies, bodies and offices could directly influence the outcome of elections. These administrative agencies, bodies and offices will be placed under direct supervision or control of UNTAC and will comply with any guidance provided by it.

6. In accordance with article 6 of the Agreement, the Secretary-General's Special Representative, in consultation with the SNC, will identify which administrative agencies, bodies, and offices could continue to operate in order to ensure normal day-to-day life in Cambodia, if necessary, under such supervision by UNTAC as it considers necessary.

7. In accordance with article 6 of the Agreement, the authority of the Secretary-General's Special Representative will include the power to:

(a) Install in administrative agencies, bodies and offices of all the Cambodian Parties, United Nations personnel who will have unrestricted access to all administrative operations and informations;

(b) Require the reassignment or removal of any personnel of such administrative agencies, bodies and offices.

8. In consultation with the SNC, UNTAC will supervise law enforcement processes throughout Cambodia to the extent necessary to ensure that law and order are maintained effectively and impartially, and that human rights and fundamental freedoms are fully protected.

9. If the Secretary-General's Special Representative deems it necessary, UNTAC, in consultation with the SNC, will undertake investigations of complaints and allegations regarding actions by the existing administrative structures in Cambodia that are inconsistent with or work against the objectives of this comprehensive political settlement. UNTAC will also be empowered to undertake such investigation on its own initiative. UNTAC will take, when necessary, appropriate corrective steps.

Section (b) *Military functions*

1. UNTAC will supervise, monitor and verify the withdrawal of foreign forces, the cease-fire and related measures in accordance with annex 2, including:

(a) Verification of the withdrawal from Cambodia of all categories of foreign forces, advisers and military personnel and their weapons, ammunition and equipment, and their non-return to Cambodia;

(b) Liaison with neighbouring Governments over any developments in or near their territory that could endanger the implementation of this Agreement;

(c) Monitoring the cessation of outside military assistance to all Cambodian parties;

(d) Locating and confiscating caches of weapons and military supplies throughout the country;

(e) Assisting with clearing mines and undertaking training programmes in mine clearance and a mine awareness programme among the Cambodian people.

2. UNTAC will supervise the regrouping and relocating of all forces to specifically designated cantonment areas in accordance with an operational timetable to be agreed upon. While the forces are in the cantonments, UNTAC will supervise the storage of their arms on site.

3. UNTAC will then initiate a phased process of arms control and reduction in such a way as to stabilize the security situation and build confidence among the parties to the conflict.

4. UNTAC will take necessary steps regarding the phased process of return to civilian life of all categories of military forces of the parties, in accordance with annex 2.

5. UNTAC will assist, as necessary, the International Committee of the Red Cross in the release of all prisoners of war and civilian internees.

Section (c) *Elections*

1. UNTAC will organize and conduct the election referred to in Part II of this Agreement in accordance with this section and annex 3.

2. UNTAC may consult with the SNC regarding the organization and conduct of the electoral process.

3. In the exercise of its responsibilities in relation to the electoral process, the specific authority of UNTAC will include the following:

(a) The establishment, in consultation with the SNC, of a system of laws, procedures and administrative measures necessary for the holding of a free and fair election in Cambodia, including the adoption of an electoral law and of a code of conduct regulating participation in the election in a manner consistent with respect for human rights and prohibiting coercion or financial inducement in order to influence voter preference;

(b) The suspension or abrogation, in consultation with the SNC, of provisions of existing laws which could defeat the objects and purposes of this Agreement;

(c) The design and implementation of a voter education programme, covering all aspects of the election, to support the election process;

(d) The design and implementation of a system of voter registration, as a first phase of the electoral process, to ensure that eligible voters have the opportunity to register, and the subsequent preparation of verified voter registration lists;

(e) The design and implementation of a system of registration of political parties and lists of candidates;

(f) Ensuring fair access to the media, including press, television and radio, for all political parties contesting in the election;

(g) The adoption and implementation of measures to monitor and facilitate the participation of Cambodians in the elections, the political campaign, and the balloting procedures;

(h) The design and implementation of a system of balloting and polling, to ensure that registered voters have the opportunity to vote;

(i) The establishment, in consultation with the SNC, of co-ordinated arrangements to facilitate the presence of foreign observers wishing to observe the campaign and voting;

(j) Overall direction of polling and the vote count;

(k) The identification and investigation of complaints of electoral irregularities, and the taking of appropriate corrective action;

(l) Determining whether or not the election was free and fair and, if so, certification of list of persons duly elected.

4. In carrying out its responsibilities under the present section, UNTAC will establish a system of safeguards to assist it in ensuring the absence of fraud during the electoral process, including arrangements for Cambodian representatives to observe the registration and polling procedures and the provision of an UNTAC mechanism for hearing and deciding complaints.

5. The timetable for the various phases of the electoral process will be determined by UNTAC, in consultation with the SNC as provided in paragraph 2 of this section. The duration of the electoral process will be —— months.

6. In organizing and conducting the electoral process, UNTAC will make every effort to ensure that the system and procedures adopted are absolutely impartial, while the operational arrangements are as administratively simple and efficient as possible.

Section (d) *Human rights*

In accordance with article 16, UNTAC will make provisions for:

(a) The development and implementation of a programme of human rights education to promote respect for and understanding of human rights;

(b) General human rights oversight during the transitional period;

(c) The investigation of human rights complaints, and, where appropriate, corrective action.

Annex 2
*Withdrawal, cease-fire and related measures**

Article I
Cease-fire

1. All Cambodian Parties (hereinafter referred to as "the Parties") agree to observe a comprehensive cease-fire on land and water and in the air. This cease-fire will be implemented in two phases. During the first phase, the cease-fire will be observed with the assistance of the Secretary-General of the United Nations through his good offices. During the second phase, which should commence as soon as possible, the cease-fire will be supervised, monitored and verified by UNTAC. The Commander of the military component of UNTAC, in consultation with the Parties, shall determine the exact time and date at which the second phase will commence. This date will be set at least four weeks in advance of its coming into effect.

2. The Parties undertake that, upon the signing of this Agreement, they will observe a cease-fire and will order their armed forces immediately to disengage and refrain from all hostilities and any deployment, movement or action that would extend the territory they control or that might lead to a resumption of fighting, pending the commencement of the second phase. "Forces" are agreed to include all regular, provincial, district, paramilitary, and other auxiliary forces. During the first phase, the Secretary-General of the United Na-

*All time-frames indicated in the present annex are included for reference only, as provided by the United Nations Secretariat.

tions will provide his good offices to the Parties to assist them in its observance. The Parties undertake to co-operate with the Secretary-General or his representatives in the exercise of his good offices in this regard.

3. The Parties agree that, immediately upon the signing of this Agreement, the following information will be provided to the United Nations:

(a) Total strength of their forces, organization, precise number and location of deployments inside and outside Cambodia. The deployment will be depicted on a map marked with locations of all troop positions, occupied or unoccupied, including staging camps, supply bases and supply routes;

(b) Comprehensive lists of arms, ammunition and equipment held by their forces, and the exact locations at which those arms, ammunition and equipment are deployed;

(c) Detailed record of their mine-fields, including types and characteristics of mines laid and information of booby traps used by them together with any information available to them about mine-fields laid or booby traps used by the other Parties.

4. Immediately upon his arrival in Cambodia, and not later than four weeks before the beginning of the second phase, the Commander of the military component of UNTAC will, in consultation with the Parties, finalize UNTAC's plan for the regroupment and cantonment of the forces of the Parties and for the storage of their arms, ammunition and equipment under UNTAC supervision. This plan will include the designation of regroupment and cantonment areas, as well as an agreed timetable. The cantonment areas will be established at battalion size or larger.

5. The Parties agree to take steps to inform their forces at least two weeks before the beginning of the second phase, using all possible means of communication, about the agreed date and time of the beginning of the second phase, about the agreed plan for the regroupment and cantonment of their forces and for the storage of their arms, ammunition and equipment and, in particular, about the exact locations of the regroupment areas to which their forces are to report. Such information will continue to be disseminated for a period of four weeks after the beginning of the second phase.

6. The Parties shall scrupulously observe the cease-fire and will not resume any hostilities by land, water or air. The commanders of their armed forces will ensure that all troops under their command remain on their respective positions, pending their movement to the designated regroupment areas, and refrain from all hostilities and from any deployment or movement or action which would extend the territory they control or which might lead to a resumption of fighting.

Article II
Liaison system and Mixed Military Working Group

A Mixed Military Working Group (MMWG) will be established with a view to resolving any problems that may arise in the observance of the cease-fire. It will be chaired by the Commander of the military component of UNTAC or his representative. Each Party agrees to designate, not later than one week prior to the date of the beginning of the second phase, an officer of the rank of brigadier or equivalent to serve on the MMWG. Its composition, method of operation and meeting places will be determined by the Commander of the military component of UNTAC, in consultation with the Parties, before the beginning of the second phase. Similar liaison arrangements will be made at lower military command levels to resolve practical problems on the ground.

Article III
Regroupment and cantonment of the forces of the Parties and storage of their arms, ammunition and equipment

1. In accordance with the operational timetable referred to in paragraph 4 of article I of the present annex, all forces of the Parties that are not already in designated cantonment areas will report to designated regroupment areas, which will be established and operated by the military component of UNTAC. These regroupment areas will be established and operational not later than one week prior to the date of the beginning of the second phase. The Parties agree to arrange for all their forces, with all their arms, ammunition and equipment, to report to regroupment areas within two weeks after the beginning of the second phase. All personnel who have reported to the regroupment areas will thereafter be escorted by personnel of the military component of UN-TAC, with their arms, ammunition and equipment, to designated cantonment areas. All Parties agree to ensure that personnel reporting to the regroupment areas will be able to do so in full safety and without any hindrance.

2. On the basis of the information provided in accordance with paragraph 3 of article I of the present annex, UNTAC will confirm that the regroupment and cantonment processes have been completed in accordance with the plan referred to in paragraph 4 of article I of this annex. UNTAC will endeavour to complete these processes within four weeks from the date of the beginning of the second phase. On the completion of the regroupment of all forces and of their movement to cantonment areas, respectively, the Commander of the military component of UNTAC will so inform each of the four Parties.

3. The Parties agree that, upon arrival in designated cantonment areas, their personnel will be instructed by their commanders to hand over all their arms, ammuni-

tion and equipment for storage on site in their own custody. Upon confirmation by UNTAC of the completion of the cantonment of all forces, such arms, ammunition and equipment will be handed over to UNTAC for storage on site in the custody of UNTAC.

4. UNTAC will check the arms, ammunition and equipment handed over to it against the lists referred to in paragraph 3 (b) of article I of this annex, in order to verify that all the arms, ammunition and equipment in the possession of the Parties have been placed under its custody.

Article IV
Resupply of forces during cantonment

The military component of UNTAC will supervise the resupply of all forces of the Parties during the regroupment and cantonment processes. Such resupply will be confined to items of a non-lethal nature such as food, water, clothing and medical supplies as well as provision of medical care.

Article V
Ultimate disposition of the forces of the Parties and of their arms, ammunition and equipment

1. In order to reinforce the objectives of a comprehensive political settlement, minimize the risks of a return to warfare, stabilize the security situation and build confidence among the Parties to the conflict, all Parties agree to undertake a phased process of return to civilian life of all categories of their military forces, and to do so within a reasonable time-frame in accordance with a detailed plan to be drawn up by UNTAC in consultation with the Parties.

2. UNTAC will continue to guard all the arms, ammunition and equipment of the Parties throughout the transitional period. The ultimate disposition of those arms, ammunition and equipment will be determined by the government that emerges through the free and fair elections in accordance with article 12 of the Agreement.

Article VI
Verification of withdrawal from Cambodia and non-return of all categories of foreign forces

1. UNTAC shall be provided no later than two weeks before the commencement of the second phase of the cease-fire with detailed information in writing regarding the withdrawal of foreign forces. This information shall include the following elements:

(a) Total strength of these forces and their organization and deployment;

(b) Comprehensive lists of arms, ammunition and equipment held by these forces, and their exact locations;

(c) A withdrawal plan (already implemented or to

be implemented), including withdrawal routes, border crossing points and time of departure from Cambodia.

2. On the basis of the information provided in accordance with paragraph 1 above, UNTAC will undertake an investigation in the manner it deems appropriate. The Party providing the information will be required to make personnel available to accompany UNTAC investigators.

3. Upon confirmation of the presence of any foreign forces, UNTAC will immediately deploy military personnel with the foreign forces and accompany them until they have withdrawn from Cambodian territory. UNTAC will also establish check-points on withdrawal routes, border crossing points and airfields to verify the withdrawal and ensure the non-return of all categories of foreign forces.

4. The Mixed Military Working Group provided for in article II of this annex will assist UNTAC in fulfilling the above-mentioned tasks.

Article VII
Cessation of outside military assistance to all Cambodian Parties

1. All Parties undertake, from the time of the signing of this Agreement, not to obtain or seek any outside military assistance, including weapons, ammunition and military equipment from outside sources.

2. The Signatories whose territory is adjacent to Cambodia, namely, the Governments of the Lao People's Democratic Republic, the Kingdom of Thailand and the Socialist Republic of Viet Nam, undertake to:

(a) Prevent the territories of their respective States, including land territory, territorial sea and air space, from being used for the purpose of providing any form of military assistance to any of the Cambodian Parties. Resupply of such items as food, water, clothing and medical supplies through their territories will be allowed but under the supervision of UNTAC;

(b) Provide written confirmation to the Commander of the military component of UNTAC not later than four weeks after the second phase of the cease-fire begins that no forces, arms, ammunition or military equipment of any of the Cambodian Parties are present on their territories;

(c) Receive an UNTAC liaison officer in each of their capitals and designate an officer of the rank of colonel or equivalent, not later than four weeks after the beginning of the second phase of the cease-fire, in order to assist UNTAC in investigating any complaints that activities are taking place on its territory that are contrary to the provisions of the comprehensive political settlement.

3. To enable UNTAC to monitor the cessation of outside assistance to all Cambodian Parties, the Parties agree that, upon signature of this Agreement, they will

provide to UNTAC any information available to them about the routes and means by which military assistance, including weapons, ammunition and military equipment, have been supplied to any of the Parties. Immediately after the second phase of the cease-fire begins, UNTAC will take the following practical measures:

(a) Establish check-points along the routes and at selected locations along the border and at airfields;

(b) Patrol the coastal and inland waterways of Cambodia;

(c) Maintain mobile teams at strategic locations within Cambodia to patrol and investigate allegations of supply of arms to any of the Parties.

Article VIII
Caches of weapons and military supplies

1. In order to stabilize the security situation, build confidence and reduce arms and military supplies throughout Cambodia, each Party agrees to provide to the Commander of the military component of UNTAC before a date to be determined by him, all information at its disposal, including marked maps, about known or suspected caches of weapons and military supplies throughout Cambodia.

2. On the basis of information received, the military component of UNTAC shall deploy verification teams to investigate each report and will destroy each cache found.

Article IX
Unexploded ordnance devices

1. Soon after arrival in Cambodia, the military component of UNTAC shall ensure as a first step that all known mine-fields are clearly marked.

2. The Parties agree that, after completion of the regroupment and cantonment processes in accordance with article III of the present annex, they will make available mine-clearing teams which, under the supervision and control of UNTAC military personnel, will leave the cantonment areas in order to assist UNTAC in removing, disarming or deactivating remaining unexploded ordnance devices. Those mines or objects which cannot be removed, disarmed or deactivated will be clearly marked in accordance with a system to be devised by the military component of UNTAC.

3. Simultaneously, UNTAC shall:

(a) Conduct a mass public education programme in the recognition and avoidance of explosive devices;

(b) Train Cambodian volunteers to dispose of unexploded ordnance devices;

(c) Provide emergency first-aid training to Cambodian volunteers.

Article X
Investigation of violations

1. Upon receipt of any information or complaint from one of the Parties relating to a possible case of non-compliance with any of the provisions of the present annex or related provisions, UNTAC will undertake an investigation in the manner which it deems appropriate. Where the investigation takes place in response to a complaint by one of the Parties, that Party will be required to make personnel available to accompany the UNTAC investigators. The results of such investigation will be conveyed by UNTAC to the complaining Party and the Party complained against, and if necessary to the SNC.

2. UNTAC will also carry out investigations on its own initiative in other cases when it has reason to believe or suspect that a violation of this annex or related provisions may be taking place.

Article XI
Release of prisoners of war

The military component of UNTAC will provide assistance as required to the International Committee of the Red Cross in the latter's discharge of its functions relating to the release of prisoners of war.

Article XII
Repatriation and resettlement of displaced Cambodians

The military component of UNTAC will provide assistance as necessary in the repatriation of Cambodian refugees and displaced persons carried out in accordance with articles 19 and 20 of the Agreement, in particular the clearing of repatriation routes and reception centres of mines and the protection of the reception centres.

Annex 3
Elections

1. The constituent assembly referred to in article 12 of the Agreement shall consist of ... members. Within (three) months from the date of the election, it shall complete its tasks of drafting and adopting a new Cambodian Constitution and transform itself into a legislative assembly which will form a new Cambodian Government.

2. The election referred to in article 12 of the Agreement will be held in Cambodia on a nation-wide basis in accordance with a system of proportional representation on the basis of lists of candidates put forward by political parties.

3. All Cambodians, including those who at the time of signature of this Agreement are Cambodian refugees and displaced persons, will have the same rights, freedoms and opportunities to take part in the electoral process.

4. Every person who has reached the age of 18 at the time of application to register, or who turns 18 during the registration period, and who either was born in Cambodia or is the child of a person born in Cambodia, will be eligible to vote in the election.

5. Political parties may be formed by any group of ... registered voters. Party platforms shall be consistent with the principles and objectives of the Agreement on a comprehensive political settlement.

6. Party affiliation will be required in order to stand for election to the constituent assembly. Political parties will present lists of candidates standing for election on their behalf, who will be registered voters.

7. Political parties and candidates will be registered in order to stand for election. UNTAC will confirm that political parties and candidates meet the established criteria in order to qualify for participation in the election. Adherence to a Code of Conduct established by UNTAC in consultation with the SNC will be a condition for such participation.

8. Voting will be by secret ballot, with provision made to assist those who are disabled or who cannot read or write.

9. The freedoms of speech, assembly and movement will be fully respected. All registered political parties will enjoy fair access to the media, including the press, television and radio.

Annex 4
Repatriation of Cambodian refugees and displaced persons

PART I
Introduction

1. As part of the comprehensive political settlement, every assistance will need to be given to Cambodian refugees and displaced persons as well as to countries of temporary refuge and the country of origin in order to facilitate the voluntary return of all Cambodian refugees and displaced persons in a peaceful and orderly manner. It must also be ensured that there would be no residual problems for the countries of temporary refuge. The country of origin with responsibility towards its own people will accept their return as conditions become conducive.

PART II
Conditions conducive to the return of refugees and displaced persons

2. The task of rebuilding the Cambodian nation will require the harnessing of all its human and natural resources. To this end, the return to the place of their choice of Cambodians from their temporary refuge and elsewhere outside their country of origin will make a major contribution.

3. Every effort should be made to ensure that the conditions that have led to a large number of Cambodian refugees and displaced persons seeking refuge in other countries should not recur. Nevertheless, some Cambodian refugees and displaced persons will wish and be able to return spontaneously to their homeland.

4. There must be full respect for the human rights and fundamental freedoms of all Cambodians, including those of the repatriated refugees and displaced persons, in recognition of their entitlement to live in peace and security, free from intimidation and coercion of any kind. These rights would include, *inter alia*, freedom of movement within Cambodia, the choice of domicile and employment, and the right to property.

5. In accordance with the comprehensive political settlement, every effort should be made to create concurrently in Cambodia political, economic and social conditions conducive to the return and harmonious integration of the Cambodian refugees and displaced persons.

6. With a view to ensuring that refugees and displaced persons participate in the elections, mass repatriation should commence and be completed as soon as possible, taking into account all the political, humanitarian, logistical, technical and socio-economic factors involved, and with the co-operation of the SNC.

7. Repatriation of Cambodian refugees and displaced persons should be voluntary and their decision should be taken in full possession of the facts. Choice of destination within Cambodia should be that of the individual. The unity of the family must be preserved.

PART III
Operational factors

8. Consistent with respect for principles of national sovereignty in the countries of temporary refuge and origin, and in close co-operation with the countries of temporary refuge and origin, full access by the Office of the United Nations High Commissioner for Refugees (UNHCR), ICRC and other relevant international agencies should be guaranteed to all Cambodian refugees and displaced persons, with a view to the agencies undertaking the census, tracing, medical assistance, food distribution and other activities vital to the discharge of their mandate and operational responsibilities; such access should also be provided in Cambodia to enable the relevant international organizations to carry out their traditional monitoring as well as operational responsibilities.

9. In the context of the comprehensive political

settlement, the Signatories note with satisfaction that the Secretary-General of the United Nations has entrusted UNHCR with the role of leadership and co-ordination among intergovernmental agencies assisting with the repatriation and relief of Cambodian refugees and displaced persons. The Signatories look to all non-governmental organizations to co-ordinate as much as possible their work for the Cambodian refugees and displaced persons with that of UNHCR.

10. The SNC, the Governments of the countries in which the Cambodian refugees and displaced persons have sought temporary refuge, and the countries which contribute to the repatriation and integration effort, will wish to monitor closely and facilitate the repatriation of the returnees. An *ad hoc* consultative body should be established for a limited term for these purposes. UNHCR, ICRC, and other international agencies as appropriate, as well as UNTAC, would be invited to join as full participants.

11. Adequately monitored short-term repatriation assistance should be provided on an impartial basis to enable the families and individuals returning to Cambodia to establish their lives and livelihoods harmoniously in their society. These interim measures would be phased out and replaced in the longer term by the reconstruction programme.

12. Those responsible for organizing and supervising the repatriation operation will need to ensure that conditions of security are created for the movement of the refugees and displaced persons. In this respect, it is imperative that appropriate border crossing points and routes be designated and cleared of mines and other hazards.

13. The international community should contribute generously to the financial requirements of the repatriation operation.

Annex 5
Principles for a new constitution for Cambodia

1. The constitution will be the supreme law of the land. It may be amended only by a designated process involving legislative approval, popular referendum, or both.

2. The constitution will contain a declaration of fundamental rights, including the rights to life, personal liberty, security, freedom of movement, freedom of religion, assembly and association [including political parties and trade unions], due process and equality before the law, protection from arbitrary deprivation of property or deprivation of private property without just compensation, and freedom from racial, ethnic, religious or sexual discrimination. It will prohibit the retroactive application of criminal law. The declaration will be consistent with the provisions of the Universal Declaration of Human Rights and other relevant international instruments. Aggrieved individuals will be entitled to have the courts adjudicate and enforce these rights.

3. The constitution will declare Cambodia's status as a sovereign, independent and neutral State, and the national unity of the Cambodian people.

4. The constitution will provide for periodic and genuine elections. It will provide for the right to vote and to be elected by universal and equal suffrage. It will provide for voting by secret ballot, with a requirement that electoral procedures provide a full and fair opportunity to organize and participate in the electoral process.

5. An independent judiciary will be established, empowered to enforce the rights provided under the constitution.

6. The constitution will be adopted by a ... majority of the members of the constituent assembly.

III. AGREEMENT CONCERNING THE SOVEREIGNTY, INDEPENDENCE, TERRITORIAL INTEGRITY AND INVIOLABILITY, NEUTRALITY AND NATIONAL UNITY OF CAMBODIA

Australia, Brunei Darussalam, Cambodia, Canada, the People's Republic of China, the French Republic, the Republic of India, the Republic of Indonesia, Japan, the Lao People's Democratic Republic, Malaysia, the Republic of the Philippines, the Republic of Singapore, the Kingdom of Thailand, the Union of Soviet Socialist Republics, the United Kingdom of Great Britain and Northern Ireland, the United States of America, the Socialist Republic of Viet Nam and the Socialist Federal Republic of Yugoslavia,

In the presence of the Secretary-General of the United Nations,

Convinced that a comprehensive political settlement for Cambodia is essential for the long-term objective of maintaining peace and security in South-East Asia,

Recalling their obligations under the Charter of the United Nations and other rules of international law,

Considering that full observance of the principles of non-interference and non-intervention in the internal and external affairs of States is of the greatest importance for the maintenance of international peace and security,

Reaffirming the inalienable right of States freely to determine their own political, economic, cultural and social systems in accordance with the will of their peoples, without outside interference, subversion, coercion or threat in any form whatsoever,

Desiring to promote respect for and observance of human rights and fundamental freedoms in conformity with the Charter of the United Nations and other relevant international instruments,

Have agreed as follows:

Article 1

1. Cambodia hereby solemnly undertakes to maintain, preserve and defend its sovereignty, independence, territorial integrity and inviolability, neutrality, and national unity; the perpetual neutrality of Cambodia shall be proclaimed and enshrined in the Cambodian constitution to be adopted after free and fair elections.

2. To this end, Cambodia undertakes:

(a) To refrain from any action that might impair the sovereignty, independence and territorial integrity and inviolability of other States;

(b) To refrain from entering into any military alliances or other military agreements with other States that would be inconsistent with its neutrality, without prejudice to Cambodia's right to acquire the necessary military equipment, arms, munitions and assistance to enable it to exercise its inherent right of self-defence and to maintain law and order;

(c) To refrain from interference in any form whatsoever, whether direct or indirect, in the internal affairs of other States;

(d) To terminate treaties and agreements that are incompatible with its sovereignty, independence, territorial integrity and inviolability, neutrality, and national unity;

(e) To refrain from the threat or use of force against the territorial integrity or political independence of any State, or in any other manner inconsistent with the purposes of the United Nations;

(f) To settle all disputes with other States by peaceful means;

(g) To refrain from using its territory or the territories of other States to impair the sovereignty, independence, and territorial integrity and inviolability of other States;

(h) To refrain from permitting the introduction or stationing of foreign forces, including military personnel, in any form whatsoever, in Cambodia, and to prevent the establishment or maintenance of foreign military bases, strong points or facilities in Cambodia, except pursuant to United Nations authorization for the implementation of the comprehensive political settlement.

Article 2

1. The other parties to this Agreement hereby solemnly undertake to recognize and to respect in every way the sovereignty, independence, territorial integrity and inviolability, neutrality and national unity of Cambodia.

2. To this end, they undertake:

(a) To refrain from entering into any military alliances or other military agreements with Cambodia that would be inconsistent with Cambodia's neutrality, without prejudice to Cambodia's right to acquire the neces-

sary military equipment, arms, munitions and assistance to enable it to exercise its inherent right of self-defence and to maintain law and order;

(b) To refrain from interference in any form whatsoever, whether direct or indirect, in the internal affairs of Cambodia;

(c) To refrain from the threat or use of force against the territorial integrity or political independence of Cambodia, or in any other manner inconsistent with the purposes of the United Nations;

(d) To settle all disputes with Cambodia by peaceful means;

(e) To refrain from using their territories or the territories of other States to impair the sovereignty, independence, territorial integrity and inviolability, neutrality and national unity of Cambodia;

(f) To refrain from using the territory of Cambodia to impair the sovereignty, independence and territorial integrity and inviolability of other States;

(g) To refrain from the introduction or stationing of foreign forces, including military personnel, in any form whatsoever, in Cambodia and from establishing or maintaining military bases, strong points or facilities in Cambodia, except pursuant to United Nations authorization for the implementation of the comprehensive political settlement.

Article 3

1. All persons in Cambodia shall enjoy the rights and freedoms embodied in the Universal Declaration of Human Rights and other relevant international human rights instruments.

2. To this end,

(a) Cambodia undertakes:

-To ensure respect for and observance of human rights and fundamental freedoms in Cambodia;

-To support the right of all Cambodian citizens to undertake activities that would promote and protect human rights and fundamental freedoms;

-To take effective measures to ensure that the policies and practices of the past shall never be allowed to return;

-To adhere to relevant international human rights instruments;

(b) The other parties to this Agreement undertake to promote and encourage respect for an observance of human rights and fundamental freedoms in Cambodia as embodied in the relevant international instruments in order, in particular, to prevent the recurrence of human rights abuses.

3. The United Nations Commission on Human Rights should continue to monitor closely the human rights situation in Cambodia, including, if necessary, by the appointment of a Special Rapporteur who would

report his findings annually to the Commission and to the General Assembly.

Article 4

The parties to this Agreement call upon all other States to recognize and respect in every way the sovereignty, independence, territorial integrity and inviolability, neutrality and national unity of Cambodia and to refrain from any action inconsistent with these principles or with other provisions of this Agreement.

Article 5

1. In the event of a violation or threat of violation of the sovereignty, independence, territorial integrity and inviolability, neutrality or national unity of Cambodia, or of any of the other commitments herein, the parties to this Agreement undertake to consult immediately with a view to adopting all appropriate steps to ensure respect for these commitments.

2. Such steps may include, *inter alia*, reference of the matter to the Security Council of the United Nations or recourse to the means for the peaceful settlement of disputes referred to in Article 33 of the Charter of the United Nations.

3. The parties to this Agreement may also call upon the assistance of the Co-Chairmen of the Paris Conference on Cambodia.

4. In the event of serious violations of human rights in Cambodia, they will call upon the competent organs of the United Nations to take such other steps as are appropriate for the prevention and suppression of such violations in accordance with the relevant international instruments.

Article 6

This Agreement shall enter into force upon signature.

Article 7

This Agreement shall remain open for accession by all States. The instruments of accession shall be deposited with the Government of the French Republic. For each State acceding to this Agreement, it shall enter into force on the date of deposit of its instrument of accession.

Article 8

The original of this Agreement, of which the Chinese, English, French, Khmer and Russian texts are equally authentic, shall be deposited with the Government of the French Republic, which shall transmit certified true copies to the Governments of the other States participating in the Paris Conference on Cambodia and to the Secretary-General of the United Nations.

IN WITNESS WHEREOF the undersigned plenipotentiaries, being duly authorized thereto, have signed this Agreement.

DONE at Paris this ... day of ..., 1990.

IV. DECLARATION ON REHABILITATION AND RECONSTRUCTION OF CAMBODIA

1. The primary objective of the reconstruction of Cambodia should be the advancement of the Cambodian nation and people, without discrimination or prejudice, and with full respect for human rights and fundamental freedom for all. The achievement of this objective requires the full implementation of the comprehensive political settlement.

2. The main responsibility for deciding Cambodia's reconstruction needs and plans should rest with the Cambodian people and the government formed after free and fair elections. No attempt should be made to impose a development strategy on Cambodia from any outside source or deter potential donors from contributing to the reconstruction of Cambodia.

3. International, regional and bilateral assistance to Cambodia should be co-ordinated as much as possible, complement and supplement local resources and be made available impartially with full regard for Cambodia's sovereignty, priorities, institutional means and absorptive capacity.

4. In the context of the reconstruction effort, economic aid should benefit all areas of Cambodia, especially the more disadvantaged, and reach all levels of society.

5. The implementation of an international aid effort would have to be phased in over a period that realistically acknowledges both political and technical imperatives. It would also necessitate a significant degree of co-operation between the future Cambodian Government and bilateral, regional and international contributors.

6. An important role will be played in rehabilitation and reconstruction by the United Nations system. The launching of an international reconstruction plan and an appeal for contributions should take place at an appropriate time, so as to ensure its success.

7. No effective programme of national reconstruction can be initiated without detailed assessments of Cambodia's human, natural and other economic assets. It will be necessary for a census to be conducted, developmental priorities identified, and the availability of resources, internal and external, determined.

To this end there will be scope for sending to Cambodia fact-finding missions from the United Nations system, international financial institutions and other agencies, with the consent of the future Cambodian Government.

8. With the achievement of the comprehensive political settlement, it is now possible and desirable to initiate a process of rehabilitation, addressing immediate needs, and to lay the groundwork for the preparation of medium- and long-term reconstruction plans.

9. For this period of rehabilitation, the United

Nations Secretary-General is requested to help co-ordinate the programme guided by a person appointed for this purpose.

10. In this rehabilitation phase, particular attention will need to be given to food security, health, housing, training, education, the transport network and the restoration of Cambodia's existing basic infrastructure and public utilities.

11. The implementation of a longer-term international development plan for reconstruction should await the formation of a government following the elections and the determination and adoption of its own policies and priorities.

12. This reconstruction phase should promote Cambodian entrepreneurship and make use of the private sector, among other sectors, to help advance self-sustaining economic growth. It would also benefit from regional approaches, involving, *inter alia*, institutions such as the Economic and Social Commission for Asia and the Pacific (ESCAP) and the Mekong Committee, and Governments within the region; and from participation by non-governmental organizations.

13. In order to harmonize and monitor the contributions that will be made by the international community to the reconstruction of Cambodia after the formation of a government following the elections, a consultative body, to be called the International Committee on the Reconstruction of Cambodia (ICORC), should be set up at an appropriate time and be open to potential donors and other relevant parties. The United Nations Secretary-General is requested to make special arrangements for the United Nations system to support ICORC in its work, notably in ensuring a smooth transition from the rehabilitation to reconstruction phases.

Annex III
Explanatory note

The role of the United Nations as envisioned in the draft agreement is based upon full respect for the sovereignty of the Cambodian nation and covers every aspect of a comprehensive political settlement. It foresees tasks with regard to the withdrawal, cease-fire and related military measures, the civil administration during the transitional period, the protection of human rights, the organization and conduct of free and fair general elections, the repatriation of Cambodian refugees and displaced persons, and the rehabilitation and reconstruction of Cambodia.

With respect to civil administration during the transitional period, the draft agreement provides that there will be three categories of entities exercising powers. The first is the Supreme National Council, which, under

article 3 of the main agreement, is the unique legitimate body and source of authority in which the sovereignty, independence and unity of Cambodia are enshrined during the transitional period.

The second is UNTAC, to which, under article 6 of the main agreement, the Supreme National Council will delegate such powers as are necessary for the implementation of the agreement in order to ensure a neutral political environment conducive to the holding of free and fair elections. Annex 1 of the draft agreement stipulates some of the tasks of UNTAC in this respect, and provides for a mechanism governing the relationship between the Supreme National Council and UNTAC. That mechanism, provided in section (a), paragraph 2, is designed to ensure that UNTAC can be provided as far as possible with guidance by the Supreme National Council on the basis of consensus. It further provides that, should the Supreme National Council be unable to provide such guidance, even-handed decisions can be taken by the Special Representative of the Secretary-General as a last resort, taking fully into account the views expressed by the members of the Supreme National Council.

The third category is the existing administrative structures. In this connection, section (a) of annex 1, provides that UNTAC will have three levels of interaction with agencies, bodies and offices of the existing administrative structures: (1) control; (2) control or supervision; (3) no control or supervision, but only investigation of complaints. The interaction will be limited to those functions and activities of the existing administrative structures, be they at the national, provincial, district or village level, which could directly influence the holding of free and fair elections in a neutral political environment. Other functions and activities will remain unaffected. An efficient and cost-effective discharge of its mandate will require UNTAC to take a pragmatic, realistic and practical approach in full consultation and co-operation with the Supreme National Council and the existing civil administration.

The first level of interaction, control, is specified in paragraph 4 of section (a) of annex 1, which provides that UNTAC will exercise such direct control as is necessary to ensure strict neutrality in the five areas already identified in paragraph 10 of the Framework document of 28 August as directly influencing the elections. In this connection, UNTAC would co-operate closely with the existing administrative structures to ensure that its tasks can be fulfilled successfully.

The second level of interaction is provided in paragraph 5, where UNTAC would exercise a lesser degree of "supervision or control" over those other administrative agencies, bodies and offices which have to be identified, in consultation with the Supreme National Council, as possibly directly influencing the outcome of elections. In this respect, the role of UNTAC would be limited to providing guidance and surveillance for the purpose of ensuring that a neutral political environment is maintained.

The third level of interaction is provided in paragraph 6. Here again, UNTAC would consult with the Supreme National Council to identify those administrative agencies, bodies and offices which could continue to operate in order to ensure normal day-to-day life in the country without any supervision or control. The role of UNTAC would be limited to investigation of complaints of actions or inactions that could affect the electoral process. These investigations would take place in accordance with the procedure specified in paragraph 9 of section (a) of annex 1. Such investigations would also be carried out with respect to complaints concerning actions or inactions by the agencies, bodies and offices of the existing administrative structures which are under UNTAC control or supervision, as defined above.

In connection with the role of UNTAC regarding civil administration, paragraph 7 of annex 1 vests UNTAC with certain personnel powers. However, these powers would only be exercised by UNTAC if it is found that certain individuals have acted in a manner inconsistent with the objectives of the settlement agreement.

Paragraph 8 of section (a) of annex 1 provides a supervisory role for UNTAC with regard to law enforcement processes throughout Cambodia, in consultation with the SNC. This is directly related to functions with respect to public security, and would encompass supervision of the maintenance of law and order and related judicial processes. It is foreseen that the civilian component of UNTAC would include police monitors. The role of these monitors would be to supervise the existing police in order to ensure that law and order are maintained effectively and impartially, and that human rights and fundamental freedoms are fully protected.

It is clear that, in the exercise of its tasks in respect of civil administration, UNTAC will work closely with the Supreme National Council and of the existing administrative structures. Without such co-operation, UNTAC will be unable to ensure that a neutral political environment conducive to the holding of free and fair elections, which is the touchstone of the role of the United Nations, can be established and maintained.

The role of the military·component of UNTAC is outlined in section (b) of annex 1 and in annex 2. Since, during the first phase of the cease-fire, the United Nations would not yet be in a position to undertake fully all the tasks provided for in paragraph 1 of section (b), it is foreseen in article 9 of the main agreement and in annex 2, article I, that the United Nations would provide "good offices" at that time. In this respect it can be envisioned that the United Nations would assist the Parties by providing liaison and communications to aid in the maintenance of the cease-fire.

Once the military component of UNTAC has been fully deployed, it would undertake the fulfilment of its tasks during the "second phase" of the cease-fire. In carrying out its functions in this respect, UNTAC will depend upon the full co-operation of all parties concerned and their implementation in good faith of the obligations they have undertaken in the comprehensive settlement agreement. This will be especially important with respect to the activities foreseen in connection with the verification of the withdrawal of all categories of foreign military forces, their non-return to Cambodia, and the cessation of military assistance.

With respect to the Cambodian armed forces, the draft agreement foresees a process of their regroupment, cantonment, disarming and eventual return to civilian life. Here again, the full co-operation of the Parties is vital. Each step can and would only be undertaken once the previous step has been completed. In this connection, article X of annex 2 foresees that, at each stage of the process, should any Party suspect that there has not been full compliance by any other Party, investigations by UNTAC would take place with the assistance of the complaining Party. The article X mechanism would also apply to all other aspects of the military obligations of the parties to the settlement agreements.

It is foreseen in article V of annex 2 that a detailed plan of phased return to civilian life of the cantoned forces within a reasonable time-frame would be drawn up in consultation with the Parties. Such a return to civilian life is essential in order to minimize the risk of return to warfare, stabilize the security situation, and build confidence among the Parties, thus to ensure the best possible prospects of the durability of the settlement. It is also essential in order to allow those Cambodians who have been cantoned to be in a position to participate freely in the electoral process, and hence to exercise their inalienable right to self-determination free from any possibility of intimidation or interference. The implementation of the detailed plan for return to civilian life would, like the other military aspects of the settlement, take into account the need to provide assurances to all Parties at each phase of the process. Certainly, it would not be possible to undertake any activities in this respect without the full co-operation of all the Cambodian Parties.

Document 7

Letter dated 21 February 1991 from France and Indonesia transmitting joint statement issued at the end of talks held at Hanoi, 1-2 February 1991, between representatives of the Paris Conference on Cambodia and Vietnamese leaders

A/46/112-S/22344, 8 March 1991

Upon the instructions of our Governments, we have the honour to transmit herewith the text of a joint statement issued at the end of the talks held at Hanoi on 1 to 2 February 1991 between Mr. Ali Alatas and Mrs. Edwige Avice, Co-Presidents of the Paris Conference on Cambodia, and Mr. Nguyen Co Thach, Vice-Chairman of the Council of Ministers and Minister for Foreign Affairs of Viet Nam (see annex).

We would be grateful if you could have the text of this letter and its annex circulated as a document of the General Assembly, under item 24 of the preliminary list, and of the Security Council.

(*signed*) Pierre-Louis BLANC
Ambassador,
Permanent Representative of France
to the United Nations

(*signed*) Nugroho WISNUMURTI
Chargé d'affaires
Ambassador,
Deputy Permanent Representative

Annex

Joint statement issued at the end of the talks held at Hanoi on 1 and 2 February 1991 between the two Co-Presidents of the Paris Conference on Cambodia and the Vietnamese leaders

The two Co-Presidents of the Paris Conference on Cambodia, Mr. Ali Alatas and Mrs. Edwige Avice, accompanied by Mr. Rafeeuddin Ahmed, Representative of the Secretary-General of the United Nations, held talks with Mr. Nguyen Co Thach, Vice-Chairman of the Council of Ministers and Minister for Foreign Affairs of Viet Nam, at Hanoi on 1 and 2 February 1991. They were also received by Mr. Vo Chi Cong, Chairman of the Council of State and by Mr. Nguyen Van Linh, General Secretary of the Communist Party of Viet Nam.

During these meetings, extensive discussions were held on the draft plan for a comprehensive political settlement of the Cambodia conflict. The Vietnamese side reiterated its acceptance of the framework document of the permanent members of the Security Council of 28 August 1990 as the basis for settling the Cambodia conflict. All sides agreed that there must be full respect for the sovereignty of the Cambodian nation.

The two Co-Presidents and the Representative of the Secretary-General of the United Nations presented comments and provided explanations on the draft agreements of 26 November 1990. The Vietnamese side welcomed the results of the meeting between the 12 members of the Supreme National Council and the two Co-Presidents and the Representative of the Secretary-General in Paris from 21 to 23 December 1990. The Vietnamese side expressed its appreciation for explanations provided by the two Co-Presidents and the Representative of the Secretary-General and reaffirmed their willingness to support the efforts of the two Co-Presidents to resolve the remaining issues. Towards this end, it was agreed that it may be useful for the two Co-Presidents to hold another meeting with the members of the Supreme National Council to pave the way for the reconvening of the Co-ordinating Committee of the Paris Conference. In order to enable the Paris Conference to be reconvened in an atmosphere propitious to national reconciliation, it is essential for all parties to the conflict to exercise genuine restraint.

The two Co-Presidents and the Vietnamese side agreed on the urgency of a comprehensive political settlement of the Cambodian conflict. They will spare no effort towards this end.

Document 8

Letter dated 22 April 1991 from France and Indonesia transmitting appeal for a voluntary cease-fire in Cambodia issued on 22 April 1991 by the Co-Chairmen of the Paris Conference on Cambodia and the United Nations Secretary-General

A/46/161-S/22552, 29 April 1991

We have the honour to transmit herewith the text of an appeal, issued on 22 April 1991 by Your Excellency and the Co-Chairmen of the Paris International Conference on Cambodia, for a voluntary cease-fire in Cambodia.

We would be grateful if you could have the text of this letter and its annex circulated as an official document of the General Assembly, under item 24 of the preliminary list, and of the Security Council.

(signed) Jean-Bernard MÉRIMÉE, Ambassador
Permanent Representative of France
to the United Nations

(signed) Nana S. SUTRESNA, Ambassador
Permanent Representative of Indonesia
to the United Nations

Annex
Appeal, issued on 22 April 1991 by the Co-Chairmen of the Paris International Conference on Cambodia and the Secretary-General, for a voluntary cease-fire in Cambodia

We, the Co-Chairmen of the Paris Conference on Cam-
bodia and the Secretary-General of the United Nations, have been following with concern the recent reports of intensified fighting in Cambodia. In this regard, we would recall that the United Nations Security Council and the General Assembly have unanimously urged all parties to the conflict to exercise maximum self-restraint, so as to create a climate conducive to the achievement of a comprehensive political settlement.

The Co-Chairmen of the Paris Conference hope to convene a meeting with the members of the Supreme National Council in Jakarta before the end of spring, in order to pursue the discussions on the draft agreements of 26 November 1990 and explore ways to resolve the pending issues. As a gesture of good faith creating a favourable environment for the success of this meeting, we would strongly appeal to all parties to the conflict to observe a temporary cessation of hostilities, from the first of May at least until the conclusion of the Jakarta meeting. We sincerely hope that this appeal will be considered seriously and will evoke a favourable response.

Document 9

Letter dated 26 June 1991 from Cambodia transmitting communiqué of the Supreme National Council meeting in Pattaya, Thailand, 24-26 June 1991

A/46/271-S/22740, 26 June 1991

I have the honour to enclose herewith, for your information, the Final Communiqué, of the meeting of the Supreme National Council of Cambodia, held from 24 to 26 June 1991 at Pattaya (Thailand) (see annex).

I should be very grateful if you could have the text of the present letter and its annex circulated as an official document of the General Assembly, under item 24 of the preliminary list, and of the Security Council.

(*signed*) SISOWATH Sirirath
Ambassador
Chargé d'affaires a.i.

Annex
Final Communiqué of the Meeting of the Supreme National Council of Cambodia in Pattaya (Thailand)

June 24-26, 1991

I.   The Supreme National Council (SNC) of Cambodia held a meeting in Pattaya (Thailand) from 24 to 26 June 1991, under the very high chairmanship of H.R.H. Samdech Norodom Sihanouk, with the participation of the Representatives of the two Co-Chairmen of the PICC and the Special Representative of the UN Secretary-General, and has come to unanimous agreements as set out in successive SNC communiques already issued. These agreements are as follows:

1/- to grant H.R.H. Samdech Norodom Sihanouk the task of convoking the SNC of Cambodia and presiding over its future meetings.

2/- to adopt the Flag and Anthem of the SNC of Cambodia, as mentioned in the proposal of H.R.H. Samdech Norodom Sihanouk dated June 22, 1991. The Flags and Anthems of the different Parties are maintained until the general elections.

3/- to implement the unlimited cease-fire and to undertake to stop receiving foreign military aids as from the 24th June 1991. The modalities of control of the United Nations will be examined during the course of further sessions of the SNC.

4/- to send a delegation of the SNC, headed by H.R.H. Samdech Norodom Sihanouk, to the next session of the UN General Assembly.

5/- to request H.R.H. Samdech Norodom Sihanouk to write on behalf of the SNC:

a) to the United Nations Secretary-General requesting the inscription of the Monuments of Angkor in the UNESCO World Heritage List;

b) to the Executive Agent of the Mekong Committee requesting the resumption of membership of Cambodia to the Mekong Committee;

c) to the World Bank and the International Monetary Fund for the sending of a SNC delegation to attend the next meeting of the World Bank and IMF in Bangkok (Thailand);

d) to the UN Secretary-General asking for humanitarian assistances and for the vocational training of Cambodians.

6/- to set up a SNC Secretariat.

7/- to set up the Headquarters of the SNC in Phnom Penh, with the following facilities and guarantees:

- Members of the SNC from each party have their own residence protected by that party's forces. The forces of members of the SNC ensure the security within the compound of their residence, while the forces of the host party ensure the security outside the compound;

- The representatives of the two Co-Chairmen of the Paris International Conference on Cambodia (PICC) have their permanent missions accredited to the SNC;

- The Special Representative of the UN Secretary-General or his representative has his own permanent mission to the SNC;

- The representatives of countries participating in the PICC or the representatives of the Perm-Five as well as the representatives of the ASEAN countries have their permanent missions accredited to the SNC.

8/- pending the setting up of the SNC Headquarters in Phnom Penh, to hold the next meeting of the SNC at the former Embassy of Cambodia in Bangkok (Thailand).

9/- to request H.R.H. Samdech Norodom Sihanouk to write to the UN Secretary-General to inform him of the Flag and Anthem of the SNC of Cambodia.

10/- to set up Working Groups to study the following items:

-Rules of procedure of the SNC;

-Electoral laws;

-Principles of the new Constitution of Cambodia.

II.   This achievement of outstanding significance cannot be reached without the wisdom, tact and moral influence that H.R.H. Samdech Norodom Sihanouk has once again conspicuously displayed during the deliberations of the SNC meeting and without His Peace Plan of June 22, 1991. This fact clearly and unquestionably confirms the spirit of national reconciliation among all Cambodians within the framework of an independent, neutral and sovereign Cambodia.

III.   The remaining issues will be discussed in the next meetings of the SNC.

IV.   The SNC wishes to take this propitious opportunity to express its warmest gratitude to His Majesty the King and Her Majesty the Queen of the Kingdom of Thailand, H.E. Mr. Anand Panyarachun, Prime Minister of the Royal Thai Government and all other Thai officials without whose generous assistance and hospitality this SNC meeting could not have been crowned with this success. The Cambodian nation and people remain profoundly indebted to the Kingdom of Thailand for her generosity, compassion and tremendous efforts she has made for the Cambodian national cause.

V.   The SNC also expresses its gratitude to all friendly countries and governments the world over who have unfailingly contributed to the search for the settlement of the Cambodia conflict over the last 12 years. The results achieved at this current meeting of the SNC cannot be separated from their long and persistent endeavors.

The SNC also addresses its gratitude to the two Co-Chairmen of the PICC and the UN Secretary-General as well as to their representatives for their co-operation.

The SNC expresses its gratitude to the Five Permanent Members of the UN Security Council for all the efforts and initiatives and to all countries participating in the PICC for their continuing concern over the plight of the Cambodian nation and people.

Done in Pattaya (Thailand), on June 26, 1991.

The 12 Members
of the Supreme National Council of Cambodia

H.R.H. Samdech NORODOM SIHANOUK
H.E. Mr. DITH MUNTY
H.E. Mr. HOR NAM HONG

H.E. Mr. HUN SEN
H.E. Mr. IENG MOULY
H.E. Mr. IM CHHUN LIM
H.E. Mr. KHIEU SAMPHAN
H.R.H. Prince NORODOM RANARIDDH
H.E. Mr. SIN SEN
H.E. Mr. SON SANN
H.E. Mr. SON SEN
H.E. Mr. TEA BANH

Document 10

Letter dated 18 July 1991 from the President of the Supreme National Council transmitting communiqué of the Council's Informal Meeting in Beijing, 16-17 July 1991

A/46/310-S/22808, 18 July 1991

I have the honour to attach herewith, for your information, the Final Communiqué of the Informal Meeting of the Supreme National Council of Cambodia, dated 17 July 1991 (see annex).

I should be very grateful if you could have the present letter and its annex circulated as an official document of the General Assembly, under item 24 of the preliminary list, and of the Security Council.

(signed) NORODOM SIHANOUK
President of the Supreme National Council of Cambodia

Annex
Final Communiqué of the Informal Meeting of the Supreme National Council of Cambodia

Beijing, 17 July 1991

I. The Supreme National Council (SNC) of Cambodia held an informal meeting in Beijing (People's Republic of China) on 16 and 17 July 1991, under the very high chairmanship of His Royal Highness Samdech NORODOM SIHANOUK. At the meeting, there were (in alphabetical order): Their Excellencies HOR NAM HONG, HUN SEN, IENG MOULY, IM CHHUN LIM, KHIEU SAMPHAN, H.R.H. Prince NORODOM RANARIDDH, Their Excellencies SON SANN and SON SEN.

The Representatives of the two Co-Chairmen of the Paris International Conference on Cambodia (PICC) and the Special Representative of the United Nations Secretary-General participated in the meeting as observers.

The Representative of the People's Republic of China participated also in the meeting as observer.

II. The SNC of Cambodia unanimously agreed:

1. To elect His Royal Highness Samdech NORODOM SIHANOUK as its President.

This important decision is a deserved homage rendered to H.R.H. Samdech NORODOM SIHANOUK who, thanks to his being above all parties, his wise and experienced leadership, is the sole Cambodian statesman in a position to achieve national reconciliation among all Cambodians and to speed up the peace process towards a comprehensive political settlement of the Cambodia conflict and towards the restoration of an independent, sovereign, peaceful, neutral, non-aligned and united Cambodia within her territorial integrity.

In order to fully implement his role as President of the Supreme National Council, H.R.H. Samdech NORODOM SIHANOUK has decided to resign from all his positions as President of the Cambodian National Resistance (CNR) and as President of the National Government of Cambodia (NGC) and has decided from now on to stand neutral acting as a conciliator, without belonging to any faction or political party.

2. To hold the next formal meeting of the SNC in Bangkok (Thailand) on 26, 27 and 28 August 1991.

3. To send a delegation to the forty-sixth session of the United Nations General Assembly, composed of:
-Head of the delegation:

H.R.H. Samdech NORODOM SIHANOUK
-Members (by alphabetical order):
  -as representatives:
  H.E. HOR NAM HONG
  H.E. HUN SEN
  H.E. KHIEU SAMPHAN

H.E. SON SANN
-as alternate representatives:
H.E. DITH MUNTY
H.E. IENG MOULY
H.E. IM CHHUN LIM
H.R.H. Prince NORODOM RANARIDDH
-a number of assistants.

4. To send to the United Nations Secretary-General a letter signed by H.R.H. Samdech NORODOM SIHANOUK in which "the SNC, reiterating once again its acceptance of the Perm Five Framework Document of 28 August 1990 in its entirety, has decided to request the United Nations to send a survey mission in order to evaluate the modalities of control and an appropriate number of United Nations personnel to control the ceasefire and the cessation of foreign military aids in cooperation with the SNC Military Working Group".

5. To send a delegation to participate in the special meeting of the Mekong Committee in mid-August 1991 as well as in its full session from 4 to 6 November 1991.

6. To appoint six officials to the SNC secretariat as follows:

MM.   CHUM BUN RONG
        Dr. MAK BEN
        PENN THOL
        SAR SAMBATH
        SOK AN
        VENG SEREYVUTH

The secretariat shall begin its work one week prior to the forthcoming SNC meeting in Bangkok (Thailand) in August 1991 at the former Cambodian Embassy, pending the installation of the SNC headquarters in Phnom Penh.

7. To set up an operational SNC working group to draft the SNC rules of procedure, the principles of the new Constitution of Cambodia and the electoral laws, and to examine the modalities of the installation of the SNC headquarters in Phnom Penh, *inter alia*:

-Situation of the headquarters at the Government Guest House,

-Sending teams of the Cambodian parties to Phnom Penh to arrange their accommodation,

-Matters pertaining to the immunity and privileges of the SNC members and the personnel of their staff.

8. To request from the United Nations Secretary-General assistance:

-to facilitate the repatriation of Cambodian refugees and displaced persons;

-to establish a mine awareness programme in Cambodia and in the refugee camps along the Cambodian border which includes:

-mass public education on the recognition and avoidance of unexploded ordnance devices;

-training of Cambodian volunteers to dispose of unexploded ordnance devices;

-emergency first aid training to Cambodian volunteers.

9. To set up a working group on repatriation which will closely work with the United Nations High Commissioner for Refugees for the preparatory work of the repatriation such as the setting up of the refugee transit centres, warehouses, road access, etc.

III.   H.R.H. Samdech NORODOM SIHANOUK, President of the SNC and all members of the SNC present in the meeting wish to express their deepest and warmest gratitude to the Government and people of the People's Republic of China, H.E. President YANG SHANG KUN and H.E. Prime Minister LI PENG as well as to all Chinese officials for their generous assistance and hospitality which have facilitated this successful meeting.

Document 11

Letter dated 29 July 1991 from the Philippines transmitting statement of the Foreign Ministers of the Association of South-East Asian Nations (ASEAN) on the Cambodian question, issued in Kuala Lumpur, 19 July 1991

A/46/328-S/22850, 29 July 1991

On behalf of the Permanent Missions to the United Nations of the States members of the Association of South-East Asian Nations (ASEAN), I have the honour to transmit to you herewith the text of a statement of the ASEAN Foreign Ministers on the Cambodian question, issued at Kuala Lumpur on 19 July 1991 (see annex).

I should be grateful if you would have the text of the present letter and its annex circulated as a document of the General Assembly, under item 24 of the provisional agenda, and of the Security Council.

(signed) Sedfrey A. ORDONEZ
Ambassador
Permanent Representative

Statement of the ASEAN Foreign Ministers on the Cambodian question, issued at Kuala Lumpur on 19 July 1991

1. The Foreign Ministers reviewed the situation in Cambodia and noted that, with the convening of the Meeting of the Supreme National Council (SNC) at Jakarta from 2 to 4 June 1991, important developments have taken place. They noted with satisfaction that the meeting of the SNC at Pattaya from 24 to 26 June 1991, convened and presided by His Royal Highness Samdech Norodom Sihanouk, had generated a momentum in advancing the peace process towards a comprehensive political settlement.

2. They welcomed the Informal Meeting of the SNC at Beijing, on 17 July 1991, to which representatives of the United Nations Secretary-General and the two Co-Chairmen of the Paris Conference on Cambodia (PCC) were invited. They were greatly encouraged by the further progress made at this meeting, particularly the unanimous election of H.R.H. Samdech Norodom Sihanouk as President of the SNC in a spirit of compromise and national reconciliation.

3. They believe that the SNC's decision to establish its headquarters in Phnom Penh should enable it to function, throughout the transitional period, as the unique legitimate body and source of authority in which the independence, sovereignty and unity of Cambodia is embodied, as stipulated in the Joint Statement of the Jakarta Informal Meeting on Cambodia of 10 September 1990.

4. The Foreign Ministers reiterated their support for the efforts of the Co-Chairmen of the PCC, the five permanent members of the United Nations Security Council and the United Nations Secretary-General, and encouraged them to continue assisting the Cambodian parties to reach agreement on the unresolved issues in the draft agreements based on the Permanent Five Framework Document. They expressed their hope that the two Co-Chairmen would be able to reconvene, as soon as feasible, the Paris Conference on Cambodia.

5. The Foreign Ministers strongly emphasized the need for national reconciliation among the Cambodian parties and called on them to intensify efforts to seek compromise among themselves to resolve the issues left outstanding after the consultations between the Co-Chairmen and the SNC members at Jakarta from 2 to 4 June 1991.

6. The Foreign Ministers look forward to the SNC assuming the Cambodian seat at the forty-sixth session of the United Nations General Assembly and welcomed the SNC's decision to send a delegation headed by H.R.H. Samdech Norodom Sihanouk to that session.

7. The Foreign Ministers emphasized that, at this crucial stage, it is important that all efforts be made to ensure that the momentum of the peace process be maintained. They noted, in particular, that it is necessary to take cognizance of the SNC, as it is now constituted and functioning, and to extend the required international support. Towards this end, the Foreign Ministers decided that all ASEAN countries would respond positively to the SNC's invitation to accredit representatives to the SNC.

Document 12

Letter dated 1 August 1991 from China, France, Indonesia, the USSR, the United Kingdom and the United States transmitting communiqué of the Co-Chairmen of the Paris Conference on Cambodia and the five permanent members of the Security Council issued in Beijing, 18 July 1991

A/46/340-S/22889, 5 August 1991

We have the honour to transmit herewith the text of the Communiqué of the Co-Chairmen of the Paris Conference on Cambodia and the five permanent members of the United Nations Security Council, issued at Beijing on 18 July 1991 (see annex).

We should be grateful if you would have the text of this letter and its annex circulated as a document of the General Assembly, under item 24 of the provisional agenda, and of the Security Council.

Co-Chairmen of the Paris Conference on Cambodia

(*signed*) Jean-Marc ROCHEREAU DE LA SABLIÈRE
Chargé d'affaires a.i. and Deputy Permanent
Representative of France to the United Nations

(*signed*) Nana SUTRESNA
Permanent Representative of the Republic
of Indonesia to the United Nations

Permanent members of the Security Council

(*signed*) LI Daoyu
Permanent Representative of China to the United Nations

(*signed*) Jean-Marc ROCHEREAU DE LA SABLIÈRE
Chargé d'affaires a.i. and Deputy Permanent
Representative of France to the United Nations

(*signed*) Valentin V. LOZINSKIY
Acting Permanent Representative of the Union of
Soviet Socialist Republics to the United Nations

(*signed*) David HANNAY
Permanent Representative of the United Kingdom
of Great Britain and Northern Ireland
to the United Nations

(*signed*) Thomas PICKERING
Permanent Representative of the United States of America
to the United Nations

Annex
*Communiqué of the Co-Chairmen of the Paris Confer-
ence on Cambodia and the five permanent members of
the United Nations Security Council, issued at Beijing on
18 July 1991*

The Co-Chairmen of the Paris Conference on Cambodia
and the five permanent members of the United Nations
Security Council met at Beijing on 17 and 18 July 1991.
The representative of the United Nations Secretary-
General was also present.

The five and Indonesia note the repeated assurances
by all Cambodian parties of their acceptance of the 28
August 1990 United Nations framework document in its
entirety, as endorsed by the Security Council in its resolution 668 (1990) and acclaimed by the General Assembly
on 15 October 1990, as the basis for settling the Cambodian conflict. They observe with satisfaction that, based
on this commitment, the Supreme National Council
(SNC) had made significant progress towards a comprehensive political settlement at meetings held recently at
Jakarta, Pattaya and Beijing.

They welcome the election of Prince Sihanouk as
President of the Supreme National Council.

These developments have created a new situation
and a new opportunity to bring lasting peace to Cambodia. The five and Indonesia thus urge the now operational

SNC to accelerate efforts to overcome the remaining
difficulties and to reach a consensus, in a continuing spirit
of reconciliation, on a comprehensive political settlement—based on the draft agreements of 26 November
1990—at its forthcoming meeting at Bangkok from 26 to
28 August 1991. Such consensus would make possible
the early reconvening of the Paris Conference on Cambodia to adopt and endorse a comprehensive political settlement which would be referred to the United Nations
for approval and implementation.

The five and Indonesia welcome the decision of the
SNC to implement an unlimited cease-fire. They also
welcome its decision to stop receiving foreign military
assistance, will respect this decision themselves and call
upon all concerned to do likewise. The five and Indonesia
also express the hope that the countries neighbouring
Cambodia will prohibit the delivery of military equipment to any of the Cambodian parties from their territory. They also reiterate that the withdrawal of foreign
military forces, the cease-fire and the cessation of outside
military assistance must be effectively verified and supervised by the United Nations.

To that end, they welcome the proposal made by the
SNC that a United Nations survey mission should be sent
to Cambodia. They agreed to recommend the dispatch of
such a mission. The mission would begin the process of
preparing for the military aspects of United Nations
Transitional Authority in Cambodia (UNTAC) and could
consider how the Secretary-General of the United Nations
can use his good offices to help maintain the unlimited
informal cease-fire now in effect.

The five and Indonesia welcome the decision taken
at the initiative of Prince Sihanouk to establish the SNC
in Phnom Penh later this year. They view positively the
sending of diplomatic representatives to the SNC after the
Council establishes itself in free and fair elections to be
held under the auspices of the United Nations, as part of
the comprehensive political settlement, in accordance
with the framework document of 28 August 1990 and as
envisaged in the 26 November 1990 draft agreements.

The five and Indonesia agreed to meet again at
Bangkok on 29 and 30 August, on which occasion they
will also hold discussions with SNC following its meeting
during the preceding days.

The participants expressed appreciation to the Government of the People's Republic of China for its excellent
arrangements in hosting the current meeting.

Document 13

Letter dated 8 August 1991 from the Secretary-General to the President of the Security Council referring to a proposal by the Supreme National Council that the United Nations send a survey mission to Cambodia, and also referring to the meeting of the Co-Chairmen of the Paris Conference on Cambodia and the five permanent members of the Security Council in Beijing, 17-18 July 1991

S/22945, 14 August 1991

I would like to draw your attention to some recent developments relating to the situation in Cambodia.

You will recall that His Royal Highness Prince Norodom Sihanouk convened a meeting of the Supreme National Council of Cambodia (SNC) in Pattaya, from 24-26 June 1991 (A/46/271-S/22740). The Co-Chairmen of the Paris Conference on Cambodia (PCC) and my Special Representative, Mr. Rafeeuddin Ahmed, were invited to attend as observers. At that meeting, a number of important decisions were taken. In particular, the SNC unanimously agreed to an immediate and unlimited cease-fire and to undertake to stop receiving outside military assistance.

You will further recall that, on 16-17 July, an informal meeting of the SNC was convened in Beijing by Prince Sihanouk (A/46/310-S/22808). The Co-Chairmen of the PCC and my Special Representative again participated as observers. At that meeting, the SNC unanimously elected Prince Sihanouk to be its President. The SNC also reiterated its acceptance of the 28 August 1990 Framework for a Comprehensive Political Settlement of the Cambodia Conflict (A/45/472-S/21689), in its entirety. In that connection, the SNC unanimously decided to request the United Nations to dispatch a survey team to Cambodia.

I have the honour to inform you that, in a letter dated 16 July addressed to me by Prince Sihanouk on behalf of the SNC, it is stated that the SNC

"has decided to request the United Nations to send a survey mission in order to evaluate the modalities of control and an appropriate number of United Nations personnel to control the cease-fire and the cessation of foreign military aids in cooperation with the SNC Military Working Group."

On 17-18 July, a meeting of the Co-Chairmen of the PCC and the five permanent members of the Security Council was held in Beijing, in the presence of my Special Representative (A/46/340-S/22889). The final communiqué of that meeting, addressing the results of the two recent SNC meetings, stated that

"The Five and Indonesia welcome the decision of the SNC to implement an unlimited cease-fire. They also welcome its decision to stop receiving foreign military assistance, will respect this decision themselves and call upon all concerned countries to do likewise. The Five and Indonesia also express the hope that the countries neighbouring Cambodia will prohibit the delivery of military equipment to any of the Cambodian parties from their territory. They also reiterate that the withdrawal of foreign military forces, the cease-fire and the cessation of outside military assistance must be effectively verified and supervised by the United Nations.

"To that end, they welcome the proposal made by the SNC that a United Nations survey mission should be sent to Cambodia. They agreed to recommend the dispatch of such a mission. The mission would begin the process of preparing for the military aspects of UNTAC and could consider how the Secretary-General of the United Nations can use his good offices to help maintain the unlimited informal cease-fire now in effect."

I wish to inform you that it is my intention to proceed with the necessary arrangements for the dispatch of a survey mission to Cambodia as soon as possible.

(*signed*) Javier PÉREZ de CUÉLLAR

Document 14

Letter dated 3 September 1991 from China, France, Indonesia, the USSR, the United Kingdom and the United States transmitting communiqué issued by the Co-Chairmen of the Paris Conference on Cambodia and the five permanent members of the Security Council at the end of their meeting in Pattaya, 29-30 August 1991

A/46/418-S/23011, 4 September 1991

We have the honour to transmit herewith the text of the communiqué of the Co-Chairmen of the Paris Conference on Cambodia and the five permanent members of the United Nations Security Council (together with its addendum), issued at the end of their meeting held at Pattaya on 29 and 30 August 1991.

We should be grateful if you would have the text of the present letter and its annex circulated as a document of the General Assembly, under item 24 of the provisional agenda, and of the Security Council.

Co-Chairmen of the Paris Conference on Cambodia:

(*signed*) Jean-Bernard MÉRIMÉE
Permanent Representative of France
to the United Nations

(*signed*) Nugroho WISNUMURTI
Chargé d'affaires a.i. and Deputy Permanent
Representative of Indonesia
to the United Nations

Permanent members of the Security Council:

(*signed*) LI Daoyu
Permanent Representative of China
to the United Nations

(*signed*) Alexander F. WATSON
Chargé d'affaires a.i. and Deputy Permanent
Representative of the United States of America
to the United Nations

(*signed*) Jean-Bernard MÉRIMÉE
Permanent Representative of France
to the United Nations

(*signed*) Yuliy M. VORONTSOV
Permanent Representative of the Union
of Soviet Socialist Republics
to the United Nations

(*signed*) David HANNAY
Permanent Representative of the United Kingdom of
Great Britain and Northern Ireland to the United Nations

Annex

Communiqué issued on 30 August 1991 by the Co-Chairmen of the Paris Conference on Cambodia and the five permanent members of the Security Council

The five permanent members of the United Nations Security Council and Indonesia met at Pattaya on 29 and 30 August 1991. The representative of the United Nations Secretary-General was also present.

The five and Indonesia also held, for the first time, a joint meeting with the Supreme National Council (SNC) of Cambodia.

The five and Indonesia express their satisfaction with the progress towards a comprehensive political settlement made at the SNC meeting on 26-29 August 1991 at Pattaya on the basis of the 28 August 1990 framework document and the 26 November 1990 draft agreement, recognizing the enhanced role of the United Nations that these documents enshrine. The outcome of this meeting demonstrates the significant progress that is being made towards national reconciliation.

They note with satisfaction the consensus reached by the SNC on how to resolve some very important remaining difficulties.

The five and Indonesia recall that they consistently envisaged a detailed plan for the phased return to civilian life of all categories of forces of the Cambodian parties. They view such an arrangement as essential to minimizing the risk of a return to warfare, stabilizing the security situation and building confidence among the parties, thus ensuring the best possible prospects of the durability of the settlement. Such an arrangement remains their fundamental commitment.

On this basis, and taking into account the progress made in the SNC and their growing spirit of cooperation, the five and Indonesia are prepared to support the formula devised by the SNC, which provides for the demobilization before the elections of 70 per cent of all forces and their arms, subject to the understandings contained in the annex to this communiqué (see addendum).

They urge the SNC to reflect further on the question of total demobilization, preferably prior to the elections.

They consider of great importance the decision of the SNC to give the final word to Prince Sihanouk on determining the advice, relevant to the implementation of the comprehensive settlement agreement, to be rendered to UNTAC when consensus is unattainable within the SNC, and they will consider further the implications of this decision for the relationship between UNTAC and the SNC.

They also note with satisfaction the declaration of the SNC that Cambodia will adopt a system of liberal, multiparty democracy and their decision to promote and encourage respect for and observance of human rights and fundamental freedoms.

They urge the SNC to reach a common position as soon as possible on the issue of the electoral system.

They agree to give sympathetic consideration to the proposal made by the SNC to request the United Nations Secretary-General to send United Nations personnel as observers to Cambodia. In this regard they urge the SNC to make every effort to resolve all remaining issues necessary to conclude a comprehensive political settlement that would facilitate a decision by the United Nations Security Council to dispatch the observer force.

In the light of the very positive progress achieved at Pattaya, the five and Indonesia consider that the time has now come to accelerate efforts to complete the comprehensive political settlement agreement for submission to the Coordinating Committee of the Paris Conference on Cambodia (PCC).

They consider it most desirable that the PCC be reconvened at ministerial level by late October and that the comprehensive political settlement be signed before the SNC, under Prince Sihanouk's chairmanship, establishes itself at Phnom Penh in mid-November.

The five and Indonesia have decided to meet again in New York in late September.

The five and Indonesia express their deep gratitude to the Government of Thailand for the excellent arrangements in facilitating the current meeting.

Addendum
Military arrangements

The five and Indonesia recall that they consistently envisaged a detailed plan for the phased return to civilian life of all categories of forces of the Cambodian parties. They view such an arrangement as essential to minimizing the risk of a return to warfare, stabilizing the security situation and building confidence among the parties, thus ensuring the best possible prospects of the durability of the settlement. Such an arrangement remains their fundamental commitment.

On this basis, and taking into account the progress made by the SNC and their growing spirit of cooperation, the five and Indonesia are prepared to support the formula devised by the SNC that provides for the demobilization before the elections of 70 per cent of all forces and their arms, subject to the following understandings:

1. It is essential to clarify as part of a comprehensive political settlement the disposition of the residual 30 per cent forces. If these forces are not demobilized prior to the election, as is the strong preference of the five permanent members of the Security Council, they will either be demobilized shortly after the elections or incorporated into a national army created by the newly elected government.

2. It is clearly understood that the definition of "forces" is that contained in paragraph 2 of article 1 of annex 2 of the draft settlement document. Forces are agreed to include all regular, provincial, district, paramilitary and other auxiliary forces. The five and Indonesia invite the Cambodian parties to furnish urgently to the representative of the United Nations Secretary-General all the information he requires to enable him to identify the various categories of forces falling under this definition.

3. All arms, ammunition and military equipment of forces covered by paragraph 2 above shall be turned over to UNTAC as such forces enter the cantonments; for forces not yet demobilized, access to their arms can only be on the basis of explicit authorization of UNTAC.

4. UNTAC will identify civil police necessary to perform law enforcement. Civil police will operate under UNTAC supervision or control.

Document 15

Letter dated 23 September 1991 from the President of the Supreme National Council transmitting final communiqué of the Council's meeting in Pattaya, 26-29 August 1991

A/46/494-S/23066, 24 September 1991

I have the honour to request Your Excellency to kindly circulate the Final Communiqué of the meeting of the Supreme National Council of Cambodia, held in Pattaya from 26 to 29 August 1991, as an official document of the General Assembly, under agenda item 24, and of the Security Council.

(*signed*) NORODOM SIHANOUK
President of the Supreme National Council of Cambodia

Annex
Final communiqué of the Supreme National Council of Cambodia

I. The Supreme National Council (SNC) of Cambodia held its meeting in Pattaya (Thailand) from 26 to 29 August 1991 under the very high chairmanship of H.R.H. Samdech NORODOM SIHANOUK, President of the SNC. The Representatives of the two Co-Chairmen of the PICC and of the Secretary-General of the United Nations were also present as observers.

The Supreme National Council unanimously agreed on the following:

1. *On the control of the cease-fire and cessation of foreign military assistance*

H.R.H. Samdech NORODOM SIHANOUK, President of the SNC, sent to the Secretary-General of the United Nations, a letter dated 26 August 1991 which reads inter alia: "The SNC of Cambodia, anxious to ensure that the Council's decision on the cessation of hostilities and of foreign military aids be fully implemented by all parties to the conflict and to speed up the UN peace process, earnestly request that Your Excellency be kind enough to do all the necessary to have at least 200 UN personnel sent to Cambodia as 'observers' in September 1991 in order to assist the SNC in controlling the cease-fire and the cessation of foreign military assistance, as a first step within the framework of a comprehensive political settlement. "

2. *On the arrangements of all forces of the Cambodian parties*

Upon the proposal of H.E. Mr. JEAN DAVID LEVITTE, Representative of France and Co-Chairman of the PICC:

- All forces of all Cambodian parties shall be reduced by 70 per cent. Arms, ammunition and equipments of these forces shall be reduced by 70 per cent as well.

- The remaining 30 per cent of these forces will be regrouped and relocated to specifically designated cantonment areas under the supervision of UNTAC. While these forces are in the cantonments, their arms, ammunition and equipments will be stored on site under UNTAC supervision. These remaining arms, ammunition and equipments should not be allowed out of cantonment areas.

3. *On the relationship between the United Nations Transitional Authority in Cambodia and the SNC*

The Supreme National Council (SNC) will offer advice to UNTAC, which will comply with this advice provided there is a consensus among the members of the SNC and provided this advice is consistent with the objectives of the Agreement on a comprehensive political settlement. The Secretary-General's Special Representative will determine whether such advice is consistent with this Agreement.

If there is no consensus on any given matter among the members of the SNC, H.R.H. Samdech NORODOM SIHANOUK, President of the SNC, should make every endeavour to reach a consensus on such a matter. In case it is still unattainable, H.R.H. Samdech NORODOM SIHANOUK, President of the SNC, shall be entitled to make the final decision, taking fully into account views expressed in the SNC.

This mechanism will be used to resolve all issues relating to the implementation of this Agreement which may arise between the Secretary-General's Special Representative and the SNC.

4. *On the political system*

- In the future, Cambodia will adopt a system of liberal democracy and multi-party. Each Cambodian citizen will enjoy the right to association and to form political parties.

- In order to be able to take part in the elections, each political party should have at least 5,000 members.

5. *On human rights and principles for a new constitution for Cambodia*

- The sub-paragraph (b) of paragraph (2) of article

15 of Part III of the 26 November 1990 Draft Agreements reads as follows: "The other Signatories to this Agreement undertake to promote and encourage respect for an observance of human rights and fundamental freedoms in Cambodia as embodied in the relevant international instruments and relevant resolutions of the UN General Assembly in order, in particular, to prevent the recurrence of human rights abuses."

- The paragraph 2 of Annex 5 of the 26 November 1990 Draft Agreements reads as follows: "Cambodia's tragic recent history requires special measures to assure protection of human rights. Therefore, the constitution will contain a declaration of fundamental rights, including the rights to life, personal liberty, security, freedom of movement, freedom of religion, assembly and association (including political parties and trade unions), due process and equality before the law, protection from arbitrary deprivation of property or deprivation of private property without just compensation, and freedom from racial, ethnic, religious or sexual discrimination. It will prohibit the retroactive application of criminal law. The declaration will be consistent with the provisions of the Universal Declaration of Human Rights and other relevant international instruments. Aggrieved individuals will be entitled to have the courts adjudicate and enforce these rights."

6. *On the question of rehabilitation and reconstruction*

The SNC requested H.R.H. Samdech NORODOM SIHANOUK, President of the SNC, to address a letter to the UN Secretary-General. The letter, dated 29 August 1991, reads inter alia:

"The SNC agreed to request Your Excellency to kindly consider the provision of assistance for the rehabilitation and reconstruction of Cambodia at the earliest possible date. This UN assistance is urgently required for the repairs and rehabilitation of roads, bridges, airport facilities, port facilities and railway lines."

7. *The SNC agreed to issue the passport of the SNC. The modalities will be determined by the Secretariat.*

II. The Supreme National Council of Cambodia expressed its warmest thanks to His Majesty the King and Her Majesty the Queen of the Kingdom of Thailand, H.E. Mr. ANAND PANYARACHUN, Prime Minister of the Royal Thai Government and all other Thai officials without whose generous assistance and hospitality this SNC meeting could not have been crowned with this success. The Cambodian nation and people remain profoundly indebted to the Kingdom of Thailand for her generosity, compassion and tremendous efforts she has made for the Cambodian national cause.

III. The SNC expressed deep appreciation and gratitude to all friendly countries and Governments the world over for their efforts in the search of a comprehensive political settlement of the Cambodia conflict.

IV. The SNC addressed its gratitude to the UN Secretary-General for sending a survey team to Cambodia in reply to the letter of 16 July 1991 of H.R.H. Samdech NORODOM SIHANOUK, President of the SNC, and to the two Co-Chairmen of the PICC as well as to their Representatives for their cooperation.

V. The SNC also expressed its gratitude to H.E. Mr. RAFEEUDDIN AHMED, Special Representative of the UN Secretary-General, H.E. Mr. JEAN DAVID LEVITTE, H.E. Mr. S. WIRYONO, Representatives of the Co-Chairmen of the PICC, and their collaborators for their assistance.

VI. The SNC expressed its gratitude to the five Permanent Members of the UN Security Council for the time and efforts they have been devoting to finding at an early date a lasting comprehensive political settlement of the Cambodia conflict.

Done in Pattaya, Thailand, 29 August 1991

- President of the SNC:
H.R.H. Samdech NORODOM SIHANOUK

- Members of the SNC:
H.E. Mr. DITH MUNTY
H.E. Mr. HOR NAMHONG
H.E. Mr. HUN SEN
H.E. Mr. IENG MOULY
H.E. Mr. IM CHHUN LIM
H.E. Mr. KHIEU SAMPHAN
H.R.H. Prince NORODOM RANARIDDH
H.E. Mr. SIN SEN
H.E. Mr. SON SANN
H.E. Mr. SON SEN
H.E. Mr. TEA BANH

Document 16

Letter dated 24 September 1991 from China, France, Indonesia, the USSR, the United Kingdom and the United States transmitting communiqué of the Co-Chairmen of the Paris Conference on Cambodia and the five permanent members of the Security Council at the end of their meeting in New York, 20-21 September 1991

A/46/508-S/23087, 27 September 1991

We have the honour to transmit herewith the text of the Communiqué of the Co-Chairmen of the Paris Conference on Cambodia and the five permanent members of the United Nations Security Council, issued at the end of their meeting, held in New York, on 20 and 21 September 1991 (see annex).

We should be grateful if you would have the text of this letter and its annex circulated as a document of the General Assembly, under agenda item 24, and of the Security Council.

Co-Chairmen of the Paris Conference on Cambodia:

(*signed*) Jean-Bernard MÉRIMÉE
Permanent Representative of France
to the United Nations

(*signed*) Nana SUTRESNA
Permanent Representative of Indonesia
to the United Nations

Permanent members of the Security Council:

(*signed*) Thomas R. PICKERING
Permanent Representative of the United States of America
to the United Nations

(*signed*) Jean-Bernard MÉRIMÉE
Permanent Representative of France
to the United Nations

(*signed*) Yuliy M. VORONTSOV
Permanent Representative of the Union of Soviet Socialist Republics to the United Nations

(*signed*) Sir David HANNAY
Permanent Representative of the United Kingdom of Great Britain and Northern Ireland to the United Nations

(*signed*) LI Daoyu
Permanent Representative of China
to the United Nations

Annex
Communiqué

New York, 21 September 1991

The five permanent members of the United Nations Security Council and Indonesia met in New York on 20 and 21 September 1991. The representative of the United Nations Secretary-General was also present.

On 20 September, the five and Indonesia held their second meeting with members of the Supreme National Council (SNC) of Cambodia under the chairmanship of Prince Norodom Sihanouk.

The five and Indonesia welcomed the informal meeting of all members of the Paris Conference on Cambodia (PCC), held on 21 September to exchange views on the latest developments in the peace process.

The five and Indonesia noted with satisfaction the decision of the SNC on the issue of the electoral system, which provides for national elections throughout Cambodia on a provincial basis in accordance with a system of proportional representation.

They also welcomed the letter of 20 September from the President of the SNC to the United Nations Secretary-General clarifying further the decision-making process.

They welcome as a further indication of the growing spirit of cooperation within the SNC the decision of all the Cambodian parties to provide the United Nations Secretariat with detailed information on their military forces at an early date to facilitate the process of preparing for the military aspects of the United Nations Transitional Authority in Cambodia (UNTAC).

They hope that the United Nations Secretary-General will shortly be able to submit for the United Nations Security Council's consideration a plan for sending a United Nations good offices mission to Cambodia soon after the comprehensive settlement agreement has been signed.

The five and Indonesia note with special satisfaction that the process of creating a comprehensive settlement agreement for Cambodia seems to have entered its final phase, thus bringing closer to realization the goal of national reconciliation and lasting peace in that country. In that connection, they express the hope that the PCC will be able to reconvene by the end of October.

Document 17

Report of the Secretary-General on proposals for a United Nations Advance Mission in Cambodia (UNAMIC)

S/23097, 30 September 1991
(including addendum, S/23097/Add.1, 30 September 1991)

Introduction

1. In my letter of 8 August 1991 to the President of the Security Council (S/22945), I stated that it was my intention to proceed with the necessary arrangements for the dispatch of a survey mission to Cambodia as soon as possible. In his reply dated 14 August 1991 (S/22946), the President of the Security Council informed me that the members of the Council agreed with the proposal contained in my letter.

2. The purpose of the present report, which has been prepared in the light of the survey mission's report, is to recommend to the Security Council that it authorize the establishment of a United Nations Advance Mission in Cambodia (UNAMIC), which would assume its functions as soon as the Agreement on a Comprehensive Political Settlement of the Cambodia Conflict is signed. Negotiations on the draft Agreement, the text of which was communicated to the Secretary-General by the Co-Chairmen of the Paris Conference on Cambodia on 8 January 1991 (S/22059), are now at an advanced stage, and it is envisaged that the Agreement will be signed around the end of October 1991.

I. Report of the survey mission

3. The mandate of the survey mission was to evaluate the modalities of control and an appropriate number of United Nations personnel to control the cease-fire and the cessation of outside military assistance and to submit recommendations for the establishment of a mine-awareness programme in Cambodia, pursuant to the requests of the Supreme National Council of Cambodia conveyed to me on 16 and 17 July 1991 by His Royal Highness Prince Norodom Sihanouk, President of the Supreme National Council. The mission was also instructed to bear in mind the communiqué dated 18 July 1991 of the Co-Chairmen of the Paris Conference on Cambodia and the permanent members of the Security Council (S/22889, annex).

4. The mission was led by my Military Adviser, Major-General Timothy Dibuama, and consisted of six military officers made available by Member States and six civilian staff members of the Secretariat. The mission visited the region from 19 August to 4 September 1991, after which it returned to New York to prepare its report.

5. The main points in the mission's report are as follows:

(a) The modalities for the control of the cease-fire and the cessation of outside military assistance have already been worked out and are described in annex 2 to the draft Agreement on a Comprehensive Political Settlement prepared by the Co-Chairmen of the Paris Conference on Cambodia and the permanent members of the Security Council (S/22059);

(b) In order to evaluate the appropriate number of United Nations personnel to implement those modalities, it would be necessary to obtain all the information referred to in article I, paragraph 3, and article VII, paragraph 3, of that annex;

(c) Certain of the Cambodian parties informed the mission that they were not at that stage ready to provide to the United Nations some of the information that would be required, and the mission was not in a position to obtain other necessary information;

(d) As a result, it was not possible for the mission to evaluate the modalities for the control of the cease-fire and the cessation of outside military assistance. The mission was also unable to begin concrete preparations for the implementation of the military aspects of the mandate foreseen for the United Nations Transitional Authority in Cambodia (UNTAC) once a comprehensive agreement is concluded;

(e) As regards the mine-awareness programme, the mission concluded that it should initially be concentrated in the north-western part of Cambodia and areas likely to be resettled by refugees on their return;

(f) Such a programme could best be provided by a small team of military personnel, who would form part of the proposed advance mission.

II. United Nations Advance Mission in Cambodia

6. At the consultations on Cambodia that took place in New York on 20 and 21 September 1991, I informed the Co-Chairmen of the Paris Conference on Cambodia and the permanent members of the Security Council that, initially, the United Nations could assist the Cambodian parties to maintain the present cease-fire by deploying in Cambodia a small advance mission consisting mainly of military liaison officers in order to help them to address and resolve any violations or alleged violations of the cease-fire. Such an advance mission could be envisaged as the first stage of the good offices

mechanism foreseen in the second paragraph of article 9 of the draft Agreement on a Comprehensive Political Settlement of the Cambodia Conflict.

7. This information was welcomed at the New York consultations and it was suggested that I should proceed with the development of a plan along those lines. Accordingly, I recommend that the Security Council should now decide to authorize the establishment of UNAMIC on the basis described in the following paragraphs.

8. UNAMIC would be under the command of the United Nations, vested in the Secretary-General under the authority of the Security Council. The mission would be led in the field by a civilian Chief Liaison Officer, appointed by the Secretary-General, who would exercise authority over all elements of UNAMIC. Command of the military elements of UNAMIC would be entrusted to a Senior Military Liaison Officer designated by the Secretary-General with the consent of the Security Council. The Senior Military Liaison Officer would report to the Secretary-General through the Chief Liaison Officer. The Secretary-General would report regularly to the Security Council on the operations of UNAMIC. All matters that might affect the nature or the continued effective functioning of the Mission would be referred to the Security Council for its decision.

9. UNAMIC would consist of civilian liaison staff, military liaison officers, a military mine-awareness unit and the necessary support personnel, who would mostly be civilian but could include some military. The military personnel of UNAMIC, who would be unarmed, would be provided by Member States at the request of the Secretary-General. The contributing countries would be selected in consultation with the parties and with the concurrence of the Security Council, bearing in mind the accepted principle of equitable geographical representation.

10. The Mission would become operational immediately after the signature of the Agreement on a Comprehensive Political Settlement of the Cambodia Conflict. The duration of the Mission's mandate would extend from the signature of the Agreement until the establishment of UNTAC by the Security Council and the adoption of its budget by the General Assembly. At that time, UNAMIC would be absorbed into UNTAC, and the good offices functions being carried out by UNAMIC would be continued and expanded by UNTAC during the first phase of the cease-fire referred to in article I, paragraph 1, of annex 2 to the draft Comprehensive Settlement Agreement. It is expected that UNAMIC will merge into UNTAC less than six months after the signature of the Agreement; in case of delay the mandate for UNAMIC might need to be extended beyond six months, subject to review by the Security Council at that time.

11. In addition to his responsibilities in relation to UNAMIC, the Chief Liaison Officer, assisted by the civilian liaison staff, would have responsibility for liaison with the Supreme National Council on the preparations for the deployment of UNTAC and on other matters related to the role of the United Nations in the implementation of the Comprehensive Political Settlement Agreement.

12. The task of the military component of UNAMIC, in its good offices role, would be to facilitate communications between the military headquarters of the four Cambodian parties in matters relating to the cease-fire. To that end, UNAMIC would establish its headquarters in Phnom Penh and would deploy liaison teams to the general military headquarters of each of the Cambodian parties. It would have its own communications network linking its headquarters and the five liaison teams. It would use its good offices, including the passing of messages between the parties and arranging meetings between them, in order to resolve difficulties, restore the status quo and determine measures to be taken to avoid any recurrence of violations.

13. In addition to his responsibilities in relation to the military elements of UNAMIC, the Senior Military Liaison Officer would undertake the tasks foreseen in article II of annex 2 to the Comprehensive Political Settlement Agreement. The Mixed Military Working Group referred to in that article would be used, as appropriate, to facilitate fulfilment of the tasks of the military component of UNAMIC.

14. In its mine-awareness role, UNAMIC would deploy small teams of military personnel with experience in training civilian populations on how to avoid injury from mines or booby traps. Initially, the teams would give priority to populations living in or close to areas of recent military confrontation. In due course, this initial programme would be expanded into those foreseen in the draft Comprehensive Political Settlement Agreement, giving priority, in consultation with the Office of the United Nations High Commissioner for Refugees (UNHCR), to repatriation routes, reception centres and resettlement areas. UNAMIC activities in this field would need to be carefully coordinated with the mine-awareness programme begun earlier in 1991 for Cambodian refugees and displaced persons in the camps along the Cambodia/Thailand border and with an information programme inside Cambodia which is to be launched shortly by the United Nations Educational, Scientific and Cultural Organization (UNESCO).

15. In order to carry out the above tasks, UNAMIC would need to be assured of the cooperation, at all times, of all the Cambodian parties. It would have to have

freedom of movement and communication and the other rights and facilities that would be necessary for the performance of its tasks. UNAMIC and its personnel would also have to be granted all relevant privileges and immunities provided for by the Convention on the Privileges and Immunities of the United Nations. In order to confirm the commitment of all the Cambodian Parties to undertake the necessary steps to enable UNAMIC to carry out its functions, I would initiate consultations on a draft Agreement on the usual lines with the Supreme National Council as soon as the Security Council had taken the decision to authorize the establishment of UNAMIC. It would also be necessary to conclude with the Government of Thailand an agreement on the status of UNAMIC personnel whose duties might require them to enter that country.

16. It is estimated that in order to carry out the mandate recommended in the present report, UNAMIC would require 8 civilian liaison staff, 50 military liaison officers, 20 other military personnel to form the mine-awareness unit, and approximately 75 international and 75 local civilian support staff. In addition, a military communications unit of some 40 persons could be provided by Australia as a voluntary contribution. An air unit of four utility helicopters and one fixed-wing aircraft would also be needed.

17. I would envisage that UNAMIC would be deployed progressively and in phases. In the first phase, the Chief Liaison Officer, with the Senior Military Liaison Officer and his staff, certain civilian advisory and administrative staff and the necessary support and logistic elements, would be deployed to Phnom Penh within 10 days of the signature of the Agreement on a Comprehensive Political Settlement. The second phase would take place as soon as the necessary vehicles, generators, accommodation, etc. had been procured and delivered to the general military headquarters of each of the Cambodian parties, whereupon the military liaison teams would be deployed together with the necessary administrative and support elements. As soon as possible thereafter, the mine-awareness unit would be deployed.

18. I shall, as soon as possible, submit a statement of the financial and administrative implications of this recommendation as an addendum to the present report. Meanwhile, it is my duty to inform the Security Council that, given the ravaged state of Cambodia's economy and infrastructure, it would be possible to obtain in Cambodia almost none of the equipment, supplies and services that the Mission would need. United Nations-provided support elements would inevitably, therefore, have to be extensive. It would also be necessary to send by air-freight to Cambodia a limited amount of the vehicles, communications, accommodation, generators, etc., required for the first phases of deployment.

III. Conclusion

19. Recent weeks have seen encouraging progress towards completion of the negotiations on a comprehensive political settlement to the long and cruel conflict in Cambodia. The international community is unanimous in wanting to see that process brought to an early and successful conclusion. I am convinced that the deployment of the advance mission recommended in the present report would help to maintain the momentum and reduce the risk of the process being disturbed by untoward developments in Cambodia. It would also demonstrate the determination of the United Nations to help the Cambodian parties and people resolve their differences in a peaceful and democratic manner.

Addendum (S/23097/Add.1)

1. In my report to the Security Council (S/23097), I indicated in paragraph 18 that I would submit, as an addendum to the report, a statement of the financial and administrative implications related to the establishment of a United Nations Advance Mission in Cambodia (UNAMIC).

2. The mandate of UNAMIC is discussed in the above-referenced report. An outline of the operational plan, general assumptions and cost estimates are provided below. In respect of the financing of the Mission, if established by the Security Council, I recommend that its full cost be considered as expenses of the organization to be borne by Member States in accordance with Article 17, paragraph 2, of the Charter. I intend to recommend to the General Assembly that the assessment to be levied on Member States be credited to a special account that would be established for this purpose.

Operational plan

3. UNAMIC would establish its headquarters at Phnom Penh and would deploy liaison teams to the General Military Headquarters of each of the Cambodian parties. In addition, the Mission would deploy teams in two forward positions, namely Battambang and Siem Reap. The latter locations would also be main bases of activities relating to the mine awareness programme. Consequently, UNAMIC would operate from six locations in the country and would have the capacity to respond rapidly to requirements elsewhere as might be required by its mandate.

4. UNAMIC would require an effective and independent round-the-clock communications system which, in addition, would be open to the Cambodian parties concerned so as to facilitate communications between them as may be necessary to resolve any difficulties that could affect the maintenance of the cease-fire.

5. UNAMIC would function as an integrated operation under the overall responsibility in the field of the

Chief Liaison Officer. Following is the summary of the main operational elements:

(a) Office of the Chief Liaison Officer headquartered at Phnom Penh, comprising eight international staff;

(b) Military Unit led by the Senior Military Liaison Officer with a strength of 70, consisting of 50 military liaison officers and 20 other military personnel to form the mine awareness unit. In addition, a unit of 40 military personnel would provide in-theatre communications for the operation. This unit would be provided by the Government of Australia as a voluntary contribution. This generous offer of the Government of Australia would allow for a more rapid deployment of personnel and for surface shipment in lieu of the more costly air lifting of most of the communications and heavy equipment required by the operation;

(c) A Civilian Unit consisting of approximately 75 international personnel and 75 local staff to provide support and technical services, including security, interpretation and translations and medical services. A detailed staffing table is provided in annex I to the present document;

(d) In view of the state of Cambodia's infrastructure, the provision at an early stage of an air unit would permit a rapid and secure deployment of Mission personnel, the establishment of the necessary supply lines as well as medical evacuation.

General assumptions

6. I have already informed the Security Council in my report (S/23097) that given the ravaged state of Cambodia's economy and infrastructure it will be nearly impossible to obtain in Cambodia the equipment, supplies and services that the Mission will need. Consequently, the financial implications take into account the necessity of providing extensive equipment and services from outside Cambodia.

7. UNAMIC would be deployed in two stages. The first group would be deployed immediately after the signature of the Agreement on a Comprehensive Political Settlement (tentatively scheduled for the end of October 1991) and before 14 November 1991. In a second stage, UNAMIC would achieve full deployment between mid-November and mid-December 1991.

Cost estimates

8. Based on the operational plan and general assumptions outlined above, it is estimated that an amount of $US 19.9 million (gross) would be required for a six-month period of operation. This amount includes the costs of start up and acquisition of capital equipment. Cost estimates broken down by major objects of expenditures are provided in annex II to the present document.

Annex I
Provisional staffing table a/

	Military personnel		Professional category and above		Field Service/ General Service personnel		Local level personnel		Total	
Substantive element										
Head of Mission			(1)	1					(1)	1
Senior political officer			(1)	1					(1)	1
Political/legal officer			(1)	1					(1)	1
Public information officer			(1)	1					(1)	1
Research assistant					(1)	1			(1)	1
Secretaries					(3)	3			(3)	3
Total substantive staff	0	0	(4)	4	(4)	4	0	0	(8)	8
Military element										
Military liaison officers	(17)	50							(17)	50
Mine-awareness personnel		20								20
Medical personnel	(3)	6							(3)	6
Military support b/	(40)	40							(40)	40
Total military element	(60)	116	0	0	0	0	0	0	(60)	116

a/ Figures in parentheses are the number of staff who would be deployed during the initial phase of the Mission, by 14 November 1991, whereas the figures without parentheses represent full deployment of the proposed number of personnel.

b/ Voluntary contribution by the Government of Australia.

	Military personnel		Professional category and above		Field Service/ General Service personnel		Local level personnel		Total	
Support element										
Senior administrative officer			(1)		1				(1)	1
Administrative officer			(1)		1				(1)	1
Personnel			(1)		1	(1)	1		(2)	2
Finance			(1)	1	(1)	2			(2)	3
Transport					(3)	10			(3)	10
Communications					(10)	12			(10)	12
Property control					(2)	4			(2)	4
Procurement and General Service			(2)	2	(13)	19			(15)	21
Security					(2)	2			(2)	2
Secretaries					(8)	8			(8)	8
Secretaries (for military)					(5)	5			(5)	5
Interpreters (local)							(10)	15	(10)	15
Other local personnel							(35)	60	(35)	60
Total support element	0	0	(6)	6	(45)	63	(45)	75	(96)	144
Total Mission staff	(60)	116	(10)	10	(49)	67	(45)	75	(164)	268

Annex II
Estimates of financial requirements

Serial	Main expenditure group	Nov.-Dec. 91 (2 months) a/	Jan.-Apr. 92 (4 months)	Total (6 months)
		(Thousands of United States dollars)		
1	*Military personnel* Estimates cover travel to the Mission area ($259,200), Mission subsistence allowance ($855,100) plus an allowance for compensation payments for service incurred injuries ($50,000) for a total of 76 military personnel, of whom 50 would be military liaison officers, 20 would be part of a mine awareness programme and 6 would be medical personnel b/	431.1	733.2	1 164.3
2	*Civilian personnel* Estimates cover gross salaries and common staff costs ($3,491,400), Mission subsistence allowance ($1,272,700), travel to the Mission ($202,500) and other official travel ($45,000) in respect of 77 international staff members and 75 locally recruited staff members	1 667.9	3 343.7	5 011.6

a/ Includes a starting-up cost of $6,230,900, covering the cost of vehicles, equipment, initial travel to the Mission of civilian and military personnel, plus positioning cost for the four helicopters to be chartered.

b/ The report of the Secretary-General (S/23097, para. 16) includes the 6 medical personnel in the total of 75 international staff.

(continued)

Serial	Main expenditure group	Nov.-Dec. 91 (2 months) a/	Jan.-Apr. 92 (4 months)	Total (6 months)
		(Thousands of United States dollars)		
3	*Construction and maintenance of premises, including utilities*	389.0	168.0	557.0

3 *Construction and maintenance of premises, including utilities*

Included under this heading are rental of premises ($165,000), cost of utilities ($45,000), purchase and erection of three prefabricated office/accommodation structures ($293,000), plus funds for general upkeep and maintenance ($54,000)

4 *Vehicle operations*   2 406.0   160.0   2 566.0

Funds are included for the acquisition of transportation equipment as follows: 18 sedans, 27 four-wheel-drive vehicles, 8 minibuses, 2 ambulances, 7 trucks, 10 mine-resistant vehicles, 7 cargo trailers, 2 forklifts and 1 container handler ($2,269,000), various workshop equipment ($50,000), the cost of petrol, oil, lubricants and spare parts ($235,000) and vehicle insurance ($12,000)

5 *Aircraft operation*   1 650.7   5 170.4   6 821.1

Estimates cover the charter of 4 utility helicopters for five months ($4,350,600), including positioning costs, the hire of a helicopter or fixed-wing aircraft as required, for about 55 hours during the initial period ($110,000) plus the charter of a medium-sized cargo aircraft for five months for transport of personnel and resupply ($1,750,000). Also included is the cost of aviation fuel ($565,500), plus ground handling charges and liability insurance ($45,000)

6 *Communications*   1 999.0   80.0   2 079.0

Estimates under this heading cover communications and test equipment ($1,916,000), communications spares and supplies ($80,000) and the cost of commercial communications ($83,000), including user charges for satellite communications and pouch services (excluding the voluntary contribution of the Government of Australia)

7 *Miscellaneous equipment*   831.2   56.0   887.2

Estimates cover the purchase of generators ($198,200), office furniture and equipment, including data processing equipment ($238,000), fuel storage tanks and pumps ($140,000), observation equipment ($70,000) and various other equipment ($165,000), including medical and water purification equipment, accommodation equipment for the outstations and refrigerators

Serial	Main expenditure group	Nov.-Dec. 91 (2 months) a/	Jan.-Apr. 92 (4 months)	Total (6 months)
		(Thousands of United States dollars)		
8	Supplies and services	149.4	76.0	225.4
	Estimated expenditures under this heading cover contractual services, medical supplies and services, stationery and office supplies, subscriptions to newspapers and periodicals, sanitation and cleaning materials, uniform items, United Nations flags and decals, electrical supplies, water and petrol jerrycans, plus miscellaneous other supplies and services			
9	Freight and related costs	80.0	60.0	140.0
	Freight charges are mostly covered under the expenditure groups for vehicles and equipment. Additional funds are included hereunder for shipment of supplies and other items for which allowance is not made elsewhere			
10				
	Support account for peace-keeping operations	141.8	284.2	426.0
	Estimates represent 8.5 per cent of the personnel costs shown under serial 2 above			
	Total of estimates (gross)	9 746.1	10 131.5	19 877.6

Document 18

Security Council resolution on UNAMIC and political settlement of the Cambodia situation

S/RES/717 (1991), 16 October 1991

The Security Council,

Recalling its resolution 668 (1990) of 20 September 1990, by which it endorsed the framework for a comprehensive political settlement of the Cambodia conflict of 28 August 1990, 1/

Taking note of the draft agreements for a comprehensive political settlement of the Cambodia conflict, 2/

Welcoming the very significant progress made, on the basis of those draft agreements, towards a comprehensive political settlement which would enable the Cambodian people to exercise its inalienable right to self-determination through free and fair elections organized and conducted by the United Nations,

Welcoming in particular the election of His Royal Highness Prince Norodom Sihanouk as the Chairman of the Supreme National Council of Cambodia,

Noting with satisfaction the other decisions taken by the Supreme National Council of Cambodia, concerning in particular the implementation of a voluntary cease-fire and the renunciation of foreign military assistance, and underlining the need for the full cooperation of the Cambodian parties,

Considering that such progress has opened the way to an early reconvening of the Paris Conference on Cambodia at the ministerial level and the signing of the agreements for a comprehensive political settlement based on the framework document of 28 August 1990, and welcoming the preparations being made by the Co-Chairmen of the Conference in that regard,

Convinced that such a comprehensive political settlement can offer at last a peaceful, just and durable solution to the Cambodia conflict,

1/ S/21689 [Document 2]
2/ S/22059 [Document 6]

Taking note of the request by His Royal Highness Prince Norodom Sihanouk for United Nations personnel to be sent to Cambodia at the earliest possible moment, 3/

Underlining the necessity of a United Nations presence in Cambodia immediately after the signing of the agreements for a comprehensive political settlement of the Cambodia conflict, pending the implementation of the arrangements set out in those agreements,

Having considered, to this end, the report of the Secretary-General of 30 September 1991 proposing the establishment of a United Nations Advance Mission in Cambodia, 4/

1. *Approves* the report of the Secretary-General of 30 September 1991; 4/

2. *Decides* to establish, under its authority, a United Nations Advance Mission in Cambodia immediately after the signing of the agreements for a comprehensive political settlement of the Cambodia conflict and in accordance with the report of the Secretary-General, with members of the mission to be sent to Cambodia immediately after the signing;

3. *Calls upon* the Supreme National Council of Cambodia, and the Cambodian parties for their part, to cooperate fully with the Mission and with the preparations for the implementation of the arrangements set out in the agreements for a comprehensive political settlement;

4. *Welcomes* the proposal of the Co-Chairmen of the Paris Conference on Cambodia to reconvene the Conference at an early date at the ministerial level to sign the agreements for a comprehensive political settlement of the Cambodia conflict;

5. *Requests* the Secretary-General to report to the Security Council by 15 November 1991 on the implementation of the present resolution, and to keep the Council fully informed of further developments.

3/ S/23066 [Document 15]
4/ S/23097 and Add.1 [Document 16]

Document 19

Letter dated 30 October 1991 from France and Indonesia transmitting, as representatives of the Co-Chairmen of the Paris Conference on Cambodia, the full texts of agreements signed in Paris, 23 October 1991, by the States participating in the Conference. Includes Final Act of the Paris Conference on Cambodia; Agreement on a Comprehensive Political Settlement of the Cambodia Conflict (with annexes); Agreement concerning the Sovereignty, Independence, Territorial Integrity and Inviolability, Neutrality and National Unity of Cambodia; and the Declaration on the Rehabilitation and Reconstruction of Cambodia

A/46/608-S/23177, 30 October 1991

In our capacity as representatives of the co-presidents of the Paris Conference on Cambodia (PCC), we have the honour to transmit to you herewith the texts of the agreements signed in Paris on 23 October 1991 by the States participating in the PCC (see annex).

We should be grateful if you could have the text of this letter and its annex circulated as a document of the General Assembly, under agenda item 24, and of the Security Council.

(*signed*) Jean-Bernard MÉRIMÉE
Permanent Representative of France
to the United Nations

(*signed*) Nugroho WISNUMURTI
Deputy Permanent Representative of Indonesia
to the United Nations,
Chargé d'affaires a.i.

Annex
Final Act of the Paris Conference on Cambodia

1. Concerned by the tragic conflict and continuing bloodshed in Cambodia, the Paris Conference on Cambodia was convened, at the invitation of the Government of the French Republic, in order to achieve an internationally guaranteed comprehensive settlement which would restore peace to that country. The Conference was

held in two sessions, the first from 30 July to 30 August 1989, and the second from 21 to 23 October 1991.

2. The Co-Presidents of the Conference were H.E. Mr. Roland DUMAS, Minister for Foreign Affairs of the French Republic, and H.E. Mr. Ali ALATAS, Minister for Foreign Affairs of the Republic of Indonesia.

3. The following States participated in the Conference: Australia, Brunei Darussalam, Cambodia, Canada, the People's Republic of China, the French Republic, the Republic of India, the Republic of Indonesia, Japan, the Lao People's Democratic Republic, Malaysia, the Republic of the Philippines, the Republic of Singapore, the Kingdom of Thailand, the Union of Soviet Socialist Republics, the United Kingdom of Great Britain and Northern Ireland, the United States of America and the Socialist Republic of Vietnam.

In addition, the Non-Aligned Movement was represented at the Conference by its current Chairman at each session, namely Zimbabwe at the first session and Yugoslavia at the second session.

4. At the first session of the Conference, Cambodia was represented by the four Cambodian Parties. The Supreme National Council of Cambodia, under the leadership of its President, H.R.H. Prince NORODOM SIHANOUK, represented Cambodia at the second session of the Conference.

5. The Secretary-General of the United Nations, H.E. M. Javier PÉREZ DE CUÉLLAR, and his Special Representative, M. Rafeeuddin AHMED, also participated in the Conference.

6. The Conference organized itself into three working committees of the whole, which met throughout the first session of the Conference. The First Committee dealt with military matters, the Second Committee dealt with the question of international guarantees, and the Third Committee with the repatriation of refugees and displaced persons and the eventual reconstruction of Cambodia.

The officers of each committee were as follows:

First Committee
Co-Chairmen: Mr. C. R. GHAREKHAN (India)
Mr. Allan SULLIVAN (Canada)
Rapporteur: Ms. Victoria SISANTE-BATACLAN (Philippines)

Second Committee
Co-Chairmen: Mr. Soulivong PHRASITHIDETH (Laos)
Dato' ZAINAL ABIDIN IBRAHIM (Malaysia)
Rapporteur: Mr. Hervé DEJEAN de la BATIE (France)

Third Committee
Co-Chairmen: Mr. Yukio IMAGAWA (Japan)
Mr. Robert MERRILLEES (Australia)
Rapporteur: Colonel Ronachuck SWASDIKIAT (Thailand)

The Conference also established an *Ad Hoc* Committee, composed of the representatives of the four Cambodian Parties and chaired by the representatives of the two Co-Presidents of the Conference, whose mandate involved matters related to national reconciliation among the Cambodian Parties. The *Ad Hoc* Committee held several meetings during the first session of the Conference.

The Coordination Committee of the Conference, chaired by the representatives of the two Co-Presidents, was established and given responsibility for general coordination of the work of the other four committees. The Coordination Committee met at both the first and second sessions of the Conference. An informal meeting of the Coordination Committee was also held in New York on 21 September 1991.

7. At the conclusion of the first session, the Conference had achieved progress in elaborating a wide variety of elements necessary for the achievement of a comprehensive settlement of the conflict in Cambodia. The Conference noted, however, that it was not yet possible to achieve a comprehensive settlement. It was therefore decided to suspend the Conference on 30 August 1989. However, in doing so, the Conference urged all parties concerned to intensify their efforts to achieve a comprehensive settlement, and asked the Co-Presidents to lend their good offices to facilitate these efforts.

8. Following the suspension of the first session of the Conference, the Co-Presidents and the Secretary-General of the United Nations undertook extensive consultations, in particular with the five permanent members of the United Nations Security Council, with the Supreme National Council of Cambodia, and with other participants in the Paris Conference. The object of these consultations was to forge agreement on all aspects of a settlement, to ensure that all initiatives to this end were compatible and to enhance the prospects of ending the bloodshed in Cambodia at the earliest possible date. The efforts of the Co-Presidents and the Secretary-General paved the way for the reconvening of the Paris Conference on Cambodia.

9. At the inaugural portion of the final meeting of the Paris Conference, on 23 October 1991, the Conference was addressed by H.E. Mr. François MITTERRAND, President of the French Republic, H.R.H. Prince NORODOM SIHANOUK, President of the Supreme National Council of Cambodia, and H.E. Mr. Javier PÉREZ DE CUÉLLAR, Secretary-General of the United Nations.

10. At the second session, the Conference adopted the following instruments:

1. *Agreement on a comprehensive political settlement of the Cambodia conflict*, with annexes on the mandate for UNTAC, military matters, elections, repatriation of Cambodian refugees and displaced persons, and the principles for a new Cambodian constitution;

2. *Agreement concerning the sovereignty, independence, territorial integrity and inviolability, neutrality and national unity of Cambodia*; and

3. *Declaration on the rehabilitation and reconstruction of cambodia.*

These instruments represent an elaboration of the "Framework for a Comprehensive Political Settlement of the Cambodia Conflicts adopted by the five permanent members of the United Nations Security Council on 28 August 1990, and of elements of the work accomplished at the first session of the Conference. They entail a continuing process of national reconciliation and an enhanced role for the United Nations, thus enabling the Cambodian people to determine their own political future through free and fair elections organized and conducted by the United Nations in a neutral political environment with full respect for the national sovereignty of Cambodia.

11. These instruments, which together form the comprehensive settlement, the achievement of which was the objective of the Paris Conference, are being presented for signature to the States participating in the Paris Conference. On behalf of Cambodia, the instruments will be signed by the twelve members of the Supreme National Council of Cambodia, which is the unique legitimate body and source of authority enshrining the sovereignty, independence and unity of Cambodia.

12. The States participating in the Conference call upon the Co-Presidents of the Conference to transmit an authentic copy of the comprehensive political settlement instruments to the Secretary-General of the United Nations. The States participating in the Conference request the Secretary-General to take the appropriate steps in order to enable consideration of the comprehensive settlement by the United Nations Security Council at the earliest opportunity. They pledge their full cooperation in the fulfilment of this comprehensive settlement and their assistance in its implementation.

Above all, in view of the recent tragic history of Cambodia, the States participating in the Conference commit themselves to promote and encourage respect for and observance of human rights and fundamental free-doms in Cambodia, as embodied in the relevant international instruments to which they are party.

13. The States participating in the Conference request the International Committee of the Red Cross to facilitate, in accordance with its principles, the release of prisoners of war and civilian internees. They express their readiness to assist the ICRC in this task.

14. The States participating in the Conference invite other States to accede to the Agreement on a Comprehensive Political Settlement of the Cambodia Conflict and to the Agreement concerning the Sovereignty, Independence, Territorial Integrity and Inviolability, Neutrality and National Unity of Cambodia.

15. Further recognizing the need for a concerted international effort to assist Cambodia in the tasks of rehabilitation and reconstruction, the States participating in the Conference urge the international community to provide generous economic and financial support for the measures set forth in the Declaration on the Rehabilitation and Reconstruction of Cambodia.

IN WITNESS WHEREOF the representatives have signed this Final Act.

DONE AT PARIS this twenty-third day of October one thousand nine hundred and ninety one, in two copies in the Chinese, English, French, Khmer and Russian languages, each text being equally authentic. The originals of ᵗhis Final Act shall be deposited with the Governments of the French Republic and of the Republic of Indonesia.

II. *Agreement on a comprehensive political settlement of the Cambodia conflict*

The States participating in the Paris Conference on Cambodia, namely Australia, Brunei Darussalam, Cambodia, Canada, the People's Republic of China, the French Republic, the Republic of India, the Republic of Indonesia, Japan, the Lao People's Democratic Republic, Malaysia, the Republic of the Philippines, the Republic of Singapore, the Kingdom of Thailand, the Union of Soviet Socialist Republics, the United Kingdom of Great Britain and Northern Ireland, the United States of America, the Socialist Republic of Vietnam and the Socialist Federal Republic of Yugoslavia,

In the presence of the Secretary-General of the United Nations,

In order to maintain, preserve and defend the sovereignty, independence, territorial integrity and inviolability, neutrality and national unity of Cambodia,

Desiring to restore and maintain peace in Cambodia, to promote national reconciliation and to ensure the exercise of the right to self-determination of the Cambodian people through free and fair elections,

Convinced that only a comprehensive political settlement to the Cambodia conflict will be just and durable and will contribute to regional and international peace and security,

Welcoming the Framework document of 28 August 1990, which was accepted by the Cambodian Parties in its entirety as the basis for settling the Cambodia conflict, and which was subsequently unanimously endorsed by Security Council resolution 668 (1990) of 20 September 1990 and General Assembly resolution 45/3 of 15 October 1990,

Noting the formation in Jakarta on 10 September 1990 of the Supreme National Council of Cambodia as the unique legitimate body and source of authority in Cambodia in which, throughout the transitional period, national sovereignty and unity are enshrined, and which represents Cambodia externally,

Welcoming the unanimous election, in Beijing on 17 July 1991, of H.R.H. Prince NORODOM SIHANOUK as the President of the Supreme National Council,

Recognizing that an enhanced United Nations role requires the establishment of a United Nations Transitional Authority in Cambodia (UNTAC) with civilian and military components, which will act with full respect for the national sovereignty of Cambodia,

Noting the statements made at the conclusion of the meetings held in Jakarta on 9-10 September 1990, in Paris on 21-23 December 1990, in Pattaya on 24-26 June 1991, in Beijing on 16-17 July 1991, in Pattaya on 26-29 August 1991, and also the meetings held in Jakarta on 4-6 June 1991 and in New York on 19 September 1991,

Welcoming United Nations Security Council resolution 717 (1991) of 16 October 1991 on Cambodia,

Recognizing that Cambodia's tragic recent history requires special measures to assure protection of human rights, and the non-return to the policies and practices of the past,

Have agreed as follows:

PART I
Arrangements during the transitional period

Section I
Transitional period

Article 1

For the purposes of this Agreement, the transitional period shall commence with the entry into force of this Agreement and terminate when the constituent assembly elected through free and fair elections, organized and certified by the United Nations, has approved the constitution and transformed itself into a legislative assembly, and thereafter a new government has been created.

Section II
United Nations Transitional Authority in Cambodia

Article 2

(1) The Signatories invite the United Nations Security Council to establish a United Nations Transitional Authority in Cambodia (hereinafter referred to as "UNTAC") with civilian and military components under the direct responsibility of the Secretary-General of the United Nations. For this purpose the Secretary-General will designate a Special Representative to act on his behalf.

(2) The Signatories further invite the United Nations Security Council to provide UNTAC with the mandate set forth in this Agreement and to keep its implementation under continuing review through periodic reports submitted by the Secretary-General.

Section III
Supreme National Council

Article 3

The Supreme National Council (hereinafter referred to as "the SNC") is the unique legitimate body and source of authority in which, throughout the transitional period, the sovereignty, independence and unity of Cambodia are enshrined.

Article 4

The members of the SNC shall be committed to the holding of free and fair elections organized and conducted by the United Nations as the basis for forming a new and legitimate Government.

Article 5

The SNC shall, throughout the transitional period, represent Cambodia externally and occupy the seat of Cambodia at the United Nations, in the United Nations specialized agencies, and in other international institutions and international conferences.

Article 6

The SNC hereby delegates to the United Nations all powers necessary to ensure the implementation of this Agreement, as described in annex 1.

In order to ensure a neutral political environment conducive to free and fair general elections, administrative agencies, bodies and offices which could directly influence the outcome of elections will be placed under direct United Nations supervision or control. In that context, special attention will be given to foreign affairs, national defence, finance, public security and information. To reflect the importance of these subjects, UNTAC needs to exercise such control as is necessary to ensure the strict neutrality of the bodies responsible for them. The United Nations, in consultation with the SNC, will identify which agencies, bodies and offices could continue to operate in order to ensure normal day-to-day life in the country.

Article 7

The relationship between the SNC, UNTAC and existing administrative structures is set forth in annex 1.

Section IV
Withdrawal of foreign forces and its verification

Article 8

Immediately upon entry into force of this Agreement, any foreign forces, advisers, and military personnel remaining in Cambodia, together with their weapons, ammunition, and equipment, shall be withdrawn from Cambodia and not be returned. Such withdrawal and non-return will be subject to UNTAC verification in accordance with annex 2.

Section V
Cease-fire and cessation of outside military assistance

Article 9

The cease-fire shall take effect at the time this Agreement enters into force. All forces shall immediately disengage and refrain from all hostilities and from any deployment, movement or action which would extend the territory they control or which might lead to renewed fighting.

The Signatories hereby invite the Security Council of the United Nations to request the Secretary-General to provide good offices to assist in this process until such time as the military component of UNTAC is in position to supervise, monitor and verify it.

Article 10

Upon entry into force of this Agreement, there shall be an immediate cessation of all outside military assistance to all Cambodian Parties.

Article 11

The objectives of military arrangements during the transitional period shall be to stabilize the security situation and build confidence among the parties to the conflict, so as to reinforce the purposes of this Agreement and to prevent the risks of a return to warfare.

Detailed provisions regarding UNTAC's supervision, monitoring, and verification of the cease-fire and related measures, including verification of the withdrawal of foreign forces and the regrouping, cantonment and ultimate disposition of all Cambodian forces and their weapons during the transitional period are set forth in annex 1, section C, and annex 2.

PART II
Elections

Article 12

The Cambodian people shall have the right to determine their own political future through the free and fair election of a constituent assembly, which will draft and approve a new Cambodian Constitution in accordance with Article 23 and transform itself into a legislative assembly, which will create the new Cambodian Government. This election will be held under United Nations auspices in a neutral political environment with full respect for the national sovereignty of Cambodia.

Article 13

UNTAC shall be responsible for the organization and conduct of these elections based on the provisions of annex 1, section D, and annex 3.

Article 14

All signatories commit themselves to respect the results of these elections once certified as free and fair by the United Nations.

PART III
Human rights

Article 15

1. All persons in Cambodia and all Cambodian refugees and displaced persons shall enjoy the rights and freedoms embodied in the Universal Declaration of Human Rights and other relevant international human rights instruments.

2. To this end,

(a) Cambodia undertakes:

-to ensure respect for and observance of human rights and fundamental freedoms in Cambodia;

-to support the right of all Cambodian citizens to undertake activities which would promote and protect human rights and fundamental freedoms;

-to take effective measures to ensure that the policies and practices of the past shall never be allowed to return;

-to adhere to relevant international human rights instruments;

(b) the other Signatories to this Agreement undertake to promote and encourage respect for and observance of human rights and fundamental freedoms in Cambodia as embodied in the relevant international instruments and the relevant resolutions of the United Nations General Assembly, in order, in particular, to prevent the recurrence of human rights abuses.

Article 16

UNTAC shall be responsible during the transitional period for fostering an environment in which respect for human rights shall be ensured, based on the provisions of annex 1, section E.

Article 17

After the end of the transitional period, the United Nations Commission on Human Rights should continue to monitor closely the human rights situation in Cambodia, including, if necessary, by the appointment of a Special Rapporteur who would report his findings annually to the Commission and to the General Assembly.

PART IV
International guarantees

Article 18

Cambodia undertakes to maintain, preserve and defend, and the other Signatories undertake to recognize and respect, the sovereignty, independence, territorial integrity and inviolability, neutrality and national unity of Cambodia, as set forth in a separate Agreement.

PART V
Refugees and displaced persons

Article 19

Upon entry into force of this Agreement, every effort will be made to create in Cambodia political, economic and social conditions conducive to the voluntary return and harmonious integration of Cambodian refugees and displaced persons.

Article 20

(1) Cambodian refugees and displaced persons, located outside Cambodia, shall have the right to return to Cambodia and to live in safety, security and dignity, free from intimidation or coercion of any kind.

(2) The Signatories request the Secretary-General of the United Nations to facilitate the repatriation in safety and dignity of Cambodian refugees and displaced persons, as an integral part of the comprehensive political settlement and under the overall authority of the Special Representative of the Secretary-General, in accordance with the guidelines and principles on the repatriation of refugees and displaced persons as set forth in annex 4.

PART VI
Release of prisoners of war and civilian internees

Article 21

The release of all prisoners of war and civilian internees shall be accomplished at the earliest possible date under the direction of the International Committee of the Red Cross (ICRC) in co-ordination with the Special Representative of the Secretary-General, with the assistance, as necessary, of other appropriate international humanitarian organizations and the Signatories.

Article 22

The expression "civilian internees" refers to all persons who are not prisoners of war and who, having contributed in any way whatsoever to the armed or political struggle, have been arrested or detained by any of the parties by virtue of their contribution thereto.

PART VII
Principles for a new Constitution for Cambodia

Article 23

Basic principles, including those regarding human rights and fundamental freedoms as well as regarding Cambodia's status of neutrality, which the new Cambodian Constitution will incorporate, are set forth in annex 5.

PART VIII
Rehabilitation and reconstruction

Article 24

The Signatories urge the international community to provide economic and financial support for the rehabilitation and reconstruction of Cambodia, as provided in a separate declaration.

PART IX
Final provisions

Article 25

The Signatories shall, in good faith and in a spirit of co-operation, resolve through peaceful means any disputes with respect to the implementation of this Agreement.

Article 26

The Signatories request other States, international organizations and other bodies to co-operate and assist in the implementation of this Agreement and in the fulfilment by UNTAC of its mandate.

Article 27

The Signatories shall provide their full co-operation to the United Nations to ensure the implementation of its mandate, including by the provision of privileges and immunities, and by facilitating freedom of movement and communication within and through their respective territories.

In carrying out its mandate, UNTAC shall exercise due respect for the sovereignty of all States neighbouring Cambodia.

Article 28

(1) The Signatories shall comply in good faith with all obligations undertaken in this Agreement and shall extend full co-operation to the United Nations, including the provision of the information which UNTAC requires in the fulfilment of its mandate.

(2) The signature on behalf of Cambodia by the members of the SNC shall commit all Cambodian parties and armed forces to the provisions of this Agreement.

Article 29

Without prejudice to the prerogatives of the Security Council of the United Nations, and upon the request of the Secretary-General, the two Co-Chairmen of the Paris Conference on Cambodia, in the event of a violation or threat of violation of this Agreement, will immediately undertake appropriate consultations, including with members of the Paris Conference on Cambodia, with a view to taking appropriate steps to ensure respect for these commitments.

Article 30

This Agreement shall enter into force upon signature.

Article 31

This Agreement shall remain open for accession by all States. The instruments of accession shall be deposited with the Governments of the French Republic and the Republic of Indonesia. For each State acceding to the Agreement it shall enter into force on the date of deposit of its instruments of accession. Acceding States shall be bound by the same obligations as the Signatories.

Article 32

The originals of this Agreement, of which the Chinese, English, French, Khmer and Russian texts are equally authentic, shall be deposited with the Governments of the French Republic and the Republic of Indonesia, which shall transmit certified true copies to the Governments of the other States participating in the Paris Conference on Cambodia, as well as the Secretary-General of the United Nations.

IN WITNESS WHEREOF the undersigned Plenipotentiaries, being duly authorized thereto, have signed this Agreement.

DONE at Paris this twenty-third day of October, one thousand nine hundred and ninety one.

Annex 1
UNTAC *mandate*

Section A. General procedures

1. In accordance with article 6 of the Agreement, UNTAC will exercise the powers necessary to ensure the implementation of this Agreement, including those relating to the organization and conduct of free and fair elections and the relevant aspects of the administration of Cambodia.

2. The following mechanism will be used to resolve all issues relating to the implementation of this Agreement which may arise between the Secretary-General's Special Representative and the Supreme National Council (SNC):

(a) The SNC offers advice to UNTAC, which will comply with this advice provided there is a consensus among the members of the SNC and provided this advice is consistent with the objectives of the present Agreement;

(b) If there is no consensus among the members of the SNC despite every endeavour of its President, H.R.H. Samdech NORODOM SIHANOUK, the President will be entitled to make the decision on what advice to offer to UNTAC, taking fully into account the views expressed in the SNC. UNTAC will comply with the advice provided it is consistent with the objectives of the present Agreement;

(c) If H.R.H. Samdech NORODOM SIHANOUK, President of the SNC, the legitimate representative of Cambodian sovereignty, is not, for whatever reason, in a positon to make such a decision, his power of decision will transfer to the Secretary-General's Special Representative. The Special Representative will make the final decision, taking fully into account the views expressed in the SNC;

(d) Any power to act regarding the implementation of this Agreement conferred upon the SNC by the Agreement will be exercised by consensus or, failing such consensus, by its President in accordance with the procedure set out above. In the event that H.R.H. Samdech NORODOM SIHANOUK, President of the SNC, the legitimate representative of Cambodian sovereignty, is not, for whatever reason, in a position to act, his power to act will transfer to the Secretary-General's Special Representative who may take the necessary action;

(e) In all cases, the Secretary-General's Special Representative will determine whether advice or action of the SNC is consistent with the present Agreement.

3. The Secretary-General's Special Representative or his delegate will attend the meetings of the SNC and of any subsidiary body which might be established by it and give its members all necessary information on the decisions taken by UNTAC.

Section B. *Civil administration*

1. In accordance with article 6 of the Agreement, all administrative agencies, bodies and offices acting in the field of foreign affairs, national defence, finance, public security and information will be placed under the

direct control of UNTAC, which will exercise it as necessary to ensure strict neutrality. In this respect, the Secretary-General's Special Representative will determine what is necessary and may issue directives to the above-mentioned administrative agencies, bodies and offices. Such directives may be issued to and will bind all Cambodian Parties.

2. In accordance with article 6 of the Agreement, the Secretary-General's Special Representative, in consultation with the SNC, will determine which other administrative agencies, bodies and offices could directly influence the outcome of elections. These administrative agencies, bodies and offices will be placed under direct supervision or control of UNTAC and will comply with any guidance provided by it.

3. In accordance with article 6 of the Agreement, the Secretary-General's Special Representative, in consultation with the SNC, will identify which administrative agencies, bodies, and offices could continue to operate in order to ensure normal day-to-day life in Cambodia, if necessary, under such supervision by UNTAC as it considers necessary.

4. In accordance with article 6 of the Agreement, the authority of the Secretary-General's Special Representative will include the power to:

(a) Install in administrative agencies, bodies and offices of all the Cambodian Parties, United Nations personnel who will have unrestricted access to all administrative operations and information;

(b) Require the reassignment or removal of any personnel of such administrative agencies, bodies and offices.

5. (a) On the basis of the information provided in Article I, paragraph 3, of annex 2, the Special Representative of the Secretary-General will determine, after consultation with the Cambodian Parties, those civil police necessary to perform law enforcement in Cambodia. All Cambodian Parties hereby undertake to comply with the determination made by the Special Representative in this regard;

(b) All civil police will operate under UNTAC supervision or control, in order to ensure that law and order are maintained effectively and impartially, and that human rights and fundamental freedoms are fully protected. In consultation with the SNC, UNTAC will supervise other law enforcement and judicial processes throughout Cambodia to the extent necessary to ensure the attainment of these objectives.

6. If the Secretary-General's Special Representative deems it necessary, UNTAC, in consultation with the SNC, will undertake investigations of complaints and allegations regarding actions by the existing administrative structures in Cambodia that are inconsistent with or

work against the objectives of this comprehensive political settlement. UNTAC will also be empowered to undertake such investigation on its own initiative. UNTAC will take, when necessary, appropriate corrective steps.

Section C. *Military functions*

1. UNTAC will supervise, monitor and verify the withdrawal of foreign forces, the cease-fire and related measures in accordance with annex 2, including:

(a) Verification of the withdrawal from Cambodia of all categories of foreign forces, advisers and military personnel and their weapons, ammunition and equipment, and their non-return to Cambodia;

(b) Liaison with neighbouring Governments over any developments in or near their territory that could endanger the implementation of this Agreement;

(c) Monitoring the cessation of outside military assistance to all Cambodian Parties;

(d) Locating and confiscating caches of weapons and military supplies throughout the country;

(e) Assisting with clearing mines and undertaking training programmes in mine clearance and a mine awareness programme among the Cambodian people.

2. UNTAC will supervise the regrouping and relocating of all forces to specifically designated cantonment areas on the basis of an operational time-table to be agreed upon, in accordance with annex 2.

3. As the forces enter the cantonments, UNTAC will initiate the process of arms control and reduction specified in annex 2.

4. UNTAC will take necessary steps regarding the phased process of demobilization of the military forces of the parties, in accordance with annex 2.

5. UNTAC will assist, as necessary, the International Committee of the Red Cross in the release of all prisoners of war and civilian internees.

Section D. *Elections*

1. UNTAC will organize and conduct the election referred to in Part II of this Agreement in accordance with this section and annex 3.

2. UNTAC may consult with the SNC regarding the organization and conduct of the electoral process.

3. In the exercise of its responsibilities in relation to the electoral process, the specific authority of UNTAC will include the following:

(a) The establishment, in consultation with the SNC, of a system of laws, procedures and administrative measures necessary for the holding of a free and fair election in Cambodia, including the adoption of an electoral law and of a code of conduct regulating participation in the election in a manner consistent with respect for human rights and prohibiting coercion or financial inducement in order to influence voter preference;

(b) The suspension or abrogation, in consultation with the SNC, of provisions of existing laws which could defeat the objects and purposes of this Agreement;

(c) The design and implementation of a voter education programme, covering all aspects of the election, to support the election process;

(d) The design and implementation of a system of voter registration, as a first phase of the electoral process, to ensure that eligible voters have the opportunity to register, and the subsequent preparation of verified voter registration lists;

(e) The design and implementation of a system of registration of political parties and lists of candidates;

(f) Ensuring fair access to the media, including press, television and radio, for all political parties contesting in the election;

(g) The adoption and implementation of measures to monitor and facilitate the participation of Cambodians in the elections, the political campaign, and the balloting procedures;

(h) The design and implementation of a system of balloting and polling, to ensure that registered voters have the opportunity to vote;

(i) The establishment, in consultation with the SNC, of co-ordinated arrangements to facilitate the presence of foreign observers wishing to observe the campaign and voting;

(j) Overall direction of polling and the vote count;

(k) The identification and investigation of complaints of electoral irregularities, and the taking of appropriate corrective action;

(l) Determining whether or not the election was free and fair and, if so, certification of the list of persons duly elected.

4. In carrying out its responsibilities under the present section, UNTAC will establish a system of safeguards to assist it in ensuring the absence of fraud during the electoral process, including arrangements for Cambodian representatives to observe the registration and polling procedures and the provision of an UNTAC mechanism for hearing and deciding complaints.

5. The timetable for the various phases of the electoral process will be determined by UNTAC, in consultation with the SNC as provided in paragraph 2 of this section. The duration of the electoral process will not exceed nine months from the commencement of voter registration.

6. In organizing and conducting the electoral process, UNTAC will make every effort to ensure that the system and procedures adopted are absolutely impartial, while the operational arrangements are as administratively simple and efficient as possible.

Section E. *Human rights*

In accordance with article 16, UNTAC will make provisions for:

(a) The development and implementation of a programme of human rights education to promote respect for and understanding of human rights;

(b) General human rights oversight during the transitional period;

(c) The investigation of human rights complaints, and, where appropriate, corrective action.

Annex 2
Withdrawal, cease-fire and related measures

Article I
Cease-fire

1. All Cambodian Parties (hereinafter referred to as "the Parties") agree to observe a comprehensive cease-fire on land and water and in the air. This cease-fire will be implemented in two phases. During the first phase, the cease-fire will be observed with the assistance of the Secretary-General of the United Nations through his good offices. During the second phase, which should commence as soon as possible, the cease-fire will be supervised, monitored and verified by UNTAC. The Commander of the military component of UNTAC, in consultation with the Parties, shall determine the exact time and date at which the second phase will commence. This date will be set at least four weeks in advance of its coming into effect.

2. The Parties undertake that, upon the signing of this Agreement, they will observe a cease-fire and will order their armed forces immediately to disengage and refrain from all hostilities and any deployment, movement or action that would extend the territory they control or that might lead to a resumption of fighting, pending the commencement of the second phase. "Forces" are agreed to include all regular, provincial, district, paramilitary, and other auxiliary forces. During the first phase, the Secretary-General of the United Nations will provide his good offices to the Parties to assist them in its observance. The Parties undertake to co-operate with the Secretary-General or his representatives in the exercise of his good offices in this regard.

3. The Parties agree that, immediately upon the signing of this Agreement, the following information will be provided to the United Nations:

(a) Total strength of their forces, organization, precise number and location of deployments inside and outside Cambodia. The deployment will be depicted on a map marked with locations of all troop positions, occupied or unoccupied, including staging camps, supply bases and supply routes;

(b) Comprehensive lists of arms, ammunition and equipment held by their forces, and the exact locations at which those arms, ammunition and equipment are deployed;

(c) Detailed record of their mine-fields, including types and characteristics of mines laid and information of booby traps used by them together with any information available to them about mine-fields laid or booby traps used by the other Parties;

(d) Total strength of their police forces, organization, precise numbers and locations of deployments, as well as comprehensive lists of their arms, ammunition and equipment, and the exact locations at which those arms, ammunition and equipment are deployed.

4. Immediately upon his arrival in Cambodia, and not later than four weeks before the beginning of the second phase, the Commander of the military component of UNTAC will, in consultation with the Parties, finalize UNTAC's plan for the regroupment and cantonment of the forces of the Parties and for the storage of their arms, ammunition and equipment, in accordance with Article III of this annex. This plan will include the designation of regroupment and cantonment areas, as well as an agreed timetable. The cantonment areas will be established at battalion size or larger.

5. The Parties agree to take steps to inform their forces at least two weeks before the beginning of the second phase, using all possible means of communication, about the agreed date and time of the beginning of the second phase, about the agreed plan for the regroupment and cantonment of their forces and for the storage of their arms, ammunition and equipment and, in particular, about the exact locations of the regroupment areas to which their forces are to report. Such information will continue to be disseminated for a period of four weeks after the beginning of the second phase.

6. The Parties shall scrupulously observe the cease-fire and will not resume any hostilities by land, water or air. The commanders of their armed forces will ensure that all troops under their command remain on their respective positions, pending their movement to the designated regroupment areas, and refrain from all hostilities and from any deployment or movement or action which would extend the territory they control or which might lead to a resumption of fighting.

Article II
Liaison system and Mixed Military Working Group

A Mixed Military Working Group (MMWG) will be established with a view to resolving any problems that may arise in the observance of the cease-fire. It will be chaired by the most senior United Nations military officer in Cambodia or his representative. Each Party agrees to designate an officer of the rank of brigadier or equivalent to serve on the MMWG. Its composition, method of operation and meeting places will be determined by the most senior United Nations military officer in consultation with the Parties. Similar liaison arrangements will be made at lower military command levels to resolve practical problems on the ground.

Article III
Regroupment and cantonment of the forces of the Parties and storage of their arms, ammunition and equipment

1. In accordance with the operational timetable referred to in paragraph 4 of article I of the present annex, all forces of the Parties that are not already in designated cantonment areas will report to designated regroupment areas, which will be established and operated by the military component of UNTAC. These regroupment areas will be established and operational not later than one week prior to the date of the beginning of the second phase. The Parties agree to arrange for all their forces, with all their arms, ammunition and equipment, to report to regroupment areas within two weeks after the beginning of the second phase. All personnel who have reported to the regroupment areas will thereafter be escorted by personnel of the military component of UNTAC, with their arms, ammunition and equipment, to designated cantonment areas. All Parties agree to ensure that personnel reporting to the regroupment areas will be able to do so in full safety and without any hindrance.

2. On the basis of the information provided in accordance with paragraph 3 of article I of the present annex, UNTAC will confirm that the regroupment and cantonment processes have been completed in accordance with the plan referred to in paragraph 4 of article I of this annex. UNTAC will endeavour to complete these processes within four weeks from the date of the beginning of the second phase. On the completion of regroupment of all forces and of their movement to cantonment areas, respectively, the Commander of the military component of UNTAC will so inform each of the four Parties.

3. The Parties agree that, as their forces enter the designated cantonment areas, their personnel will be instructed by their commanders to immediately hand over all their arms, ammunition and equipment to UNTAC for storage in the custody of UNTAC.

4. UNTAC will check the arms, ammunition and equipment handed over to it against the lists referred to in paragraph 3 b) of article I of this annex, in order to verify that all the arms, ammunition and equipment in the possesion of the Parties have been placed under its custody.

Article IV
Resupply of forces during cantonment

The military component of UNTAC will supervise the resupply of all forces of the Parties during the regroupment and cantonment processes. Such resupply will be confined to items of a non-lethal nature such as food, water, clothing and medical supplies as well as provision of medical care.

Article V
Ultimate disposition of the forces of the Parties and of their arms, ammunition and equipment

1. In order to reinforce the objectives of a comprehensive political settlement, minimize the risks of a return to warfare, stabilize the security situation and build confidence among the Parties to the conflict, all Parties agree to undertake a phased and balanced process of demobilization of at least 70 per cent of their military forces. This process shall be undertaken in accordance with a detailed plan to be drawn up by UNTAC on the basis of the information provided under Article I of this annex and in consultation with the Parties. It should be completed prior to the end of the process of registration for the elections and on a date to be determined by the Special Representative of the Secretary-General.

2. The Cambodian Parties hereby commit themselves to demobilize all their remaining forces before or shortly after the elections and, to the extent that full demobilization is unattainable, to respect and abide by whatever decision the newly elected government that emerges in accordance with Article 12 of this Agreement takes with regard to the incorporation of parts or all of those forces into a new national army. Upon completion of the demobilization referred to in paragraph 1, the Cambodian Parties and the Special Representative of the Secretary-General shall undertake a review regarding the final disposition of the forces remaining in the cantonments, with a view to determining which of the following shall apply:

(a) If the Parties agree to proceed with the demobilization of all or some of the forces remaining in the cantonments, preferably prior to or otherwise shortly after the elections, the Special Representative shall prepare a timetable for so doing, in consultation with them;

(b) Should total demobilization of all of the residual forces before or shortly after the elections not be possible, the Parties hereby undertake to make available all of their forces remaining in cantonments to the newly elected government that emerges in accordance with Article 12 of this Agreement, for consideration for incorporation into a new national army. They further agree that any such forces which are not incorporated into the new national army will be demobilized forthwith according to a plan to be prepared by the Special Representative. With regard to the ultimate disposition of the remaining forces and all the arms, ammunition and equipment, UNTAC, as it withdraws from Cambodia, shall retain such authority as is necessary to ensure an orderly transfer to the newly elected government of those responsibilities it has exercised during the transitional period.

3. UNTAC will assist, as required, with the reintegration into civilian life of the forces demobilized prior to the elections.

4. (a) UNTAC will control and guard all the arms, ammunition and equipment of the Parties throughout the transitional period;

(b) As the cantoned forces are demobilized in accordance with paragraph 1 above, there will be a parallel reduction by UNTAC of the arms, ammunition and equipment stored on site in the cantonment areas. For the forces remaining in the cantonment areas, access to their arms, ammunition and equipment shall only be on the basis of the explicit authorization of the Special Representative of the Secretary-General;

(c) If there is a further demobilization of the military forces in accordance with paragraph 2 a) above, there will be a commensurate reduction by UNTAC of the arms, ammunition and equipment stored on site in the cantonment areas;

(d) The ultimate disposition of all arms, ammunition and equipment will be determined by the government that emerges through the free and fair elections in accordance with article 12 of this Agreement.

Article VI
Verification of withdrawal from Cambodia and non-return of all categories of foreign forces

1. UNTAC shall be provided, no later than two weeks before the commencement of the second phase of the cease-fire, with detailed information in writing regarding the withdrawal of foreign forces. This information shall include the following elements:

(a) Total strength of these forces and their organization and deployment;

(b) Comprehensive lists of arms, ammunition and equipment held by these forces, and their exact locations;

(c) Withdrawal plan (already implemented or to be implemented), including withdrawal routes, border crossing points and time of departure from Cambodia.

2. On the basis of the information provided in accordance with paragraph 1 above, UNTAC will undertake an investigation in the manner it deems appropriate. The Party providing the information will be required to make personnel available to accompany UNTAC investigators.

3. Upon confirmation of the presence of any foreign forces, UNTAC will immediately deploy military personnel with the foreign forces and accompany them until they have withdrawn from Cambodian territory. UNTAC will also establish checkpoints on withdrawal routes, border crossing points and airfields to verify the withdrawal and ensure the non-return of all categories of foreign forces.

4. The Mixed Military Working Group (MMWG) provided for in article II of this annex will assist UNTAC in fulfilling the above-mentioned tasks.

Article VII
Cessation of outside military assistance to all Cambodian Parties

1. All Parties undertake, from the time of the signing of this Agreement, not to obtain or seek any outside military assistance, including weapons, ammunition and military equipment from outside sources.

2. The Signatories whose territory is adjacent to Cambodia, namely, the Governments of the Lao People's Democratic Republic, the Kingdom of Thailand and the Socialist Republic of Vietnam, undertake to:

(a) Prevent the territories of their respective States, including land territory, territorial sea and air space, from being used for the purpose of providing any form of military assistance to any of the Cambodian Parties. Resupply of such items as food, water, clothing and medical supplies through their territories will be allowed, but shall, without prejudice to the provisions of subparagraph (c) below, be subject to UNTAC supervision upon arrival in Cambodia;

(b) Provide written confirmation to the Commander of the military component of UNTAC, not later than four weeks after the second phase of the cease-fire begins, that no forces, arms, ammunition or military equipment of any of the Cambodian Parties are present on their territories;

(c) Receive an UNTAC liaison officer in each of their capitals and designate an officer of the rank of colonel or equivalent, not later than four weeks after the beginning of the second phase of the cease-fire, in order to assist UNTAC in investigating, with due respect for their sovereignty, any complaints that activities are taking place on their territories that are contrary to the provisions of the comprehensive political settlement.

3. To enable UNTAC to monitor the cessation of outside assistance to all Cambodian Parties, the Parties agree that, upon signature of this Agreement, they will provide to UNTAC any information available to them about the routes and means by which military assistance, including weapons, ammunition and military equipment, have been supplied to any of the Parties. Immediately after the second phase of the cease-fire begins, UNTAC will take the following practical measures:

(a) Establish check-points along the routes and at selected locations along the Cambodian side of the border and at airfields inside Cambodia;

(b) Patrol the coastal and inland waterways of Cambodia;

(c) Maintain mobile teams at strategic locations within Cambodia to patrol and investigate allegations of supply of arms to any of the Parties.

Article VIII
Caches of weapons and military supplies

1. In order to stabilize the security situation, build confidence and reduce arms and military supplies throughout Cambodia, each Party agrees to provide to the Commander of the military component of UNTAC, before a date to be determined by him, all information at its disposal, including marked maps, about known or suspected caches of weapons and military supplies throughout Cambodia.

2. On the basis of information received, the military component of UNTAC shall, after the date referred to in paragraph 1, deploy verification teams to investigate each report and destroy each cache found.

Article IX
Unexploded ordnance devices

1. Soon after arrival in Cambodia, the military component of UNTAC shall ensure, as a first step, that all known minefields are clearly marked.

2. The Parties agree that, after completion of the regroupment and cantonment processes in accordance with Article III of the present annex, they will make available mine-clearing teams which, under the supervision and control of UNTAC military personnel, will leave the cantonment areas in order to assist in removing, disarming or deactivating remaining unexploded ordnance devices. Those mines or objects which cannot be removed, disarmed or deactivated will be clearly marked in accordance with a system to be devised by the military component of UNTAC.

3. UNTAC shall:

(a) Conduct a mass public education programme in the recognition and avoidance of explosive devices;

(b) Train Cambodian volunteers to dispose of unexploded ordnance devices;

(c) Provide emergency first-aid training to Cambodian volunteers.

Article X
Investigation of violations

1. After the beginning of the second phase, upon receipt of any information or complaint from one of the Parties relating to a possible case of non-compliance with any of the provisions of the present annex or related provisions, UNTAC will undertake an investigation in the manner which it deems appropriate. Where the investigation takes place in response to a complaint by one of the Parties, that Party will be required to make personnel available to accompany the UNTAC investigators. The results of such investigation will be conveyed by UNTAC to the complaining Party and the Party complained against, and if necessary to the SNC.

2. UNTAC will also carry out investigations on its

own initiative in other cases when it has reason to believe or suspect that a violation of this annex or related provisions may be taking place.

Article XI
Release of prisoners of war

The military component of UNTAC will provide assistance as required to the International Committee of the Red Cross in the latter's discharge of its functions relating to the release of prisoners of war.

Article XII
Repatriation and resettlement of displaced Cambodians

The military component of UNTAC will provide assistance as necessary in the repatriation of Cambodian refugees and displaced persons carried out in accordance with articles 19 and 20 of this Agreement, in particular in the clearing of mines from repatriation routes, reception centres and resettlement areas, as well as in the protection of the reception centres.

Annex 3
Elections

1. The constituent assembly referred to in article 12 of the Agreement shall consist of 120 members. Within three months from the date of the election, it shall complete its tasks of drafting and adopting a new Cambodian Constitution and transform itself into a legislative assembly which will form a new Cambodian Government.

2. The election referred to in Article 12 of the Agreement will be held throughout Cambodia on a provincial basis in accordance with a system of proportional representation on the basis of lists of candidates put forward by political parties.

3. All Cambodians, including those who at the time of signature of this Agreement are Cambodian refugees and displaced persons, will have the same rights, freedoms and opportunities to take part in the electoral process.

4. Every person who has reached the age of eighteen at the time of application to register, or who turns eighteen during the registration period, and who either was born in Cambodia or is the child of a person born in Cambodia, will be eligible to vote in the election.

5. Political parties may be formed by any group of five thousand registered voters. Party platforms shall be consistent with the principles and objectives of the Agreement on a comprehensive political settlement.

6. Party affiliation will be required in order to stand for election to the constituent assembly. Political parties will present lists of candidates standing for election on their behalf, who will be registered voters.

7. Political parties and candidates will be registered in order to stand for election. UNTAC will confirm that political parties and candidates meet the established criteria in order to qualify for participation in the election. Adherence to a Code of Conduct established by UNTAC in consultation with the SNC will be a condition for such participation.

8. Voting will be by secret ballot, with provision made to assist those who are disabled or who cannot read or write.

9. The freedoms of speech, assembly and movement will be fully respected. All registered political parties will enjoy fair access to the media, including the press, television and radio.

Annex 4
Repatriation of Cambodian refugees and displaced persons

PART I
Introduction

1. As part of the comprehensive political settlement, every assistance will need to be given to Cambodian refugees and displaced persons as well as to countries of temporary refuge and the country of origin in order to facilitate the voluntary return of all Cambodian refugees and displaced persons in a peaceful and orderly manner. It must also be ensured that there would be no residual problems for the countries of temporary refuge. The country of origin with responsibility towards its own people will accept their return as conditions become conducive.

PART II
Conditions conducive to the return of refugees and displaced persons

2. The task of rebuilding the Cambodian nation will require the harnessing of all its human and natural resources. To this end, the return to the place of their choice of Cambodians from their temporary refuge and elsewhere outside their country of origin will make a major contribution.

3. Every effort should be made to ensure that the conditions which have led to a large number of Cambodian refugees and displaced persons seeking refuge in other countries should not recur. Nevertheless, some Cambodian refugees and displaced persons will wish and be able to return spontaneously to their homeland.

4. There must be full respect for the human rights and fundamental freedoms of all Cambodians, including those of the repatriated refugees and displaced persons, in recognition of their entitlement to live in peace and security, free from intimidation and coercion of any kind. These rights would include, inter alia, freedom of move-

ment within Cambodia, the choice of domicile and employment, and the right to property.

5. In accordance with the comprehensive political settlement, every effort should be made to create concurrently in Cambodia political, economic and social conditions conducive to the return and harmonious integration of the Cambodian refugees and displaced persons.

6. With a view to ensuring that refugees and displaced persons participate in the elections, mass repatriation should commence and be completed as soon as possible, taking into account all the political, humanitarian, logistical, technical and socio-economic factors involved, and with the co-operation of the SNC.

7. Repatriation of Cambodian refugees and displaced persons should be voluntary and their decision should be taken in full possession of the facts. Choice of destination within Cambodia should be that of the individual. The unity of the family must be preserved.

PART III
Operational factors

8. Consistent with respect for principles of national sovereignty in the countries of temporary refuge and origin, and in close co-operation with the countries of temporary refuge and origin, full access by the Office of the United Nations High Commissioner for Refugees (UNHCR), ICRC and other relevant international agencies should be guaranteed to all Cambodian refugees and displaced persons, with a view to the agencies undertaking the census, tracing, medical assistance, food distribution and other activities vital to the discharge of their mandate and operational responsibilities; such access should also be provided in Cambodia to enable the relevant international organizations to carry out their traditional monitoring as well as operational responsibilities.

9. In the context of the comprehensive political settlement, the signatories note with satisfaction that the Secretary-General of the United Nations has entrusted UNHCR with the role of leadership and co-ordination among intergovernmental agencies assisting with the repatriation and relief of Cambodian refugees and displaced persons. The Signatories look to all non-governmental organizations to coordinate as much as possible their work for the Cambodian refugees and displaced persons with that of UNHCR.

10. The SNC, the Governments of the countries in which the Cambodian refugees and displaced persons have sought temporary refuge, and the countries which contribute to the repatriation and integration effort, will wish to monitor closely and facilitate the repatriation of the returnees. An ad hoc consultative body should be established for a limited term for these purposes. The UNHCR, the ICRC, and other international agencies as appropriate, as well as UNTAC, would be invited to join as full participants.

11. Adequately monitored short-term repatriation assistance should be provided on an impartial basis to enable the families and individuals returning to Cambodia to establish their lives and livelihoods harmoniously in their society. These interim measures would be phased out and replaced in the longer term by the reconstruction programme.

12. Those responsible for organizing and supervising the repatriation operation will need to ensure that conditions of security are created for the movement of the refugees and displaced persons. In this respect, it is imperative that appropriate border crossing points and routes be designated and cleared of mines and other hazards.

13. The international community should contribute generously to the financial requirements of the repatriation operation.

Annex 5
Principles for a new constitution for Cambodia

1. The constitution will be the supreme law of the land. It may be amended only by a designated process involving legislative approval, popular referendum, or both.

2. Cambodia's tragic recent history requires special measures to assure protection of human rights. Therefore, the constitution will contain a declaration of fundamental rights, including the rights to life, personal liberty, security, freedom of movement, freedom of religion, assembly and association including political parties and trade unions, due process and equality before the law, protection from arbitrary deprivation of property or deprivation of private property without just compensation, and freedom from racial, ethnic, religious or sexual discrimination. It will prohibit the retroactive application of criminal law. The declaration will be consistent with the provisions of the Universal Declaration of Human Rights and other relevant international instruments. Aggrieved individuals will be entitled to have the courts adjudicate and enforce these rights.

3. The constitution will declare Cambodia's status as a sovereign, independent and neutral State, and the national unity of the Cambodian people.

4. The constitution will state that Cambodia will follow a system of liberal democracy, on the basis of pluralism. It will provide for periodic and genuine elections. It will provide for the right to vote and to be elected by universal and equal suffrage. It will provide for voting

by secret ballot, with a requirement that electoral procedures provide a full and fair opportunity to organize and participate in the electoral process.

5. An independent judiciary will be established, empowered to enforce the rights provided under the constitution.

6. The constitution will be adopted by a two-thirds majority of the members of the constituent assembly.

III. *Agreement concerning the sovereignty, independence, territorial integrity and inviolability, neutrality and national unity of Cambodia*

Australia, Brunei Darussalam, Cambodia, Canada, the People's Republic of China, the French Republic, the Republic of India, the Republic of Indonesia, Japan, the Lao People's Democratic Republic, Malaysia, the Republic of the Philippines, the Republic of Singapore, the Kingdom of Thailand, the Union of Soviet Socialist Republics, the United Kingdom of Great Britain and Northern Ireland, the United States of America, the Socialist Republic of Vietnam and the Socialist Federal Republic of Yugoslavia,

In the presence of the Secretary-General of the United Nations,

Convinced that a comprehensive political settlement for Cambodia is essential for the long-term objective of maintaining peace and security in South-East Asia,

Recalling their obligations under the Charter of the United Nations and other rules of international law,

Considering that full observance of the principles of non-interference and non-intervention in the internal and external affairs of States is of the greatest importance for the maintenance of international peace and security,

Reaffirming the inalienable right of States freely to determine their own political, economic, cultural and social systems in accordance with the will of their peoples, without outside interference, subversion, coercion or threat in any form whatsoever,

Desiring to promote respect for and observance of human rights and fundamental freedoms in conformity with the Charter of the United Nations and other relevant international instruments,

Have agreed as follows:

Article 1

1. Cambodia hereby solemnly undertakes to maintain, preserve and defend its sovereignty, independence, territorial integrity and inviolability, neutrality, and national unity; the perpetual neutrality of Cambodia shall be proclaimed and enshrined in the Cambodian constitution to be adopted after free and fair elections.

2. To this end, Cambodia undertakes:

(a) To refrain from any action that might impair the sovereignty, independence and territorial integrity and inviolability of other States;

(b) To refrain from entering into any military alliances or other military agreements with other States that would be inconsistent with its neutrality, without prejudice to Cambodia's right to acquire the necessary military equipment, arms, munitions and assistance to enable it to exercise its inherent right of self-defence and to maintain law and order;

(c) To refrain from interference in any form whatsoever, whether direct or indirect, in the internal affairs of other States;

(d) To terminate treaties and agreements that are incompatible with its sovereignty, independence, territorial integrity and inviolability, neutrality, and national unity;

(e) To refrain from the threat or use of force against the territorial integrity or political independence of any State, or in any other manner inconsistent with the purposes of the United Nations;

(f) To settle all disputes with other States by peaceful means;

(g) To refrain from using its territory or the territories of other States to impair the sovereignty, independence, and territorial integrity and inviolability of other States;

(h) To refrain from permitting the introduction or stationing of foreign forces, including military personnel, in any form whatsoever, in Cambodia, and to prevent the establishment or maintenance of foreign military bases, strong points or facilities in Cambodia, except pursuant to United Nations authorization for the implementation of the comprehensive political settlement.

Article 2

1. The other parties to this Agreement hereby solemnly undertake to recognize and to respect in every way the sovereignty, independence, territorial integrity and inviolability, neutrality and national unity of Cambodia.

2. To this end, they undertake:

(a) To refrain from entering into any military alliances or other military agreements with Cambodia that would be inconsistent with Cambodia's neutrality, without prejudice to Cambodia's right to acquire the necessary military equipment, arms, munitions and assistance to enable it to exercise its inherent right of self-defence and to maintain law and order;

(b) To refrain from interference in any form whatsoever, whether direct or indirect, in the internal affairs of Cambodia;

(c) To refrain from the threat or use of force against the territorial integrity or political independence of Cambodia, or in any other manner inconsistent with the purposes of the United Nations;

(d) To settle all disputes with Cambodia by peaceful means;

(e) To refrain from using their territories or the territories of other States to impair the sovereignty, independence, territorial integrity and inviolability, neutrality and national unity of Cambodia;

(f) To refrain from using the territory of Cambodia to impair the sovereignty, independence and territorial integrity and inviolability of other States;

(g) To refrain from the introduction or stationing of foreign forces, including military personnel, in any form whatsoever, in Cambodia and from establishing or maintaining military bases, strong points or facilities in Cambodia, except pursuant to United Nations authorization for the implementation of the comprehensive political settlement.

Article 3

1. All persons in Cambodia shall enjoy the rights and freedoms embodied in the Universal Declaratlon of Human Rights and other relevant international human rights instruments.

2. To this end,

(a) Cambodia undertakes:

- to ensure respect for and observance of human rights and fundamental freedoms in Cambodia;

- to support the right of all Cambodian citizens to undertake activities that would promote and protect human rights and fundamental freedoms;

- to take effective measures to ensure that the policies and practices of the past shall never be allowed to return;

- to adhere to relevant international human rights instruments;

(b) The other parties to this Agreement undertake to promote and encourage respect for and observance of human rights and fundamental freedoms in Cambodia as embodied in the relevant international instruments in order, in particular, to prevent the recurrence of human rights abuses.

3. The United Nations Commission on Human Rights should continue to monitor closely the human rights situation in Cambodia, including, if necessary, by the appointment of a Special Rapporteur who would report his findings annually to the Commission and to the General Assembly.

Article 4

The parties to this Agreement call upon all other States to recognize and respect in every way the sovereignty, independence, territorial integrity and inviolability, neutrality and national unity of Cambodia and to refrain from any action inconsistent with these principles or with other provisions of this Agreement.

Article 5

1. In the event of a violation or threat of violation of the sovereignty, independence, territorial integrity and inviolability, neutrality or national unity of Cambodia, or of any of the other commitments herein, the parties to this Agreement undertake to consult immediately with a view to adopting all appropriate steps to ensure respect for these commitments and resolving any such violations through peaceful means.

2. Such steps may include, *inter alia*, reference of the matter to the Security Council of the United Nations or recourse to the means for the peaceful settlement of disputes referred to in Article 33 of the Charter of the United Nations.

3. The parties to this Agreement may also call upon the assistance of the Co-Chairmen of the Paris Conference on Cambodia.

4. In the event of serious violations of human rights in Cambodia, they will call upon the competent organs of the United Nations to take such other steps as are appropriate for the prevention and suppression of such violations in accordance with the relevant international instruments.

Article 6

This Agreement shall enter into force upon signature.

Article 7

This Agreement shall remain open for accession by all States. The instruments of accession shall be deposited with the Governments of the French Republic and the Republic of Indonesia. For each State acceding to this Agreement, it shall enter into force on the date of deposit of its instrument of accession.

Article 8

The original of this Agreement, of which the Chinese, English, French, Khmer and Russian texts are equally authentic, shall be deposited with the Governments of the French Republic and the Republic of Indonesia, which shall transmit certified true copies to the Governments of the other States participating in the Paris Conference on Cambodia and to the Secretary-General of the United Nations.

IN WITNESS WHEREOF the undersigned plenipotentiaries, being duly authorized thereto, have signed this Agreement.

DONE at Paris this thirty-first day of October, one thousand nine hundred and ninety one.

IV. *Declaration on the rehabilitation and reconstruction of Cambodia*

1. The primary objective of the reconstruction of Cambodia should be the advancement of the Cambodian nation and people, without discrimination or prejudice, and with full respect for human rights and fundamental freedom for all. The achievement of this objective requires the full implementation of the comprehensive political settlement.

2. The main responsibility for deciding Cambodia's reconstruction needs and plans should rest with the Cambodian people and the government formed after free and fair elections. No attempt should be made to impose a development strategy on Cambodia from any outside source or deter potential donors from contributing to the reconstruction of Cambodia.

3. International, regional and bilateral assistance to Cambodia should be co-ordinated as much as possible, complement and supplement local resources and be made available impartially with full regard for Cambodia's sovereignty, priorities, institutional means and absorptive capacity.

4. In the context of the reconstruction effort, economic aid should benefit all areas of Cambodia, especially the more disadvantaged, and reach all levels of society.

5. The implementation of an international aid effort would have to be phased in over a period that realistically acknowledges both political and technical imperatives. It would also necessitate a significant degree of co-operation between the future Cambodian Government and bilateral, regional and international contributors.

6. An important role will be played in rehabilitation and reconstruction by the United Nations system. The launching of an international reconstruction plan and an appeal for contributions should take place at an appropriate time, so as to ensure its success.

7. No effective programme of national reconstruction can be initiated without detailed assessments of Cambodia's human, natural and other economic assets. It will be necessary for a census to be conducted, developmental priorities identified, and the availability of resources, internal and external, determined.

To this end there will be scope for sending to Cambodia fact-finding missions from the United Nations system, international financial institutions and other agencies, with the consent of the future Cambodian Government.

8. With the achievement of the comprehensive political settlement, it is now possible and desirable to initiate a process of rehabilitation, addressing immediate needs, and to lay the groundwork for the preparation of medium- and long-term reconstruction plans.

9. For this period of rehabilitation, the United Nations Secretary-General is requested to help co-ordinate the programme guided by a person appointed for this purpose.

10. In this rehabilitation phase, particular attention will need to be given to food security, health, housing, training, education, the transport network and the restoration of Cambodia's existing basic infrastructure and public utilities.

11. The implementation of a longer-term international development plan for reconstruction should await the formation of a government following the elections and the determination and adoption of its own policies and priorities.

12. This reconstruction phase should promote Cambodian entrepreneurship and make use of the private sector, among other sectors, to help advance self-sustaining economic growth. It would also benefit from regional approaches, involving, *inter alia*, institutions such as the Economic and Social Commission for Asia and the Pacific (ESCAP) and the Mekong Committee, and Governments within the region; and from participation by non-governmental organizations.

13. In order to harmonize and monitor the contributions that will be made by the international community to the reconstruction of Cambodia after the formation of a government following the elections, a consultative body, to be called the International Committee on the Reconstruction of Cambodia (ICORC), should be set up at an appropriate time and be open to potential donors and other relevant parties. The United Nations Secretary-General is requested to make special arrangements for the United Nations system to support ICORC in its work, notably in ensuring a smooth transition from the rehabilitation to reconstruction phases.

Document 20

Note by the Secretary-General concerning the adoption of the Paris Agreements by the Paris Conference on Cambodia

S/23179, 30 October 1991

1. On 23 October 1991, the Paris Conference on Cambodia adopted the following instruments:

(a) Final Act of the Paris Conference on Cambodia;

(b) Agreement on a Comprehensive Political Settlement of the Cambodia Conflict, with annexes on the mandate for the United Nations Transitional Authority in Cambodia, military matters, elections, repatriation of Cambodian refugees and displaced persons, and the principles for a new Cambodian constitution;

(c) Agreement Concerning the Sovereignty, Independence, Territorial Integrity and Inviolability, Neutrality and National Unity of Cambodia;

(d) Declaration on the Rehabilitation and Reconstruction of Cambodia.

2. By a letter dated 30 October 1991, the Permanent Representative of France to the United Nations and the Chargé d'Affaires a.i. of the Permanent Mission of Indonesia to the United Nations, on behalf of the Co-Presidents of the Paris Conference on Cambodia, requested circulation of these instruments (S/23177).

3. In accordance with the request addressed to me in paragraph 12 of the Final Act of the Paris Conference, I am hereby drawing the attention of the Security Council to this matter, in order to enable it to consider the comprehensive political settlement of the Cambodia conflict at the earliest opportunity.

Document 21

Security Council resolution on political settlement of the Cambodia situation

S/RES/718 (1991), 31 October 1991

The Security Council,

Recalling its resolutions 668 (1990) of 20 September 1990 and 717 (1991) of 16 October 1991,

Welcoming the meeting in Paris, from 21 to 23 October 1991, of the Paris Conference on Cambodia at the ministerial level, at which the agreements for a comprehensive political settlement of the Cambodia conflict were signed, 1/

Having considered the agreements for a comprehensive political settlement of the Cambodia conflict signed in Paris on 23 October 1991,

Noting that those agreements provide, *inter alia*, for the designation of a special representative of the Secretary-General and the establishment of a United Nations Transitional Authority in Cambodia,

Noting also that it is the intention of the Secretary-General to send a survey mission to Cambodia as soon as possible to prepare a plan for implementing the mandate envisaged in the agreements, for submission to the Security Council,

Underlining the necessity for the full cooperation of the Supreme National Council of Cambodia, and all Cambodians for their part, in the implementation of the agreements,

1. *Expresses its full support* for the agreements for a comprehensive political settlement of the Cambodia conflict, signed in Paris on 23 October 1991; 1/

2. *Authorizes* the Secretary-General to designate a special representative for Cambodia to act on his behalf;

3. *Welcomes* the intention of the Secretary-General to send a survey mission to Cambodia as soon as possible to prepare a plan for implementing the mandate envisaged in the agreements;

4. *Requests* the Secretary-General to submit to the Security Council at the earliest possible date a report containing his implementation plan, including in particular a detailed estimate of the cost of the United Nations Transitional Authority in Cambodia, on the understanding that this report would be the basis on which the Council would authorize the establishment of the Authority, the budget of which is to be subsequently considered and approved in accordance with the provisions of Article 17 of the Charter of the United Nations;

1/ S/23177 [Document 19]

5. *Calls upon* all Cambodian parties to comply fully with the cease-fire that entered into force at the time of the signature of the agreements;

6. *Calls upon* the Supreme National Council of Cambodia, and all Cambodians for their part, to cooperate fully with the United Nations in the implementation of the agreements on a comprehensive political settlement of the Cambodia conflict.

Document 22

Report of the Secretary-General on UNAMIC

S/23218, 14 November 1991

1. On 16 October 1991, the Security Council adopted resolution 717 (1991), the operative paragraphs of which read as follows:

"1. *Approves* the report of the Secretary-General;

"2. *Decides* to establish, under its authority, a United Nations Advance Mission in Cambodia immediately after the signing of the agreements for a comprehensive political settlement and in accordance with the report of the Secretary-General, with members of the mission to be sent to Cambodia immediately after the signing;

"3. *Calls upon* the Supreme National Council of Cambodia, and the Cambodian parties for their part, to cooperate fully with the United Nations Advance Mission in Cambodia and with the preparations for the implementation of the arrangements set out in the agreements for a comprehensive political settlement;

"4. *Welcomes* the proposal of the Co-Chairmen of the Paris Conference on Cambodia to reconvene the Conference at an early date at ministerial level to sign the agreements for a comprehensive political settlement of the Cambodia conflict;

"5. *Requests* the Secretary-General to report to the Security Council by 15 November 1991 on the implementation of the present resolution, and to keep the Council fully informed of further developments."

2. The Agreements on a Comprehensive Political Settlement of the Cambodia Conflict referred to in paragraph 2 of the above-mentioned resolution were signed in Paris on 23 October at the final meeting of the Paris Conference on Cambodia. The arrangements for the establishment of the United Nations Advance Mission in Cambodia (UNAMIC) have accordingly entered into force.

3. In accordance with the plan described in my report of 30 September 1991 (S/23097 and Add.1), I have appointed Mr. A. H. S. Ataul Karim (Bangladesh) as Chief Liaison Officer of UNAMIC. With the consent of the Council (see S/23206), Brigadier General Michel Loridon (France) has been designated Senior Military Liaison Officer.

4. On 9 November, Mr. Karim, accompanied by three military liaison officers, assumed his functions in Phnom Penh, where a number of civilian support staff members had already arrived. On 12 November, Brigadier General Loridon assumed the command of the military elements of UNAMIC. On the same day, the air operations unit contributed by France also arrived in Phnom Penh, joining the military communications unit contributed by Australia, which had arrived on 10 November.

5. I am pleased to report that UNAMIC is now operational. Deployment of the remaining civilian and military personnel will now proceed rapidly and is expected to be completed on schedule by mid-December 1991.

Document 23

General Assembly resolution on the situation in Cambodia

A/RES/46/18, 20 November 1991

The General Assembly,

Having considered the item entitled "The situation in Cambodia",

Recalling its resolution 45/3 of 15 October 1990 and Security Council resolutions 668 (1990) of 20 September 1990, 717 (1991) of 16 October 1991 and 718 (1991) of 31 October 1991,

Recalling also the support and assistance of the

international community, the participants in the Paris Conference on Cambodia and all interested States and parties, especially the humanitarian aid rendered to the Cambodian people since 1978,

Welcoming the agreements on a comprehensive political settlement of the Cambodia conflict, signed at the Paris Conference on Cambodia on 23 October 1991, 1/

Taking note of the report of the Secretary-General, 2/

Noting with appreciation the continuing efforts of the Secretary-General and his staff towards the implementation of the agreements on a comprehensive political settlement of the Cambodia conflict,

1. *Expresses its full support* for the agreements on a comprehensive political settlement of the Cambodia conflict, hereinafter referred to as the "Paris Agreements", which, *inter alia*, would maintain, preserve and guarantee the sovereignty, independence, territorial integrity and inviolability, neutrality and national unity of Cambodia;

2. *Supports* the efforts of the Secretary-General to set up an effective United Nations Transitional Authority in Cambodia as soon as possible, with the aim of restoring peace and stability in Cambodia and to implement the Paris Agreements;

3. *Welcomes* the fact that commitment to self-determination for the Cambodian people through free and fair elections organized and conducted by the United Nations and full respect for human rights have been incorporated in the provisions of the settlement;

4. *Calls upon* all parties concerned to ensure respect for and full observance of the human rights and fundamental freedoms of the Cambodian people and to assist them to exercise their right to self-determination through free and fair elections, as provided for in the Paris Agreements;

5. *Also calls upon* all parties concerned to comply fully with the cease-fire that entered into force at the time of the signature of the Paris Agreements;

6. *Urges* all parties concerned to implement fully the terms of the Paris Agreements, in close cooperation with the United Nations Transitional Authority in Cambodia;

7. *Expresses its deep appreciation* to the international community, the Co-Presidents of the Paris Conference on Cambodia, the permanent members of the Security Council, States in the region, other States and the Cambodian parties themselves, in particular His Royal Highness Samdech Norodom Sihanouk, for their invaluable contributions over the past decade to restore and maintain peace and unity in Cambodia and to promote national reconciliation;

8. *Expresses its deep appreciation also* to donor countries, the United Nations agencies and other national and international humanitarian organizations that have rendered assistance to the Cambodian people and urges them to continue their support for the process of repatriation of the Cambodian refugees and displaced persons under the leadership and coordination of the United Nations High Commissioner for Refugees, and for the rehabilitation and reconstruction of Cambodia;

9. *Reiterates its deep appreciation* to the Secretary-General and his staff for their continuing efforts in helping to implement the Paris Agreements;

10. *Reiterates also its deep appreciation* to the Secretary-General for his efforts in coordinating humanitarian relief assistance and in monitoring its distribution, and requests him to continue such efforts as necessary.

1/ A/46/608-S/23177 [Document 19]
2/ A/46/617

Document 24

Letter dated 28 December 1991 from France transmitting statement on Cambodia by the five permanent members of the Security Council, issued in New York, 28 December 1991

A/47/63-S/23335, 28 December 1991

I have the honour to transmit to you the text of a statement on Cambodia by the five Permanent Members of the Security Council, issued at New York on Saturday, 28 December 1991 (see annex).

On behalf of my colleagues, the other Permanent Members, I should be grateful if you would have this text ciculated as a document of the forty-seventh session of the General Assembly, under the item entitled "The situation in Cambodia", and of the Security Council.

(signed) Jean-Bernard MÉRIMÉE

Annex
Statement of the Five on Cambodia,
issued on 28 December 1991

The Five permanent members of the Security Council highly appreciate the efforts being made by His Royal Highness Samdech Preah Norodom Sihanouk, Head of State and President of the Supreme National Council of Cambodia, to assure progress towards peace in Cambodia. In particular, they took note with satisfaction that the SNC Secretariat has become operational under the personal leadership of H.R.H. Samdech Preah Norodom Sihanouk and that the Mixed Military Working Group has begun to take shape.

The Five welcome and support the statement made by H.R.H. Samdech Preah Norodom Sihanouk concerning the convening of an SNC meeting before the end of the current year, as well as his declaration, dated 27 December 1991, on measures to be taken in order to consolidate and expedite the peace process in Cambodia.

They appeal to all Cambodian parties to contribute to the development of the process of national reconciliation and the maintenance of peace, by strictly respecting all agreements, including those related to assuring all necessary conditions for the normal functioning of the SNC in Phnom Penh.

Document 25

Report of the Secretary-General on the expansion of UNAMIC's mandate

S/23331, 30 December 1991
(including addendum, S/23331/Add.1, 6 January 1992)

1. In resolution 717 (1991) adopted on 16 October 1991, the Security Council decided to establish, under its authority, a United Nations Advance Mission in Cambodia (UNAMIC). It further decided that UNAMIC should be deployed immediately after the signing of the Agreements on a Comprehensive Political Settlement of the Cambodia conflict, in accordance with the recommendations contained in my report S/23097 of 30 September 1991.

2. The Agreements on a Comprehensive Political Settlement of the Cambodia Conflict were signed in Paris on 23 October 1991. In resolution 718 (1991) adopted on 31 October, the Security Council noted that the Agreements provided for the establishment of a United Nations Transitional Authority in Cambodia (UNTAC). It expressed its full support for the Agreements and requested the Secretary-General to submit, at the earliest possible date, a report containing his plan for implementing the mandate envisaged in the Agreements, on the understanding that this report would be the basis on which the Council would authorize the establishment of UNTAC.

3. On 14 November 1991, I reported to the Council (S/23218) that UNAMIC had begun to discharge its functions and that its deployment was expected to be completed by mid-December. The mandate of UNAMIC provides, inter alia, for the establishment of a mine-awareness programme which is to be implemented by small teams of military personnel with experience in training civilian populations on how to avoid injuries from mines or booby-traps. Initially, the teams are to give priority to populations living in or close to areas of recent military confrontation. In due course, this initial programme is to be expanded into those foreseen in the Paris Agreements, giving priority, in consultation with the United Nations High Commissioner for Refugees (UNHCR), to repatriation routes, reception centres and resettlement areas.

4. In this connection, annex 1, section C, paragraph 1 (e), of the Paris Agreements provides that UNTAC would undertake, among other measures, "assisting with clearing mines and undertaking training programmes in mine clearance and a mine-awareness programme among the Cambodia people". 1/

5. Annex 2, article IX, of the same Agreements provides that:

"1. Soon after arrival in Cambodia, the military component of UNTAC shall ensure, as a first step, that all known minefields are clearly marked.

"2. The Parties agree that, after completion of the regroupment and cantonment processes in accordance with Article III of the present annex, they will make available mine-clearing teams which, under the supervision and control of UNTAC military personnel, will leave the cantonment areas in order to assist in removing, disarming or deactivating remaining unexploded ordnance devices. Those mines or objects which cannot be removed, disarmed

1/ A/46/608 [Document 19]

or deactivated will be clearly marked in accordance with a system to be devised by the military component of UNTAC.

"3. UNTAC shall:

"(a) Conduct a mass public education programme in the recognition and avoidance of explosive devices;

"(b) Train Cambodian volunteers to dispose of unexploded ordnance devices;

"(c) Provide emergency first-aid training to Cambodian volunteers." 2/

6. Since the adoption of the Paris Agreements and the entry into force of a formal cease-fire, there has been a growing sense in the international community of the need to undertake, on an urgent basis, a major de-mining effort in Cambodia. It has been suggested that such an effort should begin even before the establishment of UNTAC, so as to take advantage of the present dry season and to prepare the ground for the safe and orderly repatriation of Cambodian refugees and displaced persons under United Nations auspices.

7. I have accordingly decided to recommend to the Security Council that the mandate of UNAMIC be expanded to include training in mine clearance and the initiation of a de-mining programme. These activities would be undertaken on the following basis: the existing UNAMIC mine-awareness programme would immediately be developed to include training of Cambodian personnel in mine detection and mine clearance; for this purpose the strength of the existing unit would be increased with additional expert personnel contributed by Member States. Concurrently, a de-mining programme would be initiated by a specialized military unit provided by a Member State on an urgent basis, with a view to taking maximum advantage of the present dry season. This programme would be concentrated in the northwestern part of Cambodia and would give priority, in consultation with UNHCR, to repatriation routes, reception centres and areas where refugees and displaced persons will be resettled. The programme would also incude an engineering (construction) component, to repair the roads which have been cleared of mines and to ensure that the roads and bridges to be used by returnees are safe and able to sustain the expected increase in the volume of traffic.

8. As members of the Security Council are aware, I recently despatched a military survey mission to Cambodia in order to prepare a plan for implementing the mandate envisaged for the military component of UNTAC in the Paris Agreements. The mission, which was led by my Military Adviser, Major-General Timothy K. Dibuama, has advised me, in the light of the information provided by the Cambodian parties and of its discussions with a UNHCR mission which was currently in Cambodia to identify possible resettlement areas, that, in order to undertake the mine training and de-mining tasks described above, UNAMIC would need:

(a) A planning and liaison unit at its headquarters in Phnom Penh. This unit would liaise with the National Mine Clearance Commission recently established by the Supreme National Council of Cambodia, as well as with UNHCR, other international organizations, Governments and non-governmental organizations concerned, in order to gather all available information on land mines in Cambodia and facilitate the marking of all known minefields as a matter of urgency. The proposed unit would develop a training programme for Cambodians in the fields of mine-detection and mine-clearance. It would also elaborate plans for de-mining activities, determine the priorities for their execution and allocate the work to be undertaken by de-mining units;

(b) A field engineer battalion to initiate the mine-clearing of repatriation routes, reception centres and resettlement areas, and to carry out emergency repair and rehabilitation work of roads and bridges which had been cleared of mines. First priority would be given to those roads that are to be used by the first group of returnees;

(c) Expert training teams to train Cambodian military personnel, who would be made available by the four Cambodian parties, to participate under supervision of UNAMIC in the mine-clearing of repatriation routes, reception centres and resettlement areas;

(d) Logistic support personnel to meet the second line transport and fuel requirements of the engineer unit and the mine-clearing training teams and to provide the necessary communications support.

9. It is estimated that approximately 40 military personnel would be required for the planning and liaison unit at UNAMIC headquarters. The engineer unit would need a total strength of about 700. The expert training and supervisory teams would require about 200 all ranks. About 150 logistic support personnel would be required. These military personnel, totalling approximately 1,000, would be provided by Member States. The engineer unit would need to be an integrated unit with all the equipment required for its activities. It has to be emphasized, however, that, in Cambodia's present devastated condition, the movement of the engineer unit and its heavier equipment to its place of operation in Cambodia would give rise to formidable difficulties. It would also be necessary for the unit concerned to enjoy a very high level of self-sufficiency in supply, shelter, transport and communications.

10. I shall submit as soon as possible, as an addendum to the present report, a statement of the financial and administrative implications of the proposed expan-

2/ A/46/608 [Document 19]

sion of UNAMIC's mandate. Meanwhile, it is my duty to inform the Security Council that, in view of the present financial situation of the Organization, it will not be possible to undertake the activities proposed in this report until the necessary cash resources become available.

11. It is generally recognized that a major de-mining effort is needed in Cambodia. While the total eradication of mines will necessarily be a long-term endeavour, the initial programme recommended in this report should be undertaken on an urgent basis, in order to make an early start to tackle this problem before the beginning of the rainy season in May. This would enable UNAMIC to reduce the threat posed by mines to the civilian population and to begin to prepare the ground for a safe and orderly repatriation of the refugees and displaced persons under United Nations auspices. It would also facilitate the timely deployment of UNTAC and the discharge of its responsibilities throughout Cambodia.

Addendum (S/23331/Add.1)

1. In paragraph 10 of my report to the Security Council (S/23331), I indicated that I would submit an addendum setting out the financial and administrative implications of the proposed expansion of UNAMIC's mandate to include training in mine clearance and the initiation of a demining programme.

2. As stated in paragraphs 8 and 9 of the report, in order to carry out these added responsibilities, UNAMIC would need an additional 1,090 military personnel for: a planning and liaison unit (40), a field engineering battalion (700), expert training and supervisory teams (200) and logistics support personnel (150). In addition, 34 civilian staff would be required to provide additional administrative, transport, communication, procurement, security and interpretation support to UNAMIC. There would also be additional requirements for premises/accommodation, transport, communication and miscellaneous equipment, and miscellaneous supplies and services.

3. Should the Security Council decide to expand the mandate of UNAMIC on the basis of my recommendation as set out in the main part of the present report, it is estimated that the cost of the expansion through the end of UNAMIC's present mandate on 30 April 1992 would be approximately $24.7 million. This takes into account a phased deployment of the military and civilian personnel beginning mid-January 1992. A breakdown of the estimated cost by main objects of expenditure is provided for information purposes in the annex to this addendum.

4. It would be my recommendation to the General Assembly, should the Security Council decide to expand UNAMIC's mandate, that the additional cost relating thereto should be considered an expense to the Organization to be borne by Member States in accordance with Article 17, paragraph 2, of the Charter of the United Nations and that the assessments to be levied on Member States be credited to the UNAMIC Special Account.

Annex

Cost estimates by objects of expenditure

Objects of expenditure	Total (In thousands of US dollars)
1. Military component	
(a) Planning and liaison unit and expert training and supervisory teams	3 663.8
(b) Field engineer and logistic support personnel	4 702.2
(c) Contingent-owned equipment	437.5
(d) Death and disability	400.0
2. Civilian personnel, including travel to mission area	1 049.9
3. Construction and maintenance of premises, including utilities	2 573.5
4. Vehicle operations	2 401.6
5. Aircraft operation, including rental and fuel	3 671.0
6. Communications	2 127.5
7. Miscellaneous equipment	2 202.1
8. Miscellaneous supplies, services, freight and support costs	1 499.2
Total estimates (gross)	24 728.3

Document 26

Security Council resolution on UNAMIC

S/RES/728 (1992), 8 January 1992

The Security Council,

Recalling its resolutions 668 (1990) of 20 September 1990, 717 (1991) of 16 October 1991 and 718 (1991) of 31 October 1991,

Welcoming the fact that the United Nations Advance Mission in Cambodia has become operational as reported by the Secretary-General in his report of 14 November 1991, 1/

Welcoming also the progress that has been made in implementing the provisions of the agreements on a comprehensive political settlement of the Cambodia conflict signed in Paris on 23 October 1991 2/ relating to the functioning of the Supreme National Council of Cambodia under the chairmanship of His Royal Highness Prince Norodom Sihanouk and the maintenance of the cease-fire,

Concerned that the existence of mines and minefields in Cambodia poses a serious hazard to the safety of people in Cambodia, as well as an obstacle to the smooth and timely implementation of the agreements, including the early return of Cambodian refugees and displaced persons,

Noting that the Mission's mandate as approved by the Security Council in its resolution 717 (1991) provides, *inter alia*, for the establishment of a mine-awareness programme, and that the agreements provide for the United Nations Transitional Authority in Cambodia to undertake, *inter alia*, a programme of assisting with clearing mines and undertaking training programmes in mine clearance and a mine-awareness programme among the Cambodian people,

Considering that the establishment of training programmes in mine clearance, in addition to the existing mine-awareness programme undertaken by the Mission, and the early initiation of mine clearance are required for the effective implementation of the agreements,

Having considered the report of the Secretary-General proposing that the mandate of the Mission be expanded to include training in mine clearance and the initiation of a mine-clearance programme,

1. *Approves* the report of the Secretary-General on Cambodia of 30 December 1991 and 6 January 1992, 3/ especially the provision of assistance in mine clearing by Cambodians;

2. *Calls upon* the Supreme National Council of Cambodia, and all the Cambodian parties, to continue to cooperate fully with the United Nations Advance Mission in Cambodia, including in the discharge of its expanded mandate;

3. *Reiterates its call* to all the Cambodian parties to comply scrupulously with the cease-fire and to lend all necessary assistance to the Mission;

4. *Requests* the Secretary-General to keep the Security Council informed of further developments.

1/ S/23218 [Document 22]
2/ S/23177 [Document 19]
3/ S/23331 and Add.1 [Document 25]

Document 27

Letter dated 18 January 1992 from the Secretary-General to the President of the Security Council referring to Security Council resolution 718 (1991) concerning the financing of the United Nations Transitional Authority in Cambodia (UNTAC)

S/23458, 24 January 1992

I have the honour to refer to Security Council resolution 718 (1991) of 31 October 1991. In it the Council, *inter alia,* expressed its full support for the Agreements on a Comprehensive Political Settlement of the Cambodia Conflict and requested the Secretary-General to submit

at the earliest possible date a report containing his implementation plan, including in particular a detailed estimate of the cost of the United Nations Transitional Authority in Cambodia (UNTAC), on the understanding that this report would be the basis on which the Council would authorize the establishment of UNTAC, the budget of UNTAC to be subsequently considered and approved in accordance with the provisions of Article 17 of the Charter of the United Nations.

In accordance with resolution 718 (1991), survey missions have been sent to Cambodia to collect the information required for the formulation of the plan of implementation of UNTAC's mandate. On the basis of this information, the report requested by the Security Council in resolution 718 (1991) is under preparation and it will be presented to the Council as soon as possible.

The President of the Supreme National Council, H.R.H. Prince Norodom Sihanouk, the Cambodian parties and the international community have repeatedly stressed the need for the urgent establishment and deployment of UNTAC, in order to prevent any erosion of the peace process. I fully share these concerns.

Members of the Security Council are aware that the United Nations procedures relating to the establishment of new operations and the steps that must be taken before funds are committed and allotted to such operations represent a time-consuming process. Experience has shown that the launching of an effective operation requires funds to be committed several months prior to its planned deployment date to enable such preliminary actions as contracting for services, equipment procurement and delivery, establishment of advance parties and commissioning and installation of equipment and stores. In the case of UNTAC, the anticipated size and scope of the operation, the degraded state of Cambodia's infrastructure and climatic conditions would compound the problem of adequate lead time, which, unless it is resolved, could create serious logistic problems and cause delay in deployment.

While the full and precise cost of deploying UNTAC has not yet been determined, there is no question that the current level of commitment authority available to the Secretary-General—either with the concurrence of the Advisory Committee on Administrative and Budgetary Questions or on his own—prior to the finalization of the budget would fall far short of the amount that would be required to initiate preparations for a timely deployment of UNTAC once the Security Council has authorized its establishment.

In order to enable me to prepare for the first phase of UNTAC's deployment, I have decided to submit to the General Assembly a proposal for the provision of an initial appropriation of US$ 200 million, which, upon the approval by the Security Council of my report on the implementation plan, should be made available immediately for the procurement of accommodation, transportation, communication and other support equipment and services. This amount would represent an assessment of initial requirements and would be taken into account against the full assessments to be levied against Member States once the budget of UNTAC has been approved by the General Assembly.

I am convinced that this approach will facilitate the timely deployment of UNTAC, thus enhancing the prospects for the restoration of a durable peace in Cambodia.

I should be grateful if you would bring this matter to the attention of the members of the Security Council.

(*signed*) Boutros BOUTROS-GHALI

Document 28

Letter dated 20 January 1992 from the Secretary-General to Prince Norodom Sihanouk of Cambodia concerning the deployment of UNTAC and the broadening of the mandate of UNAMIC

Not issued as a United Nations document; original in French

Having taken note of the press release issued by the Supreme National Council of Cambodia (SNC) following its meeting on 11 January, I wish to thank you for the favourable reception by SNC of my decision to appoint Mr. Yasushi Akashi as my Special Representative for Cambodia. In this capacity, Mr. Akashi will be responsible for establishing and leading the United Nations Transitional Authority in Cambodia (UNTAC).

I share with you and SNC the desire that UNTAC take up its position in Cambodia as soon as possible and assume fully the responsibilities conferred upon it under the Paris Agreements. A plan for implementation of the UNTAC mandate is currently being prepared, bearing in mind the recommendations made by the survey missions which have recently visited Cambodia. The plan will be submitted as soon as possible to the Security Council, which will then authorize the creation of UNTAC. The budget for the operation will then be considered and approved by the General Assembly, in accordance with the provisions of Article 17 of the Charter of the United Nations.

Meanwhile, the efforts undertaken by my predecessor to strengthen the United Nations presence in the field will be actively pursued. The broadening of the mandate of the United Nations Advance Mission in Cambodia (UNAMIC), as confirmed under Security Council resolution 728 (1992), is a part of this process. This resolution, adopted on 8 January, provides for the deployment of some one thousand military experts to initiate a mine-clearance programme and to train Cambodians in that skill. Deployment of the experts should begin shortly.

It is also planned to establish a preparatory unit for the gathering of the technical information required for the planning of elections. The first officers of this unit, which will report to UNAMIC, should also begin to arrive at Phnom Penh in the course of next month. A team of legal officers has also been given the task of drawing up a draft electoral law and a code of conduct, which will be the subject of consultations with SNC in accordance with the provisions of the Paris Agreements, which confer upon the United Nations responsibility for organizing and conducting the elections.

Furthermore, I have just informed the Security Council of my intention to request that the General Assembly approve an appropriation of 200 million United States dollars in order to purchase the equipment and logistical supplies required for implementation of the first phase of UNTAC's deployment.

I shall continue to do everything in my power to accelerate, as far as possible, the deployment of UNTAC as soon as the Security Council and the General Assembly have taken the necessary decisions.

The mission of UNTAC in Cambodia can, however, only be fulfilled if SNC fully performs the functions entrusted to it under the Paris Agreements. Since your historic return to Phnom Penh on 14 November 1991, the international community has been following with admiration the remarkable efforts you have made to ensure that SNC can begin operating and to endow it with the necessary structures. Despite the difficulties which have arisen in this connection, I am sure it is essential that these efforts, under your wise guidance, be continued. Indeed, the President of the Supreme National Council stands at the very heart of the institutional framework foreseen in the Paris Agreements. He has a crucial role to play in the decision-making process within SNC, in the Council's relations with UNTAC and in the promotion of a genuine national reconciliation, without which peace in Cambodia could well prove ephemeral.

I wish to assure you that you can rely on my support and cooperation. I have asked Mr. Akashi to discuss with you what measures might be taken before UNTAC is deployed to support your efforts and to facilitate your task.

Accept, Sir, the assurances of my highest consideration.

(*signed*) Boutros BOUTROS-GHALI

Document 29

Letter dated 23 January 1992 from Prince Norodom Sihanouk to the Secretary-General concerning implementation of the Paris Peace Agreements

Not issued as a United Nations document; original in French

His Excellency Mr. Yasushi Akashi, your Special Representative, yesterday afternoon kindly conveyed to me your noble and very important letter of 20 January 1992. I am extremely grateful to you.

On behalf of the Cambodian people, of its Supreme National Council (SNC) and of myself, I express my deepest and most admiring gratitude to you for the many significant measures you have taken and will take to ensure that more progress is made each month in resolving the difficult problems which we have had or shall have to confront in the process of implementing in full the Paris Peace Agreements dated 23 October 1991.

In Cambodia, UNAMIC and its Head of Mission, H.E. Mr. Ataul Karim, continue to make enormous efforts, with excellent results. The same goes for the remarkable work done by the senior representatives of the five permanent members of the Security Council and of Indonesia, the International Committee of the Red Cross (ICRC) and other international bodies.

There is no doubt that Mr. Yasushi Akashi will, on your behalf, make an invaluable and historic contribution to saving the Cambodian people and nation.

The SNC and myself fully support your Special Representative and will cooperate faithfully and whole-heartedly with him.

Accept, Sir, the assurances of my highest consideration.

(*signed*) NORODOM SIHANOUK

Document 30

Report of the Secretary-General on Cambodia containing his proposed implementation plan for UNTAC, including administrative and financial aspects

S/23613, 19 February 1992
(including addendum, S/23613/Add.1, 26 February 1992)

1. By its resolution 718 (1991) of 31 October 1991, the Security Council, inter alia, expressed full support for the Agreement on a comprehensive political settlement of the Cambodia conflict, signed in Paris on 23 October 1991, 1/ (hereinafter referred to as the Agreement), and requested the Secretary-General to submit at the earliest possible date a report containing his implementation plan, including in particular a detailed estimate of the cost of the United Nations Transitional Authority in Cambodia (UNTAC), whose establishment was provided for in the Agreement. The Security Council made that request on the understanding that the present report would be the basis upon which the Council would authorize the establishment of UNTAC, the budget of UNTAC to be subsequently considered and approved in accordance with the provisions of Article 17 of the Charter of the United Nations. The Security Council also authorized the Secretary-General to designate a special representative for Cambodia.

2. The present report, which contains the Secretary-General's proposed implementation plan, is submitted pursuant to Security Council resolution 718 (1991). An addendum to the report, covering indicative administrative and financial aspects of the proposed plan will be issued as soon as possible.

3. In formulating these proposals, the Secretary-General has been guided by information gathered by a number of survey missions sent to Cambodia, the most recent three, which visited Cambodia in October to December 1991, being the following: one on elections, one on military arrangements and one on civil administration, police and human rights. It should be noted however that, in spite of the efforts made by these missions, the information obtained cannot be regarded as complete and current assessments regarding priorities and deployment may prove to be inaccurate, as circumstances in Cambodia change. The specific recommendations contained in the present report may therefore need to be re-examined in the light of experience, once UNTAC is in place.

I. Introduction

4. The Agreement invites the Security Council to establish UNTAC with civilian and military components under the direct responsibility of the Secretary-General of the United Nations, and to provide it with a mandate in conformity with the Agreement. The general framework of UNTAC's mandate is provided in Annex 1 to the Agreement, with specific elements provided in other annexes. Elements are also contained in the Declaration on the Rehabilitation and Reconstruction of Cambodia, adopted by the Paris Conference on Cambodia on 23 October 1991 as part of the comprehensive political settlement of the Cambodia conflict. 2/

5. The mandate foreseen for UNTAC under the Agreement includes aspects relating to human rights, the organization and conduct of free and fair general elections, military arrangements, civil administration, the maintenance of law and order, the repatriation and resettlement of the Cambodian refugees and displaced persons, and the rehabilitation of essential Cambodian infrastructures during the transitional period. The transitional period is defined in article 1 of the Agreement as the period commencing with the entry into force of the Agreement and terminating when the constituent assembly elected in conformity with the Agreement has approved the new Cambodian Constitution and transformed itself into a legislative assembly, and thereafter a new Cambodian Government has been created. The Agreement entered into force upon signature, on 23 October 1991.

6. The focal point of the United Nations relationship in Cambodia is the Supreme National Council, which, under the Agreement, is the "unique legitimate body and source of authority in which, throughout the transitional period, the sovereignty, independence and unity of Cambodia are enshrined". By virtue of article 6 of the Agreement, the Supreme National Council of Cambodia has delegated to the United Nations "all powers necessary" to ensure the implementation of the Agreement. The Special Representative of the Secretary-General would be the head of UNTAC and would maintain an ongoing dialogue with the Supreme National Council regarding UNTAC's activities in implementing its mandate.

7. UNTAC would consist of seven distinct com-

1/ S/23177 [Document 19]
2/ S/23177 [Document 19]

ponents, as follows: the human rights component, the electoral component, the military component, the civil administration component, the police component, the repatriation component and the rehabilitation component. The level of the activities of the different components of UNTAC will vary during the course of the transitional period and will be coordinated, as necessary, in order to allow for the most efficient and cost-effective use of resources.

II. The components

A. *Human rights component*

1. *Functions*

8. Article 15 of the Agreement provides the framework within which activities to promote and protect human rights in Cambodia will be undertaken. In particular, the article states that Cambodian authorities must ensure respect for and observance of human rights and fundamental freedoms, including support of the right of all citizens to undertake human rights activities, effective measures to ensure no return to the policies and practices of the past and adherence to the relevant international human rights instruments.

9. The Cambodians themselves thus clearly have the obligation to promote and protect human rights and fundamental freedoms in Cambodia. Others have the responsibility to encourage their respect and observance in order to prevent the recurrence of human rights abuses. In this connection, under article 16 of the Agreement, UNTAC is given responsibility during the transitional period for fostering an environment in which respect for human rights is ensured.

10. One measure that would foster such an environment would be the ratification or accession by the Supreme National Council of the relevant human rights instruments on behalf of Cambodia. This would provide a framework in Cambodian law within which Cambodians could undertake activities for the protection and promotion of their rights and freedoms. It would also greatly facilitate UNTAC's efforts to enhance respect for the rule of law.

11. Other measures for fostering the proper environment are stipulated in section E of annex 1 to the Agreement. These include making provisions for the development and implementation of a human rights education programme to promote respect for and understanding of human rights, the exercise of general human rights oversight and the investigation of complaints and allegations of human rights abuses and, where appropriate, corrective action.

12. The development and dissemination of a human rights education programme is foreseen as the cornerstone of UNTAC's activities in fostering respect for human rights and fundamental freedoms, for Cambodians must fully understand both the content and the significance of those rights and freedoms in order to be in a position to know when and how to protect them properly. This is especially important in an environment in which the framing of a new Cambodian Constitution containing human rights guarantees will be on the national agenda.

13. Such a civic education programme would be developed in a manner that is culturally sensitive and generally "accessible" to Cambodians. Its dissemination would rely upon all channels of communication available in the country, including printed materials (words and pictures), cultural events and presentations, radio and television media, videocassette distribution, mobile teaching units, etc. It is foreseen that UNTAC would also work closely with existing educational administrative structures in Cambodia to ensure that human rights education is appropriately included in the curriculum at all levels, including children, adults and special groups. The latter would include those individuals best placed to be further disseminators of information, such as teachers and community leaders. UNTAC would also expect to collaborate with non-governmental organizations (NGOs) operating in Cambodia for this purpose as well as to encourage the establishment of indigenous human rights associations.

14. It is foreseen that the civic education programme content would vary, stressing different "clusters" of rights at different times, and that it would be responsive to current events. However, particular themes will be emphasized throughout, notably relating to the exercise of rights in an electoral environment, the existence of mechanisms for remedial action, rights related to protection of the person and other rights enshrined in the Universal Declaration of Human Rights. Complementary training and monitoring initiatives would be supported.

15. Coordination of the human rights programme content with other civic education programmes being disseminated, especially in relation to the elections and to repatriation, would be a priority. To the extent possible, programme production would take place inside Cambodia. This would allow optimum responsiveness to the actual situation, including evaluation of programme impact and immediate adjustment, as necessary. In this way, the efficiency and effectiveness of programmes can be maximized.

16. The second element of UNTAC's activities for fostering an environment in which human rights and fundamental freedoms would be respected is the exercise of general human rights oversight in all of the existing administrative structures in Cambodia. In this connec-

tion, special guidelines and materials targeted to civil servants would be produced to promote education and human rights awareness among them. Some training in the application of these materials could also be foreseen within the context of training and orientation courses contemplated under the civil administration mandate.

17. Certain of the existing structures are more susceptible to human rights concerns than others. This category would include, but is not limited to, those agencies, bodies and offices exercising law-enforcement and judicial functions. Special attention would be focused on these groups, for which the Agreement foresees control or supervision in any case. Codes of conduct pertaining to law enforcement officials and the judiciary would be developed, adapted and applied, and supported with supplementary training, especially in the area of fundamental criminal procedure. A higher ratio of UNTAC staff to local administrative personnel in these areas is already foreseen elsewhere in the present plan. Parallel training for UNTAC personnel operating in these areas is also recommended in order to facilitate their effective functioning.

18. The third element of UNTAC's human rights mandate is the provision of a mechanism for the investigation of allegations of human rights abuses occurring during the transitional period in Cambodia. In this respect, UNTAC would undertake investigations of its own accord in instances where the Special Representative has reason to believe that such abuses have occurred or may be imminent.

19. When investigation is called for, UNTAC would rely upon the investigation mechanism established in conformity with section B, paragraph 6, of annex 1 to the Agreement. The implementation of that mechanism would be monitored by UNTAC human rights liaison officers, who would accompany investigators, as appropriate. Special attention would be paid to the "susceptible" areas, where effective measures must be devised. UNTAC would naturally retain the right to order or to take corrective action, as appropriate. In this connection, UNTAC may choose to associate the Supreme National Council with its proceedings, if necessary, in order to promote effective redress. UNTAC may also wish to associate indigenous human rights monitoring groups with its proceedings, with the agreement of the parties concerned.

20. Special provisions would be made by UNTAC, within the ambit of its mandate to organize and conduct elections, to ensure the immediate redress of violations relating to participation in the electoral process.

2. Structure

21. A human rights office established at headquarters will be the central policy-making and coordinating body in this area. The staff of that office would include specialists in human rights advocacy, civic education and investigation, as well as an officer in charge of liaison with human rights NGOs. The number of human rights officers required may be modest, since all UNTAC staff, operating in all areas of the mandate, would be charged with carrying out human rights functions, as an integral part of their primary duties. In this respect, special human rights materials and training are envisaged for all UNTAC staff. In addition, periodic human rights reports would be submitted to the central human rights office, in order to enable the latter to maintain an overall perspective of the situation in the country.

22. No staff devoted exclusively to human rights is foreseen at the provincial or lower levels, although headquarters staff could be called upon to undertake field visits as warranted. Rather, the substantive officers at the provincial level and below, operating in the areas of civil administration, information and monitoring of the local police, would be specifically called upon to carry out human rights functions on a primary basis as well.

B. Electoral component

1. Functions

23. Under article 13 of the Agreement, UNTAC is entrusted with the task of organizing and conducting free and fair general elections in Cambodia. The objective of UNTAC's work would be to facilitate the broadest possible participation of Cambodians in the election of their representatives. Of the estimated 8.7 million Cambodians, approximately half will be eligible to vote in accordance with the criteria established in paragraph 4 of annex 3 to the Agreement.

24. In planning the electoral process, UNTAC is governed by the provisions of section D of annex 1, and of annex 3 to the Agreement. Those provisions charge UNTAC with designing and implementing a system for every phase of the election of 120 members to the constituent assembly. Paragraph 2 of annex 3 directs that all electoral processes will take place only on Cambodian soil. This is consistent with considerations of simplicity, efficiency and economy. Candidates will stand for provincial seats in the constituent assembly and results would be tabulated on a provincial basis using a proportionality formula.

(a) Legal framework

25. UNTAC's first task is to establish, in consultation with the Supreme National Council, a legal framework that would consist of an electoral law and regulations to govern the electoral process. It is foreseen that an integral part of the legal framework would be the electoral code of conduct provided by UNTAC.

26. The Agreement stipulates that the election is to

be held on a provincial basis. Owing to the significant demographic changes that have occurred since the last systematic and comprehensive census was carried out, adequate statistics regarding the size and location of the Cambodian electorate are not available. Accordingly, the allocation of seats in the constituent assembly per province should be made only after registration of voters has been completed, it being understood that each province would elect at least one representative. By waiting until the registration of voters has been completed, a more consistent ratio of voters per representative in the constituent assembly can be ensured. The electoral law would therefore stipulate the system to be used for designation of the number of seats at the appropriate time, that system being the same as would be used for determining the results of the elections, i.e. the proportionality by largest remainder formula.

(b) *Civic education and training*

27. An important element of the electoral effort will be a large-scale campaign addressed to the general public on the purposes and importance of the elections and, particularly, the integrity of the ballot. General and detailed information on each phase of the election would be provided at appropriate times throughout the process. Video, other audiovisual, radio and printed materials would be used to assist in this process. The establishment of radio broadcast and print facilities and of distribution networks, including access to community radio and/or televisions and mobile video units, may be foreseen.

28. In addition, the ultimate effectiveness of the electoral process depends upon the understanding and skill of those who are charged with carrying it out. In this respect, it is foreseen that orientation and/or training would be required for international staff, locally recruited staff and political party agents, in the functions to be carried out and the procedures to be applied at each of the various stages of the electoral process. Such training should range from quite basic (e.g. clerical procedures) to quite sophisticated (e.g. election management). It should be noted that the requirement for training is not limited to the electoral process, although the amount of training required for this purpose would be the largest.

(c) *Registration of voters*

29. The criteria of eligibility and the right to vote are specified in paragraphs 3 and 4 of annex 3 to the Agreement. Every person who has reached the age of 18 years and who was born in Cambodia or is the child of a person born in Cambodia will be eligible to vote.

30. Registration of voters would be carried out over a period of three months, on the understanding that some flexibility may be required in order to ensure that all of the approximately 4.3 million eligible Cambodians will have the opportunity to be registered. Voters must be registered in order to vote. Registration stations (fixed, temporary and mobile) would be located throughout Cambodia, taking into account population density and accessibility. At each station, it is expected that the Cambodian political parties would provide agents to observe the proceedings. Registered voters would be issued UNTAC registration cards. Challenge and appellate procedures would be provided at the registration stations and at the provincial levels. Registration of the military forces that have not been demobilized would take place in the cantonments.

31. It is estimated that about 800 five-man registration teams, relying upon local personnel to the extent possible, would be required. It is further foreseen that an additional 200 two-man internationally staffed supervisory teams, or more if necessary, would be required to canvass all districts in Cambodia. The coordination of the work of the teams would be handled at the provincial level. It may be necessary for the UNTAC military or police component to provide security arrangements for the registration stations in certain circumstances.

(d) *Political parties and candidates*

32. The Agreement provides for a multiparty electoral system. Paragraphs 5, 6, 7 and 9 of annex 3 to the Agreement provide a framework for the formation and rights of political parties and candidates. Political parties must provide verifiable membership lists of at least 5,000 registered voters. In accordance with the electoral law and procedures to be established, political parties would designate agents whose participation as observers in the voter registration and polling processes would enhance the freeness and fairness of the elections.

33. All political parties must be formally registered by UNTAC in order to participate in the elections; UNTAC will establish eligibility criteria which should be met in order to qualify for registration. Such criteria will include the stipulation that party platforms must be consistent with the objects and principles of the Agreement and that there be strict adherence to a code of conduct for the elections. Similar criteria will be established for qualification as a candidate, including the fact that all candidates must be registered voters.

34. In order to ensure that political parties can actively participate in voter registration, a system of provisional or temporary registration of parties prior to the voter registration processes is envisaged. UNTAC will design procedures for provisional party registration. Once a party has been provisionally registered, it could benefit from special training and orientation courses related to participation in the electoral processes. The provisional registration will subsequently be confirmed (i.e. the party would be officially registered) once UNTAC

has verified that all of the established criteria have been met. Only officially registered parties would be permitted to campaign actively. The duration of the campaign period could be six to eight weeks. A political party would be required to be officially registered in order for its symbol to appear on the ballot.

35. The electoral code of conduct provided by UNTAC would be designed to ensure, *inter alia*, that freedom of speech, assembly and movement would be fully respected. In addition, UNTAC will ensure that a system is put into place that would allow all registered political parties fair access to the media, including print, audio and visual media.

(e) *Polling*

36. The voting process would be designed to permit all registered voters to exercise their franchise rights conveniently and in the absence of fear, while preventing fraud.

37. Polling stations would be established, wherever possible in the same location as registration stations. It will not be possible to determine the number of polling stations required until the registration of voters is completed and the size and distribution of the electorate is known. It is none the less estimated that the establishment of approximately 8,000 polling teams would be required, with each comprising about seven persons. The polling teams would be supervised by approximately 1,400 internationally recruited polling officers. In more densely populated areas, more than one polling team may operate at a particular polling station. Should it be determined that more than 1,400 polling stations are necessary, more polling supervisors would need to be recruited. Political parties contesting in the elections may appoint polling agents to observe the polling processes. The presence of foreign observers is also foreseen, as called for in section D, paragraph 3 (i) of annex 1 to the Agreement.

38. Weighing carefully a large number of considerations, not least of which are the agricultural and migratory cycles that result from climatic conditions in Cambodia, it is felt that polling should be held in late April or early May 1993, shortly after the Cambodian New Year, when the majority of Cambodians are expected to be gathered at their respective home locations. The duration of the polling period should be no longer than three days at the most, on the understanding that there should be a single day of polling only in any one location, and that no ballot counting would take place prior to the final day of voting in all locations.

39. Voting will be for political parties and not for individuals, i.e. only party names and symbols will appear on the ballot. However, the list of party candidates for each province would be publicized widely prior to polling day and would be posted prominently at polling stations.

Voting will be by secret ballot. Provision would be made for "tendered ballots". A tendered ballot would be issued to a voter only in instances when a voter is voting in a province other than the one in which he is registered or when there may be some doubt surrounding his right to vote. In both cases, the voter's eligibility would be subject to verification prior to recording his vote. Safeguards to protect the integrity of the polling will be provided, including the use of indelible ink to mark voters' fingers.

40. Ballot boxes would be sealed and transported to storage/counting stations. UNTAC would design and provide adequate security arrangements for transportation, storage and counting of ballots. Challenge and appellate procedures for each step of the balloting and counting process are foreseen. The results of the election should be tabulated, verified, compiled and officially declared by UNTAC as quickly as possible after the close of polling.

2. *Structure and the need for computerization*

41. The Special Representative would have the task of organizing and conducting the elections. He would be assisted by a chief electoral officer. This officer would be headquartered in Phnom Penh, which would also be the seat of the Special Representative's Electoral Advisory Committee. This Committee would be composed of three international staff appointed by the Special Representative and would have the responsibility to ensure the prevention and control of election irregularities. There would be a total of 72 international electoral staff at headquarters, who would be deployed in March/April 1992.

42. The civic education, training and computer elements would also be based in Phnom Penh. However, the bulk of the responsibilities for actually conducting and coordinating the various phases of the electoral process would lie with the 21 provincial-level offices. For each provincial-level office, the provincial electoral officer would be assisted by officers in charge of electoral operations, information, training, communications, compliance and complaints, and coordination. There would be a total of 126 international electoral staff at the provincial level, who would be deployed in March/April 1992.

43. Approximately 200 district offices are foreseen, headed by 400 district electoral supervisors and answering to the provincial offices. The 400 international electoral staff would be deployed in May 1992. The district offices would have the responsibility, *inter alia*, of supervising the work of the 800 registration and 8,000 polling teams. For this purpose, the district personnel should be highly mobile. During the polling, the 400 district electoral supervisors would act as polling supervisors. Their number would be augmented by approximately 1,000 international personnel seconded from

Governments for two to three weeks in April 1993. Their presence during the polling period would allow for one polling supervisor per polling station. The number of interpreters required during the polling period would consequently also be increased.

44. To maximize efficiency and consequently minimize costs, the electoral process should be computerized. The specific areas subject to computerization are voter registration, logistical arrangements, compilation of polling results and administrative activities ancillary to the planning and conduct of registration, polling and counting. A total of 12 computer support staff has been included in the 72 international electoral staff at headquarters referred to in paragraph 41 above.

45. The computerized voter registration system should consist of two linked subsystems. The first would be used to account for and control the movement of voter registration cards and associated materials, thereby ensuring that such cards and materials cannot find their way into the hands of persons not entitled to vote. The second would record the particulars of individuals who have been registered to vote, in order to produce lists of registered voters and cancelled registration cards and for inventory control of registration materials. The computerized voter registration system should accommodate both roman and Khmer script input, and should produce printed output in each.

46. The scale of the tasks of organizing staffing and equipping registration teams and polling stations dictates that logistical arrangements should be computerized as well. Separate database systems would be required for registration and polling. Records of staff and equipment allocated to each polling station, including information such as serial numbers of ballot boxes, seals and ballot papers, would be required in order to generate statistical reports of total allocations country-wide, provincially and subprovincially. The input of overall registration data by interlinking the various systems would allow the most efficient allocation of international and local staff and of equipment and vehicles. Communications capabilities would also be enhanced by computerization.

47. By computerizing the compilation of polling results, speed and accuracy are greatly enhanced. The system could be programmed to apply the appropriate proportional representation formula to determine the candidates winning those seats in each province. However, any such system should be carefully tested and verified prior to its application.

48. Systems development should commence as early as possible. The need for computerization is not specific to the electoral component, but the heaviest demands on the system would emanate from the electoral process. Computers should be available to electoral staff throughout the process, down to the district level.

3. Calendar

49. The election is the focal point of the comprehensive settlement. The manner in which the elections are conducted would be, and must be seen to be, absolutely impartial. To be effective, sufficient time would be required for each phase of the process to be completed. This naturally presupposes that UNTAC's other activities would be carried out in a timely manner, in order to ensure that a climate conducive to holding free and fair elections is created.

50. The registration of voters must be as complete as possible, so that the maximum number of voters can cast their votes. Therefore, registration and voting periods should be selected in those parts of the year in which there are no large-scale agricultural activities and no major festivals, so that Cambodians are most likely to be in their normal places of residence and would need to do the least amount of travelling in order to participate in the electoral process. Also for reasons of stability, it is extremely important that all electoral activities proceed in a planned sequence without interruption, in accordance with a predetermined calendar of operations. This calendar must take into account information and training needs, in order to enable each particular step in the electoral process to be carried out as efficiently and effectively as possible.

51. Taking into account all factors, it is recommended that registration of voters commence in October 1992 and proceed for three months, discretion being allowed to the Special Representative to extend the period if necessary to ensure that the electoral roll is as complete as possible. Elections should be scheduled for sometime during the period extending from the end of April to the beginning of May 1993. A detailed proposed calendar is contained in annex I to the present document.

C. Military component

1. Functions

52. The Agreement deals with the military aspects of UNTAC's mandate in three sets of provisions. Article 11 of the Agreement provides the general framework; section C of annex 1 to the Agreement enumerates the main functions; and annex 2 contains the detailed provisions regarding the specific undertakings of the Cambodian parties and neighbouring States and the role and activities of the military component of UNTAC.

53. The objectives of the military arrangements during the transitional period are to stabilize the security situation and build confidence among the parties to the conflict. The achievement of these objectives is a necessary precursor to the successful conduct of the functions

of the other components and, in particular, the repatriation programme.

54. The main functions of the military component of UNTAC can be grouped into four categories, as follows:

(a) Verification of the withdrawal and non-return of all categories of foreign forces and their arms and equipment;

(b) Supervision of the cease-fire and related measures, including regroupment, cantonment, disarming and demobilization;

(c) Weapons control, including monitoring the cessation of outside military assistance, locating and confiscating caches of weapons and military supplies throughout Cambodia, storing of the arms and equipment of the cantoned and the demobilized military forces;

(d) Assisting with mine-clearance, including training programmes and mine awareness programmes.

55. In addition, under the Agreement, the military component is charged with the task of undertaking investigations, on complaint from one of the parties or on its own, of alleged non-compliance with any of the provisions relating to military arrangements (art. X of annex 2 to the Agreement). It is also called upon to provide assistance in relation to the release of prisoners-of-war (art. XI of annex 2 to the Agreement) and in the repatriation of Cambodian refugees and displaced persons (art. XII of annex 2 to the Agreement).

56. To ensure the smooth carrying out of the military component's responsibilities, the Agreement calls for the establishment of a mixed military working group, on which military representatives of all Cambodian parties are represented. The working group has already been established and is currently functioning under the chairmanship of the Senior Military Liaison Officer of the United Nations Advance Mission in Cambodia (UNAMIC). Once UNTAC has been established, the Commander of the military component of UNTAC, or his designated representative, would chair the working group. As the scale of UNTAC's activities increases, similar liaison arrangements would be made at other command levels.

(a) *Verification of the withdrawal and non-return of foreign forces*

57. As of the entry into force of the Agreement on 23 October 1991, all foreign forces, advisers and military personnel remaining in Cambodia, together with their weapons, ammunition and equipment, were to have been withdrawn from Cambodia. Once the UNTAC military component is deployed, it would have a continuing role in verifying the non-presence and non-return of any foreign forces.

58. This would be accomplished in two ways. First, UNTAC would post military observers at fixed locations where foreign forces would be likely to enter Cambodia. Twenty-four such ingress/egress points have been identi-fied and, subject to further assessment, would be as follows: seven along the border with Thailand, nine along the border with Viet Nam, two along the border with the Lao People's Democratic Republic, one each at the ports of Kompong Som and Phnom Penh and one each at the airports at Phnom Penh, Battambang, Siem Reap and Stung Treng. The military observers manning the fixed stations at these locations would also have responsibility for monitoring the cessation of outside military assistance to the Cambodian parties (see para. 76 below). These teams would report to UNTAC headquarters in Phnom Penh regarding any movement of combatants or arms into Cambodia.

59. Second, UNTAC would deploy mobile monitoring teams of military observers to investigate allegations of the presence of foreign forces. These mobile teams would, at the same time, be charged with the investigation of allegations of other violations of the military provisions of the Agreement.

60. In order to assist it in carrying out its mandate in this area, UNTAC would deploy liaison officers to the capitals of the States neighbouring Cambodia. These liaison officers would have the responsibility for maintaining the necessary contacts between UNTAC and the neighbouring States, with a view to assisting in the discharge of UNTAC's mandate in Cambodia. The liaison officers would carry out their functions with due respect for the sovereignty of the neighbouring States.

(b) *Cease-fire and related measures*

61. The first phase of the cease-fire entered into effect with the signing of the agreements on 23 October 1991 and the good offices mechanism provided in the Agreement has been in place since 9 November 1991, when UNAMIC was deployed. Upon the deployment of UNTAC, UNAMIC will be absorbed into it and the good offices functions would be continued and expanded.

62. The exact time and date at which the second phase of the cease-fire begins would be determined by the Commander of the military component of UNTAC, in consultation with the parties. UNTAC would supervise, monitor and verify the second phase of the cease-fire.

63. The regroupment, cantonment, disarming and demobilization of the military forces of the Cambodian parties are essential elements both for the cease-fire and for the achievement of the other objectives of UNTAC. Moreover, timely completion of these elements is indispensable if UNTAC is to be able to carry out its mandate in an effective and cost-efficient manner. In this connection, it is noted that paragraph 1 of article V of annex 2 to the Agreement foresees the balanced demobilization of at least 70 per cent of the military forces of the parties prior to the end of the process of registration for the elections and their subsequent total demobilization.

64. In accordance with paragraph 2 of article V of annex 2 to the Agreement the Secretary-General continues to believe that full demobilization of the military forces of the Cambodian parties prior to the end of the process of registration for the elections would enhance the prospects of free and fair elections and enduring peace. It is pointed out further that complete demobilization would greatly enhance efficiency and would produce significant savings in UNTAC's operation by enabling the closure of cantonment areas, the consequent reduction in the number of UNTAC military personnel and the reallocation of resources that would otherwise be required for the continued administration of the cantoned forces. Furthermore, demobilized forces would benefit from vocational retraining under paragraph 3 of article V of annex 2 to the Agreement (see para. 154 below) and would be assisted in their reintegration into Cambodian life as productive citizens and enabled to participate in the electoral process. The Secretary-General therefore strongly urges the Cambodian parties to agree to the complete demobilization of their military forces prior to the end of the election registration process and calls upon the Security Council to join him in so doing.

65. During the visit of the military survey mission to Cambodia in November-December 1991, information provided by the four Cambodian parties revealed that their regular military forces totalled over 200,000, deployed in some 650 separate locations. In addition, militias, totalling some 250,000, operate in almost all villages throughout the country. These forces are armed with over 300,000 weapons of all types and some 80 million rounds of ammunition.

66. While the Agreement provides that all forces of the parties, with their weapons, should be regrouped and cantoned, the magnitude of the forces indicated above would mean that the regroupment and cantonment of all forces, including the militias, would necessitate a massive deployment of UNTAC military personnel for an extended period. It would also entail a serious disruption of the social and economic life of Cambodia, since most of the militia members are engaged in farming and other civilian activities while being organized and armed to protect their communities. In order to achieve economy in the operation of UNTAC and in order not to cripple the economy of Cambodia, practical arrangements have been worked out and agreed to by the parties whereby the militia forces would not be physically cantoned but would be disarmed in the following manner. The members of the militia forces would report to the nearest local headquarters (to be designated by UNTAC) in order to hand over their weapons to UNTAC. UNTAC would collect all weapons and transfer them to more secure centralized locations.

67. With respect to the regrouping and cantonment of the regular forces of the four parties, the military survey mission obtained the acceptance by the respective commanders-in-chief of the forces of the Cambodian parties to reduce the number of regroupment areas from their desired total of 325 to 95 and the number of cantonment areas from their desired total of 317 to 52. This reduction is expected significantly to enhance efficiency and economy in carrying out this task of the UNTAC military component. The 95 regroupment areas and 52 cantonment areas would comprise the following:

(a) 48 regroupment areas and 33 cantonments for the Cambodian People's Armed Forces;

(b) 30 regroupment areas and 10 cantonments for the National Army of Democratic Kampuchea;

(c) 8 regroupment areas and 6 cantonments for the Khmer People's National Liberation Armed Forces;

(d) 9 regroupment areas and 3 cantonments for the National Army of Independent Kampuchea.

68. Soon after the start of phase two of the cease-fire, regroupment of forces would begin and, as agreed by the Cambodian parties and in accordance with the timetable to be drawn up by the Commander of the military component of UNTAC, would proceed on a simultaneous basis country-wide. The regrouped forces would then proceed with their commanders to the designated cantonment areas. The forces of the four Cambodian parties would use separate regroupment and cantonment areas. The four parties are expected to produce all troops, weapons, ammunition and equipment declared by them. There would be no demobilization of regular forces by any of the parties without the supervision of UNTAC. When the Commander of the military component of UNTAC has satisfied himself that proper account has been rendered by all parties, the demobilization process would begin and be conducted according to the timetable to be drawn up by UNTAC in consultation with the parties.

69. The naval forces of the Cambodian People's Armed Forces comprise a maritime branch and a riverine branch, totalling some 4,000 and equipped with 18 naval and 38 riverine vessels. These naval forces would be regrouped and cantoned in the same manner as the regular land forces, except that a limited number would be retained to patrol coastal and riverine areas, under the close supervision and control of UNTAC (see para. 76 below).

70. In addition, engineer and logistic units, although they would be regrouped and cantoned in the same manner as other units of the regular forces, would be subject to special arrangements in view of their role in the Cambodian demining programme as well as in supplying and supporting the cantoned forces.

71. These special arrangements for the retention of

some naval units, as well as engineer and logistic units, would reduce the number of UNTAC military personnel who would otherwise be required. These retained units would be counted as part of the up to 30 per cent of forces that might be kept at the end of the demobilization to be completed prior to the end of the process of registration for the elections.

72. The Ministry of Defence and its personnel located in Phnom Penh would also require special arrangements as far as the regroupment and cantonment processes are concerned. Since Phnom Penh will be the hub of all political activity in the country, every effort must be made to ensure that the Ministry of Defence and its military personnel there do not constitute and are not seen to pose a threat to any of the parties. At the same time, it would be necessary to allow the Ministry of Defence as well as the command groups of the forces of the other three parties to continue to exercise command of and provide support to the troops being regrouped and cantoned in the field under UNTAC supervision.

73. In order to reconcile these conflicting requirements as far as military personnel in Phnom Penh are concerned, the Commander of the military component of UNTAC would, before the start of the second phase of the cease-fire and in consultation with the appropriate military authorities, select a number of locations in and around Phnom Penh and draw up a timetable for the regroupment and cantonment of the military personnel deployed in the Phnom Penh area. All such personnel would be required to report to one of these locations in accordance with the timetable. Commanders of the various departments and units of the Ministry would be required to account for all military personnel, arms, ammunition and equipment under their command. In accordance with the provisions of the Agreement, all such arms, ammunition and equipment would be placed in the custody of UNTAC. On completion of the accounting process, all those involved in command and providing essential logistic and support services to the troops cantoned in the field would be allowed to resume their functions under the control and supervision of UNTAC.

74. The specific tasks which the military component would need to perform in relation to the regroupment and cantonment processes are as follows:

(a) Ensuring the demining of envisaged regroupment and cantonment areas, as necessary;

(b) Establishing the regroupment and cantonment areas and supervising their operation;

(c) Recording and verifying numbers of personnel of the military forces of the Cambodian parties and escorting them from the regroupment to the cantonment areas;

(d) Ensuring that all of the military forces are cantoned and disarmed;

(e) Monitoring and supervising the cantonments;

(f) Implementing a phased demobilization of 70 per cent (or more, if possible) of the cantoned forces prior to the end of the process of registration for the elections, as well as their subsequent demobilization in accordance with an agreed schedule.

75. In the regroupment and cantonment processes, the possible need to assist the parties with transporting their personnel to the regroupment areas, constructing shelters to accommodate the cantoned troops and resupplying or feeding them might require special attention. UNTAC may be required in particular to provide food. The UNTAC rehabilitation component would also play a role in vocational retraining and reintegration of the demobilized forces (see para. 154 below).

(c) *Weapons control*

76. The UNTAC military component would have ongoing duties to monitor the cessation of outside military assistance. This would be accomplished in part through the manning of fixed posts at ingress/egress points, as discussed above, and in part through the monitoring and investigative activities of the mobile teams, also discussed above. The naval unit within the military component would supervise the patrolling of coastal areas and inland waterways by the retained units of the naval forces (see paras. 69 and 71 above). In addition, UNTAC military liaison officers stationed in neighbouring States would support activities in this area of UNTAC's mandate (see para. 60 above).

77. UNTAC mobile teams of engineers would be responsible for promptly investigating reports of caches of weapons and military supplies inside Cambodia. Any such caches found would be confiscated and destroyed.

78. Reduction and control of weapons in Cambodia is a major element of the cease-fire and related measures. The military component would undertake the following sequence of activities:

(a) Disarming the militia;

(b) Ensuring that all of the cantoned military forces are disarmed and that no weapons, ammunition or equipment is subsequently brought into the cantonments;

(c) Ensuring that all of the reported arms, ammunition and equipment are placed under UNTAC custody;

(d) Once in custody, ensuring that the arms, ammunition and equipment are secure;

(e) Implementing a phased reduction of the arms, ammunition and equipment held in custody at the cantonments and their progressive transfer to designated areas, in keeping with the phased demobilization of the forces, and ensuring their security during the transfer process.

79. In order to accomplish these tasks, secure facilities would be established at the 52 cantonment areas,

where the weapons, ammunition and equipment of the forces would be deposited into UNTAC custody. This number may be reduced over time as the demobilization process proceeds and cantonment areas are consolidated or closed.

(d) Mine programmes

80. In accordance with the mandate provided to it by the Security Council on 16 October 1991, and expanded on 8 January 1992 (see resolution 728 (1992)), UNAMIC is already charged with the task of undertaking mine-awareness, mine-recording and marking and mine-clearance training programmes, as well as providing assistance in mine-clearance itself. Once UNTAC is established and deployed, these programmes will be taken over by its military component and expanded. Continuation and management of these programmes would be entrusted to the engineer unit within the military component. The magnitude of the mine problem in Cambodia requires that a sizeable and intense effort should be undertaken in the very early stages to facilitate UNTAC's deployment and its manifold activities.

2. Factors that would affect the execution of tasks of the military component

81. In order to carry out the above tasks, the military component of UNTAC would need to be assured that all the Cambodian parties will scrupulously fulfil the commitments they have made in signing the agreements and will extend full cooperation to UNTAC at all times. The military component would need to have full freedom of movement and communication and other rights and facilities that would be necessary for the performance of its tasks.

82. Given the scale and complexity of its tasks and the sense of distrust that the belligerents continue to harbour about each other's intentions, it is essential that the military component of UNTAC should be provided with the personnel and resources to enable it to establish immediately an effective and credible presence.

83. In broad terms UNTAC's military component would need to canton about 200,000 soldiers, disarm about 450,000 soldiers (including militia), secure more than 300,000 weapons of various types, and monitor the security of the borders and territorial waters of Cambodia. At the same time, it would have to establish a nationwide mine-training programme of unprecedented proportions and assist with mine-clearance. Its logistic elements would also be required to provide support to the other components of UNTAC, in an integrated support system.

84. The effective execution of these enormous tasks as well as the rate at which they can proceed depends upon the timely availability of resources and the capacity of the infrastructure, including roads, airfields, ports, fuel supply, power supply, communications, warehousing space and personnel accommodation, as well as the necessary repair and maintenance capacities. Taking into account the state of the existing infrastructure in Cambodia, it would be essential for a sizeable and concerted engineering effort to be deployed urgently to restore basic infrastructure before the onset of the rainy season in May.

3. Structure, operation and calendar

85. Based on the recent reconnaissance on the ground and information obtained from the parties, it is considered that the military component of UNTAC would require a strength of about 15,900 all ranks to carry out the assigned tasks. This will consist of:

(a) Force headquarters and sector headquarters staff of 204;

(b) Military observer group of 485;

(c) An infantry element of 10,200, consisting of 12 enlarged infantry battalions of 850 (all ranks) each;

(d) An engineer element of 2,230 (all ranks);

(e) An air support group of 326 (all ranks) to operate and maintain 10 fixed-wing aircraft (2 communication and liaison aircraft, 4 short take-off and landing aircraft and 4 heavy transport aircraft) and 26 helicopters (2 heavy transport, 6 medium and 18 utility helicopters);

(f) A signals unit of 582 (all ranks);

(g) A medical unit of 541 (all ranks);

(h) A composite military police company of 160 (all ranks);

(i) A logistic battalion of 872 (all ranks);

(j) A naval element of 376 (all ratings) to operate 6 sea patrol boats, 9 river patrol boats, 3 landing craft and 12 special boats (LFPB). All the craft, except the 12 special boats, will be provided by Cambodia.

The numbers indicated represent the total UNTAC requirements and include those personnel and equipment already deployed or planned for UNAMIC.

86. In making this assessment of the resources required, account has been taken of the specific geographic and economic conditions prevailing in Cambodia. These include, in particular, the varied nature of the topography and vegetation, climatic conditions, the nature of warfare which has been waged and the disposition of the forces of the parties and, above all, the degradation or non-existence of infrastructure. All these factors individually or collectively affect the resources required to enable the UNTAC military component to carry out effectively the tasks assigned to it under the Agreement. UNTAC, with its civilian and military components, would have an integrated logistic support system. While the signals unit and medical unit identified above would probably be adequate to support UNTAC as a whole, the air support group, logistics elements and engineers may

need to be strengthened to support the various civil components.

4. *Concept of operations*

87. Annex 2 to the Agreement describes in some detail the *modus operandi* of the military component of UNTAC and the general time-frame by which important aspects of its tasks should be accomplished. The concept of operations of the military component of UNTAC has been elaborated under the four major functions discussed in paragraphs 57 to 80 above. Additional considerations that apply to the operations of the military component are discussed below.

88. As already noted, UNAMIC will be absorbed into UNTAC on the establishment of the latter. Some of the military staff officers deployed in UNAMIC headquarters are carrying out detailed planning in the field regarding the deployment of UNTAC. It is planned to deploy the military component of UNTAC progressively (see annex II to the present report), starting with the early deployment of essential engineer units to continue and expand the mine programme and to undertake rehabilitation of vital infrastructure, followed by the arrival of logistic units to establish a firm logistic base for UNTAC. This process would culminate in the deployment of almost all the remaining military personnel by one week prior to the start of the second phase of the cease-fire. The bulk of these latter personnel would be deployed at the designated regroupment and cantonment areas of the forces of the parties. At the same time other military personnel of UNTAC would be deployed at other locations, mainly the ingress/egress points:

(a) To verify withdrawal from Cambodia and non-return of all categories of foreign forces;

(b) To monitor the cessation of outside military assistance to the Cambodian parties;

(c) To carry out all the other tasks assigned to it under the Agreement.

The peak strength of the military component would be reached prior to the regroupment and cantonment exercise and last for a period not exceeding six months.

89. As the demobilization of forces proceeds, a progressive reduction of the strength of UNTAC military personnel engaged in the regroupment and cantonment process can be anticipated, with the numbers of military observers and infantry personnel being reduced to approximately 330 and 5,100 respectively soon after the completion of the demobilization process. However, the sizes of the signals unit, air support group, engineer element and logistics and medical units would probably not change significantly, as their services would continue to be required by the other components of UNTAC throughout this period. Following election day, it may be possible to reduce considerably the size of each of the elements of the military component. Phased deployment geared to the tasks to be performed would allow for maximum economy in this aspect of the operation.

5. *Proposed organization and deployment*

90. To carry out its assigned tasks effectively, the following organization and deployment for the military component of UNTAC is envisaged. Force headquarters would be located at Phnom Penh. For operational purposes, Cambodia would be divided into nine sectors. Each sector would have its share of infantry personnel and military observers and would be supported by appropriate engineer, aviation, signal, medical and logistic subunits. In seven of the sectors, one battalion each would be deployed. Two of the sectors, where two battalions each would be deployed, would require the establishment of a separate sector headquarters. The proposed deployment and a summary of tasks to be performed by each element of the force are outlined below.

(a) *Headquarters.* A total of 204 officers, drawn from contingents contributed to UNTAC, would be required to man the force headquarters and two sector headquarters. The force headquarters would comprise the traditional branches of military staff of an operational-level headquarters;

(b) *Infantry battalions.* Twelve self-sufficient battalions (850 all ranks each) capable of supporting themselves for at least 60 days without resupply would be fielded. These must have their integral first-line and second-line support in all respects. The units would be responsible for, among other things:

(i) Establishment and manning of 95 regroupment and 52 cantonment areas around the country;

(ii) Escort of about 200,000 troops from regroupment to cantonment areas;

(iii) Disarming of about 450,000 troops (including the militia);

(iv) Escort of about 92,000 weapons and a large quantity of ammunition belonging to the militias from subdistrict and district headquarters to more secure and centralized facilities at the provincial level;

(v) Custody of about 300,000 weapons and some 80 million rounds of ammunition of different types and calibre and a large amount of equipment of the parties at some 52 locations around the country throughout the transitional period;

(vi) Monitoring of cessation of outside military assistance to the troops deployed in the cantonment areas;

(vii) Provision of protection at reception centres of Cambodian refugees and displaced persons;

(viii) Supervision of the resupply of all forces of the parties during the regroupment and cantonment process;

(c) *Military observers.* A total of 485 military observers would be responsible, among other things, for:

(i) Physically checking the number of troops that report to each cantonment area and all the weapons turned in at each cantonment area to ensure that these numbers agree with data previously reported for each unit by the parties;

(ii) Supervising the demobilization process;

(iii) Establishing a number of verification teams, which would investigate, upon complaints received from the parties or on their own, allegations of non-compliance with any of the provisions of annex 2 to the Agreement;

(iv) Establishing check-points along routes and at selected locations along the Cambodian side of the border as well as at airfields and ports inside Cambodia to monitor cessation of outside military assistance to all Cambodian parties and to verify the withdrawal from Cambodia and non-return of all categories of foreign forces;

(v) Establishing a liaison office in each of the capitals of the States neighbouring Cambodia, namely, the Lao People's Democratic Republic, Thailand and Viet Nam (see para. 60 above);

(d) *Signals unit.* A total of 582 (all ranks) would be deployed throughout the mission area. This unit would be responsible for the establishment of the force communication net, including ground-to-air communications. In addition, in coordination with civilian communications staff, the unit would assist with the provision of communication to the civilian components of UNTAC;

(e) *Engineer unit.* An engineer element of 2,230 (all ranks) would be responsible, among other things, for:

(i) Continuation and expansion of the mine programme already established by UNAMIC, namely:

    a. Conduct of mass education programme in the recognition and avoidance of explosive ordnance devices;

    b. Training of Cambodian volunteers to dispose of unexploded ordnance devices;

    c. Rendering of assistance with mine-clearing;

(ii) Disposal of unexploded ordnance devices and destruction of arm caches;

(iii) Provision of assistance to infantry battalions with all engineer tasks beyond the capacity of organic unit engineers; these tasks, for organic and engineer units, would include water-purification, site preparation for, erection and repair of accommodation and minor maintenance of tracks and roads. In addition, the engineer unit might need to repair and improve airfields, helicopter landing sites, ports, etc.;

(f) *Air support group.* A total of 326 (all ranks) would operate and maintain 10 fixed-wing aircraft and 26 helicopters (see para. 85 above). The air support group would be responsible for providing support to all components of UNTAC. This would include reconnaissance tasks, troop technical support, logistic support and overall air support to the civilian component;

(g) *Naval unit.* A total of 376 (all ratings) would be responsible for:

(i) Patrolling the coastal and inland waterways of Cambodia to monitor cessation of outside military assistance to all Cambodian parties;

(ii) Discharging all duties relating to the regroupment, cantonment and demobilization of the naval forces;

(h) *Logistic battalion.* A total of 872 (all ranks) would provide logistic support to the military component and assist the civilian component as required;

(i) *Medical unit.* A total of 541 (all ranks) would provide medical support to all components of UNTAC;

(j) *Military police company.* This would be a composite unit comprising a total of 160 (all ranks) to be drawn from the Member States contributing formed units to UNTAC.

6. *Calendar*

91. In order to ensure that all aspects of the military mandate can be fulfilled in a timely manner, taking into account UNTAC's other responsibilities, it is recommended that full deployment of the military component be accomplished by the end of May 1992. The regroupment and cantonment processes, as well as the demobilization of at least 70 per cent of the cantoned forces, should be completed by the end of September 1992. A proposed schedule of deployment of UNTAC military component is attached in annex II to the present document.

D. Civil administration component

1. Functions

92. Article 6 of the Agreement contains the general provisions governing UNTAC's mandate in civil administration. In this article, it is stipulated that the objective is to "ensure a neutral political environment conducive to free and fair general elections". The specific framework within which UNTAC is to carry out its civil administration mandate is provided in section B of annex 1 to the Agreement.

93. In accordance with the Agreement, UNTAC would have three levels of interaction with the agencies, bodies and offices of the existing administrative structures in all parts of Cambodia. However, the difficulties of following a rigidly segmented approach should be noted, as it is exceedingly problematic in practice to classify a particular administrative act as falling exclusively within one level of activity. Rather, the overall consideration should be the level of interaction which would be required to ensure that the objectives of article 6 are fulfilled, without contravening the terms of the Agreement. In other words, flexibility should be applied, with UNTAC reserving the possibility of making a final determination as to the level of interaction, in consultation with the Supreme National Council as circumstances warrant. It is assumed, for these purposes, that all of Cambodia's administrative functions would be carried out inside the country during the period of UNTAC's presence. If it is found that this is not in fact the case, it will be necessary for UNTAC to take the steps required to ensure that its mandate is fulfilled.

94. The first level of interaction is "direct control", as provided in section B, paragraph 1, of annex 1 to the Agreement, which is to be exercised "as necessary to ensure strict neutrality". Five fields for scrutiny are identified, namely foreign affairs, national defence, finance, public security and information. It is the United Nations alone that has the responsibility for determining what will be necessary in these fields, in both the identification of agencies, bodies and offices and in the implementation of its mandate. In this respect, a functional analysis will yield an identification of the existing administrative structures concerned. However, the application of the functional approach reveals that there are sometimes overlaps between the five areas indicated in the Agreement. Flexibility should accordingly be maintained.

95. In terms of implementation, UNTAC would rely upon codes of conduct and guidelines for management, especially regarding ethical conduct, measures to counter corruption, measures to ensure non-discrimination and other principles of accountability. Specific discipline-related directives and guidelines would be provided, as appropriate. In addition, UNTAC has been accorded the right to issue binding directives on an ad hoc basis, as necessary.

96. In the area of foreign affairs, the main concerns relate to the issuance of passports and visas, the receipt and distribution of foreign assistance and other important aspects relating to foreign policy. In relation to the first concern, each of the Cambodian parties is issuing or has issued Cambodian travel documents and/or visas. In addition, the Supreme National Council has announced that it will do the same. UNTAC foreign affairs liaison officers would have to be present at the sites where decisions are taken regarding the issuance and honouring of passports and visas, to ensure the proper (non-discriminatory) formulation and application of policies and procedures. In relation to the second concern, UNTAC's mandate in foreign affairs would be carried out in close collaboration with UNTAC liaison staff exercising direct control over the area of finance. In relation to the third concern, UNTAC would exercise general scrutiny to ensure that the objectives and purposes of the Agreement were not transgressed in the execution of foreign policy by the existing administrative structures and would rely heavily upon its complaints and investigation mechanism for this purpose.

97. In the areas of national defence, UNTAC's role under its civil administration mandate would be carried out in close collaboration with the work of the military component. Its mandate under section B of annex 1 to the Agreement would, however, require UNTAC to exercise scrutiny over the military structures of the Cambodian parties from an administrative point of view. In this connection, UNTAC's functions in the areas of finance and foreign affairs would also be implicated, in the former with respect to military expenditures, and in the latter bearing in mind the Agreement concerning the Sovereignty, Independence, Territorial Integrity and Inviolability, Neutrality and National Unity of Cambodia. 3/

98. In the area of finance, the fiscal policy and allocation/utilization of funds have important political connotations, as politically motivated changes or aberrations in their application could have adverse effects on the electoral process. A functional analysis reveals that control over planning, comprising allocation of resources and budgeting, is required. The budgeting process has a significant political dimension, for the budget is the instrument whereby various administrative functions are funded. The formulation of budget priorities will therefore entail decisions that may have a direct impact upon the electoral process. Similarly, the systems of accounting for expenditures should indicate correlation with the priorities identified.

99. Areas of finance over which scrutiny is called for also include banking, customs, the release and utilization of funds and commodities, taxation, public enterprises and wage and salary policies, the manipulation of any of which could affect strict neutrality. Financial operational guidelines would be provided to the existing administrative structures at all levels. The presence of UNTAC finance liaison officers would be required at the central and provincial levels. In addition, as in the other areas of scrutiny, reliance would be placed upon complaints and investigation mechanism for detecting violations at lower levels.

3/ S/23177 [Document 19]

100. In the area of public security, the maintenance of law and order is the key not only to the creation of a neutral political environment in which all Cambodians may exercise their political rights to participate in the electoral process but also to the effective implementation by UNTAC of all aspects of its mandate. In other words, in order to ensure the success of the transitional arrangements, UNTAC must be able to work as a partner with all of the existing administrative structures charged with public security.

101. In addition to the activities of the UNTAC civil police component *vis-à-vis* the local police forces at all levels, the presence of UNTAC administrative liaison staff would be required in the agencies, bodies and offices dealing with public security at the highest levels. Since the maintenance of law and order is the responsibility of the Cambodian police forces, UNTAC's functions would include ensuring that public security policy is formulated in a manner consistent with, and meet the needs of, the objectives and purposes of the Agreement. Similarly, execution of policy, administration and coordination should be followed closely by UNTAC staff.

102. Notwithstanding the primary importance of the effective maintenance of law and order, as narrowly defined, a broader view of functions in the field of public security must be taken to embrace the protection of other fundamental freedoms. A consistent and integrated reading of the Agreement would reveal that UNTAC's scrutiny should encompass functions to ensure human rights and the effective redress of grievances. This aspect of UNTAC's mandate is reinforced in paragraph 5 (b) of section B of annex 1 to the Agreement, which calls for UNTAC supervision of all law enforcement and judicial processes. It would entail principally the provision of codes of conduct, directives and training, although an UNTAC liaison presence is also envisaged.

103. In addition, the proper and effective application of the law requires the prior existence and knowledge of the law. Hence, as an immediate step, an examination of the law should be initiated by UNTAC to determine, first, what the law is and, second, that it is in all cases consistent with not only the letter of, but also the objectives and purposes of, the Agreement. Such an exercise is consistent with paragraph 3 (b) of section D of annex 1 to the Agreement, which calls for a review of Cambodian law.

104. In the area of information, there is a very close interrelationship between UNTAC's responsibilities of direct control and its activities in the area of dissemination of information, civic education and the elections. The direct-control aspect would include monitoring of the information sector and ensuring fair access to it and the other aspects would include utilizing the information sector and complementing existing information channels

as necessary. The supervision and monitoring functions would include reviewing printed and broadcast materials (radio and television), vetting public statements and generally ensuring that publicity or information dissemination by the parties satisfies the stipulations of the Agreement and of the appropriate codes of conduct and guidelines (including the electoral code of conduct). The placement of UNTAC liaison officers in all information structures, at the central, provincial and lower levels, is envisaged.

105. It would be essential for UNTAC to have its "finger on the pulse" of the Cambodian information sector, a task which would be greatly complicated by language concerns and the paucity of facilities and supporting infrastructures in the country. In this connection, it should be noted that UNTAC's scrutiny must extend to all sources of information, since it is not possible to limit the flow of information territorially. Given the paramount importance of information in the maintenance of law and order, the protection of human rights and the conduct of free and fair elections, very high priority must be placed upon UNTAC's needs in this area.

106. For those areas not identified in article 6 of the Agreement, paragraphs 2 and 3 of section B of annex 1 to the Agreement direct UNTAC to enter into consultations with the Supreme National Council for the purpose of identifying those administrative structures that could influence the outcome of the elections and over which a lesser degree of scrutiny would be exercised. For example, the education, communications and health sectors may fall within this category. It is noted that, in some cases, UNTAC human rights liaison or rehabilitation staff may already be involved in these sectors, in which case they would be called upon to also exercise scrutiny under the civil administration mandate.

107. While some UNTAC liaison presence may be warranted in certain areas, subject to the outcome of the consultations with the Supreme National Council, reliance would be placed upon the use of codes of conduct and guidelines, as well as upon the complaints and investigation mechanism foreseen in paragraph 6 of section B of annex 1 to the Agreement. In connection with the codes of conduct and guidelines, training would be extended to Cambodian administrative personnel in order to ensure that those instruments are understood and observed, thus reducing the need for UNTAC intervention in the long run.

108. In connection with the complaints mechanism, the Agreement permits UNTAC to take corrective action, as appropriate. Complaint and investigation procedures should be commenced at the appropriate (field) level pertaining to the area of administration concerned, where the appropriate UNTAC liaison personnel would try to resolve the problem. Should this not prove possible, for what-

ever reason, UNTAC headquarters complaints personnel would be seized of the matter. The complaints personnel would also be charged with monitoring the progress and disposition of all complaints, to enable an ongoing assessment of the political climate and the detection of any patterns of violations which may become apparent.

2. Structure

109. The overall direction and implementation of UNTAC's mandate in civil administration would lie with the Special Representative of the Secretary-General. Offices would be established to deal with each of the five areas identified for direct control, one for those other areas that may require a lesser degree of scrutiny, one for training and one for complaints and investigation. The close interrelationship between certain of UNTAC's civil administration responsibilities and its other activities, notably those of the human rights, the civil police, the electoral and the rehabilitation components, as well as UNTAC's other information activities, necessitate a high degree of cooperation and collaboration among UNTAC's operational staff.

110. Twenty-one provincial offices would be established at provincial and municipal centres, paralleling the existing structures in the country. At each provincial office, five to seven international staff would be assigned duties under the civil administration mandate, in addition to other related duties, as appropriate. For example, a staff member performing supervision or control of information may also have responsibilities relating to dissemination of UNTAC information and human rights. ·

111. It is also foreseen that there will be about 200 subprovincial offices, located mostly at the district level and operating mostly in the areas of public security (civil police) and information, although other functions for these offices may be warranted in certain cases. In areas other than public security, the subprovincial offices will rely mainly, although not exclusively, upon locally recruited staff.

E. Police component

1. Public order considerations

112. Paragraph 5 (a) of section B of annex 1 to the Agreement stipulates that, after consultation with the Cambodian parties, the Special Representative will determine those civil police necessary to perform law enforcement in Cambodia. The responsibility for management of the police forces would continue to rest with the Cambodian Parties. However, paragraph 5 (b) provides that the civil police will operate under UNTAC supervision or control, in order to ensure that law and order are maintained effectively and impartially, and that human rights and fundamental freedoms are fully protected.

113. The number of Cambodian civil police, their deployment and the degree of supervision and control that may be required will depend on the law and order situation that may exist during the transitional period. In this respect, there are a number of factors to be taken into account. There has reportedly been no arms control and it would appear that there are a considerable number of weapons in "non-official" hands all over the country. Moreover, the demobilization of the armed forces would release a considerable number of persons whose only skills relate to the handling of weapons. All of these factors may result in deterioration of the law and order situation, with an increase in brigandage, robbery, violence and theft, although the vocational retraining programme, which is recommended in accordance with article V, paragraph 3 of annex 2 to the Agreement, would be likely to mitigate the risks to society. It should be noted, in this context, that electoral processes are inherently antagonistic in nature, which could stretch the existing public order machinery.

114. The initial assessment of the strength of the existing civil police indicates that there are a total of over 47,000 police personnel of the Cambodian People's Party. The Cambodian People's Party police force includes border police, traffic police, maritime and riverine police, customs police, security guards and other specialized police. No distinction is made by the Cambodian People's Party between administrative personnel who perform duties in the public security agencies and the patrolmen charged with the maintenance of law and order in the field, all of whom figure in the reported strength of the police forces. However, the former would be subject to direct control by UNTAC public security liaison officers under the civil administration mandate, while the latter would be supervised or controlled by UNTAC civilian police monitors.

115. At the provincial level and below, the Cambodian People's Party police forces number around 40,000 men, with about one third at the provincial and about two thirds at the district and commune levels. The Cambodian People's Party maintains 1,147 "administrative police posts", whose jurisdiction is usually a commune or group of villages. In addition, 84 border posts are maintained by the Cambodian People's Party, of which 83 are along the Vietnamese border and one is along the border with Thailand.

116. The "A-3" forces of the Cambodian People's Party have reportedly been disbanded and allocated to the administrative police posts. However, it would appear that these forces could be reconstituted at short notice. Continuous monitoring of the structure of the internal security forces would, therefore, be necessary.

117. The strength of the civil police force of the

Party of Democratic Kampuchea is reportedly over 9,000 men, most of whom are evidently in the field, with the strengths of the units varying from 12 to 60 depending on the size of the village. The Party of Democratic Kampuchea police force also controls four points along the Thai border. The Party of Democratic Kampuchea police force is scarcely distinguishable from the military forces.

118. Though there is no formal civil police structure under the control of the United National Front for an Independent, Neutral, Peaceful and Cooperative Cambodia, it would appear that there is a small force of around 150 military police in the areas controlled by this party. Similarly, although there is no formal Khmer People's National Liberation Front (KPNLF) civil police structure, it would appear that there is a small force of some 400 military police in the areas controlled by the Khmer People's National Liberation Front.

119. The strength of the civil police that each Party may retain during the transitional period would have to be determined bearing in mind the law and order situation, local security requirements during the elections, the undesirability of excessive disbanding of existing police forces and the ability of UNTAC civilian police monitors to supervise and control a large force spread all over the country. Taking rough population estimates, it is possible to determine a reasonable ratio of Cambodian police responsible for the maintenance of law and order per person. Special circumstances are present in Cambodia, such as lack of roads and communications facilities, as well as the need to maintain law and order effectively throughout the transitional period.

120. On a comparative basis and subject to further verification, it is assessed that the strength of the civil police in the area controlled by the United National Front for an Independent, Neutral, Peaceful and Cooperative Cambodia should be around 1,700 men and in the area controlled by KPNLF around 1,000 men. The strength of the police force in the Party of Democratic Kampuchea of over 9,000 men, in comparison, would appear high; subject to further verification, a strength of about 5,000 men would seem sufficient. Further consideration of these levels would be undertaken only after investigation of the situation on the ground, including location and accessibility of the villages, population density and distribution, convenient points of location of supervisory personnel and an assessment of the law and order situation.

121. The United National Front for an Independent, Neutral, Peaceful and Cooperative Cambodia and the Khmer People's National Liberation Front would have to constitute police forces, while the Party of Democratic Kampuchea force would have to be reorganized as a civil police force. The UNTAC civilian police personnel deployed in the areas controlled by these parties could be

actively associated with this process. Guidelines for recruitment, reorganization and training could be formulated in consultation with UNTAC; however the costs of recruitment would have to be borne by the parties themselves.

122. The total number of Cambodian civil police that UNTAC civilian police monitors are expected to be responsible for supervising would be some 50,000, subject to further verification. The total number of police posts or stations in the field is estimated to be about 1,500. Policing of the waterways and the coast should be envisaged. The strengthening of the local coastal police should be considered in greater detail, bearing in mind the requirements for customs control along the coast.

123. With the deployment of senior UNTAC civilian police staff, a more detailed study would be carried out, including further investigation of the existing structures, strength, arms and equipment, and deployments of the civil police forces of all of the parties. Such a study is required in order to ensure that, during the transitional period, the maintenance of law and order, and its supervision, are adequate and effective.

2. *Functions*

124. The main function of the UNTAC civilian police monitors is provided in section B, paragraph 5 (b) of annex 1 to the Agreement, i.e. to supervise or control the local civil police in order to ensure that law and order are maintained effectively and impartially, and that human rights and fundamental freedoms are fully protected. In order to do so effectively, UNTAC civilian police monitors must be deployed in the field down to the district levels. They will be required to be mobile so that they can cover the subdistrict level. Their activities will focus upon the activities of the local civil police functioning out of the existing or established police posts or stations.

125. The civilian police monitors at both the provincial and the district levels would have to tour their jurisdictions continuously in order to ensure that the local police are functioning in the desired manner. This would also enhance public confidence and help in fostering an atmosphere conducive to free and fair elections. This touring would be an effective way of gathering information on the situation at the commune and village levels. In this connection, the establishment of frequent contact with village leaders would be useful, for they are reportedly the principal agents for the maintenance of law and order at the village level at present.

126. To assist the UNTAC monitors in carrying out their functions, use will be made as appropriate of codes of conduct and other operational guidelines developed by the United Nations. As the functions that the local police personnel had been called upon to perform

in the past may have had a political character that would no longer be appropriate in the transitional period, orientation and training courses should be organized for all levels of the existing police hierarchy, in order to ensure an understanding of the role of UNTAC and an appreciation of the functions that the local police would be called upon to perform. In particular, it would be necessary to familiarize local police personnel with the concepts of human rights and fundamental freedoms, with the provisions of specific codes of conduct and with the manner in which these should be respected and implemented.

127. Although the main function of the UNTAC civilian police monitors would be to control and supervise the Cambodian police forces, they would also need to assume other responsibilities relating to the elections and to security requirements within UNTAC itself. Some of the security functions may necessitate the full-time assignment of UNTAC civilian police or may require civilian police monitors to play a dual role in the exercise of their functions, especially in connection with the electoral processes.

3. *Structure*

128. The structure of the UNTAC civilian police component would include a policy and management unit at headquarters, 21 units at the provincial level and 200 district-level units. There would be a total of about 3,600 UNTAC civilian police monitors.

129. The headquarters composition would include a monitoring unit for carrying out inquiries as necessary, for emergency liaison with the UNTAC units in the field and for similar duties as may be assigned to it. Specific decisions regarding deployment away from headquarters, especially at subprovincial levels, would depend upon an assessment on the spot of public order needs. Considerations in this regard may include not only UNTAC's ability to discharge responsibilities efficiently and effectively but also factors related to instilling confidence in the public. Priority in deployment would be given, however, to areas in which Cambodian refugees and displaced persons have been resettled.

130. The UNTAC civilian police personnel at the provincial level would be called upon to guide and supervise the UNTAC monitors at the district levels and below, to control and supervise the local civil police at the provincial level and to respond to emergency situations. The continuous monitoring and reporting of the law and order situation would be the responsibility of the provincial level.

131. The UNTAC civilian police monitors at the subprovincial level would be called upon to supervise and coordinate the activities of the local civil police in the field. The 200 district-level UNTAC units would consist

of mobile teams. The tasks of the mobile teams would include touring the district regularly and periodically visiting the local police posts and stations, for the purpose of ensuring that law and order are maintained impartially and effectively. In order to ensure adequate supervision, one team, consisting of two UNTAC police officials, should be assigned to each police post or station. Based on the estimate of 1,500 police posts or stations, a total of 3,000 UNTAC civilian police monitors in the field would be required. This would give an estimated ratio of one UNTAC police monitor in the field to approximately 15 local civil police, or one UNTAC police monitor to approximately 3,000 Cambodians.

F. *Repatriation component*

132. Article 20 of the Agreement provides that all Cambodian refugees and displaced persons shall have the right to return to Cambodia and to live in safety, security and dignity, free from intimidation or coercion of any kind, and that their repatriation in conditions of safety and dignity should be facilitated under the overall authority of the Special Representative and as an integral part of UNTAC. It is noted in annex 4 to the Agreement that the repatriation and resettlement processes will entail an inter-agency effort. Paragraph 9 of that annex reaffirms the Secretary-General's designation of the Office of the United Nations High Commissioner for Refugees (UNHCR) as the lead agency in this respect.

133. Annex 4 to the Agreement provides the framework within which the repatriation and resettlement processes will be undertaken. In particular, it is stipulated that Cambodians must return to their homeland voluntarily, that they should be allowed to return to the place of their choice and that their human rights and fundamental freedoms must be fully respected. The fulfilment of these conditions has important implications for UNTAC's information programmes.

134. Paragraph 12 of annex 4 notes that, in ensuring that conditions of security are created for the movement of refugees and displaced persons, appropriate border crossing-points and routes must be designated and cleared of mines and other hazards.

135. Based on guidelines provided in that annex, UNHCR signed a memorandum of understanding with the Royal Thai Government and the Supreme National Council on 21 November 1991. The memorandum defines the modalities of cooperation on all aspects of the repatriation operation.

136. UNHCR has determined that there are more than 360,000 potential returnees, of whom over 90 per cent are under the age of 45 and almost half under the age of 15 years. The population is divided almost equally by gender and the family unit consists, on average, of 4.4

persons. There is a high rate of illiteracy, and most of the potential returnees were originally farmers, 60 per cent of whom came from the Cambodian provinces along the border with Thailand. Over two thirds of the population has lived in the camps along the Thai border for over 10 years. Of the total population, around 90 per cent are expected to elect to return to Cambodia under United Nations auspices, with the rest returning spontaneously.

137. The following objectives have been set for the repatriation and resettlement of the refugees and displaced persons from the camps along the Thai border:

(a) The organized repatriation of the refugees and displaced persons within a nine-month period;

(b) The identification and provision of agricultural and settlement land, installation assistance and food for an average of one year for up to 360,000 returnees. Depending on the experience gained, this period could be extended up to 18 months, notably through introduction of food-for-work projects;

(c) The provision of installation assistance and food for up to 12 months for up to 30,000 "spontaneous" returnees;

(d) The provision of limited reintegration assistance for up to 360,000 returnees and upgrading of services in returnee-concentrated areas through quick-impact projects. Infrastructural improvements are envisaged by the United Nations Development Programme (UNDP) outside the framework of the repatriation budget.

138. The objectives specified in paragraph 137 should be met subject to adequate funding and the solution of mine-related problems. In order to meet these objectives, it is foreseen that the UNTAC plan for repatriation, under the lead of UNHCR, would entail three stages, as follows:

(a) The movement of the returnees from the border camps to the final destinations of their choice in Cambodia by:

(i) Movement from border camps to staging areas for final registration and boarding of buses and trucks;

(ii) Transportation by bus and truck through one or more crossing-point to reception centres inside Cambodia;

(iii) Brief transit of up to one week at reception centres;

(iv) Onward movement by truck from reception centres to final destinations.

(b) The provision of immediate assistance (shelter, materials, household kits) and food for an average period of 12 months (subject to adjustment);

(c) A reintegration programme that includes quick-impact projects and medium- to long-term area development projects. Modalities for development and

coordination and implementation of the reintegration phase has been defined in a memorandum of understanding signed between UNDP and UNHCR at their meeting from 10 to 14 January 1992.

139. The preregistration has now been completed and information-sharing with the camp population has been intensified. Preliminary data show that the majority (57.3 per cent) of the eventual returnees wish to settle in Battambang province. The next largest group (14 per cent) wishes to return to destinations in Banteay Meanchey, with 17.7 per cent opting for destinations in other provinces, while approximately 11 per cent of the potential returnees have indicated that they wish to leave the choice of province to the United Nations.

140. It is foreseen that the movement of returnees from the border camps in Thailand to their destinations in Cambodia under United Nations auspices will be organized through the Poipet border crossing via six reception centres in Cambodia. However, new border crossing points via additional reception facilities could be set up under the agreed safeguards and conditions. The departure of an average of 8,500 to 10,000 persons per week should be envisaged. The rate of flow from the border camps would be determined by the absorption capacity at the destinations inside Cambodia.

141. Given an average family size of 4.4 persons, about two hectares of land per family would be required for self-sufficiency. This would indicate a need for the identification and allocation of some 150,000 hectares of land inside Cambodia for resettlement. Land so allocated must be determined to be free of mines, for which purpose detailed mine verification is required prior to the land being designated as suitable for resettlement. A UNHCR land identification mission using remote-sensing techniques has identified 240,000 hectares of potentially suitable unclaimed land in the provinces of main interest to returnees. Seventy thousand hectares have been surveyed for demining purposes and some 30,000 hectares have been classified as probably not mined. This land is now being verified more thoroughly to confirm its suitability.

142. It should be noted that actual demining is a very lengthy process, requiring years of work with no guarantee of complete clearance. However, as a priority, the areas around the reception centres and access roads must be demined. In addition, the constitution of verification teams with limited demining capability is necessary to enable the timely identification of suitable resettlement sites that are "probably not mined".

143. While identification of suitable agricultural land proceeds, three alternative courses of action can be foreseen and proposed to prospective returnees. They are as follows:

(a) To arrange the voluntary return to specific destinations of choice for those returnees who would opt to make their own arrangements for land. They would be provided with food and standard resettlement kits and, where possible, they would enjoy the benefits of quick-impact projects in their resettlement areas;

(b) Temporarily to relocate a number of returnees to villages near the potentially available land pending its further preparation or clearance of mines;

(c) To establish a mechanism, through NGO partners, to assist those families who opt for non-agricultural income-generating activities.

144. Resettlement packages to be provided to each returnee family would include a set of basic housing materials for use at final destinations, consisting of sawn timber, poles, bamboo and plastic tarpaulin sheeting, as well as construction tools, including nails, wire, handsaws, files, post-hole diggers and pliers. Returning families will need to provide themselves with additional thatch or similar material to complete walls and eventually to replace the plastic sheeting.

145. Each family will also be supplied with a kit of household items and agricultural tools, including water buckets, mosquito nets, axes, machetes, hoe heads, spades, knives, sickle blades, and rope. An additional US$ 15 per household will be provided to supplement the resettlement kits with local purchases of needed additional items.

146. It is foreseen that food assistance would be provided for an average period of 12 months at distribution points proximate to the final destinations of the returnees. The food basket would include 500 grams/day of oil and 10 grams/day of salt. The duration of food assistance will be reviewed after six months in the light of the experience gained.

147. Transportation and warehousing space throughout Cambodia will be required to enable the prepositioning of building materials, food and household kits for repatriation and resettlement purposes.

148. The repatriation and resettlement of Cambodian refugees and displaced persons would be headed by a Director for repatriation, who will be appointed by the Secretary-General, on the recommendation of the United Nations High Commissioner for Refugees. The Director would report to the Special Representative, as well as to the High Commissioner.

149. The repatriation and resettlement would be funded from voluntary contributions. Since the implementation and integrity of the electoral process is dependent upon the prior repatriation of Cambodian refugees and displaced persons, UNTAC's schedule of operations would be seriously jeopardized if sufficient funds were not made available in full and in a timely manner.

G. Rehabilitation component

1. Functions

150. The Declaration on the Rehabilitation and Reconstruction of Cambodia 2/ was one of the three instruments comprising the comprehensive political settlement of the Cambodia conflict signed in Paris on 23 October 1991. Paragraph 8 of the Declaration notes that, with the achievement of the comprehensive settlement, the initiation of a process of rehabilitation, addressing immediate needs and laying the groundwork for future plans, is desirable. Paragraph 10 stipulates that particular attention should be given in the rehabilitation phase to food security, health, housing, training, education, the transport network and the restoration of Cambodia's existing basic infrastructure and public utilities.

151. Chronologically, the rehabilitation phase would run from the signature of the Agreement and the establishment of UNTAC until the formation of a new Cambodian Government following free and fair elections. Paragraph 2 of the Declaration recognizes the principal responsibilities of that new Cambodian Government in determining Cambodia's reconstruction needs and plans.

152. The overall need for as much coordination as possible of international, regional and bilateral assistance to Cambodia is noted in paragraph 3 of the Declaration. For this purpose, the Secretary-General is requested under paragraph 9 to appoint a rehabilitation programme coordinator. The Rehabilitation Coordinator will be the head of the rehabilitation component of UNTAC. In Cambodia, where resources are scarce, circumstances are expected to be changing rapidly and UNTAC is expected to be present in almost every domain, it will be essential to coordinate rehabilitation efforts within the framework of activities being carried out by UNTAC in the implementation of its mandate.

153. The urgent needs to be met during the rehabilitation phase include the following:

(a) Humanitarian needs in terms of food, health, housing and other essential needs, of all Cambodians and particularly the disadvantaged, the handicapped, and women and children;

(b) Resettlement needs, comprising essential agricultural inputs, improved access, drinking water supplies, health and education facilities, vocational training and food security as necessary, in order to meet:

(i) The resettlement and reintegration needs of the 350,000 Cambodians returning to their original or chosen places of habitation and livelihood, the 170,000 internally displaced persons, and the estimated 150,000 or more Cambodian military forces to be demobilized by the military component of UNTAC;

(ii) The essential needs of the populations in all

Cambodian communities, especially rural communities, with special focus on areas where resettlement will take place;

(c) Essential restoration, maintenance and support of basic infrastructure, institutions, utilities and other essential services, such as major roadways, railways, seaports and river ports, airports, telecommunications, health, education, banking, etc., as well as training related to the efficient operation of the various sectors.

154. In respect of the demobilized military forces of the Cambodian parties, the provision by UNTAC of reintegration assistance, as required, is stipulated in paragraph 3 of article V of annex 2 to the Agreement. This would mainly take the form of training programmes in small-scale enterprise development, including training in small-scale production, basic finance, accounting and marketing and the development of small-scale credit facilities. In addition, vocational and managerial training would be provided, *inter alia*, in vehicle maintenance and repair, woodworking, carpentry and basic food processing. It is estimated that a total of US$ 9 to 14 million would be required for this reintegration assistance, to be funded as part of UNTAC's regular operating budget.

155. With regard to other activities undertaken in the rehabilitation phase, it is estimated that the resource needs would amount to about US$ 800 million, to be funded from voluntary donor contributions.

2. *Structure*

156. The rehabilitation effort would be headed by a Coordinator for Rehabilitation in Cambodia, appointed by the Secretary-General, who would report to the Special Representative. It would be the Coordinator's responsibility to make ongoing assessments of needs, to ensure that needs are being met without duplication or overlap and generally to ensure efficient and effective coordination. In addition, he would have responsibilities related to raising resources through donor consultations in order to meet identified needs.

157. In carrying out his functions, the Coordinator would establish the necessary consultative and coordinating bodies, comprised of representatives from United Nations agencies, donor Governments and NGOs, consolidating and building upon the already established coordination mechanisms in Cambodia, with which the appropriate Cambodian officials could be associated.

III. Computerization, information, training and recruitment requirements

158. Given the magnitude of UNTAC's mandate, and in order to operate efficiently, there will be a need for computerization of all of UNTAC's components. The election component has been mentioned in paragraphs 44

to 48 above. In relation to the military component, it will be necessary to keep detailed inventories of the personnel, arms and equipment of the Cambodian forces throughout the regroupment, cantonment, disarming and demobilization phases. The need to facilitate UNTAC's own deployment and logistical requirements will also be vast. All these elements should be integrated, in order to enhance the efficiency of the allocation and control of resources throughout the transitional period.

159. Special needs in the information sector will be presented in Cambodia. The rapid and effective flow of information between UNTAC and the grass-roots is essential to the successful fulfilment by UNTAC of its mandate. Radio appears to be the most efficient method of dissemination of the spoken word, but the radio broadcast facilities inside Cambodia are antiquated and deteriorated and at present the broadcast range covers only about half the Cambodian territory. Television would normally be the most effective means of dissemination, but broadcast facilities in Cambodia have a range of only about 75 kilometres from Phnom Penh. Video parlours are, however, very popular in the countryside. Print media are present, but printing facilities, supplies and distribution networks are inadequate and the impact of the written word is, in any case, hindered by low literacy rates. Print media are therefore most effective in urban areas and among school children.

160. All of the components of UNTAC will have information needs that are specific in nature and that cannot be adequately and effectively met under existing conditions. Certain of UNTAC's major information requirements in Cambodia can be immediately identified and include massive civic education campaigns in human rights, mine awareness and electoral matters. An additional major requirement will be programming to acquaint Cambodians with the Agreement, with UNTAC, its purposes, its activities and goals (generally and at specific stages of the process), its structure and personnel, etc. The object of this programming would be to establish and maintain UNTAC's credibility and thus to enhance its effectiveness and provide a vital means for fulfilling its mandate. Experience has shown that this is a key element enabling the success of missions of this type.

161. Because of the inadequacy of the existing infrastructure and facilities for meeting the very large information needs presented by UNTAC's mandate, it is foreseen that an important office within the UNTAC structure would be the UNTAC information office.

162. The information office at UNTAC headquarters would serve as the sole production point and conduit for information to be disseminated to the Cambodian population by UNTAC. By centralizing the information service in this way, it is expected that efficiency can be

enhanced. In addition to its overall programming coordination and review functions, the information office would be comprised of a production section, an audio-visual section, and a translation section. It is foreseen that the translation into Khmer of all materials for dissemination should also be centralized, in order to ensure consistency of terminology and message.

163. It is foreseen that the production and distribution/dissemination of radio and television programming, video cassettes, magazines, posters, fliers, textbook and other educational materials, the staging of cultural events and simulations, and the deployment of mobile information units (loudspeakers, video monitors, etc.) would be used by UNTAC in order to ensure that the message reaches Cambodians at all levels of society and in all parts of the country. By relying to a large extent upon the logistical facilities that will have to be provided to UNTAC generally in order to enable it to function at all, realistic, effective and cost-efficient UNTAC information machinery can be put into place.

164. Another of UNTAC's special needs will be for training. In this respect, a distinction must be drawn between that training which will fall within the UNTAC rehabilitation scheme generally and that which is essential to UNTAC in order to enable it to carry out its mandate. It is the scale of the latter which posits training as a special need of UNTAC. Indeed, as noted in various parts of the present report, training will be required at all levels in order to enable UNTAC to fulfil its mandate effectively and efficiently.

165. For international staff, general orientation regarding the mandate, structure, and procedures of UNTAC will be required, as well as specific training, as necessary, in the individual functions to be performed. Particular attention will be paid to the procedures and techniques to be applied for human rights oversight. Some mine-awareness and first-aid training will also be required. In addition, Khmer language training for international staff is foreseen.

166. Similar programmes will be required for locally recruited staff, although they will need to be undertaken on a much larger scale and their orientation may be somewhat different. Language training will be essential for local staff, especially for upgrading interpretation techniques. Clerical training, including the use of computers, will also be needed. Some managerial or other job-related training may also be required for certain levels of local staff, especially for the execution of the civil administration and elections mandates. Indeed, the electoral process will place heavy demands upon training in general, as mentioned above.

167. Training for non-UNTAC staff is also foreseen. The training in demining procedures will be carried out by the military component. On the civilian side, the training of political party agents regarding their role in the electoral process will be required. In the area of civil administration, some training in the content and application of the codes of conduct and guidelines to be provided is foreseen, including those related to human rights. Training of the civil police forces will be required, in law enforcement techniques and in human rights norms, as well as in the application of election-related regulations to be established by UNTAC.

168. It is foreseen that a training unit would be established at UNTAC headquarters and charged with development, implementation and coordination of all training needs. To the extent possible, a "train the trainers" approach would be followed. All manner of training materials, including manuals, other textual and audio-video materials, would be utilized. Classroom teaching and field training are both foreseen.

169. Another special need relates to recruitment. In this area, it may be necessary to resort to innovative means to ensure that UNTAC is fully and appropriately staffed. Conscious of the need to be as cost-effective as possible, heavy reliance will be placed upon locally available personnel. Considerations relating to language skills will have a bearing on this question, especially in the light of the fact that the number of Cambodians who speak a language other than Khmer is extremely low.

170. The staffing of the military component and of the component of UNTAC police monitors will follow the usual procedures. On the civilian side, every effort will be made to provide UNTAC with personnel from within the Organization. However, given the number of staff required, the disciplines and backgrounds needed, and the nature and duration foreseen for the mission, it may not be possible to staff UNTAC adequately from within the Organization. It may be possible to find some personnel with the appropriate qualifications in the specialized agencies of the United Nations system, with whom arrangements for secondment can be made. In other cases, Member States may be able to provide personnel to UNTAC.

171. Some of the staffing needs would be filled through the United Nations Volunteers programme. It is foreseen that the United Nations Volunteers would provide 400 volunteers to serve as the district electoral supervisors referred to in paragraph 43 above. The costs of these volunteers is taken into account in the information given in the addendum to the present report.

IV. Concluding remarks

172. Four essential conditions must be met if UNTAC is to be able to discharge its responsibilities effectively and with complete impartiality:

(a) First, UNTAC must at all times have the full support of the Security Council;

(b) Second, it must operate with the full cooperation, at all times, of the Cambodian parties and all other parties concerned;

(c) Third, it must enjoy full freedom of movement and communications. This should be embodied in separate status-of-mission agreements, to be concluded with the Supreme National Council and with the Governments of the neighbouring States in which UNTAC may be located;

(d) Fourth, the necessary financial resources must be provided by Member States in full and in a timely manner.

In this connection, the Secretary-General recommends that, should the Council decide to establish UNTAC, with the exceptions noted in the present report, the expenditures of the Mission should be considered as expenses of the Organization to be borne by Member States in accordance with Article 17, paragraph 2, of the Charter of the United Nations. The Secretary-General would therefore recommend to the General Assembly that the assessments to be levied on Member States should be credited to a special account to be established for this purpose.

Addendum (S/23613/Add.1)

Introduction

1. In paragraph 2 of my report to the Security Council on Cambodia 1/ I indicated my intention to issue as soon as possible an addendum to the report covering indicative administrative and financial aspects of the proposed plan. Given the complexity, size and scope of the United Nations Transitional Authority in Cambodia (UNTAC) the formulation of a detailed estimation of costs as requested by the Council in its resolution 718 (1991) of 31 October 1991 would necessarily be a time-consuming process. It was for this reason *inter alia* that I informed the Council of my intention to seek an initial appropriation of some US$ 200 million, which the General Assembly approved on 14 February 1992, so as to facilitate the timely deployment of UNTAC.

2. The estimates provided in the present addendum are preliminary and solely indicative of the order of magnitude of the eventual budget of UNTAC. These are subject to variations in the light of the ongoing collection and analysis of relevant data. It is my hope that these preliminary estimates would enable the Security Council to proceed with its consideration of the proposed implementation plan and authorize the establishment of UNTAC as soon as possible.

I. *Preliminary cost estimates*

3. The preliminary indicative costs of UNTAC, inclusive of the initial appropriation of US$ 200 million, are estimated at approximately $1,900 million gross ($1,876 million net). The costs of the repatriation programme are excluded from these estimates. I intend to launch a separate appeal for the further financing of this operation. I may, however, recommend alternative arrangements if there was to be a shortfall in funding the repatriation component. The annex to the present document contains a breakdown by major objects of expenditure.

General considerations and assumptions

4. The transitional period is defined in article I of the Agreement. 2/ Paragraph 1 of annex III to the Agreement foresees the creation of a new Cambodian Government within three months of the date of the election scheduled for late April–early May 1993, i.e. by 31 July 1993. Consequently, the estimates cover a period of approximately 15 months.

5. Based on the implementation plan and the reports of the survey missions, the structure and personnel requirements of UNTAC are as follows:

(a) UNTAC will be headed by the Special Representative of the Secretary-General, assisted by a deputy, an executive management, coordination and liaison team, human rights, political, legal and economic advisers and an information service. The number of international personnel required is estimated at 76, including support staff. In addition, UNTAC will have an administrative support division of some 450 international staff;

(b) The human rights and civil administration components, consisting of some 224 specialists, assisted by 84 international support staff, will exercise the functions outlined in sections II A and D of the implementation plan. They will operate at the central levels, from offices to be established at the 21 provincial and municipal centres and, particularly as regards dissemination of information and civic education, from offices at all of the estimated 200 districts in the country;

(c) The military component, headed by a Force Commander, will have a strength of about 15,900 all ranks, consisting of a force headquarters and sector headquarters staff, a military observer group of 485, an infantry element of 10,200 all ranks, a naval element of 376 and logistics and specialized support elements of about 4,500. The infantry element and the observer group will be reduced from 10,200 and 485 to 5,100 and 300 respectively by 30 September 1992 (see para. 89 of the implementation plan). A further gradual reduction would take place shortly after the elections;

1/ S/23613 [Document 30]
2/ S/23177 [Document 19]

Annex I UNTAC Election Calendar

ID	Name	1992												1993			
		Jan	Feb	Mar	Apr	May	Jun	Jul	Aug	Sep	Oct	Nov	Dec	Jan	Feb	Mar	Apr
1	Preparation of Legal Framework		▮														
2	Civic Education Programme Development			▮													
3	Conduct Civic Education Campaign																▮
4	Recruit International Staff (3 Waves)			▮				▮									
5	Train/Field Internat. Staff (3 Waves)				▮				▮								▮
6	Organization of Headquarters				▮												
7	Organization of Regional Offices					▮											
8	Deploy Internat. Teams, District Level									▮							
9	Final Location Registr. Places/Routes				▮												
10	Preparation of Training Programmes						▮										
11	Selection of Trainers						▮										
12	Training of Trainers								▮								
13	Select National Registration Officials						▮										
14	Train National Registration Officials								▮								
15	Registration of Voters										▮						
16	Temporary Registr. of Political Parties				▮												
17	Challenges (& Reserve Time for Registr.)												▮				
18	Train Party Observers									▮							
19	Formal Registration Political Parties											▮					
20	Registration of Candidates													▮			
21	Electoral Campaign														▮		
22	Cooling-off Period																▬
23	Selection of National Polling Officials														▮		
24	Training of National Polling Officials																▮
25	Election																▮ *

Annex II Proposed Schedule of Deployment - Military Component of UNTAC

	PREPARATORY STAGE							CANTONMENT AND DEMOBILIZATION PHASE				ELECTORAL PHASE							POST ELECTORAL PHASE	
	Nov 91	Dec 91	Jan 92	Feb 92	Mar 92	Apr 92	May 92	Jun 92	Jul 92	Aug 92	Sep 92	Oct 92	Nov 92	Dec 92	Jan 93	Feb 93	Mar 93	Apr 93	May 93	Jun 93	Jul 93
					D-12	D-8	D-4	D-Day										E-Day			
HQs									204												
INF BN*									10,200	or 12 batt				5,100	or 6 batt					2,550	or 3 batt
MILOBs**			50						485					330						50	
SIGNALS		38		63					582											38	
AIR		80							326											111	
ENGINEER		20		940					2,230											20	
LOGISTICS				125					872											125	
MEDICAL		6		15					541											6	
NAVY									376												
MILITARY POLICE									160					120						60	
TOTAL			UNAMIC 1,273						15,873			REGISTRATION		10,578						3,164	

D-Day Phase 2 Cease-fire starts (31 May 92)
D + 20 Demob 70% complete (30 Sep 92)
E-Day Election Day (end Apr 93)
*INF BN = Infantry battalions
**MILOBs = Military observers

(d) The police component will consist of some 3,600 civilian police monitors operating throughout the territory from offices to be established in 21 provincial/municipal centres and in some 200 district offices;

(e) The electoral component will consist of 72 international personnel operating from headquarters and 126 personnel at 21 provincial and municipal centres. Under the supervision of headquarters and provincial electoral personnel, 400 United Nations Volunteers will operate from each of the 200 districts. Electoral personnel will be supplemented by 800 Cambodian teams (4,000 personnel) during the three- to four-month period of registration of voters and, for the polling process, by 1,000 international supervisors and 8,000 Cambodian polling teams (56,000 personnel). The electoral component will be phased out shortly after the certification of the results of the election to be held late April/early May 1993.

6. All UNTAC components will be assisted by an estimated 7,000 locally recruited support personnel, including some 2,500 interpreters and by additional temporary staff as may be required for the conduct of the electoral process and other tasks.

II. *Concluding remarks*

7. It is my intention to ensure optimum efficiency in resource utilization. Accordingly, the activities of the support elements of UNTAC will be coordinated and integrated to the fullest extent possible. A coordination mechanism will be established to ensure a proper pooling of resources and planning of tasks on the basis of priority requirements of the whole mission.

Annex I
United Nations Transitional Authority in Cambodia
Provisional estimates of financial implications
(In thousands of United States dollars)

Summary statement

Serial	Main expenditure group	
1.	Military personnel costs	
(a)	Pay, allowances and travel	
	(i) Reimbursement to Governments for pay and allowance, at standard costs	200 650
	(ii) Daily allowance for troops	7 040
	(iii) Subsistence allowance for military observers, including travel	24 190
	(iv) Deduction for provision of accommodation	(1 580)
	(v) Troop emplacement, rotation and repatriation	24 300
	(vi) Welfare, leave allowance for troops	4 300
		258 900

Serial	Main expenditure group	
(b)	Other costs pertaining to military personnel	
	(i) Ration cost for troops	4 200
	(ii) Depreciation of contingent-owned equipment	50 700
	(iii) Compensation claims for death and disability	15 000
		106 900
	Subtotal 1	365 800
2.	Civilian personnel costs	
(a)	Civilian police monitors	
	(i) Subsistence allowance, including travel	195 750
	(ii) Deduction for provision of accommodation	(40 000)
		155 750
(b)	Staff members (and volunteers)	
	(i) Net salaries—international staff	60 600
	(ii) Net salaries—locally recruited staff	38 090
	(iii) Compensation—United Nations Volunteers	24 480
	(iv) Common staff costs, including travel to/from area	52 430
	(v) Other official travel	550
	(vi) Subsistence allowance	64 010
	(vii) Deduction for provision of accommodation	(14 300)
	(viii) Staff assessment	23 540
	(ix) Support account for peace-keeping operations at 8.5 per cent of total of items (i) to (viii)	21 200
		270 600
	Subtotal 2	426 350

3. Air operations
Provision is made for 18 fixed-wing aircraft (8 heavy cargo, 8 STOL-type and 2 command/liaison aircraft) and 32 helicopters (26 utility and 6 medium-lift helicopters) plus an additional 12 utility helicopters during the election period.

(a)	Charter cost for helicopters and fixed-wing aircraft	186 500
(b)	Aviation fuel	14 910
(c)	Air traffic control and navigational equipment, various airport services and ground handling charges	15 500
(d)	Additional air support during the election period	2 690
	Subtotal 3	219 600

Serial	Main expenditure group		Serial	Main expenditure group	

4. Transport operations
   - (a) Vehicle acquisition, including freight — 153 200
   - (b) Rental of vehicles — 2 160
   - (c) Spare parts, repairs and maintenance, for all vehicles, including contingent-owned — 25 000
   - (d) Petrol, oil and lubricants — 15 270
   - (e) Vehicle insurance — 1 500
   - (f) Workshop equipment — 6 000
   - (g) Water transportation
     - (i) Acquisition of patrol boats — 6 000
     - (ii) Hire of vessels — 5 000
     - (iii) Maintenance and operation of vessels — 1 500
     - (iv) Dredging and navigational supplies — 1 000
     - (v) Fuel for operation of vessels — 1 200
       - 14 700
   - Subtotal 4 — 217 830

5. Construction and maintenance of premises
   - (a) Acquisition of prefabricated buildings for offices and accommodation—including ablution and mess facilities, furniture, generators and waterpurification equipment plus freight and installation — 354 800
   - (b) Repairs of essential infrastructures, including bridge replacement — 36 500
   - (c) Engineer equipment — 17 740
   - (d) Rental of premises — 2 250
   - (e) Supplies and services for upkeep and maintenance — 4 500
   - (f) Utilities, including fuel for generators — 2 250
   - Subtotal 5 — 418 040

6. Communications
   - (a) Communications equipment — 44 460
   - (b) Communications spares and supplies, including contractual services for installations — 19 150
   - (c) Test and workshop equipment — 1 500
   - (d) Electrical supplies and hardware — 3 150
   - (e) Commercial communications costs, including pouch services — 5 940
   - Subtotal 6 — 74 200

7. Miscellaneous equipment
   - (a) Office furniture and equipment — 5 820
   - (b) Data-processing equipment — 10 505
   - (c) Observation equipment — 860
   - (d) Medical and dental equipment — 400
   - (e) Field defence equipment — 300
   - (f) Petrol tanks, pumps and metering devices — 2 400
   - (g) Generators for electoral registration teams — 160
   - (h) Miscellaneous other equipment — 2 400
   - (i) Parts for repair and maintenance of equipment — 2 010
   - (j) Equipment for public information — 3 145
   - Subtotal 7 — 28 000

8. Supplies and services
   - (a) Contractual services — 7 740
   - (b) Claims and adjustment — 1 000
   - (c) General stores — 15 660
   - (d) Clothing, uniforms and accoutrements — 1 800
   - (e) Medical and dental supplies — 1 900
   - (f) Field defence stores — 4 000
   - Subtotal 8 — 32 100

9. Assistance to factions a/
   - (a) Rehabilitation assistance to the demobilized military forces — 14 000
   - (b) Provision of food to the forces of the Cambodian parties, including transportation and distribution — 27 340
   - Subtotal 9 — 41 340

10. Training requirements
   - (a) For UNTAC personnel (see para. 164 of the implementation plan) — 5 350

11. Pre-implementation costs
   - (a) Requirements for the United Nations Advance Mission in Cambodia (UNAMIC), allocation for period up to 30 April 1992 — 33 640

a/ Reference is made to paragraph 154 of the implementation plan with respect to item (a) and paragraph 75 with respect to item (b).

(continued)

Serial	Main expenditure group		Serial	Main expenditure group	
12.	Air and surface freight		13.	Allowance for contingencies	
(a)	Charter of vessels for deployment and redeployment of vehicles, equipment and supplies of military contingents	17 250	(a)	Approximately 0.3 per cent of gross estimates	5 200
(b)	Airlift for deployment (other than personnel)	12 600		Grand total (gross)	1 900 000
(c)	Air and surface freight plus clearing charges, not included elsewhere in the estimates	3000	14.	Less—income from staff assessment	(24 000)
	Subtotal 12	32 850			
	Subtotal 1-12	1 894 800		Grand total (net)	1 876 000

Document 31

Security Council resolution on UNTAC and implementation of the Paris Agreements

S/RES/745 (1992), 28 February 1992

The Security Council,

Reaffirming its resolutions 668 (1990) of 20 September 1990, 717 (1991) of 16 October 1991, 718 (1991) of 31 October 1991 and 728 (1992) of 8 January 1992,

Reaffirming also its full support for the agreements signed in Paris on 23 October 1991 on a comprehensive political settlement of the Cambodia conflict, 1/

Taking note of the report of the Secretary-General on Cambodia of 19 and 26 February 1992 submitted pursuant to resolution 718 (1991), 2/

Desiring to contribute to the restoration and maintenance of peace in Cambodia, to the promotion of national reconciliation, to the protection of human rights and to the assurance of the right to self-determination of the Cambodian people through free and fair elections,

Convinced that free and fair elections are essential to produce a just and durable settlement to the Cambodia conflict, thereby contributing to regional and international peace and security,

Mindful of Cambodia's recent tragic history and determined that the policies and practices of the past will not be repeated,

Expressing appreciation for the work of the United Nations Advance Mission in Cambodia in the maintenance of the cease-fire, in mine awareness and mine clearance, and in preparation for the deployment of a United Nations Transitional Authority in Cambodia,

Noting with appreciation the efforts of His Royal Highness Prince Norodom Sihanouk and the Supreme National Council of Cambodia under his chairmanship in regard to the implementation of the provisions of the agreements,

Welcoming the appointment by the Secretary-General of a Special Representative for Cambodia to act on his behalf,

1. *Approves* the report of the Secretary-General on Cambodia of 19 and 26 February 1992 2/ containing his plan, which is subject to re-examination in the light of experience, for implementing the mandate envisaged in the agreements on a comprehensive political settlement to the Cambodia conflict signed in Paris on 23 October 1991; 1/

2. *Decides* that the United Nations Transitional Authority in Cambodia shall be established under its authority in accordance with the above-mentioned report for a period not to exceed eighteen months;

3. *Decides* that it is vital that elections be held in Cambodia by May 1993 at the latest as recommended by the Secretary-General in paragraph 38 of his report;

4. *Requests* the Secretary-General to deploy the Authority as rapidly as possible to implement the above decision, urges that both the deployment and the further implementation of his plan be done in the most efficient and cost-effective way possible, and invites him to that end to keep the operation under continuous review, bearing in mind the fundamental objectives of the agreements;

5. *Calls upon* the Supreme National Council of Cambodia to fulfil its special responsibilities set out in the agreements;

6. *Also calls upon* all parties concerned to comply scrupulously with the terms of the agreements, to cooperate fully with the Authority in the implementation of

1/ S/23177 [Document 19]
2/ S/23613 [Document 30]

its mandate, and to take all necessary measures to ensure the safety and security of all United Nations personnel;

7. *Further calls upon* the Supreme National Council of Cambodia and all Cambodians on behalf of the host country to provide all necessary assistance and facilities to the Authority;

8. *Strongly urges* the Cambodian parties to agree to the complete demobilization of their military forces prior to the end of the process of registration for the elections as well as to the destruction of the weapons and ammunition deposited into the Authority's custody in excess of those, if any, which may be deemed necessary by the Authority for the maintenance of civil order and national defence, or which may be required by the new Cambodian Government;

9. *Appeals* to all States to provide all voluntary assistance and support necessary to the United Nations and its programmes and specialized agencies for the preparations and operations to implement the Agreements, including for rehabilitation and for the repatriation of refugees and displaced persons;

10. *Requests* the Secretary-General to report to the Security Council by 1 June 1992 and subsequently to report to the Council in September 1992, January 1993, and April 1993 on progress to date in the implementation of the present resolution and on tasks still to be performed in the operation, with particular regard to the most effective and efficient use of resources;

11. *Decides* to remain seized of the matter.

Document 32

Letter dated 8 March 1992 from Prince Norodom Sihanouk to the Secretary-General pledging support for Security Council resolution 745 (1992) on the implementation of the provisions of the Paris Agreements

Not issued as a United Nations document; original in French

On behalf of the Supreme Council of Cambodia, the Cambodian people and myself, I express our deepest gratitude to you and the United Nations Security Council for resolution 745 (1992), which was adopted unanimously by the Council at its 3057th meeting on 28 February 1992.

We Cambodians for our part shall do everything possible to ensure specific support for and full implementation of this resolution, which is of such great importance and benefit for both the present and the future of our country and our nation.

Accept, Sir, the assurances of my highest consideration.

(signed) NORODOM SIHANOUK

Document 33

First progress report of the Secretary-General on UNTAC

S/23870, 1 May 1992

Introduction

1. By paragraphs 1 and 2 of its resolution 745 (1992), the Security Council approved the Secretary-General's report of 19 February 1992 (S/23613) containing my plan for implementing the mandate envisaged in the Agreements on a Comprehensive Political Settlement of the Cambodia Conflict, and established the United Nations Transitional Authority in Cambodia (UNTAC) under its authority to carry out the plan.

2. By paragraph 10 of the same resolution, the Council requested the Secretary-General to report to the Security Council at stated intervals on progress made in the implementation of the resolution and on tasks still to be performed in the operation, with particular regard to the most effective and efficient use of resources.

3. The first report of the Secretary-General was to be submitted by 1 June 1992. However, on the basis of my visit to Cambodia from 18 to 20 April 1992, I believe that this is an appropriate juncture for this first progress report.

I. Progress made to date in the implementation of resolution 745 (1992) and tasks still to be performed

A. *General*

4. UNTAC has made a generally good start in Cambodia. A constructive working relationship has been established with the Supreme National Council (SNC) and with its President, HRH Prince Norodom Sihanouk; the repatriation of refugees from the border camps began on 30 March 1992 and is continuing without major hindrance; the cease-fire has been restored in Kompong Thom province, which had recently been the scene of armed clashes, and United Nations troops have been deployed there to monitor the separation of forces; efforts have been made to reassure Cambodians that protection of their human rights will receive high priority; a country-wide survey has begun to gather the information required for the planning of the electoral process; and, during my visit to Cambodia, I issued an appeal for voluntary funds required to meet the rehabilitation needs of Cambodia. Also during my visit, I issued an appeal for States which had not yet done so to adhere to the Paris Agreements.

5. The arrival in Phnom Penh on 15 March 1992 of my Special Representative for Cambodia marked the initial deployment of UNTAC, which thereupon absorbed UNAMIC, the United Nations Advance Mission in Cambodia. Military units and personnel from a number of troop-contributing States have already arrived in the country and more are being deployed. UNTAC is therefore working towards an early start to Phase II of the cease-fire process (cantonment and demobilization phase). The date for this depends on the progress of military deployment and on the cooperation of the Cambodian parties.

6. The Phnom Penh authorities have agreed to provide some lodging facilities for the use of the Military Component, while the Party of Democratic Kampuchea has begun to remove restrictions on access by UNTAC to areas controlled by it and is permitting UNTAC to proceed with the reconnaissance and identification of sites for the regroupment and cantonment of forces.

B. *Relations with the Supreme National Council*

7. In accordance with article 3 of the Agreement on a Comprehensive Political Settlement of the Cambodia Conflict, signed in Paris on 23 October 1991, 1/ the SNC is the unique legitimate body and source of authority in which, throughout the transitional period, the sovereignty, independence and unity of Cambodia are enshrined. By article 6 of the Agreement, the SNC delegated to the United Nations all powers necessary to ensure the implementation of the Agreement, as described in annex 1 to the Agreement.

8. Proceeding on the basis of the relevant provisions of the Agreement, my Special Representative has taken the initiative in drawing up, in close consultation with Prince Norodom Sihanouk, President of the SNC, agendas for the SNC's meetings and in making proposals for consideration and adoption by the SNC. The SNC has also agreed, on the proposal of my Special Representative, to establish Technical Advisory Committees in a number of areas of UNTAC's responsibilities to function as subsidiary organs of the SNC with a view to recommending to it specific courses of action. Each Technical Advisory Committee will be chaired by a senior UNTAC official.

9. Since UNTAC began its deployment in Cambodia on 15 March 1992, the SNC has held a total of five meetings (on 16 March, 1 and 6 April, and two meetings on 20 April). As a result of initiatives taken by UNTAC at these meetings, the SNC has reached agreement on a number of matters necessary for the implementation of the plan. In addition, as a confidence-building measure and at the request of the SNC, UNTAC established on 1 April 1992 a "hot line" service linking the Special Representative and the Force Commander with a representative of each of the four Cambodian parties.

10. A more detailed report on progress achieved so far and tasks still to be performed by each component of UNTAC can be found below.

C. *Human rights component*

11. Following reports of violent incidents involving political figures, my Special Representative issued a statement on 19 March 1992 stressing UNTAC's determination, in accordance with article 16 of the Paris Agreement, to foster an environment in which human rights would be assured so as to permit the exercise of fundamental freedoms, including the right to participate in free and fair elections. In particular, it was stressed that preventing attacks on individuals, especially if they were politically motivated, and punishing those responsible for attacks that do occur, must be an important priority for the local authorities under UNTAC's supervision and control.

12. UNTAC has established a quick-response mechanism for investigating alleged human rights violations, composed of members of the human rights, civil administration and police components as appropriate. Some investigations have been completed and others are under way or pending.

13. The human rights component commenced its first training programmes for UNTAC police monitors in April and will use similar programmes, adapted as necessary, for local officials in the coming months.

1/ S/23177 [Document 30]

14. On 20 April 1992, I attended a meeting of the SNC at which its members, including Prince Norodom Sihanouk, signed instruments of accession to the International Covenant on Civil and Political Rights and the International Covenant on Economic, Social and Cultural Rights. This formal legal undertaking is the first of a series of measures designed to create a free and neutral political environment within Cambodia. At the meeting, I emphasized that it was now up to the Cambodian parties to take necessary measures to ensure that the principles contained in the Covenants are applied in a concrete manner.

D. *Electoral component*

15. My Special Representative presented the draft electoral law drawn up by UNTAC to the SNC at its meeting on 1 April. In accordance with the terms of the Paris Agreement, the draft deals specifically with those matters which, under section D of annex 1 to the Paris Agreement, will be the subject of legal prescription.

16. At the SNC meeting on 6 April, members discussed the draft and made comments to which my Special Representative replied in writing on 13 April 1992. A further round of comments was made at the second SNC meeting on 20 April 1992. This process of consultation will be completed as soon as possible and the draft law will thereafter be promulgated by UNTAC in accordance with paragraph 3 (a) of section D of annex 1 to the Paris Agreement.

17. Initial work on the compilation of socio-demographic and cartographic data required for the detailed planning of the election process is being undertaken by the Advance Election Planning Unit, which was established in late 1991 and has now been integrated into the electoral component of UNTAC. The Unit has now completed initial visits to 19 of the 21 provinces of Cambodia, and visits to the remaining two provinces (Koh Kong and Kompong Thom) will have been completed by the end of April.

18. By 1 May 1992, 10 regional coordinators will be deployed to follow up on these activities and begin the actual data collection needed for voter registration.

19. Planning and preparation for voter registration and polling is also proceeding. However, the arrangements made for the purchase of major items of equipment are hampered by the need to ensure compliance with the existing rules governing purchases, which could result in a deferral for some weeks of the commencement of voter registration.

E. *Military component*

20. As of the end of April 1992, the total number of troops deployed within Cambodia was 3,694. The functions of the military component were summarized in paragraph 54 of my report to the Security Council on the implementation of UNTAC (S/23613). Its activities to date are described below.

1. *Verification of the withdrawal and non-return of all categories of foreign forces and their arms and equipment*

21. As of the entry into force of the Agreement on 23 October 1991, all foreign forces, advisers and military personnel remaining in Cambodia, together with their weapons, ammunition and equipment, were to have been withdrawn. UNTAC's role in this connection is twofold: to set up a number of check-points along Cambodia's borders, including maritime surveillance through coastal and riverine operations, and to deploy mobile monitoring teams of military observers to investigate allegations of the presence of foreign forces.

22. In document S/23613 it was foreseen that, subject to further assessment, 24 check-points would be established as follows: seven along the border with Thailand, nine along the border with Viet Nam, two along the border with the Lao People's Democratic Republic, one each at the ports of Kompong Som and Phnom Penh and one each at the airports at Phnom Penh, Battambang, Siem Reap and Stung Treng. However, it may be necessary to modify either the total number of check-points to be established or their distribution along the various borders. A decision on this matter will be made once the detailed reconnaissance of all proposed sites which is now under way is complete. In the meantime, three check-points have already been established along the border with Viet Nam. In accordance with the plan, the military observers manning these check-points will be responsible for monitoring the cessation of outside military assistance to the Cambodian parties and the non-return of foreign forces.

2. *Supervision of the cease-fire and related measures, including regroupment, cantonment, disarming and demobilization*

23. The cease-fire has generally been maintained with the exception of Kompong hom, where forces of all four Cambodian parties are present and where a number of armed clashes have occurred since mid-January 1992. On 26 February, an UNTAC helicopter on a reconnaissance mission in that area came under fire and an officer of the Australian contingent was wounded. UNTAC investigation indicated that members of the National Army of Democratic Kampuchea (NADK) had been responsible for the incident. NADK has said that its own investigation showed that its members were not responsible. UNTAC subsequently restored the cease-fire in Kompong Thom and 200 United Nations troops were deployed in the town of Kompong Thom to verify it while opposing forces effected a withdrawal. The situation has since remained generally quiet. The United Nations pres-

ence in Kompong Thom has been expanded and now stands at a total of 244 United Nations troops.

24. Progress has also been made in the establishment of regroupment and cantonment areas. While a total of 52 cantonment areas were envisaged in document S/23613, following discussions with the Cambodian parties, it has been agreed to establish a total of 55 cantonment areas, as follows:

-33 cantonments for the Cambodian People's Armed Forces;

-14 cantonments for the National Army of Democratic Kampuchea;

-5 cantonments for the Khmer People's National Liberation Forces;

-3 cantonments for the National Army of Independent Kampuchea.

The Party of Democratic Kampuchea has begun to remove some of the restrictions it had been placing on UNTAC's freedom of movement in areas under its control. However, it is not yet certain whether UNTAC will have the full freedom of movement it requires in these areas to reconnoitre and identify regroupment and cantonment areas.

3. *Mine programmes*

25. As noted in document S/23613, "The magnitude of the mine problem in Cambodia requires that a sizeable and intense effort should be undertaken in the very early stages to facilitate UNTAC's deployment and its manifold activities" (para. 80). It should be pointed out that the prevalence of unexploded mines will be a problem in Cambodia for many years to come and must be addressed increasingly by Cambodians themselves.

26. With this in mind, at its meeting on 20 April 1992, the Supreme National Council agreed to the establishment of the Cambodian Mine Action Centre under the presidency of Prince Norodom Sihanouk and the vice-presidency of my Special Representative. The Cambodian Mine Action Centre will assist in undertaking, *inter alia*, long-term programmes in mine awareness, mine-marking and mine-clearance. It is to be managed by a 10-member Governing Council, which was established by the end of April 1992, with 5 Cambodian members to be appointed by Prince Norodom Sihanouk and 5 other members to be appointed by my Special Representative.

27. UNTAC has also deployed six mine-clearing training teams in north-western Cambodia with a further four teams preparing to commence training. Graduates of these courses have already begun mine-clearing operations, and it is estimated that 5,000 Cambodians will have been trained in mine-clearing by the end of the year. In accordance with the implementation plan, many of these will be former soldiers of the forces of the four Cambodian parties. Training and deployment of these demobilized soldiers will be an important element in rehabilitation and the creation of employment, as well as in the prevention of banditry.

28. It has become apparent that the United Nations will need to pay and equip these newly trained mine-clearing personnel. Funds will be required not only for monthly wages, but also for compensation for families in the case of death or disablement.

4. *Other activities*

29. In addition, the military component of UNTAC has provided security assistance for the repatriation of refugees from the camps on the Thai border in the form of convoy escorts and a security presence in each of the reception centres. It is anticipated that this requirement will decrease as the UNTAC military and police presence becomes more pervasive.

30. A good start has been made on the repair of roads and bridges in the north-western provinces with priorities based on the need to ensure access for all UNTAC components throughout the imminent rainy season. Work has commenced on the other urgent priority of preparing the airfields in Phnom Penh and the central and northern provinces for UNTAC use.

F. *Civil administration component*

31. Article 6 of the Agreement contains the general provisions governing UNTAC's mandate in civil administration. In this article, it is stipulated that the objective is to "ensure a neutral political environment conducive to free and fair general elections". The specific framework within which UNTAC is to carry out its civil administration mandate is provided in section B of annex 1 to the Agreement.

32. The civil administration component has initiated contacts with the existing administrative structure in order to prepare the control functions provided for in article 6 and in section B of annex 1 to the Agreement and to determine which other agencies should be placed under UNTAC supervision and control.

33. Recruitment of the staff required by this component has begun, but is proceeding rather slowly because of the high degree of specialization in the functions required to be performed. In the meantime, the SNC has substantially approved operating procedures for the exercise of the right of assembly and freedom of association drawn up by the civil administration component and proposed to the SNC by the Special Representative.

34. Control of the agencies, bodies and offices dealing with the Cambodian information media began by late April, when technical means for monitoring Cambodian broadcast news media were in place. The potential to monitor other Cambodian news media is to be fully realized by June. Meanwhile, UNTAC plans to establish a Cambodian media committee under its chairmanship

and with participation by Cambodian political groups in May. Also in May, UNTAC hopes to promulgate a code of media conduct to help ensure that freedom of the press and access to the media are fully respected in Cambodia and are not abused.

G. Police component

35. As of the end of April, a total of 193 civilian police monitors had arrived in Cambodia, and, in accordance with the recommendations contained in my implementation plan (S/23613), priority in their deployment has been given to Sisophon and Battambang, where Cambodian refugees and displaced persons are being resettled. Further deployments will take place in consultation with the Office of the United Nations High Commissioner for Refugees (UNHCR) as the repatriation process unfolds. In addition, civilian police monitors have been posted at the three border check-points established by the military component of UNTAC (see para. 22 above), and the remainder have been deployed in the Phnom Penh area. Additional deployment can be initiated as soon as the necessary logistic support is secured.

36. As noted in paragraph 113 of document S/23613, a number of factors are likely to affect the precarious security situation in Cambodia during the transitional period. The presence of United Nations civilian police monitors should, however, help to stabilize the situation. To date, Member States have agreed to provide a total of 1,903 police monitors. It is my earnest hope that, with the cooperation of Member States, the full complement of 3,600 personnel needed for the police component will be secured in view of its crucial role in the creation of an environment conducive to the holding of free and fair elections.

H. Repatriation component

37. As noted above, repatriation began on 30 March 1992 with the return to Cambodia of 526 men, women and children. They were welcomed at the reception centre at Sisophon in north-west Cambodia by Prince Norodom Sihanouk, my Special Representative and staff of UNHCR, which is organizing the operation.

38. During the first 10 days of April, repatriation proceeded at a reduced pace to test the logistical arrangements as well as the absorption capacity in Cambodia. After a brief interruption for the Cambodian new year, repatriation movements resumed on 21 April 1992 and arrival rates will be increased. As of the end of April, a total of 5,763 persons had returned.

39. However, the difficulty of finding suitable mine-free land for the returnees, the congestion of urban areas, the unsatisfactory health situation within the country and the delays expected to arise during the rainy season have raised concerns that a number of refugees and displaced persons will not be able to return to their homes in time to take part in the electoral process. Since, as noted in paragraph 149 of document S/23613, "the implementation and integrity of the electoral process is dependent upon the prior repatriation of Cambodian refugees and displaced persons", it is clear that maximum flexibility will have to be exercised in the search for viable options for reintegration if the refugees and displaced persons are to return in time to register for the election. A geographical widening of land settlement options and diversification of non-agricultural solutions offered to returnees are being actively pursued.

I. Rehabilitation component

40. The Paris Agreements include a Declaration on the Rehabilitation and Reconstruction of Cambodia and established guidelines for the resumption of international assistance to support the peace process and the institution of a democratic Government.

41. On 20 April 1992, in Phnom Penh, I formally launched the appeal to the international donor community to provide $593 million to Cambodia. The funds will be used for food, health services, shelter, education, training and the restoration of the country's basic infrastructure, public utilities and supportive institutions to initiate the process of rehabilitation during the transition period. Also included is the cost of repatriating the refugees from Thailand, which was the subject of an earlier appeal in the amount of $116 million.

42. Resource requirements for the rehabilitation period include $81 million for the resettlement and reintegration of the repatriated refugees as well as internally displaced persons and demobilized soldiers. In the category of essential services, $44 million is required for food security, seeds, draft animals and agricultural equipment; $40 million for health, nutrition, potable water and sanitation and $33 million for education and training. Another $150 million will be needed for repair and restoration of public utilities, roads, ports, railways and other major infrastructural works. Finally, in order to avert runaway inflation and the disintegration of the civil service, the appeal seeks $111 million in commodity aid and balance-of-payments support in order to help stabilize the economic and social situation in the country.

43. In order to amplify the coordinating role of the SNC in rehabilitation, a Technical Advisory Committee on rehabilitation has been set up. Cooperating agencies and bilateral donors will be encouraged to address their proposals to this Technical Advisory Committee, which will make recommendations to the plenary meeting of the SNC.

J. Information requirements

44. With regard to the dissemination of UNTAC information, an UNTAC information bulletin will begin

publication in May, and UNTAC will have access to existing radio transmission facilities in South-East Asia through which it will be able to broadcast UNTAC information and education programmes. At the same time, work will continue to identify the best means of disseminating UNTAC's message to the Cambodian population at large and to ensure that the public is fully informed of its rights and responsibilities in the matter of human rights and the electoral process as the mission unfolds. UNTAC radio programming will be produced by its information service in cooperation with other relevant components of UNTAC.

45. The staffing of the UNTAC information component has begun and is expected to accelerate rapidly beginning in late April.

II. Concluding remarks

46. In this first progress report, it can be stated that UNTAC has begun to establish itself both politically and militarily in Cambodia. Work on all aspects of the mission's activities is proceeding at varying rates and some successes have been recorded by each component. During my visit to Cambodia, I was impressed to observe the high calibre and efficiency of the troops who were already there. In that connection, I wish to express my appreciation to the Governments which so speedily provided these contingents. At the same time, UNTAC has faced difficulties and delays in deployment which, if not remedied,

could have a negative effect on the operation.

47. Since the arrival in Cambodia of my Special Representative on 15 March 1992, all senior officials of UNTAC have assumed their duties. However, the slow pace of the recruitment and deployment of civilian staff at the second and third echelons, particularly of the civil administration component, could impair UNTAC's ability to exercise adequate supervision and control where required. The pace of recruitment has, however, now accelerated.

48. The slower than expected pace of arrival of military contingents, and in particular the considerable difficulty experienced in securing and emplacing the equipment they need to bring with them, could also have an adverse impact on UNTAC's ability to maintain its tight schedule of operations. This would be the more regrettable in that much progress has been made in securing the cooperation of the parties.

49. Every effort is being made to address the difficulties mentioned in the present report and to discharge UNTAC's complex tasks within the time-frames envisaged in the implementation plan. However, I wish to note that the experience of mounting a large and complex United Nations operation such as UNTAC may point to the possible need to re-examine the manner in which existing financial and administrative rules and regulations of the Organization are applied to such operations.

Document 34

Note verbale dated 10 June 1992 from Viet Nam transmitting two notes dated 30 May 1992 sent to UNTAC by the Ministry of Foreign Affairs of Viet Nam

S/24082, 10 June 1992

The Permanent Representative of the Socialist Republic of Viet Nam to the United Nations presents his compliments to the Secretary-General of the United Nations and has the honour to request the latter to circulate as a document of the Security Council two notes dated 30 May 1992 and sent to the United Nations Transitional Authority in Cambodia by the Ministry of Foreign Affairs of the Socialist Republic of Viet Nam.

The full texts of the two notes are attached.

Annex I

Note verbale dated 30 May 1992 from the Ministry of Foreign Affairs of Viet Nam addressed to the United Nations Transitional Authority in Cambodia

The Ministry of Foreign Affairs of the Socialist Republic of Viet Nam presents its compliments to the United Nations Transitional Authority in Cambodia and has the honour to inform the latter of the following:

As early as 1982, Viet Nam started the partial withdrawal of its army volunteers out of Cambodia, and by 26 September 1989, Viet Nam completed the withdrawal of all Vietnamese volunteers, weapons and military equipment out of Cambodia. Since then, Viet Nam has had no military forces, weapons and military equipment on Cambodian territory. Neither has it reintroduced its forces, weapons and military equipment in any form into Cambodia.

This is Viet Nam's act of good will which constitutes an important contribution to the signing of the international agreement on a comprehensive political solution to the Cambodian problem in Paris on 23 October 1991.

At the 21 October 1991 session of the coordinating committee of the Paris International Conference on Cambodia, Mr. Rafeeuddin Ahmed, United Nations Under-Secretary-General explained that article 6, annex 2 which provides for information that should be supplied to UNTAC only concerns foreign forces present in Cambodia at the time of the signing of this agreement. Co-President of the International Conference on Cambodia, French Foreign Minister Roland Dumas also reaffirmed this in the conference closing speech. Therefore, article 6, annex 2 of the agreement does not concern Viet Nam.

The Ministry of Foreign Affairs of the Socialist Republic of Viet Nam wishes to inform UNTAC of these facts so that the latter can complete its documents for the second phase of the cease-fire.

The Ministry of Foreign Affairs of the Socialist Republic of Viet Nam avails itself of this opportunity to, once again, resolutely reject all allegations of the presence of Vietnamese troops in Cambodia which are aimed at covering up attempts to undermine the implementation of the Paris Agreement.

Annex II
Note verbale dated 30 May 1992 from the Ministry of Foreign Affairs of Viet Nam addressed to the United Nations Transitional Authority in Cambodia

The Ministry of Foreign Affairs of the Socialist Republic of Viet Nam presents its compliments to the United Nations Transitional Authority in Cambodia and has the honour to bring to the latter's notice that:

By way of implementing paragraph B, article 7, annex 2 of the Paris Agreement on a comprehensive political settlement of the Cambodian conflict signed on 23 October 1991 and as a signatory to the agreement and a neighbour which shares border with Cambodia, Viet Nam wishes to reaffirm that:

Viet Nam has ceased its military assistance to Cambodia since September 1989 and has not allowed any country to use its territory for the purpose of providing military assistance to the Cambodian parties.

On Vietnamese territory, there are no military forces, weapons, ammunition and military equipment of any Cambodian parties.

Document 35

Special report of the Secretary-General on UNTAC and phase II of the cease-fire

S/24090, 12 June 1992

1. In my first progress report on the United Nations Transitional Authority in Cambodia (UNTAC) of 1 May 1992 (S/23870 and Corr.1 and 2), I stated that UNTAC, under the leadership of my Special Representative, Mr. Yasushi Akashi, had made a generally good start in Cambodia. I referred, *inter alia*, to the fact that the cease-fire had been restored in Kompong Thom Province, which had been the scene of recent armed clashes, and that the Party of Democratic Kampuchea had begun to remove restrictions on access by UNTAC to areas controlled by it. I added, however, that it was not yet certain whether UNTAC would have the full freedom of movement it required in those areas to reconnoitre all the locations selected for regroupment and cantonment of the forces of the Party of Demo-

cratic Kampuchea, the National Army of Democratic Kampuchea (NADK).

2. Subsequently, on 9 May, the Commander of the military component of UNTAC, Lieutenant-General John Sanderson, announced that phase II of the cease-fire would begin on 13 June 1992 at 0800 hours. General Sanderson took this step in consultation with the four Cambodian parties and after having obtained from each of them assurances that it would:

(a) Grant freedom of movement to UNTAC personnel, vehicles and aircraft;

(b) Mark minefields in the areas under its control;

(c) Provide to UNTAC by 20 May 1992 information on its troops, arms, ammunition and equipment;

(d) Adhere to the Paris Agreement (S/23177, annex) and in particular:

(i) Not interfere with troops moving to regroupment and cantonment areas;

(ii) Inform its troops of the plan for regroupment and cantonment and the dates and times specified therein.

3. However, in the days following General Sanderson's announcement, it became increasingly clear that the Party of Democratic Kampuchea was not taking the steps necessary to enable it to honour the assurances that it had given. In particular, there was continuing interference with UNTAC's freedom of movement, including obstruction of the deployment of the Netherlands battalion in areas controlled by NADK. At the meeting of the Supreme National Council of Cambodia held on 26 May 1992, my Special Representative again underlined the crucial need for all the Cambodian parties scrupulously to fulfil their obligations as set forth in the Paris Agreements in order to ensure the successful implementation of phase II. He called on the four parties, and the Party of Democratic Kampuchea in particular, to show that they were prepared to enter phase II by taking the following steps:

(a) Permit full and unrestricted freedom of movement to UNTAC in the zones they control;

(b) Refrain from further violations of the cease-fire in Kompong Thom, Kompong Cham and elsewhere;

(c) Mark minefields as required and not to undertake renewed mining;

(d) Stand down from their aggressive postures in Kampot;

(e) Cooperate fully with UNTAC in the reconnaissance of the remaining cantonment sites;

(f) Provide forthwith detailed information on the troops, arms and ammunition to be committed to regroupment and cantonment;

(g) Refrain from including in their radio broadcasts misinformation about UNTAC activities and intentions;

(h) Establish proper commander-to-commander relationships at UNTAC's request;

(i) Inform their forces by using all possible means of communication that phase II will begin at 0800 hours on 13 June and to tell their forces what to do in order to meet the requirements of phase II;

(j) Ensure that all their troops maintain their present positions pending movement to the designated regroupment areas;

(k) Arrange for all their forces, with all their arms, ammunition and equipment, to report to regroupment areas by 27 June, that is, within two weeks from the beginning of phase II;

(l) Then undertake a phased and balanced demobilization of at least 70 per cent of their forces.

Mr. Akashi called on the representatives of the parties to provide at the next meeting of the Supreme National Council on 5 June, if not before, assurances of full compliance with the provisions of the Paris Agreement relating to phase II of the cease-fire and detailed information on the steps they had taken to implement the 12 points.

4. The Party of Democratic Kampuchea's response to this appeal was not reassuring. In particular, in an incident on 30 May 1992, when my Special Representative, the Force Commander, and other senior UNTAC officials were visiting Pailin in the west of the country, NADK personnel prevented them from proceeding from Pailin to the Thai border. On 3 June, I addressed a personal appeal to H.E. Mr. Khieu Samphan, member of the Supreme National Council, urging that the Party of Democratic Kampuchea take the steps necessary to enable UNTAC to begin implementation of phase II on 13 June. I, of course, informed HRH Prince Norodom Sihanouk of this action. A reply from Mr. Khieu Samphan was received on 5 June, which, to my regret, did not contain the requested assurances from the Party of Democratic Kampuchea.

5. At the meeting of the Supreme National Council held on 5 June 1992, my Special Representative once again called on the parties in the strongest terms for full compliance with the provisions of the Paris Agreements and requested them to inform him of the steps they had taken to implement the 12 points. Positive responses were forthcoming from three of the parties, but the Party of Democratic Kampuchea failed to provide the information requested.

6. On 9 June, my Special Representative received a letter from the Party of Democratic Kampuchea stating that it was not in a position to allow UNTAC forces to proceed with their deployments in the areas under its control.

7. At the most recent meeting of the Supreme National Council, on 10 June 1992, my Special Representative reaffirmed the need for the parties to honour the obligations which they had accepted when they signed the Agreements in Paris. He also recalled the importance the international community attached to those Agreements and their full and correct implementation and the significant resources it was contributing to the restoration of peace and stability in Cambodia. He called once more on the Party of Democratic Kampuchea to meet in full its obligations under the Paris Agreements, to comply with the 12 points he had listed at the meeting of the Supreme National Council on 26 May and to enter phase II of the cease-fire on 13 June as agreed. The representative of the Party of Democratic Kampuchea again failed to respond positively.

8. I have taken advantage of the presence of many world leaders at the United Nations Conference on Environment and Development in Rio de Janeiro to convey to a number of them my deep concern about the problems that have arisen over implementation of phase II and I have sought their help in support of my own efforts to ensure that the timetable will be strictly adhered to by all the Cambodian parties.

9. Implementation of the Paris Agreements has thus reached a critical stage. I find it necessary to draw this to the Security Council's attention so that the Council can consider what action it might appropriately take to ensure that UNTAC receives the cooperation it needs and in particular that the timetable for implementation is adhered to.

10. The vital importance of starting phase II on 13 June as announced cannot be overemphasized. This is crucial in order to ensure that various interrelated processes—cantonment, disarmament and demobilization, repatriation and elections—can proceed within the timeframe envisaged in the implementation plan (S/23613) and that free and fair elections take place, as scheduled, in April/May 1993. To that end, every possible effort has been made to overcome major logistic difficulties and to deploy the bulk of the military component of UNTAC in Cambodia before 13 June. As of 12 June, over 10,000 troops have arrived in Cambodia, with a further 1,000 scheduled to arrive by 13 June, and more scheduled to arrive by the end of June.

11. However, UNTAC's ability to adhere to the timetable is gravely compromised by lack of cooperation from the Party of Democratic Kampuchea. Two of the other parties have provided, as required and on time, the necessary information on the number of their troops, arms, ammunition and equipment to be cantoned and the third has made a bona fide effort to comply substantially. The Party of Democratic Kampuchea on the other hand has failed to provide this information to UNTAC. NADK has also continued to deny full access and freedom of movement to UNTAC, preventing it from conducting reconnaissance of 6 of the 16 cantonment sites envisaged for NADK. It has also failed to mark minefields in areas under its control and has remined some areas. UNTAC believes NADK to have been responsible for many of the cease-fire violations that have continued to occur in the provinces of Kompong Thom, Kompong Cham and elsewhere.

12. In explanation of its failure to comply with UNTAC's requirements, the Party of Democratic Kampuchea has asserted that foreign military personnel remain present in Cambodia and that, until their withdrawal and non-return has been verified by UNTAC, its own security requires that fulfilment of the above-men-tioned obligations must be deferred. While firmly rejecting this view, UNTAC has taken a number of steps designed to help to allay any legitimate security concerns. It has established 10 border checkpoints, one more than envisaged in the implementation plan, on the Cambodia-Viet Nam border at an earlier date than specified in the Agreement. It has invited the representatives of the four parties to participate in manning the checkpoints. On 30 May it launched mobile military teams empowered to carry out investigations of any alleged violations of the provisions of annex 2 to the Paris Agreement, including allegations of the presence of foreign forces, and invited the parties to submit any such allegations to it. On 1 June, the Party of Democratic Kampuchea submitted in writing a list of allegations regarding the presence of foreign forces in Cambodia. In accordance with annex 2, article VI, paragraph 2, of the Paris Agreement, UNTAC requested the Party of Democratic Kampuchea to make personnel available to accompany UNTAC's investigations of these allegations. The Party of Democratic Kampuchea has so far failed to comply with that request.

13. Following the unsatisfactory outcome of the meetings of the Supreme National Council on 5 and 10 June 1992, the question arose of whether 13 June 1992 should be maintained as the date for implementation of phase II of the cease-fire, given that it depends critically on the cooperation of all parties and would not be sustainable for more than a brief period without such cooperation. After careful consideration, I have concluded that phase II of the cease-fire must proceed as scheduled on 13 June. Any significant delay in the implementation of the military aspects of the plan would result in a loss of the momentum that has been carefully built up in recent weeks and would jeopardize UNTAC's ability to organize and conduct the elections by April or May 1993. My Special Representative is accordingly consulting the three parties which have expressed their readiness to begin the regroupment and cantonment of their forces, in order to ensure that this process is conducted in a manner which would minimize any military disadvantage they would suffer *vis-à-vis* the fourth party.

14. However, this can be only a short-term solution and it is imperative that all efforts should now be made to persuade the Party of Democratic Kampuchea to join the other parties, in good faith, in implementing the comprehensive political settlement to which the international community has committed so much diplomatic effort and such substantial human and material resources. The Security Council may itself wish to consider what action it could take to achieve this objective.

Document 36

Statement by the President of the Security Council concerning difficulties encountered by UNTAC in implementation of the Paris Agreements

S/24091, 12 June 1992

Having read the report of the Secretary-General (S/24090), the Security Council is deeply concerned by the difficulties that the United Nations Transitional Authority in Cambodia (UNTAC) is encountering in the implementation of the Paris Agreements, 1/ on the eve of moving to the second phase of the cease-fire. In particular, the Council notes that, during the meeting of the Supreme National Council on 10 June 1992, one party was not able to allow the necessary deployment of UNTAC in areas under its control. The Council believes that any delay could jeopardize the whole peace process to which all Cambodian parties have agreed under the auspices of the United Nations and the Paris Conference.

The Council reaffirms the importance of the full and timely implementation of the Paris Agreements. The Council commends the efforts of the Secretary-General's Special Representative and UNTAC in this regard. It reaffirms that the Supreme National Council, under the chairmanship of HRH Prince Norodom Sihanouk, is the unique legitimate body and source of authority in which, throughout the transitional period, the sovereignty, independence and unity of Cambodia are enshrined. In this regard, section III of part I of the Paris Agreements should be implemented as soon as possible.

The Council stresses the need that the second phase of the military arrangements should begin on 13 June 1992, as determined in accordance with the Agreements. In this connection, the Council urges the Secretary-General to accelerate the deployment of the full UNTAC peace-keeping force to Cambodia and within the country.

The Council calls upon all parties to comply strictly with the commitments they have accepted, including cooperation with UNTAC. It specifically calls upon all parties to respond affirmatively to the latest demands for cooperation in implementation of the Agreements put to them by UNTAC.

1/ S/23177

Document 37

Letter dated 24 June 1992 from Japan transmitting Tokyo Declaration on the Cambodia Peace Process and the Tokyo Declaration on the Rehabilitation and Reconstruction of Cambodia, issued at the conclusion of the Ministerial Conference on the Rehabilitation and Reconstruction of Cambodia, 22 June 1992

A/47/285-S/24183, 25 June 1992

I have the honour to transmit herewith the texts of the Tokyo Declaration on the Cambodia Peace Process (annex I) and the Tokyo Declaration on the Rehabilitation and Reconstruction of Cambodia (annex II), issued at the conclusion of the Ministerial Conference on the Rehabilitation and Reconstruction of Cambodia on 22 June 1992.

I should be grateful if the text of the present letter and its annexes were circulated as a document of the General Assembly, under item 126 of the preliminary list, and of the Security Council.

(*signed*) Yoshio HATANO

Ambassador Extraordinary and Plenipotentiary

Permanent Representative of Japan
to the United Nations

Annex I

Tokyo Declaration on the Cambodia Peace Process, issued at the conclusion of the Ministerial Conference on the Rehabilitation and Reconstruction of Cambodia on 22 June 1992

We, the representatives of Australia, Austria, Belgium, Brunei Darussalam, Cambodia, Canada, China, Denmark, Finland, France, Germany, India, Indonesia, Ireland, Italy, Japan, the Lao People's Democratic Republic, Malaysia, the Netherlands, New Zealand, Norway, the Philippines, Portugal, the Republic of Korea, the Russian Federation, Singapore, Spain, Sweden, Switzerland, Thailand, the United Kingdom of Great Britain and Northern Ireland, the United States of America, Viet Nam, the European Community, and the Special Representative of the Secretary-General of the United Nations for Cambodia,

Meeting at the Ministerial Conference on the Rehabilitation and Reconstruction of Cambodia (MCRRC) on 20 and 22 June 1992, hosted by the Government of Japan and co-chaired by the host and the United Nations Development Programme (UNDP),

Adopted the following declaration:

1. We exchanged views on and assessed the status of the implementation of the Paris Agreements ("the Agreements").

We note that, despite all the difficulties involved, substantial progress has been made in the implementation of the Agreements. In this regard, we pay high tribute to the eminent role played by His Royal Highness Prince Norodom Sihanouk as the President of the Supreme National Council of Cambodia (SNC), and commend the efforts of Mr. Yasushi Akashi, the Special Representative of the Secretary-General of the United Nations for Cambodia and the Head of the United Nations Transitional Authority in Cambodia (UNTAC) and his staff.

2. We stress the imperative need for the Cambodian parties to renew their commitment to the cease-fire and related measures under the Agreements, and call upon all Cambodian parties concerned to refrain from hostilities and to resolve, in good faith and in a spirit of cooperation, any disputes through peaceful means.

3. We welcome the accession of the SNC, signed by all its members, to the International Covenants on Civil and Political Rights and on Economic, Social and Cultural Rights, and reaffirm the importance of safeguarding respect for and observance of human rights and fundamental freedoms in Cambodia.

4. (a) We reaffirm the vital importance of holding free and fair elections in the spring of 1993 as scheduled, and welcome the progress that UNTAC, in cooperation with SNC, is making in preparing a new electoral law and taking other steps necessary for the holding of free and fair elections;

(b) We stress the importance of the repatriation and resettlement of Cambodian refugees and displaced persons, particularly in relation to the elections set for the next spring. In this connection, we note with appreciation the efforts of the Office of the United Nations High Commissioner for Refugees (UNHCR) as lead agency, in close coordination with other international organizations, the countries concerned, and relevant nongovernmental organizations, for the repatriation and resettlement of Cambodian refugees and displaced persons. We recognize the extremely difficult circumstances under which repatriation and resettlement are being conducted and pledge our continued support for such efforts.

5. (a) Mindful of the statement of the President of the Security Council of the United Nations of 12 June 1992, we stress the importance of the full and timely implementation of the Agreements and the need for compliance by all the signatories with the provisions of the Agreements to allow UNTAC to exercise, in consultation with SNC, all the powers with which it is mandated by the Agreements, in accordance with the mechanisms and time schedule set therein;

(b) We welcome the commencement of the second phase of the cease-fire on 13 June. We, however, express our serious concern over the difficulties UNTAC is encountering in the implementation of the Agreements, in particular over the refusal of one party to allow the necessary deployment of UNTAC prior to and since the commencement of the second phase of the cease-fire in the areas under its control. We call upon that party to cooperate with UNTAC in the full and timely implementation of the second phase of the cease-fire and to meet promptly its obligations under the Agreements;

(c) We emphasize the need for the Secretary-General of the United Nations to accelerate the deployment of the full UNTAC peace-keeping forces to Cambodia and within the country.

6. We stress the need for UNTAC to exercise its mandate under articles 6 and 7 of the Agreement on a Comprehensive Political Settlement of the Cambodia Conflict, and under sections A and B, among others, of annex 1 to that Agreement, to ensure a neutral political environment.

To this end, we urge the Secretary-General of the United Nations to recruit and deploy in Cambodia all essential United Nations civil administration personnel as soon as possible.

7. We confirm that we will render, in accordance with the Agreements, all necessary support and cooperation so that UNTAC may fulfil its mandate and that the second phase may proceed as scheduled. In this respect,

we stress the importance of timely financial contributions and the provision of personnel.

8. We call upon the Security Council of the United Nations, the Secretary-General of the United Nations and the two Co-Presidents of the Paris Conference to continue to monitor carefully the implementation of the Agreements, as provided by the Agreements.

9. Through this Declaration, we intend to give a clear signal that there is full international support for the peace process and to reaffirm the importance we attach to its effective and expeditious implementation.

Annex II

Tokyo Declaration on the Rehabilitation and Reconstruction of Cambodia, issued at the conclusion of the Ministerial Conference on the Rehabilitation and Reconstruction of Cambodia on 22 June 1992

We, the representatives of Australia, Austria, Belgium, Brunei Darussalam, Cambodia, Canada, China, Denmark, Finland, France, Germany, India, Indonesia, Ireland, Italy, Japan, the Lao People's Democratic Republic, Malaysia, the Netherlands, New Zealand, Norway, the Philippines, Portugal, the Republic of Korea, the Russian Federation, Singapore, Spain, Sweden, Switzerland, Thailand, the United Kingdom of Great Britain and Northern Ireland, the United States of America, Viet Nam, the European Community, the United Nations Transitional Authority in Cambodia (UNTAC), the United Nations Children's Fund (UNICEF), the United Nations Development Programme (UNDP), the World Food Programme (WFP), the Office of the United Nations High Commissioner for Refugees (UNHCR), the International Labour Organisation (ILO), the Food and Agriculture Organization of the United Nations (FAO), the United Nations Educational, Scientific and Cultural Organization (UNESCO), the World Health Organization (WHO), the World Bank, the International Monetary Fund (IMF) and the Asian Development Bank (ADB),

Meeting at the Ministerial Conference on the Rehabilitation and Reconstruction of Cambodia (MCRRC) on 20 and 22 June 1992, hosted by the Government of Japan and co-chaired by the host and UNDP,

Adopted the following declaration:

Socio-economic situation in Cambodia

1. We recognize that Cambodia suffers from the devastation of a 20-year-long war, which resulted in the destruction of its basic infrastructure, deterioration of living standards, lack of human resources and a serious fiscal deficit. In order to undertake full-scale rehabilitation and reconstruction which would bring about economic and social stability in Cambodia, external assistance, both technical and financial, is indispensable.

Guidelines for assistance in Cambodia

2. We consider that the following points must be taken note of in proceeding to assist in the rehabilitation and reconstruction of Cambodia:

(a) Successful implementation of the rehabilitation and reconstruction assistance effort for Cambodia as a whole is highly dependent on strict adherence to the Agreements reached at the Paris Conference on 23 October 1991;

(b) The main responsibility for the rehabilitation and reconstruction of Cambodia rests with the Cambodian people, and international assistance for rehabilitation and reconstruction should be supportive of the self-help efforts of the Cambodian people themselves;

(c) Assistance for rehabilitation and reconstruction should be made available impartially, with full regard for Cambodia's sovereignty, benefit all regions of Cambodia and reach all levels of society and the most needy sectors of the population;

(d) During the transitional period, as referred to in the Agreements, in addition to emergency humanitarian assistance—including de-mining—and rehabilitation assistance with quick impact, ground work for longer-term assistance, which addresses priority needs, should be initiated;

(e) Contributors should take into consideration the priorities identified in paragraph 10 of the Paris Declaration on the Rehabilitation and Reconstruction of Cambodia (food security, health, housing, training, education, the transport network and the restoration of Cambodia's existing basic infrastructure and public utilities) and developed in the report entitled "Cambodia, socio-economic situation and immediate needs", which was jointly prepared by UNDP, the World Bank, IMF and ADB and based on the results of special missions carried out by these four organizations and other agencies, and the consolidated appeal, issued on 20 April 1992 by the United Nations Secretary-General, concerning the rehabilitation of Cambodia;

(f) In the implementation of assistance programmes, due regard should be paid to possible adverse effects on the environment; due consideration should also be given to measures which will improve the social and cultural conditions of the Cambodian people, in particular those of disadvantaged groups, and the roll of women.

Achievements to date

3. (a) We welcome the substantial and generous sums pledged during the MCRRC for the rehabilitation and reconstruction of Cambodia. We take note of the fact that the Secretary-General's consolidated appeal for Cambodia's needs of April 1992 outlined the most urgent needs to be met during the rehabilitation period. The

pledges made at the MCRRC, including ongoing commitments, amount to US$ 880 million, including medium-term needs. This is a clear manifestation of the determination and willingness of the international community to assist in the rehabilitation of Cambodia. We express our resolve to implement without delay the commitments already made and we sincerely hope that the rehabilitation and reconstruction of Cambodia will proceed in a timely and satisfactory manner;

(b) We highly appreciate the role of the non-governmental organizations, which have been extensively engaged in activities to meet the humanitarian needs in Cambodia. We express our strong hope that the experience and expertise of the non-governmental organizations will continue to be utilized in the process of rehabilitation and reconstruction.

International support mechanism

4. During the transitional period, the authority representing Cambodia regarding international assistance is the Supreme National Council of Cambodia (SNC), in accordance with the terms of the Paris Agreements. We welcome the statement by UNTAC regarding the procedure for the clearance of rehabilitation projects, as expressed at the SNC meeting of 10 June 1992, which also stressed the need to maintain the closest dialogue with all the Cambodian parties in helping to coordinate all assistance. We encourage the countries and organizations concerned to provide the necessary information and to consult with the UNTAC Director for Rehabilitation at Phnom Penh, so that during the transitional period the assistance of bilateral and international organizations will be implemented effectively and without duplication. The Director will monitor such assistance in order to advise contributors on the overall progress of the rehabilitation programme.

5. We agree to establish a consultative body to be called the "International Committee on the Reconstruction of Cambodia" (ICORC), which will be an international mechanism for coordinating, in consultation with the Government of Cambodia when formed after free and fair elections, the medium- and long-term assistance for the reconstruction of Cambodia, the framework of which is described in the appendix to the present declaration. ICORC will be open to countries and international organizations contributing to the medium- and long-term reconstruction of Cambodia, bilaterally, multilaterally, or through tripartite or other arrangements. It will be chaired by Japan, and in principle will be convened annually, with the venue normally alternating between Tokyo and Paris. The first meeting of ICORC will be convened by the chair-country at an appropriate time prior to the holding of elections.

6. We welcome the recent initiative taken by the international financial community towards supporting the normalization of Cambodia's relations with international financial institutions.

We also welcome the announcement made by the representative of Cambodia at the Conference to take the necessary steps to facilitate the normalization of its relationships with the international financial institutions.

Issues for the development of Cambodia's economy in the future

7. International financial institutions stressed the importance of market-based reforms in Cambodia to increasing output in major sectors of the economy, which has yet to regain the levels of nearly a quarter of a century ago. In Cambodia, there remain fundamental institutional and policy-related constraints to further economic progress which must be addressed promptly. We stress our resolve and willingness to extend appropriate assistance, including technical assistance, to Cambodia during the rehabilitation period, as well as the reconstruction phase, through appropriate approaches that ensure and strengthen Cambodia's own capacity to sustain its development.

8. We are hopeful that, with the assistance now envisaged for the rehabilitation period, as well as the reconstruction phase, Cambodia can expand and diversify its external trade and investment relationships, so that it will be integrated into the dynamic economic development of the Asia-Pacific region and of the world.

Appendix
Framework of the International Committee on the Reconstruction of Cambodia

1. The International Committee on the Reconstruction of Cambodia (ICORC) will be a long-term consultative body that will provide a forum through which contributors can exchange views and information with the Cambodian authorities, with the objective of coordinating better the international assistance for the reconstruction of Cambodia.

2. ICORC is expected to enable the Government of Cambodia, to be formed after free and fair elections, to put its views before the contributors and to facilitate its planning, with advance notice of aid levels and aid priorities to be provided by the contributors. It is also expected to enable the contributors to consult with and advise the Cambodian authorities on development requirements, which would be helpful for the contributors in setting their own aid levels and priorities for the benefit of Cambodia.

3. An important role of ICORC will be to provide an occasion for the coordination of assistance to Cambodia to develop an institutional economic and social planning and aid-management capacity necessary for the

successful implementation of the reconstruction programme.

4. The membership of ICORC will be open to all countries and international organizations contributing to the long-term reconstruction of Cambodia.

5. After its formation, the Government of Cambodia will be represented at all meetings of ICORC.

6. During the transitional period, Cambodia will be represented by a delegation representing the Supreme National Council of Cambodia. The Special Representative of the Secretary-General of the United Nations for Cambodia will also be represented.

7. Representatives of non-governmental organizations active in Cambodia, and nominated by the NGO Coordination Committee for Cambodia, will be welcome to present their views as observers at meetings of ICORC.

8. Japan will convene and chair the meetings of ICORC, which will be conducted annually, unless the convener, in consultation with participating countries and international organizations, agrees otherwise.

9. During the transitional period, UNDP, in cooperation with UNTAC and other relevant international agencies, will provide technical and secretariat support to ICORC. This role will subsequently be assumed by an international organization or organizations invited to do so by the Government of Cambodia, formed after free and fair elections.

10. The venue for ICORC meetings will normally alternate between Tokyo and Paris. The convener, in consultation with participating countries and international organizations, may determine to convene meetings in other venues, such as Phnom Penh.

Document 38

Letter dated 27 June 1992 from Mr. Khieu Samphan, member of the Supreme National Council, transmitting proposal of the Party of Democratic Kampuchea (PDK) on cooperation between UNTAC and the Supreme National Council

Not issued as a United Nations document

The talks and proceedings in Tokyo, in conjunction with the Ministerial Conference on the Reconstruction and Rehabilitation of Cambodia, have led to the identification of a certain number of points in common in the efforts for the fair and impartial implementation of the Paris Agreements.

The Party of Democratic Kampuchea sincerely appreciates this development.

I have the honour to submit herewith for your consideration the proposals of the Party of Democratic Kampuchea concerning the measures to be taken to promote close and effective cooperation between UNTAC and the Supreme National Council of Cambodia in implementation of the Paris Agreements.

Accept, Sir, the assurances of my highest consideration.

(*signed*) Khieu SAMPHAN

SNC member

President of the Party of
Democratic Kampuchea

**Proposal of the Democratic Kampuchea Party
on the cooperation between UNTAC and the SNC**

27 June 1992

I. *Common grounds reached at Tokyo*

The Cambodian parties and other concerned parties, taking advantage of the time available at the Tokyo Ministerial Conference on Rehabilitation and Reconstruction of Cambodia, held discussions on 21 and 22 June 1992.

1. A consensus has emerged that the Paris Agreement is a law for all of us. The 3 fundamental objectives of the Agreement are peace, independence and national reconciliation. Any measures to favour its loyal and impartial implementation must be taken in conformity with the provisions as well as with the letter and spirit of the Agreement.

2. It has been admitted that the concerns about the implementation of the Agreement, especially its two key provisions, are legitimate. Those two key provisions refer to:

(i) The verification of the withdrawal from Cambodia of all categories of foreign forces and their non-return to the country;

(ii) The measures to be taken to enable the SNC to carry out its mandate as "the unique legitimate body and source of authority in Cambodia" during the transitional period.

As far as the first key provision is concerned, it has been admitted that the representatives of all the Cambodian parties will participate in the activities of the checkpoints as well as the Mobile Investigating Team for the verification of the withdrawal from Cambodia of all categories of foreign forces and their non-return to the country, of the cease-fire and the cessation of outside military assistance to all the Cambodian parties.

As for the second key provision, it has been admitted that the SNC will play a more active role in its close cooperation with UNTAC in the implementation of the Paris Agreement. To this end, consultative mechanisms will be considered and created as need be.

The Democratic Kampuchea party welcomes those view-points.

II. *Proposal of the Democratic Kampuchea Party on the cooperation between UNTAC and the SNC*

1. *There is no government in Cambodia during the transitional period*

a/ The Paris Agreement clearly stipulates that:

(i) The SNC is the unique legitimate body and source of authority in Cambodia. It embodies the sovereignty, independence and unity of Cambodia. It represents Cambodia externally. (Preambular Para. 5 and Articles 3 and 5)

(ii) The SNC delegates to the United Nations all powers necessary to ensure the implementation of the Agreement. (Article 6)

b/ According to the letter and spirit of the Agreement:

(i) The authority in Cambodia during the transitional period emanates from the cooperation between UNTAC and the SNC;

(ii) The SNC is not a government;

(iii) There is no government in Cambodia during the transitional period;

(iv) The existing administrative structures continue to function under the control and/or supervision of UNTAC.

2. *Creation of Consultative Committees of the SNC within the existing administrative structures*

The loyal and impartial implementation of all the provisions of the Paris Agreement requires a close and efficient cooperation between UNTAC and the SNC. In his report of 19 February 1992, the Secretary-General of the United Nations points out the following:

"The focal point of the United Nations relationship in Cambodia is the Supreme National Council ... The Special Representative of the Secretary-General would be the head of UNTAC and would maintain an ongoing dialogue with the SNC regarding UNTAC's activities in implementing its mandate."

The existing administrative structures of the 4 Cambodian parties maintained and continue to operate in conformity with the provision of the Agreement. The Agreement also spells out the conditions under which the forces of civil police of the 4 Cambodian parties function.

To ensure a close and efficient cooperation between UNTAC and the SNC in these fields, to create and maintain transparency and mutual confidence among all the Cambodian parties, and to achieve a genuine national reconciliation so as to create a neutral political environment conducive to free, democratic and fair general elections.

It is necessary that, within the existing administrative structures and the police forces of all the Cambodian parties, Consultative Committees of the SNC be set up. It is understood that the control and/or supervision of those existing administrative structures shall be exerted by UNTAC, in conformity with the provisions of the Paris Agreement.

Document 39

Letter dated 7 July 1992 from the Secretary-General to Mr. Khieu Samphan, member of the Supreme National Council, referring to letter of 27 June and concerning implementation by UNTAC of the provisions of the Paris Agreements

Not issued as a United Nations document; original in French

I thank you for your letter of 27 June 1992 concerning the consultations held in connection with the Tokyo Ministerial Conference on the Rehabilitation and Reconstruction of Cambodia. I believe that the outcome of the consultations is encouraging and that the "non-paper" prepared on that occasion provides the basis for an equitable solution to the difficulties that have arisen in the implementation of the second phase of the cease-fire provided for in the Paris Agreements. In view of your discussions with my Special Representative, it should be possible to reach agreement on the relaunching of the peace process, in keeping with the commitments made by all parties on 23 October 1991 in Paris. I am counting on your understanding, support and cooperation in order to achieve this goal in the near future.

I wish to assure you that UNTAC will make every effort to implement, with complete impartiality, the provisions of the Paris Agreements, including the verification of the withdrawal of foreign forces and their non-return to Cambodia. My Special Representative will also take the necessary steps to accelerate the deployment of UNTAC personnel responsible for civil administration and to enable them to carry out all their responsibilities relating to the control and supervision of the existing administrative structures. He will also ensure that cooperation between UNTAC and the Supreme National Council is strengthened, so that the Council may perform fully its proper role in restoring peace, promoting national reconciliation and creating a neutral political environment that will enable the Cambodian people to determine their own future, freely and independently.

However, the time we have at our disposal in order to complete this exhilarating task is limited. We must therefore work together so that we can keep to the timetable for the implementation of the Paris Agreements set by the Security Council and thus meet the expectations of the international community and the Cambodian people.

I trust that I can count on your cooperation. Accept, Sir, the assurances of my highest consideration.

(*signed*) Boutros BOUTROS-GHALI

Document 40

Proposal dated 12 July 1992 of the Party of Democratic Kampuchea on the implementation of phase II of the cease-fire and the regroupment and cantonment of the forces of the PDK

Not issued as a United Nations document

1. The fundamental objective of the Paris Agreements of 23 October 1991 is to restore the sovereignty, independence, territorial integrity and inviolability, neutrality and national unity of Cambodia through the integral and loyal implementation of the Agreements by all the signatories.

That objective can only be obtained by the implementation of the two-key provisions, namely the withdrawal under the control and supervision of UNTAC of all categories of foreign forces from Cambodia and their non-return to the country, and the measures to be taken so as to enable the Supreme National Council (SNC) to carry out its mandate in accordance with the Paris Agreements as "the unique legitimate body and source of authority in Cambodia" during the transitional period.

The Democratic Kampuchea party firmly supports that objective as well as all measures set forth in the Agreements in order to have the above-cited two-key provisions fully implemented.

2. Inspired by that sincere intention, the Democratic Kampuchea party, as a signatory to the Paris Agreements, has always affirmed that there must be no "government" in Cambodia during the transitional period.

The Democratic Kampuchea party deems it necessary that measures should be taken without delay to enable the existing administrative structures of the 4 Cambodian parties to function free from the directives and policies of any "government", which must no longer exist ever since the signing of the Paris Agreements.

In this spirit and in order to facilitate the implementation of Phase II of the supervised cease-fire and the regroupment and cantonment of the forces of the four Cambodian parties, the Democratic Kampuchea party would like to make the following proposal as measures to be taken by itself and by the Phnom Penh party:

1st week: The Democratic Kampuchea party will accept the regroupment and cantonment of 10 per cent of its armed forces once

The Phnom Penh party accepts to de-politicize the Ministries of National Defence and Public Security. There will be therefore no Ministers and Vice-Ministers in those two fields.

2nd week: The Democratic Kampuchea party will accept the regroupment and cantonment of another 20 per cent of its armed forces once

The Phnom Penh party accepts to de-politicize the Ministries of Foreign Affairs and Finance. There will be therefore no Ministers and Vice-Ministers in those fields.

3rd week: The Democratic Kampuchea party will accept the regroupment and cantonment of another 30 per cent of its armed forces once

The Phnom Penh party accepts to de-politicize the Ministry of Information. There will be therefore no Minister and Vice-Minister in that field.

4th week: The Democratic Kampuchea party will accept the regroupment and cantonment of the remaining 40 per cent of its armed forces once

The Phnom Penh party accepts to de-politicize the "People's Assembly", the chairmanship of the Council of Ministers, the presidency of the so-called "State of Cambodia" and other ministries. There will be therefore no Prime Minister, Deputy Prime Ministers, Ministers, Vice-Ministers, President and other attributes of the State or Government.

Along with those measures, it is necessary that within the existing administrative structures and the police forces of all the Cambodian parties, *Consultative Committees of the SNC* be set up.

It is understood that the control and/or supervision of those existing administrative structures should be carried out by UNTAC in conformity with the provisions of the Paris Agreements.

It is also necessary that the qualified representatives of the 4 Cambodian parties be associated in the process of regroupment and cantonment of the armed forces.

The Democratic Kampuchea party earnestly hopes that the above-cited measures be seriously taken into consideration by all the concerned parties.

Document 41

Second special report of the Secretary-General on UNTAC and phase II of the cease-fire

S/24286, 14 July 1992

1. In my special report dated 12 June 1992 (S/24090), I noted that, in accordance with the Paris Agreements, the Force Commander of the military component of the United Nations Transitional Authority in Cambodia (UNTAC) had determined that the second phase of the cease-fire should begin on 13 June. In order to comply with the Agreements, the four Cambodian parties were obliged to take a number of steps, including the regroupment and cantonment of their armed forces.

2. I also noted in my report, however, that it was becoming increasingly clear that one party, the Party of Democratic Kampuchea (PDK), was not taking the steps necessary to enable it to honour the assurances that it had given. That party has still failed to comply with the Agreements and has refused to canton any of its forces.

3. As of 10 July, the number of troops cantoned by each of the four Cambodian parties was as follows:

Cambodian People's Armed Forces (CPAF)	9 003
National Army of Independent Kampuchea (ANKI)	3 187
Khmer People's National Liberation Armed Forces (KPNLAF)	1 322
National Army of Democratic Kampuchea (NADK)	0
Total	13 512

4. Furthermore, PDK has failed to take a number of other measures incumbent upon it for the proper implementation of the Paris Agreements. These involve failure to grant free and unrestricted access to UNTAC and to mark minefields in the zones they control, and to refrain from further violations of the cease-fire.

5. In explanation of its position, PDK has introduced its own interpretations of the provisions of the Paris Agreements relating to the verification of the withdrawal and non-return of foreign forces and to the role and powers of the Supreme National Council. PDK asserts that these provisions have not been implemented, and that until they are it is not in a position to proceed with the implementation of the other provisions.

6. At the Ministerial Conference on the Rehabilitation and Reconstruction of Cambodia, held at Tokyo on 22 June 1992, an informal "proposal for discussion" was drawn up by representatives of the five permanent members of the Security Council, the co-Chairmen of the Paris Conference and other participants in the Conference, including my Special Representative. This proposal, which is reproduced in the annex to the present report, sets out a number of measures designed to meet some of the concerns expressed by PDK and thus to facilitate its participation in the full implementation of the Paris Agreements without further delay.

7. At an extraordinary meeting of the Supreme National Council convened at Tokyo on the same day, the four Cambodian parties were asked to respond to the proposal for discussion. Three of them accepted it. PDK did not reject the proposal, but promised to consider it and to make known its views at a later stage.

8. On 2 July 1992, in the absence of His Royal Highness Prince Norodom Sihanouk, a working session of the Supreme National Council was held at UNTAC headquarters at Phnom Penh. The Tokyo proposal was discussed and again three of the Cambodian parties expressed agreement with it. However, PDK expressed no opinion on the proposal; instead, it introduced its own proposals regarding the role and powers of the Supreme National Council and the administrative structures in the zone under the control of the Cambodian People's Party.

9. On 8 July 1992, a further meeting of the Supreme National Council was held under the Chairmanship of Prince Sihanouk, at which my Special Representative again pressed the Party of Democratic Kampuchea, represented at the meeting by Mr. Khieu Samphan, the President of the party, for a clear and positive response to the Tokyo proposal. Mr. Khieu Samphan did not respond to that request, but repeated his own proposals. Moreover, in a letter addressed to me on 9 July, he again took the same position.

10. In addition to the meetings of the Supreme National Council, my Special Representative has met three times with Mr. Samphan in the last two weeks in an endeavour to secure the agreement of PDK to the Tokyo proposal and to persuade it to take the necessary steps to comply with the Paris Agreements.

11. UNTAC has also taken a number of steps designed to meet the concerns of PDK. In particular, UNTAC has strengthened its verification mechanisms, such as border checkpoints and mobile military investigation teams in order to follow up, as required, on any evidence that might be presented to it regarding the presence of foreign forces or the provision of outside military assistance. It is hoped that, with the assistance and cooperation of the neighbouring countries, UNTAC will soon be able to complete the establishment of border checkpoints so that it may fully implement the provisions of annex 2, articles VI and VII of the Agreements. In addition, UNTAC is giving top priority to the recruitment and deployment of its civil administration staff as rapidly as possible, in order to exercise its mandate under the Agreements of direct control over existing administrative structures in the areas of foreign affairs, national defence, finance, public security and information, as well as its supervision in other areas.

12. UNTAC has also actively sought agreement with PDK on the establishment of a mechanism for keeping the four Cambodian parties informed and involved with regard to UNTAC exercise of direct control over the five areas named above. Consideration is being given, *inter alia*, to establishing working groups under UNTAC chairmanship or other appropriate consultative mechanisms.

13. At these meetings, Mr. Khieu Samphan has elaborated his party's position *vis-à-vis* the relationship between the Supreme National Council and UNTAC and the question of UNTAC exercise of authority in Cambodia, and has called for the dissolution of the main institutions and structures established by the Cambodian People's Party in the zone under its control. However, it is clearly understood in the Paris Agreements that UNTAC control should be exercised through the "existing administrative structures" of each of the four Cambodian parties. As my Special Representative has explained to Mr. Samphan, the Phnom Penh authorities form part of these "existing administrative structures" and cannot be abolished or dismantled.

14. Phase II commenced on 13 June 1992. In accordance with the Paris Agreements, UNTAC was to have endeavoured to complete the regroupment and cantonment process within four weeks, i.e., by 11 July. In fact, as a result of the refusal of one party to take part in that process, and because of the need to ensure that this process is undertaken in such a way as to maintain the military balance between the four parties, barely 5 per cent of the estimated 200,000 soldiers had been cantoned by that date.

15. Since my last special report to the Security Council, UNTAC military deployment has been proceeding and is now almost complete, with some 14,300 troops in the country and the remainder en route. Other aspects of the UNTAC operation are also moving forward to the greatest possible extent under the circumstances. A total of 50,000 refugees and displaced persons have been repatriated; 1,780 UNTAC civilian police monitors have been deployed throughout the country to supervise the fair and impartial enforcement of law and order; more

than 100 cases of human rights investigations have been successfully carried out in the last few weeks in the zones under control of the Cambodian People's Party, and investigations will soon begin as necessary in the zones of the United Nations Front for an Independent, Neutral, Peaceful and Cooperative Cambodia (FUNCINPEC) and KPNLF; extensive discussions have taken place over the electoral law submitted to the Supreme National Council on 1 April; and the Ministerial Conference at Tokyo resulted in pledges of $880 million, substantially in excess of the sum I called for in my appeal. In all of these spheres, however, UNTAC has been denied access to operate in the zones controlled by PDK.

16. As far as civil administration is concerned, my Special Representative announced on 26 June comprehensive plans to introduce, throughout the territory of Cambodia, United Nations control of the existing administrative structures of each of the four parties. While three of the parties have, pursuant to the request of my Special Representative, submitted lists of their laws for review by UNTAC, PDK has failed to do so. Work is now proceeding on the review of the laws of the three parties in compliance.

17. In the five areas over which UNTAC is mandated to assume direct control, efforts to recruit and deploy staff with the necessary qualifications and experience have been accelerated. Control over the administrative structures of the Cambodian People's Party dealing with foreign affairs and national defence was established on 1 July 1992. In finance, control will be progressively introduced between 1 July and 1 September; in public security, the staff concerned will be fully deployed by 15 July, following which the service will be completely operational; and in information, UNTAC established a Media Working Group composed of representatives of the four parties on 10 June 1992, and the Director of the Information Division has now visited the broadcasting facilities of three of the parties.

18. In my special report of 12 June, I stated that the successful implementation of phase II of the cease-fire depended on the cooperation of all parties and would not be sustainable for more than a brief period without such cooperation. I also noted that the implementation of the Paris Agreements had reached a critical stage. I found it necessary to draw this to the attention of the Security Council so that the Council could consider what action it might appropriately take to ensure that UNTAC received the cooperation it needed, and in particular that the timetable for implementation was adhered to.

19. Since then, phase II of the cease-fire has begun on time, and three of the parties have shown themselves willing to participate in the regroupment and cantonment process, but PDK has not. That party has also failed to respond to repeated requests from my Special Representative to comply with the 12 points he listed on 26 May 1992 to ensure implementation of the Paris Accords, or to accept the proposal for discussion drawn up by participants in the Ministerial Conference at Tokyo. As a result, the ability of UNTAC to adhere to the timetable set by the Security Council has been seriously compromised. In these circumstances, there are two possible courses of action: the first is to suspend the operation until all parties can be persuaded to fulfil their obligations under the Paris Agreements. The second is to pursue the process and thus demonstrate that, despite the lack of cooperation of one party, the international community remains determined to assist the Cambodian people in their quest for peace and stability. I am convinced that the latter approach is the most appropriate.

20. Accordingly, I have asked my Special Representative to press forward with the regroupment and cantonment process wherever possible. UNTAC will do this cautiously and selectively, while taking great care to maintain security in the countryside and ensuring that the parties cooperating with UNTAC do not suffer a military disadvantage *vis-à-vis* the party that is not. It will concentrate, for instance, on areas where there is no military confrontation. Some cantoned troops may also be permitted to keep their weapons until the situation is clarified. However, UNTAC efforts to continue with the regroupment and cantonment process with the cooperation of only three of the parties cannot go on indefinitely. Indeed, I am convinced that any further delay in the full implementation by all parties of this essential aspect of the Paris Agreements is likely to affect the ability of UNTAC to organize and conduct the elections on schedule and that it could ultimately jeopardize the whole peace process.

21. I therefore believe that every effort should continue to be made to persuade PDK to join phase II and to cooperate with UNTAC and the other three parties. To this end, I wrote on 7 July to Mr. Samphan. I assured him that my Special Representative would pursue his efforts to take into account, on the basis of the Tokyo Proposal, the legitimate concerns expressed by PDK, as well as those of the other three parties. I have also taken advantage of my visits to certain capitals, including most recently Paris and London, to share with leaders my concern about the implementation of the Paris Agreements and to enlist their support.

22. In conclusion, the main questions that need to be addressed at this juncture are, in my view, the following: (a) what steps might be taken to persuade PDK to comply with its obligations under the Paris Agreements; (b) what action should be taken to underscore the determination of the international community to implement the Agreements, in accordance with the timetable set

forth in my implementation plan (S/23613); and (c) how to obtain the full and active support of the signatories of the Paris Agreements for UNTAC efforts to carry out the various aspects of the mandate entrusted to it by the Security Council.

Annex
Proposal for discussion

1. The principles embodied in the Paris Agreements, to which all signatories, including the Cambodian parties, have committed themselves, represent the only viable means of restoring peace and prosperity to all the people of Cambodia.

2. The first requirement at this juncture is a full and timely implementation of the Paris Agreements and, in particular, that the Cambodian parties carry out immediately the obligations relating to phase II of the cease-fire, as set out by the Special Representative of the Secretary-General for Cambodia on 26 May 1992.

3. What follows requires as of this day a binding undertaking by all Cambodian Parties to assure full and effective cooperation with the United Nations Transitional Authority in Cambodia (UNTAC) and immediate access to and freedom of movement throughout their respective areas for all military and civilian personnel of UNTAC.

4. After careful consideration of the views of His Royal Highness Prince Norodom Sihanouk and high representatives of the four Cambodian parties, the following measures, within the letter and spirit of the Paris Agreements and preserving their integrity, may assist the full implementation of the comprehensive settlement without further delay.

5. The Supreme National Council will assume a more active role in developing advice to the Special Representative in implementing the Agreements, including the implementation of phase II. It will cooperate more closely with the various parts of UNTAC implementation efforts. Meetings of the Supreme National Council will be held frequently. Other consultative mechanisms can also be considered.

6. Each of the Cambodian parties shall cooperate actively with UNTAC in the fulfilment of UNTAC responsibilities under the Agreements for the investigation, verification and reporting of allegations of the presence of foreign forces in Cambodia, and of allegations of cease-fire violations and formally confirming the cessation of outside military assistance not permitted under the Agreements. To this end, the Supreme National Council will give advice to UNTAC on further verification activities. Observers from each of the Cambodian parties shall also be attached to the Mobile Investigation Teams set up by UNTAC. It is a fundamental principle that each of the Mobile Verification Teams, including observers from each of the Cambodian parties, shall have free and unrestricted access to all areas controlled by each Cambodian Party.

7. In order to ensure a neutral political environment, UNTAC must accelerate the recruitment and deployment of its civil administration personnel into all existing administrations. Special attention shall be given to the five key areas identified in the Agreements. Likewise, all of the Parties accept without further delay the deployment of those personnel, including members of the UNTAC police component. UNTAC, in consultation with the Supreme National Council, will ensure that its control of each of the five key areas will be applied with equal vigour to the administrations of the four Parties.

8. The Supreme National Council will discuss all high-level visits of foreign dignitaries to Cambodia. Reception of high foreign guests should be conducted in the name of the Supreme National Council with close cooperation from the existing administrations.

9. All foreign trade and investment agreements by all Cambodian Parties shall be reported to the Supreme National Council secretariat and subject to UNTAC oversight in consultation with the Supreme National Council.

10. After consultation with the Supreme National Council regarding procedures and qualifications, UNTAC, through its civil administration control, will supervise the issuance of visas to all foreigners seeking to enter any part of Cambodian territory. The Supreme National Council shall consider the issue of a uniform stamp, in the name of the Supreme National Council, to validate on request passports, travel documents and identity cards of Cambodians.

11. It is a fundamental principle that multilateral assistance and budget support activities coordinated through UNTAC during the rehabilitation period shall be designated to the Supreme National Council and shall be disbursed, when UNTAC can supervise the delivery of assistance or expenditure of money. In any United Nations documents referring to assistance or budget support for "Cambodia" or for "the Cambodian authorities", it is clearly understood that these terms refer to the whole territory of Cambodia or to the administrations of all Cambodian parties. It is also clearly understood that budgetary support to pay or subsidize the salaries of teachers, administrators, officials, health workers, etc., in "Cambodia" is applicable according to need to the territory or administration controlled by each Cambodian Party.

Document 42

Security Council resolution on implementation of the Paris Agreements

S/RES/766 (1992), 21 July 1992

The Security Council,

Reaffirming its resolutions 668 (1990) of 20 September 1990, 717 (1991) of 16 October 1991, 718 (1991) of 31 October 1991, 728 (1992) of 8 January 1992, and 745 (1992) of 28 February 1992,

Recalling the statement made by the President of the Security Council on 12 June 1992, 1/

Recalling also that any difficulty arising in the implementation of the agreements on a comprehensive political settlement to the Cambodia conflict signed in Paris on 23 October 1991 2/ should be settled through close consultation between the Supreme National Council of Cambodia and the United Nations Transitional Authority in Cambodia and must not be allowed to undermine the principles of these agreements, or to delay the timetable for their implementation,

Taking note of the second special report of the Secretary-General dated 14 July 1992 on the United Nations Transitional Authority in Cambodia, 3/ and in particular of the fact that the Cambodian People's Party, the Front uni national pour un Cambodge indépendant, neutre, pacifique et coopératif and the Khmer People's National Liberation Front have agreed to proceed with phase II of the cease-fire as laid down in annex 2 of the Agreement on a Comprehensive Political Settlement of the Cambodia Conflict and that the Party of Democratic Kampuchea has so far refused to do so,

Taking note also of the Tokyo Declaration on the Cambodia Peace Process issued on 22 June 1992, 4/ and the other efforts made at Tokyo by the countries and parties concerned for the implementation of the Paris agreements,

1. *Expresses its deep concern* at the difficulties met by the United Nations Transitional Authority in Cambodia in the implementation of the agreements on a comprehensive political settlement to the Cambodia conflict signed in Paris on 23 October 1991; 2/

2. *Underlines* that all signatories of the Paris agreements are bound by all their obligations thereunder;

3. *Deplores* the continuing violations of the cease-fire and urges all parties to cease all hostilities forthwith, to cooperate fully with the Authority in the marking of all minefields and to refrain from any deployment, movement, or other action intended to extend the territory they control or which might lead to renewed fighting;

4. *Reaffirms* the international community's firm commitment to a process under which the Authority, operating freely throughout all of Cambodia as authorized by the Paris agreements, can verify the departure of all foreign forces and ensure full implementation of the agreements;

5. *Demands* that all parties respect the peaceful nature of the Authority's mission and take all necessary measures to ensure the safety and security of all United Nations personnel;

6. *Urges* all parties to cooperate with the Authority in broadcasting information helpful to implementation of the Paris agreements;

7. *Strongly deplores* the continuing refusal by one of the parties to permit the necessary deployment of all components of the Authority to the areas under its control to enable the Authority to carry out its full functions in the implementation of the Paris agreements;

8. *Urges* all States, in particular neighbouring States, to provide assistance to the Authority to ensure the effective implementation of the Paris agreements;

9. *Approves* the efforts of the Secretary-General and his Special Representative for Cambodia to continue to implement the Paris agreements despite the difficulties;

10. *Invites* in particular the Secretary-General and his Special Representative to accelerate the deployment of the Authority's civilian components, especially the component mandated to supervise or control the existing administrative structures;

11. *Demands* that the Party that has failed so far to do so permit without delay the deployment of the Authority in the areas under its control, and implement fully phase II of the Plan as well as the other aspects of the Paris Agreements;

12. *Requests* the Secretary-General and his Special Representative to ensure that international assistance to the rehabilitation and reconstruction of Cambodia from now on benefits only the parties which are fulfilling their obligations under the Paris agreements and cooperating fully with the Authority;

13. *Decides* to remain actively seized of the matter.

1/ S/24091 [Document 36]
2/ S/23177 [Document 19]
3/ S/24286 [Document 41]
4/ S/24183 [Document 37]

Document 43

Letter dated 27 July 1992 from the Special Representative of the Secretary-General for Cambodia to the Secretary-General concerning the situation in Cambodia

Not issued as a United Nations document

I would like to bring you up to date on the Cambodian situation since I know that this is one of your major preoccupations. I am very pleased with the unanimous adoption last week of Security Council Resolution 766, and am monitoring the extent to which it might have any visible impact on the PDK. However, as of now, only the other three of the four Cambodian factions have said that they respect Resolution 766 and it would seem to me that the Party of Democratic Kampuchea (so-called Khmer Rouge) will feel the impact only when a stronger resolution is adopted by the Council.

The military situation has somewhat worsened, with the DK taking aggressive action in the north of Cambodia, as well as in some parts of the centre and the south. The acceptance of cantonment under UNTAC supervision by the three parties has created a vacuum, which DK is exploiting. We have therefore been forced to be selective and flexible with regard to the tempo of cantoning other troops. At the same time, some DK soldiers have also shown interest in being cantoned and joining their families, but their leaders have managed to keep tight control and have flatly refused to cooperate with UNTAC. With more energetic information activities we should be able to encourage the defection of the rank and file DK soldiers.

The SNC continues to function as well as can be expected under the circumstances, mostly on our own initiative. Prince Sihanouk is cooperating with us in full. He is, however, sometimes discouraged and despondent. I am glad that at my request he took a decision on 16 July for the first time to break a deadlock on rehabilitation programmes without asking me to do so as in the past. I have encouraged inter-Khmer talks, but these meetings appear to be worse than when UNTAC is present with them. I have tried to hold more informal discussions with the parties but have not achieved much of a result.

At the Supreme National Council Khieu Samphan speaks for the record and not to enlarge areas of agreement. I have tried to address issues of genuine concern to the DK, holding bilateral talks, some of them quite lengthy, with Khieu Samphan already five times since the Tokyo Ministerial Conference.

In the first of the two areas of DK concern, that is, the alleged presence of Vietnamese forces, we have tried to meet their concern through the prompt establishment of border checkpoints and the launching of mobile investigation teams, and have repeatedly appealed to them to give us relevant verifiable information. No cooperation has been forthcoming in this regard. In the meantime, DK radio engages in vicious propaganda, linking UNTAC with the State of Cambodia and Vietnam.

In the second area of concern to DK we have repeatedly emphasized the importance of SNC as the genuine interlocutor and partner of UNTAC. My recent statement at the Kandal Province and our care to present a new protocol, enhancing the importance of SNC, seems to have somewhat pleased DK. We are now working on a new passport to be issued by SNC. At the same time, we have taken a firm line that no body can tinker with the Paris Agreement and that "the existing administrative structures", including the Phnom Penh administration, has to function if complete chaos is to be avoided.

By probing Khieu Samphan I have ascertained that a mere change of designation of ministries or ministers in the Hun Sen administration would not satisfy DK, who want a radical "depolitisation" giving a crippling blow to the Phnom Penh regime. I am also satisfied that replacing the Dutch battalion with an ASEAN battalion in the DK zones will not change their non-cooperation with us. I am thus forced to the conclusion that DK is trying to gain what it could not get either in the battlefield or in the Paris negotiations, that is, to improve its political and military power to such an extent that the other parties will be placed at a distinctive disadvantage when UNTAC leaves.

So long as we stand firm on the strict implementation of the Paris Accord, there is not too much we can do to satisfy DK, except to make our control of civil administration more effective, ameliorate the protocol and a few other matters. We are doing all of these and will continue doing so. While professing its fidelity to the Paris Accord, DK in reality defies it openly and consistently by ignoring the cease-fire, by refusing cantonment and free access to their areas and by boycotting the Mixed Military Working Group, a statutory body.

While we continue talking with Khieu Samphan, DK seems determined to expand its influence in as many parts of Cambodia as possible in order to increase the areas of cultivation by its supporters and increase the number of its potential voters at the forthcoming elections. Their willingness to accept pro-DK refugees into their zones of control is along this line of policy.

There is a view held by close observers here that DK is impervious to international public opinion but will start cooperating with UNTAC towards the end of the rainy season in September or October after attaining the above objectives. The question for us is whether, in that event, we can still adhere to our original timetable set out in the Secretary-General's plan of February, or have to revise it and if so to what degree. In this respect we will have to guard against the criticism that we are going through the motion of free and fair elections in a superficial manner. We will also examine the possibility of holding elections outside the DK zones. I intend to come back to these points in a few days in greater detail.

My basic approach, for which I believe I will have your support, is to combine patient persuasion with sustained pressure. We will continue to work with the SNC, where we can count on the consistent support of Prince Sihanouk as well as the three factions. At the same time we will do our best not to alienate DK as the permanent disgruntled minority. We will adhere to an impartial stand, while criticizing any acts in violation of the Paris Agreement.

The security situation in the countryside worsens with increased acts of banditry and murders of peasants and Vietnamese residents. The economic situation is precarious with the imminent hyper-inflation. UNTAC is grappling with the gigantic task to keep this country afloat and to have Cambodians focussed on their common national priorities rather than on their sectarian differences or ethnic hatred toward the Vietnamese.

It is increasingly evident that Khieu Samphan is little more than a glorified mouthpiece of DK, repeating the fixed lines of argument dictated to him by the "mysterious Pol Pot" (words of Thai Prime Minister Anand to me) and his small "committee". Pol Pot seems to be dedicated to the doctrine of simultaneously "talk and fight". Nevertheless, we keep our door open to DK so that we will be able to seize a new opportunity quickly whenever their policy or tactics changes.

Several Member States can help us in this situation. *Thailand* obviously has a key role. They can do a lot by cutting off its ties with the DK. But I doubt the capacity of the Thai civilian government in Bangkok to impose its will upon Thai military in the border areas, even if its intentions to cooperate with UNTAC are unmistakable. *China* still enjoys the confidence of DK, although its large influence is probably diminishing since the cessation of its military assistance to the DK.

Other countries which are important for us are

Indonesia, the Co-Chairman of the Paris Conference, *Japan* because of its huge economic clout, *the United States* because of its military and political weight, and lastly, *France* because of its long links with Cambodia as well as its chairmanship of the Paris Conference. (France has, however, antagonized the DK by its strong advocacy of anti-DK sanctions.) We need to work with all these countries if pressure on DK is to be kept. It is particularly important that the ASEAN countries are with us, rather than argue for an unspecified "Asian approach".

Last, but not least, the *Security Council* has to be kept au courant about our efforts through you and Mr. Goulding at Headquarters. I am doing my bit in Phnom Penh through frequent meetings with the Expanded Group of Permanent Five, which includes Indonesia, Japan, Germany, Australia and now Thailand.

In the likely event that DK's non-cooperation with UNTAC continues unabated, you may wish to consider presenting another report to the Security Council in about a month's time. At that time we would need a stronger resolution with particular emphasis on economic pressures against DK. This should not however involve any spectacular action, but rather a steady strengthening of our border checkpoints adjacent to the DK zones, in order to control the inflow of arms and petroleum and the outflow of gems and logs, a major source of DK's income. Thailand has promised to cooperate in the establishment and functioning of our checkpoints, several of which can only be supplied from the Thai side. Our military people are working on the details of these checkpoints with expanded terms of reference. Thailand will certainly have to do more than it has done in the past. So far it has not even signed a Status Agreement with us. Gen. Sanderson will visit Bangkok soon to follow up on my talks there on 17 July.

Through such steady external pressures and through a combination of UNTAC's even-handed approach and the solid common front of three factions, DK may well change their tune in two months or so and agree to our entry into their zones and start cantoning its troops. If it does so, it will also try to hide weapons in the forest and convert some of its best soldiers into temporary citizens. In the event, we may have to compress or shorten some of the steps towards free elections while complying with the Paris Agreement.

I am well aware of the financial implications of any delay in adhering to our timetable set out in your February plan of implementation. At the same time, we must be free from any accusations that we are going through the "motion" of democratic elections in a superficial manner, allowing DK or other anti-democratic elements to surface soon after the elections and UNTAC's departure.

The prospects are daunting, but I remain basically optimistic. I feel that the UN has a substantial reservoir of resources and goodwill at its disposal, not to speak of the unanimous support of the entire international community. A great majority of Cambodians want to build a new, peaceful country before the sympathy and generosity of the world towards their country dissipates. In the meantime, we will try to persuade the DK to pursue their ambitions through parliamentary means set out in the Paris Agreement rather than through the use of violence.

Yasushi AKASHI
Special Representative of the Secretary-General for Cambodia

Document 44

"Cambodia: next steps": Australian paper dated 16 September 1992

Not issued as a United Nations document

1. Australia remains convinced that the Paris Agreements as signed last October remain the best basis for a durable peace in Cambodia because they represent a comprehensive settlement which includes all the Cambodian parties and have the support of all members of the P5 and the key regional countries. The momentum of economic and social reconstruction under the Agreements is increasing: achievement of these objectives is vital for Cambodia's future.

2. Despite the international community's concerted and sympathetic approach to Khmer Rouge (DK) concerns, including the non-paper produced at the Tokyo meeting and the recent Thai, Japanese, and Chinese initiatives, the DK continue deliberately to withhold their participation in phase II of the peace process.

-All the P5, core group and ASEAN countries have agreed that the DK demands are not in strict accord with the actual terms of the Paris Agreements.

3. Given the damaging slippage in the timetable for implementation of the settlement, there is now an urgent need for a strategy for the coming months which takes account of the need to achieve optimum results in relation to the goals of the peace settlement.

4. In dealing with the current problems in the process we believe the international community should aim to:

-preserve the basic integrity of the comprehensive settlement,

-maintain pressure on the DK by demonstrating the international community's resolve to implement that settlement according to the UN-agreed timetable, with or without DK participation,

-leave the way open for the DK to return to the process at any time (and particularly before the proposed 1 December deadline),

-endeavour to ensure as safe an internal security environment as possible,

-maintain international consensus in dealing with the DK problem, and

-maintain the momentum of social and economic rehabilitation, increasing the flow of foreign funding into non-DK areas (particularly to prevent the Cambodian economy from total collapse, which would undermine the whole process: this side of the settlement has worked too slowly, and budget support is urgently required).

5. A powerful incentive for the DK to return to the settlement will be the demonstration of the international community's continued resolve to have UNTAC press on with implementation of the settlement including the elections, as fully as possible and according to the UN-agreed timetable, with or without the DK.

6. It is essential to establish a clear timetable for the achievement of this goal in order to end the current drift in the peace process:

-a proposed timetable along these lines is set out at the end of this paper.

7. Australia believes the course of action most likely to achieve optimal results in terms of the key objectives of the peace settlement would be:

- to apply article 29 of Agreement 1, which reads as follows:

"Without prejudice to the prerogatives of the Security Council of the United Nations, and upon the request of the Secretary-General, the two Co-Chairmen of the Paris Conference on Cambodia, in the event of a violation or threat of violation of this Agreement, will immediately undertake appropriate consultations, including with members of the Paris Conference on Cambodia, with a view to taking appropriate steps to ensure respect for these commitments",

-at the same time for the Security Council to proceed to firmer measures against the DK, in particular by setting a date for the imposition of sanctions,

-if these steps failed to bring a positive response from the DK, for the implementation of the Paris Agreements, including elections, to proceed without the DK in accordance with the approved timetable.

8. The application of article 29, providing for intervention of PICC Co-Chairmen at this crucial stage, could serve a number of useful purposes:

- article 29 provides a mechanism which might serve to break the deadlock and reintegrate the DK into the process at this crucial time,

- if the article 29 consultations took place within the firmly fixed timetable referred to below, they could not become yet another means for the DK to delay implementation of the settlement,

-if the DK did not take the opportunity of such consultations to re-join the process, then the wording of article 29 is wide enough in our judgement to support the continuation of the settlement, regardless of DK violations

: "appropriate steps" can be extended to include deciding to continue application of the settlement as far as possible, without the DK.

9. Given the time constraints, it would be preferable if the PICC Co-Chairmen consulted with PICC countries through normal diplomatic channels. Because of his presence in the region, Mr Alatas might take responsibility for consulting directly with the Cambodian factions.

10. The major problems associated with this plan of action would be those of security:

-the armed forces of the three other factions (the CPAF, ANK and the KPNLAF) would need to be kept intact as far as possible

: they would be necessary to hold the front line and prevent the DK from further expanding their territory,

: but in keeping with the need for a neutral political environment in the lead-up to the elections, the three armed forces would then need to come under some form by supervision by UNTAC,

-Prince Sihanouk and others believe it is unlikely the DK would mount a campaign of violence to disrupt elections outside their own territory

: but as a precaution UNTAC infantry battalions would need to be redeployed to co-operate with the three factions' forces to protect the voter registration and election process throughout non-DK territory

: this may mean an increase in the UNTAC military

budget, as the number of UNTAC battalions in Cambodia could not be scaled back from December onwards as originally planned.

11. If, against expectation, the DK did mount a sustained military attack on UNTAC forces following their exclusion from the settlement this would clearly place the situation outside the current mandate of the UNTAC peace-keeping force.

-it would then be up to the Security Council to decide whether to move from a Chapter VI to a Chapter VII mandate (presumably very unlikely), or to withdraw from Cambodia operations entirely, leaving concerned countries to come to agreement on some form of joint action outside the terms of the Paris Agreements

: presumably in support of a Sihanouk-Hun Sen administration in which FUNCINPEC and the KPNLF would co-operate.

-However, even in the worst-case scenario of a UN withdrawal (and given the UN's stake in the Cambodia operation this is to be avoided if at all possible), the Paris settlement will have had a major impact in the political and military situation in Cambodia

: the DK will find itself internationally isolated, without any materiel and diplomatic support

: international recognition and support would have shifted overwhelmingly to the DK's opponents.

12. If the settlement is to be implemented without the DK, UNTAC's responsibility to create a neutral political environment in preparation for the elections remains as important as ever. Matters needing urgent attention in this area include:

-a review of whether the planned total of 157 senior administrators is adequate to fulfill credibly UNTAC's civilian administrative mandate,

-UNTAC acceptance of responsibility for measures to control the entry of foreigners (including both Vietnamese and Thais) by a border checkpoint system. The Vietnamese settlers question is ultimately one for an elected Cambodian Government to resolve, but there are real dangers—including the outbreak of anti-Vietnamese violence during the transitional period—should the numbers of Vietnamese entering Cambodia continue: a situation for which UNTAC would, under its mandate, be responsible,

-UNTAC information and public awareness activities will be even more important if implementation proceeds without the DK. There is an urgent need for a dedicated UNTAC radio station with programming, power and repeaters, to take UNTAC's message into every part of Cambodia 24 hours a day: it is not enough to counter anti-UNTAC propaganda from DK radio with the occasional use of time on Voice of America or some Thai stations.

Canberra/Bangkok
10 September 1992

Proposed timetable

I. By end of September (U/L four)

The UN Security Council, in response to the report to be presented by the Secretary-General's Special Representative, adopts a resolution which:

1) Requests the Secretary-General, in accordance with article 29 of Agreement I, to request the Paris Conference (PICC) Co-Chairs to "undertake appropriate consultations, including with members of the Paris Conference on Cambodia, with a view to taking appropriate steps to ensure respect" for the parties' commitment to the settlement,

2) Requests that the PICC Co-Chairmen report back to the Security Council through the Security-Council on their findings by mid-October

: this would be just before the due date for UNGA consideration of the second tranche of UNTAC funding,

3) Sets a date (third week of October) for the imposition of sanctions and describes the type of sanctions (which would probably consist primarily of control of the road access into DK territory) that would be applied should the DK continue to refuse compliance with the terms of the settlement.

II. Third week of October (U/L four)

On the basis of the PICC Co-Chairmen's report, assuming that this report finds no change in the DK position, a further meeting of the UN Security Council decides to impose sanctions and adopts a resolution which:

1) Formally imposes those sanctions as a binding Security Council decision,

2) Gives notice that, unless the DK have complied by 1 December, the implementation of the agreement,

including the UN-organised elections, would proceed without them

- subject to the views of other parties, the resolution could go so far as to formally exclude the DK from the implementation of the settlement,

3) Gives notes that, in that event, the Security Council would on 1 December also have to declare a formal suspension of phase II military arrangements (cantonment, disarmament, suspension, demobilization) for the other three factional armies.

III. Late October (U/L two)

The General Assembly approves the second tranche of funding for UNTAC for the period 1 November-14 December, with approval of third tranche scheduled for mid-December, after expiry of the final deadline for DK participation.

IV. Early December (U/L two)

In the event of continued DK non-compliance, agreement by the Security Council, after due consultation with all the concerned parties, on a revised plan consequent to the non-participation of the DK from the agreement. This might include:

-a revised budget

-a formal suspension of the cantonment, disarmament and demobilization of the armed forces of the three co-operating factions

-formal suspension of the DK participation in the mixed military working groups and other UNTAC-SNC liaison bodies (and possibly—although arguably not desirably—in the SNC itself)

In the meantime, UNTAC would be proceeding to implement the settlement in all the territory of Cambodia not under direct DK control in accordance with the approved timetable:

-including voter registration, starting from October, and

-disbursement of UN rehabilitation funds in non-DK areas.

V. April-May 1993 (U/L4)

Conduct of UN-organised and supervised elections for a constituent assembly and (very probably) for a president of Cambodia.

Document 45

Second progress report of the Secretary-General on UNTAC

S/24578, 21 September 1992

Introduction

1. On 1 May 1992, I submitted to the Security Council my first progress report on the United Nations Transitional Authority in Cambodia (UNTAC) (S/23870). I subsequently submitted two special reports (S/24090 of 12 June 1992 and S/24286 of 14 July 1992). The first of these led to a statement by the President of the Security Council on 12 June 1992 (S/24091) and the second formed the basis for deliberations by the Council that resulted in the adoption of resolution 766 (1992) of 21 July 1992. The present second progress report is submitted pursuant to paragraph 10 of resolution 745 (1992).

I. Progress made to date in the implementation of resolutions 745 (1992) and 766 (1992) and tasks still to be performed

A. *General*

2. UNTAC is now close to full deployment throughout almost the whole territory of Cambodia. However, the continuing refusal of the Party of Democratic Kampuchea (PDK) to grant UNTAC personnel access to the zones it controls or to commit its forces to cantonment as called for in the implementation plan (S/23613) gives grounds for serious concern. As explained in my second special report, PDK has introduced its own interpretations of the provisions of the Paris Agreements relating to the verification of the withdrawal and non-return of foreign forces and to the role and powers of the Supreme National Council (see S/23177, annex). PDK asserts that these provisions have not been implemented and that, until they are, it is not in a position to proceed with the implementation of the other provisions. In line with this assertion, PDK has issued a series of proposals laying down conditions under which it would be prepared to participate fully in the peace process. Although my Special Representative has carefully studied all these proposals with a view to identifying ways of accommodating PDK's concerns, it has not been possible to accept them because they are inconsistent with the Paris Agreements.

3. In other respects, however, the implementation of the mission is proceeding apace. The electoral law was adopted on 5 August 1992. Provisional registration of political parties has begun and preparations are under way for the registration of voters. It is still intended that elections will be held not later than May 1993. The repatriation of refugees and displaced persons is making steady progress; more than 115,000 had returned to Cambodia by 15 September 1992 without serious incident. The progressive installation of United Nations civilian officials in the administrative structures of the three Cambodian parties that are complying with the peace process has enabled UNTAC to establish supervision and control in accordance with its mandate. The work of the human rights and civilian police components has been extended to every province. A number of rehabilitation assistance programmes have been approved by the Supreme National Council.

B. *Relations with the Supreme National Council*

4. UNTAC continues to enjoy the full cooperation and support of the President of the Supreme National Council, His Royal Highness Prince Norodom Sihanouk. Twelve Council meetings have taken place since my first progress report. At these meetings, on the initiative of UNTAC, the Supreme National Council adopted a number of measures related to various aspects of UNTAC's work, as discussed below.

5. The Supreme National Council continues to function along the lines laid down in the Comprehensive Political Settlement and its relationship with UNTAC has generally been harmonious and productive, despite the constraints resulting from the failure of PDK to participate fully in the peace process. At the Council meeting held on 7 May 1992, Prince Sihanouk and the other members present signed the agreement on the legal status of UNTAC in Cambodia. In accordance with the Paris Agreements, UNTAC has kept the Supreme National Council fully informed about its activities.

C. *Human rights component*

6. Promotion of a better understanding of and respect for human rights and fundamental freedoms is essential in order to create an environment in which free and fair elections may take place. To achieve this, the component is active in three broad areas. First, it has encouraged the Supreme National Council to adhere to relevant international human rights instruments and has undertaken a review of the existing judicial and penal systems in the light of their provisions. Secondly, it has begun an extensive human rights information and education campaign in close cooperation with the Information/Education Division of UNTAC. Thirdly, it has

investigated human rights-related complaints and taken corrective measures where necessary.

7. As of 18 September, human rights officers had been deployed in 15 of the 21 provinces. They will be deployed in three more provinces by 25 September and in the remainder by early October. In addition, two officers had been deployed in the zones controlled by the United National Front for an Independent, Neutral, Peaceful and Cooperative Cambodia (FUNCINPEC) and the Khmer People's National Liberation Front (KPNLF). The component has not yet been granted access to the zone controlled by PDK.

8. Following the Supreme National Council's ratification, on 20 April 1992, of the International Covenants on Civil and Political Rights and on Economic, Social and Cultural Rights, 1/ it agreed on 10 September to accede to the Convention against Torture and Other Cruel, Inhuman or Degrading Treatment or Punishment; 2/ the International Convention on the Elimination of All Forms of Discrimination against Women; 3/ the Convention on the Rights of the Child; 4/ and the Convention 5/ and Protocol 6/ relating to the Status of Refugees.

9. In order to support indigenous human rights groups, the component has organized training sessions for local organizations, teachers, school administrators and others. It is also planning to organize in Phnom Penh an International Symposium on Human Rights in Cambodia, from 30 November to 1 December 1992.

10. More than 250 complaints of harassment and intimidation, arbitrary arrest, wrongful death, destruction of property and wrongful injury have been filed with the component. One hundred and thirty of these have been referred to other components of UNTAC, 13 have been found to be unsubstantiated, and the remainder have been investigated by the human rights component. In all investigations, the component works closely with the civilian police component.

11. Work has also begun on prison reform, although so far only in the prisons controlled by the Phnom Penh authorities. A Prisons Control Commission has been established and its review led to the release in May of 108 prisoners detained without trial and of an additional 150 such prisoners in August. In addition, the component has provided human rights briefings to UNTAC civilian police officers and United Nations Volunteers.

D. Electoral component

12. The electoral component has deployed some 150 international staff at UNTAC headquarters and in the provinces. An additional 20 are expected to arrive by the end of September. The 400 United Nations Volunteers have been almost fully deployed to the district level, while the deployment of some 1,000 locally recruited staff is also under way.

13. The electoral law, which had been submitted by UNTAC on 1 April 1992, was adopted by the Supreme National Council on 5 August and was promulgated on 12 August. It differs from the draft submitted in April in two respects. Following intensive discussions, it was decided that, in order to meet the concern expressed by the parties that the franchise be restricted to "Cambodian persons", the text of the Paris Agreements should be interpreted as giving the right to register to "every Cambodian person", defined as follows:

(a) A person born in Cambodia, at least one of whose parents was born in Cambodia; or

(b) A person, wherever born, at least one of whose parents is or was a Cambodian person within the meaning of paragraph (a).

14. Secondly, the draft law was amended to permit overseas Cambodians to vote at one polling station in Europe, one in North America and one in Australia. However, registration of voters is still to take place exclusively in Cambodia.

15. The provisional registration of political parties began on 15 August, and 14 organizations have so far expressed interest in registration. UNTAC has prepared the necessary documentation. The electoral law requires UNTAC to guarantee the right of political parties to open offices throughout the country. In discussions with UNTAC, the Phnom Penh authorities have agreed to reverse their policy of not permitting other parties to open offices in areas under their control. On 10 September 1992, my Special Representative informed the Supreme National Council that the electoral regulation giving political parties the right to open offices throughout Cambodia had come into effect. At the same meeting, Mr. Hun Sen announced that parties other than PDK would be allowed to open offices in the areas under the control of his administration. PDK would be allowed to open an office when it granted UNTAC access to its zone.

16. The registration of voters is scheduled to begin in October 1992, as called for in the implementation plan (S/23613). According to the latest population estimates, the voting population appears to be about 5 million, which is somewhat larger than the 4.3 million estimated in the implementation plan. However, UNTAC will make

1/ General Assembly resolution 2200 A (XXI), annex.
2/ General Assembly resolution 39/46, annex.
3/ General Assembly resolution 34/180, annex.
4/ General Assembly resolution 44/25, annex.
5/ United Nations, *Treaty Series*, vol. 189, No. 2545.
6/ United Nations, *Treaty Series*, vol. 606, No. 8791.

every effort to hold to the planned figure of around 800 registration stations. The other modalities for the electoral process are likely to remain as described in the implementation plan.

17. Uncertainty over PDK's intentions is having an adverse effect on the electoral component's planning. Moreover, it may no longer be possible to make practical arrangements for voter education, training and registration in the PDK-controlled areas if UNTAC gains access to those areas only after the electoral process has reached an advanced stage.

18. The component is currently examining a proposal to hold a presidential election simultaneously with the election for a constituent assembly. Much support for this idea has been voiced by the Cambodian parties and by Prince Sihanouk himself, who take the view that such an election would have a stabilizing effect in the period after the elections. However, a presidential election is not provided for in the Paris Agreements or the implementation plan. It would therefore require Security Council authorization, as well as the provision of additional resources.

E. *Military component*

19. The UNTAC military component is now almost fully deployed in Cambodia at just below its projected strength of 15,900, with 12 infantry battalions, military observers, engineer, signals, naval, air and other elements, totalling about 15,100 all ranks.

20. The component has established nine checkpoints on Cambodia's border with Viet Nam, two on the border with the Lao People's Democratic Republic and seven on that with Thailand. Checkpoints have also been established at the airports and at the port of Sihanoukville, as well as on major routes within the country. These checkpoints are supplemented by regular patrols with the purpose of discovering and discouraging unauthorized movements of armed persons and weapons, deterring banditry and establishing UNTAC's presence. In accordance with the Paris Agreements, the component is also engaged in investigating cease-fire violations and the possible presence of foreign forces and in locating arms caches.

21. Although cease-fire violations since the first progress report have been minor in nature, the refusal of PDK to allow UNTAC access to its zone and to canton its forces has seriously hampered the military component's operations. There have, in particular, been a number of cases of firing at UNTAC helicopters, most of them from areas believed to be under the control of the armed forces of PDK. My Special Representative and the Force Commander have been in regular contact with the President of PDK and his colleagues in order to seek a solution to these problems, as described in my first and second special reports. On 27 August, a senior PDK spokesman announced that the National Army of Democratic Kampuchea (NADK) was prepared to enter cantonment even before full verification of the withdrawal and non-return of foreign forces, without, however, setting a date for the entry into cantonment. The spokesman also announced NADK's intention to rejoin the Mixed Military Working Group after an absence of some three months. This took place on 17 September and is a positive development.

22. The non-cooperation of PDK has not prevented the military component from beginning the regroupment, cantonment and disarmament of the armed forces of the three factions that are complying with their obligations under the Paris Agreements. By 10 September UNTAC had cantoned more than 50,000 troops, as follows:

Cambodian People's Armed Forces	42 368
National Army of Independent Kampuchea	3 445
Khmer People's National Liberation Armed Forces	6 479
National Army of Democratic Kampuchea	—
Total	52 292

UNTAC has also taken custody of approximately 50,000 weapons.

23. About 38,000 of the cantoned troops have been granted agricultural leave in order to harvest the rice crop after having handed over their weapons and identification cards. All are subject to recall at two weeks' notice to ensure 100 per cent cantonment before the process of formal demobilization begins.

24. The component continues to train members of the Cambodian parties in mine-clearance. Eleven mine-clearance training centres have been established and some 850 soldiers have now been fully trained. The length of each training course has been doubled from two to four weeks for safety reasons. No casualties have been sustained by the trainees. About 350 are currently employed by UNTAC in mine-clearance activities, especially those directly supporting the repatriation and rehabilitation programmes and those required in connection with the continued establishment of the UNTAC infrastructure. For instance, an area of some 22,000 square metres, east of route 69 in sector 2, has been cleared of more than 1,000 mines.

F. *Civil administration component*

25. UNTAC's civil administration activities are governed by the Paris Agreements and the implementation plan, as well as being guided by the proposal for discussion ("non-paper") drawn up by participants in the

Tokyo Ministerial Conference on the Rehabilitation and Reconstruction of Cambodia (see S/24286, annex).

26. Over 800 members of the civil administration component—some 200 international and 600 locally recruited staff—have been deployed. Like the other components of UNTAC, civil administration personnel have so far been denied access to the PDK-controlled areas. However, the component has drawn up a plan for control of the PDK administrative structures that can be implemented as soon as UNTAC gains access to them. Contact has been established with the administrations of two other Cambodian parties, FUNCINPEC and KPNLF, and civilian controllers were sent to their zones at the end of August. However, most of the civil administration personnel have been deployed in the administrative structures of the Phnom Penh authorities.

27. The goal of direct control is to ensure a neutral environment permitting the holding of free and fair elections. To meet this goal in operational terms, the civil administration component is using three complementary means of control: control a posteriori, control a priori and appraisal. Control a posteriori is achieved through the receipt of all documentation dealing with the operation of the existing administrative structures, including the lines of decision-making, personnel policies and *matériel* questions. Control a priori is achieved through the component's authority to obtain prior knowledge of all decisions reached by the structures, as well as the authority to change decisions dealing, for instance, with personnel, finance and the sale of assets. Control by appraisal is achieved through the proposal of improvements in the operations of the existing administrative structures. On a day-to-day basis, these three means of direct control are exercised in various ways, including the physical presence of civil administration personnel alongside their highest-ranking counterparts in the existing administrative structures, weekly meetings between UNTAC staff and these individuals and the establishment of clear lines of decision-making so that civil administration personnel can exert a priori control over decisions.

28. In accordance with paragraphs 102 and 103 of the implementation plan, the civil administration component asked each of the four Cambodian parties to submit a list of their current laws for review by UNTAC. With the exception of PDK, all parties complied. At the initiative of UNTAC, the Supreme National Council, at its meetings on 20 April and 5 June 1992, adopted laws enshrining the rights of freedom of association and of assembly. At its meeting on 10 September, the Supreme National Council also approved a set of principles relating to the legal system, penal law and penal procedure. The object of these was to establish uniform standards for the judiciary and for substantive law that would be applicable throughout Cambodia and would be in accordance with instruments adopted by the United Nations.

29. On 1 July 1992, the civil administration component began to exercise full control over the five key areas in the Phnom Penh administration, as specified in the Paris Agreements: foreign affairs, national defence, public security, finance and information. In Phnom Penh, between one and three civil administration personnel are currently deployed in the ministries of defence, national security, foreign affairs, consular affairs and finance and in the national bank. By 15 July, UNTAC civil administration offices had been established in all 21 provinces. At the present time there are approximately 95 international staff in the Phnom Penh office and 123 in the provinces. In addition, in accordance with annex 1, section B, paragraphs 2 and 3 of the Agreements, UNTAC has established optional control over a number of areas that have been identified as having some direct influence over the outcome of the elections.

1. *Civil administration activities in Phnom Penh*

(a) *Foreign affairs*

30. Paragraph 10 of the Proposal for Discussion states:

"After consultation with the Supreme National Council..., UNTAC, through its civil administration control, will supervise the issuance of visas to all foreigners seeking to enter any part of Cambodian territory. The Supreme National Council shall consider the issue of a uniform stamp, in the name of the Supreme National Council, to validate on request passports, travel documents and identity cards of Cambodians."

31. UNTAC has now established a seven-day-a-week presence at Pochentong International Airport, Phnom Penh, in order to help to resolve any immigration problems that may arise there. The civil administration component's Foreign Affairs Service has also proposed to the Phnom Penh authorities that the requirement for exit visas for Cambodians be abolished. The proposal is being considered. UNTAC has also provided Prince Sihanouk and his household, as well as the members and secretariat of the Supreme National Council, with Supreme National Council passports.

32. In addition, the component has assumed control over the receipt and distribution of foreign aid. This involves not only supervision of the relevant officials in the foreign ministry, but also officials of administrative bodies and agencies operating in this area, such as the "*Comité de Réception de l'Aide Humanitaire*" and the "Cambodian Red Cross".

(b) National defence

33. Officials of the component's Defence Service have inspected the Phnom Penh administrative structure dealing with defence and plan shortly to visit the FUNC-INPEC and KPNLF structures. Their inspections and inquiries have revealed a high level of political activity by the Cambodian People's Party (CPP) within the armed forces of the Phnom Penh authorities. Measures are being developed to limit this activity. As of 1 September, the Service was fully staffed; periodic inspections are now being replaced by full-time and direct control over decisions. The Service has also requested that an inventory of assets be prepared.

(c) Public security

34. The exercise of control over public security, in collaboration with the civilian police and human rights components, has reached an advanced stage. In addition to compiling all existing laws and modifying those found to be incompatible with the Paris Agreements, the Public Security Service has drafted codes of conduct. The Public Security Working Group, which comprises representatives of the four parties under UNTAC chairmanship, meets twice a month.

(d) Finance

35. Direct control over this field was instituted on 1 July 1992 and was fully established in the first part of September. As regards the Phnom Penh authorities, financial controllers are present in each of the ministries, in the National Bank of Cambodia and, with six exceptions that will soon be corrected, in all provincial administrations. Specific mechanisms are in place, which enable UNTAC to examine and approve individual expenditure items. Emphasis is also being given to the most important sources of revenue, such as customs duties. As regards FUNCINPEC and KPNLF, control of expenditure and revenue is being exercised. No control can at present be exercised over PDK.

(e) Information

36. The Director of the Information/Education Division has established a working group composed of representatives of the Cambodian parties and the media in order to keep them involved in, and informed of, the actions UNTAC is taking to exercise direct control in the field of information. The Division has presented the working group with a draft media charter, which was prepared in cooperation with the human rights component. The aim of the charter is to lay down principles for the exercise of freedom of the press and of the rights and obligations of media organizations and administrative agencies, bodies and offices operating in the field of information, especially in the context of elections. Measures to ensure fair access to the media, in accordance with the Paris Agreements, will be a priority matter for discussion in the media working group. The Information Director has also visited the radio stations and press facilities of three of the four parties, the exception being PDK.

(f) Inquiries and complaints

37. In keeping with its mandate (see S/23613, para. 108), the civil administration component has also established an Inquiries and Complaints Service, which works in close collaboration with the civilian police, electoral and human rights components. The Service has already taken up some 50 complaints.

(g) Optional control

38. On 26 May the Supreme National Council agreed to an UNTAC proposal to identify, in addition to the five areas specified in the Paris Agreements, administrative agencies, bodies and offices which could directly influence the outcome of the elections and which should therefore be placed under the direct supervision or control of UNTAC. This was done in accordance with annex 1, section B, paragraph 2, of the Paris Agreements. It was agreed that the organs in question should be those dealing with public health, education, agriculture, maritime and riverine fisheries, communications and posts, energy production and distribution, navigable waters and public transport, tourism and historical monuments, mines and general administration. It was further agreed that all administrative agencies, bodies and offices other than those listed above should, in accordance with annex 1, section B, paragraph 3, of the Agreements, be subject to general supervision.

2. Civil administration activities in the provinces

39. Provincial headquarters have been established and are now operating in all 21 provinces, including the cities of Phnom Penh and Sihanoukville. The typical provincial headquarters comprises a Director, a Deputy Director, a Finance Officer and a Human Rights/Information Officer, together with support staff. As noted above, electoral officials, who work in close cooperation with civil administration personnel, have also been deployed in all provinces.

40. On 28 August 1992, UNTAC convened a meeting in Phnom Penh with the provincial governors appointed by the Phnom Penh authorities to discuss issues that had emerged in various provinces as a result of the supervision and control exercised by the UNTAC provincial directors. These included the right of non-CPP political parties to open offices in the zone controlled by the

Phnom Penh authorities, land and property questions, freedom of movement and so on.

G. *Civilian police component*

41. Some 2,500 police officers have now been deployed out of the 3,600 provided for in the implementation plan. Arrangements for the deployment of more than half of the remaining police personnel are already in hand and consultations are being undertaken with Member States to ensure that the full authorized strength of the civilian police component is achieved as soon as possible.

42. In spite of this delay in its full deployment, the component has been able to extend its activities to all provinces. It has established a highly visible presence in Phnom Penh and at the provincial level, and is in the process of establishing police stations in the districts, as well as conducting regular patrols in the villages. It has a permanent presence in the zones of the FUNCINPEC and KPNLF in order to train and supervise their civilian police forces. At the press conference on 27 August mentioned above (para. 21), the PDK spokesman indicated that the party would send representatives to cooperate with UNTAC civilian police in seven Cambodian provinces. That cooperation has now begun.

43. The civilian police component works in close cooperation with the human rights, electoral, military, civil administration and repatriation components, and many of its activities have been referred to under those headings.

44. The component's duties also include directing the efforts of the local police force against the growing problem of banditry in the interior. In cooperation with the military component, it is discussing the supervision of checkpoints and patrols operated by the existing police forces in sensitive areas. A number of weapons have already been handed in to UNTAC civilian police monitors, who help to man UNTAC's border checkpoints.

45. In addition to his regular contacts with the Phnom Penh official responsible for public security, the UNTAC Police Commissioner also chairs a committee on traffic control with the participation of all parties except PDK. Since the arrival of UNTAC, the volume of traffic in Phnom Penh has greatly increased, causing congestion and confusion among drivers unaccustomed to heavy traffic. A number of accidents have occurred, and UNTAC's civilian police have introduced better training and traffic control procedures for police officers in the capital, as well as training courses for provincial police forces.

46. In addition to these substantive activities, the component's presence throughout the country supports the military component in "showing the flag" and assuring Cambodians of UNTAC's commitment to the peace process. The police presence, like that of the military,

promotes the creation of a neutral political environment by making Cambodians aware that arbitrary abuse of power will not be tolerated. It was UNTAC civilian police officers, for example, who played a leading role in securing the release of Mr. Ieng Mouly, a KPNLF member of the Supreme National Council, when he was arrested in July by the police of the Phnom Penh authorities. On several occasions also, NADK members have presented themselves with their weapons to civilian police personnel.

H. *Repatriation component*

47. Since the repatriation exercise began on 30 March 1992, more than 115,000 Cambodian refugees and displaced persons have returned to their country under the auspices of UNTAC's repatriation component with the Office of the United Nations High Commissioner for Refugees (UNHCR) acting as the lead agency. This has been accomplished without any major incidents. Some 250,000 remain to be repatriated, less those who return spontaneously without UNTAC/UNHCR assistance. UNHCR is making every effort to advise refugees on the situation prevailing in their communes of final destination, particularly when they are unsafe or inaccessible.

48. After a relatively slow start, during which the country's absorption capacity was tested, the monthly rate of return has now risen to more than 30,000 and is expected to increase to as much as 40,000 during the coming dry season. Given this rate of return, the continuing cooperation of the Thai authorities and the increasing eagerness of the border population to return to their homeland, the likelihood that most returnees will be home in time to take part in the electoral process is very high. Repatriation is being carried out by air, road, rail and, especially during the current rainy season, by boat.

49. Despite efforts to diversify the options for the returnees—e.g., offering them cash instead of land and building materials—the shortage of available and safe land still gives rise to concern. The slow pace of mine-clearing and continuing disputes over the ownership of land contribute to this scarcity, which is compounded by the prevalence in some parts of the country of banditry and malaria. However, the search for land has now been extended to the centre and east of the country, which are proving quite promising. In July 1992 UNHCR signed with the non-governmental organization Handicap International an agreement that provides for the recruitment of Cambodian mine clearance personnel trained and supervised by UNTAC.

50. The speed of return is such that the three smaller camps on the border—O'Trao, Site K and Sok

Sann—will be closed during October 1992. PDK has made no attempt to obstruct or interfere with the 35,000 or so persons who have returned to Cambodia from camps controlled by it. Indeed, PDK has in some respects been cooperative with the repatriation component of UNTAC. UNHCR has also taken steps to address the security situation at the largest refugee camp, Site 2, which has suffered from chronic law-and-order problems.

51. While most returnees so far have been repatriated to areas administered by the Phnom Penh authorities, more than 6,000 have been transported directly, at their request, to the KPNLF zone and movements of returnees wishing to go to the FUNCINPEC zone will soon begin. As long as UNTAC has no free access to the PDK zone, there are no plans to transport and assist returnees there. However, some may be going there of their own accord.

I. Rehabilitation component

52. Shortly after the establishment of UNTAC in Cambodia, a Technical Advisory Committee of the Supreme National Council was set up under the chairmanship of the UNTAC Director of Rehabilitation in order to facilitate the approval of projects with the consensus of the four parties. PDK initially refused to cooperate with the work of the Technical Advisory Committee because it considered that many of the projects under consideration tended de facto to support the Phnom Penh authorities through balance-of-payments and budgetary support, to the detriment of the other parties. However, since the Tokyo Ministerial Conference on the Rehabilitation and Reconstruction of Cambodia held in June 1992, at which the international community pledged nearly $880 million in aid to Cambodia, PDK has adopted a more positive attitude.

53. UNTAC has always made clear that international aid would be applied under its general direction, and would be designed to improve the lives of all Cambodians irrespective of party affiliation. In this respect, it is guided by paragraph 11 of the proposal for discussion elaborated at the Tokyo Conference, which states:

"It is a fundamental principle that multilateral assistance and budget support activities coordinated through UNTAC during the rehabilitation period shall be designated to the Supreme National Council and shall be disbursed when UNTAC can supervise the delivery or expenditure of money. In any United Nations documents referring to assistance or budget support for 'Cambodia' or for 'the Cambodian authorities', it is clearly understood that these terms refer to the whole territory of Cambodia or to the administrations of all Cambodian parties. It is also clearly understood that budgetary support to pay or subsidize the salaries of teachers, administrators, officials, health workers, etc., in 'Cambodia' is applicable according to need of the territory or administration controlled by each Cambodian Party."

The rehabilitation component is also guided by paragraph 12 of resolution 766 (1992).

54. At the Supreme National Council meeting of 16 July, UNTAC presented a list of 10 programmes totalling more than $187 million. The largest of these were the United Nations Children's Fund (UNICEF) programme of cooperation ($89 million), a three-year programme funded and executed by UNICEF and aimed at improving drinking water supply and sanitation, schools, health services and food security, as well as support for disadvantaged women and assistance to handicapped and disadvantaged children. The second major programme proposed was an aide-mémoire for an Asian Development Bank (ADB) soft loan for $74.4 million covering projects in transport, power, agriculture and education. The four Cambodian parties supported 9 of the 10 proposed programmes, but PDK opposed borrowing from an international financial institution until such time as the issue of the role and powers of the Supreme National Council was resolved. In the event, all ten programmes were approved by the President of the Supreme National Council, in accordance with the powers granted to him under the Paris Agreements.

55. On 24 August 1992, the Supreme National Council approved seven other programmes with a total funding of over $15 million and on 10 September a further six totalling some $27 million.

56. The activities of the rehabilitation component are also guided by paragraph 9 of the Tokyo proposal for discussion, which reads as follows:

"All foreign trade and investment agreements by all Cambodian parties shall be reported to the Supreme National Council secretariat and subject to UNTAC oversight in consultation with the Supreme National Council."

57. The attention of the Supreme National Council had been drawn to the problem of the overexploitation of Cambodia's natural resources. At its 7 May meeting, the Deputy Special Representative had pointed out that the rapid depletion of the country's timber stock and gem mines could not only have grave environmental consequences but could also affect the vital interests and the future of Cambodia in other ways. He invited the Supreme National Council to consider the possibility of establishing a mechanism for reviewing and examining the different contractual arrangements relating to the exploitation of natural resources.

58. Following the renewed attention given to this matter in the Tokyo proposal for discussion, the Supreme National Council decided on 23 July to set up another Technical Advisory Committee, also under the chairmanship of UNTAC's Director of Rehabilitation, to formulate and recommend to the Supreme National Council specific measures for dealing with the issue. The Technical Advisory Committee is now considering the merits of recommending to the Supreme National Council that it declare, *inter alia*, a country-wide moratorium on the export of logs from Cambodia.

J. Information/Education Division

59. The role of the Information/Education Division of UNTAC is to explain to Cambodians throughout the country the essence of the Paris Agreements and UNTAC's nature, objectives and activities. After two decades of fighting and international isolation, many Cambodians are little aware of the international community's efforts to assist their country. Many are sceptical about the applicability in Cambodia of basic concepts of human rights, including free and fair elections and multiparty political campaigning.

60. All four Cambodian Parties maintain their own broadcasting stations, each of which offers its audience a more or less one-sided version of current affairs. While the radio stations of three of the parties have cooperated with UNTAC by broadcasting information on the peace process and the United Nations role, the PDK radio has become increasingly hostile towards UNTAC and PDK has declined to broadcast UNTAC information and public awareness programmes.

61. The Division has undertaken a range of other activities to get its message across to Cambodians in all parts of the country and to counteract negative propaganda aimed at UNTAC. These include the production of audiovisual material in the Khmer language, which is distributed throughout the country by UNTAC military, police and civilian personnel.

62. The main vehicle for spreading the UNTAC message, however, is medium wave (AM) radio. Plans to acquire more equipment for producing UNTAC radio materials are now considerably advanced, and it is hoped that UNTAC's own broadcasting capacity will begin in October and reach its full operational potential by December. UNTAC plans to use one of the powerful transmitters of the Phnom Penh authorities as the core of its own operations beginning in October; but as that transmitter does not cover the entire country, relay transmitters for the provinces will be necessary. In the meantime, arrangements have been made with the Thai Foreign Ministry and Voice of America (VOA) for a VOA transmitter in Thailand to broadcast UNTAC materials at prime time twice daily.

63. The production of information is hampered by the language barrier. The great majority of Cambodians speak only Khmer, which requires the translation into that language of all information materials. Strenuous efforts are being made to identify and recruit properly qualified translators, but the number of these remains very limited.

64. The provision of information about UNTAC to Cambodians will continue to be important, particularly if PDK's non-cooperation continues. UNTAC will also have to ensure that all registered political parties have free access to the media and that detailed information is available to voters on the registration and voting procedures for the elections.

II. Conclusions and recommendations

65. UNTAC has made substantial strides towards its goals in the six months since its inception despite constraints imposed by the refusal of PDK to participate fully in the peace process, in particular the second phase of the cease-fire. Following the adoption of the electoral law, provisional registration of parties has begun and registration of voters is about to begin. Extensive military deployment across most of the country and a strong police presence extending to the village level have been established. More than 115,000 refugees and displaced persons have been safely repatriated. The international community has pledged $880 million to meet the essential rehabilitation needs of the country. Supervision and control over the existing administrative structures of three of the parties have been established and are being strengthened. UNTAC continues to inform Cambodians of their human rights and to foster the protection of those rights. All UNTAC's activities are becoming increasingly familiar to Cambodians throughout the country as a result of the information and public awareness campaign. UNTAC has thus acquired a powerful momentum that has enabled it to move ahead simultaneously on many fronts. Its presence has already had a profound and probably lasting impact on Cambodia. These achievements would not have been possible without the continuing support of the Security Council and the international community, the full cooperation of His Royal Highness Prince Sihanouk and the positive attitude and goodwill of the great majority of Cambodians.

66. Having carefully reviewed what UNTAC has accomplished so far, as well as the obstacles it has faced, I remain determined that the electoral process should be carried out in accordance with the timetable laid down in the implementation plan. While the attitude of PDK has limited implementation of the plan, UNTAC has

consistently stressed that the door is still open to PDK to participate fully and constructively in the peace process and that the military component stands ready to undertake the cantonment of NADK forces. My Special Representative has also made it clear that, in accordance with the Paris Agreements, UNTAC must be given unhindered access to PDK-controlled areas and that all its components must be allowed to operate as required in those areas in order to discharge their respective functions.

67. Meanwhile, UNTAC will press forward with the implementation of all the provisions of the Paris Agreements, including those concerning the verification of the withdrawal and non-return of foreign forces and the cessation of outside military assistance to the Cambodian parties. This may require an increase in the number of checkpoints within the country and along its borders with one or more of the neighbouring countries, as well as appropriate modifications in the manning of those checkpoints and an updating of their terms of reference. More intensive military investigations and patrols may also be required.

68. That said, the persistent failure of the PDK to meet the obligations it assumed when it signed the Paris Agreements obstructs the full implementation of those Agreements. The present drift in the peace process cannot be allowed to continue without seriously impairing UNTAC's ability to carry out its mandate within the time-frame set by the Security Council. It is clear that the time is approaching when some difficult decisions regarding ways and means of pursuing this operation will have

to be seriously considered. Naturally such decisions should be taken only when the international community is satisfied that every effort to resolve the present difficulties has been made. UNTAC will therefore continue to work closely with the parties and the Supreme National Council to identify possible solutions within the framework of the Paris Agreements.

69. For UNTAC to achieve its objectives, the continuing support of the international community, particularly of neighbouring countries as called for in resolution 766 (1992), will be invaluable, not least in helping to communicate to the leadership of PDK the firm resolve of the United Nations that UNTAC should implement its mandate vigorously and to the full. The support of the Security Council itself is of special importance. The Council may wish to take further action to impress upon the parties the international community's firm determination to press ahead with the implementation of the settlement, so as to bring peace to Cambodia and enable the Cambodian people to look to a better and more stable future.

70. In this connection, I intend, subject to the approval of the Security Council, to request the co-Chairmen of the Paris Conference to undertake, within a definite time-frame, consultations as provided for by article 29 of the Paris Agreements. These consultations would be carried out in close cooperation with myself and my Special Representative, with the aim of finding a way out of the present impasse or, if that should prove impossible, exploring appropriate steps to ensure the realization of the fundamental objectives of the Paris Agreements.

Document 46

Statement by the Foreign Ministers of the five permanent members of the Security Council following a meeting with the Secretary-General, 25 September 1992

S/24587, 25 September 1992

We have the honour to enclose the text of the statement issued following the meeting which you held on 25 September 1992 with our Ministers of Foreign Affairs. We should be grateful if you would arrange for it to be circulated as a document of the Security Council.

(*Signed*) LI Daoyu
Permanent Representative of China
to the United Nations

(*Signed*) Jean-Bernard MÉRIMÉE
Permanent Representative of France
to the United Nations

(*Signed*) Yuli M. VORONTSOV
Permanent Representative of the Russian Federation
to the United Nations

(*Signed*) David HANNAY
Permanent Representative of the United Kingdom of
Great Britain and Northern Ireland
to the United Nations

(*Signed*) Edward J. PERKINS
Permanent Representative of the United States of America
to the United Nations

Annex

Statement issued on 25 September 1992 by the Ministers for Foreign Affairs of the five permanent members of the Security Council following a meeting with the Secretary-General

On 25 September 1992, the Ministers for Foreign Affairs of the five permanent members of the Security Council were the guests at a luncheon given by the Secretary-General of the United Nations, H.E. Dr. Boutros Boutros-Ghali. Taking part were the State Councillor and Minister of Foreign Affairs of the People's Republic of China, H.E. Mr. Qian Qichen; the Minister of State, Minister of Foreign Affairs of France, H.E. Mr. Roland Dumas; the Minister for Foreign Affairs of the Russian Federation, H.E. Mr. Andrei V. Kozyrev; the Permanent Representative of the United Kingdom of Great Britain and Northern Ireland to the United Nations, H.E. Sir David Hannay, KCMG, representing the Secretary of State for Foreign and Commonwealth Affairs of the United Kingdom of Great Britain and Northern Ireland, H.E. Mr. Douglas Hurd; and the Acting Secretary of State of the United States of America, H.E. Mr. Lawrence S. Eagleburger.

The Ministers, meeting the Secretary-General in continuation of their close consultation as permanent members of the Security Council, noted that during the past year the United Nations efforts to maintain peace and security, to prevent and settle regional disputes brought real results. The Organization has become an increasingly effective instrument of collective efforts in maintaining international peace and security. The Security Council summit meeting in January 1992 demonstrated the high profile of the United Nations and the determination of the Council to build a safer and fairer world.

The Ministers noted with appreciation the report of the Secretary-General, "An agenda for peace". They welcomed the report which contains many interesting concepts and proposals as a forward-looking attempt to meet the challenges facing the United Nations in the 1990s. They look forward to further discussion of the report in the relevant bodies with a view to rapid and concrete follow-up.

The Ministers stressed the importance of the role of the United Nations in the field of emergency humanitarian assistance, in particular through effective coordination.

The Ministers expressed their deep concern over the situation in the former Yugoslavia. They called upon all the parties in Bosnia and Herzegovina to stop immediately military actions and to put an end to violations of the Geneva Convention of 12 August 1949 and breaches of International Humanitarian Law. They demand that necessary measures be taken for ensuring the safety of United Nations personnel and other personnel engaged in the delivery of humanitarian assistance. They noted with satisfaction that the London stage of the International Conference on the former Socialist Federal Republic of Yugoslavia had established a framework for the political settlement of the crisis in all its aspects.

The Ministers deplored persistent Iraqi non-compliance with resolution 687 (1991) and other relevant resolutions of the Security Council, and Iraq's failure to implement resolutions 706 (1991) and 712 (1991). They expressed their deep concern at the deteriorating conditions affecting the safety of United Nations personnel and the personnel of non-governmental organizations in Iraq and their support for the Secretary-General's continued efforts in relation to the humanitarian programmes in Iraq.

The Ministers welcomed the Secretary-General's efforts to ensure Libyan compliance with the relevant Security Council resolutions and urged him to continue his efforts.

The Ministers noted with satisfaction the constructive approach being taken by the parties in the Arab-Israeli negotiations within the framework of the Middle East Peace conference, and their readiness to discuss the core problems with a view to achieving a comprehensive, just and lasting peace based on resolutions 242 (1967) and 338 (1973) of the Security Council.

While reviewing the progress made by the United Nations Transitional Authority in Cambodia in implementing the Paris Agreements on a comprehensive settlement of the Cambodia conflict, the Ministers stressed their adherence to complete and timely implementation of these Agreements. They also expressed their deep concern over the difficulties which UNTAC faces in securing the full implementation of the Paris Agreements as described in the Secretary-General's report of 14 July 1992 and addressed in Security Council resolution 766 (1992). The Ministers assured the Secretary-General of their firm determination to support his efforts not to allow these difficulties to undermine the principles of the Agreements or delay their implementation. They noted with appreciation the efforts being made by the countries concerned to overcome the difficulties.

The Ministers expressed their support for the measures taken by the Secretary-General to assist fact-finding and reconciliation of the parties in Moldova, Georgia and Nagorno-Karabakh. They welcomed the efforts of the Commonwealth of Independent States together with those of regional organizations to establish collective mechanisms for the maintenance of peace on the territory of the former USSR.

The Ministers expressed their appreciation for the efforts of the Secretary-General to secure a peaceful transition of power to the Government of the Islamic State of Afghanistan. They support the continuation of international efforts aimed at ending the bloodshed and bringing stability in Afghanistan.

The Ministers called for the earliest resolution of related humanitarian problems including release of all prisoners of war from the former Soviet Union and return of Afghans who remain outside their country.

The Ministers commended the Secretary-General for his continuing efforts to achieve a comprehensive and just settlement to the Cyprus problem. They support the settlement of that problem on the basis of the Secretary-General's "Set of Ideas", including the map of territorial adjustments.

The Ministers welcomed the Secretary-General's report on the question of South Africa of 7 August 1992. They expressed deep concern about the recent escalation of violence and urged the Government of South Africa to take effective measures to stop it. They called upon all parties in South Africa to cooperate in combating violence through effective implementation of the National Peace Accord, and expressed the hope that observers deployed in South Africa under the terms of Security Council resolution 772 (1992) would be able to make a worthwhile contribution in this connection. They also underlined the importance of the resumption of the negotiating process leading to a peaceful transition to a democratic, non-racial and united South Africa.

The Ministers expressed their deep concern about the human tragedy in Somalia. They urged the Secretary-General to continue, in close cooperation with the Organization of African Unity, the League of Arab States and the Organization of the Islamic Conference, his efforts in search of a political settlement to the crisis in Somalia and called upon all parties, movements and factions in that country to facilitate the efforts of the United Nations, its specialized agencies and humanitarian organizations in providing urgent coordinated emergency assistance to the affected Somalia population.

The Ministers also reviewed with the Secretary-General some other regional disputes and expressed full support for his efforts for their settlement.

-They expressed their support for United Nations efforts in facilitating the implementation of the Peace Accords for Angola, in particular with respect to elections to be held on 29 and 30 September 1992.

-The Ministers encouraged the Secretary-General to assist the parties in Mozambique as they implement the peace settlement in this country.

-They call upon both parties in the Western Sahara conflict to cooperate fully with the Secretary-General and his Special Representative in their efforts to implement the settlement plan and to conduct an early self-determination referendum.

-The Ministers urge the Government of El Salvador and the FMLN to demonstrate good faith in implementing the agreements, fully to abide by the agreed time-limits, to exert every effort to bring about national reconciliation and to implement the process of demobilization and reform.

The Ministers supported the initial efforts of the Secretary-General to restructure the United Nations Secretariat with the aim of increasing its effectiveness and capability. They look forward to his continuing efforts to reform and improve the operation of the Secretariat and the overall United Nations system. In this context they noted the importance which the Secretary-General attached to the effective institutional follow-up of the United Nations Conference on Environment and Development, held in June 1992 in Rio de Janeiro.

At the meeting the Ministers noted with satisfaction a high degree of interaction and cooperation between the Secretary-General and the five permanent members of the Security Council. The Ministers expressed their confidence that this interaction will continue to develop in the interests of the United Nations and the whole international community.

The Ministers expressed their deep appreciation to the Secretary-General for his active contribution to ensuring peace and international security. They thanked the Secretary-General for his invitation to their meeting, which they consider to be very useful and constructive. They also agreed to continue consultations.

Document 47

*Letter dated 29 September 1992 from Mr. Khieu Samphan,
member of the Supreme National Council, to the Secretary-General
referring to "Cambodia: next steps", Australian paper*

Not issued as a United Nations document

May I be permitted to express our profound gratitude to Your Excellency for allowing me at the last Summit of the Non-aligned Movement to have with you a thorough exchange of views on the implementation stage of the Paris Agreement, particularly on how to overcome the difficulties that we are now facing. Since then, there have been practical approaches from all sides aimed at narrowing the positions that so far remain apart.

1. However, we have just been informed that Australia has lately elaborated and distributed a paper entitled: "Cambodia: next steps" to various missions and embassies accredited to the Supreme National Council in Phnom Penh. The document, which could be formally presented in the near future, suggests among other things "the implementation of the Paris Agreement without the Democratic Kampuchea party", the maintaining of the Phnom Penh regime and army; and the formation of "an administration" in which the two other parties would be included in the framework of the Phnom Penh regime, installed by Vietnam and used as a tool for its aggression and occupation of Cambodia since 1979.

We have also learnt that efforts have been made at different levels to have the United Nations adopt and carry out "the steps" outlined in the above-mentioned document. In this regard, we humbly solicit Your Excellency and all United Nations Members States committed to peace and justice to examine that document and form their views: are these suggestions contained in the paper conformed with the spirit and letter of the Paris Agreement, particularly its objective?

2. The Paris Agreement, to which we remain firmly committed, containing basic elements as follows:

-the verification of the withdrawal of all categories of foreign forces from Cambodia and their non-return;

-the formation of the Supreme National Council as "the unique legitimate body and source of authority in Cambodia" during the transitional period;

-the regroupment, cantonment, total disarmament and demobilization of up to seventy per cent, as a first step, of all Cambodian parties' armed forces;

-the organization and conduct by UNTAC of free and fair elections to enable the Cambodian people to exercise their sacred right to self-determination and to have a government of their own choosing in line with the regime of liberal democracy and pluralism within the framework of a free market economy and of an independent, peaceful and neutral Cambodia.

Clearly enough, the issues of verification of the withdrawal of foreign forces and the Supreme National Council being the unique legitimate body and sources of authority in Cambodia predominate over the others. The primary objective of the Paris Agreement is "to maintain, preserve and defend the independence, territorial integrity and national unity of Cambodia" and "to restore peace and promote national reconciliation" among all the Cambodian people regardless of their political affiliations and without discrimination or prejudice. UNTAC and the SNC are mandated to ensure the implementation of this Agreement and the fulfillment of its objective.

3. If those measures described in the above-mentioned document were accepted and implemented, would they be in line with the spirit and letter of the Agreement and serve its fundamental purpose? Obviously, those steps, if implemented, would not only jeopardize the integrity of the Agreement but also run counter to the profound aspirations of the Cambodian people for peace, national concord and reconciliation among the four existing forces presently in the country, Cambodia would not be able to free herself from foreign occupation, since there would be no participation of the four Cambodian parties in the verification process of the withdrawal of foreign forces and their non-return.

Those measures are clear attempts to deny any role and means to the SNC which groups all the four Cambodian parties while maintaining the Phnom Penh regime by associating "FUNCINPEC and KPNLF" with that party and by providing "urgent budget support" to prevent its "total collapse". It is known to all that that regime was installed by Vietnam more than thirteen years ago and has been served as a tool of its occupation ever since. In that condition, can there be effective verification of the withdrawal of all categories of foreign forces from Cambodia? Certainly not. On the contrary, that regime would be legitimized and Cambodia would be forever occupied by Vietnam.

4. From our part, inspired by a sincere desire to circumvent difficulties that have stood in the way of the implementation of the Paris Agreement, the Democratic

Kampuchea party has advanced successive proposals, the latest dated 22 August 1992, the contents of which have already been brought to Your Excellency's attention. We would like to solicit Your Excellency and all UN Members States committed to peace and justice to form their views: do the measures suggested in those proposals run counter to the spirit and letter of the Paris Agreement and its objective? What the Democratic Kampuchea party has asked for is only the strengthening of the role of the SNC by conferring upon it necessary powers and means needed to carry out its mandate as "the unique legitimate body and source of authority" in order to cooperate closely with UNTAC to ensure the implementation of the Accord, and the setting up of consultative committees within the existing administrative structures of the Cambodian parties so as to enable the latter together with UNTAC to control each other. Are these demands contrary to the spirit of the Agreement? We would be willing to enter into phase II as soon as measures are taken to enable the SNC to cooperate with UNTAC to exercise effective control in all aspects, especially the withdrawal of foreign forces from Cambodia.

It is a matter of common knowledge that foreign forces in various form— soldiers, advisers and experts— still remain in Cambodia in disguise as soldiers of the Phnom Penh party or civilian "advisers" or "experts" working in the administrative structure of that regime or civilians merged with the Vietnamese settlers or ordinary persons living in the countryside and the cities. Therefore, measures taken in the military aspect alone would not be sufficient and effective. Those measures, though necessary, should be within the framework of an all-aspect control by UNTAC in close cooperation with the SNC.

If the SNC composed of the four Cambodian parties continues to be denied of any substantive role, can UNTAC alone be in a position to exercise effective control both in the military and administrative aspects? The experiences of the past eleven months clearly testify that UNTAC, being out of touch with the Cambodian reality notwithstanding its goodwill, could not perform any effective control. It has not been able to verify the withdrawal of all categories of foreign forces from Cambodia and their non-return. Each Cambodian party continues to act at will in the areas it controls. A neutral political environment indispensable for the organization of free and fair elections has not been created. Insecurity has pervaded throughout Phnom Penh and other areas under the Phnom Penh party's control.

We sincerely trust that Your Excellency and countries committed to peace and justice would discern who have made every efforts to ensure the implementation of the Paris Agreement in its integrality, particularly the verification of the withdrawal of all categories of foreign

forces from Cambodia and the enhanced role of the SNC, and who have persistently refused the full implementation of the Paris Accord, and any effective role for the SNC making it impossible to cooperate with UNTAC in verifying the withdrawal of all foreign forces and their non-return.

5. Your Excellency has been well aware that, being an important component of the Cambodian National Resistance, the Democratic Kampuchea party has made all kinds of sacrifices and carried out for the past more than thirteen years arduous and hard-fought struggle along side with all Cambodian patriotic forces: Our sole objective is to ensure a complete withdrawal of all categories of foreign forces from Cambodia so that peace and independence could be restored and national reconciliation could be realized. As part of the then Coalition Government of Democratic Kampuchea, we have always actively worked for the overwhelming support of the United Nations General Assembly resolutions on the "Situation in Cambodia" which call for an end to foreign occupation and invasion, the withdrawal of foreign forces, the realization of national reconciliation among the Cambodian parties and the respect of the right to self-determination of the Cambodian people. The Paris Agreement of 23 October 1991 which incorporates all the principles laid down in those UN General Assembly resolutions was a source of delight for all the Cambodian people, including the Democratic Kampuchea party. We have therefore no reason whatsoever to prevent the Paris Agreement, obtained through long and difficult struggle, from being fully implemented. On the contrary, we have every interest and done our utmost to ensure the implementation of the Agreement in its integrality because it responds to the objective of our struggle as well as to the profound aspirations and the ardent wish of the Cambodian people.

At the same time, the Democratic Kampuchea party has no interest to oppose any UN involvement. On the contrary, we see the imperative need of the United Nations presence in Cambodia to ensure together with the SNC, the implementation of all provisions of the Paris Agreement without selectivity or discrimination. Your Excellency and countries committed to peace and justice the world over have not been unaware of the Democratic Kampuchea party's insistence for an enhanced role of the United Nations in cooperation with the four Cambodian parties to ensure the settlement of the Cambodian problem through a comprehensive and political solution; of who have strenuously opposed any United Nations role, and United Nations involvement in the verification of the withdrawal of foreign forces from Cambodia, and national reconciliation among all Cambodian parties.

Before the signing of the Paris Agreement in October 1991, these people had refused any settlement that called for the withdrawal of all foreign forces and the participation of all the four Cambodian parties. They had instead attempted to form a bi-partite coalition "administration" in the framework of the Vietnamese-installed regime in order to legitimize the Vietnamese occupation of Cambodia. These attempts have continued still even after the adoption of the Agreement by refusing true verification of the withdrawal of all categories of foreign forces from Cambodia and any effective role of the SNC composed of the four Cambodian parties. That is, Your Excellency, the real cause which has made the Paris Agreement largely unimplemented more than eleven months after its coming into force. In the face of such a situation, we sincerely hope that Your Excellency as the custodian of peace and the principles of the United Nations Charter together with all peace- and justice-loving countries the world over would redouble their efforts and contribute to an early implementation of the Paris Agreement in its integrality in order to achieve its noble objectives clearly enunciated in the Accord, namely the restoration of peace, independence and the promotion of real national reconciliation among all the Cambodian parties regardless of their political tendencies and without discrimination or prejudice.

Please accept, Your Excellency, the renewed assurances of my highest consideration.

KHIEU SAMPHAN
President of the Democratic Kampuchea Party
Member of the SNC

Document 48

Contribution dated 30 September 1992 by Mr. Son Sann, member of the Supreme National Council, to the search for a solution to the deadlock in the implementation of the Paris Agreements

Not issued as a United Nations document

It would be useful to recall that since 1979 the UNO voted each year with an increasing majority the draft Resolutions on Cambodia presented by the ASEAN countries asking particularly for: first, the withdrawal from Cambodia of all *foreign forces*; second, the non-return of the universally condemned practices and policies.

The October 23, 1991, Paris Agreement on Cambodia precisely mentioned—after the withdrawal of "foreign forces" and their non-return—disarmament and demobilisation of 70% of the armed forces of the four Cambodian parties, cantonment of the remaining 30%, then the organisation of general, free and fair elections all over Cambodia, in a really neutral environment. Which implies:

1) The re-instatement of Cambodia in its genuine borders, those recognized by the neighbouring countries. *Cambodia's territorial integrity* being guaranteed by the Paris Agreement;

2) *The withdrawal of all "foreign forces"* and their non-return; Now, since 1979, the so-called Vietnamese settlers have entered Cambodia in a great number, freely, without passport or visa, following on the Vietnamese invading troops. Since the signing of the Paris Agreement, those illegal Vietnamese settlers continue to arrive freely, to grab fertile lands, trades and jobs in town, fishing in our Great Lakes, management of our rubber plantations...

Most of them are demobilized Vietnamese soldiers, they are young and armed... A great many of them hold Cambodian identity cards and would have the possibility to vote in Cambodia... The presence of about one million Vietnamese is very badly accepted by the Cambodian people. Not to take into consideration this Cambodian popular feeling would be a mistake which might be important. To state that there is no evidence of the presence of Vietnamese troops in Cambodia is equivalent to the declaration by the Cambodians that there is no evidence of the total withdrawal of the Vietnamese troops. The 1949 Geneva Convention forbids the immigration of all those Vietnamese settlers during wartime, following the Vietnamese invading troops. All those illegal settlers must return to Viet-Nam before the May 1993 elections which will have to take place in a really neutral environment.

3) *The strict respect of Human Rights,* the end to abuses by force, intimidations, terrorism, etc... used as means to administrate. The UNTAC has worked very hard to try and make order, security and respect of Human Rights prevail. Nevertheless, the Cambodian people have not yet confidence. Reprisals and murders are still practised...

4) *Dismantling of all special police organizations* that are more or less led by Vietnamese advisors;

The Cambodian people will be reassured only when all powers are held by the SNC with the agreement of the UNTAC. When they feel really safe, they will give all the information needed about the presence of the Vietnamese "forces" in Cambodia.

5) *The redressment of all injustices* such as the impossibility for the Cambodians abroad to come and be registered in Cambodia to be able to vote. The same for the Kampuchea Krom (Cambodians from South Vietnam) who must be allowed to vote because they are Cambodians when in Cambodia.

When all these five conditions mentioned in the previous paragraphs are met, H.E. Khieu Samphan will have no more acceptable reason not to implement cor-

rectly, like the other signatories, the October 23, 1991 Paris Agreement.

We must avoid the interpretation of this Agreement in favour or against such or such Cambodian party. It is necessary to take into consideration the higher interest of the Cambodian people. This agreement aims at bringing a *durable peace* back to Cambodia, and to set up an environment truly neutral in order *to enable the Cambodian people to decide on their own fate thanks to the really free and fair elections, and above all to national reconciliation.*

SON SANN
President of the KPNLF and
Member of the SNC of Cambodia

Document 49

Security Council resolution on implementation of the Cambodia peace process

S/RES/783 (1992), 13 October 1992

The Security Council,

Reaffirming its resolutions 668 (1990) of 20 September 1990, 71 (1991) of 16 October 1991, 718 (1991) of 31 October 1991, 728 (1992) of 8 January 1992, 745 (1992) of 28 February 1992 and 766 (1992) of 21 July 1992,

Recalling the statement made by the President of the Security Council on 12 June 1992 (S/24091),

Recalling also the declaration on the Cambodia peace process adopted in Tokyo on 22 June 1992 (S/24183),

Paying tribute to His Royal Highness Prince Norodom Sihanouk, President of the Supreme National Council, for his efforts to restore peace and national unity in Cambodia,

Taking note of the cooperation extended to UNTAC, by the parties of SOC, FUNCINPEC and KPNLF, and of the fact that the PDK still fails to meet obligations it assumed when it signed the Paris Agreements, as reflected in the report of the Secretary-General dated 21 September 1992 (S/24578),

Reaffirming that UNTAC must have full and unrestricted access to the areas controlled by each of the parties,

Welcoming the achievements of UNTAC in the implementation of the Paris Agreements, concerning, *inter alia*, military deployment almost throughout the whole country, the promulgation of the electoral law, the

provisional registration of political parties, the beginning of voter registration, safe repatriation of over 150,000 refugees, progress in rehabilitation programmes and projects and the campaign in favour of respect for human rights,

Welcoming the accession of the SNC to a number of international human rights conventions,

Welcoming also the progress made by UNTAC in strengthening supervision and control over administrative structures as set out in the Paris Agreements, and recognizing the importance of this part of UNTAC's mandate,

Welcoming further the fact that the SNC functions in accordance with the Paris Agreements,

Expressing appreciation to the States and international financial institutions which announced, during the Tokyo Conference on 22 June 1992, financial contributions to Cambodia's reconstruction and rehabilitation,

Expressing its gratitude to the Governments of Thailand and Japan for their efforts to find solutions to the current problems relating to the implementation of the Paris Agreements,

Deeply concerned by difficulties faced by UNTAC caused in particular by security and economic conditions in Cambodia,

1. *Approves* the report of the Secretary-General (S/24578);

2. *Confirms* that, in conformity with paragraph 66

of the report, the electoral process shall be carried out in accordance with the timetable laid down in the implementation plan and thus that the election for a constituent assembly will be held no later than May 1993;

3. *Supports* the intention of the Secretary-General, expressed in paragraph 67 of his report, concerning the checkpoints in the country and along its borders with neighbouring countries;

4. *Expresses* its gratitude to the Secretary-General and his Special Representative for their efforts as well as to Member States which have cooperated with UNTAC in order to solve the difficulties it has met and *urges* all States, in particular neighbouring countries, to provide assistance to UNTAC to ensure the effective implementation of the Paris Agreements;

5. *Deplores* the fact that the PDK, ignoring the requests and demands contained in its resolution 766/(1992), has not yet complied with its obligations;

6. *Demands* that the party mentioned in paragraph/5 fulfil immediately its obligations under the Paris Agreements; that it facilitate without delay full deployment of UNTAC in the areas under its control; and that it implement fully phase II of the plan, particularly cantonment and demobilization, as well as all other aspects of the Paris Agreements, taking into account that all parties in Cambodia have the same obligations to implement the Paris Agreements;

7. *Demands* full respect for the cease-fire, *calls upon* all parties in Cambodia to cooperate fully with UNTAC to identify minefields and to refrain from any activity aimed at enlarging the territory under their control, and *further demands* that these parties facilitate UNTAC investigations of reports of foreign forces, foreign assistance and cease-fire violations within the territory under their control;

8. *Reiterates* its demands that all parties take all necessary measures to ensure the safety and security of all United Nations personnel and refrain from any threat or violent act against them;

9. *Emphasizes*, in accordance with article/12 of the Paris Agreements, the importance of the elections being held in a neutral political environment, *encourages* the Secretary-General and his Special Representative to continue their efforts to create such an environment, and in that context *requests*, in particular, that the UNTAC radio broadcast facility be established without delay and with access to the whole territory of Cambodia;

10. *Encourages* the Secretary-General and his Special Representative to make use fully of all possibilities offered by UNTAC's mandate, including annex 1, section B, paragraph 5 (b), of the Paris Agreements to enhance the effectiveness of existing civil police in resolving the growing problems relating to the maintenance of law and order in Cambodia;

11. *Invites* States and international financial institutions to make available as soon as possible the contributions they had already announced during the Tokyo Conference on 22 June 1992, giving priority to those which produce quick impact;

12. *Invites* the Governments of Thailand and Japan, in cooperation with the Co-Chairmen and in consultation with any other Government as appropriate, to continue their efforts to find solutions to the current problems relating to the implementation of the Paris Agreements and to report to the Secretary-General and the Co-Chairmen of the Paris Conference by 31 October 1992 on the outcome of their efforts;

13. *Invites* the Secretary-General, in accordance with the intention expressed in paragraph 70 of his report (S/24578), to ask the Co-Chairmen of the Paris Conference immediately on receipt of the report referred to in paragraph/12 of this resolution to undertake appropriate consultations with a view to implementing fully the peace process;

14. *Requests* the Secretary-General to report to the Security Council as soon as possible, and no later than 15 November 1992, on the implementation of this resolution and, if the present difficulties have not been overcome, *undertakes* to consider what further steps are necessary and appropriate to ensure the realization of the fundamental objectives of the Paris Agreements;

15. *Decides* to remain actively seized of the matter.

Document 50

*Letter dated 2 November 1992 from the Secretary-General to
Mr. Roland Dumas, Minister for Foreign Affairs of France and
Co-Chairman of the Paris Conference on Cambodia, referring to
Security Council resolution 783 (1992) and requesting that the
Co-Chairmen undertake consultations with a view to implementing
the peace process*

Not issued as a United Nations document; original in French

I have the honour to refer to resolution 783 (1992) adopted by the Security Council on 13 October. As you know, paragraph 12 of the resolution invites the Governments of Japan and Thailand, in cooperation with the Co-Chairmen of the Paris Conference and in consultation with any other Government, as appropriate, to continue their efforts to find solutions to the current problems relating to the implementation of the Paris Agreements and to report to the Secretary-General and the Co-Chairmen of the Conference by 31 October 1992 on the outcome of their efforts.

I have now received the report from the Governments of Japan and Thailand on their efforts to implement paragraph 12 of resolution 783 (1992). [Document 54.] You will note when you read the report that the two Governments have not been able to solve the current difficulties.

Consequently, in accordance with paragraph 13 of the resolution and paragraph 70 of my report of 21 September 1992 (S/24578), I should like to ask you and His Excellency the Minister for Foreign Affairs of Indonesia, in your capacity as Co-Chairmen of the Paris Conference, to undertake appropriate consultations with a view to implementing fully the peace process.

In this connection, I wish to recall that in paragraph 14 of resolution 783 (1992) the Security Council requested me to report to it as soon as possible, and no later than 15 November 1992, on the implementation of the resolution. The Council undertook, if the present difficulties had not been overcome, to consider what further steps were necessary and appropriate to ensure the realization of the fundamental objectives of the Paris Agreements.

Accept, Sir, the assurances of my highest consideration and my warmest regards.

(Signed) Boutros BOUTROS-GHALI

Document 51

*Letter dated 2 November 1992 from the Secretary-General to
Mr. Ali Alatas, Minister for Foreign Affairs of Indonesia and
Co-Chairman of the Paris Conference on Cambodia, referring to
Security Council resolution 783 (1992) and requesting that the
Co-Chairmen undertake consultations with a view to implementing
the peace process*

Not issued as a United Nations document

I have the honour to refer to resolution 783 (1992) adopted by the Security Council on 13 October. You will recall that paragraph 12 of this resolution invited the Governments of Thailand and Japan, in cooperation with the Co-Chairmen of the Paris Conference and in consultation with any other Government as appropriate, to continue their efforts to find solutions to the current problems relating to the implementation of the Paris Agreements and to report to the Secretary-General and the Co-Chairmen of the Paris Conference by 31 October 1992 on the outcome of their efforts.

I have now received the report of the Governments of Thailand and Japan on the efforts which they undertook in implementation of that provision. [Document

54.] Your Excellency will note from the copy of the report conveyed to you that the two Governments were unable to resolve the current difficulties.

I now have the honour, pursuant to paragraph 13 of the resolution, and as I had indicated in paragraph 70 of my report of 21 September 1992 (S/24578), to ask Your Excellency and His Excellency the Foreign Minister of France, the Co-Chairmen of the Paris Conference, to undertake appropriate consultations with a view to implementing fully the peace process.

In this connection, Your Excellency may wish to bear in mind that, by paragraph 14 of its resolution 783 (1992), the Security Council has requested me to report to it as soon as possible, and no later than 15 November 1992, on the implementation of that resolution. If the present difficulties have not been overcome, the Council has undertaken to consider what further steps are necessary and appropriate to ensure the realization of the fundamental objectives of the Paris Agreements.

Accept, Excellency, the assurances of my highest consideration and my personal warmest regards.

(*Signed*) Boutros BOUTROS-GHALI

Document 52

Letter dated 2 November 1992 from the Secretary-General to Prince Norodom Sihanouk transmitting report by Governments of Japan and Thailand in accordance with paragraph 12 of Security Council resolution 783 (1992)

Not issued as a United Nations document; original in French

I have the honour to transmit to you herewith a copy of the report presented to me by the Governments of Japan and Thailand in accordance with paragraph 12 of resolution 783 (1992) adopted by the Security Council on 13 October. [Document 54.]

The report confirms that the two Governments have been unable to solve the difficulties that have arisen in the implementation of the Paris Agreements on Cambodia. Consequently, in accordance with paragraph 13 of resolution 783 (1992), I have asked the Co-Chairmen of the Paris Conference to undertake consultations to consider ways of overcoming the difficulties in question. Attached you will find copies of the letters sent to them by me on the subject.

I am convinced that you can make a fundamental contribution to these consultations. I was pleased to learn in this connection that you plan to meet with the Co-Chairmen in Peking on 7 and 8 November 1992 and that you have invited the members of the Supreme National Council (SNC) to take part in the talks. I very much hope that all the members of the SNC will agree to cooperate fully with you in your efforts and in the efforts undertaken by the Co-Chairmen with a view to implementing the Paris Agreements and relaunching the peace process. I assure you that you may count on my personal support and on the support of my Special Representative.

I should also like on the occasion of your birthday to present to you my best wishes for happiness, health and success in your tireless action to achieve peace, stability and national reconciliation in Cambodia.

Accept, Your Royal Highness, the assurances of my highest consideration.

(*Signed*) Boutros BOUTROS-GHALI

Document 53

*Letter dated 12 November 1992 from Prince Norodom Sihanouk
to the Secretary-General concerning consultations in Beijing,
7-8 November 1992*

Not issued as a United Nations document; original in French

Thank you very much for your important letter dated 2 November 1992 and the documents that were enclosed.

As you already know, the consultations between Their Excellencies Messrs. Roland Dumas and Ali Alatas and Mr. Khieu Samphan of the Party of Democratic Kampuchea in Peking on 7 and 8 November 1992 did not lead to the result we (Your Excellency, the two Co-Chairmen of the Paris Conference on Cambodia, the international community, the immense majority of my fellow countrymen and I myself) had hoped for.

As you also know, I have always done my utmost to support and assist UNAMIC and your Special Representative, and His Excellency Mr. Yasushi Akashi, in the performance of their historic and extremely difficult mission in Cambodia. I shall continue wholeheartedly to support H.E. Mr. Yasushi Akashi and UNTAC in their noble mission, which is vital for Cambodia and its people.

Allow me to take this opportunity to again pay warm tribute to you for all you have done and continue to do for the well-being of my people and my country. We, Khmer, will never forget your kindness and your historic contribution to the rescue of Cambodia and its wretched people.

I thank you and urge you to accept the assurances of my highest and admiring consideration.

(Signed) Samdech Preah NORODOM SIHANOUK

Document 54

*Report of the Secretary-General on the implementation of Security
Council resolution 783 (1992) on the Cambodia peace process. Also
contains a brief overview of the main developments in Cambodia
since second progress report dated 21 September 1992; a report dated
31 October 1992 by Japan and Thailand to the Secretary-General and
the Co-Chairmen of the Paris Conference; and a report and statement
by the Co-Chairmen*

S/24800, 15 November 1992

1. The present report is submitted to the Security Council in pursuance of paragraph 14 of resolution 783 (1992) of 13 October 1992. It also contains a brief overview of the main developments in Cambodia since my second progress report dated 21 September (S/24578).

2. By paragraph 12 of resolution 783 (1992), the Security Council invited the Governments of Thailand and Japan, in cooperation with the Co-Chairmen of the Paris Conference on Cambodia and in consultation with any other Government as appropriate, to continue their efforts to find solutions to the problems relating to the implementation of the Paris Agreements (S/23177, annex) and to report to the Secretary-General and the Co-Chairmen by 31 October 1992 on the outcome of their efforts. In their report (see annex I), the Governments of Thailand and Japan informed me that they had had consultations with the Party of Democratic Kampuchea (PDK) on 22 and 29 October. The two Governments expressed disappointment that PDK had "refused to address the contents" of the suggestion that was presented to that Party with a view to "meeting the concerns repeatedly raised" by it on the role of the Supreme National Council. The two Governments concluded that, although PDK had not stated that it rejected their suggestion, "it was clear, in view of the response by PDK, that the tripartite consultation was no longer the appropriate means to address the impasse in the peace process".

3. As invited under paragraph 13 of the same resolution, I wrote on 2 November to the Co-Chairmen of the Paris Conference and asked them to undertake appropriate consultations with a view to implementing fully the peace process. I also wrote to His Royal Highness Prince Norodom Sihanouk, President of the Supreme National Council, to apprise him of these developments.

4. Pursuant to that request, the Foreign Ministers of France and Indonesia, the Co-Chairmen of the Paris Conference, met in Beijing with Prince Sihanouk, members of the Supreme National Council representing the four Cambodian parties and representatives of the five permanent members of the Security Council, as well as Australia, Germany, Japan and Thailand. My Special Representative also participated in the Beijing consultations.

5. The Co-Chairmen subsequently presented to me a report, which is attached as annex II. In that report the Co-Chairmen informed me that it had become clear, during the consultations, that three of the Cambodian parties "remained fully committed to continue cooperating in the implementation of the peace process". PDK, on the other hand, had confirmed that it was "still not prepared to cooperate in the further implementation of the Paris Agreements". Furthermore PDK had also indicated its intention "not to take part in the electoral process and in the subsequent elections, so long as, according to [that Party], a neutral political condition as provided for in the Paris Agreements was not ensured". It therefore appears, on the basis of the report of the Co-Chairmen, that PDK is not prepared, under present conditions, to comply with paragraph 6 of resolution 783 (1992).

6. In a declaration released after the Beijing consultations (annex III), the Co-Chairmen reaffirmed that no party was entitled to withdraw from its obligations on the pretext of any complaint it might have regarding the implementation of the Paris Agreements. The Co-Chairmen also considered that PDK non-compliance with phase II of the cease-fire required an adjustment of the implementation plan, particularly as regards the activities of the Military Component of the United Nations Transitional Authority in Cambodia (UNTAC).

7. The difficulties that have arisen in the implementation of the second phase of the cease-fire have led to the effective suspension of the cantonment, disarmament and demobilization process. Nevertheless, UNTAC continues to make steady progress in the discharge of the other aspects of its mandate. Indeed, in Phnom Penh and in much of the countryside, the process of peaceful change and emergence from isolation has rapidly evolved over the last few months. Scattered violations of the cease-fire and of human rights continue. In this connection, there has recently been a disturbing number of what seem to be politically motivated acts of harassment, intimidation and violence, as well as an increase in banditry and urban crime. But the widespread presence of UNTAC and the significant volume of international private investment in Cambodia since March 1992 have transformed both the physical environment of the country and the attitudes of its people. The latter is most evident in the voter registration exercise.

8. Since the opening of voter registration in Phnom Penh on 5 October 1992, about a million Cambodians, or almost a quarter of the estimated 4.5 million qualified to do so, have now been duly registered. The initiation of the registration process in each province has been staggered as follows: Kandal, Svay Rieng, Prey Veng and Kampong Cham on 19 October; Kampong Speu, Kampong Chhnang, Sihanoukville, Pursat and Takeo on 26 October; and Kampot, Kratie, Mondulkiri, Ratanakiri, Stung Treng, Koh Kong, Kampong Thom, Battambang and Siem Reap on 9 November. The process will be launched in the remaining two provinces, Banteay Meanchey and Preah Vihear, on 23 November 1992. Registration has so far proceeded successfully. The UNTAC-trained Cambodian registration teams, working under international supervision, are hard-working and enthusiastic, and the voters have displayed a high level of patience and commitment to the process.

9. In order to ensure the continued success of voter registration and of the subsequent elections, UNTAC will further pursue its efforts to create and maintain a neutral political environment, in accordance with paragraph 9 of resolution 783 (1992) and the relevant provisions of the Paris Agreements. This will require continued emphasis, *inter alia*, on respect for human rights and fundamental freedoms, as well as the fostering of a feeling of security on the part of all Cambodians.

10. On 9 November, UNTAC Radio began broadcasting from a Phnom Penh-based transmitter loaned for UNTAC's exclusive use by the Party of the State of Cambodia (SOC). The broadcasts concentrate on information regarding voter registration and the electoral process, but also feature human rights and other aspects of the UNTAC mandate. Preparations are proceeding for the acquisition and installation of booster stations to ensure that the UNTAC message can be beamed to all parts of Cambodia.

11. By paragraph 10 of its resolution 783 (1992), the Security Council encouraged the Secretary-General and his Special Representative to make use fully of all possibilities offered by UNTAC's mandate, including annex 1, section B, paragraph 5 (b), of the Paris Agreements to enhance the effectiveness of existing civil police in resolving the growing problems relating to the maintenance of law and order in Cambodia.

12. The UNTAC Civilian Police Component, which is responsible for supervising and controlling the local police, has now reached almost full deployment with the arrival in Cambodia of some 3,400 of the 3,600 provided for. About 60 to 65 per cent of police personnel are engaged full-time in directly assisting the voter registration process.

13. In addition, the Component is training the local police in basic police methods throughout the zones to which it has access. This includes investigation and traffic control, as well as giving special instruction to police officers and judges in the implementation of the new penal code adopted by the Supreme National Council on 10 September 1992. The Component is also working in close cooperation with the Human Rights and Civil Administration Components on public security-related issues.

14. I remain concerned, however, about the military situation in the country. After a period of relative quiet in the rainy season, tension has again increased in the central and northern parts of Cambodia following a series of artillery exchanges. These are generally of an indecisive character with few casualties on either side, and no overall pattern is evident. In the opinion of UNTAC the responsibility for these cease-fire violations is divided between the two largest factions, PDK and SOC. I sincerely hope, however, that these violations do not constitute a prelude to the resumption of dry-season military activity by any of the parties. My Special Representative recently issued a call for military restraint. I too appeal to all parties to respect the cease-fire scrupulously and to refrain, in accordance with article 9 of the Paris Agreements, from any activity which is aimed at enlarging the territory they control or which might lead to renewed fighting.

15. Another disturbing development, in direct violation of paragraph 8 of resolution 783 (1992), is an increase in attacks on UNTAC personnel and helicopters. On 5 November, an UNTAC helicopter flying from Siem Reap to Samrong suffered a loss in hydraulic pressure as a result of small-arms fire above the village of Phum Damari Slap and was forced to land. Another helicopter arrived within minutes and picked up the 11 passengers and crew, but was itself fired upon and hit by 3 bullets.

16. On 7 November, an attack took place on the village of Choan Khsan in the province of Preah Vihear. UNTAC was obliged to evacuate an electoral team and 11 civilian Police Monitors. There were no casualties, and the nearby UNTAC check-point was subsequently reinforced by the Military Component. These attacks took place in areas where PDK is known to be present. That party is also believed to be responsible for the destruction of two bridges, on routes 6 and 21, on 13 October.

17. In the cantonment process, which began in June with the declaration of phase II of the cease-fire, some 55,000 troops of the three participating factions, or approximately a quarter of the estimated total number of troops, have entered the cantonment sites and handed over their weapons. Some 40,000 of them were subsequently released, subject to recall by UNTAC, on agricultural leave. PDK has, however, refused to participate and ordered its troops not to canton, although some 200 personnel of the National Army of Democratic Kampuchea (NADK) have spontaneously presented themselves to UNTAC. Under the circumstances, it has not been possible to continue the cantonment process towards its conclusion.

18. UNTAC has devoted and will continue to devote serious attention to the question of foreign forces. The Strategic Investigation Team established under annex II, article X of the Agreements will shortly submit to a special session of the Supreme National Council an interim report on its investigations of allegations or suspicions of the presence of foreign forces in Cambodia. To date, UNTAC has not found evidence of the presence of any formed units of such forces in areas to which it has access. In this context, I wish to call on all parties to facilitate, in accordance with paragraph 7 of resolution 783 (1992), UNTAC investigations of reports of foreign forces, foreign military assistance and cease-fire violations within the territory under their control.

19. The issue of foreign residents and immigrants is a matter which deeply concerns many Cambodians. The recent killings of Vietnamese-speaking villagers and fishermen in Tuk Meas village and in Koh Kong province have aroused serious concern about public security as well as about their implications for the creation of a neutral political environment. UNTAC investigations indicate that units of NADK were responsible for both incidents. While the issue of foreign residents is a matter for discussion between the future government of Cambodia and the Governments of neighbouring countries, UNTAC is considering the establishment of a Technical Advisory Committee to the Supreme National Council to gather factual information as a basis for such discussion.

20. In accordance with paragraph 3 of resolution 783 (1992), by which the Security Council supported the intention of the Secretary-General concerning the checkpoints in the country and along its borders with neighbouring countries, UNTAC has drawn up plans to strengthen border controls. The effective implementation of these plans, however, will require the close cooperation of neighbouring countries, as called for in paragraph 4 of resolution 783 (1992) and in the relevant provisions of the Paris Agreements.

21. I have carefully noted the Co-Chairmen's views regarding the discussions held in Beijing on the proposal for holding an election to designate a Cambodian head of State on the basis of direct universal suffrage. It will be recalled that, in my second progress report, I had indicated that UNTAC was examining this proposal. I share the Co-Chairmen's assessment that the holding of a presidential election would contribute to the process of national reconciliation and help to reinforce the climate of stability which will be needed during the delicate period when the Constituent Assembly will have the task of drafting and adopting the new Cambodian constitution. I have therefore asked my Special Representative to make contingency plans for the organization and conduct of such an election by UNTAC, on the understanding that it would require, in due course, the authorization of the Security Council and the provision of additional resources. It should be stressed, however, that the presidential election would need to be held within a time-frame that was realistic and practicable and did not compromise the election of a Constituent Assembly, which is the central objective of the Paris Agreements and the culminating event of the peace process.

Conclusions

22. I sincerely regret that PDK has not found it possible so far to cooperate with UNTAC in the implementation of the provisions of the Paris Agreements or to heed the unanimous appeals contained in Security Council resolutions 766 (1992) of 21 July and 783 (1992) of 13 October. I also regret that the commendable efforts undertaken successively by the Governments of Japan and Thailand and by the Co-Chairmen of the Paris Conference have not convinced PDK to fulfil its obligations under the agreements it solemnly signed a year ago.

23. It is worth recalling, in this context, that all Cambodian parties unequivocally accepted, under section A of annex I to the Paris Agreements, that the Secretary-General's Special Representative would determine, in all cases, whether advice or action of the Supreme National Council, and therefore of its members, was consistent with the Agreements. The participants in the Paris Conference had felt that this specific provision, as well as others relating to the resolution of all issues concerning the implementation of the Agreements, was essential to avoid a paralysis of the peace process. This is precisely the danger with which the Security Council, the international community, and above all, the Cambodian people, are now confronted.

24. This situation presents the Security Council with two difficult decisions. First there is the question of what further action should be taken to persuade PDK to comply with its obligations under the Paris Agreements.

Considerable diplomatic efforts have been undertaken to that end by my Special Representative, by the other Cambodian parties, by Japan and Thailand and most recently by the Co-Chairmen of the Paris Conference. A number of measures, which have been taken by UNTAC in support of these diplomatic efforts, are referred to in this report and its annexes. Regrettably, these efforts have not succeeded. I have hitherto favoured patient diplomacy and I continue to believe that this is the best means of getting the peace process back on track. I am aware of the fact that there have been discussions on whether the Security Council should adopt a different approach and decide on specific measures to get PDK to honour its commitments. The feasibility of such measures would depend critically on the full cooperation of neighbouring countries and other Member States. I do not, however, recommend such an approach at this stage.

25. Secondly, it is necessary for the Security Council to decide whether to press on with implementation of as much as possible of the Paris Agreements, within the agreed timetable which calls for elections not later than May 1993, notwithstanding the non-cooperation of PDK. The alternatives would be either to put the process on hold until, by one means or another, PDK's cooperation was obtained or to conclude that it was not possible to pursue the operation under present conditions and that UNTAC should therefore be withdrawn. The latter course is clearly unacceptable after so much has been achieved and so many hopes raised that Cambodia will at last achieve peace and democracy. The idea of putting the process on hold must also be rejected. Neither the political nor the economic situation in Cambodia would sustain a prolonged transitional period. In addition, it would require the international community to maintain indefinitely a large and very costly operation, whose recurrent costs are now running at almost $100 million per month.

26. I therefore concur with the Co-Chairmen of the Paris Conference that the implementation of the peace process must continue and that the timetable, leading to the holding of free and fair elections no later than May 1993, must be maintained. But it is necessary to spell out what this will entail if—as I still hope will not be the case—PDK maintains its non-cooperation with UNTAC. The election will take place while a substantial part of the forces of the Cambodian parties remains under arms. Few of these troops will have been cantoned and the Paris Agreements' requirement that at least 70 per cent of them should have been demobilized will not have been met. This does not by itself mean that a free and fair election cannot be held; but it will add to UNTAC's difficulties both in organizing the election and in ensuring, as best it can, the security of candidates, voters and electoral offi-

cials throughout the electoral process. It also has to be observed that if UNTAC continues to be denied access to PDK-controlled areas, the people living in those areas are likely to be deprived of the opportunity to exercise their right to register and to vote.

27. In this connection, I have considered the possibility of organizing in these areas by-elections which would take place after the Constituent Assembly elections, provided UNTAC was given the access and freedom of movement required to ensure a free and fair process. I have, however, concluded that this idea is not worth pursuing for a number of reasons. Unless UNTAC had access to the population concerned and had been able to estimate its size, it would be technically difficult to devise an acceptable formula for calculating the number of seats to be kept vacant in the Constituent Assembly, especially since annex III, paragraph 2, of the Paris Agreements provides that the elections must be held "on a provincial basis in accordance with a system of proportional representation on the basis of list of candidates put forward by political parties". The holding of by-elections to fill the vacant seats would also lead to a delay in the Constituent Assembly's work and in the adoption of the new Cambodian constitution. This would in turn require an extension of the transitional period and would prolong UNTAC's costly presence in the country. In addition, this proposal could appear to give an unfair reward to a party that had failed to comply with essential provisions of the Paris Agreements, at the expense of other parties that had so complied. UNTAC will nevertheless continue to engage in an active dialogue with PDK, in an effort to meet any legitimate concerns that party may have and to persuade it to comply with its obligations under the Paris Agreements. In the hope that these efforts will succeed, UNTAC will remain prepared to accommodate PDK's entry into the process as long as this is practically feasible.

28. In the meantime, the various components of UNTAC will vigorously pursue the activities they have undertaken to implement, as far as possible, their respective mandates. The large number of Cambodians registering to vote is a significant sign of the change that has already taken place in the country. It demonstrates that Cambodians support UNTAC's efforts to achieve this change through peaceful means. UNTAC will therefore proceed with the preparations for the holding of the elections, in accordance with paragraph 2 of resolution 783 (1992).

29. UNTAC will give high priority to the creation and maintenance of a neutral political environment. In this context, it will actively support the right of any Cambodian to move freely throughout the country to exercise his or her right to register and to vote. UNTAC will broadcast to the widest possible audience the right

of each individual Cambodian, wherever he or she lives, to take part in the process, and the importance of exercising that right.

30. UNTAC will also continue to supervise and control the activities of the existing civil police forces to ensure that law and order are maintained effectively and impartially and that human rights and fundamental freedoms are protected. It will pursue the repatriation of refugees and displaced persons as well as the rehabilitation assistance programmes approved by the Supreme National Council. In the area of civil administration, UNTAC will continue to extend, as necessary, its supervision and control over the existing administrative structures. The cooperation extended by the parties of Front Uni National pour un Cambodge Indépendant, Neutre, Pacifique et Coopératif (FUNCINPEC), Khmer People's National Liberation Front (KPNLF) and SOC has so far been generally satisfactory. I wish to express my appreciation to these parties for their cooperation. At the same time, I wish to stress that the non-cooperation of one party should not be invoked by any other party as a pretext for withdrawing from its obligations under the Paris Agreements.

31 Given the continuing failure of PDK to enter phase II of the cease-fire and the resulting obstacle to the continuation of the cantonment and demobilization process, I have approved my Special Representative's recommendation that UNTAC should adjust the deployment of its Military Component, with a view to fostering a general sense of security among the Cambodian people and enhancing its ability to protect the voter registration and, subsequently, the polling process, particularly in remote or insecure areas. I am convinced, in this connection, that the projected reduction of the strength of the Military Component, as envisaged in my implementation plan of 19 February 1992 (S/23613), is no longer feasible. Accordingly, I propose that its present level of deployment be maintained until the elections. The financial implications of this adjustment to the implementation plan will be detailed in my forthcoming report to the General Assembly on the financing of UNTAC.

32. For UNTAC to achieve these goals effectively, the continuing support, commitment and cooperation of Prince Sihanouk, the Supreme National Council, the Cambodian people and neighbouring countries, is indispensable. The Security Council has a critical role to play in this regard. I hope that the Council will consider the adoption of measures that will facilitate UNTAC's mission and impress upon the parties concerned the firm determination of the international community to ensure the realization of the fundamental objectives of the Paris Agreements, so as to enable the Cambodian people to determine their own political future and open the way to

the peace, freedom, stability and prosperity to which they have aspired for so long.

Annex I

Report by the Governments of Japan and Thailand addressed to the Secretary-General of the United Nations and the Co-Chairmen of the Paris International Conference on Cambodia dated 31 October 1992

Introduction

1. The Governments of Japan and Thailand undertook consultations with the Party of Democratic Kampuchea (PDK) on 22 and 29 October 1992 on the basis of paragraph 12 of Security Council resolution 783 (1992) of 13 October 1992. The present report is submitted to the Secretary-General of the United Nations and to the Co-Chairmen of the Paris Conference on Cambodia, as called for by the resolution. The report describes the situation that led to the consultations, the result of the consultations and the assessment by the Governments of Japan and Thailand of the consultations.

Consultations by Japan and Thailand with the Party of Democratic Kampuchea

2. At the Ministerial Conference on the Rehabilitation and Reconstruction of Cambodia, held in Tokyo on 22 June 1992, an informal proposal for discussion consisting of 11 points was drawn up in order to meet some of the concerns expressed by PDK. a/ The proposal was discussed at the Supreme National Council meeting held on 8 July 1992 in Phnom Penh, and was accepted by the Party of the State of Cambodia (SOC), the Front Uni National pour un Cambodge Indépendant, Neutre, Pacifique et Coopératif (FUNCINPEC) and Khmer People's National Liberation Front (KPNLF), but not by PDK. PDK, in the meantime, issued a series of proposals (27 June, 3 July, 12 July) describing its perception on the implementation of the peace process and conditions under which it was prepared to participate fully in the peace process, including the entering into the second phase of the cease-fire.

3. Against this background, the Governments of Japan and Thailand decided to hold an informal dialogue with PDK to hear out its claims and concerns. The first of such consultations was held at Bangkok on 17 July 1992. At the meeting, the representatives of PDK stated its basic positions describing its perception of the problems in the implementation of the peace process. PDK stressed two main points as essential:

(a) Verification of the withdrawal from Cambodia of all categories of foreign forces and their non-return to the country;

(b) Strengthening of the role of the Supreme National Council and the effective supervision and control of the existing administrative structures.

In the dialogue, PDK noted that considerable progress had been made by the United Nations Transitional Authority in Cambodia (UNTAC) in meeting the first point, but that measures taken by UNTAC to address the second point were unsatisfactory.

4. The Governments of Japan and Thailand carefully assessed the contention of PDK. Both Governments were of the view that, if the claims of PDK could be met by the measures that fell within the framework of the Paris Peace Agreements, then those measures should be suggested for implementation. Recognizing that PDK was concerned mainly with the strengthening of the role of the Supreme National Council and the effective supervision and control of existing administrative structures, the two Governments proposed the establishment of an Administrative Consultative Body in their "suggestion" (see appendix I), which was conveyed to PDK at the second tripartite consultation on 22 August 1992 in Bangkok. PDK had also prepared its own proposal dated 22 August 1992 for the meeting and suggested the establishment of Consultative Committees (see appendix II).

5. The third tripartite consultation was held on 27 August 1992 in Bangkok. PDK had merged the Thai-Japanese suggestion with their own proposal and came up with the new proposal (see appendix III). Japan and Thailand stressed to PDK that any new proposal must conform strictly to the Paris Agreements and that, in their views, the establishment of the Consultative Committees within the respective existing administrative structures as proposed by PDK went beyond the framework of the Paris Agreements. The Governments of Japan and Thailand instead suggested that the Consultative Committees be established as regional subsidiary bodies of the Administrative Consultative Body.

6. The Security Council adopted resolution 783 (1992) on 13 October 1992 after deliberating on the Secretary-General's report of 21 September 1992 (S/24578). In the resolution, the Council invited the Governments of Thailand and Japan, in cooperation with the Co-Chairmen and in consultation with any other Government as appropriate, to continue their efforts to find solutions to the current problems relating to the implementation of the Paris Agreements and to report to the Secretary-General and the Co-Chairmen of the Paris Conference by 31 October 1992 on the outcome of the efforts.

7. Immediately following the adoption of Security Council resolution 783 (1992), the Governments of

a/ S/24286 [Document 41]

Japan and Thailand began their work on revising their suggestion. The full responsibility for the revised suggestion (see appendix IV) rests with the Governments of Japan and Thailand, but the countries concerned and the United Nations Transitional Authority in Cambodia were consulted for their opinions prior to finalizing the text. The revised suggestion of Japan and Thailand was handed to PDK on 22 October 1992 in Phnom Penh, and it was agreed that both sides would meet again on 29 October 1992 to hear the views of PDK.

8. The fourth tripartite consultation between Japan, Thailand and PDK took place on 29 October 1992 in Phnom Penh. The representatives of the Co-Chairmen and UNTAC were invited to attend the consultation as observers.

9. (a) In the consultation, it was explained by Thailand and Japan to PDK that the meeting would be the last of the tripartite consultations, and that the consultation was conducted on the basis of Security Council resolution 783 (1992);

(b) Contrary to its position during the 22 and 27 August 1992 tripartite meetings, where PDK sought to address specific issues with a view to returning to the peace process, PDK stated that, in order to resolve the present impasse, it was necessary to discuss and come to a common understanding on the general situation concerning the implementation of the Paris Agreements and that, if a common understanding could be reached, then it would be easier to find specific measures to address the issues at hand. PDK then went on to reiterate its basic positions at great length, stressing that the most important aspect of the Paris Agreements, in its view, was to realize the withdrawal of all foreign forces from Cambodia. With regard to the revised suggestion by Japan and Thailand, PDK stated that, although it had studied the suggestion carefully, it did not consider that it addressed the deep aspiration of the Cambodian people. PDK further criticized UNTAC, in strong terms, saying that UNTAC cooperated with one of the Cambodian parties rather than the Supreme National Council in its implementation of the Paris Agreements. It further criticized recent UNTAC decisions and measures by saying that they had been taken without taking into consideration the role of the Supreme National Council;

(c) Both Japan and Thailand expressed their disappointment at the reaction of PDK, stressing, *inter alia*, that:

(i) In the previous consultations in August, PDK had explicitly confirmed that the strengthening of the role of the Supreme National Council and the establishment of the Consultative Committees were the only requirements on its part to enter into the second phase of the cease-fire;

(ii) The two Governments had, from the beginning of the consultations, tried to address the central concern of PDK as explained to them by PDK;

(iii) The broader context which PDK insisted as the fundamental issue to be addressed went beyond the scope of the efforts of Japan and Thailand called for by the Security Council and could not be addressed in the tripartite consultation;

(d) Japan and Thailand sought to obtain PDK's clearer reaction with regard to the revised suggestion of the two countries, but PDK only reverted to its previous statement without discussing the Thai-Japanese suggestion;

(e) In closing, the two countries expressed their hope that a solution might be found through further dialogue.

Observations by Japan and Thailand

10. With regard to our assessment of this latest and final round of talks with PDK, the two countries are disappointed at the outcome in that (a) PDK has refused to address the contents of the Thai-Japanese suggestion, which is aimed precisely at meeting the concerns repeatedly raised by PDK on the role of the Supreme National Council; and (b) that PDK has once again gone back to talking about the broader situation concerning the implementation of the Paris Agreements, which has made it difficult, if not impossible, to pinpoint specific remedial measures. In this respect, PDK had backtracked on its earlier position in its proposals of 22 and 27 August 1992.

11. With regard to the revised Thai-Japanese suggestion, although PDK had not stated that it rejected the suggestion and although the elements in the suggestion may be relevant in addressing some of the concerns raised by PDK, it was clear, in view of the response by PDK, that the tripartite consultation was no longer the appropriate means to address the impasse in the peace process.

12. The Governments of Japan and Thailand firmly believe that the election for a constituent assembly should be held no later than May 1993, and that the Co-Chairmen of the Paris Conference should embark upon appropriate consultations as called for in Security Council resolution 783 (1992) with a view to implementing the peace process fully.

13. The Governments of Japan and Thailand remain ready to cooperate with the Co-Chairmen, His Royal Highness Samdech Preah Norodom Sihanouk, the United Nations and all parties concerned in the imple-

mentation of the Paris Agreements to bring about a lasting peace in Cambodia.

Appendix I
Suggestion by Thailand and Japan

1. In addition to the 11 points contained in the Tokyo "non-paper" (see S/24286, annex), it is suggested that a new body be set up to deliberate on any requests, suggestions as well as possible complaints regarding all administrative matters that are related to the control and supervision by UNTAC of existing administrative structures stipulated in the Paris Agreements.

2. The Supreme National Council delegates to UNTAC all the necessary powers for the implementation of the Paris Agreements and, accordingly, the existing administrative structures must be placed under control of UNTAC according to the Paris Agreements.

3. The body shall be called the "Administrative Consultative Body" and shall be placed under the auspices of UNTAC (see attachment for the details).

4. The Administrative Consultative Body is designed to address administrative issues with a view to ensuring the neutrality of administrative actions leading to the holding of free and fair elections in Cambodia and will make recommendations to UNTAC for decision. All policy matters relating to the implementation of the Paris Agreements shall be handled by UNTAC in consultation with the Supreme National Council.

5. The functions of the Administrative Consultative Body shall be in strict conformity with the terms of the Paris Agreements.

6. The Administrative Consultative Body shall be established when all the Cambodian parties enter into phase II of the cease-fire.

Attachment
Administrative Consultative Body

1. *Objective*: Act as a coordinating body for consideration of any requests made by any of the Cambodian parties regarding administrative matters relating to the implementation of the Paris Agreements.

2. *Composition*:

(a) Representatives of the four Cambodian parties: the ratio of representation is to be the same as that for the Supreme National Council;

(b) Representatives of UNTAC;

(c) One representative from the five permanent members of the Security Council, plus, as an observer with the right to speak, on a rotational basis in the alphabetical order of the following countries: Australia, China, France, Indonesia, Japan, Russian Federation, Thailand, United Kingdom of Great Britain and Northern Ireland and United States of America;

(d) The meetings are to be chaired by the Director for Civil Administration of UNTAC to be appointed by the Special Representative of the Secretary-General of the United Nations.

3. The Administrative Consultative Body shall be convened on a regular basis.

4. *Functions of the Administrative Consultative Body: screening of the requests*:

(a) If the requests warrant deliberations:

(i) Hearing of the party making the request and the party to which the request is directed will be conducted;

(ii) The Administrative Consultative Body may make recommendations to UNTAC for decision;

(b) If the requests do not merit further deliberation by UNTAC, the requesting party will be told of the conclusion together with the reasoning.

Appendix II
Proposal of the Party of Democratic Kampuchea on the role of the Supreme National Council and the implementation of phase II dated 22 August 1992

The Cambodian people and the international community have always reaffirmed the need for respecting the inalienable right of the Cambodian people freely to determine their destiny without outside pressure or interference.

They deem it necessary that the 23 October 1991 Paris Agreement on a Comprehensive Political Settlement of the Cambodia conflict be implemented loyally, impartially and in a balanced manner, especially its following two key provisions:

(a) The verification of the withdrawal of all categories of foreign forces from Cambodia and their non-return to the country;

(b) The appropriate measures to be taken so as to enable the Supreme National Council to fulfil its mandate as "the unique legitimate body and source of authority in Cambodia" during the transitional period.

The Cambodian people and the international community as a whole and the Association of South-East Asian Nations (ASEAN) in particular have expressed their earnest hope to see the Supreme National Council with His Royal Highness Samdech Norodom Sihanouk, Head of State, as its President, play its eminent role as "the unique legitimate body and source of authority in Cambodia", and called on all parties concerned to safeguard the integrity of the Supreme National Council.

His Excellency Yasushi Akashi, Special Representative of the Secretary-General and head of UNTAC, who, together with the Supreme National Council, has been entrusted by the Paris Agreement to see to it that the Agreement is implemented loyally, impartially and in a balanced manner, recognized at the Supreme National Council meeting in Siem Reap on 5 August 1992 that "there should be no government in Cambodia during the transitional period", that "all authority rests between UNTAC and the Supreme National Council", and that "the Cambodian sovereignty lies with the Supreme National Council".

The Party of Democratic Kampuchea, deeply devoted to peace, independence and national reconciliation, would like to express once again its unswerving commitment to the Paris Agreement.

Anxious to have the peace process move forward and the Paris Agreement implemented loyally, impartially and in a balanced manner by all parties concerned, the Party of Democratic Kampuchea:

(a) Expresses its readiness to enter phase II if appropriate measures are taken to confer upon the Supreme National Council all power and means to fulfil its mandate as "the unique legitimate body and source of authority in Cambodia" so as to enable the Supreme National Council with His Royal Highness Samdech Preah Norodom Sihanouk, Head of State, as its President, to take initiatives and actions aimed at achieving progressively national reconciliation and at the same time creating propitious conditions for fruitful cooperation between the Supreme National Council and UNTAC in the implementation of the Paris Agreement, all this in accordance with the unanimous wish of all and in keeping with the spirit and letter of the Paris Agreement;

(b) Wishes in this spirit that, among appropriate measures to be taken, the Consultative Committees of the Supreme National Council to be chaired by UNTAC be set up within the existing administrative structures and the police forces of all the Cambodian parties. Those Consultative Committees will assist UNTAC in its tasks of control and/or supervision of the existing administrative structures and the police forces of all the Cambodian parties, with a view to establishing and maintaining transparency and mutual confidence among all the Cambodian parties and achieving genuine national reconciliation and a neutral political environment conducive to the organization and conduct of free, democratic and fair general elections.

We also deem it necessary that the representatives of the four Cambodian parties be associated in the process of regroupment and cantonment of the armed forces of the four Cambodian parties.

The Party of Democratic Kampuchea hopes that this proposal, inspired by sincere goodwill to have the implementation of the Paris Agreement move forward, be seriously taken into consideration by all parties concerned.

Appendix III
Proposal of the Party of Democratic Kampuchea on the role of the Supreme National Council and the implementation of phase II dated 27 August 1992

The Cambodian people and the international community have always reaffirmed the need for respecting the inalienable right of the Cambodian people freely to determine their destiny without outside pressure or interference.

They deem it necessary that the 23 October 1991 Paris Agreement on a Comprehensive Political Settlement of the Cambodia conflict be implemented loyally, impartially and in a balanced manner, especially its following two key provisions:

(a) The verification of the withdrawal of all categories of foreign forces from Cambodia and their non-return to the country;

(b) The appropriate measures to be taken so as to enable the Supreme National Council to fulfil its mandate as "the unique legitimate body and source of authority in Cambodia" during the transitional period.

The Cambodian people and the international community as a whole and the Association of South-East Asian Nations (ASEAN) in particular have expressed their earnest hope to see the Supreme National Council with His Royal Highness Samdech Preah Norodom Sihanouk, Head of State, as its President, play its eminent role as "the unique legitimate body and source of authority in Cambodia", and called on all parties concerned to safeguard the integrity of the Supreme National Council.

His Excellency Yasushi Akashi, Special Representative of the Secretary-General and head of UNTAC, who, together with the Supreme National Council has been entrusted by the Paris Agreement to see to it that the Agreement is implemented loyally, impartially and in a balanced manner, recognized at the Supreme National Council meeting in Siem Reap on 5 August 1992 that "there should be no government in Cambodia during the transitional period", that "all authority rests between UNTAC and the Supreme National Council", and that "the Cambodian sovereignty lies with the Supreme National Council".

The Party of Democratic Kampuchea, deeply devoted to peace, independence and national reconciliation, would like to express once again its unswerving commitment to the Paris Agreement.

Anxious to have the peace process moved forward

and the Paris Agreement implemented loyally, impartially and in a balanced manner by all parties concerned, the Party of Democratic Kampuchea would like to make the following proposal:

(a) The Party of Democratic Kampuchea expresses its readiness to enter phase II if appropriate measures are taken to confer upon the Supreme National Council all power and means to fulfil its mandate as "the unique legitimate body and source of authority in Cambodia" so as to enable the Supreme National Council with His Royal Highness Samdech Preah Norodom Sihanouk, Head of State, as its President, to take initiatives and actions aimed at achieving progressively national reconciliation and at the same time creating propitious conditions for fruitful cooperation between the Supreme National Council and UNTAC in the implementation of the Paris Agreement, all this in accordance with the unanimous wish of all and in keeping with the spirit and letter of the Paris Agreement;

(b) Among appropriate measures, to set up:

(i) The Administrative Consultative Body or ACB (see attachment);

(ii) The Consultative Committees within the existing administrative structures and the police forces of all the Cambodian parties (see attachment).

We also deem it necessary that the representatives of the four Cambodian parties be associated in the control and verification process of the regroupment and cantonment of the armed forces of the four Cambodian parties.

Attachment

I. *The Administrative Consultative Body or ACB*

1. *Objective*: To address administrative issues with a view to ensuring the neutrality of administrative actions and a neutral political environment leading to the holding of free and fair general elections in Cambodia and to make recommendations to UNTAC and the Supreme National Council for decision.

2. *Composition*:

(a) Representatives of the four Cambodian parties: ratio of representation is the same as that for the Supreme National Council;

(b) Representatives of UNTAC;

(c) One representative from the five permanent members of the Security Council, plus, as an observer with the right to speak, on a rotational basis in the alphabetical order of the following countries: Australia, China, France, Indonesia, Japan, Russian Federation, Thailand, United Kingdom of Great Britain and Northern Ireland and United States of America;

(d) The meetings are to be chaired by the Director

for Civil Administration of UNTAC to be appointed by the Special Representative of the Secretary-General of the United Nations.

3. *Meetings*: The Administrative Consultative Body shall be convened on a regular basis.

4. *Function of the Administrative Consultative Body*: To make recommendations to UNTAC and the Supreme National Council for decision.

II. *The Consultative Committees or CCs*

1. *Composition*:

(a) Representatives of the four Cambodian parties;

(b) Representatives of UNTAC, who will be the Chairmen of the Consultative Committees.

2. *Functions of the Consultative Committees*: To assist the Administrative Consultative Body in achieving its objective.

Appendix IV
Revised suggestion by Thailand and Japan

In addition to the 11 points contained in the Tokyo "non-paper" (see S/24286, annex), the following are suggested to contribute to ensuring the neutrality of administrative actions.

A. *Establishment of the Administrative Consultative Body and the Consultative Committees*

1. It is suggested that a system of bodies be set up to deliberate on any requests, suggestions as well as possible complaints regarding all administrative matters that are related to the control and supervision by UNTAC of existing administrative structures stipulated in the Paris Agreements.

2. The Supreme National Council delegates to UNTAC all the necessary powers for the implementation of the Paris Agreements and, accordingly, the existing administrative structures must be placed under control of UNTAC according to the Paris Agreements.

3. The system of bodies will consist of the "Administrative Consultative Body" and "Consultative Committees" which will be the regional subsidiary bodies of the Administrative Consultative Body (see attachment for details).

4. The Administrative Consultative Body and the Consultative Committees are designed to address administrative issues with a view to ensuring the neutrality of administrative actions relevant to the holding of free and fair elections in Cambodia. The Administrative Consultative Body and the Consultative Committees will have consultative role, and will refer matters through the Administrative Consultative Body to UNTAC and the Supreme National Council. Decisions on the matters referred will be made in accordance with annex I to the

Agreement on a Comprehensive Political Settlement of the Cambodia Conflict. All policy matters relating to the implementation of the Paris Agreements will be directly handled by UNTAC and the Supreme National Council in accordance with the Paris Agreements.

5. The functions of the Administrative Consultative Body and the Consultative Committees will be in strict conformity with the terms of the Paris Agreements.

6. The Administrative Consultative Body as well as the Consultative Committees will be established when all the Cambodian parties enter into phase II of the cease-fire.

B. *Transparency*

Besides the proposed establishment of the Administrative Consultative Body and the Consultative Committees, it is suggested that UNTAC inform the Supreme National Council monthly of its activities concerning the control and supervision of existing administrative structures, *inter alia*, the activities of the working groups and technical advisory groups and the work of UNTAC personnel installed in administrative agencies, bodies and offices of the existing administrative structures.

Attachment
Administrative Consultative Body

1. *Objective:* Act as a coordinating body for consideration of any requests made by any of the Cambodian parties regarding administrative matters related to the control and supervision by UNTAC of existing administrative structures stipulated in the Paris Agreements.

2. *Composition:*

(a) Representatives of the four Cambodian parties: the ratio of representatives is to be the same as that for the Supreme National Council;

(b) Representatives of UNTAC;

(c) The meetings are to be chaired by the Director for Civil Administration of UNTAC, or by another official to be appointed by the Special Representative of the Secretary-General of the United Nations.

3. The Administrative Consultative Body will be convened on a regular basis, in principle once a week.

4. *Functions of the Administrative Consultative Body:*

(a) If the requests warrant deliberations:

(i) The Administrative Consultative Body will hold a hearing of the party making the request and the party to which the request is directed;

(ii) After deliberations, the Administrative Consultative Body may refer the matter to UNTAC and the Supreme National Council. Decisions on the matters referred will be made in accordance with

annex I to the Agreement on a Comprehensive Political Settlement of the Cambodia Conflict;

(b) If the requests do not merit further deliberation by the Supreme National Council and UNTAC, or when the appeals by a party on the conclusions of the Consultative Committees are dismissed, the requesting party will be told of the conclusion together with the reasons.

5. *Consultative Committees:*

(a) A Consultative Committee will be established in each zone controlled by respective administrative structures of the four Cambodian parties;

(b) The Consultative Committees will act as regional offices of the Administrative Consultative Body. Each Consultative Committee will consider requests made by any of the Cambodian parties regarding administrative matters that are related to the control and supervision by UNTAC of existing administrative structures within its zone;

(c) The Consultative Committees may refer the matter to the Administrative Consultative Body for further consideration. Any party may make an appeal to the Administrative Consultative Body if it finds the conclusion of the Consultative Committees to be unsatisfactory by providing the reason for its dissatisfaction;

(d) The Consultative Committees will be composed of the representatives of the four Cambodian parties whose ratio of representation is to be the same as that for the Supreme National Council, and of the representatives of UNTAC. They will be chaired by the Senior Representative of UNTAC;

(e) The meetings of the Consultative Committees will be held in the location to be chosen by their Chairman as appropriate in consideration of the subject in question, which could eventually include the office of the respective administrative structures whose functional jurisdiction covers the matter being brought to the Consultative Committees;

(f) The Consultative Committees may seek relevant information from the parties concerned and may have hearings.

Annex II
Report of the Co-Chairmen of the Paris Conference on Cambodia

In your letter dated 2 November 1992, you asked us, in our capacity as Co-Chairmen of the Paris Conference and according to paragraph 13 of Security Council resolution 783 (1992) adopted on 13 October 1992, to undertake appropriate consultations with a view to implementing fully the peace process in Cambodia.

In response to that request, the two Co-Chairmen undertook consultations in Beijing on 7 and 8 November with the President of the Supreme National Council of Cambodia, His Royal Highness Prince Norodom Sihanouk, your Special Representative H.E. Mr. Yasushi Akashi, as well as with His Royal Highness Prince Ranariddh representing the FUNCINPEC, H.E. Mr. Son Sann representing the Khmer People's National Liberation Front (KPNLF), H.E. Mr. Khieu Samphan representing the Party of Democratic Kampuchea (PDK) and H.E. Mr. Hun Sen representing the Party of the State of Cambodia (SOC). Consultations were also conducted with the representatives of the permanent members of the Security Council, as well as of Japan, Thailand, Australia and Germany.

To make this meeting most profitable, we conducted on 7 November 1992, throughout the day, consultations which enabled us to gather the views of His Royal Highness Prince Sihanouk, Mr. Akashi, each of the Cambodian factions, the representatives of the permanent members of the Security Council, and the representatives of the above-mentioned other Governments. On the following day, 8 November 1992, the Supreme National Council of Cambodia convened a special session under the chairmanship of His Royal Highness Prince Norodom Sihanouk, in which the two Co-Chairmen, your Special Representative and the representatives of the above-mentioned countries also participated.

As a result of these meetings, we have the honour to present the following observations:

(a) It was generally agreed that, in many respects, encouraging progress was being made in the implementation of the Paris Agreements:

(i) The Supreme National Council, under the chairmanship of His Royal Highness Prince Norodom Sihanouk, has been meeting on a regular basis and has adopted many important decisions;

(ii) Preparations for elections have been started: 11 parties have been provisionally registered so far; the registration of voters, which started on 5 October 1992, is proceeding well and should be completed by January 1993. 500,000 Cambodians have been registered so far, thus showing the desire of the Cambodian people to participate actively in the elections;

(iii) The repatriation of more than 170,000 refugees and displaced persons, out of a total of 350,000, has proceeded satisfactorily. It can now be expected that all the refugees will be repatriated before the May 1993 elections;

(iv) Supervision and control over existing administrative structures has been established throughout the Cambodian territory, except in areas under the control of the Party of Democratic Kampuchea;

(v) Finally, disbursement of assistance for the rehabilitation of Cambodia as decided at the Tokyo Conference in June 1992 has started throughout the country for the benefit of the Cambodian people;

(b) We pay tribute to His Royal Highness Prince Norodom Sihanouk, for his tireless efforts to restore peace and national unity in Cambodia. We welcome your action, as well as the contribution of your Special Representative and of all those who made such a significant progress possible;

(c) During the talks that we held with the representatives of the four Cambodian parties, it became clear that three of those parties remained fully committed to continue cooperating in the implementation of the peace process. On the other hand, PDK confirmed that it was still not prepared to cooperate in the further implementation of the Paris Agreements so long as what they claim to be the improper implementation of certain aspects of those agreements, specifically, regarding verification of foreign (Vietnamese) troops withdrawal and their non-return and regarding the status and functioning of the Supreme National Council, were not resolved. As is known, this party continues to oppose UNTAC deployment in the areas under its control and has so far not complied with its obligations under phase II of the ceasefire and military arrangements (i.e. regroupment, cantonment, disarmament and demobilization of the military forces of all four Cambodian parties). Furthermore, in response to our questions, Mr. Khieu Samphan, President of PDK, also clearly indicated the intention of his Party not to take part in the electoral process and in the subsequent elections, so long as, according to him, a neutral political condition as provided for in the Paris Agreements was not ensured. In justifying his position, the President of PDK reiterated the arguments he had previously submitted to your Special Representative as well as to the representatives of Japan and Thailand when the two countries were earlier endeavouring, unsuccessfully, to find a solution to the deadlock. According to him, the plan of implementation of the Paris Agreements constituted an integral whole; the provisions of the Paris Agreements pertaining to the withdrawal of foreign forces were not implemented properly since, according to him, Vietnamese forces were still in Cambodia; moreover, he believed that the Supreme National Council had not been given the necessary means to fulfil its mandate as stipulated in the Paris Agreements. In response, we recalled the various measures taken by UNTAC to address the concerns expressed by PDK. Thus, in order to verify the withdrawal of foreign troops, the following measures were taken: early establishment of checkpoints at the Vietnamese border; setting-up of mobile military investigation teams, to which all parties were invited to designate representatives, to check on any presence of foreign troops; calling on all Cambodian parties to provide information on the subject; and the establishment of a strategic investigation team to follow up on any allegations and suspicions on foreign forces. In spite of these measures, UNTAC had not been provided with any information indicating the presence of foreign forces. We also recalled the measures taken by your Special Representative to strengthen the Supreme National Council, *inter alia*, through the creation of technical advisory committees (on repatriation of refugees, rehabilitation, territorial integrity) in addition to the Mixed Military Working Group, and the establishment of working groups open to all parties in the five areas of the existing administrative structures over which UNTAC exercises control and supervision. In spite of these explanations, PDK maintained its position. We reminded PDK that the Security Council in its resolutions 766 (1992) and 783 (1992) had clearly stated that this attitude represented a violation of the Paris Agreements. We also drew the attention of Mr. Khieu Samphan to the fact that the Security Council remained seized with the matter and would have to consider what further measures needed to be taken in the light of these developments;

(d) Indeed, as you underlined in your above-mentioned letter dated 2 November, the Security Council in paragraph 14 of resolution 783 (1992) requested the Secretary-General to report to the Security Council as soon as possible and no later than 15 November 1992 on the implementation of that resolution and to consider what further steps were necessary and appropriate for the realization of the fundamental objectives of the Paris Agreements. Without prejudice to your report, we believe it may be useful for the Security Council to consider the following points:

(i)   Reaffirming solemnly that the Cambodian peace process must continue to be implemented and that the timetable leading to elections in April-May 1993 must be maintained;

(ii)   Calling again upon the party that has not yet complied with its obligations, in particular with phase II of the peace plan, to do so;

(iii)   Specifying, however, that should this party maintain its present position, the process shall be continued with the cooperation of the three other parties, while still leaving the door open to the non-participating party to rejoin the process;

(iv)   Adjusting some aspects of the implementation plan with a view to ensuring the realization of the fundamental objectives of the Paris Agreements;

(v)   Requesting the Secretary-General to take all necessary measures to complete the establishment of

checkpoints as required in paragraph 3 of Security Council resolution 783 (1992);

(vi)   Including an appeal to the general public and all parties to take all necessary measures to ensure the safety and security of all United Nations personnel and to refrain from any threats or violent acts against them, and to create a neutral political environment for the conduct of free and fair elections;

(vii)   Defining measures to be implemented against PDK should it hamper the continuation of the peace plan.

Concerning the next Security Council meeting, we note that in the course of the meeting of the Supreme National Council on 8 November, Mr. Khieu Samphan, President of PDK, expressed the wish to be authorized to state the position of his party to the members of the Security Council. However, His Royal Highness Prince Sihanouk, President of the Supreme National Council, as well as Mr. Yasushi Akashi, your Special Representative, expressed the view that it would perhaps be more appropriate for the President of the Supreme National Council to represent the Supreme National Council in the Security Council and that the position of individual factions could be presented in written form as an attachment to the President's statement;

(e) In conclusion, we should like to invite your attention also to an important matter that was raised in the course of the consultations in Beijing. We noted the strong interest expressed by three of the four Cambodian parties (SOC, FUNCINPEC and KPNLF) that, in addition to the scheduled general elections for a constituent assembly, elections should also be held for a Cambodian head of State on the basis of direct universal suffrage. It was felt that such a presidential election would contribute significantly to the process of national reconciliation as well as provide an anchor of stability in the interim period after the general elections and before a new Government of Cambodia could emerge. We noted, however, that the fourth Cambodian party, without raising objections in principle, did not join the consensus on this subject. Nevertheless, we believe that it may be useful to keep this idea in mind, since such an election would help implement the peace process.

Roland DUMAS

Ali ALATAS

Annex III
Statement by the two Co-Chairmen of the Paris Conference on Cambodia

Pursuant to Security Council resolution 783 (1992), adopted unanimously on 13 October 1992, the Supreme

National Council of Cambodia met at Beijing on 8 November 1992 under the leadership of His Royal Highness Prince Norodom Sihanouk, with the participation of the Co-Chairmen of the Paris Conference, Mr. Roland Dumas, Minister of State and Minister for Foreign Affairs of the French Republic, and Mr. Ali Alatas, Minister for Foreign Affairs of the Republic of Indonesia, as well as Mr. Yasushi Akashi, Special Representative of the Secretary-General for Cambodia.

The two Co-Chairmen paid tribute to His Royal Highness Prince Norodom Sihanouk, President of the Supreme National Council, for his tireless efforts to restore peace and national unity in Cambodia.

They then presented to the Council a mixed assessment of the results of the peace plan at the halfway point in its implementation.

(a) Some aspects are unquestionably positive:

(i) The deployment of approximately 16,000 troops and 5,000 civilians has been completed;

(ii) Supervision and control over existing administrative structures have been established in all the sectors concerned and almost throughout the whole country, with the exception of the areas controlled by Democratic Kampuchea;

(iii) The Supreme National Council, in which all parties in Cambodia participate under the leadership of Prince Sihanouk, has adopted important decisions at each of its meetings;

(iv) Preparations for the elections are well under way: 11 political parties have been provisionally registered; the registration of all those eligible to vote, initiated on 5 October 1992, is proceeding smoothly, and should be completed in January 1993; 500,000 Cambodians have already been registered in voter registration lists, which testifies to the Cambodian people's desire to participate in the elections in overwhelming numbers;

(v) The repatriation of more than 170,000 refugees, out of a total of 350,000, has taken place under satisfactory circumstances. It is now virtually certain that all the refugees will be resettled before the elections in May 1993;

(vi) Lastly, the financial contributions to Cambodia's rehabilitation decided on at the Tokyo Conference ($800 million) have begun to be distributed in the country for the benefit of the Cambodian people;

(b) On the other hand, the military aspects of the United Nations peace plan have been stalled since 13 June 1992, because of Democratic Kampuchea's refusal to implement phase II of the plan and to allow the United Nations to have access to the areas under its control. In view of that situation, the Co-Chairmen recalled the decisions adopted by the Special Representative in response to the concerns expressed by Democratic Kampuchea with regard to the alleged presence of foreign troops;

(i) The early establishment of checkpoints along the country's border with Viet Nam;

(ii) The creation of mobile military fact-finding units to investigate reports of foreign forces;

(iii) An appeal to all parties in Cambodia to provide all relevant information on the subject, and the establishment of a strategic investigation team in which all parties had been invited to participate.

The Co-Chairmen also recalled the decisions already adopted by the Special Representative to strengthen the powers of the Supreme National Council through the establishment of technical advisory committees and working groups (on the repatriation of refugees, rehabilitation, territorial integrity, information, public safety and finances), in addition to the Mixed Military Working Group.

The two Co-Chairmen expressed regret that the efforts made by Japan and Thailand had not succeeded; they believed that the non-implementation of phase II of the plan now made it necessary to revise the mandate of the military component of the United Nations Transitional Authority in Cambodia.

They further reaffirmed that no party had the right to default on its obligations on the ground of complaints relating to the implementation of the plan. Such an attitude could not be tolerated.

They urgently appealed to all parties in Cambodia to show full respect for the cease-fire and the military status quo. In particular, they demanded strict guarantees of the safety and security of all United Nations personnel.

(c) In accordance with Security Council resolution 783 (1992), the two Co-Chairmen will report to the Secretary-General within the next few days on the overall results of their efforts, so that the Secretary-General may, as requested, report to the Security Council no later than 15 November 1992. The Council will then be able to consider what further steps are necessary and appropriate to ensure the realization of the fundamental objectives of the Paris Agreements and the holding of the elections on the scheduled date, no later than May 1993.

Document 55

Security Council resolution on implementation of Cambodia peace process

S/RES/792 (1992), 30 November 1992

The Security Council,

Reaffirming its resolutions 668 (1990) of 20 September 1990, 717 (1991) of 16 October 1991, 718 (1991) of 31 October 1991, 728 (1992) of 8 January 1992, 745 (1992) of 28 February 1992, 766 (1992) of 21 July 1992 and 783 (1992) of 13 October 1992,

Taking note of the report of the Secretary-General of 15 November 1992 1/ on the implementation of resolution 783 (1992),

Paying tribute to His Royal Highness Prince Norodom Sihanouk, President of the Supreme National Council of Cambodia, for his continuing efforts to restore peace and national unity in Cambodia,

Reaffirming its commitment to implement the agreements on a comprehensive political settlement of the Cambodia conflict signed at Paris on 23 October 1991 2/ and its determination to maintain the implementation timetable of the peace process, leading to elections for a constituent assembly in April/May 1993, the adoption of a constitution and the formation of a new Cambodian government thereafter,

Recognizing the need for all Cambodian parties, the States concerned and the Secretary-General to maintain close dialogue in order to implement the peace process effectively,

Recalling that all Cambodians have, in accordance with article 12 of the Agreement on a Comprehensive Political Settlement of the Cambodia Conflict, the right to determine their own political future through the free and fair election of a constituent assembly and that political parties wishing to participate in the election can be formed in accordance with paragraph 5 of annex 3 to the Agreement,

Noting the discussion during the consultations held in Beijing on 7 and 8 November 1992 by the Co-Chairmen of the Paris Conference on Cambodia regarding a presidential election, and the views of the Co-Chairmen shared by the Secretary-General that such an election could contribute to the process of national reconciliation and help to reinforce the climate of stability in Cambodia,

Welcoming the achievements of the Special Representative of the Secretary-General for Cambodia and of the United Nations Transitional Authority in Cambodia in the implementation of the Paris agreements,

Welcoming in particular the progress made in voter registration,

Welcoming also the efforts of the Authority to strengthen its relationship with the Supreme National Council of Cambodia and its supervision and control over the existing administrative structures, *inter alia*, to ensure the widest possible agreement on essential regulations for elections, natural resources, rehabilitation, national heritage and human rights, on relations with the international financial institutions, and on the question of foreign residents and immigrants,

Noting the efforts of the Authority to address the concerns raised by the Party of Democratic Kampuchea, including steps to verify the withdrawal of all foreign forces, advisers and military personnel from Cambodia, close cooperation between the Authority and the Supreme National Council as the embodiment of Cambodian sovereignty, the creation of technical advisory committees to advise the Supreme National Council and the Authority, the extension of Authority supervision and control over the five key administrative areas mandated in the Paris agreements in the areas to which the Authority has access, and the creation of working groups in these areas to enable the parties to be involved in and informed about the Authority's activities in these five key areas,

Expressing its appreciation to Japan and Thailand for their efforts to find solutions to current problems relating to the implementation of the Paris agreements,

Expressing also its appreciation for the efforts of the Co-Chairmen of the Paris Conference on Cambodia, in consultation with all parties, pursuant to resolution 783 (1992) to find a way to implement fully the Paris agreements,

Deploring the failure of the Party of Democratic Kampuchea to meet its obligations under the Paris agreements, notably as regards unrestricted access by UNTAC to the areas under the control of the Party of Democratic Kampuchea for voter registration and other purposes of the agreements and as regards the application of phase II of the cease-fire concerning cantonment and demobilization of its forces,

Deploring recent violations of the cease-fire and their implications for the security situation in Cambodia,

1/ S/24800 [Document 54]
2/ S/23177 [Document 19]

emphasizing the importance of maintaining the cease-fire and calling on all parties to comply with their obligations in this regard,

Condemning attacks against the Authority, in particular the recent firings upon Authority helicopters and on electoral registration personnel,

Concerned by the economic situation in Cambodia and its impact on the implementation of the Paris agreements,

1. *Endorses* the report of the Secretary-General dated 15 November 1992 1/ on the implementation of Security Council resolution 783 (1992);

2. *Confirms* that the election for a constituent assembly in Cambodia will be held not later than May 1993;

3. *Notes* the decision of the Secretary-General to instruct his Special Representative for Cambodia to make contingency plans for the organization and conduct by the United Nations Transitional Authority in Cambodia of a presidential election, and moreover, noting that such an election must be held in conjunction with the planned election for a constituent assembly, requests the Secretary-General to submit any recommendations for the holding of such an election to the Council for decision;

4. *Calls* upon all Cambodian parties to cooperate fully with the Authority to create a neutral political environment for the conduct of free and fair elections and prevent acts of harassment, intimidation and political violence;

5. *Determines* that the Authority shall proceed with preparations for free and fair elections to be held in April/May 1993 in all areas of Cambodia to which it has full and free access as at 31 January 1993;

6. *Calls on* the Supreme National Council of Cambodia to continue to meet regularly under the chairmanship of His Royal Highness Prince Norodom Sihanouk;

7. *Condemns* the failure by the Party of Democratic Kampuchea to comply with its obligations;

8. *Demands* that the Party of Democratic Kampuchea fulfil immediately its obligations under the agreements on a comprehensive political settlement to the Cambodia conflict, signed in Paris on 23 October 1991, 2/, that it facilitate without delay full deployment of the Authority in the areas under its control, that it not impede voter registration in those areas, that it not impede the activities of other political parties in those areas, and that it implement fully phase II of the cease-fire, particularly cantonment and demobilization, as well as all other aspects of the Paris agreements, taking into account that all parties in Cambodia have the same obligations to implement the Paris agreements;

9. *Urges* the Party of Democratic Kampuchea to join fully in the implementation of the Paris agreements, including the electoral provisions, and requests the Secretary-General and States concerned to remain ready to continue dialogue with the Party of Democratic Kampuchea for this purpose;

10. *Calls on* those concerned to ensure that measures are taken, consistent with the provisions of Article VII of annex 2 to the Agreement on a Comprehensive Political Settlement of the Cambodia Conflict to prevent the supply of petroleum products to the areas occupied by any Cambodian party not complying with the military provisions of this Agreement and requests the Secretary-General to examine the modalities of such measures;

11. *Undertakes* to consider appropriate measures to be implemented should the Party of Democratic Kampuchea obstruct the implementation of the peace plan, such as the freezing of the assets it holds outside Cambodia;

12. *Invites* the Authority to establish all necessary border checkpoints, requests neighbouring States to cooperate fully in the establishment and maintenance of those checkpoints and requests the Secretary-General to undertake immediate consultations with States concerned regarding their establishment and operation;

13. *Supports* the decision of the Supreme National Council dated 22 September 1992 to set a moratorium on the export of logs from Cambodia in order to protect Cambodia's natural resources, requests States, especially neighbouring States, to respect this moratorium by not importing such logs, and requests the Authority to take appropriate measures to secure the implementation of such moratorium;

14. *Requests* the Supreme National Council to consider the adoption of a similar moratorium on the export of minerals and gems in order to protect Cambodia's natural resources;

15. *Demands* that all parties comply with their obligations to observe the cease-fire and calls upon them to exercise restraint;

16. *Requests* the Authority to continue to monitor the cease-fire and to take effective measures to prevent the recurrence or escalation of fighting in Cambodia, as well as incidents of banditry and arms smuggling;

17. *Demands* also that all parties take all action necessary to safeguard the lives and the security of Authority personnel throughout Cambodia including by issuing immediate instructions to this effect to their commanders forthwith and reporting their action to the Special Representative of the Secretary-General;

18. *Requests* the Secretary-General to consider the implications for the electoral process of the failure by the Party of Democratic Kampuchea to canton and demobi-

lize its forces and, in response to this situation, to take all appropriate steps to ensure the successful implementation of the electoral process;

19. *Also requests* the Secretary-General to investigate and report upon the implications for security in post-election Cambodia of the possible incomplete implementation of the disarmament and demobilization provisions of the Paris agreements;

20. *Invites* the States and international organizations providing economic assistance to Cambodia to convene a meeting to review the current state of economic assistance to Cambodia in the wake of the Ministerial Conference on Reconstruction and Rehabilitation of Cambodia held at Tokyo on 20 and 22 June 1992;

21. *Further invites* the Secretary-General to report to the Security Council as soon as possible and no later than 15 February 1993 on the implementation of the present resolution, and on any further measures that may be necessary and appropriate to ensure the realization of the fundamental objectives of the Paris agreements;

22. *Decides* to remain actively seized of the matter.

Document 56

Letter dated 30 November 1992 from Thailand outlining the position of the Royal Thai Government with regard to Security Council resolution 792 (1992)

S/24873, 30 November 1992

Upon the instructions of my Government, in connection with Security Council resolution 792 (1992) on Cambodia which was adopted on 30 November 1992, I would like to convey to you the position of the Royal Thai Government on the matter (see annex).

I would be grateful if you would kindly arrange for this letter and its annex to be circulated as a document of the Security Council.

(*Signed*) Nitya PIBULSONGGRAM
Ambassador
Permanent Representative

Annex
Position of the Royal Thai Government with regard to Security Council resolution 792 (1992) on Cambodia

1. Thailand as a neighbouring country wishes to see genuine and lasting peace in Cambodia which will not only return normalcy to the border areas but will also create stability and prosperity to the region as a whole.

2. Genuine and lasting peace in Cambodia can be brought about only through the participation of all Cambodian parties in the peace process. Thailand has therefore supported all efforts to persuade the Party of Democratic Kampuchea (PDK) to comply with its obligations under the Paris Agreements and feels that the door should not be closed to negotiation with the PDK.

3. Thailand shares the view of the Secretary-General in his latest report (document S/24800 dated 15 November 1992) that "patient diplomacy" was the best means of getting the peace process back on track.

4. On the specific measures cited in Security Council resolution 792 (1992), Thailand is of the opinion that these measures must be realistic, implementable and consistent with the realities of the present situation. As a member in good standing of the United Nations, Thailand will comply with measures that may have effect on Thailand so long as these measures do not contravene Thai law or Thai sovereignty and territorial integrity. Furthermore, in devising detailed plans for the implementation of specific measures, neighbouring countries should be closely consulted in accordance with the provisions of Article 50 of the Charter of the United Nations.

5. With regard to the question of border checkpoints referred to in paragraph 12 of resolution 792 (1992), Thailand is of the view that such checkpoints must be established strictly in accordance with the terms of the Paris Agreements. Article VII, paragraph 3 (a) of the Agreements stipulates that checkpoints shall be established "along the routes and at selected locations along the *Cambodian side of the border* and at airfields *inside Cambodia*." Previous Security Council resolutions including resolution 783 (1992) of 13 October 1992 also referred to the "checkpoints in the country (Cambodia) and along its borders with neighbouring countries."

Document 57

Statement by the President of the Security Council on the increasing number of attacks against United Nations personnel serving in peace-keeping operations

S/24884, 2 December 1992

The members of the Security Council wish to express their deep concern and outrage about the increasing number of attacks against United Nations personnel serving in various peace-keeping operations.

A number of serious incidents affecting military and civilian personnel serving with United Nations Angola Verification Mission II, the United Nations Transitional Authority in Cambodia and the United Nations Protection Force have occurred during the last few days.

On 29 November in Uige, northern Angola, a Brazilian police observer with the United Nations Angola Verification Mission II was killed as a result of an outbreak of hostilities between the National Union for the Total Independence of Angola and Government forces, during which the Mission's camp was caught in the cross-fire. The members of the Council convey their deep sympathy and condolences to the Government of Brazil and to the bereaved family,

The situation in the United Nations Protection Force, which has already suffered over 300 casualties, 20 of them fatal, remains deeply troubling. On 30 November 1992, two Spanish Force soldiers in Bosnia and Herzegovina were seriously injured in a mine attack and a Danish Force soldier was abducted by armed men today.

On 1 December, two British military observers and four naval observers of the United Nations Transitional Authority in Cambodia, two from the Philippines, one from New Zealand and one from the United Kingdom, on patrol in Kompong Thom province, were illegally detained by forces belonging to the National Army of Democratic Kampuchea. An Authority helicopter, sent to assist in the discussions for their release, was fired upon, and a French military observer on board was injured. Moreover, today, six Authority civilian police monitors, three Indonesians, two Tunisians and one Nepalese, were injured in two land mine incidents in Siem Reap province.

The members of the Council condemn these attacks on the safety and security of United Nations personnel and demand that all parties concerned take all necessary measures to prevent their recurrence. The members of the Council consider the abduction and detention of United Nations peace-keeping personnel as totally unacceptable and demand the immediate and unconditional release of the United Nations Transitional Authority in Cambodia and United Nations Protection Force personnel concerned.

Document 58

Letter dated 20 December 1992 from Mr. Khieu Samphan, member of the Supreme National Council, to the Secretary-General transmitting statement by PDK on violations by UNTAC of the PDK-controlled zones

Not issued as a United Nations document

I have the honour to transmit to you, herewith, for your information, the statement by the Party of Democratic Kampuchea and the National Army of Democratic Kampuchea regarding the repeated violations by UNTAC of areas under the control of the Party of Democratic Kampuchea.

Accept, Sir, the renewed assurances of my highest consideration.

Khieu SAMPHAN
President of the Party of Democratic Kampuchea
Member of the Supreme National Council

Statement by the Democratic Kampuchea Party and the National Army of Democratic Kampuchea on the repeated violations by UNTAC of the DKP-controlled zones

1. The representative of UNTAC at the Mixed Military Working Group (MMWG) Secretariat had informed the DKP in Phnom Penh that on 18 December 1992 the NADK detained certain numbers of UNTAC personnel of a helicopter which landed at Stung Tror village in Prek Prasap district, Kratie province.

Furthermore, some foreign radios on 19 December 1992 broadcast news distorting the truth of that event.

2. It should be noted that these events have taken place almost daily, and that they have not been provoked by the DKP. As a matter of fact, it is not the DKP which has sent its forces to arrest or detain UNTAC personnel in the zones of the Phnom Penh party or in areas where UNTAC is stationed. In all events that have taken place recently, it is UNTAC personnel that have entered the DKP-controlled zones without informing the latter beforehand.

Moreover, deliberately-distorted news have been broadcast on the so-called arrest by the DKP of 15 then 46 Indonesian personnel of UNTAC. In fact, the Indonesian forces working with UNTAC stationed in those areas have always maintained good relations with the population and the NADK for already almost a year.

All this is a propaganda aimed at misleading the world public opinion which is not well informed of the real situation in Cambodia. It is also a smear campaign and a plan designed to mislead the United Nations Security Council into enforcing sanctions against the DKP.

Nothing could justify the landing of the UNTAC helicopter at Stung Tror village in Prek Prasap district, Kratie province. As a matter of fact, that area is very remote and is a plateau of dense forest. The truth is that that is an ill political intention designed to provoke shootings at the helicopter, and then place the responsibility for the incident on the DKP.

3. In the face of this situation, the DKP and the NADK wish to underline that the incidents that took place in Stung Sen region, Kompong Thom province on 1 December 1992, and those occurred at O Salar village, north of Kompong Thom provincial town on 15 December 1992, and which have been disseminated as "the NADK holding hostage 15 and 46 Indonesian forces", are part and parcel of the provocative plan as described above. Today, a new incident is deliberately created by sending an UNTAC helicopter to land at an area of dense forest, very remote, in the district of Prek Prasap, without informing the NADK beforehand. This incident is also part of the same provocative plan.

The DKP and the NADK would like to draw the attention of the national and world public opinion as well as that of the Secretary-General of the United Nations on these facts.

Consequently, the DKP and the NADK urge H.E. Mr. Yasushi Akashi and H.E. Lieutenant-General John Sanderson to put an end to all these activities.

We would like to reiterate once again that the DKP and the NADK would enter into Phase II of the cease-fire as soon as UNTAC correctly implements the 23 October 1991 Paris Agreement in its totality, particularly concerning the following points:

-the SNC must be in a position to fulfill its mandate as the unique legitimate body and source of authority in Cambodia during the transitional period;

-UNTAC in cooperation with the SNC must control the withdrawal of all categories of Vietnamese forces from Cambodia;

-UNTAC must, in cooperation with the SNC, control the 5 fields.

These are necessary conditions for the cantonment, disarmament and demobilization of the forces of the 4 Cambodian parties.

But for more than a year already, UNTAC has not implemented correctly the Paris Agreements of 23 October 1991. Indeed, UNTAC:

1. has done nothing so that the SNC could exercise its mandate;

2. has not controlled the withdrawal of all categories of Vienamese forces, and has only repeated that "there are no Vietnamese forces in Cambodia";

3. has not placed the 5 fields under its control.

The nation, the people and the national resistance forces of Cambodia, most notably His Royal Highness Samdech Preah Norodom Sihanouk, Head of State and President of the SNC, FUNCINPEC, KPNLF, DKP and even several members of UNTAC have stressed on many occasions these facts.

On the contrary, UNTAC in connivance with Vietnam and its puppets tries by all means to lure the DKP into regrouping its forces in cantonment areas, to neutralize them and thereby putting the nation and people of Cambodia in jeopardy.

In these conditions, the DKP and the NADK wish to reiterate that UNTAC is authorized to enter the DKP-controlled zones after having consulted the DKP representatives within the MMWG or the liaison offices. It should be recalled that the principles of holding consultation beforehand have already been accepted.

With regard to those liaison offices, it should be recalled that UNTAC represented by General John Sanderson and the 4 Cambodian parties have already decided that each Cambodian party would send 2 representatives to those offices. However, the DKP liaison officers which had been once in Kompong Thom have been prevented until now from returning to their posts. Furthermore, the liaison officers of the DKP have also been barred from going to their posts at Stung Treng, Kampot, Kompong Som, Kratie, in the naval forces and others, although the relevant principle has already been adopted for almost a year.

In the above-mentioned conditions and at the present time when the Vietnamese and the puppet forces are carrying out their dry-season military operations, UNTAC takes full responsibility in case it enters the DKP-controlled zones without obtaining authorization beforehand.

(*Signed*) KHIEU SAMPHAN
President of the DKP
Member of the SNC

(*Signed*) SON SEN
Vice-President of the DKP
Commander-in-Chief of the NADK
Member of the SNC

Document 59

Statement by the President of the Security Council concerning illegal detention of UNTAC personnel in Cambodia by elements of the PDK

S/25003, 22 December 1992

The Security Council strongly condemns the illegal detention of United Nations Transitional Authority in Cambodia personnel by elements of the Party of Democratic Kampuchea and acts of threat and intimidation against these personnel. It demands that such actions and any other hostile acts against the Authority cease immediately, and that all parties take all action necessary to safeguard the lives and the security of Authority personnel.

The Council urges all the parties to abide scrupulously by their obligations under the agreement on a comprehensive political settlement of the Cambodia conflict signed in Paris on 23 October 1991 to cooperate fully with the Authority and to respect all the relevant resolutions of the Council.

Document 60

Letter dated 30 December 1992 from Mr. Nguyen Manh Cam, Minister for Foreign Affairs of Viet Nam, to the Secretary-General concerning violence against Vietnamese residents in Cambodia

S/25053, 5 January 1993

Upon instruction from my Government, I have the honour to request you kindly to circulate as a document of the Security Council, a letter dated 30 December 1992, addressed to you by His Excellency Mr. Nguyen Manh Cam, Minister for Foreign Affairs of Viet Nam, concerning the recent acts of terrorism and barbarous massacre against Vietnamese residents in Cambodia (see annex).

(*Signed*) TRINH XUAN LANG
Ambassador
Permanent Representative

Annex
Letter dated 30 December 1992 from the Minister for Foreign Affairs of Viet Nam addressed to the Secretary-General

With deep concern, I send you this letter regarding Democratic Kampuchea's repeated acts of terrorism and barbarous massacre against Vietnamese who are living legally in Cambodia.

As you have been aware, at 2130 hours on 27 December 1992, a group of soldiers of Democratic Kampuchea attacked a fishing village along the Tonle Sap River in Kom Pong Tralach district, Kom Pong Chnang province, in search of Vietnamese so as to murder them. There, they killed 14 people, including 12 Vietnamese, and injured 14 others. On 29 December 1992, Mr. Eric Berman, Deputy spokesman of the United Nations Transitional Authority in Cambodia (UNTAC), reaffirmed that Democratic Kampuchea's forces were responsible for the above-mentioned massacre.

These acts by Democratic Kampuchea constitute a new massacre in a series of its acts of terrorism and massacre against Vietnamese in the recent period, especially since July 1992. These barbarous massacres against Vietnamese residents in Cambodia by Democratic Kampuchea's forces are a challenge to mankind's conscience and international public opinion.

These barbarous acts are in serious violation of the purposes and principles of the Charter of the United Nations, the Universal Declaration of Human Rights and other related international documents, including the right to security of person provided for in article 5 of the International Convention on the Elimination of All Forms of Racial Discrimination and the right of minority communities to safety and protection. These acts are also in extreme flagrant violation of the Paris Agreement on Cambodia and its relevant annexes.

The Democratic Kampuchea faction's violation of human rights and its obstinate refusal to enter the second phase of the cease-fire in Cambodia have placed the political settlement of the Cambodia problem in very critical danger, challenging the international community and jeopardizing peace and stability in South-East Asia.

The Government of the Socialist Republic of Viet Nam strongly condemns these barbarous acts of terrorism committed by the Democratic Kampuchea faction against innocent Vietnamese residents in Cambodia. The Government of the Socialist Republic of Viet Nam requests the United Nations, UNTAC, the two Co-Chairmen of the International Conference on Cambodia, the signatories to the Paris Agreement on Cambodia, as well as the Supreme National Council of Cambodia and the international community to take resolute measures so as to put an immediate end to these bloody acts by the Democratic Kampuchea faction.

I am confident that, with your authority and responsibility, you will take urgent and strong steps so as to put an end to the serious violation of human rights being committed by Democratic Kampuchea in Cambodia and compel it to implement the Paris Agreement on Cambodia.

(*Signed*) NGUYEN MANH CAM
Minister for Foreign Affairs
Socialist Republic of Viet Nam

Document 61

Letter dated 5 January 1993 from Mr. Hun Sen, member of the Supreme National Council, to the Secretary-General transmitting declaration by the State of Cambodia

Not issued as a United Nations document; original in French

I have the honour to transmit to you herewith the declaration by the State of Cambodia, and to ask you kindly to consider seriously the state of the repeated and increasingly aggressive and arrogant violations of the Paris Agreements and of the cease-fire by the Party of Democratic Kampuchea-Khmer Rouge over the past fourteen months and just months before the elections provided for in the Paris Agreements.

This exceptionally serious situation calls into question not only the organization of the forthcoming elections which the Party of Democratic Kampuchea-Khmer Rouge is already rejecting, but also the very life of the Cambodian nation and people. In so doing, the Khmer Rouge remain ever true to their essential and constant strategic objective, namely, to regain power no matter what the price, even if it means challenging the international community by violating with impunity the Agreements they have signed and the appeals and successive resolutions of the Security Council of the United Nations.

The exceptional gravity of the situation in my view fully merits application of the appropriate measures provided for in article 29 of the Agreement on a Comprehensive Political Settlement of the Cambodia Conflict and, if necessary, of Chapter VII of the Charter of the United Nations.

Accept, Sir, the assurances of my highest consideration.

(*Signed*) HUN SEN
Member of the Supreme National Council of Cambodia
President of the Council of Ministers
of the State of Cambodia

Declaration of the State of Cambodia

From the day the Paris Agreements were signed on October 23, 1991 and now, just a few months away from the election which is regarded as the key and the back-bone of these Accords, the present situation, resulting from the PDK-Khmer Rouge's non-compliance and violations, constitutes the most serious threat to peace and to the existence of the Cambodian people.

By refusing to comply with the Accords they signed and by violating them every day and in the most arrogant and provocative way, while the other parties, in particular, the party of the State of Cambodia, have been cooperating with the UN Transitional Authorities and implementing the Agreements, the PDK-Khmer Rouge have accumulated substantial military and political profits.

Having taken advantage of the regroupment, cantonment and planned demobilisation of the armed forces of the party of the State of Cambodia and of other complying parties, the Khmer Rouge have expanded the zones under their control, enabling them to further expanding their infiltration into other areas and even closer to towns and cities. This expansion of the Khmer Rouge controlled areas places the complying parties in risky defensive positions when it comes to protecting the population. UNTAC's operating arena will be further reduced, the voter's turnout will be less and less as a result of the Khmer-Rouge refusal to allow UNTAC's access to their zones and the people to vote.

Greater danger will soon come from the fact that the Khmer Rouge will use the zones they have thus grabbed as stepping stones for launching military offensives, and as base-areas from which to infiltrate, to sabotage and to expand further what they called their semi-liberated zones and their guerrilla-zones, and combined with agents they infiltrated all over the country, to create unrest, to commit acts of terrorism and to collect intelligence information for military purposes. It is necessary to recall that lately, the Khmer Rouge are now in a position to fire artillery shells into towns and cities, to threaten UNTAC's voter registration teams, to force them to evacuate, to destroy and burn the voter's registration cards, to intimidate the people from going to register or to vote, to repress the civilian population, to commit multiform acts of terrorism, to take UNTAC officers hostages and to fire at UNTAC, etc. All this constitutes a very serious threat to the further implementation of the Agreements.

The State of Cambodia is therefore drawn to the conclusion that, if this situation is allowed to evolve in its present course, the upcoming election will run into great difficulties, even to the point that no election can be held at all. The Khmer Rouge have no interest in letting the election to proceed peacefully.

It is also not irrelevant to recall that, as members of the Supreme National Council, the PDK-Khmer Rouge have taken advantage of their presence in this body and its institutions to score some benefits as well as to obstruct the peace process as defined by the Paris Agreements. They put up obstacles at every meeting. They made use of their positions as SNC members to maintain their legitimacy as well as to make profits from it, so much so that their military officers appointed to the military co-ordinating committees waste no time in this capacity to collect intelligence information useful for the military offensives.

Confronted with this most serious danger for Cambodia and for all Cambodians, the party of the State of Cambodia, in its capacity as a signatory of the Paris Agreements, wishes to submit the following requests to the consideration of the Co-Chairmen of the Paris International Conference on Cambodia and to the UN Security Council:

1. To take every measures aimed at putting an end to all Khmer Rouge military violations, to stop them from expanding the territory any further, otherwise, the zones in which election can be held will shrink, and the voter's turnout will be smaller. These measures should also aim at ensuring the safety of voter registration and that of the scheduled election. To this end, the party of the State of Cambodia proposes that UNTAC exercise its mandate as provided for by the Paris Agreements and by UNSC Resolution 792. If this mandate is proved ineffective, the party of the State of Cambodia proposes that the UN Security Council rectify it in response to the changing situation brought about by the PDK-Khmer Rouge.

2. In order to ensure that the upcoming election proceed in a free, fair and democratic manner, it is absolutely essential to set a deadline for the Khmer Rouge participation in the election on 31 January 1993 in conformity with paragraph 5 of the UNSC Resolution 792. Otherwise, these elections will not be fair, and not in conformity with the letter and spirit of the Paris Agreements if the Khmer Rouge were allowed to participate at the last minute, since their controlled zones have always stayed out of UNTAC's control and supervision, hence: no neutral political environment over there. The population under Khmer Rouge control would not have registered as voters. Election in such a situation is simply not fair.

We can never accept a biased implementation of the Paris Agreements.

3. If the PDK-Khmer Rouge continue to defy the Paris Accords and to stay out of the planned election beyond the above deadline, the question is why should the Khmer Rouge be allowed to stay in the SNC so that

they could benefit more from it until they achieve their goal of regaining power by every means?

If this is the case, the party of the State of Cambodia is of the views that the PDK-Khmer Rouge, legally and logically speaking, have forfeited their rights to be part of the SNC, because the fact is that they have already excluded themselves from the peace process. The party of the State of Cambodia demands that the Khmer Rouge be evicted from the peace process of the Paris Agreements and be declared insurgents and out-laws in accordance with their deeds.

Election held in Cambodia in a situation in which the PDK-Khmer Rouge not only stay out of it, but keep on violating the Agreements, and yet they can maintain their legitimacy, their controlled zones, their armed forces, their political representation in the SNC, would only help to solidify further the de-facto partitioning of Cambodia, politically, psychologically and legally, even if this partitioning is only temporary.

4. In order to further consolidate national reconciliation and unity of Cambodia, and to ensure political stability before and after the Constitutional Assembly election, the party of the State of Cambodia requests with insistence that a clear date be set for the anticipated presidential election.

On behalf of the State of Cambodia, may we then request LL.EE. the Co-Chairmen of the Paris International Conference on Cambodia and H.E. the UN Secretary-General to closely watch this very dangerous situation, and to take appropriate and necessary actions before it is too late, in order to safeguard the Cambodian people from the second Khmer Rouge genocide and to rescue the Paris Agreements.

Document 62

Letter dated 5 January 1993 from Prince Norodom Ranariddh, member of the Supreme National Council, to the Secretary-General concerning the political situation in Cambodia

Not issued as a United Nations document; original in French

Allow me to thank you very warmly for the efforts you are making to restore peace and a liberal and pluralistic democracy to our dear Cambodia.

The dramatic deterioration of the political situation in Cambodia at this time is none the less disturbing. UNTAC's wait-and-see policy which numerous observers have unfortunately noted is a source of growing concern.

As HRH Samdech Préah Norodom Sihanouk, Head of State and President of the Supreme National Council of Cambodia, rightly pointed out in his letter of 3 January 1993 to your Special Representative in Cambodia, Mr. Yasushi Akashi, "can there be democratic elections worthy of that name with a certain degree of 'legality' if Cambodia reverts to what it was, following the coup d'état of 18 March 1970, a country that fears neither God nor man?"

Sir, the repeated, politically motivated terrorist attacks which have been perpetrated with complete impunity on members of the FUNCINPEC Party, of which I have the honour to be President, is intolerable. Since 2 November 1992, because of UNTAC's weakness there have been 18 attacks on FUNCINPEC, in which 18 people have died, all of them members of the Party, and 22 have been wounded, 7 of them seriously.

My decision to put a stop to all working relations with UNTAC as from 5 January 1993 must be seen as a sign of my steadfast resolution, on the one hand, to see the Paris Agreements of 23 October 1991 implemented in their totality and, on the other, to achieve the ultimate goal set by those agreements, namely the holding of elections to ensure the self-determination of the Cambodian people.

The FUNCINPEC Party has always abided faithfully by these Agreements and has always demonstrated its unswerving determination to achieve the "comprehensive political settlement" proposed and wished for by the distinguished permanent members of the Security Council and the Co-Chairmen of the Conference.

It is, therefore, quite natural that I should turn to you today in order that we may seek together what can be done to preserve the essential, namely, a rapid return to a neutral political environment conducive to free and fair elections. Is it not up to UNTAC, which has the means but lacks the grim determination, "to establish true democracy and peace in my country", to use the very fitting words used by HRH Samdech Préah Norodom Sihanouk?

Sir,

In view of the urgency of the situation, I am taking the liberty of informing you of my intention to ask the Co-Chairmen of the Conference to speak to you about this very serious situation of which wretched Cambodia is a victim.

In these critical times, UNTAC needs decisive ac-

tions, and your assistance may be invaluable in contributing thereto.

Accept, Sir, the assurances of my highest consideration.

(*Signed*) NORODOM RANARIDDH
President of FUNCINPEC
Member of the Supreme Council of Cambodia

Document 63

Letter dated 19 January 1993 from Prince Norodom Ranariddh, Mr. Ieng Mouly, Mr. Sam Rainsy and Mr. Son Sann, members of the Supreme National Council, to the Secretary-General concerning the electoral registration of Cambodians residing abroad

Not issued as a United Nations document; original in French

As members of the Supreme National Council of Cambodia representing the FUNCINPEC and KPNLF Parties, we are taking the liberty of writing to you directly to ask you to intervene decisively in order to settle, reasonably and equitably, a specific and important problem concerning the elections which are soon to be held in our country under the supervision of UNTAC.

It concerns the electoral registration of Cambodians residing abroad, specifically overseas; it should be possible to carry out this operation in a few major cities in the United States, Canada, France and Australia, so as to enable the Cambodians living overseas, who constitute an integral part of the Cambodian nation and an important segment of the electorate, to participate fully in the ongoing electoral process leading to the self-determination of the Khmer people.

The Electoral Law promulgated on 12 August 1992 by your Special Representative, His Excellency Mr. Yasushi Akashi, does provide for the opening of polling places abroad for these Cambodians living overseas, but it requires the latter to first come and register in Cambodia in order to have the right to cast a vote on election day. This provision is unrealistic and unjust, for only a very small proportion (less than 1 per cent) of the 250,000 to 300,000 Cambodian electors resident abroad who meet the criteria of the Electoral Law have been able, or will be able, to go to Cambodia in order to complete the required registration formalities, due to a variety of insurmountable financial, administrative, professional and family problems.

In practice, therefore, the vast majority of Cambodians resident overseas have been excluded from the ongoing electoral process and this will certainly cast serious doubts on the fairness of the forthcoming elections and may, quite rightly, prompt a large proportion of the electorate to protest the outcome of the elections. Furthermore, on the question of principle, the current formula in effect introduces electoral segregation on the basis of money (only those who can afford a relatively expensive trip to Cambodia will be able to vote), and we do not think that the United Nations can be in favour of any type of voting system based on a poll tax.

The decisions taken in Cambodia and for Cambodia concern Cambodians first and foremost. These same Cambodians must be the first to be consulted, and it is their opinion which must, ultimately, prevail. The most famous Cambodian, the father of the Cambodian nation, Samdech Préah Sihanouk, speaking as Head of State and President of the Supreme National Council, has already expressed his views several times regarding the need to give Cambodians living overseas all practical facilities necessary to enable them to participate fully in the ongoing electoral process. FUNCINPEC and KPNLF wholeheartedly support the just, wise and generous position taken by Samdech Préah Norodom Sihanouk. The Party of Democratic Kampuchea also expressed a similar viewpoint in a letter dated 22 July 1992 from His Excellency Mr. Khieu Samphan, President of PDK and member of the Supreme National Council, to His Excellency Mr. Yasushi Akashi (a copy of which is enclosed). As for the party of the State of Cambodia, it has never officially opposed this position, which has been clearly formulated by the three other Cambodian parties.

For your information on this question of electoral

registration of Cambodians living overseas, we should like to convey to you the following documents:

Letter dated 19 November 1992 from His Excellency Mr. Yasushi Akashi to FUNCINPEC;

Letter dated 23 November 1992 from FUNCINPEC to His Excellency Mr. Yasushi Akashi;

Letter dated 30 November 1992 from FUNCINPEC to His Excellency Mr. Reginald Austin, who is in charge of elections in UNTAC;

Statement by FUNCINPEC dated 8 December 1992;

Communiqué of FLNPK dated 8 December 1992;

Note from FUNCINPEC dated 8 January 1993;

Letter from His Royal Highness Prince Norodom Ranariddh, President of FUNCINPEC and member of the Supreme National Council, to His Excellency Mr. Yasushi Akashi.

We wish to draw your attention to the fact that despite all our written communications which we have mentioned above and sent to UNTAC, and despite the many interventions and verbal requests made by FUNCINPEC and KPNLF to UNTAC, to date we have received no detailed, written reply to the question we have raised. We have simply been given orally, and in a rather confused manner, some fragmentary and sometimes contradictory information, giving us to understand that our request could not be taken into consideration.

That is why FUNCINPEC and KPNLF, which have always been extremely cooperative and loyal partners of UNTAC in the implementation of the United Nations peace plan since the signing of the Paris Agreements on 23 October 1991, have decided to approach you jointly so that UNTAC may be able promptly to take a correct decision on this question of electoral registration of Cambodians living overseas.

When you have looked at the enclosed documents you will see that the electoral registration of Cambodians residing abroad can be completed in a very short period of time (one week instead of four months in Cambodia itself) and that it can take place under much easier conditions than on Cambodian soil itself.

It is true that, since the elections are to be held before the end of May 1993, there is not much time. However, it is not too late, as yet, to take the necessary correct decision. During the remaining four months it would be quite possible to prepare simultaneously for the vote in Cambodia (where the registration operations are already practically completed) and for the registration abroad of Cambodians living overseas. The latter operations could very well be held in February or March 1993. The main thing is to ensure that all the electoral rolls are drawn up before the scheduled date of the elections.

I thank you for your kindness to our compatriots overseas and extend to you our profound gratitude for your sense of fairness.

Accept, Sir, the assurances of our highest consideration.

IENG MOULY
Member of the Supreme National Council

NORODOM RANARIDDH
President of FUNCINPEC
Member of the Supreme National Council

SAM RAINSY
Member of the Supreme National Council

SON SANN
President of FNLPK
Member of the Supreme National Council

Document 64

Letter dated 20 January 1993 from Singapore transmitting, on behalf of the Permanent Representatives to the United Nations of the States members of ASEAN, statement on the holding of a presidential election in Cambodia, issued 15 January 1993

S/25133, 21 January 1993

On behalf of the Permanent Representatives to the United Nations of the States members of the Association of South-East Asian Nations (ASEAN), I have the honour to transmit to you herewith the text of a statement by the ASEAN Foreign Ministers on the holding of a presidential election in Cambodia issued on 15 January 1993.

I would be grateful if you could arrange to have the present statement circulated as a document of the Security Council.

(*Signed*) CHEW Tai Soo

Annex
Statement by the ASEAN Foreign Ministers on the holding of a presidential election in Cambodia

1. We, the Foreign Ministers of the Association of South-East Asian Nations (ASEAN), view with deep concern the current impasse in the Cambodian peace process.

2. We are particularly concerned over the intensified military activities in violation of the cease-fire arrangements and the increasing incidents of political harassment, intimidation and even assassinations perpetrated against personalities and political workers of especially the Front uni national pour un Cambodge indépendant, neutre, pacifique et coopératif (FUNCINPEC) and the Khmer People's National Liberation Front (KPNLF), which could eventually lead to renewed large-scale fighting in Cambodia. We are also gravely concerned over the recent spate of killings of residents of Vietnamese origin. We call on all Cambodian parties to cooperate with the United Nations Transitional Authority in Cambodia (UNTAC) and to contribute to ensuring a peaceful and neutral political environment so that there can be free and fair elections as stipulated in the Paris Peace Agreements.

3. We welcome and fully support His Royal Highness Prince Samdech Norodom Sihanouk's announcement of 8 January 1993 that he is ready to be a candidate in a presidential election to be held in April or May 1993. We believe that His Royal Highness Prince Samdech Norodom Sihanouk will be able to play a pivotal role in bringing about national reconciliation among all Cambodians, which is essential if genuine and lasting peace in Cambodia is to be attained.

4. We are of the view that Cambodia needs political stability prior to and after the general elections of the members of the Constituent Assembly scheduled to be held in May 1993. An elected President would facilitate the conduct of the general elections and would also provide an anchor of stability in the period after the general elections. He would effectively serve as the unifying force of the country pending the completion of the drafting of the new Cambodian Constitution and the establishment of a new Cambodian Government. We believe that such a presidential election would help to reinforce the overall peace process and overcome the present impasse in the implementation of the Paris Peace Agreements. We therefore strongly urge all the Cambodian parties to agree to the holding of a presidential election.

5. We call on all the Cambodian parties to cooperate in the spirit of national reconciliation and to exercise self-restraint in order to prevent the situation from deteriorating any further. We also call on all the Cambodian parties to comply with their obligations under the Paris Peace Agreements. They should ensure the safety of UNTAC personnel who are performing their duties. In particular, we call on the Party of Democratic Kampuchea (Khmer Rouge) to comply fully with all its obligations under the Paris Peace Agreements.

Document 65

Third progress report of the Secretary-General on UNTAC

S/25154, 25 January 1993

Introduction

1. By paragraph 10 of its resolution 745 (1992), the Security Council requested the Secretary-General to report to the Council at stated intervals on progress made in the implementation of the resolution and on tasks still to be performed in the operation, with particular regard to the most effective and efficient use of resources. In accordance with this provision and in response to subsequent resolutions and to developments in Cambodia, I have submitted reports on 1 May (S/23870), 12 June (S/24090), 14 July (S/24286), 21 September (S/24578) and 15 November 1992 (S/24800).

2. Resolution 745 (1992) calls for a further progress report in January 1993. This third progress report is submitted to the Security Council in pursuance of that request. It describes the activities of the United Nations Transitional Authority in Cambodia (UNTAC) up to 10 January 1993.

3. By paragraph 21 of resolution 792 (1992) adopted on 30 November 1992, the Council requested the Secretary-General to report not later than 15 February 1993 on the implementation of that resolution and on any further measures that might be necessary and appropriate to ensure the realization of the fundamental objec-

tives of the Paris Agreements (see S/23177). A report in pursuance of that resolution will be submitted at that time.

I. Implementation of resolution 745 (1992)

A. *General*

4. UNTAC has pursued its implementation of the peace process despite the setbacks described in my earlier reports. The refusal of the Party of Democratic Kampuchea (PDK) to fulfil its obligations under the Paris Agreements by participating fully in the peace process made it impossible to implement phase II of the cease-fire. This has meant the effective suspension of the cantonment, disarming and demobilization of the armed forces of the four factions, with the result that those forces remain under arms in the field. Since the beginning of the dry season in November 1992, cease-fire violations—including the movement of troops for strategic advantage and armed clashes between the forces of the two largest factions, the National Army of Democratic Kampuchea (NADK) and the Cambodian People's Armed Forces (CPAF)—have increased and tension has risen in some parts of the country.

5. On the other hand, the success of voter registration has clearly demonstrated that the peace process has the support of the overwhelming majority of the Cambodian people. By the end of December 1992, nearly 4.4 million Cambodians had been registered, representing about 96 per cent of the estimated total number of those qualified to vote in the zones to which UNTAC has access. Registration is effectively complete in most provinces of Cambodia, although it is still continuing in the northern provinces where it began only in November.

6. By the end of December 1992, close to 240,000 refugees and displaced persons—about two thirds of the total—had been safely repatriated to Cambodia. From 30 November to 2 December 1992, UNTAC hosted the first ever international human rights symposium in Phnom Penh. The Supreme National Council has, since my last progress report, approved a dozen rehabilitation projects worth more than $110 million. Progress made and tasks still to be performed by each of the Components and Divisions of UNTAC are described in detail below.

B. *Relations with the Supreme National Council*

7. Since my last progress report, issued on 21 September 1992 (S/24578), the Supreme National Council has held a total of five meetings or working sessions (22 September, 20 October, 8 November (in Beijing) and 8 and 10 December (at UNTAC headquarters)). "Working sessions" are meetings which, because of the absence from Phnom Penh of the President of the Supreme National Council, His Royal Highness Prince Norodom Sihanouk, are held informally under the chairmanship of my Special Representative, Mr. Yasushi Akashi.

8. The agenda at those meetings included such matters as principles to be incorporated into the post-election Constitution, the territorial integrity of Cambodia, relations between the Supreme National Council and multilateral financial institutions, direct control by UNTAC in the field of finance, the exploitation of Cambodia's natural resources, the establishment of the Cambodian National Heritage Protection Authority, the questions of foreign forces and foreign residents and immigrants and the approval of rehabilitation projects.

9. The results of the special Supreme National Council meeting held in Beijing on 8 November 1992 were described in my report on the implementation of resolution 783 (1992) and, in particular, in its annexes II and III (S/24800). Since then, Prince Sihanouk has stayed in Beijing, where he is receiving medical treatment. The two working sessions which, in his absence, my Special Representative chaired on 8 and 10 December respectively, were not attended by some members. The recommendations agreed by those present at the meetings were conveyed to Prince Sihanouk, who approved them.

10. The 10 December meeting was devoted mainly to the question of the verification of the withdrawal and non-return of foreign forces, a matter in which UNTAC was entrusted with specific responsibilities under annex 2, article VI of the Paris Agreement. As reported in document S/24800 (para. 18), UNTAC has not so far found evidence of any formed units of foreign forces in areas of Cambodia to which it has access. The strategic investigation teams established by UNTAC to investigate the foreign forces question submitted an interim report on their activities to the working session of the Supreme National Council held on 10 December. The report described investigations into allegations or suspicions of the presence of foreign forces, all of which had proved inconclusive. Members of the Supreme National Council were invited to provide additional information to support claims that such forces did exist in Cambodia. No additional information has yet been provided.

11. The influence exerted in Cambodia by its two larger neighbours has traditionally been a matter of deep concern to Cambodians. While the Paris Agreement refers only to "foreign forces, advisers and military personnel", there has been a tendency to interpret this provision in much wider terms than a purely military presence and to try to involve UNTAC in matters that fall outside its mandate. In a statement on 14 December 1992, Prince Sihanouk stated that "certain neighbouring countries" had advanced their borders with Cambodia to the detriment of Cambodia's territorial integrity, and spoke of the "occupation" and "exploitation" of Cambodian districts

or villages by nationals of those countries. That exploitation, he said, had led to "the irreversible annihilation of the natural resources of Cambodia, particularly the woods, the precious stones and fish and crustaceans".

12. UNTAC's efforts to address these problems have included the establishment of a Technical Advisory Committee to the Supreme National Council on territorial integrity and a proposal to set up another on foreign residents and immigrants in order to establish the facts of a situation which the new Government formed after the elections may decide to address. In accordance with resolution 792 (1992), UNTAC is also taking appropriate measures to secure implementation of the moratorium on the export of logs decided by the Supreme National Council on 22 September 1992.

13. On 20 December 1992, Prince Sihanouk announced that, following consultations with the parties concerned, a second representative of the Front Uni National pour un Cambodge Indépendant, Neutre, Pacifique et Coopératif (FUNCINPEC) would become a member of the Supreme National Council, thus increasing the total number of members to 13. The new member was later named as Mr. Sam Rainsy. Prince Sihanouk has indicated that this step was taken in order to allow FUNCINPEC to be represented, like the Khmer People's National Liberation Front (KPNLF) and PDK, by two members.

14. On 4 January 1993, Prince Sihanouk informed Mr. Akashi that he was obliged to cease cooperation with UNTAC and with the Party of the State of Cambodia because of the persistent violent attacks on FUNCINPEC offices and staff. Mr. Akashi visited the Prince in Beijing on 8 January 1993 and reported to him regarding recent developments in Cambodia, including the measures taken by UNTAC to promote a neutral political environment. At that meeting, Prince Sihanouk expressed his readiness to hold a meeting of the Supreme National Council in Beijing on 28 January 1993. The Prince also confirmed that he would be a candidate in the presidential elections referred to in paragraph 3 of resolution 792 (1992).

15. On 5 January 1993, Prince Norodom Ranariddh, leader of FUNCINPEC, informed my Special Representative that, in view of the deterioration of the political situation, he would suspend working relations with UNTAC until effective measures were taken to put an end to the current climate of violence (see also sect. I.K below). However, at a subsequent meeting with my Special Representative, Prince Ranariddh expressed gratitude for UNTAC's efforts to address this problem and stressed that FUNCINPEC had always cooperated with UNTAC and would continue to do so.

C. *Human Rights Component*

16. In pursuance of its basic mandate, UNTAC has continued to expand its human rights education and training programmes, both in Phnom Penh and in the provinces. As part of its efforts to promote the development of an independent judiciary, a major programme of training for judges and defence lawyers/public defenders has been initiated. The first course for 60 defenders was completed in November 1992.

17. Formal human rights training has now been introduced into the Cambodian education system. UNTAC has distributed a set of curricular materials throughout the country, and primary and secondary school teachers in the Phnom Penh administration are being trained in their use. Human rights officers are using the materials for training in FUNCINPEC and KPNLF zones. The curriculum of Phnom Penh University also now includes human rights studies, and a course began on 27 October 1992 for 210 law students. Denial of access has made it impossible to extend this programme to the zones controlled by PDK.

18. UNTAC is also stepping up human rights training outside the school system. Training sessions for officials of the existing administrative structures and professional or activist groups have been undertaken in almost every province. More than 4,000 people have attended training sessions in Phnom Penh alone, and an average of 100 people in each of the provinces. The Component has also provided human rights training to members of various UNTAC components.

19. UNTAC's human rights information campaign has set up mobile video units in each province to show videos on basic human rights concepts. Additional radio programmes are also being produced. Together with the United Nations Educational, Scientific and Cultural Organization (UNESCO), UNTAC has organized a team of traditional singers who tour the provinces with a performance featuring human rights messages.

20. Collaboration with indigenous human rights organizations is an important aspect of UNTAC's work. There are now five such organizations with offices in nearly all provinces and with a combined membership reportedly approaching 50,000. UNTAC has provided them with materials, training and expertise as well as small grants for basic office expenses. UNTAC is also setting up a resource centre and library for all the organizations to use collectively. There is also close cooperation with international non-governmental human rights organizations represented in Cambodia.

21. A large majority of persons currently detained in civilian prisons administered by the Phnom Penh authorities have not been accorded due process in the determination of the charges against them. Some prisoners have been detained for up to 10 years without trial, and others claim that their detention is due to their political allegiance rather than to any criminal action on

their part. UNTAC is actively investigating all cases of prisoners who are members of other parties in order to determine whether or not their detention is politically motivated.

22. Conditions of detention in civil prisons throughout Cambodia continue to be closely monitored. Health conditions in some prisons remain poor, partly because of inadequate rations. The use of cells lacking light and ventilation persists at several prisons. UNTAC has pressed the local authorities to improve the situation to the extent possible within the means available to the prison administration.

23. An International Symposium on Human Rights in Cambodia was held in Phnom Penh from 30 November to 2 December 1992, with the participation of representatives of each of the Cambodian human rights organizations. Also participating were some 25 representatives from human rights organizations in Europe, North America and the Asia/Pacific region and of the United Nations Centre for Human Rights and other organizations of the United Nations system. The opening session included presentations on the future of human rights in Cambodia by three of the four Cambodian parties who are signatories to the Paris Agreements.

24. The primary purpose of the Symposium was to examine ways in which the international community might best assist indigenous human rights organizations and structures in the coming years. The Symposium expressed concern at the recent increase in political violence, as described in section I.K below. International and regional human rights organizations agreed to provide resources and expertise, both during the transitional period and afterwards, to assist Cambodian human rights organizations and to complement and continue UN-TAC's efforts in this field. The Symposium also called for a continued United Nations presence in Cambodia following the withdrawal of UNTAC, including possibly an operational presence by the Centre for Human Rights.

25. For Human Rights Day, 10 December, UNTAC organized various events in Phnom Penh and the provinces, including a nationwide drawing contest for children.

D. Electoral Component

26. In paragraph 51 of the implementation plan (S/23613), it was proposed that the registration of voters should begin in October 1992 and last for three months, with a provision for extension if the need arose to ensure the registration of the maximum number of voters. On 21 December, my Special Representative announced the extension of the registration period until 31 January 1993. Given the success of voter registration so far, as well as the current rate of registration in every province

in Cambodia, UNTAC is confident of being able to register at least 97 per cent of the estimated eligible population throughout the country by the end of January 1993.

27. As reported below, it is anticipated that the repatriation of refugees and displaced persons will not be completed until about March 1993. Special arrangements are therefore being made for the registration of those who could not be registered in Cambodia by the end of the original period of registration. This will be done, in addition to extending the period for registration within Cambodia as referred to above, by providing a special facility for refugees only. On the basis of the data currently available, the number of refugees to be accommodated in this way would be between 40,000 and 60,000.

28. In view of the unwillingness of PDK to guarantee access to zones under its control, UNTAC has adopted the practice of registering all applicants in non-PDK areas before moving gradually into districts in which NADK is known to operate. Electoral teams in these districts carry out their tasks in close cooperation with the Civilian Police and Military Components, whose functions, as described below, have been modified to enable them to protect electoral staff if the need arises.

29. So far, many electoral teams operating in or around zones where NADK is present have been permitted to register applicants and have reported high levels of interest in and commitment to the electoral process among the population of those zones. In some cases, residents have been permitted to leave the zones to register at registration points located outside them. In other cases, however, NADK units have refused to allow teams to carry out registration and have requested them to leave. The teams complied, but they will keep trying wherever possible until the completion of the registration process at the end of January. Since UNTAC has not been allowed access to all the PDK-controlled areas, it is unable to estimate the size of the population of those areas or the number of potential voters living there who have not been registered. However, the PDK-controlled areas are generally considered to be sparsely populated, comprising only about 5 per cent of the total population.

30. Since the promulgation of the electoral law in August 1992, 20 political parties have provisionally registered and acquired the right to place their agents in the registration points. This right applies to all of the 834 points and in some cases up to 4 or 5 parties are represented. One of the rights of the party agents is to object to applicants they consider to be unqualified to register. This is a particularly sensitive issue in view of the claim repeatedly made by some Cambodian parties that "Vietnamese" would try to register and vote. To date, however, only about 0.3 per cent of all applicants have been the

subject of challenges by party agents. Where parties have pursued these objections, they have in general failed to file effective grounds for rejecting those registered or evidence to support their disqualification. It can be concluded that the system has been effective in deterring unqualified applicants. In accordance with the electoral law, applicants who are refused registration may appeal to the UNTAC District Electoral Supervisor. The number of such appeals has also been minimal.

31. The computer system for controlling voter registration, described in paragraph 45 of the implementation plan (S/23613), is working well. About 280 Cambodian data-entry clerks, working in three 8-hour shifts per day to ensure a round-the-clock service, use 110 Khmer-language keyboards to enter into the central computer information on cards received from the registration points. The system is designed to support the entering and tracking of up to 5.2 million voter registration records and to produce the lists of registered voters that will be issued to political parties. All the data-entry clerks were trained by four Cambodian trainers, who themselves received instruction at United Nations Headquarters in New York. Owing to communications difficulties and rough terrain, there is a time-lag in the recovery of registration information by the computer centre. While the total number of registration cards issued has now exceeded 4 million, the number of cards so far logged in stands at about 2.6 million.

32. At a date to be determined in accordance with the Electoral Law, my Special Representative will invite political parties already provisionally registered to apply for official registration. This will require those parties to submit a list containing the names, signatures, voter registration numbers and addresses of at least 5,000 registered voters who are members of the party. On 30 November 1992, Mr. Khieu Samphan, Mr. Son Sen and other members of PDK announced that they had established the founding committee of a new party, the National Unity of Cambodia Party (NUCP). In a statement issued the same day, my Special Representative indicated that such a party should register under the Electoral Law and participate fully in the electoral process by, *inter alia*, granting access to other parties and to UNTAC, so that it can discharge its functions in accordance with the Paris Agreements. However, UNTAC has not so far been advised of the creation of this new party.

33. At the Supreme National Council working session of 10 December 1992, representatives of FUNCIN-PEC and KPNLF pressed strongly for two revisions of the Electoral Law approved by the Supreme National Council and promulgated by UNTAC in August 1992. One would extend the franchise to the so-called Khmer Krom residents in Cambodia, that is, ethnic Cambodians born, or with a parent born, in southern Viet Nam. The second would allow Cambodians living overseas to register outside Cambodia (at present the law allows such Cambodians to vote overseas but they must register as voters in Cambodia).

34. My Special Representative has had extensive discussions on these two proposed revisions of the Electoral Law with the parties concerned. On the basis of his reports, I have given careful consideration to these two issues, especially in view of the support expressed for them by Prince Sihanouk. However, I have regretfully come to the conclusion that the extension of the franchise on purely ethnic grounds to persons who were not born in Cambodia would not be consistent with the letter or the spirit of the Paris Agreements. Furthermore, at a time when the registration process is nearing completion, the printing of additional registration cards and other necessary documentation would create such delays that it would make it practically impossible to hold the elections in May 1993, in accordance with the time-table set by the Security Council. The same can be said of the complex problems arising from any attempt to allow Cambodians to register overseas. I have therefore told my Special Representative that, unless the Security Council decides otherwise, he should not approve these two proposed revisions of the Electoral Law.

E. Military Component

1. Cease-fire violations

35. In my report of 15 November 1992 (S/24800, paras. 14-18), I expressed concern over the military situation in Cambodia. There has recently been an increase in the daily count of cease-fire violations but with no clear gain to either of the forces of the two largest factions, NADK and CPAF. Most cease-fire violations take place in Kompong Thom, Siem Reap and Battambang provinces in central and north-west Cambodia. They typically take the form of artillery duels, which drive villagers from their homes without causing extensive casualties on either side. In other cease-fire violations, six bridges in central and northern Cambodia have been blown up since mid-October 1992.

36. The Party of the State of Cambodia (SOC), claiming that NADK has made territorial gains, has called on my Special Representative to restore the military balance. Reports from United Nations military and naval observers in the countryside do not conclusively confirm this claim, but rather indicate that the armed forces of SOC (CPAF) are attempting to recover territory over which NADK extended its influence during the recent rains, while NADK is attempting to consolidate its gains and interrupt CPAF's communications. This pattern is illustrated by the increased state of readiness of NADK

forces in Kompong Thom, where United Nations observers report that NADK lines of communication and supply have been shortened and combat training intensified.

37. On 4 November 1992, my Special Representative issued a call for military restraint, urging all parties to respect the peace process and to refrain from building up their forces, making aggressive military moves or attacking one another. He stressed that no Cambodian party had the right to deny the Cambodian people the right to take control over their country and their destiny through free and fair elections. In my report of 15 November 1992, I also appealed to all parties to respect the cease-fire scrupulously and to refrain, in accordance with article 9 of the Paris Agreements, from any activity which is aimed at enlarging the territory they control or which might lead to renewed fighting.

38. However, in December there occurred two very serious cease-fire violations. Frequent exchanges of shelling took place between NADK and CPAF throughout the month in the Bavel area of Battambang province, causing about 15,000 local residents to flee their homes. Many of these were assisted by the Office of the United Nations High Commissioner for Refugees (UNHCR) with the help of the World Food Programme (WFP), the United Nations Children's Fund (UNICEF) and the International Committee of the Red Cross (ICRC). On 24 and 25 December NADK artillery shells landed near a location occupied by UNTAC troops from the Bangladesh battalion in Svay Leu district 50 kilometres north-east of Siem Reap. An UNTAC electoral registration team supported by UNTAC military and civilian police personnel had been deployed there a few days earlier. The area came under shelling again on 31 December. In total, about 20 rounds fell near the UNTAC camp. The UNTAC personnel were evacuated, but have since returned. Bavel is still being subjected to sporadic shelling, but Svay Leu appears to be currently calm.

2. Redeployment of the Military Component

39. As stated in article 11 of the Paris Agreement, the objectives of the Military Component are to "stabilize the security situation and build confidence among the parties to the conflict, so as to reinforce the purpose of this agreement and to prevent the risks of a return to warfare". This was to have been done through the cantonment and demobilization of the forces of all four factions. However, the refusal of the PDK to participate in that process has made it necessary to redeploy the Military Component in order to fulfil the requirements of Security Council resolution 792 (1992).

40. The Military Component will continue to perform many of the tasks entrusted to it since the beginning of the mission, including weapons control and assistance to the Repatriation Component, as well as its essential engineering, demining, logistics, communications and other functions. The Component will continue its patrolling, observation and monitoring duties by land and water and its civic action programmes to build confidence in the countryside.

41. However, the priority task of the Component in the coming months, as described in paragraph 31 of my report of 15 November 1992 (S/24800), is to enhance UNTAC's ability to protect voter registration and, subsequently, the electoral and polling processes, particularly in remote or insecure areas.

42. In order to accomplish this, the original deployment pattern of the Military Component, which was based on the requirements of regroupment and cantonment, has been realigned to correspond with the borders of the Cambodian provinces. This will conform with the deployment of electoral teams and shorten the time taken to respond to potential threats to them. The new deployment, which was completed on 31 December 1992, is also designed to foster a sense of security among Cambodians in those areas with a higher potential for conflict. Similarly, military observers now accompany electoral teams in order to negotiate, where necessary, with local authorities or forces that try to hinder registration. While some incidents have occurred, as described below, the military observers have often succeeded in such negotiations. In addition, with the winding down of the voter registration exercise, the Military Component will be asked to assist in UNTAC's efforts to promote a neutral political environment, as described in section I.K below.

43. The Military Component's mine-clearance programme will also continue to receive high priority. The number of trained mine-clearance personnel has now reached 1,323, with a further 160 under training. Since there is a shortage of supervisors, only 542 of these are employed, 352 directly by UNTAC and 190 by other agencies. In order to resolve this problem, some UNTAC trainers have been requested to act as supervisors while some of the trained mine clearers are receiving additional training as supervisors.

3. Attacks on UNTAC personnel and aircraft

44. Since my second progress report of 21 September 1992, 14 UNTAC personnel have been injured as a result of military activity by one or other faction. These include nine military, police and civilian personnel injured in land-mine explosions in Banteay Meanchey, Kratie and Siem Reap provinces. In addition, one soldier and three civilian electoral staff were injured by gunfire in two separate incidents, and an officer was injured when his helicopter was fired upon.

45. The latter incident was 1 of 11 involving attacks on helicopters, mostly over Siem Reap, Kompong Thom and Preah Vihear provinces, with 1 incident taking place over Kompong Speu Province. Most of these did not result in injury, although in one case a helicopter was forced to land because of damage caused by small-arms fire, as described in paragraph 15 of my report of 15 November 1992 (S/24800).

46. A total of 21 UNTAC personnel have died by accident or from natural causes since the beginning of the mission, including 10 since my report of 21 September 1992.

47. During December, a number of incidents occurred in which UNTAC military and other personnel were detained in the countryside by units of NADK, each apparently acting in isolation. The incidents took place while UNTAC military and naval observers and other military personnel were exercising their right to move freely throughout the territory of Cambodia in order to carry out their duties, including election-related duties. In all cases UNTAC personnel were released unconditionally and unharmed.

48. On 2 December, six United Nations military observers were detained by a unit of NADK and held for two days before being released unharmed. My Special Representative subsequently issued a statement in which he noted that the PDK leadership had been cooperative in securing the observers' release, but that their troops had acted quite wrongly in detaining them in the first place. The statement also referred to the statement of the President of the Security Council of 2 December 1992 (S/24884) expressing the members' deep concern and outrage at this and other serious incidents involving United Nations peace-keeping personnel. The latter statement demanded that the parties concerned take all necessary measures to prevent the recurrence of such incidents. It also stressed that the abduction and detention of United Nations peace-keeping personnel was totally unacceptable.

49. On 15 December 1992, two military observers accompanying an electoral team near the village of O Sala in Kompong Thom Province entered into negotiations with a local NADK commander to ensure the safety of the team. They were obliged to stay overnight with the NADK unit and were joined the next day by two more military observers and a company of one of UNTAC's two Indonesian battalions. After further discussions, and a further night at the scene, the 4 observers and several members of the Indonesian battalion were allowed to leave for Kompong Thom City, while 8 Indonesian soldiers remained at O Sala, with a further 40 or so stationed about 400 metres away. On 18 December, all of them were allowed to leave O Sala unconditionally.

50. Another incident occurred in Kratie Province on 18-19 December 1992 involving the overnight detention of 10 members of UNTAC's Uruguayan battalion, 3 Russian helicopter crew members and a Russian military observer. NADK representatives did not appear for a previously arranged rendezvous with a unit of NADK and, in ensuing attempts to make contact with them, the UNTAC group inadvertently landed in a NADK defensive position. Negotiations through established mechanisms led to peaceful resolution of the incident but confirmed the need to formalize liaison between NADK field commanders and UNTAC, through the deployment of NADK liaison officers in the provincial capitals. Discussions with all factions continue with a view to gaining agreement to procedures that will allow this deployment to occur.

51. On 20 December 1992, Mr. Khieu Samphan addressed a letter to my Special Representative, enclosing a declaration of PDK and NADK jointly signed by himself and Mr. Son Sen, which asserted, *inter alia*, that UNTAC should not enter PDK-controlled zones without prior authorization and that UNTAC must assume full responsibility for incidents that occurred as a result of its failure to obtain such authorization. On 22 December 1992, my Special Representative and the Force Commander replied, pointing out the distortions contained in the declaration. On the same day, the President of the Security Council issued a statement (S/25003) in which the Council strongly condemned the illegal detention of UNTAC personnel by elements of PDK.

4. *Other developments*

52. In its resolution 792 (1992), the Security Council adopted a number of measures relating to the full implementation of the Paris Agreements and of decisions taken or to be taken by the Supreme National Council. In particular, the Council invited UNTAC to establish all necessary border check-points, requested neighbouring States to cooperate fully in the establishment and maintenance of those check-points and requested the Secretary-General to undertake immediate consultations with States concerned regarding their establishment and operation.

53. As reported in paragraph 20 of my second progress report, UNTAC has established nine check-points on Cambodia's border with Viet Nam, two on the border with the Lao People's Democratic Republic and seven on that with Thailand. In accordance with my original implementation plan (S/23613), additional check-points have been established at ports, airports and major routes inside Cambodia.

54. The border check-points already in place give UNTAC the capacity to observe activities in zones con-

trolled by FUNCINPEC, KPNLF and SOC. To supplement them, a further eight check-points are to be established along the Thai border in the zone controlled by PDK. Consultations are currently taking place between UNTAC representatives and the Royal Thai Government with a view to agreeing on modalities for the cooperation called for in paragraph 12 of resolution 792 (1992) regarding the establishment and operation of those check-points.

55. Originally, the border check-points were put in place pursuant to articles VI and VII of annex 2 of the Paris Agreement governing the verification of the withdrawal from Cambodia and the non-return of all categories of foreign forces and the cessation of outside military assistance to all Cambodian parties. In addition to these duties, check-point personnel are also now required to assist in the implementation of paragraphs 10 and 13 of resolution 792 (1992) and ultimately in the implementation of paragraph 14. In accordance with paragraph 21 of that resolution, more detailed information on its implementation will be contained in the report to be submitted to the Security Council by 15 February 1993.

F. Civil Administration Component

1. General

56. The extension of UNTAC supervision and control over the existing administrative structures of the three parties in compliance with the peace plan has continued despite the deteriorating security situation, which complicates UNTAC's task. In particular, progress has been achieved in the further development of the expenditure control procedure, the establishment of a border control mechanism, the planning of specialized control operations in telecommunications and civil aviation and the measures taken to promote a neutral political environment (see sect. I.K below). In addition, UNTAC has decided to extend its control to the "council of ministers" of the Phnom Penh administration, since a number of decisions affecting the activities of other "ministries" are taken at that level. On the other hand, UNTAC has been unable to gain access to the administrative structure of PDK, and this inability has given rise to a hardening of the position of the Phnom Penh authorities *vis-à-vis* the supervision and control exercised by UNTAC over them in nearly all fields. This has been particularly evident since the beginning of October 1992.

2. Foreign affairs

57. During September, following the submission of the second progress report, UNTAC supervised the abolition of entry and exit visas for the holders of passports issued by the Phnom Penh authorities, the abolition of the policy of retaining those passports after their holders had returned to Cambodia, the streamlining of immigration procedures at Phnom Penh Airport, and the simplification and expediting of procedures for obtaining passports from the Phnom Penh authorities. On 22 September, the Supreme National Council declared that all Cambodian passports shared the same status as the newly issued Supreme National Council passports when endorsed by the Supreme National Council seal. An increase of corruption in the issuance of passports, however, has recently been detected. Efforts to secure the cooperation of the "ministry of foreign affairs" of SOC have not so far been successful and, if this persists, UNTAC may soon have to take firmer action to remedy the situation.

58. UNTAC has focused its attention on the distribution of food aid in order to prevent its use in influencing voters and has dealt with a number of cases of embezzlement.

59. A border-control mechanism has been developed by the Civil Administration, Civilian Police and Military Components. This is of particular significance in view of the concerns many Cambodians express about the influx of Vietnamese into Cambodia and the adoption by the Supreme National Council on 22 September 1992 of a moratorium on the export of round logs from the country. The operation of the mechanism will rely on the UNTAC border check-points already established and those to be established in accordance with the Paris Agreements and with resolution 792 (1992).

3. National defence

60. On 14 October, the "minister of defence" of SOC signed a declaration outlining the principal modalities of UNTAC's direct control in the field of defence. One of these is a priori control, which allows UNTAC to examine decisions by the "ministry" before they are finalized. On 21 October, the "minister of defence" approved an information circular proposed by UNTAC concerning measures to be taken with regard to immovable property assets and underlining the distinction between private and public assets. This is a significant issue in that land and property disputes in general, and disputes over land and property owned by the administrations in particular, are extremely widespread and complex in Cambodia.

61. All incoming and outgoing correspondence of the SOC "ministry" of defence is monitored by UNTAC in order to control any actions that might impair the neutrality of the political environment. Similar correspondence of the FUNCINPEC and KPNLF administrations is also monitored. The removal from populated areas of munitions dumps thought to be in a dangerous condition has been secured and the sale for scrap of unserviceable weapons after their destruction by the Mili-

tary Component has been approved. The use of funds from such sales is monitored.

62. A draft directive is now in preparation to be signed by the leaders of CPAF, Army of National Campuchea Independence (ANKI) and the Khmer People's National Liberation Armed Forces (KPNLAF) governing political activity by military personnel. Consideration is being given to drawing up a similar code of conduct for other categories of officials, including civil servants and police officers.

4. Public security

63. Following the adoption by the Supreme National Council on 10 September 1992 of transitional provisions relating to the judiciary and criminal law and procedures, known as the "interim penal provisions", a training programme was launched on 2 November for about 200 local magistrates, police officers, prosecutors and public defenders from three of the four Cambodian parties. This was done in collaboration with the Human Rights and Civilian Police Components. The latter also worked with the Civil Administration Component in establishing a working group on road safety, which has produced videos and a booklet on traffic rules and an interim traffic code, and a working group on banditry. Prison visits have been conducted, without prior authorization, to ensure that the provisions are being properly applied.

64. However, the public security situation throughout Cambodia is still unsatisfactory. The special measures now under consideration in order to create and maintain a neutral political environment conducive to free and fair elections are discussed below.

5. Finance

65. UNTAC is experiencing difficulty in exercising the controls it has sought to put in place over the Phnom Penh authorities as a result of the increasing resistance from them referred to above. Efforts are nevertheless continuing to strengthen UNTAC's control over expenditure, all sources of revenue (e.g., taxes and customs), the central bank functions and the sale of public assets. Techniques and methodology for financial control have also been discussed with the FUNCINPEC and KPNLF administrations.

66. Another dimension is the stabilization of the country's economy in order to reduce possible causes of unrest that might have an adverse effect on the electoral environment. In particular, UNTAC has been involved in efforts undertaken by external donors such as the World Bank International Monetary Fund (IMF) and the Asian Development Bank (AsDB), as well as bilateral donors whose financial assistance programmes have macroe-

conomic implications. An AsDB loan agreement of $74 million was recently approved, and in October 1992 the Netherlands agreed to provide $2 million in short-term assistance for the importation of rice and other goods.

67. In conjunction with the World Bank, the new budget of SOC has been introduced to enhance clarity and transparency and to eliminate budget elements relating to party political activity.

68. In its efforts to assert control over the national bank, UNTAC is monitoring the issue of currency on a weekly basis. Efforts are now under way to set up a system to monitor the bank's position vis-à-vis the currency reserves and liabilities of the Phnom Penh administration and to help to forecast economic trends.

69. A workshop for all provincial financial controllers was held on 23 and 24 November in Phnom Penh on various aspects of control techniques, and seminars for tax officials and customs officers of the Phnom Penh administration have been organized.

6. Information

70. In October 1992, UNTAC published media guidelines drafted in the Media Working Group established by the Information/Education Division. The guidelines aim at lifting legal restrictions and encouraging the operation of a free and responsible press. To foster this process, UNTAC has helped to launch a Cambodian Media Association of all Cambodian journalists, which had met twice by mid-December. Fair access to the media by all political parties during the forthcoming electoral campaign will also be ensured.

71. UNTAC has enjoyed limited success in its efforts to exercise control over the existing administrative structures dealing with information. No access has been granted to the structures of PDK. The "ministry of information" of SOC has resisted UNTAC's attempts to effect a priori control. Information officers have sought, but failed, to attend editorial meetings of some of its information entities, including its press agency and its television station, "TV Kampuchea". The latter organization has also refused to show one UNTAC video that it considers not to be neutral vis-à-vis SOC, but it has regularly broadcast other UNTAC information materials without difficulty.

7. Complaints and investigations

72. More than 140 complaints have now been received, mostly concerning land disputes, evictions and allegations involving interference or abuse by local officials that are not human rights violations.

73. As already noted, many land and property disputes involve the "ministry of defence" of SOC. At the

instigation of UNTAC, the "ministry" has now established two committees whose objectives are to prepare an inventory of all real estate owned by the "ministry" and to take disciplinary action against soldiers found to be trespassing on either public property or private property owned by others.

8. *Specialized control*

74. In accordance with annex 1, section B, paragraph 2, of the Paris Agreement, the Supreme National Council agreed at its meeting on 26 May 1992 to UNTAC's "optional" or "second-level" control over a number of fields, including public health, education, agriculture, fishing, transport, energy, tourism, historic monuments, mines and general administration.

75. As of 3 October, an UNTAC naval officer was given the responsibility of monitoring the activities of the Phnom Penh "ministries" involved in the civil administration of the ports of Cambodia.

76. A health sector technical working group was established to examine health-related questions such as ensuring equal access for Cambodians to health services and setting a standard for qualifications of healthcare workers. The group, which includes representatives of the Cambodian parties, UNTAC Medical Services, the World Health Organization (WHO), UNHCR, UNICEF, ICRC and the International Federation of Red Cross and Red Crescent Societies (IFRC), met on 5 October 1992 to discuss control of the spread of the acquired immune deficiency syndrome in Cambodia.

G. *Civilian Police Component*

77. The Civilian Police Component (CIVPOL) has now effectively reached full deployment with the arrival in Cambodia of some 3,550 officers out of the authorized strength of 3,600, with the final 50 due to arrive soon. The activities of the Component, both in general and in response to paragraph 10 of resolution 783 (1992), are described in paragraphs 11 to 13 of my report on the implementation of that resolution (S/24800). Activities of the component in promoting a neutral political environment of Cambodia are described in section I.K below.

78. On 27 November 1992, in implementation of its mandate to organize training courses for the local police, UNTAC awarded graduation certificates to 84 Cambodian police officers who had completed its course on basic police methods. The graduates included members of KPNLF and KPNLAF, as well as 24 officers from PDK. UNTAC has decided to deploy civilian police monitors in areas controlled by PDK to help to protect returning refugees who wish to settle there with assistance from the Repatriation Component. Both Components have

been promised full access to those areas where repatriation is to take place.

H. *Repatriation Component*

79. About two thirds of the refugees and displaced persons—a total of some 240,000—had been repatriated without serious incident by the end of December 1992. A total of 34,400 persons were repatriated during the month of December and movements are expected to exceed 40,000 in January 1993. The repatriation of all 360,000 or so refugees by May 1993 is confidently expected. Following the closure in October 1992 of three border camps, Sok Sann, Site K and O'Trao, Site B camp was closed on 14 December 1992. Site 8 is scheduled to close in late January 1993, Site 2 in late March and Khao-I-Dang as soon as possible thereafter.

80. More than 10 per cent of the returnees have been repatriated to the Thmar Puok area presently under the control of KPNLF. Some 3,000 persons have also been repatriated to the zone administered by FUNCINPEC. Preparations for movements to the area under the control of PDK are continuing and the first movement to one of the proposed settlement sites is scheduled to take place around some time in January 1993. A few thousand persons have registered their desire to return to this area.

81. The general deterioration of the security situation has, however, affected the repatriation operation, albeit to a limited extent for the time being. Recurrent fighting in the Bavel district of Battambang Province, for instance, has forced returnees as well as the receiving population to become internally displaced persons. As a result, UNTAC has now declared the district insecure and unsuitable for repatriation purposes.

82. The programme of quick impact projects, jointly managed with the United Nations Development Programme (UNDP), is progressing successfully. To date some $3.4 million has been disbursed out of a total of more than $9 million earmarked for quick impact projects in the UNHCR programme. The main areas of activity are infrastructure, health, provision of water, agriculture and education.

83. One of the limiting factors in the reintegration into Cambodia of the returnees is the shortage of safe, available land. With this in mind, the Director of the Repatriation Component has also been named as the Director a.i. of the Cambodian Mine Action Centre, whose Governing Council held its first meeting on 4 November 1992. In accordance with the statute adopted by the Supreme National Council in June 1992, Prince Sihanouk is the President of the Governing Council of the Centre and my Special Representative serves as Vice-President. Each has appointed five members to serve on

the Governing Council and, in addition, UNTAC has appointed a Treasurer. The 4 November meeting approved an eight-month operations plan to June 1993 and a draft budget. The Centre will pursue four objectives: increasing mine awareness, collecting mine information and marking minefields, clearing mines and unexploded ordnance and training Cambodians in mine-clearance skills.

84. A group of 398 Vietnamese Montagnards, called the "Front Uni de Libération des Races Opprimées" (United Front for the Liberation of Oppressed Races) (FULRO), who had been living for more than 15 years in the forests of Mondolkiri Province, laid down their arms and were transported on 10 October 1992 to an UNTAC transit centre, near Phnom Penh, for screening by United States officials. The process proceeded smoothly, and all of them were accepted for resettlement in North Carolina, United States of America. They travelled to the United States, via Bangkok, in nine groups, between 18 November and 2 December 1992.

85. Out of some 11,000 Cambodian refugees living in Viet Nam since 1975, 850 have requested to be repatriated. The first convoy of 101 returnees took place on 15 November 1992. As of 15 December, a total of 456 returnees had come back.

I. *Rehabilitation Component*

86. At the two Supreme National Council meetings held in Phnom Penh on 22 September and 20 October 1992, four rehabilitation projects totalling $11.7 million were approved. These involved technical assistance in the rehabilitation of public finances and in humanitarian and development-related matters, the safeguarding of Angkor Wat and the promotion and development of agro-related metalworking industries. A further nine projects worth more than $100 million were approved at the Supreme National Council working session held on 8 December. As a result, a total of 35 projects representing over $340 million have been approved by the Supreme National Council since the Tokyo Ministerial Conference on the Rehabilitation and Reconstruction of Cambodia held in June 1992.

87. In collaboration with UNESCO, UNTAC proposed to the Supreme National Council at its meeting on 20 October 1992 the establishment of a National Heritage Protection Authority of Cambodia to coordinate efforts aimed at protecting and administering the physical and cultural heritage of Cambodia. This was approved unanimously by the Supreme National Council. In December 1992, UNESCO decided that the site of Angkor Wat, together with its monuments and its archaeological zones, should be officially inscribed on the list of monuments to be preserved by the international community.

88. At its meeting on 22 September 1992, the Supreme National Council, acting on the initiative of UNTAC, adopted a moratorium on the export of untreated logs as from 31 December 1992 in order to protect Cambodia's natural resources. By paragraph 13 of its resolution 792 (1992), the Security Council supported that decision; requested States, especially neighbouring States, to respect the moratorium by not importing such logs; and requested UNTAC to take appropriate measures to secure the implementation of such a moratorium.

89. At its working session on 8 December 1992, the Supreme National Council reviewed without objection a plan for the implementation of the moratorium, which involves the Civil Administration, Military and Civilian Police Components, as well as the Rehabilitation Component. The plan requires a review of existing logging contracts concluded with the four Cambodian parties, the development of legal penalties for illegal trade in logs and sawn timber and provisions for UNTAC supervision of the enforcement of the moratorium by the border police and customs authorities of the existing administrative structures. Since 1 January 1993, in accordance with that plan and pursuant to resolution 792 (1992), UNTAC personnel at the border check-points have been monitoring and reporting any illegal export of logs and sawn timber so that the administrative structures concerned and the countries of destination can be informed. My Special Representative has called on countries adjacent to Cambodia to assist in the implementation of the moratorium.

90. In accordance with paragraph 14 of resolution 792 (1992), proposals are being drawn up for submission to the Supreme National Council regarding a moratorium on the export of minerals and gems in order to protect Cambodia's natural resources.

J. *Information/education*

91. UNTAC produces a variety of videos, posters, information leaflets, flyers and large banners and advertisements for public display to encourage full participation in voter registration and to illustrate the work of UNTAC, especially the Human Rights Component. Radio production will increase from four to nine new half-hour programmes per week as the new Khmer direct-production staff begin independent scriptwriting and recording. Programmes are repeated throughout the day at local peak times. The programmes are broadcast from a transmitter in Phnom Penh and reach most of Cambodia, and the addition of relay transmitters, for which tenders were closed in December 1992, will ensure

that UNTAC broadcasts can be heard throughout the country. These efforts are complemented by the dissemination in the provinces of 43,000 radios donated by the Japanese people through a non-governmental organization and by a Japanese political party. Another 100,000 transistor radios are in the pipeline. An UNTAC Information Centre was opened in Phnom Penh in mid-November 1992 for Cambodians wishing to read UNTAC materials and watch the video products and as a venue for meetings of Cambodian journalists and for media-related seminars.

92.   Translations and analyses of the Khmer-language radio and print output of all four Cambodian parties are provided to my Special Representative and all UNTAC components. Information officers also conduct regular opinion surveys among Cambodians of all categories and occupations in Phnom Penh and the country-side to assess the impact of UNTAC's information programme and to monitor the attitude of the people towards UNTAC and its implementation of the peace process.

93.   UNTAC is now preparing for more intensified activity during the electoral campaign, which will include informing Cambodians of the events of the campaign and their significance, disseminating information on the various political party platforms, building confidence in the secrecy of the ballot and instructing voters in voting procedures.

K.   *Creation and maintenance of a neutral political environment*

94.   One of UNTAC's most important tasks is the creation and maintenance of a neutral political environment conducive to the holding of free and fair elections, as called for in article 6 of the Paris Agreement. This environment is to be achieved through UNTAC control of the existing administrative structures, as well as by promoting respect for human rights as provided for in article 16 of the Paris Agreement. As my Special Representative has informed the Supreme National Council, such an environment does not yet exist. A spate of violent incidents over the last few months has heightened a sense of insecurity among Cambodians. UNTAC's Human Rights, Civilian Police and Civil Administration Components have jointly taken the lead in developing measures to prevent and deal with threats to public order so that electoral activity can proceed in peaceful and orderly conditions.

95.   Threats to public order in Cambodia can be divided into three categories: politically motivated attacks on political party offices and staff; attacks on Vietnamese-speaking persons; and killings which seem to have no particular political motivation but which spread a climate of fear and intimidation. Although there are provinces where basic political rights are by and large respected, there are others where this is far from being the case. The local administrative agencies, bodies and offices that are in a position to influence the outcome of the election have in many instances not responded properly to their obligation to ensure respect for human rights and fundamental freedoms and to accept UNTAC control and supervision. The existing administrative structures are not providing effective protection to some political parties, nor do officials of those parties believe they are receiving adequate protection from the authorities.

96.   In recent weeks there have been more than 40 attacks on political party offices and workers throughout Cambodia. Most of these are directed against FUNCINPEC and the Buddhist Liberal Democratic Party (political wing of KPNLF). The worst incidents have taken place in Battambang, Kandal, Sihanoukville, Pursat, Prey Veng, Svay Rieng, Koh Kong, Siem Reap and Kampot. In most cases, unknown assailants driving past the offices or homes of party members by night throw grenades or fire automatic weapons at them before speeding off. All these incidents have been investigated or are currently under investigation by the Civilian Police Component in collaboration with the Human Rights Component, but UNTAC's efforts are hampered by the lack of witnesses.

97.   In addition to the killings of Vietnamese-speaking persons in Tuk Meas Village and Koh Kong Province which I described in paragraph 19 of my 15 November report (S/24800), four other violent incidents took place in October and November in which the victims were of Vietnamese origin. Three of these, involving kidnapping, murder and the destruction of property, took place in Sihanoukville. The fourth concerned the abduction, rape and murder of Vietnamese nationals, apparently by a group of Cambodian men, early in November. On 17 November 1992, on the basis of a Civilian Police and Human Rights investigation into the murders in Koh Kong Province, my Special Representative wrote to Mr. Khieu Samphan, President of PDK, seeking his cooperation in locating 10 members of NADK who had been identified as suspects in the killings. No cooperation has been forthcoming.

98.   On 16 December, UNTAC was informed that three fishermen of Vietnamese origin had been missing from their home in Hang Kasoun village, Stung Treng province, since 8 December. The bodies of the victims were found floating in the Mekong. UNTAC investigations subsequently established that the three had been killed by NADK soldiers, whose names were given to the investigators. On 27 December a group of about 24

soldiers attacked Taches village in Kompong Chhnang Province. The soldiers who, according to witnesses, belonged to NADK, asked villagers to identify "Vietnamese" residents and killed 14 people pointed out to them. They wounded 14 others, of whom one has since died. The victims included six women and four children. As in the case of the earlier attacks, there is strong evidence that this incident was racially motivated.

99. Summary executions of groups of persons have also caused considerable concern. In two separate incidents in November, a total of 10 bodies were found in shallow graves in Battambang and Kompong Cham provinces. The victims, all young men, were bound and they had been stabbed, beaten or shot to death. Some were in uniform. UNTAC Civilian Police and Human Rights investigations into the cases strongly indicate the involvement of CPAF personnel in the Battambang case, but the identity of the perpetrators in the Kompong Cham case is still unclear.

100. On 19 November 1992, my Special Representative publicly stated that a free and fair election could not be held in circumstances where people faced threats to their lives, property and personal security for attempting to exercise their political rights. He strongly reaffirmed UNTAC's full commitment to the creation and maintenance of a neutral political environment.

101. In order to foster such an environment, UNTAC has announced that it will give priority to protecting three freedoms: freedom from intimidation, freedom of party affiliation and freedom of action for political parties. The attention of the four parties has also been drawn to paragraph 4 of resolution 792 (1992), which calls on them to cooperate fully with UNTAC to create a neutral political environment for the conduct of free and fair elections and prevent acts of harassment, intimidation and political violence.

102. In November, at the request of UNTAC, senior public security officials of the Phnom Penh administration issued a public statement condemning acts of political intimidation and transmitted instructions accordingly to their subordinates. UNTAC Provincial Directors have also informed the Phnom Penh administration officials responsible for each province, their deputies and heads of districts or communes that, if investigation so warranted, they could be held personally responsible by UNTAC for all acts of intimidation, all threats and all violent actions perpetrated against the agents of the parties active in their province. UNTAC has made it clear to the local authorities that any allegations of intimidation and violence directed against political parties will be vigorously investigated.

103. In mid-December 1992, UNTAC's Civilian Police and Military Components instituted intensive patrols and static guard duty to improve the security of political party offices thought to be most vulnerable to attack, and these measures were further refined early in January 1993. On 6 January, in accordance with articles 6 and 16 and sections B and E of annex I of the Paris Agreements, my Special Representative issued a directive establishing procedures for the prosecution of persons responsible for human rights violations. Pursuant to this directive, UNTAC has assumed powers to arrest, detain and prosecute suspects in cases involving serious human rights violations. These powers will be exercised in accordance with the Provisions relating to the Judiciary and Criminal Law and Procedure Applicable in Cambodia during the Transitional Period, which were adopted by the Supreme National Council on 10 September 1992.

II. Concluding observations

104. Some of the developments which have occurred in Cambodia since my last progress report are encouraging, while others are cause for concern.

105. On the positive side, there is no doubt that the voter registration exercise has been a remarkable success. It also demonstrates that the overwhelming majority of the Cambodian people support the peace process and UNTAC's efforts to implement the mandate entrusted to it under the Paris Agreements. It testifies to the confidence of the Cambodian people in the democratic process. In accordance with its mandate and with paragraph 5 of Security Council resolution 792 (1992), UNTAC will therefore continue to make every effort to prepare for the holding of free and fair elections by May 1993, in all areas of Cambodia to which it has access as at 31 January 1993. I sincerely hope that all parties will respect the unmistakable wish of the Cambodian people to be given the opportunity to decide freely their own future, in a peaceful and secure environment.

106. I am also encouraged by the progress of the repatriation process. Two thirds of the 360,000 Cambodian refugees and displaced persons have now been safely repatriated and I am confident that, under present conditions, this process will be completed in time to enable all eligible returnees to take part in the elections.

107. On the other hand, there have been a number of negative developments that have created obstacles to the full implementation of the Paris Agreements. As the members of the Security Council are aware, PDK's refusal to participate in the second phase of the cease-fire has made it impossible for UNTAC to carry out the cantonment, disarmament and demobilization of the factions' armed forces. The continuing existence of large and sometimes undisciplined armies, as well as attempts by some of them to improve their positions on the ground,

has had an adverse effect on the security situation in the country. There has been an increase in violations of the cease-fire, and there have also been a number of attacks on UNTAC personnel and helicopters. Last month, for the first time, members of the UNTAC Military Component were temporarily detained by elements of NADK in three separate incidents.

108.   Another disturbing feature of the present situation is the growing climate of violence resulting from politically motivated acts of intimidation and attacks against party offices and party workers, as well as from apparently deliberate killings of persons of Vietnamese descent. There also seems to be a growing reluctance on the part of some of the existing administrative structures to accept the control and supervision functions entrusted to UNTAC. It is worth reiterating in this connection that non-compliance by one party should not be invoked by any other party as a pretext for failing to honour its obligations under the Paris Agreements. In addition, the Supreme National Council has not met as frequently as it should, and the level of participation of some of the parties in its meetings has been disappointing.

109.   These developments have seriously hampered UNTAC's efforts to create and maintain the neutral political environment needed for the holding of free and fair elections. The measures recently announced by my Special Representative to deter attacks against political party offices and to arrest and prosecute those thought to be responsible for acts of violence, in combination with some other measures under consideration by UNTAC, should contribute to improving the political atmosphere in the country and promoting a climate of security and stability.

110.   I am convinced, however, that the best way of overcoming the present difficulties is for all parties to remain actively involved in the peace process and to engage in constructive dialogue within the Supreme National Council, in accordance with their obligations under the Paris Agreements. Clearly, peace in Cambodia cannot be achieved without the continuing support of the Cambodian parties, and UNTAC cannot succeed in its mission unless they cooperate in ensuring that the mechanisms set up by the Paris Agreements function in an effective manner.

111.   I fully understand the serious concerns recently expressed by Prince Sihanouk about the many challenges that the peace process faces. I am encouraged by the constructive discussions he had with my Special Representative on 8 January and by his decision, despite continuing health problems, to host a meeting of the Supreme National Council in Beijing on 28 January 1993. At this critical juncture, his leadership and moral authority are more than ever needed. Prince Sihanouk remains the sole figure capable of uniting Cambodians of all political persuasions. I am confident that, his health permitting, he will continue to work actively towards peace, stability and national unity in Cambodia and to support UNTAC's endeavours to contribute to the achievement of these goals.

112.   In this context, I am gratified that Prince Sihanouk confirmed to my Special Representative that he intended to participate in the presidential election referred to in paragraph 3 of resolution 792 (1992). I am convinced that the holding of a presidential election, in conjunction with the planned election for a constituent assembly, could contribute to national reconciliation and that it could provide an essential element of stability during the rest of the transitional period. I have therefore asked my Special Representative to proceed immediately with the necessary technical preparations. I trust that, in view of the time constraints, the members of the Council will support this course of action. I will submit to the Council, in my next report, further recommendations regarding the modalities for the organization and conduct of such an election.

113.   In the meantime, UNTAC will continue to do its best to resolve the difficulties that have arisen, so that it can pursue the implementation of its complex mandate in an improved and more secure environment. I am aware that further challenges lie ahead and that the coming weeks may be critical in this regard. I therefore intend to visit the region next month to review the situation personally and study what further measures might usefully be taken to reinforce the peace process and ensure the best possible implementation of the Paris Agreements. In the final analysis, however, this can be achieved only with the active cooperation and support of the Cambodian parties.

114.   In conclusion, I wish to express my appreciation to the Governments contributing military and civilian police personnel to UNTAC. I take this opportunity to pay tribute to Mr. Yasushi Akashi, my Special Representative for Cambodia, and to all the men and women—civilian, military and police—of UNTAC. They have performed with efficiency and devotion to duty under difficult conditions the important tasks assigned to them by the Security Council.

Document 66

Letter dated 28 January 1993 from the Secretary-General to
Prince Norodom Ranariddh, member of the Supreme National Council,
concerning the situation in Cambodia and the role of UNTAC

Not issued as a United Nations document; original in French

I thank you for your letter of 5 January 1993. I share your concerns regarding the political situation in Cambodia and vehemently deplore the recent attacks on representatives of certain political parties, in particular, your own.

The Paris Agreements clearly define the responsibilities of all involved. It is the duty of each Cambodian party to ensure that law and order are maintained in the zone under its control. UNTAC, for its part, is responsible for verifying that the existing administrative structures carry out this task impartially and that human rights and fundamental freedoms are protected.

As you know, UNTAC has on numerous occasions called upon the administrative structures concerned to assume their responsibilities in this regard. In addition, my Special Representative recently announced specific measures to prevent attacks on the personnel and premises of political parties. He also authorized UNTAC to arrest alleged perpetrators of acts of violence and to institute legal proceedings against them.

I wish to assure you that my Special Representative will not hesitate to take any further step to help enhance public safety and establish a climate of trust. In accordance with its mandate, UNTAC also will continue to accord special importance to the creation of a neutral political environment in which the Cambodian people will be able freely to determine their future in the elections to be held in May 1993. In the final analysis, however, this goal can be attained only if the Cambodian parties continue to cooperate with UNTAC in overcoming the difficulties which have arisen regarding the implementation of the Paris Agreements.

Accept, Sir, the assurances of my highest consideration.

(Signed) Boutros BOUTROS-GHALI

Document 67

Letter dated 29 January 1993 from the Secretary-General to
Mr. Hun Sen, member of the Supreme National Council, referring to
letter of 5 January 1993 concerning the situation in Cambodia

Not issued as a United Nations document; original in French

I thank you for your letter of 5 January 1993 and for the statement of the same date which you transmitted to me.

I understand your concerns regarding the situation in Cambodia and the refusal of the Party of Democratic Kampuchea to honour its obligations under the Paris Agreements. The Security Council clearly stated its position on this matter when it adopted resolution 792 (1992) on 30 November 1992.

However, I wish to emphasize that all the Cambodian parties are required to comply with and implement the Paris Agreements. Violations by one of the parties may not be invoked by another party as grounds for failing to honour the obligations and responsibilities which it has agreed to assume.

I am confident that the Party of the State of Cambodia will continue to cooperate with UNTAC in implementing the Paris Agreements and creating a neutral political environment in which the Cambodian people will determine their future in the elections to be held in May 1993. In particular, I am counting on your cooperation to put an end to the acts of intimidation and violence recently perpetrated against the representatives of certain political parties in the regions controlled by the Party of the State of Cambodia.

Indeed, it is the duty of each Cambodian party to ensure that order is maintained in the zone under its control. Under the Paris Agreements, UNTAC, for its part, is responsible for verifying that the existing administrative structures carry out that task impartially and that human rights and fundamental freedoms are protected.

With reference to article 29 of the Paris Agreements and Chapter VII of the United Nations Charter, I wish to assure you that I am in permanent contact with the Co-Chairmen of the Paris Conference. However, the authority to adopt measures under Chapter VII of the Charter rests with the Security Council, not with the Secretary-General. As you are aware, the Council is con-tinuing to follow developments in Cambodia closely. I am confident that it will take whatever step proves necessary at the appropriate time.

Accept, Sir, the assurances of my highest considera-tion.

(Signed) Boutros BOUTROS-GHALI

Document 68

Letter dated 1 February 1993 from the Secretary-General addressed to the President of the Security Council concerning the holding of a presidential election in Cambodia

S/25273, 10 February 1993

It is my intention to present shortly to the Security Council a report on the implementation of resolution 792 (1992) and on any further measures that may be neces-sary or appropriate to ensure that the fundamental objectives of the Paris Agreements on Cambodia are achieved. Paragraph 21 of this resolution requests me to report to the Council no later than 15 February 1993.

Meanwhile, I wish to inform the members of the Security Council of certain important decisions taken at the meeting of the Supreme National Council (SNC) held on 28 January 1993 at Beijing under the chairman-ship of His Royal Highness Prince Norodom Sihanouk.

At that meeting, it was decided that the election for the constituent assembly would be held from 23 to 25 May 1993.

Prince Sihanouk also informed the SNC that the presidential election mentioned in paragraph 3 of resolution 792 (1992) should take place, in accord-ance with the Paris Agreements, after the constituent assembly adopted the new constitution of Cambodia. He also assured the members of SNC that he would continue in the meantime to cooperate actively with the United Nations Transitional Authority in Cambodia (UNTAC) in the implementation of the Paris Agreements.

I should be grateful if you would bring this informa-tion to the attention of the members of the Security Council.

(Signed) Boutros BOUTROS-GHALI

Document 69

Report of the Secretary-General on the implementation of Security Council resolution 792 (1992)

S/25289, 13 February 1993

1. The present report is submitted to the Security Council in pursuance of paragraph 21 of resolution 792 (1992), by which the Council requested me to report no later than 15 February 1993 on the implementation of that resolution and on any further measures that might be necessary and appropriate to ensure the realization of the fundamental objectives of the Paris Agreements on Cambodia (see S/23177, annex).

2. In accordance with paragraph 10 of resolution 745 (1992), I submitted to the Security Council on 25 January 1993 my third progress report on the United Nations Transitional Authority in Cambodia (UNTAC) (S/25124). The present report should be read in conjunc-tion with the third progress report.

I. Meetings of the Supreme National Council

3. On 28 January 1993, His Royal Highness Prince Norodom Sihanouk chaired a meeting of the Supreme National Council of Cambodia in Beijing. Dur-ing this meeting, the Supreme National Council agreed that, in accordance with paragraph 5 of resolution 792 (1992), the elections for the constituent assembly should

be held from 23 to 25 May 1993 (see sect. VII below). The Supreme National Council also approved seven additional rehabilitation projects totalling $25 million, reviewed the status of the implementation of the moratorium on the export of logs and considered a similar moratorium on the export of minerals and gems (see sect. V below).

4. In addition, the Supreme National Council discussed the possibility of issuing a declaration denouncing all acts of violence, urging self-restraint on the Cambodian parties and calling for an end to violence directed against UNTAC. The representative of the Party of Democratic Kampuchea (PDK) objected to the adoption of such a declaration, but Prince Sihanouk decided that he would issue a statement in his own name, noting that three of the four Cambodian parties supported it (see annex I).

5. Prince Sihanouk also used the occasion to express renewed support for UNTAC and assured the meeting that he would continue to cooperate with the United Nations in the implementation of the Paris Agreements. He informed my Special Representative that he would be returning to Phnom Penh on 9 February 1993.

6. On 10 February 1993 the Supreme National Council met again in Phnom Penh, for the first time since October 1992. The agenda of the meeting, which was chaired by Prince Sihanouk, included items on a neutral political environment and the preservation of Cambodia's natural resources. The results of that meeting, as well as those of the meeting of 28 January, are discussed in more detail below.

II. The military situation

7. Since my third progress report, the Cambodian People's Armed Forces (CPAF), the army of the Party of the State of Cambodia (SOC), have launched attacks on the National Army of Democratic Kampuchea (NADK), the armed forces of PDK, in a number of districts. Exchanges of artillery and mortar fire between CPAF and NADK as well as movements of troops by the two forces have also occurred. These activities focused on two broad areas: west-central Battambang province and northwestern Kompong Thom south-central Preah Vihear provinces. Smaller actions have taken place in Kratie and Siem Reap provinces. Using combinations of artillery, armoured vehicles and tanks, CPAF has drawn closer to the PDK-held district town of Pailin in the province of Battambang. UNTAC has protested these moves which, taken together, constitute a serious cease-fire violation. My Special Representative has called on SOC to desist from violating the cease-fire and to exercise self-restraint. CPAF has since drawn back from the furthest point of its advance and, while tension persists and cease-fire viola-

tions continue to occur, the situation is now calmer. Mr. Hun Sen has called for UNTAC forces to interpose themselves between the two sides as a "buffer zone", but this could be done only with the consent and cooperation of both parties. PDK has reiterated its position that it will not permit UNTAC to establish itself in its zone unless its conditions for joining the peace process are met.

8. It should be recalled in this context that PDK has failed to comply with the military provisions of the Paris Agreements and that NADK, as noted in my third progress report (S/25124, para. 36), had attempted to consolidate its gains and interrupt CPAF's communications. Under such circumstances, the Phnom Penh authorities have asserted that they had the right to protect themselves against any offensive action by NADK. UNTAC has pointed out, however, that CPAF's recent moves have exceeded the bounds of self-defence.

9. Over the past few weeks, and especially since the CPAF attacks in the Pailin area, NADK has tightened restrictions on the group of 12 UNTAC personnel deployed in the town, who include military observers, mine-clearance personnel, signals staff and interpreters. At one time they were subject to virtual house arrest. These restrictions have eased somewhat following UNTAC protests, but the situation is not yet satisfactory. My Special Representative has made it clear to PDK that the UNTAC personnel in Pailin must be permitted to carry out their normal duties without let or hindrance.

10. Paragraph 18 of resolution 792 (1992) requests me to consider the implications for the electoral process of the failure by PDK to canton and demobilize its forces and, in response to this situation, to take all appropriate steps to ensure the successful implementation of the electoral process.

11. Paragraphs 39 to 43 of my third progress report describe the steps taken by the Military Component when it became clear that it would not be possible to implement cantonment and disarmament. The most important aspects of the resulting redeployment involved the protection of the registration exercise and activities in support of a neutral political environment. They are described in the relevant sections. The Military Component's dispositions for the protection of the election itself will be discussed in more detail in the fourth progress report, which is due in April 1993.

III. Creation and maintenance of a neutral political environment

12. Paragraph 95 of my third progress report described the three categories into which threats to public order in Cambodia can be divided: politically motivated attacks on political party offices and staff; attacks on Vietnamese-speaking persons; and killings that seem to

have no particular political motivation but which spread a climate of fear and intimidation. Subsequent paragraphs of that report described the violent incidents that had occurred, as well as the measures undertaken by UNTAC to counter them. On 1 February 1993, as a further refinement of these measures, UNTAC Civilian Police, in consultation with the Military Component and with the cooperation of the Cambodian police, instituted static guarding of political party offices considered to be most at risk during the hours of darkness, when attacks are most likely.

13. Scores of incidents of political or ethnic violence, which have resulted in some 60 deaths since August 1992, as well as acts of harassment and intimidation, have also been reported to UNTAC officials. Responsibility for the killings of Vietnamese-speaking persons has generally been attributed to NADK elements, while investigations carried out by UNTAC indicate that the great majority of attacks on political party offices and members are attributed to soldiers, police or supporters of SOC. The broad picture that emerges from the figures is that incidents of violence and intimidation peaked in December 1992, after rising through October and November, but fell significantly in January 1993. However, political violence seems to have increased somewhat in early February with the detention of four members of the Front uni national pour un Cambodge indépendant, neutre, pacifique et coopératif (FUNCINPEC) in Battambang and an attack on Bakan district, Pursat Province, on the night of 8-9 February 1993, which caused the deaths of five local civilians. UNTAC premises and property were also damaged in the attack, but there were no UNTAC casualties. Many of the incidents have been concentrated in the provinces of Battambang and Kompong Cham, and the victims in the vast majority of cases were members of FUNCINPEC.

14. Other acts of violence that may or may not be politically motivated continue. Late at night on 12 January, an armed band of some 40 men attacked the village of Phum Angkrong in Siem Reap Province, killing three Cambodians, including two UNTAC electoral workers. My Special Representative condemned the attack, which was carried out by persons unknown. On 27 January 1993, approximately 3 kilometres north-east of Phum Angkrong, about 10 to 15 armed assailants killed 8 Cambodians—4 men and 4 women—and injured 12 others. UNTAC Civilian Police are investigating these attacks amid indications that NADK elements may have been responsible for both of them.

15. As described in my third progress report (para. 103), my Special Representative established on 6 January a special UNTAC office with powers to arrest, detain and prosecute persons accused of politically motivated crimi-

nal acts and human rights violations. UNTAC has since instituted proceedings against two suspects arrested by it and now held in its custody. The first is a police officer of SOC, who has been charged with the murder of a FUNCINPEC party official. The second is a member of NADK, who is charged, on the basis of his confession, with the murder of 13 ethnic-Vietnamese Cambodians and 2 other Cambodians.

16. Following the discussions my Special Representative had with Mr. Hun Sen in January, Mr. Chea Sim, president of the "national assembly" of SOC, called on the local authorities to take all necessary measures to protect offices of political parties, thwart all forms of criminal activity and safeguard public security. My Special Representative has urged leaders of all political parties to help to create in the minds of their followers tolerance for peaceful political competition and to ensure adherence to the code of conduct during the forthcoming political campaign.

17. Maintenance of a neutral political environment has also been tested by a propaganda campaign by the Phnom Penh administration against UNTAC through television, radio and the party newspaper. While attacks against UNTAC on the PDK radio have been common and have become increasingly hostile for several months, the SOC campaign began fairly recently. The motive appears to be to spread the message that only SOC can defend the country against PDK and so deserves electoral support, while UNTAC cannot be trusted to protect Cambodians. In fact, the Military Component has strengthened its anti-banditry patrols in the remoter parts of the country and reinforced its support for other components and for the electoral process. It is deployed in some 270 locations throughout Cambodia. Military patrols are also supplementing the other measures taken by UNTAC to protect political party offices deemed to be at risk of attack. Civic action programmes undertaken by the Military Component in the more remote regions of the countryside reinforce these messages of UNTAC's commitment to the Cambodian people.

IV. Non-cooperation of the Party of Democratic Kampuchea

18. On 27 January 1993, my Special Representative met in Beijing with Mr. Khieu Samphan, President of PDK, in a renewed effort to secure his party's cooperation with UNTAC. Mr. Akashi recalled the relevant provisions of Security Council resolution 792 (1992), especially paragraph 5, which stated that UNTAC should proceed to conduct free and fair elections in all parts of Cambodia to which it had full access as at 31 January 1993. He stressed that the elections were designed to produce a peaceful, stable and united Cam-

bodia and that it was in the long-term interests of PDK to take part. However, Mr. Khieu Samphan insisted that the conditions stated by his party—the removal of foreign forces from Cambodia, the granting of greater powers to the Supreme National Council and full UNTAC control over the five areas of foreign affairs, national defence, public security, finance and information specified in the Paris Agreements—be fulfilled before his party would join the peace process.

19. As noted in my third progress report, PDK has remained unwilling to guarantee access to the zones under its control for the purpose of voter registration. However, on some occasions NADK soldiers and officers registered and assisted or allowed other people living in PDK zones to register. Neither PDK nor the political party whose formation it announced in November 1992, the National Unity of Cambodia Party (NUCP), applied for official registration to take part in the elections for the constituent assembly.

V. Border control and the preservation of Cambodia's natural resources

20. By paragraphs 10, 12, 13 and 14 of its resolution 792 (1992), the Security Council adopted a number of measures aimed at protecting the natural resources of Cambodia, particularly timber, minerals and gems, and at improving the implementation of article VII of annex 2 of the Paris Agreement.

21. In accordance with those provisions, UNTAC appealed to neighbouring countries to assist in the implementation of the moratorium. Towards the end of December 1992, the Governments of the Lao People's Democratic Republic, Thailand and Viet Nam all announced that they would impose a complete ban on the import of logs from Cambodia beginning 1 January 1993. In a letter dated 5 January 1993, Mr. Hun Sen also informed UNTAC that the necessary orders had been given to all competent organs of the Phnom Penh authorities regarding the ban on the export of logs.

22. In addition, UNTAC deployed border control teams to monitor closely any violations of the moratorium by land or sea. Regrettably, numerous and large-scale violations, by both routes, have continued to occur, as indicated below. Furthermore, UNTAC's efforts to establish an additional 9 check points along the border with Thailand, which would raise to 17 the number of check points on that border, have proved unavailing. The part of the border which remains to be covered lies within the zone controlled by PDK, which has refused to permit the establishment of check points there. The figures below therefore do not include the bulk of log exports from the PDK zone.

23. United Nations observers at the check points recorded a total of 46 violations of the moratorium between 1 January and 5 February 1993, with 46,507 cubic metres of logs being transported by personnel belonging to three of the Cambodian parties to seven known destinations, as follows:

Party	Number of consignments	Volume of wood (cubic metres)
SOC	42	46 042
PDK	3	150
FUNCINPEC	1	315
Khmer People's National Liberation Front	0	0
Total	46	46 507

Destination	Number of consignments	Volume of wood (cubic metres)
Thailand	21	21 802
Viet Nam	7	1 871
Lao People's Democratic Republic	4	5 018
Japan	3	11 600
Singapore	1	1 500
Pakistan	1	3 114
Hong Kong	1	30
Unknown	8	1 572
Total	46	46 507

24. In approving the moratorium on log exports on 22 September 1992, the Supreme National Council agreed at the same time to place the export of sawn timber under the control and monitoring of UNTAC in close consultation with the Supreme National Council. At the meeting of the Supreme National Council on 10 February 1993 it was agreed, on the proposal of UNTAC, that the Technical Advisory Committee dealing with this question should determine a ceiling on the export of sawn timber in 1993 which would result in a significant decrease in the number of trees felled.

25. At the meeting on 28 January 1992, UNTAC proposed, in pursuance of paragraph 14 of resolution 792 (1992), the adoption by the Supreme National Council of a moratorium on the export of minerals and gems from Cambodia, to enter into force as from 28 February 1993. This draft declaration, amended on the proposal of FUNCINPEC to include the commercial extraction of mineral resources onshore and offshore, had received the support of three of the four Cambodian parties in the Technical Advisory Committee, but objections were expressed by PDK. The question was raised again at the Supreme National Council meeting on 10 February 1993,

and it was decided to adopt the moratorium despite continued objection by PDK.

26. By paragraph 10 of its resolution 792 (1992), the Security Council called on those concerned to ensure that measures were taken to prevent the supply of petroleum products to the areas occupied by any Cambodian party not complying with the military provisions of the Paris Agreements, and requested me to examine the modalities of those measures.

27. As noted in my previous reports, PDK has failed to comply with the military provisions contained in the Paris Agreements, especially cantonment and disarmament. Accordingly, UNTAC has entered into discussions with the Government of Thailand, which borders on most of the zones controlled by PDK, regarding the implementation of that provision.

28. Pursuant to those discussions, the Thai authorities have announced that petroleum shipments from Thailand to Cambodia have been suspended. Procedures are being put in place that would allow, under UNTAC monitoring, a controlled volume of petroleum from Thailand to enter the zones of those parties fulfilling their responsibilities under the Paris Agreements. Shipments through other borders will continue, but will be closely monitored. Internal movements of petroleum products will be controlled by SOC. To deter violations of the ban, all roads into the relevant areas are to be patrolled and mobile check points established under UNTAC monitoring.

29. In the broader context of border control, UNTAC's involvement will be diversified with the deployment of Civil Administration staff to monitor other areas such as customs and immigration control. The 23 check points now in operation are each manned by an UNTAC team comprising military observers, armed soldiers and civilian police with communication support facilities. All the Cambodian parties have been invited to send representatives and all except PDK are represented at the check points.

VI. Rehabilitation assistance

30. By paragraph 20 of its resolution 792 (1992), the Security Council invited the States and international organizations providing economic assistance to Cambodia to convene a meeting to review the current state of such assistance, in the wake of the Ministerial Conference on Reconstruction and Rehabilitation of Cambodia held in Tokyo in June 1992.

31. At the Supreme National Council meeting of 28 January 1993 held in Beijing, my Special Representative announced that some $540 million of the $880 million pledged at the Conference had now been committed for specific rehabilitation activities. He informed the Supreme National Council, however, that UNTAC was concerned about the actual level of disbursements, which currently stand at $95 million. The lack of funding for certain sectors of specific activities, including training and the maintenance of essential social services, also gave rise to concern that those deficiencies might compromise the overall rehabilitation effort.

32. To address those concerns, and in pursuance of Security Council resolution 792 (1992), informal consultations were held with donors in New York and Phnom Penh to discuss the holding of a meeting to review rehabilitation efforts. As a result of these consultations, it was agreed that a technical-level meeting of donors should be held in Phnom Penh on 25 February 1993 with the participation of the Cambodian parties and of all countries and organizations providing assistance to Cambodia, including non-governmental organizations. The meeting will assess the commitments made by the end of January 1993 against the pledges made in Tokyo; review the constraints in the disbursement of these commitments; and consider the priority needs that had emerged since the Tokyo Conference. The meeting will also prepare the ground for the holding, following the Cambodian elections, of the first session of the International Committee on the Reconstruction of Cambodia (ICORC), in accordance with the Tokyo Declaration of 22 June 1992 (S/24183).

VII. Electoral matters

33. At the meeting of the Supreme National Council on 28 January 1993, Prince Norodom Sihanouk announced that he had decided not to advance his candidacy for presidential elections before or simultaneously with the constituent assembly elections. Instead, he wished to wait until the new Constitution had been adopted before holding the elections, so that the President could be elected in accordance with the modalities, the term of office and powers laid down in the Constitution.

34. As regards the elections for the constituent assembly, the members of the Supreme National Council agreed that they would be held from 23 to 25 May 1993. It is foreseen that, during this period, there will be voting at fixed polling stations. UNTAC anticipates, however, that two additional days of voting at mobile polling stations will be required in order to ensure that every registered voter has the chance to vote. It is therefore expected that polling will take place from 23 to 27 May.

35. As indicated in my third progress report, voter registration ended on 31 January 1993, except for the registration of those refugees and displaced persons who

have not yet been able to return to Cambodia. Of the 360,000 refugees and displaced persons who were in the border camps, some 80,000 remain, of whom about half are eligible to vote. Special arrangements are being made to enable the latter to register. In addition, registration was extended in a limited number of locations in Cambodia for a few days, in order to accommodate villagers who had not had the chance to register.

36. The voter registration exercise was extremely successful, with a provisional total of 4,640,000 voters registered throughout Cambodia. In many cases the number of voters registered exceeded the estimated total calculated by the Advance Electoral Planning Unit in its nationwide survey conducted in the first half of 1992. This is the result partly of undercounting in the statistics on which the survey was based and partly of the influx of returnees. While it is possible that multiple registration by some applicants may have been a further factor, it has been made clear to the Cambodians that strict voting procedures will ensure that no one can vote more than once, irrespective of how many times he or she may have registered.

37. As explained in the third progress report, there is a time-lag in the recovery and input of registration information by the UNTAC electoral computer centre. By 1 February, some 4,029,000 registrants had been entered into the Electoral Component computers. Data-entry clerks are now entering about 250,000 registrants into the system each week, and it is anticipated that the finalized and verified voters' list will be produced by mid-April.

38. On 27 January, a total of 20 out of the 22 provisionally registered political parties had applied for official party registration in accordance with the Electoral Law. The official registration process involves the submission of the names and voter registration numbers of 5,000 registered voters who are members of the party concerned. The Electoral Component is now in the process of verifying those names and numbers. When verification is complete, the names of the parties that have successfully completed the registration procedure will be announced and those parties will be entitled to appear on the ballot paper. The Cambodian People's Party (SOC), FUNCINPEC and the Buddhist Liberal Democratic Party (Khmer People's National Liberation Front (KPNLF)), representing three of the four Cambodian parties which were signatories to the Paris Agreements, have applied for official registration but, as noted above, PDK did not do so. The name of that party will therefore not appear on the ballot paper. The registered parties have been requested to name lists of candidates for each province.

39. Much thought has been given to the timing and duration of the political campaign. According to the implementation plan (S/23613), the duration of the campaign was set tentatively at six weeks, beginning in early March. However, now that the date of the election has been set for late May, it is necessary either to extend the campaign or to start later. Divergent considerations bear on this question. The longer the campaign goes on, the greater the risk that it may be marred by interparty violence. On the other hand, a short campaign may give an advantage to one party to the detriment of others. At the 10 February Supreme National Council meeting, therefore, UNTAC announced that it had decided that the campaign would begin on 7 April 1993 and last until 19 May 1993, when a four-day cooling-off period would take place before polling. UNTAC would make its information and broadcasting facilities available to all political parties in order to ensure fair access to the media.

VIII. Post-electoral security

40. In paragraph 19 of its resolution 792 (1992) the Security Council requested me to investigate and report upon the implications for security in post-election Cambodia of the possible incomplete implementation of the disarmament and demobilization provisions of the Paris Agreements. It is obviously of the greatest importance that peaceful conditions should prevail during the three months which the Paris Agreements give the Constituent Assembly to complete its tasks of drafting and adopting a new Cambodian Constitution and transforming itself into a legislative assembly, which will form a new Cambodian Government.

41. Under the Paris Agreements it was envisaged that peaceful conditions during this period would be assured by the cantonment of all the forces of the parties, the demobilization of at least 70 per cent of them before the end of voter registration and the continuing cantonment of the remainder, pending their demobilization before or shortly after the elections or their incorporation into a new national army, as decided by the newly elected Government. Regrettably, the decision of PDK not to enter into phase II of the cease-fire will almost certainly make it impossible to apply the above-described arrangements. The elections seem likely to take place at a time when the two biggest armed forces of the parties will remain largely intact and the other two parties will also still have some of their forces in the field. Recent weeks have demonstrated the risk that this state of affairs can lead to major hostilities; evidently that risk could become greater after the elections.

42. The Paris Agreement, in article V of annex 2, provides that the ultimate disposition of any forces which have not been demobilized by the time the newly elected Government formed in accordance with article 12 of that

Agreement takes office will be a matter for decision by that Government. The Agreement further provides that such forces should either be incorporated into a new national army or be demobilized forthwith according to a plan to be prepared by my Special Representative. It is to be assumed that the new Constitution will contain provisions for the formation of the new national army, as well as transitional provisions for disposing of non-demobilized forces in accordance with the Paris Agreements, including the role foreseen therein for UNTAC.

43. As regards the interim period between the elections and the formation of the new Government, there are broadly two possibilities:

(a) All four Cambodian parties agree, belatedly, to implement the cantonment and demobilization procedures provided for in annex 2 of the Paris Agreement;

(b) All four parties, to a greater or lesser extent, maintain their forces in the field, as at present, and UNTAC continues to use its best endeavours to ensure that the cease-fire is respected.

In either case, the maintenance of law and order would remain the responsibility of the civil police of the existing administrative structures, under the supervision and control of UNTAC.

44. Of these two possibilities, the first is clearly the preferable one. I shall continue to use my good offices, in consultation with the Co-Chairmen of the Paris Conference and other interested Member States, to make it possible. If those efforts fail, it will be necessary to keep UNTAC's Military and Civilian Police Components in being, at a greater strength than previously foreseen, until the Constituent Assembly has completed its work and the new Government has been formed. I shall, in due course, present appropriate recommendations to the Security Council in this regard, on the basis of my Special Representative's assessment of the military and police personnel he would require for this purpose. The Security Council may also find it necessary, at a later stage, to consider whether the elected Government should, if it so wishes, continue to receive international support in maintaining internal security after the new Government is formed and, in accordance with the Paris Agreements, the transitional period and UNTAC's mandate come to an end.

IX. Observations

45. Although the peace process continues to encounter serious problems, progress has been made in implementing resolution 792 (1992). Dates have been set for a constituent assembly election in May, and UNTAC is proceeding on schedule with electoral preparations in all areas of Cambodia to which it had access as at 31 January 1993; the Supreme National Council has resumed meetings in Phnom Penh under the chairmanship of His Royal Highness Prince Norodom Sihanouk; measures are being taken to prevent the supply of petroleum to PDK, since it has failed to comply with the military provisions of the Paris Agreements; and UNTAC has strengthened its border control system and its monitoring of compliance with the provisions relating to the export of logs. In the last-mentioned matter, UNTAC has requested full cooperation from neighbouring States, and expects that such cooperation will be forthcoming so that this important decision of the Supreme National Council can be implemented.

46. However, the response of some of the Cambodian parties to resolution 792 (1992) has not been satisfactory. I must stress in this context that, as signatories to the Paris Agreements, the Cambodian parties have the primary responsibility for their implementation and that the future stability and well-being of Cambodia depends on the Cambodians themselves. While the United Nations, acting principally through UNTAC, will continue to do everything in its power to assist them, the Cambodian parties cannot expect the international community to succeed where they themselves fail.

47. Prince Sihanouk, in issuing a Declaration condemning all acts of violence against Cambodians or foreigners, including United Nations personnel, has set a lead for all Cambodian parties to follow. The Security Council may wish to issue a similar call, broadening the demand that was contained in paragraph 17 of its resolution 792 (1992). The Council may wish further to call on the three parties which aligned themselves with the Declaration to continue their close cooperation with UNTAC and prevent or punish acts of violence, particularly when they are politically motivated.

48. SOC has offered substantial cooperation to UNTAC since the operation began, but in more recent months there have been serious difficulties relating to the maintenance of law and order in the areas under its control and the protection of the staff and offices of other political parties engaged in lawful political activity. CPAF has also launched military attacks against NADK, which go beyond its right to defend itself against hostile action by the latter. SOC should desist from any further offensive military action and redouble its efforts to prevent attacks and intimidation directed against other political parties.

49. As for PDK, by failing to admit UNTAC to its zones and to register for the elections within the relevant time-frames, that party has again failed to avail itself of the many opportunities offered to it by UNTAC and the international community to keep the door open for it to rejoin the peace process. The United Nations position regarding the PDK's two main conditions for rejoining

the peace process has been repeatedly stated in my previous reports and elsewhere. It goes without saying that UNTAC will continue to exert its best efforts to fulfil its mandate under the Paris Agreements in all its aspects.

50. At the same time, I think it important to resist any pressure to exclude PDK representatives from the Supreme National Council. The framework of the Paris Agreements, despite the damage done to it by the failure of some of the Cambodian signatories to meet their obligations in full, still offers, I am convinced, the best hope for a solution to the problems of Cambodia. This is particularly so with regard to the need to promote national reconciliation.

51. In my third progress report, I informed the members of the Security Council that, in view of Prince Sihanouk's intention to participate in the presidential election referred to in paragraph 3 of resolution 792 (1992), I had asked my Special Representative to proceed immediately with the necessary technical preparations. I also stated that I would submit to the Council, in the present report, further recommendations regarding the modalities for the organization and conduct of such an election. However on 28 January 1993, as indicated in section VII above, Prince Sihanouk informed the members of the Supreme National Council that he had decided that the presidential election should be held after the adoption of the new Cambodian Constitution by the Constituent Assembly. I informed the President of the Security Council of this development in a letter which I addressed to him on 1 February 1993 (S/25273).

52. I continue to believe that the holding of a presidential election, in conjunction with the constituent assembly elections scheduled to be held from 23 to 27 May 1993, could have enhanced the prospects for national reconciliation in Cambodia and provided a critical element of stability during the rest of the transitional period. However, I understand and respect the reasons that have led Prince Sihanouk to conclude that the holding of a presidential election should be deferred. The preparations undertaken by UNTAC in this regard have therefore been put on hold.

53. The imperative need for UNTAC now is to maintain the momentum towards the holding of constituent assembly elections starting on 23 May. To that end, UNTAC will redouble its efforts to improve the political environment and to prevent further cease-fire violations.

I have also instructed my Special Representative to assess post-election security requirements and submit his recommendations to me. UNTAC will also continue to encourage and assist the Supreme National Council in its work on the constitutional principles so as to prepare a foundation for the new Government.

54. As the implementation of the Paris Agreements, to which the international community has devoted so much effort and resources, approaches a crucial stage, it is ever more essential that all the Cambodian parties comply fully with their obligations under those Agreements. Only thus will the Cambodian people be enabled to exercise the right to determine their own future and restore Cambodia to peace and stability.

Annex I

Statement by Norodom Sihanouk, Chief of State and President of the Supreme National Council of Cambodia *(Beijing, 28 January 1993)*

At the conclusion of today's important working meeting of the Supreme National Council-UNTAC-representatives of the "permanent 5", I have the honour to make the following statement, both in my own name and on behalf of the Supreme National Council members belonging to KPNLF-BLDP, to FUNCINPEC, and to the Cambodian People's Party (State of Cambodia):

I. We, the President of the Supreme National Council and members of the Council belonging to the three above-mentioned factions and parties, condemn all acts and all forms of violence (politically motivated assassinations, racist crimes, harassments, intimidation, threats, political terrorism, etc.) against Cambodians or foreign persons in Cambodia. And we ask all political parties, all armed or non-armed factions and everyone constantly to display self-restraint in their attitudes, their acts and their relations *vis-à-vis* or with others.

II. We condemn any act which threatens the dignity, fundamental freedoms, rights, security and personal safety of any member of UNTAC, whether civilian or military.

We ask all political parties and all armed or non-armed factions in Cambodia scrupulously to respect the life, safety and fundamental freedoms of all UNTAC civilian and military members, at all levels.

Document 70

Commission on Human Rights resolution requesting the Secretary-General to ensure a continued United Nations human rights presence in Cambodia after the end of the UNTAC mandate, including through the operational presence of the United Nations Centre for Human Rights

E/CN.4/RES/1993/6, 19 February 1993

The Commission on Human Rights,

Guided by the principles embodied in the Charter of the United Nations, the Universal Declaration of Human Rights and the International Covenants on Human Rights,

Recalling its decision 1992/102 of 21 February 1992,

Bearing in mind the role and responsibilities of the United Nations and the international community in the process of the rehabilitation and reconstruction of Cambodia, which will continue after the transitional period,

Recognizing that Cambodia's tragic recent history requires special measures to assure the protection of human rights and the non-return to the policies and practices of the past,

Taking note of the Agreement on a Comprehensive Political Settlement of the Cambodian Conflict signed on 23 October 1991, including Part III relating to human rights,

Noting the decision to hold elections in Cambodia from 23 to 25 May 1993, and the consequent ending, three months thereafter, of the mandate of the United Nations Transitional Authority in Cambodia,

Welcoming the signature by Cambodia on 20 April 1992 of the International Covenants on Human Rights and its accession on 20 September 1992 to the Convention against Torture and Other Cruel, Inhuman or Degrading Treatment or Punishment, the Convention on the Elimination of All Forms of Discrimination against Women, the Convention on the Rights of the Child and the Convention relating to the Status of Refugees and the Protocol thereto,

Noting the summary and proposals contained in the report on the International Symposium on Human Rights in Cambodia held in Phnom Penh from 30 November to 2 December 1992 (E/CN.4/1993/Add.1),

Welcoming the establishment of the Trust Fund for the Programme in Human Rights Education for Cambodia, which calls for intensive collaboration between United Nations and non-governmental organizations active in the field of human rights,

1. *Takes note with appreciation* of the report of the Secretary-General (E/CN.4/1993/19);

2. *Requests* the Secretary-General to ensure a continued United Nations human rights presence in Cambodia after the expiry of the mandate of the United Nations Transitional Authority in Cambodia, including through the operational presence of the Centre for Human Rights, in order to:

(a) Manage the implementation of educational and technical assistance and advisory services programmes and to ensure their continuation;

(b) Assist the Government of Cambodia established after the election, at its request, in meeting its obligations under the human rights instruments recently acceded to, including the preparation of reports to the relevant monitoring committees;

(c) Provide support to bona fide human rights groups in Cambodia;

(d) Contribute to the creation and/or strengthening of national institutions for the promotion and protection of human rights;

(e) Continue to assist with the drafting and implementation of legislation to promote and protect human rights;

(f) Continue to assist with the training of persons responsible for the administration of justice;

3. *Recognizes* the constraints on the financial resources of the Centre for Human Rights;

4. *Requests* the Secretary-General to provide appropriate additional resources, within existing overall United Nations resources, to fund the operational presence of the Centre for Human Rights within the framework of other United Nations activities in Cambodia after the expiry of the mandate of the United Nations Transitional Authority in Cambodia;

5. *Strongly urges* Governments and interested organizations to consider contributing to the Trust Fund for the programme in Human Rights Education for Cambodia;

6. *Requests* the Secretary-General to appoint a special representative to:

(a) Maintain contact with the Government and people of Cambodia;

(b) Guide and coordinate the United Nations human rights presence in Cambodia;

(c) Assist the Government in the promotion and protection of human rights;

(d) Report to the General Assembly at its forty-eighth session and the Commission on Human Rights at its fiftieth session under the agenda item entitled "Advisory services in the field of human rights";

7. *Decides* to review the respective programmes and mandates set out in the present resolution at its fifty-first session;

8. *Requests* the Secretary-General to communicate the contents of the present resolution to, and seek the consent and cooperation of, the newly elected Government of Cambodia to facilitate the tasks of the Special Representative and the Centre for Human Rights in the fulfilment of their respective mandates.

Document 71

Security Council resolution on the election for the constituent assembly in Cambodia

S/RES/810 (1993), 8 March 1993

The Security Council,

Reaffirming its resolutions 668 (1990) of 20 September 1990 and 745 (1992) of 28 February 1992 and other relevant resolutions,

Taking note of the report of the Secretary-General of 13 February 1993,

Paying tribute to His Royal Highness Prince Norodom Sihanouk, Chairman of the Supreme National Council, for his continuing efforts to restore peace and national unity in Cambodia,

Recalling that under the agreements on a comprehensive political settlement to the Cambodia conflict signed in Paris on 23 October 1991 the Cambodian people have the right to determine their own political future through the free and fair election of a constituent assembly, which will draft and approve a new Cambodian constitution and transform itself into a legislative assembly, which will create the new Cambodian government,

Welcoming the achievements of the Secretary-General and the United Nations Transitional Authority in Cambodia in the implementation of the Paris agreements, in particular regarding voter registration and refugee repatriation, and reaffirming its continuing support for the activities of the Authority,

Welcoming the decision taken by the Supreme National Council at its meeting on 10 February 1993 to adopt a moratorium on the export of minerals and gems and to consider limits on the export of sawn timber from Cambodia in order to protect Cambodia's natural resources,

Deploring the violations of the cease-fire by the Party of Democratic Kampuchea and the Party of the State of Cambodia,

Concerned by the increasing number of acts of violence perpetrated on political grounds, in particular in areas under the control of the Party of the State of Cambodia, and on ethnic grounds, and by the negative implications of such acts for the implementation of the Paris agreements,

Underlining the importance of measures by the Authority in order to ensure a neutral political environment in Cambodia,

Condemning attacks, threats and intimidation against the Authority, in particular the recent detention of Authority personnel,

Deploring the failure of the Party of Democratic Kampuchea to meet its obligations under the Paris agreements, notably as regards unrestricted access by the Authority to the areas under its control and as regards the application of phase II of the cease-fire, and urging the party concerned to join fully in the implementation of the Paris agreements,

Expressing strong concern at recent reports by the Authority of a small number of foreign military personnel serving with the armed forces of the Party of the State of Cambodia in violation of the Paris agreements, calling on all parties to cooperate fully with Authority investigations of reports of foreign forces within the territory under their control, and emphasizing the importance of the immediate removal of all foreign forces, advisers and military personnel from Cambodia,

1. *Approves* the report of the Secretary-General of 13 February 1993; 1/

2. *Endorses* the decision by the Supreme National Council that the election for the constituent assembly shall be held from 23 to 27 May 1993;

1/ S/25289 [Document 69]

3. *Underlines* the crucial importance of national reconciliation for the attainment of lasting peace and stability in Cambodia;

4. *Urges* all Cambodian parties to cooperate fully with the United Nations Transitional Authority in Cambodia in the preparation and holding of the election for the constituent assembly;

5. *Expresses its satisfaction* at the extent of voter registration;

6. *Calls on* the Authority to continue to make every effort to create and maintain a neutral political environment conducive to the holding of free and fair elections, and requests the Secretary-General to inform the Security Council by 15 May 1993 of the conditions and preparations for the election;

7. *Urges* all Cambodian parties to help create in the minds of their followers tolerance for peaceful political competition and to ensure adherence to the code of conduct during the forthcoming political campaign;

8. *Urges in particular* all Cambodian parties to take all necessary measures to ensure freedom of speech, assembly and movement, as well as fair access to the media, including the press, television and radio, for all registered political parties during the electoral campaign starting on 7 April 1993, and to take all necessary steps to reassure the Cambodian people that the balloting for the election will be secret;

9. *Demands* that all Cambodian parties take the necessary measures to put an end to all acts of violence and to all threats and intimidation committed on political or ethnic grounds, and urges all those parties to cooperate with the Authority's Special Prosecutor's Office in investigations of such acts;

10. *Expresses its full confidence* in the ability of the Authority to conduct an election that is free and fair and its readiness to endorse the results of the election provided that the United Nations certifies it free and fair;

11. *Calls on* all Cambodian parties to abide by their commitment under the agreements on a comprehensive political settlement to the Cambodia conflict signed in Paris on 23 October 1991 2/ to respect those results;

12. *Recognizes* that the Cambodians themselves bear primary responsibility for the implementation of the Paris agreements and for the future stability and well-being of Cambodia;

13. *Recognizes in particular* that the Cambodians have the responsibility, after the election for the constituent assembly, to agree on a constitution and to create a government within three months, and emphasizes the importance of completing that task on time;

14. *Expresses its readiness* to support fully the constituent assembly and the process of drawing up a constitution and establishing a new government for all Cambodia;

15. *Takes note* of the remarks of the Secretary-General in paragraph 44 of his report concerning the security situation in Cambodia during the period between the election for the constituent assembly and the end of the mandate of the Authority upon the creation of a government, and welcomes his intention to submit recommendations in that connection;

16. *Commends* the decision of the Supreme National Council at its meeting on 10 February 1993 to adopt measures for the protection of Cambodia's natural resources, and supports steps taken by the Technical Advisory Committee on Management and Sustainable Exploitation of Natural Resources to implement these decisions;

17. *Reiterates its demand* that all parties honour in full their obligations under the Paris agreements, in particular to desist from all offensive military activity;

18. *Demands* that all parties take all action necessary to safeguard the lives and the security of Authority personnel throughout Cambodia, and desist from all threats or intimidation against Authority personnel and from any interference with them in the performance of their mandate;

19. *Requests* the Secretary-General to report to the Council in the context of his fourth progress report in April 1993 on the implementation of the present resolution and on any further measures that may be necessary and appropriate to ensure the realization of the fundamental objectives of the Paris agreements;

20. *Decides* to remain actively seized of the matter.

2/ S/23177 [Document 19]

Document 72

Letter dated 12 March 1993 from Viet Nam transmitting 11 March 1993 statement by the Ministry of Foreign Affairs concerning armed attacks committed on 10 March 1993 by the armed forces of the PDK against Vietnamese residents of the village of Chong Kneas, Cambodia

S/25409, 13 March 1993

Upon instructions from my Government, I have the honour to transmit to you herewith a statement made on 11 March 1993 by the Ministry of Foreign Affairs of the Socialist Republic of Viet Nam, strongly denouncing the most barbarous acts of massacre committed by Democratic Kampuchea forces against Vietnamese residents in Cambodia, and request you to kindly circulate the statement as a document of the Security Council.

(*Signed*) TRINH XUAN LANG
Permanent Representative

Annex
Statement dated 11 March 1993 from the Ministry of Foreign Affairs of the Socialist Republic of Viet Nam

According to the latest news, on 10 March 1993 a force of the "Democratic Kampuchea" attacked the fishing village of Chong Kneas, 10 kilometres south of Siem Riep of Cambodia, killing 33 Vietnamese of whom 8 were children, and wounding 29 others of whom 26 were Vietnamese and 3 Cambodians. On the morning of 11 March, a spokesman for the United Nations Transitional Authority in Cambodia (UNTAC) confirmed the above-mentioned incident.

Following a series of barbarous acts of terrorism against Vietnamese residents in Cambodia in recent times, this is the largest massacre of Vietnamese residents in Cambodia conducted by the "Democratic Kampuchea" faction since the signing of the Paris Agreements on a Comprehensive Political Settlement of the Cambodia conflict. This massacre is a new and extremely blatant challenge to mankind's conscience, crudely encroaching upon international documents on human rights, and inciting national hatred between Cambodia and Viet Nam. This is also a blatant violation of the Paris Agreements on Cambodia and its appendices.

The savage massacre of Vietnamese residents by the "Democratic Kampuchea" in Siem Riep on 10 March is a very dangerous escalations step in a series of their acts of undermining the peace process and stability in Cambodia. If resolute measures are not taken there will be a danger of recurrence of massacre in Cambodia, the consequences of which are unforeseeable.

The Government of the Socialist Republic of Viet Nam strongly condemns the new, bloody act of the "Democratic Kampuchea", and demands that it put an immediate end to such acts. The Government of the Socialist Republic of Viet Nam earnestly urges the justice-loving public opinion the world over to resolutely condemn this savage act and to raise their voice to protect the human rights of the Vietnamese residents in Cambodia.

The Government of the Socialist Republic of Viet Nam demands that the United Nations, the co-chairmen of and the parties to the Paris Agreements on Cambodia, the Supreme National Council and particularly the UNTAC in their power and functions as stipulated by the Paris Agreements take urgent measures to immediately stop the savage massacre of Vietnamese residents and defend their peaceful life in accordance with the spirit of the Paris Agreements as well as international documents on human rights, including the right to personal safety stated in the Convention on the Elimination of All Forms of Racial Discrimination and the right of minority communities.

Document 73

Statement by the President of the Security Council concerning attacks on UNTAC resulting in five deaths on 2 April 1993

S/25530, 5 April 1993

The Security Council strongly condemns all attacks on the United Nations Transitional Authority in Cambodia (UNTAC), particularly the recent attacks which have resulted in the death of two Bangladeshi members of UNTAC and the cowardly assassination of three members of the Bulgarian contingent of UNTAC on 2 April 1993.

The Council expresses its strong support for UNTAC in carrying out its mandate within the framework of the Paris agreements. It demands that all hostile acts against UNTAC cease immediately and that all parties take measures to safeguard the lives and the security of UNTAC personnel.

It expresses its condolences to the Governments of Bangladesh and Bulgaria and to the families of the victims; it pays tribute to the latter for their courage and dedication. It requests the Secretary-General to report urgently to the Council on the circumstances of these murderous acts and the responsibility for them.

The Council also expresses its determination that the election for the constituent assembly should be held on the dates decided by the Supreme National Council and endorsed by the Security Council in its resolution 810 (1993) of 8 March 1993. In this respect, the Council stresses the importance of ensuring a neutral political environment in Cambodia, as well as the cessation of acts of violence and of all threats and intimidation committed on political or ethnic grounds.

Document 74

Letter dated 7 April 1993 from Denmark transmitting statement issued by the European Community concerning implementation of the peace process in Cambodia and acts of violence against UNTAC personnel and others

S/25563, 8 April 1993

I have the honour to transmit herewith the text in English and French of a statement on Cambodia issued by the European Community and its member States on 7 April 1993.

I should be grateful if you would have the present letter and its annex circulated as a document of the Security Council.

(*Signed*) Bent HAAKONSEN
Ambassador
Permanent Representative of Denmark to
the United Nations

Annex

Statement on Cambodia

The European Community and its member States refer to Security Council resolution 810 on Cambodia, which stipulates the official start as of today, 7 April 1993, of the campaign for the elections to the Constituent Assembly on 23-27 May 1993.

The Community and its member States express their continued strong support for the implementation of the Paris Agreements. They congratulate the Secretary-General, his Special Representative and UNTAC on their success in implementing the provisions of the Agreements to the fullest extent possible, particularly in electoral registration and the return of refugees and displaced persons to Cambodia.

It is of utmost importance that the remaining phase of the election process organized by the United Nations be implemented in a peaceful and secure environment, without political intimidation and harassment, to ensure free and fair elections. The Community and its member States call on all parties to cooperate with UNTAC towards this objective and to respect fully their obligations under the Paris Agreements. They also urge the parties to commit themselves to accept and abide by the outcome of the elections.

In underlining the need for a peaceful climate for free and fair elections in Cambodia, the European

Community and its member States express their deep concern at the continued cease-fire violations, in particular the recent increase in attacks on both UNTAC military and civilian personnel and the brutal attacks against groups of Vietnamese origin. They strongly condemn these actions and urge all Cambodian parties to work for an immediate cessation of such activities.

Document 75

Letter dated 14 April 1993 from the Special Representative of the Secretary-General for Cambodia to Mr. Khieu Samphan, member of the Supreme National Council, concerning the latter's decision to leave Phnom Penh for security reasons

Not issued as a United Nations document

Your letter to His Royal Highness Prince Norodom Sihanouk has been brought to my attention, in which you informed Monseigneur of your decision to leave your Headquarters in Phnom Penh, because of fears about security.

I deeply regret this decision, since I feel that the critical juncture the peace process has now reached requires even greater dialogue between UNTAC and all Cambodian parties. Your absence from Phnom Penh is certainly not conducive to such discussion.

I therefore wish to inform Your Excellency that UNTAC will be glad to ensure your security if you decide to return to Phnom Penh. Please do not hesitate to contact me or the UNTAC Liaison Office in Bangkok if you wish to accept this offer. I will be at your disposal to discuss the concrete modalities on security measures required.

I also wish to indicate my desire to continue our discussions in my constant endeavour to find a common ground with Your Excellency.

Accept, Excellency, the assurances of my highest consideration.

Yasushi AKASHI
Special Representative of the Secretary-General for Cambodia

Document 76

Statement by the President of the Security Council concerning attacks on UNTAC

UN Press Release SC/5597/Rev.2, 22 April 1993

The members of the Security Council have learned of the deaths of two United Nations Protection Force (UNPROFOR) soldiers in recent days—a Slovak soldier today, 22 April, as a result of artillery shelling of Sector South in Croatia; and a Ukrainian soldier, on 16 April, struck by an artillery fragment in Sarajevo, Bosnia and Herzegovina.

Their deaths bring to 30 the total of UNPROFOR soldiers killed in the course of duty since May 1992. In addition, the United Nations Transitional Authority in Cambodia (UNTAC) has suffered a further casualty with the killing of another Bulgarian soldier by NADK firing on 19 April.

The members of the Security Council unequivocally condemn the killings of the United Nations peace-keeping personnel and demand that attacks on United Nations peace-keepers cease forthwith. They express their condolences to the bereaved families of the soldiers concerned and to the Governments of Bulgaria, the Slovak Republic and Ukraine.

Document 77

Letter dated 23 April 1993 from France and Indonesia, as Co-Chairmen of the Paris Conference on Cambodia, transmitting statement by the signatory States of the Paris Agreements concerning implementation of peace process in Cambodia and acts of violence

S/25658, 23 April 1993

In our capacity as representatives of the co-presidents of the Paris Conference on Cambodia, we have the honour to transmit to you herewith the statement made by the signatory States of the Paris Conference on Cambodia.

We should be grateful, if you could provide for the distribution of this statement as a document of the Security Council.

(Signed) Jean-Bernard MÉRIMÉE
Représentant permanent de la France
auprès de l'Organisation des Nations Unies

(*Signed*) Witjaksana SOEGARDA
Chargé d'Affaires,
Représentant permanent adjoint de l'Indonésie
auprès de l'Organisation des Nations Unies

Annex
Statement on Cambodia

At the initiative of the co-chairmen of the Paris Conference on Cambodia, the signatory States of the agreements on a comprehensive political settlement of the Cambodia conflict declare their firm determination to support the electoral process under way in that country. In particular, they support unreservedly the decision of the Supreme National Council of Cambodia that the elections shall be held on 23/27 May 1993. They call on UNTAC to continue to make every effort to create and maintain a neutral political environment conducive to the holding of free and fair elections, and support UNTAC's endeavours in this respect. For this purpose, the signatory States pledge their full support to the Special Representative of the Secretary-General, M. Yasushi Akashi, in implementing the Paris agreements, in cooperation with the SNC. They associate themselves with resolution 810 as well as other relevant Security Council resolutions.

The signatory States of the Paris agreements vigorously condemn all acts of violence committed on political or ethnic grounds whoever the perpetrators and the victims may be. In particular, they express their indignation at the cowardly assassinations of civilian and military personnel of UNTAC who came to Cambodia on a mission of peace. They demand that all Cambodian parties take measures necessary to end all acts of violence and to ensure particularly the safety of all United Nations civilian and military personnel.

They call upon all Cambodian parties to abide by their commitment under the Paris agreements to respect the results of the elections provided they are certified free and fair by the United Nations. They express their readiness to support fully the Constituent Assembly and the process of drawing up the Constitution and establishing a new Government for all Cambodia.

The signatory States of the Paris agreements express their support for and confidence in His Royal Highness Prince Norodom Sihanouk, head of State and President of the Supreme National Council of Cambodia, for his crucial role in carrying out the peace process and in promoting national reconciliation. They pledge their full support for the determination of Prince Norodom Sihanouk and the people of Cambodia to achieve a comprehensive political settlement and to proceed with the election. They also support fully the vital role of Prince Norodom Sihanouk and the people of Cambodia in securing the assistance and active engagement of the international community in post election reconstruction and peace-building in Cambodia.

Finally, the signatory States reiterate their full commitment to implement the Paris agreements.

Document 78

Letter dated 26 April 1993 from the Secretary-General to the President of the Security Council transmitting information relating to recent incidents which resulted in the deaths of members of UNTAC

S/25669, 27 April 1993

Pursuant to the request contained in the statement made by the President of the Security Council on 5 April 1993 (S/25530), I have the honour to submit the following information relating to recent incidents which resulted in the deaths of members of the United Nations Transitional Authority in Cambodia (UNTAC).

On 27 March 1993 at approximately 1950 hours, an UNTAC post in Angkor Chum district in Siem Reap Province occupied by a unit of the Bangladesh contingent came under mortar and small-arms fire. The attackers advanced to within 200 to 300 metres. The UNTAC soldiers returned fire from their trenches, using small-arms fire and grenades. They were able to stop the attackers' advance and the attackers gradually retreated. The attack lasted for about one hour followed by intermittent firing of small arms and mortars. Evidence subsequently came to light that two of the attackers had been killed.

Early in the attack, a Bangladeshi soldier was wounded. He was evacuated by air to UNTAC Field Hospital in Siem Reap but he subsequently died from his wounds in the early hours of the following day. Four Cambodian civilians were also injured in the incident.

Investigation by UNTAC strongly indicates that the attack was deliberately directed against the UNTAC position by members of the National Army of Democratic Kampuchea (NADK). It appears that members of the Cambodian People's Armed Forces (CPAF), who were located some 1,000 metres away, may also have returned fire against the attackers.

On 29 March 1993 at approximately 2300 hours, a Bangladeshi civilian member of UNTAC was shot through the head and killed as the car in which he was a passenger passed a group of CPAF soldiers in central Phnom Penh.

The victim was travelling in an unmarked car with two other Bangladeshi nationals, one of whom was a member of the UNTAC Civilian Police Component; the other was a non-UNTAC civilian. The CPAF soldiers were apparently manning a check-point and fired on the car when it passed. The CPAF authorities have since arrested two soldiers and charged them with the murder of the UNTAC staff member.

In the evening of 2 April 1993, at an UNTAC post at Phum Prek in Kompong Speu Province, the local NADK commander, accompanied by two soldiers, joined the 11 members of the Bulgarian battalion stationed there for dinner. Relations between the Bulgarian soldiers and the local NADK members had previously been good.

After dinner the NADK commander left and returned at about 2305 hours with 10 to 15 armed soldiers. The NADK members then opened fire on the unarmed Bulgarian soldiers with automatic weapons and hand grenades, killing three and wounding three others, before withdrawing.

Later that night and until dawn of the next day the Bulgarian camp again came under NADK mortar and small-arms fire, but there were no further UNTAC losses.

The six casualties were transported by road to the nearby Bulgarian contingent position at Amelean, also in Kompong Speu Province, where the three wounded were airlifted to Phnom Penh. One is being treated in the UNTAC Field Hospital in Phnom Penh and the other two have been evacuated to Bangkok for further treatment.

On the night of 5 April 1993 at approximately 2345 hours, the Bulgarian position at Amelean came under machine-gun fire and a sentry was wounded in the abdomen. The wounded soldier was evacuated for medical treatment to Bangkok, where it was determined that his spinal cord was damaged, resulting in the paralysis of both legs.

On the morning of 8 April 1993 at approximately 0745 hours, a United Nations Volunteer of Japanese nationality in the UNTAC Electoral Component and his Cambodian interpreter were detained by armed and uniformed men as they were travelling by car in Prasat Sambo District, Kompong Thom Province. They were shot and died of their wounds. UNTAC has not been able to determine responsibility for this act, which took place in an area contested by the forces of different factions, and investigations are proceeding on an urgent basis.

On 19 April 1993 at approximately 0230 hours, the UNTAC District headquarters in Oaral District, Kompong Speu Province, came under attack. The office is in the vicinity of a CPAF camp. An Indonesian Civilian Police monitor who, together with four Bulgarian soldiers, was in the District headquarters at the time radioed for assistance and a Fast Response Team was dispatched from a nearby Bulgarian company position to the scene. This consisted of an armoured personnel carrier (APC) with seven soldiers.

When the APC was approximately 1.5 kilometres from the District headquarters, it came under fire from both sides. One anti-tank grenade hit the vehicle from the right side and penetrated the armour. One Bulgarian soldier was killed instantly and five others were wounded, one of them seriously.

The attackers ransacked, looted and caused serious damage to the UNTAC District office, and the nearby District Civil Administration office also came under attack. In addition, the attackers, who were said to number about 100, destroyed a total of seven buildings belonging to local people. In the course of the attack on the UNTAC office, an Indonesian Civilian Police monitor and a Cambodian interpreter were also injured.

Preliminary investigations by UNTAC indicate that members of NADK were responsible for the attack. In view of the fact that the UNTAC offices were located adjacent to a CPAF camp and that non-UNTAC buildings were also destroyed in the attack, it cannot be concluded that UNTAC was the target, or at least the sole target of the attack.

(Signed) Boutros BOUTROS-GHALI

Document 79

Fourth progress report of the Secretary-General on UNTAC

S/25719, 3 May 1993

1. By paragraph 10 of its resolution 745 (1992), the Security Council requested the Secretary-General to report to the Council at stated intervals on progress made in the implementation of the resolution and on tasks still to be performed in the operation, with particular regard to the most effective and efficient use of resources. In accordance with this provision and in response to subsequent resolutions and to developments in Cambodia, I have submitted three progress reports as well as other reports on 1 May (S/23870 and Corr.1 and 2), 12 June (S/24090), 14 July (S/24286), 21 September (S/24578) and 15 November 1992 (S/24800) and 25 January (S/25124) and 13 February 1993 (S/25289).

2. The present report is in compliance with the Council's request in resolution 745 (1992) for a fourth progress report in April 1993. It also reports, in response to a further request in resolution 810 (1993), on the implementation of that resolution and on measures to ensure the realization of the fundamental objectives of the Paris Agreements of 23 October 1991 (see S/23177, annex). It describes the activities of the United Nations Transitional Authority in Cambodia (UNTAC) up to 3 May 1993.

3. By paragraph 6 of resolution 810 (1993), the Security Council requested the Secretary-General to inform the Council by 15 May 1993 of the conditions and preparations for the election. While that additional report will be devoted to that matter, and to the broader question of the creation and maintenance of acceptable conditions for a free and fair election, the present report also contains the latest information relating to the organization and conduct of the elections.

I. Implementation of resolution 745 (1992)

A. *General*

4. The main obstacle to the implementation of UNTAC's mandate since its establishment in Cambodia on 15 March 1992 has been the refusal of one of the parties, the Party of Democratic Kampuchea (PDK), to meet the obligations it assumed in signing the Paris Peace Agreements. That Party has neither demobilized its armed forces, nor has it granted UNTAC personnel access to the zones it controls in the thinly populated north and west of the country. To the contrary, in violation of the cease-fire it has sought to extend the territory it controls and has blown up bridges and carried out other military operations. On many occasions its units in the field have temporarily detained United Nations military observers and other UNTAC personnel, all of whom were, however, released unharmed after negotiation. PDK Radio has launched increasingly vitriolic attacks on UNTAC and its senior officials and has directed violent propaganda against Vietnamese-speaking persons living in Cambodia. Members of the National Army of Democratic Kampuchea (NADK), the armed forces of PDK, have been implicated in massacres of Vietnamese-speaking persons. Since the latter part of March 1993 members of UNTAC have been the subject of several attacks, many of them in circumstances that strongly indicate the involvement of PDK.

5. In response to what it described as encroachment by the NADK, the military force of the Party of the State of Cambodia (SOC), the Cambodian People's Armed Forces (CPAF), have launched attacks on NADK, which in UNTAC's view also constitute violations of the cease-fire. Furthermore, since political parties contesting the election for a constituent assembly began opening offices last September in the SOC-controlled zone, which comprises some 80 per cent of the country, SOC has been blamed for organizing or condoning violent attacks on the personnel and offices of those parties. Most of those attacks, which reached a peak last December, have been directed at the Front uni national pour un Cambodge indépendant, neutre, pacifique et coopératif (FUNCINPEC) and, to a lesser extent, at the Khmer People's National Liberation Front (KPNLF), the other two Cambodian factions which signed the Paris Agreements. Despite the responsibility of the existing administrative structures to maintain law and order in their respective zones, SOC has so far made only a handful of arrests in any of these cases.

6. As a result of these developments, UNTAC has been obliged, with the approval of the Security Council, to modify its activities in implementation of the Paris Agreements, especially the deployment and the tasks of its Military Component. These modifications have been described in detail in earlier reports listed above. As reported earlier, PDK's non-cooperation made it necessary for UNTAC to suspend the cantonment of the armed forces of the three other factions, after some 55,000 troops had been disarmed under UNTAC supervision, and the Military Component, in close cooperation with the Civilian Police and other components of UNTAC, has redirected its efforts to ensuring the security of the electoral process and the safety of the Cambodian political parties and of UNTAC staff under conditions of instability which are not in consonance with the original implementation plan. Thus, the UNTAC Military Component was redeployed to provide security for the voter registration teams, while the Civilian Police Component mounted static guard and mobile patrols around political party offices considered to be at risk.

7. Given the distortions that have arisen in the implementation of the peace plan, UNTAC has endeavoured to create and maintain the best possible conditions for the holding of free and fair elections starting on 23 May 1993. The measures described above led to a marked reduction between December 1992 and March 1993 in the levels of politically motivated violence, though subtler and non-violent forms of intimidation continued. However, an upsurge in violence directed against ethnic minorities during the month of March triggered a migration of thousands of Vietnamese-speaking persons seeking greater safety from such attacks.

8. On 7 and 8 April 1993 I paid my second visit in a year to UNTAC at the start of the six-week electoral campaign. In an address to His Royal Highness Prince Sihanouk, President of the Supreme National Council (SNC), and the members of the SNC, I reminded them of their responsibilities under the Paris Agreements and stressed that they must do their utmost to help themselves and to help UNTAC. I also stated that, bearing in mind the measures UNTAC had taken since December to improve the security situation, it was my judgement, with all due caution, that the basic acceptable conditions for the conduct of an electoral campaign did exist. However, the situation in Cambodia still gives grounds for serious concern and UNTAC will be scrutinizing developments with great care and attention until the end of the election itself in order to ensure that those conditions are closely monitored and improved as far as possible. It is encouraging that, so far, despite an atmosphere of tension, electoral campaigning is being conducted peacefully with the participation of tens of thousands of Cambodians.

B. *Relations with the Supreme National Council*

9. The meeting of the Supreme National Council held at Beijing on 28 January 1993 was described in my report of 13 February 1993 on the implementation of Security Council resolution 792 (1992) (S/25289, paras. 3-6). Since then, SNC has held three plenary meetings (on 10 February and 4 and 10 April 1993) under the chairmanship of Prince Sihanouk and four working sessions (on 9 and 20 March and 21 and 29 April 1993) under the chairmanship of my Special Representative, Mr. Yasushi Akashi, in the absence from Phnom Penh of Prince Sihanouk. The meetings dealt with recent developments, including military developments in Cambodia, the creation and maintenance of a neutral political environment, the implementation of the SNC moratoriums on the export of timber and gems, the work of various technical advisory committees (TACs), constitutional principles and other matters. Further details can be found under the relevant sections below.

10. On 4 April 1993, Mr. Khieu Samphan, President of PDK, formally announced to SNC that his party would not be participating in the elections, asserting that "Vietnamese forces of aggression" continued to occupy Cambodia and that a neutral political environment did not exist.

11. On 7 April 1993, Mr. Hun Sen, "Prime Minister" of the Phnom Penh authorities, wrote to me requesting that he and the Security Council take measures together with the existing administrative structures to ensure that the elections could proceed in a neutral po-

litical environment and with sufficient security. The accompanying memorandum accused PDK of serious violations of human rights and of the Paris Agreements and requested authorization to take the necessary means in cooperation with UNTAC to prevent PDK from taking further advantage of the situation, to safeguard the electoral process and "to protect the elected government and the Cambodian people from a second genocide".

12. In a letter dated 3 April 1993, Prince Sihanouk informed my Special Representative that he would resign from the Presidency of SNC on 28 May 1993, after the election. At our meeting on 7 April, I strongly urged the Prince to reconsider, saying that Cambodia needed his leadership before, during and after the election. He thereupon agreed to continue to serve as President of SNC throughout the transitional period.

13. On 13 April 1993 Mr. Khieu Samphan wrote to Prince Sihanouk to announce that he could no longer attend the Supreme National Council in Phnom Penh because there was insufficient security and that PDK was withdrawing "temporarily" from Phnom Penh. The following day, my Special Representative wrote to Mr. Khieu Samphan offering to provide him with UNTAC security, but this offer was declined.

C. *Human Rights Component*

14. Despite the various activities of the Human Rights Component described in earlier reports, notably my third progress report (S/25124), the human rights situation in Cambodia continues to give rise to deep concern. The persistence of politically and ethnically motivated attacks is obviously a serious threat to the protection of human rights as well as to the creation and maintenance of a neutral political environment. This issue is treated under section K below.

15. The development and dissemination of a human rights education programme was accelerated during the period under review, with particular reference to teacher training, dissemination of relevant international instruments, education of health professionals, training of public and political officials and support for local human rights organizations.

16. Teams of human rights trainers travelled to Kompong Som, Banteay Meanchey, Kompong Chhnang, Kratie, Ratanakiri, Pursat, Kompong Speu, Prey Veng, Kompong Thom, Battambang, Koh Kong and Stung Treng for week-long courses for the following audiences: representatives of political parties, members of human rights associations, teacher trainees and justice officials. Another team was deployed in Phnom Penh and Kompong Thom to teach courses in teacher training colleges. In consultation with the officials of the health administration of the party of the State of Cambodia, a new course

was begun on human rights for students in the Medical Faculty, complementing the course taught last year at the Law School.

17. A special course was conducted for human rights advocates. Several training activities were organized for the human rights associations, including a training programme on United Nations human rights procedures and a special training programme in Phnom Penh dealing with human rights issues in the electoral process.

18. Considerable human rights education activity was carried out by the provincial human rights officers and their training assistants. Such courses have been addressed to commune leaders, district electoral supervisors, teachers, women's associations, monks, soldiers, police, political parties and human rights associations. The number of persons reached by these courses range in the thousands in Banteay Meanchey, Kampot, Kandal, Koh Kong and Pursat, and in the hundreds in Kompong Cham, Kompong Chhnang, Kompong Som, Kompong Speu, Siem Reap and Stung Treng, Svay Rieng and Takeo.

19. Educational materials, posters, leaflets, stickers and other printed materials prepared in previous reporting periods were reproduced for further dissemination. In addition, a 400-page compilation of human rights instruments applicable in Cambodia was printed in 10,000 copies for wide dissemination among educators and practitioners.

20. On another front, the United Nations Commission on Human Rights adopted a resolution at its spring session at Geneva providing for the first time for the operational involvement of the Centre for Human Rights in Cambodia in the post-UNTAC period, thus providing an important support mechanism for the Cambodian human rights organizations. The resolution also requests the Secretary-General to appoint a special representative on human rights in Cambodia. However, no specific reference was made to article 17 of the Paris Agreements, which calls on the Commission on Human Rights to continue to monitor closely the human rights situation in Cambodia including, if necessary, by the appointment of a Special Rapporteur who would report to the Commission and to the General Assembly.

D. *Electoral Component*

21. Following completion of voter registration, including the registration of returning refugees, and the compilation of the computerized voters' list, the number of registered voters has now been set at nearly 4.7 million, or some 96 per cent of the estimated eligible population. All 20 political parties which had provisionally registered (S/25124, para. 30) have now officially registered to take

part in the election. The Party of Democratic Kampuchea is not among them.

22. In my report on the implementation of resolution 792 (1992) (S/25289, para. 34), I stated that it was expected that polling would take place from 23 to 27 May 1993, including three days of voting in static polling stations and a further two days in mobile stations. Following further intensive study, UNTAC has concluded that the reorganization of staff from static to mobile teams will itself require a full day. Polling therefore will be extended to 28 May.

23. Since the last report (S/25289) was issued, my Special Representative has promulgated a number of minor revisions to the original Electoral Law in order to respond to security or other considerations as they have arisen or been anticipated. These revisions include a ban on public meetings before the election campaign officially opened on 7 April, a ban on public opinion polls, which, it was considered, might have an intimidatory effect, a ban on the placing of party seals on ballot boxes at the time of polling, and revised provisions for the removal of names from the lists of candidates.

24. On 11 March 1993, my Special Representative met with the leaders of the 20 political parties registered to take part in the election. Saying that he considered them the stewards and guardians of democracy in Cambodia, he informed them of their rights and responsibilities as party leaders under the Electoral Law.

25. In my third progress report (S/25124, paras. 33-34), I described the strong pressure from FUNCINPEC and the KPNLF for revisions of the Electoral Law to extend the franchise to the so-called Khmer Krom residents in Cambodia and to allow overseas Cambodians to register outside Cambodia as well as the reasons for which I decided that, unless the Security Council decided otherwise, these two proposed revisions should not be approved. My Special Representative therefore also took the opportunity to stress to the political party leaders that UNTAC rejected in advance arguments by some of the Cambodian parties aimed at providing grounds for refusing to accept the election results, alleging that the results of the election might have been different if these proposed revisions had been accepted. My Special Representative also rejected allegations that many "Vietnamese" had registered to vote. The registration process was scrutinized by representatives of the political parties with the right to challenge registrants whom they deemed to be unqualified. Challenges were issued in respect of only a fraction of 1 per cent of registrants, and none has been confirmed by the evidence. A further change to the law permitted the establishment of polling stations in the United States, France and Australia in order to accommodate Cambodians living overseas, though the law also required that those individuals come to Cambodia to register to vote. Arrangements are being made for these overseas polling stations to be located in Paris, New York and Sydney.

26. On the basis of the number of registered voters, the 120 seats for the Constituent Assembly have been allocated to the 21 provinces and the Phnom Penh special district as follows:

Allocation of seats by province

Banteay Meanchey	6
Battambang	8
Kompong Cham	18
Kompong Chhnang	4
Kompong Speu	6
Kompong Thom	6
Kompot	6
Kandal	11
Koh Kong	1
Kratie	3
Mondolkiri	1
Phnom Penh	12
Preah Vihear	1
Prey Veng	11
Pursat	4
Ratanak Kiri	1
Siem Reap	6
Sihanoukville	1
Stung Treng	1
Svay Rieng	5
Takeo	8
Total	120

27. All 20 political parties contesting the election have submitted their list of candidates. The lists for 3 of the parties were published on 13 April and the lists for 13 more on 22 April 1993. The lists for the remaining four parties, which are being held back at their request, will be published before the election.

28. Preparations for the conduct of the election are now well under way. The necessary equipment and supplies, including the ballot papers and boxes, are already in Cambodia and delivery schedules have been established to ensure that all the necessary materials will be in place before the opening of polling. The selection of more than 50,000 Cambodian electoral staff has been completed, and their recruitment and subsequent training has been programmed so that they can take up their duties when polling begins. The number of polling stations, originally envisaged to be about 1,400, has been reviewed in the light of the security situation, but is likely to remain about the same. Some of the polling stations were to be divided into two sites, close to each other; and the number

of secondary sites may be somewhat reduced. Polling stations are divided into large, medium or small static stations—consisting of eight, six and three polling teams respectively—as well as mobile stations. Each polling station will have a Cambodian Presiding Officer in charge and one international polling station officer to provide support and assist the Presiding Officer. Polling will begin at static stations in the more populated areas during the first three days of the polling period so that the maximum number of votes will be cast during this period to create a momentum.

29. Plans have also been made for the recruitment of approximately 1,000 international polling station officers from more than 30 countries, who should be arriving in Cambodia in May for training in the United Nations Electoral Law before reporting for duty at polling stations throughout the country. Eleven countries were requested to provide a total of 50 fingerprint and 5 handwriting experts to check the tendered ballots, i.e., those cast by voters who had lost their cards, had them illegally confiscated or who were voting in a province other than that in which they had registered. Responses to this request have been slow. It is hoped that Governments will be able to provide UNTAC with this important capability.

30. UNTAC also has encouraged the Cambodian parties to examine constitutional principles and different forms of constitutions that the members of the constituent assembly may wish to consider. The question of constitutional principles was first placed on the agenda of SNC in September 1992 and has since been discussed at regular intervals. In November 1992 UNTAC sponsored a seminar for party representatives of the Technical Advisory Committee on constitutional principles, and in January 1993 international experts were invited to assist in discussions on the matter. A further six-day constitutional seminar took place from 29 March to 3 April 1993, concentrating on four main features: constitutions and conflicts; Cambodia's constitutional history; crucial issues facing the Constituent Assembly; and developing procedures for debate. The meeting was attended by members of SNC and its secretariat, all political parties registered to contest the election, selected non-governmental organizations, the main United Nations agencies operating in Cambodia and international experts.

31. The killing in Kompong Thom Province on 8 April 1993 of a district electoral supervisor, a Japanese national and a Cambodian interpreter has raised concern about security. The 465 United Nations Volunteers who serve as district electoral supervisors, deployed throughout the country, have played a vital role in the training of Cambodian electoral staff and in the programme of civic education about the election in the countryside as well as in convincing the electorate that their vote will be secret. Following the incident of 8 April, UNTAC has instituted emergency provisional arrangements to improve security. All United Nations Volunteers, including district electoral supervisors, in 10 central and western provinces considered to present security risks were instructed to withdraw from the countryside and not to travel without an armed escort until further notice. Those district electoral supervisors have been brought back to Phnom Penh for extensive debriefing while an inter-component security plan utilizing armed escorts and ready reaction forces is refined. Some 40 United Nations Volunteers have decided to leave their post, but most have indicated their intention to stay. A proposal to allow UNTAC Civilian Police members to carry weapons was carefully considered, but my Special Representative, on the recommendation of the UNTAC Police Commissioner, has decided not to do so at this time.

32. At the same time, as already noted, since the election campaign began on 7 April, scores of public meetings and rallies have taken place without incident throughout Cambodia with the participation of all parties.

E. *Military Component*

1. *Cease-fire violations*

33. The military situation in Cambodia continues to be marked by persistent, but low-intensity and small-scale, violations of the cease-fire, particularly in the central and western parts of the country. As noted in earlier reports, these usually take the form of clashes or exchanges of fire between the armed forces of PDK and SOC. These clashes, however, have not been sustained for more than a few days at a time.

34. However, security problems arise also from the spread of acts of banditry, usually perpetrated by former soldiers or serving troops who have not been adequately paid or paid at all, which contribute to a sense of insecurity in the countryside.

35. One of the most serious violations of the cease-fire occurred on 3 May 1993. In the early morning hours of that day, groups of armed men, allegedly belonging to NADK, attacked the town of Siem Reap in the Siem Reap Province from several directions using rocket launchers, small arms and grenades. They attacked a CPAF garrison as well as the Siem Reap airport and ransacked buildings belonging to UNTAC and to the local civilian population. The airport suffered no damage. CPAF police and military reinforcements countered the attack and the attackers withdrew from the town. UNTAC suffered no casualties, but casualties were reported among the civilian population as well as among the attackers.

2. Redeployment of the Military Component

36. In my report on the implementation of Security Council resolution 792 (1992) (S/25289, para. 11), I stated that the disposition of the Military Component for the protection of the election would be discussed in more detail in the fourth progress report.

37. The Component's coordination with the Civilian Police Component has been strengthened. Teams of military observers are working with UNTAC Civilian Police in monitoring political rallies and gatherings throughout the country, and personnel from both components are assisting electoral staff with the civic education campaign. Security arrangements are now being finalized in order to provide for the fullest possible security during the polling both for static and mobile teams, especially in those parts of the country considered relatively unstable. In addition, in collaboration with the Civilian Police Component, the Military Component has concluded agreements for providing security for the polling period with the armed forces of the three factions which are in compliance with the peace process SOC, FUNCINPEC and KPNLF. The central feature of these arrangements is that the security of the polling stations and their vicinity will be provided by UNTAC alone. UNTAC will be solely responsible for all security measures to be taken in the immediate vicinity of a polling station, as well as United Nations personnel and property. The armed forces of the factions will be responsible for assisting UNTAC, conveying information on possible or actual threats to the election and ensuring security in the zones under their control.

38. The tightening of restrictions by NADK on UNTAC liaison personnel stationed in Pailin has been a matter of concern. For some time NADK has frequently confined the military observers and other staff to their houses while preventing UNTAC from resupplying them with fuel, preventing resupply by air and creating obstacles to their replacement and rotation. Despite my Special Representative's repeated protests to Mr. Khieu Samphan, President of PDK, these measures have not been relaxed. UNTAC has endeavoured to maintain their deployment in Pailin as long as possible while continuing its efforts to resupply them. However, these UNTAC personnel were withdrawn from Pailin on 30 April 1993. UNTAC is negotiating with NADK to open an alternate liaison channel at nearby Sok Sann.

3. Attacks on UNTAC personnel

39. Circumstances of incidents between 27 March and 19 April 1993 resulting in eight fatalities among UNTAC military and civilian personnel and responsibility for them have been described in the letter I addressed to the President of the Security Council on 26 April 1993 (S/25669). Since that letter was sent, UNTAC has reported, in respect of the incident of 8 April in Kompong Thom Province, that evidence appeared to rule out the involvement of any Cambodian faction as such. The incident of 27 March 1993 in which a Bangladeshi soldier was killed appears to be the first deliberate attack against UNTAC personnel.

40. As a result of these attacks all units of the Military Component in all locations were directed to increase vigilance and enhance their security measures and procedures. Instructions were issued forbidding the approach to UNTAC positions by unknown armed men. The Military Component has been reinforcing its defensive positions all over Cambodia, particularly in Siem Reap and Kompong Thom Provinces. These positions have been expanded to allow the construction of bunkers and overhead protection as well as firing bays, which are defensive pits from which soldiers can return fire. Where UNTAC assets are located in isolated locations, permanent guards and/or mobile patrols are used to improve the physical security of the premises. Security at UNTAC headquarters has also been strengthened by heightening the walls around the compound, tightening control over approaching traffic, improving the illumination along the walls and instituting better verification of the identification of visitors and staff. Military personnel, in cooperation with Civilian Police monitors, have also been manning checkpoints and roadblocks to confiscate illegally held weapons (see para. 84 below).

41. Since I reported on the incidents referred to in paragraph 39 above, I regret to say that several more attacks on UNTAC personnel have occurred. On 30 April, at about 9.30 p.m., in Kompong Cham Province, unknown armed assailants fired at an UNTAC vehicle carrying three Civilian Police Monitors. One Colombian officer was killed and a Malaysian officer was seriously injured. The latter has been evacuated to Kuala Lumpur for medical treatment. Also on 30 April at approximately 9 p.m., a detachment of the Uruguayan battalion in Kratie Province was attacked by unknown assailants and two Uruguayan soldiers were slightly injured. On 1 May at about 10.40 p.m., unidentified persons threw three handgrenades at a Dutch battalion camp in Banteay Meanchey Province. One Dutch soldier was injured and evacuated to Bangkok. On 3 May, an UNTAC patrol consisting of two vehicles was ambushed in Kompong Cham Province and five members of the Indian battalion were injured, one seriously. UNTAC investigation indicates that this attack was carried out by NADK. Since the beginning of UNTAC, 11 UNTAC civilian and military personnel have been killed as a result of hostile action. Thirty-nine others have died from other causes.

4. Withdrawal and non-return of foreign forces

42. Article VI of annex 2 to the Paris Agreements relates to the verification of the withdrawal from Cambodia and the non-return of all categories of foreign forces. This question is of particular significance to the implementation of the Paris Agreements because the Party of Democratic Kampuchea cites the alleged presence of "foreign forces", that is, Vietnamese forces, in Cambodia to justify its refusal to comply with its obligations under the Agreements.

43. In May 1992, acting under article VI as well as article X of annex 2 to the Paris Agreements, in accordance with which UNTAC is authorized to investigate violations on its own initiative, UNTAC established Strategic Investigation Teams (SITs) to follow up allegations of the continued presence of foreign forces in Cambodia. At that time, and repeatedly since then, UNTAC has called on the Cambodian parties to furnish it with verifiable information relating to foreign forces, and to provide liaison officers to facilitate UNTAC's investigation, as is required under the Agreements. No such information or cooperation has been received to date.

44. In my report to the Security Council dated 15 November 1992 (S/24800, para. 18), I stated that UNTAC had not found evidence that there were any formed units of foreign forces in Cambodia. This continues to be the case. The Government of Viet Nam has repeatedly stated that it had withdrawn its troops from Cambodia in September 1989.

45. On 10 December 1992, at the working session of the Supreme National Council, UNTAC issued an interim report on the work of the SITs stating that at that point none of its investigations had yielded conclusive evidence of the presence of foreign forces, but that it was continuing its work. The Cambodian parties were again urged to supply UNTAC with information on the presence of foreign forces, but none did so.

46. On 1 March 1993, UNTAC announced that three of the persons who had been under investigation by the SITs were Vietnamese and that they had served with the Vietnamese armed forces in Cambodia; they were, therefore, "foreign forces" within the meaning of the definition approved by SNC at its meeting on 20 October 1992. Two of the men were serving with CPAF and the third was a former member. All three had been issued identity cards by the Phnom Penh authorities. Therefore, UNTAC asked the Phnom Penh authorities to discharge the two still serving from their armed forces and to withdraw the identity cards of all three men. UNTAC also requested the Government of Viet Nam to accept the three men back as Vietnamese nationals, but the latter has so far declined to do so. A further four men have since

been identified as "foreign forces" and the SIT investigations are continuing.

47. At the same time UNTAC has made the complexities of the situation as clear as possible. The three men originally identified were all married to Cambodian women and had children, and there was no suggestion that they were in any way under the control of the Vietnamese authorities. The explanation of such considerations is considered necessary in view of the widespread popular resentment among Cambodians directed against Vietnamese nationals and Vietnamese-speaking persons. This resentment, which has its roots in the history of the relations between Cambodia and Viet Nam, has been deliberately and systematically whipped up not only by the Party of Democratic Kampuchea but also, to a lesser extent, by FUNCINPEC and KPNLF.

48. UNTAC has accordingly been at pains to make it clear that members of "foreign forces" as specified in the Paris Agreements, and with regard to whom UNTAC has specific responsibilities, are different from foreign residents and immigrants, e.g., persons who had migrated from Viet Nam to Cambodia for economic and other reasons. UNTAC has also made clear its view that persons born in Cambodia of Vietnamese descent, many of whom have lived in Cambodia for two or three generations, represent a separate category. UNTAC has no special responsibility under the Paris Agreements for foreign residents or immigrants and considers that these questions are long-term matters that can be resolved only by discussions between the future Government of Cambodia and the Government of Viet Nam. UNTAC has also publicly criticized what it considers to be racist utterances by some of the Cambodian parties and emphasized the responsibility of the local authorities to maintain law and order in the zones they control and to assure the safety and security of their citizens.

49. The aspects of this question that affect the environment in which elections are to be held are discussed in section K below on the creation and maintenance of a neutral political environment.

5. Engineering and rebuilding of infrastructure

50. Since the beginning of the mission, UNTAC's five engineering units, supplemented by the engineer platoons in 11 of the 12 infantry battalions, have been improving and restoring the roads, bridges and airfields which are indispensable for the safe and rapid movement of UNTAC personnel throughout the country. These operations have also greatly improved the infrastructure for the Cambodian population, particularly in the countryside.

51. The engineering units—from China, France, Japan, Poland and Thailand—have repaired hundreds of

bridges and improved scores of kilometres of roads, as well as airfields at Pochentong (Phnom Penh) and Stung Treng.

6. *Mine awareness and mine clearance*

52. The Mine Clearance Training Unit (MCTU) teaches Cambodians to identify, locate and destroy land mines and to mark minefields. MCTU, which comprises 183 officers and men, also promotes mine awareness among the general public. Each of the eight national contingents in MCTU is organized into mine clearance training teams, which teach the courses, and mine clearance supervisory teams, which supervise the mine clearance work of the teams that have been trained. In the past year, the Unit has trained more than 2,000 Cambodians, of whom about 600 are actually employed in mine clearance activities, either directly by UNTAC or by four non-governmental organizations (HALO Trust, Mine Awareness Group, Norwegian People's Aid and Handicap International) involved in mine clearance in Cambodia. The main barrier to employing more trained mine-clearance staff is the shortage of supervisory teams.

53. In the past year, MCTU has been instrumental in clearing more than 1.6 million square metres of land and disposing of more than 15,000 mines and other pieces of unexploded ordnance. The Unit has also addressed schoolchildren and villagers throughout the countryside and lectured UNTAC military and police personnel on mine awareness and mine avoidance. None the less, 17 UNTAC staff have been injured because of mines or other types of ordnance since the beginning of the mission, and numerous Cambodians continue to suffer injuries.

54. As noted in my third progress report (S/25124, para. 83), the Governing Council of the Cambodian Mine Action Centre (CMAC) held its first meeting on 4 November 1992 and adopted the short-term plan of operations. The Governing Council met again on 16 March 1993 to consider its work to date and the problems still to be faced.

55. UNTAC is now working to "Cambodianize" CMAC in order to equip it to function after the end of the UNTAC mandate. Five Cambodians have already been recruited to commence training on the computer-assisted mine database, and the recruitment of Cambodians to take eventual responsibility for the four main branches, information and policy, operations, training and administration, is now proceeding.

56. The other major priority is fund-raising. CMAC will not be able to fulfil its intended role as Cambodia's national mine-clearance body independent of UNTAC's financial and institutional support unless international funding is made available as a matter of urgency. A document outlining the financial requirements for CMAC's short-term plan of operations has been widely distributed among the donor community, but the response so far can only be described as disappointing. Mines pose a grave and long-term threat to the well-being of the Cambodian people. I appeal strongly to the international community to render assistance in this area.

F. *Civil Administration Component*

1. *General*

57. Since my last report, the most significant development in the exercise of UNTAC civil administration control over the five areas specified in the Paris Agreements—foreign affairs, national defence, public security, finance and information—has been the activity of the Control Team, established in January 1993. The Control Team supplements the regular supervision that UNTAC exercises over the existing administrative structures, particularly outside Phnom Penh, which otherwise would tend to be inadequate because of the relatively small number of UNTAC personnel devoted to each province.

58. Each Control Team is headed by an Inspector assisted by representatives of the Military and Civilian Police components, staff from the Finance and Public Security Services of the Civil Administration Component and analysts and interpreters from the Information/Education Division. They act on the basis of a Mission Order signed by the Deputy Special Representative of the Secretary-General and following an interview with the Provincial Governor. Their purpose is to verify if, at the provincial, district and village levels, the local administration is being conducted in a politically neutral manner during the electoral process. To achieve this purpose, the team exercises its right under the Paris Agreements to have unrestricted access to documents.

59. The Control Teams have carried out operations in zones controlled by SOC in the provinces of Kandal, Prey Veng, Takeo and Kompong Cham, and the translation and in-depth analysis of the documents made available to UNTAC by the local administration are now under way. A further operation was carried out in April in the FUNCINPEC zone at Ampil. Analysis of the SOC documents to which UNTAC has gained access indicates widespread and persistent use of the SOC state apparatus to conduct political campaign activities of the Cambodian People's Party (CPP) in which state employees—police, armed forces and civil servants—are mobilized for CPP electioneering. UNTAC is now undertaking an in-depth review of the documentary evidence of SOC's attitudes and practices towards opposition political parties, indigenous human rights organizations and repatriated refugees in order to coordinate appropriate responses.

60. As an initial step, Civil Administration staff

have been instructed to try to prevent local authority officials from conducting political party activities during their normal working hours, to prevent the use of public buildings and local authority vehicles for partisan purposes and to emphasize the secrecy of the ballot.

2. *Foreign affairs*

61. In accordance with the declaration by the Supreme National Council that all Cambodian passports shared the same status as SNC passports, work began in January 1993 to endorse applicants' passports with the SNC seal to ensure equal treatment. By 1 April, some 9,000 passports, including diplomatic, ordinary and service passports, had been endorsed with the seal.

62. In coordination with the UNTAC Military and Civilian Police Components, the staff of the UNTAC Civil Administration Component have also assumed greater supervision and control over the various border functions, such as immigration, customs and the implementation of the moratoriums on timber, gems and minerals. As part of the civilian operation, a Border Control Unit has been established which will be responsible for liaison between UNTAC components and the existing administrative structures, civilian field operations, civilian logistical support and other activities. Efforts are now being made to recruit and deploy 30 border control officers to the checkpoints and to major immigration and customs centres to work with the military observers and civilian police already there.

63. During March 1993, UNTAC began a series of training seminars for Cambodian immigration and border control officers on the implementation of procedures agreed with the three parties cooperating with UNTAC.

3. *Defence*

64. In late January 1993, the leaders of the armed forces of the three factions complying with the Paris Agreements, CPAF, KPNLAF and the Army of National Kampuchea Independence (ANKI), signed the directive prepared by UNTAC regulating the political activity of military personnel. The three factions also signed early in 1993 similar directives on the political activity of members of the police force and civil administration, respectively. These directives are discussed in section K below. Also at the request of UNTAC, the SOC "First Vice-Minister of Defence", the highest-ranking officer responsible for political affairs, signed a directive in late February prohibiting the wearing of CPP insignia on uniforms and the display of CPP posters on military buildings.

65. In response to the spate of politically motivated intimidation and violence, much of which was attributed to soldiers of CPAF, in early February UNTAC estab-lished a system to bring to the attention of the SOC "ministry of defence" cases where CPAF members are alleged to have taken part in illegal activity. At the request of UNTAC, the "ministry" established a special committee to investigate these allegations, and by the end of March 1993 UNTAC had been provided with a list of CPAF personnel responsible for investigations into allegations of misconduct in each province and each unit. However, the "ministry" has admitted the guilt of its personnel in only a small number of cases and punishments are rare.

4. *Public security*

66. In early 1993 UNTAC began training magistrates and police officers of the existing administrative structures in the implementation of the Penal Code adopted by the SNC in September 1992 on UNTAC's initiative. This phase of training followed earlier phases in which about 200 judges, prosecutors and police officers of the three Cambodian parties complying with the peace process were trained in the Code during the latter part of 1992. The directive issued by my Special Representative in March 1993 prohibiting the illegal possession and carrying of weapons and explosives is discussed in paragraph 84 below.

67. In cooperation with the Human Rights and Civilian Police components, the staff of the Civil Administration Component are continuing a programme of regular prison visits designed to effect the implementation of the relevant provisions of the Penal Code. Some progress has been made in this area, principally in improvements to prison conditions. Through working with a major programme by the International Committee of the Red Cross (ICRC) to improve the water and sanitation services in the Phnom Penh and provincial prisons, marked improvements in the physical conditions of those prisons have been achieved.

68. Unfortunately, problems of the use of shackles in several provincial prisons and in police stations continue despite UNTAC's repeated attempts to end this practice. Problems with shortages of food continue to cause major concern in many of the provincial prisons. Physical mistreatment of prisoners remains a concern in a number of provincial prisons, and also in police cells.

69. A programme of bringing prisoners before the courts for determination of the legality of their detention has been commenced to endeavour to break the control of the security forces over issues of detention. Applications for the release of prisoners held for long periods without trial have been made in Phnom Penh and in several provincial courts, although a lack of appellate courts hampers the effectiveness of this programme. Where appropriate, *démarches* to the existing adminis-

trative authorities are also made for the release of long-term prisoners.

5. Finance

70. Since the latter part of March 1993, the value of the Cambodian riel has become extremely unstable, with the exchange rate falling from about 2,500 riels to the United States dollar to more than 4,000. This instability has been accompanied by a steep rise in prices, particularly of rice, which now costs three or four times what it did before the slump in the riel. The fluctuations in the value of the riel cannot be attributed to any action or error on the part of the Phnom Penh financial authorities, whose operations are closely controlled and supervised by UNTAC; nor has UNTAC been able to ascertain the economic reasons for the fluctuations. However, it does appear that the other three Cambodian parties—PDK, FUNCINPEC and KPNLF—are unwilling to support the riel, whose collapse would have serious implications for the Phnom Penh authorities.

71. UNTAC's efforts to stabilize the riel, which is the currency used by the great majority of the Cambodian people, are, therefore, hampered by political considerations in that direct support for the currency would be seen as partiality towards the Phnom Penh authorities. On the other hand, the economic and social difficulties caused by rapid and severe inflation would obviously have negative implications for the environment in which elections are to be held, particularly given the damage already caused to that environment by the acts of violence described above. UNTAC has, therefore, taken measures to introduce additional rice supplies into the market to discourage hoarding and to bring down the price in an effort to avert social unrest. However, it may take some time to accomplish this.

72. The other important development in this field concerns negotiations for the loan to Cambodia pledged by the World Bank at the Tokyo Conference of June 1992. The Cambodian parties have failed to endorse the draft credit agreement despite UNTAC's repeated assurances that the loan would be politically neutral, it would have no effect on the electoral process, no money could be disbursed until the new Cambodian Government was in place, the new Government would have to endorse any agreement with the Bank and the loan was intended to benefit the Cambodian people as a whole and not one or another party. UNTAC has also pointed out to the Cambodian parties a substantial time-lag between the signing of an agreement and the actual financial transaction.

73. At its meeting on 10 April 1993, SNC, on the recommendation of UNTAC, adopted a financial control directive prepared by my Special Representative on the transfer of public assets in order to introduce orderly and transparent procedures into the process of privatization of property owned by the existing administrative structures.

74. In mid-February 1993, a week-long mission was sent by UNTAC to the zones administered by KPNLF and FUNCINPEC in northern Cambodia. Detailed financial reviews were conducted of all administrative activity and of bilaterally funded health programmes. These were found to be generally in order. Discussions were also undertaken with representatives of those two parties on logging, the petroleum embargo, customs, the proposed UNTAC procedure on the sale of public assets, the resettlement of returnees and other activities in their zones.

6. Information

75. Any assessment that the election had been free and fair would depend heavily on the perception that the political parties had fair access to the media. In addition to making its own television/video, radio and other information facilities available to the 20 parties contesting the election, UNTAC has also exercised its right to control the existing administrative structures directly in order to secure access for all parties to the public media facilities of the Phnom Penh authorities, and to the radio stations of the FUNCINPEC and KPNLF parties. My Special Representative accordingly issued a directive on fair access to the media during the electoral campaign setting out the responsibilities of UNTAC and the existing administrative structures in this respect, that is, primarily the media facilities of the Phnom Penh authorities.

76. In accordance with that directive, Radio UNTAC shall:

(a) Broadcast daily electoral programmes;

(b) Offer to every registered political party each week segments for the broadcast of political material;

(c) Allow a "right of response" where a political party, its candidate or official believes it has been unfairly attacked or its public statements misrepresented.

77. It was also agreed that the television station of the Phnom Penh authorities, TVK, would broadcast one hour a day of election-related material from UNTAC and the political parties, as is set forth in the directive.

7. Specialized control

78. In the sector of preserving cultural and historical monuments, the Steering Committee for the UNESCO Zoning and Environmental Management Plan for the Angkor area held its first meeting at Siem Reap in March 1993. A group of 23 technical experts is involved in developing the plan.

79. The Specialized Control Service has also established a Health Sector Technical Working Group to enable the four Cambodian parties to work together with

international and United Nations agencies to resolve problems of health service delivery within the existing administrative structures.

G. *Civilian Police Component*

80. In mid-December 1992, following a steep rise in attacks with hand-grenades and automatic weapons against the offices of political parties, the UNTAC Civilian Police Component in collaboration with other UNTAC components launched a special operation to curb the attacks. All political party offices were regularly visited and checked by 24-hour Civilian Police patrols. There are now more than 600 offices, and it would not be possible for UNTAC with its limited resources to provide security for all of them. Protection methods have therefore been refined in close cooperation with the parties concerned. A list of 60 party offices considered to be most at risk was drawn up and the UNTAC Civilian Police and Military components provided protection, initially on a 24-hour-a-day basis and then during the hours of darkness only. Since then, no office thus guarded has been attacked and the number of attacks against offices in general declined markedly in February and the first part of March. However, as the political parties opened additional offices down to the commune and village levels, the number of attacks began to rise again.

81. Much of the daily work of the Civilian Police Component is focused on the main part of its mandate, namely, supervision or control of local police activities. At present, an important part of this work is the monitoring of political rallies and meetings during the campaign period. Since the opening of the electoral campaign on 7 April, about 200 political rallies and meetings have taken place in 16 of Cambodia's 21 provinces, primarily by the larger and better-organized parties. In nearly every case the organizing party complied with the United Nations Electoral Law and the related security regulations for the planning and conduct of the meeting. Not a single case of disruption or harassment of a meeting has been reported, nor has there been any clash between members of different parties.

82. Apart from the supervision of investigations carried out by local police, UNTAC Civilian Police have undertaken independently hundreds of investigations into serious crimes, particularly those which are considered to be politically or ethnically motivated. In about 60 to 70 per cent of cases such allegations turn out to be groundless. In others the investigations are inconclusive because of the inadequate state of the local authorities' public security structures in much of the countryside. In a number of cases, as discussed below in section K, the Special Prosecutor has enough evidence to issue a warrant. Where the crime involves political or ethnic consid-erations, my Special Representative also raises the matter in the Supreme National Council and, where appropriate, in private meetings with and letters to the leaders of the Cambodian parties concerned. However, as noted below, crime control activities are hampered by the lack of a functioning court system in any of the zones to which UNTAC has access, as well as by the poor conditions in the prisons.

83. Preparations are also being made to contribute to the security arrangements for the election, when UNTAC Civilian Police monitors will be present at all polling stations.

84. UNTAC Civilian Police personnel have also been closely involved with other UNTAC activities relating to the establishment and maintenance of acceptable conditions for the conduct of free and fair elections, and this matter is examined in more detail in section K below. To this end, my Special Representative signed on 17 March 1993 a directive prohibiting the possession and carrying of firearms and explosives by unauthorized persons. After a three-week amnesty during which such persons were permitted to hand in prohibited materials, offenders were to be subject to terms of imprisonment and to the confiscation of weapons and explosives in their possession. The directive has proved very effective as a crime control measure both in Phnom Penh and in the provinces. Joint checkpoints manned by UNTAC Civilian Police and the local police since 5 April 1993 have resulted in the confiscation of a total of 71 high-powered firearms such as AK-47 rifles, 65 low-powered firearms such as pistols and revolvers, 7 rocket launchers and hundreds of rounds of assorted ammunition. In Phnom Penh, 14 random checkpoints are mounted each day and an average of about 15 firearms are confiscated each week. These are stored for a time to enable the holders to justify their possession by producing documents and, if this is not done, eventually destroyed. This has led to a significant decrease in reported crime in Phnom Penh. Serious crimes of all kinds, including murder, rape, armed robbery, the causing of explosions and the illegal discharge of firearms, totalled 66 in January and rose to 82 in February. In March the total fell to 65, and the April total was 35.

85. In accordance with paragraph 123 of the implementation plan (S/23613) and in order to ensure effective supervision by UNTAC of the police forces of the parties, the Civilian Police Component undertook a comprehensive study of the size, organization and equipment of the police forces of the three Cambodian factions complying with the peace accords. No access has been granted to the zone controlled by PDK. It was confirmed that the two smaller parties, FUNCINPEC and KPNLF, have limited operating police forces, while SOC has some

48,500 police officers, though inadequately trained and equipped.

86. Since the beginning of the mission the Component has provided training for the local police. It has conducted courses in basic training, operational training, traffic control, human rights, criminal law, criminal investigation, the roles of UNTAC and the Civilian Police Component, crime prevention, demonstration and riot control and the code of conduct. This training, which is ongoing, has taken place both in Phnom Penh and the provinces, and has to date involved some 2,000 SOC police officers.

87. As indicated in the third progress report (S/25124, para. 78), UNTAC Civilian Police have also been engaged in providing basic police training for the other factions. This training took place in Ampil and Osmach in the FUNCINPEC zone and in Thmar Pouk in the zone controlled by KPNLF. To date, more than 450 police officers have successfully completed their training courses, including 28 from PDK. The first police instructors' course for these three factions began in the UNTAC Khmer Police Training School in Thmar Pouk during April 1993.

H. *Repatriation Component*

88. The movement phase of the repatriation of some 365,000 Cambodian refugees and displaced persons from camps on the Thai border and elsewhere will have been completed by the end of April 1993. On 30 March 1993, exactly one year after the operation commenced, the United Nations High Commissioner for Refugees, Mrs. Sadako Ogata, presided over the official closing ceremony at the largest and last of the refugee camps, Site 2. The few thousand remaining refugees and displaced persons have now been repatriated, with the exception of about 600 who have refused to be repatriated. The Government of Thailand informed UNTAC that they would be deported.

89. The monthly rate of return rose from 4,000 in April 1992 to 20,000 in June 1992. By July, some 30,000 Cambodians were returning home each month. Although the rains made travelling conditions difficult, this was largely overcome by the use of rail and, in some cases, waterways. The rate of return rose to 35,000 a month by November and reached a peak of 40,000 in the months of January and February 1993. Though the great bulk of the returnees came from Thailand, some 2,000 were also repatriated from Indonesia, Viet Nam and Malaysia.

90. With respect to the reintegration sites within Cambodia, all four Cambodian parties have scrupulously respected the freedom of choice of the returnees. Most people chose to settle in areas controlled by the Phnom Penh authorities. Of the rest, about 33,000 chose to settle in the KPNLF zone, while several thousand settled in the PDK and FUNCINPEC zones. More than half of the returnees have settled in the northern provinces of Banteay Meanchey and Battambang, while many others have settled in Siem Reap, Kandal and Pursat provinces.

91. In addition to rations for 400 days and a domestic kit, returnees had the choice of several forms of assistance, including agricultural land, a housing plot and a cash grant in lieu of building materials. Most returnees, some 88 per cent, chose the cash grant.

92. In order to assist in reintegration, the Office of the United Nations High Commissioner for Refugees (UNHCR), the lead agency for repatriation, together with UNDP and various non-governmental organizations, implemented more than 60 quick-impact projects (QIPs) to help communities absorb the returnees. These include road and bridge repair, mine clearance, agricultural development, digging of wells and water ponds and improvement and construction of sanitation, health and education facilities.

93. Since electoral registration began in October 1992, all eligible returnees were given the opportunity to be registered for elections on their return to their homeland, either in their final destination along with the local population or in the six reception centres. In January 1993, as the deadline for the end of the electoral registration period was approaching, a special arrangement was made between the Repatriation and Electoral components to enable registration of the remaining eligible population in the border camps. They were temporarily "listed" in Thailand during the month of January and received their registration cards upon return to Cambodia.

94. In cooperation with other UNTAC components, United Nations agencies and non-governmental organizations, UNHCR has established a country-wide mechanism for monitoring the condition of returnees. The main objective is to survey the security situation as well as the reintegration of returnees. Information will be collected by UNHCR coordinators in Cambodia who will analyse the information and try to address any problems that have arisen. With a view to the gradual phasing out of UNHCR international staff in the months ahead, the intention is to "Cambodianize" the system, using trained Cambodians in the near future. The training of such staff is currently progressing.

I. *Rehabilitation Component*

95. During 1992, the Supreme National Council, acting on the recommendation of UNTAC, approved a total of 35 rehabilitation projects worth $340 million. Since the beginning of 1993, SNC has approved a further 10 projects worth about $26 million. However, by March

1993 only about $100 million of the $880 million pledged at the Ministerial Conference on the Rehabilitation and Reconstruction of Cambodia held at Tokyo in June 1992 had been disbursed.

96. The Donors' Meeting held at Phnom Penh on 25 February 1993 reaffirmed donors' commitments to the principles for rehabilitation and reconstruction made at the Tokyo Conference. Donors reiterated the pledges they had made at that conference and expressed their desire to address Cambodia's immediate needs. They declared their willingness to speed up disbursements over the pre-election period. More than 30 donors, including international and non-governmental agencies, are implementing their assistance programmes with disbursements scheduled over the next few months in key sectors such as health and education. Support is also being provided for institutional capacity-building with UNTAC's Rehabilitation Component and the Economic Adviser's Office preparing seminars and training programmes in priority areas of public sector management and civil service reform, investment planning and natural resource development.

97. Part of the rehabilitation support was a $75 million International Development Association emergency rehabilitation credit from the World Bank for health, education, transport, agriculture and public utilities. At the working session of SNC held on 8 December 1992 an *aide-mémoire* concerning the proposed loan was approved and it was decided that negotiations should open immediately with the World Bank to take up the loan. However, despite protracted and intensive negotiations it has since become clear that the Cambodian parties are unable to reach a meeting of minds on the credit agreement. In order to break the stalemate the matter was again brought to the plenary of SNC at its meeting on 4 April 1993, but no decision was reached.

98. The Rehabilitation Component, in close coordination with UNTAC military observers, Civil Administration and Civilian Police personnel deployed at border checkpoints, has continued to monitor the extent of compliance with the SNC moratorium on the export of timber adopted on 22 September 1992. The figures available show a continued decline in the number of violations and the quantity of logs exported, as follows:

Month	No. of violations	Volume of timber (in cubic metres)
January	46	48,049
February	11	12,370
March	5	2,345

99. In all five cases the faction responsible for the violation was the SOC. It should be made clear, however, that UNTAC still has no access to the zones controlled by PDK, nor is it permitted to station observers on the Thai side of the border to monitor violations that may be occurring in those zones.

100. On 10 February 1993, in addition to the 22 September 1992 moratorium on logs, SNC adopted supplementary measures aimed at discouraging further tree felling by reducing the volume of sawn timber allowed to be exported from Cambodia. It was agreed that the volume of sawn timber exported during the first five months of 1993 should not exceed five twelfths (5/12) of the absolute quota to be determined for 1993.

101. In the absence of a consensus among the Cambodian parties as to what that quota should be, my Special Representative determined that the overall forest exploitation target for the zone controlled by the State of Cambodia should be 215,000 cubic metres for 1993. This figure represents an overall decrease of 30 per cent from the 1991 level of forest exploitation, which was 309,891 cubic metres. Within this figure, the export of sawn timber for 1993 should not exceed 160,000 cubic metres.

102. At its working session on 9 March, SNC approved the UNTAC draft action plan on the implementation of the Declaration on Mining and Export of Minerals and Gems from Cambodia. The Declaration placed a moratorium on the commercial extraction of mineral resources on land and offshore and on the export of minerals and gems from Cambodia, effective 28 February 1993.

103. The Action Plan is to be implemented by the collection and dissemination of information, legislative measures, enforcement by the local authorities under UNTAC supervision and the support of the international community, particularly the countries adjacent to Cambodia. A special appeal has been made to the Government of Thailand to request the Thai-registered companies operating in Cambodia to cease operations and remove their equipment from the country. I personally took up this matter with the Foreign Minister of Thailand during my recent visit to Bangkok. However, response to this appeal is still awaited.

J. Information/education

104. A general overview of UNTAC's activities in this area was given in the third progress report (S/25124, paras. 70-71 and 91-93), while its efforts to ensure fair access to the media are addressed in paragraphs 75-77 above.

105. While, in accordance with paragraph 8 of resolution 810 (1993), the main emphasis of UNTAC's information/education efforts during the electoral campaign is on the secrecy of the ballot (and on the production of political party campaign material for broadcasting), UNTAC is prepared to respond flexibly to

rapidly changing circumstances by adjusting its broadcast messages. These would concern, for example, the importance of the election for the future of Cambodia and the importance of voting for individual Cambodians and, in particular, the need not to be intimidated.

106. The recent establishment of radio relay stations has helped expand the audience and bring the UNTAC message to all parts of the country. This has been supplemented by the distribution of hundreds of thousands of radios donated by the Japanese Government and Japanese non-governmental organizations.

107. In addition, UNTAC information videos on various aspects of the electoral process, including roundtable discussions involving representatives of the 20 political parties contesting the election, have been shown on Phnom Penh television and distributed throughout the country. Though relatively few households outside the capital can receive Phnom Penh television directly, there is in most population centres a video parlour where villagers gather to watch videos and UNTAC provincial staff regularly give screenings of videos produced by UNTAC. Billboards to accommodate the posters of all the political parties have also been erected, as well as special banners and posters preparing voters for the election.

K. Creation and maintenance of a neutral political environment

108. A major challenge to the creation and maintenance of a neutral political environment has been posed by the various acts of violence and intimidation. At its working session on 9 March 1993, my Special Representative was obliged to inform the SNC that the election cannot be free and fair unless the basic minimum acceptable conditions are in place.

109. During the month of March about 100 persons, including many of Vietnamese descent, were killed in Cambodia. The victims included members of all four Cambodian parties. Though many acts of violence had apparent political or ethnic overtones, some killings had no identifiable motivation and took place in an environment where, after years of war, there is an oversupply of weapons and violence is only too common.

110. The deteriorating security situation has rendered difficult the investigation of politically and racially motivated violence in provinces such as Kampong Thom, Siem Reap, Banteay Meanchey and Battambang.

111. Warrants were issued by the UNTAC Special Prosecutor for the arrest of 12 people during the period under review. These include 7 CPAF officers wanted in connection with the abduction and subsequent disappearance of 4 FUNCINPEC members in Battambang, 2 SOC officials wanted in connection with the murder of a

Buddhist Liberal Democratic Party (BLDP) member in Prey Veng, and an NADK officer wanted in connection with the massacre at Chong Kneas in Siem Reap.

112. Efforts to maintain a neutral political environment have also been hampered by the surveillance conducted by the authorities of the Cambodian parties at all levels aimed at identifying political opponents and the harassment and intimidation of perceived opponents. All three existing administrative structures to which UNTAC has access have been mobilizing their resources to promote political support. Such activity by the Phnom Penh authorities, by virtue of the larger resources at their disposal, is a matter of particular concern to UNTAC. My Special Representative has repeatedly complained about this practice and stressed that it militates against the freeness and fairness of the election.

113. Early this year, a series of directives prepared by UNTAC dealing with the issue of political activities by members of existing administrative structures was signed by the three Cambodian parties complying with the Paris Agreements. The Directives prohibit the use of members of the armed forces, the police force and civil administration, respectively, for partisan purposes and permit these persons to engage in political activity only if this is conducted outside working hours and out of uniform.

114. UNTAC has devoted considerable efforts to easing the restrictions on freedom of expression and on freedom of movement in many areas of the country. Freedom of association with political parties and human rights groups, particularly at the provincial and district levels, has also traditionally been restricted. In order to dispel the climate of fear and intimidation UNTAC has pressed for an active political campaign by all the duly registered political parties with fair access to the media and the right to hold public meetings and rallies in safety.

115. Three aspects of the current wave of violence are addressed in the following paragraphs: attacks on Vietnamese-speaking persons, including those born in Cambodia of ethnic Vietnamese descent; attacks on political party members and offices; and attacks on UNTAC military and civilian personnel.

1. Attacks on Vietnamese-speaking persons

116. On 10 March 1993 a group of some 20 armed men attacked a floating village at Chong Kneas, Siem Reap Province, inhabited primarily by Cambodian-born persons of Vietnamese descent who fish on the Tonle Sap lake, killing 33 people including 12 children. A further 24 people were injured in the attack, and two of the assailants were themselves killed. UNTAC investigations concluded that the attackers were members of an NADK unit led by a Mr. Loeung Dara. UNTAC issued a warrant

for his arrest and my Special Representative wrote to Mr. Khieu Samphan, President of the Party of Democratic Kampuchea, requesting that he be surrendered to UNTAC custody. No reply has been received to that request.

117. On 24 March 1993 a group of 10-20 assailants attacked three fishing boats at Chnok Tru village, Kompong Chhnang Province killing five adults and three children. Investigations have revealed evidence of NADK involvement, but UNTAC has so far not been able to make any arrests.

118. On the night of 29 March 1993, in Phnom Penh, at least four premises frequented or owned by Vietnamese-speaking persons were attacked by unidentified persons in a coordinated manner with hand-grenades, resulting in two deaths and at least 20 injuries.

119. As a result of these attacks, several thousand members of the Vietnamese community in Cambodia, many of whom have lived there for two or three generations, began to migrate from their homes towards the Vietnamese border, many of them by boat down the Tonle Sap and the Bassac River. UNTAC naval units supplemented by armed marines closely monitored these movements on the rivers in order to ensure that the local authorities assumed their responsibility to protect the migrants. The UNTAC Civilian Police did the same on land.

120. Since the exodus began in late March, 21,659 ethnic Vietnamese persons had, as of 28 April 1993, been recorded crossing the border into Viet Nam at border checkpoints manned by UNTAC personnel. It is not known how many more may have crossed at illegal or unmanned crossing points. The movement, however, has now been considerably reduced.

121. On 5 April 1993 Mr. Vu Khoan, Vice-Minister of Foreign Affairs of Viet Nam, met with my Special Representative and conveyed to him the profound disquiet of his Government at what he described as the acts of sabotage of the Paris Agreements and the terrorist acts directed against Vietnamese-speaking persons by the Party of Democratic Kampuchea. He vigorously condemned the massacres that had taken place. The Vice-Minister urged UNTAC to take all possible measures to ensure the security of the Vietnamese population in Cambodia.

122. My Special Representative informed the Vice-Minister of UNTAC's determination to do all in its power to put an end to violence in Cambodia. However, it was made clear that the primary responsibility for the protection of civilians in the zone controlled by the Phnom Penh authorities rested with those authorities. UNTAC would do its utmost to ensure that they complied with their responsibilities, but UNTAC's own resources were insufficient to provide full protection to the Vietnamese population while at the same time carrying out their priority task of protecting the electoral process. UNTAC also explained its position on foreign forces, foreign residents and immigrants, and persons born in Cambodia of foreign ancestry, as well as its efforts to maintain the distinction between those three categories.

123. During my visit to Viet Nam on 11 and 12 April 1993, I discussed the matter with the Government and stated that UNTAC would do its utmost to ensure the protection of the ethnic Vietnamese community in Cambodia. UNHCR is also taking all necessary precautions to help Viet Nam should there be an influx of ethnic Vietnamese from Cambodia.

2. Attacks on political party members and offices

124. Since political party activity began in September 1992, party members have been subjected to various kinds of threats, intimidation and violent attacks. On the basis of complaints made by political parties as well as reports from UNTAC components, UNTAC has kept records on various forms of interference with political activity, including allegations of harassment and intimidation as well as murders and armed attacks. Verbal threats and intimidation, including such acts as tearing down posters and notice-boards, have also occurred. Verbal threats are taken seriously because experience has shown that such threats are often carried out. Many of these attacks and incidents have been attributed to members or supporters of SOC.

125. During the first part of March there was a slight downward trend in politically motivated attacks in comparison with the number of incidents recorded during the corresponding period in February. However, the latter part of March was marked by a comparative increase in the number and the violent character of such incidents.

126. Efforts to gather, classify and interpret information on attacks alleged to be politically motivated are made difficult by the second-hand or unreliable nature of many of the allegations, the inadequacy of record keeping by the local authorities and the inadequate resources available to UNTAC to investigate and follow up allegations that are made. None the less, it can be said that the level of politically motivated violence has fallen since the high point reached in December 1992, that the level for the month of April so far tends to indicate a further fall and that this decline can be attributed at least in part to efforts directly undertaken by UNTAC as well as actions taken by the local authorities at UNTAC's urging. Whether that apparent improvement is real, and whether it can be sustained during the election campaign, has yet to be seen.

3. *Attacks on UNTAC military and civilian personnel*

127. Details of the incidents that resulted in the death of UNTAC civilian and military personnel are contained in the letter of 26 April 1993 which I addressed to the President of the Security Council in response to a request made in the statement of the President on the safety and security of UNTAC staff issued on 5 April 1993 (S/25530). Since then, evidence gathered in UNTAC's investigation of the killing of an UNTAC district electoral supervisor and his interpreter on 8 April appears to rule out the involvement in this incident of any Cambodian party as such and indicates that the motive for the killings may have been connected with decisions made in the recruitment of local electoral staff. UNTAC has not yet been able to determine the precise responsibility for this act, and investigation is continuing on an urgent basis.

128. During my visit to Cambodia on 7 and 8 April, I issued an urgent appeal for an end to violence. This was reiterated by my Special Representative at the SNC meeting on 10 April 1993, as well as by the Ambassadors to SNC of countries particularly concerned with the Cambodian situation.

129. Prince Sihanouk issued a strong declaration demanding of his "armed compatriots" that they refrain from acts of violence against UNTAC. That declaration was endorsed in writing by representatives of SOC, KPNLF and FUNCINPEC, but PDK declined to endorse it.

II. Concluding observations

130. The members of the Security Council are aware of the scope of the Paris Agreements on Cambodia, and of the complexities of the peace process which have been accentuated due to the attitudes and actions of certain signatories. Consequently, it has not proved possible to implement fully all aspects of the Paris Agreements in accordance with the implementation plan which I submitted to the Security Council in February 1992 (S/23613). The non-cooperation of the Party of Democratic Kampuchea has persisted and all efforts by the Security Council, by UNTAC and by others to persuade it to assume the responsibilities it undertook in signing the Agreements have been unavailing. The PDK's refusal to open its zones to UNTAC and to canton and disarm its troops as it had committed itself to do led to the suspension of the demobilization of the armed forces of the other three factions. SOC and CPAF personnel have also taken part in politically motivated attacks against opposition parties in order to intimidate them. Moreover, the massacres of Vietnamese-speaking persons and deliberate attacks on UNTAC members reflect the growing hostility of PDK to the peace process and to the elections. Though cease-fire violations are generally on a small scale and though UNTAC has achieved some successes in reducing political violence, the election will clearly not be taking place in an environment as disarmed and politically neutral as was envisaged in the Paris Agreements and in the implementation plan.

131. These conditions have naturally given rise to serious concerns as to whether or not the election could or should proceed, and to what extent its results could be said to reflect the free expression of the will of the Cambodian people. If it is to go forward, as I believe it must, consideration has to be given to how it can be conducted most democratically and with the least possible risk to Cambodian and international electoral staff.

132. The Cambodian people as a whole have shown that they desire an election. Nearly 5 million Cambodians, or about 96 per cent of the eligible population, registered to vote in the registration exercise UNTAC conducted between October 1992 and January 1993. Twenty political parties completed the formalities for registration to compete in the election and in so doing have undertaken to accept the results. This is strong evidence of commitment to the electoral process. More convincing still is the evidence, as noted above, that tens of thousands of Cambodians throughout the country are engaging peacefully in public meetings and political rallies without violence or clashes. The three Cambodian parties cooperating with UNTAC, too, have pledged themselves to accept the election results.

133. It is clear, therefore, that the United Nations is called upon to do its utmost to proceed with the election. To do otherwise would be to neglect a duty to the Cambodian people that has been entrusted to the United Nations by the international community through the Paris Agreements and the Security Council. Not to proceed would mean ceding to unacceptable threats and giving the right of veto over the peace process to an armed group that has rejected its commitment under the Paris Agreements.

134. It is equally clear, however, that the election will not be proceeding in the way originally envisaged. The events since March make it prudent to assume that further violence is likely against individual Cambodians, against political parties and against UNTAC personnel. The danger is that such attacks will have an impact on the voter turnout. UNTAC has been tightening security measures in the provinces most affected. However, such measures could also lower the turnout, yet cannot assure the complete safety of voters or of local and international staff if armed and violent individuals are determined to hinder the election.

135. As noted in paragraph 2 above, resolution

810 (1993) of the Council requests the Secretary-General to report in the context of the fourth progress report on any further measures that may be necessary and appropriate to ensure the realization of the fundamental objectives of the Paris Agreements.

136. In my report of 15 November 1992 (S/24800, para. 31), I had proposed that, given the altered conditions for UNTAC's operation, the level of deployment of its Military Component, which under the original implementation plan was to have been reduced after the completion of the cantonment and demobilization process, should be maintained until the election. Further, in my report of 13 February 1993 (S/25289, para. 44), I had indicated my intention, in due course, to present appropriate recommendations to the Security Council on the level of deployment of UNTAC's Military and Civilian Police Components that would be needed for the remainder of the transitional period. As the members of the Security Council are aware, that level would depend to a significant extent on the outcome of the election and the conditions that would prevail after the election, and it would not be possible to make an adequate assessment at this time. It would therefore be my intention to submit to the Security Council after the election a further report on the activities of UNTAC including my assessment and recommendation on this subject. Pending that report, I again propose that UNTAC's Military and Civilian Police Components be maintained at the present level.

137. It has become quite evident that some of the Cambodian parties that signed the Paris Agreements have been less than consistent in applying those Agreements and have not given UNTAC the cooperation required under them. I therefore think it worth restating that the primary responsibility for implementing the Agreements rests squarely on the Cambodian parties themselves. This includes the obligation of each of the parties to maintain security in the zones it controls and to contribute to the creation and maintenance of a neutral political environment. The State of Cambodia must prevent or punish politically motivated crimes committed in its zone and desist from using the State apparatus for party political ends. The Party of Democratic Kampuchea risks international and internal isolation if it is seen to have attempted to disrupt the Cambodian elections. That Party must also be held responsible for the attacks it has carried out against Cambodians, including those of Vietnamese ancestry, and against UNTAC personnel, as well as for any future attacks it may carry out. The Parties of FUNCINPEC and KPNLF must persist in their determination to campaign peacefully without giving in to intimidation.

138. If the holding of a free and fair election in Cambodia is a test for the United Nations, it is also a test for Cambodians themselves. Neither peace nor elections nor national reconciliation can be imposed by force, nor indeed is UNTAC mandated or equipped to use force. As I have remarked in an earlier report, Cambodian parties cannot expect the international community to succeed where they themselves fail.

139. Under the circumstances, the United Nations faces a difficult decision. One alternative is to proceed with the best possible election under imperfect conditions, in the knowledge that that is what the majority of Cambodians desire and in the hope that the authentic voice of Cambodia will be heard and obeyed. The other choice would be to declare that the basic acceptable conditions for free and fair elections do not exist in Cambodia because of the climate of violence and hostility, and because violence may worsen further after the elections, whatever the results.

140. Taking all these circumstances into consideration, there is no doubt in my mind that UNTAC must continue to carry out its mandate as well as it can. It must do so with all caution and prudence and with the greatest possible concern for the safety of its own staff and the well-being of Cambodians. It may well be, in the light of the sobering experience of the last 13 months, that the expectations originally entertained for ensuring that the election is free and fair and for the success of national reconciliation were overly optimistic. Nevertheless, given Cambodia's recent tragic history, it would probably be neither realistic nor fair to hold it to prevailing standards in stable democratic countries. Conditions for an election in Cambodia have never been perfect and may not be so for a long time, any more than they are in many other countries. That is no reason to hold back an election which, after all, is not the end of the process of Cambodia's renewal but the beginning.

141. In the last analysis, it is on the shoulders of the Cambodian people and the Cambodian parties, which are members of the Supreme National Council and signatories of the Paris Agreements, as well as the political parties taking part in the election, that responsibility for Cambodia's future rests. The situation in Cambodia remains uncertain and the way ahead for the peace process and for UNTAC will not be smooth. Nevertheless, UNTAC will continue to do its utmost to assist the Cambodian people in carrying out their obligations under the Paris Agreements and achieving a future of peace, stability and self-determination.

Document 80

Letter dated 7 May 1993 from Mr. Hun Sen, member of the Supreme National Council, to the Special Representative of the Secretary-General for Cambodia, concerning the electoral process

Not issued as a United Nations document

Excellency,

I have the honour to refer to the two Cambodian People's Party letters N. 20 CPP/C/UN/93 dated 17 April 1993 and N. 23 CPP/C/UN/93 dated 3 May 1993 respectively on the subject of the Management System of Ballot Boxes and the poll irregularities sent to H.E. Mr. Reginald Austin, and to the statements of the CPP representatives made at the two last meetings between UNTAC Electoral Component and the political parties consecutively held pursuant to Article 4 (12), the Electoral Law Annex 1—Code of Conduct, on 3 and 6 May 1993 at UNTAC Headquarters and Human Rights Component Head Office.

Hereby, I kindly request you to consider the following:

First: On the matter of guarding the ballot boxes at the end of each polling and counting day, I propose that wherever the ballot boxes are to be stored be it polling stations or UNTAC premises (civilian or military), *my Party agent(s) must be allowed to keep permanently an eye on them (ballot boxes).*

Second: With regard to the transportation of ballot boxes either by land, water or air, I propose that *at least one of my Party agents be permitted to accompany them.*

Third: Since we have solid information on the *election rigging* as proved by the document we enclosed with our above-said letter of 3 May 1993, I object to the initiative and proposal of the representative of the FUNCINPEC Party concerning the use of curtain to surround the booth (voting compartment) to prevent what he said "the omnipresent Organisation" from seeing the prospective voters place their tick on the ballot paper. In fact, the curtain enclosure is not part of the original UNTAC electoral administration plan, because from the technical point of view, the booth designed by UNTAC and its placement against the wall or not is more than enough to ensure that the voters could mark their tick without anyone sight. On the contrary, the proposal to put the curtain coincides with the contents of the FUNCINPEC document we just discovered. Therefore, if such a proposal is accepted, it will greatly facilitate that *Party's ballot switching trick.*

Excellency,

While reassuring you that the Cambodian People's Party has put every confidence in UNTAC in terms of conducting and organizing the upcoming elections, I also would like to stress that I could not accept in case if my Party agents are only allowed to monitor the ballot boxes during the polling and counting hours while at the end of each operational day, they don't have any idea about the whereabouts of the ballot boxes.

If we want an election which is really fair and free from all kinds of eventual tricks, UNTAC must accept my two proposals, the aim of which is only to provide an essential complementary element of strengthening the free and fair character of the whole electoral process in Cambodia.

Finally, I would like to draw your attention to the fact that we must not open more room for the contesting political parties so that they could use it as additional excuses to reject the election results.

As the polling days draw nearer, I look forward to hearing from you soon.

Please accept, Excellency, the assurances of my highest consideration.

HUN SEN
Vice President of the
Cambodian People's Party

Document 81

Report of the Secretary-General in pursuance of paragraph 6
of Security Council resolution 810 (1993) on preparations for
the election for the constituent assembly in Cambodia

S/25784, 15 May 1993

1. The Security Council, by paragraph 6 of its resolution 810 (1993) of 8 March 1993, called on the United Nations Transitional Authority in Cambodia (UNTAC) to continue to make every effort to create and maintain a neutral political environment conducive to the holding of free and fair elections. It also requested me to inform the Council by 15 May 1993 of the conditions and preparations for the election. The present report is submitted in response to that request.

2. I have previously reported to the Security Council on the activities of UNTAC in a series of progress reports and special reports, most recently in the fourth progress report (S/25719) of 3 May 1993. The present report should be read in conjunction with those reports.

3. As the election to be held from 23 to 28 May approaches, the overwhelming majority of the voters in Cambodia, as well as political parties and factions, have made manifest their commitment to the election as the culmination of the peace process. As reported earlier, more than 4.7 million Cambodians, or some 96 per cent of the estimated voters, have registered to vote. At a meeting called on 6 May in Beijing by His Royal Highness Prince Norodom Sihanouk, three of the four factions—Front uni national pour un Cambodge indépendant, neutre, pacifique et coopératif (FUNCINPEC), Khmer People's National Liberation Front (KPNLF) and the Party of the State of Cambodia(SOC)—reaffirmed their support for the election, a commitment that was reiterated by them at a working session of the Supreme National Council (SNC) on 10 May. At the latter meeting, Mr. Son Sann, the leader of KPNLF/Buddhist Liberal Democratic Party (BLDP— a political party of KPNLF) proposed the suspension of the electoral process and postponement of the election, but the SNC did not pursue the proposal and BLDP has continued to campaign.

4. Since the official start of the electoral campaign on 7 April, the 20 political parties registered to contest the election have campaigned actively and vigorously. Scores of political meetings and rallies have been held daily and peacefully with the participation of tens of thousands of people in virtually all parts of Cambodia. Although FUNCINPEC and the BLDP have complained that SOC has sought to prevent their supporters from attending their meetings, in UNTAC's view, neither such attempts nor political attacks and intimidation to which they have been subjected have prevented these parties from conducting an active campaign. UNTAC itself has also organized multi-party meetings.

5. Technical preparations for the election have been virtually completed. Some 900 International Polling Station Officers recruited from 44 countries and the Inter-Parliamentary Union have arrived to take part in a three-day training course being held from 13 to 15 May in Thailand. They will be joined by 130 from the United Nations Secretariat as well as about 370 detailed from within UNTAC and will arrive at their duty stations in Cambodia by 18 May. Their duties, and the polling process in general, are described in section D of my fourth progress report.

6. At the meeting of the Supreme National Council held on 21 April 1993, my Special Representative expressed the view that the freeness and fairness of the election would be judged in accordance with three main criteria: the extent to which the campaign and voting are marred by violence, intimidation and harassment; the extent to which SOC, which controls the largest zones and has the most extensive administrative structure, enjoys unfair advantages, whether by using its administrative apparatus for its own political ends or by denying other political parties access to the public media; and the technical conduct of the poll. While these are addressed in the present report, the final assessment will be made after the election.

7. The measures taken by UNTAC to control the existing administrative structures have been described in detail in my previous reports. UNTAC's more recent efforts to promulgate a code of conduct for military and police personnel and civil servants and to prevent the Cambodian People's Party (CPP) from using the resources and staff of the administrative apparatus for electoral purposes have also been described. UNTAC has vigorously raised the issue of the separation of party and State several times both in public and in private meetings with the leading figures of the Phnom Penh authorities. My Special Representative recently announced that an officer of the Cambodian People's Armed Force (CPAF) and a district chief of the CPP had been removed from the register of voters for improper conduct in violation of the Electoral Law.

8. UNTAC has taken particular issue with the Phnom Penh authorities over the access of other political parties to the media and their right to freedom of movement. As a result of strong intervention by UNTAC, FUNCINPEC was able to obtain the release from SOC of the television broadcasting equipment it had imported for campaign purposes. All political parties have had access to UNTAC information media, and three parties—FUNCINPEC, BLDP and the Neutral Democratic Party of Cambodia—have requested and been granted assistance from UNTAC with air transport facilities for campaign purposes.

9. Radio UNTAC now broadcasts 15 hours a day. This has enabled it to intensify a message central to UNTAC's electoral education campaign, namely, that all votes are secret. The leaders of all three factions participating in the election have agreed to my Special Representative's proposal to appear with him on television to reassure voters about the secrecy of the ballot. UNTAC is satisfied that its electoral procedures fully protect the secrecy of the ballot, and that this message has been conveyed to Cambodian voters.

10. It is evident that incidents of violence can have a disruptive effect on even a carefully prepared election especially through their destabilizing psychological effects. Following the killing of a United Nations Volunteer serving as a District Electoral Supervisor and his interpreter in Kompong Thom Province on 8 April, some 60 United Nations Volunteers have withdrawn from their posts. Since document S/25669, in which I reported on a number of incidents of attacks against UNTAC personnel, and my fourth progress report (S/25719) were issued, the security situation in Cambodia has been marked by further acts of violence. While it is not possible to classify all acts of violence or to determine who was responsible, there are essentially four categories of violence: (a) killings of Cambodians, including those of Vietnamese ancestry, by the forces of PDK, the National Army of Democratic Kampuchea (NADK), in an effort both to disrupt the election and, evidently, to pressure those of Vietnamese ancestry to leave Cambodia; (b) attacks and harassment by SOC elements aimed at intimidating other political parties, primarily FUNCINPEC; (c) attacks on UNTAC personnel; and (d) random violence associated with banditry and lawlessness.

11. Since the beginning of April, despite initial indications of a relative decline in violence during that month, UNTAC investigations have confirmed that 110 Cambodians, including those of Vietnamese descent, have died as victims of violence and a further 179 have been injured. A large number of these casualties have resulted from attacks on civilians and on SOC by NADK and by unidentified groups, and attacks on other political parties by SOC and unidentified groups. UNTAC will publish shortly the results of all its investigations into serious acts of violence, harassment and intimidation since 1 March 1993.

12. I regret to report that further attacks against UNTAC personnel have occurred since the issuance of the fourth progress report on UNTAC. On 4 May 1993, an UNTAC convoy was ambushed by an unidentified armed group in Banteay Meancheay Province. In the evening of the same day, NADK elements attacked the Chinese Engineering Company and the Polish Logistics Company in Kompong Thom Province with rockets and small arms fire. In the early hours of 7 May 1993 a group of unidentified armed men attacked the UNTAC office in Thpong district in Kompong Speu Province with mortars, rockets and small arms fire. On 8 May 1993, a Pakistani Company came under fire at Choam Khsan in Preah Vihear Province by NADK elements. On 11 May, two unidentified men threw two hand grenades towards a car driven by a Civilian Police officer in Sisophon.

13. In these incidents, two UNTAC personnel died and 17 others were wounded, several of them seriously. Since the inception of UNTAC, 13 UNTAC civilian and military personnel have lost their lives and 52 have been wounded as a result of hostile action; 39 have died from other causes.

14. In the light of PDK's repeatedly expressed intention to oppose the election, including by violent means, as well as in response to the incidents described above, UNTAC has further refined and elaborated its security plans. Thus, no polling will be conducted in the areas controlled by PDK, to which UNTAC has not been permitted access, as well as some remote areas in which NADK have been operating. These areas, mainly located in Siem Reap and Kompong Thom provinces, are thinly populated. Other parts of the country have been designated as high-, medium- and low-risk zones, with low-risk zones predominating in the heavily populated south and east of the country, including the capital, Phnom Penh. The status of every district in the country is being reviewed on a daily basis by sector commanders of the Military Component, who have overall responsibility for all UNTAC personnel in the sector, and electoral officials on the basis of the latest security information; this daily review will continue during the election itself.

15. Different levels of security measures have been established for each level of risk involving fixed guards, mobile patrols and general area security in accordance with the security arrangements described in the fourth progress report (S/25719, para. 37). In high-risk zones, armed UNTAC military personnel will be stationed at and around polling stations. Physical fortifications have

been strengthened and staff will be issued protective gear. Quick Reaction Forces and medical support units have also been identified for the high-risk sites.

16. In response to the heightened threat in Kompong Thom Province, UNTAC civilian personnel have been withdrawn from some locations and the number of polling sites has been reduced from 102 to 51. Civilian staff, including Civilian Police monitors, can now seek direct protection from the Indonesian Battalion of the Military Component in the towns of Kompong Thom, Stung and Baray. In Siem Reap Province, personnel of all components can now be accommodated with military units every evening. Similar arrangements can be made in other provinces if necessary.

17. The first, precautionary stage of the five-stage Mission Security Plan, has now been declared for the entire country. Movement in the provinces is now subject to authorization and monitoring by sector commanders of the UNTAC Military Component and, where possible, takes place in convoys.

18. In order to further strengthen security during the election, urgent consultations have been held in recent days with a number of Governments on the provision of additional equipment for UNTAC. In this connection, I would like to express my appreciation to the Governments of Australia, Japan, Malaysia, Namibia and the United States of America for the additional material assistance and voluntary financial contributions they have provided. Discussions are continuing with a number of other Governments. Meanwhile, essential items for enhanced security have been shipped to the mission.

19. While evidently there can be no guarantee of total safety, all possible steps have been taken to ensure the maximum security that are consistent with UNTAC's character as a peace-keeping operation and with the need to attract the highest possible voter turnout. None the less, it bears repeating that it is on the Cambodian parties that the primary responsibility rests for the maintenance of security in the zones they control. In this connection, the three Cambodian factions supporting the election have recently requested that UNTAC return to them the weapons they deposited with it in implementation of the second phase of the cease-fire in accordance with the Paris Agreements. In view of its implications, especially regarding the security situation, I am giving this request urgent and close consideration.

20. It is now evident that, despite the demonstrated interest of the Cambodian people to determine their future at the polls, and the meticulous preparations by UNTAC for the election, the conditions for the election are not those anticipated in the Paris Agreements. This results from the unfortunate attitude of PDK, which, having progressively withdrawn from the peace process starting with the military provisions, has now moved from boycotting the election to attempts to actively disrupt it through violence. Such actions constitute a clear breach of solemn commitments. I am certain that the members of the Security Council share my determination not to allow these actions to deny Cambodians this opportunity, carefully nurtured by the international community, to secure peace through the democratic process.

21. It is regrettable that SOC also has contributed, although to a lesser extent, towards the climate of violence by resorting to intimidation of other political parties. Further, it has not responded satisfactorily to UNTAC's efforts to prevent the use of its administrative structure for political purposes.

22. It therefore must be borne in mind that the approaching election in Cambodia is likely to be affected by continuing violence, although UNTAC will continue to do its utmost in providing security measures. Unfortunately, this is a feature in many other countries even when elections are held in far more favourable conditions, rather than in the wake of a prolonged and bitter conflict that has left a legacy of tensions and deep distrust as is the case in Cambodia. As noted in paragraph 140 of my fourth progress report, it would be unrealistic to hold Cambodia to standards valid in countries that enjoy stability or established democratic traditions. UNTAC, therefore, will be conducting the most impartial election that is possible in conditions that are not susceptible to its full control. It would be ingenuous to expect that a postponement would bring improved conditions—the contrary is more probable.

23. It is appropriate to recall that H.R.H. Prince Norodom Sihanouk, who has guided his country through far more difficult times, has supported the election, and recently has encouraged his compatriots to participate in this singular opportunity. This lends further credibility to the electoral process. I remain convinced that he has a crucial role to play at this critical juncture in fostering national reconciliation and promoting stability in the post-election period.

24. It is clear to me that it is the will and intent of the Security Council as well as of the vast majority of the Cambodian people that the election be held as scheduled. With this and all the preceding considerations in view, I have directed that this should be done.

Document 82

Letter dated 18 May 1993 from Singapore transmitting statement by the ASEAN Foreign Ministers on the elections in Cambodia

S/25794, 18 May 1993

On behalf of the Permanent Representatives to the United Nations of the States Members of the Association of Southeast Asian Nations (ASEAN), I have the honour to transmit to you herewith the text of a statement issued by the Foreign Ministers of ASEAN on the elections in Cambodia.

I should be grateful if you could arrange to have the statement circulated as a document of the Security Council.

(*Signed*) CHEW Tai Soo

Annex
Statement by ASEAN Foreign Ministers on the elections in Cambodia

1. We, the Foreign Ministers of the Association of Southeast Asian Nations (ASEAN), note with deep concern the attempts to disrupt the forthcoming elections in Cambodia.

2. We hold firmly that the elections should proceed as scheduled under the Paris Agreements.

3. We call on all the Cambodian parties to live up to the spirit of national reconciliation for the sake of Cambodia's sovereignty, independence, territorial integrity and inviolability, neutrality and national unity.

We again urge them to comply fully with all their obligations under the Paris Agreements. We regret that the Party of Democratic Kampuchea (Khmer Rouge) has chosen not to participate in the forthcoming elections.

4. We also call on all Cambodian parties to respect the result of the forthcoming elections as declared by the United Nations. We are ready to support fully the Constituent Assembly, the drafting of a Constitution and the formation of a new government, resulting from the elections in Cambodia.

5. We reiterate our full support for His Royal Highness Samdech Norodom Sihanouk, Head of State and President of the Supreme National Council of Cambodia, and for his pivotal role in achieving peace and national reconciliation in the period prior to, during and after the elections.

6. We deplore the acts of violence against the personnel of UNTAC. We call for the further strengthening of security measures for all UNTAC personnel including the International Polling Station Officers, electoral officials and United Nations volunteers. We further reaffirm our support for UNTAC and emphasize the need for all Member States of the United Nations contributing personnel to UNTAC to maintain their personnel in Cambodia as planned.

Document 83

Security Council resolution on the election for the constituent assembly in Cambodia

S/RES/826 (1993), 20 May 1993

The Security Council,

Reaffirming its resolutions 668 (1990) of 20 September 1990, 745 (1992) of 28 February 1992, 810 (1993) of 8 March 1993 and other relevant resolutions,

Taking note of the reports of the Secretary-General of 3 May 1993 and 15 May 1993,

Expressing its strong support for the almost five million Cambodians who, in spite of violence and intimidation, have registered to vote in the election of a constituent assembly, and have broadly and actively participated in the electoral campaign,

Recognizing the great importance of His Royal Highness Prince Norodom Sihanouk, Chairman of the Supreme National Council, continuing his invaluable efforts in Cambodia to achieve national reconciliation and restore peace,

1. *Approves* the reports of the Secretary-General of 3 May 1993 1/ and 15 May 1993; 2/

2. *Expresses its satisfaction* with the arrangements made by the United Nations for the conduct of the election for the constituent assembly in Cambodia described in the report of the Secretary-General of 15 May 1993;

3. *Demands* that all the parties abide by the agreements on a comprehensive political settlement to the Cambodia conflict signed in Paris on 23 October 1991 3/ and give the United Nations Transitional Authority in Cambodia the full cooperation required under them;

4. *Commends* those participating in the election campaign in accordance with the Paris agreements despite the violence and intimidation in order that the Cambodian people may have an opportunity to choose freely their own government;

5. *Deplores* all acts of non-cooperation with the Paris agreements and condemns all acts of violence committed on political and ethnic grounds, intimidation and attacks on Authority personnel;

6. *Expresses its full support* for the measures taken by the Authority to protect the safety of its personnel and underlines the need for the Authority to continue its efforts in this regard;

7. *Demands* that all parties take all actions necessary to safeguard the lives and the security of Authority personnel throughout Cambodia, and desist from all threats or intimidation against Authority personnel and from any interference with them in the performance of their mandate;

8. *Expresses its appreciation* for the positive efforts and the achievements of the Authority in preparation for the elections, in respect both of the registration of candidates and parties and of the holding of the electoral campaign, albeit under difficult conditions;

9. *Fully supports* the decision of the Secretary-General that the election be held as scheduled in accordance with the decision of the Supreme National Council endorsed by the Security Council in its resolution 810 (1993);

10. *Calls on* the Authority to continue to work in accordance with resolution 810 (1993) to ensure a neutral political environment conducive to the holding of free and fair elections;

11. *Reaffirms* its determination to endorse the results of the election for the constituent assembly provided that the United Nations certifies it free and fair;

12. *Reminds* all the Cambodian parties of their obligation under the Paris agreements fully to comply with the results of the election;

13. *Warns* that the Council will respond appropriately should any of the parties fail to honour its obligations;

14. *Reaffirms* its readiness to support fully the constituent assembly and the process of drawing up a constitution and establishing a new government for all Cambodia and to support subsequent efforts to promote national reconciliation and peace-building;

15. *Recognizes* that the Cambodians themselves bear primary responsibility for the implementation of the Paris agreements and for the political future and well-being of their own country, and reaffirms that all Cambodian parties are expected to honour their obligations under the Paris agreements and participate constructively and peacefully in the political process after the election;

16. *Requests* the Secretary-General to report promptly to the Council on the holding and results of the election, including on the conduct of the parties as regards their obligations under the Paris agreements and, if necessary, to recommend any initiative and/or measures conducive to ensuring their full respect by all parties;

17. *Decides* to remain actively seized of the matter.

1/ S/25719 [Document 79]

2/ S/25784 [Document 81]

3/ S/23177 [Document 19]

Document 84

Statement by the President of the Security Council concerning the act of violence against UNTAC on 21 May 1993

S/25822, 22 May 1993

The Security Council strongly condemns the shelling on 21 May 1993 of the United Nations Transitional Authority in Cambodia (UNTAC), during which the Chinese engineering detachment suffered two deaths and seven wounded. It expresses its condolences to the Chinese Government and to the families of the victims; it pays tribute to the latter for their courage and dedication.

The Council takes note of the preliminary report by

the Secretariat indicating that the shelling was carried out by the National Army of Democratic Kampuchea. It requests the Secretary-General to investigate further and to report urgently to the Council.

The Council expresses its strong support for UNTAC in carrying out its mandate within the framework of the Paris agreements. It strongly condemns all attacks against UNTAC and demands that those responsible cease forthwith all hostile acts against UNTAC and take immediate measures to safeguard the lives and the security of UNTAC personnel.

The Council recalls the warning contained in its resolution 826 (1993) of 20 May 1993 that it would respond appropriately should any of the parties fail to honour its obligations. It further warns that it will not countenance the use of violence to interfere with or overturn the democratic process in Cambodia and will take further appropriate measures against any of the parties failing to honour its obligations.

The Council also expresses its determination that the election for the constituent assembly should be held on the dates decided by the Supreme National Council and endorsed by the Security Council in its resolution 810 (1993) of 8 March 1993 and reaffirms its commitment to resolution 826 (1993). The Council calls upon the Cambodian people fully to exercise their right to vote in the forthcoming elections. In this respect, the Council stresses the importance of ensuring the cessation of acts of violence and of all threats and intimidation, as well as of ensuring a neutral political environment in Cambodia.

Document 85

Letter dated 28 May 1993 from the Secretary-General to Prince Norodom Sihanouk on the conduct of the election in Cambodia

Not issued as a United Nations document; original in French

On this auspicious day, when the Khmer people are celebrating the successful outcome of the elections just held in Cambodia, I wish to express to you my profound gratitude for your precious assistance to the United Nations and to UNTAC both before and during the polling.

I am convinced that your return to Phnom Penh just before the elections helped considerably to strengthen the confidence of Cambodians in the ability of UNTAC to ensure that polling would take place smoothly, in an atmosphere of freedom and relative calm.

Through you, I wish to congratulate the Khmer people for having exercised their right to vote on such a large scale. This exceptional participation rate confounded—as nothing else could—defeatists and other prophets of doom who were predicting that the Cambodians would not have the courage to vote, solely because one of the Cambodian parties to the Paris Agreements was calling upon them to boycott the elections.

Encouraged by your dedication and your self-sacrifice, the Cambodian people have fully justified the confidence that UNTAC has always had in them.

However, the smooth conduct of these democratic elections must not make us forget the considerable amount of work that remains to be done over the coming weeks.

In that connection, in view of the assurances you gave me when I visited Phnom Penh on 7 and 8 April 1993, I am pleased to know that my Special Representative, Mr. Yasushi Akashi, and UNTAC will be able to count on generous support from you throughout the forthcoming phase of the political process.

For my part, I can assure you that we shall work in close cooperation with you and with the members elected to the Constituent Assembly.

I wish to express to you once again my profound gratitude for your invaluable support.

Accept, Your Royal Highness, the assurances of my highest consideration.

(Signed) Boutros BOUTROS-GHALI

Document 86

*Letter dated 28 May 1993 from the Secretary-General to the
President of the Security Council reporting further on the shelling
in Kompong Cham Province, Cambodia, 21 May 1993*

S/25871, 1 June 1993

In the statement issued by the President of the Security Council on 22 May 1993 relating to the activities of the United Nations Transitional Authority in Cambodia (UNTAC) (S/25822), the Council took note of the preliminary report by the Secretariat on the shelling that had taken place on 21 May 1993 in Kompong Cham Province and requested me to investigate the incident further and to report urgently to the Council.

The information contained in this letter is submitted in response to that request and is based on reports of investigations undertaken by UNTAC including by its Strategic Investigation Team.

On 21 May 1993 at about 11.30 p.m. local time, approximately 15-20 members of the National Army of Democratic Kampuchea (NADK), the forces of the Party of Democratic Kampuchea (PDK), attacked a police position of the party of the State of Cambodia (SOC) which is located directly south and about 150 metres from the position of a Chinese Engineer Company in Skon village in Kompong Cham Province. Small arms and rockets were used in the attack. SOC police retaliated immediately using small arms, mortars and rockets.

Three rockets were fired by NADK from approximately 100 to 150 metres further south of the SOC position. The first of these, probably a B40.5 rocket, overshot the SOC position and went through an open window of one of the barracks of the Chinese company, which was located in the line of fire. One Chinese soldier was killed instantly. Another suffered serious injuries and died about two and a half hours later. Seven other soldiers were injured. All of the injured soldiers were evacuated to Phnom Penh. A sentry of the Chinese company observed the other two rockets overshoot both the SOC position and the Chinese camp and fall into a pond at the rear of the barracks. The exchanges of fire between NADK and SOC police lasted approximately 45 minutes before NADK withdrew to the south.

Following investigations by the Strategic Investigation Team, UNTAC has confirmed its initial finding that it is unlikely that the Chinese company was the intended target of the attack; one section of the Chinese company is located east of the SOC police position and closer to the source of fire but this section was not hit. UNTAC's assessment is that a rocket aimed at the SOC police position hit the Chinese camp due to inaccuracy of fire and the location of the camp which is in the same line of fire as the SOC position.

(Signed) Boutros BOUTROS-GHALI

Document 87

*Letter dated 31 May 1993 from Prince Norodom Sihanouk to
the Secretary-General concerning the election in Cambodia
and paying tribute to UNTAC*

Not issued as a United Nations document; original in French

I wish to express to you my sincere and profound gratitude for your eloquent letter of 28 May 1993.

My satisfaction with respect to the scale of the participation of the Khmer people in the electoral process is equalled only by your own.

This very gratifying outcome is attributable to the constant attention that you have given to the difficult and very complex Cambodian problem.

This result represents the consecration of the courageous, painstaking and ultimately effective action taken by all the United Nations officials and Members of the United Nations that have been playing a very active role on the ground: your Special Representative, Mr. Yasushi Akashi, his distinguished UNTAC colleagues, the brave military and police contingents and all the international observers.

I wish to pay a generous tribute to them.

ou may be assured of my unswerving support throughout the forthcoming phase of the political process.

Accept, Sir, the assurances of my highest consideration.

(*Signed*) NORODOM SIHANOUK

Document 88

Letter dated 2 June 1993 from the Secretary-General transmitting statement made by the Special Representative of the Secretary-General for Cambodia at Supreme National Council meeting on 29 May 1993; endorses the statement of the Special Representative that the conduct of the election was free and fair.

S/25879, 2 June 1993

I have the honour to bring to your attention the statement made by my Special Representative for Cambodia at a meeting of the Supreme National Council of Cambodia on 29 May 1993 after the conclusion of the polling period in the election in Cambodia from 23 to 28 May 1993. In this statement, which I endorse fully, my Special Representative declared that the conduct of the election had been free and fair.

After the completion of the counting of votes, which is now proceeding, a determination will be made, as provided under the Paris Agreements, on the freeness and fairness of the entire election process.

(*Signed*) Boutros BOUTROS-GHALI

Annex
Statement by the Special Representative of the Secretary-General for Cambodia at the Supreme National Council of Cambodia

29 May 1993

Your Royal Highness, distinguished members of the Supreme National Council, Your Excellencies, ladies and gentlemen,

Last night the six-day polling period of the Cambodian elections ended. As I speak, the counting of the ordinary ballots and the verification and counting of the tendered ballots is proceeding. The ordinary ballots are being counted in provincial centres and in Phnom Penh. The tendered ballots are being verified and counted in Phnom Penh only. We will be announcing figures twice a day in each Province starting later today, and I would expect that we can complete the count of ordinary ballots nationwide by early next week.

The verification and counting of the tendered ballots will take a little longer. However, since tendered ballots accounted for only about 7 per cent of the total, and since tendered ballots were cast in most cases because voters

were voting outside the Province in which they had registered rather than because they had lost their cards, verification can be completed in a relatively short time. The total vote count can probably therefore be completed and announced within the week.

At our last meeting, which took place on 20 May, after the end of the electoral campaign but before the beginning of the polling, I announced that acceptable conditions existed for the holding of the election, on the basis of the conduct of the campaign and the peaceful holding of public meetings and rallies by hundreds of thousands of Cambodians.

The polling began on schedule on Sunday, 23 May. It proceeded without serious incident until Friday, 28 May. For the first three days fixed polling stations operated in tandem with smaller mobile teams, and for the last three days mobile teams only were in operation.

The election took place in every district of every Province of Cambodia, except for two districts in Siem Reap Province. According to the latest figures, a total of 4,242,454 registered voters, representing some 89.04 per cent of the electorate exercised their right to cast their ballots. In our view, they did so without fear in an atmosphere of calm that was almost completely free of violence and intimidation. There was no significant disruption of the polling.

Some technical difficulties arose. These included the rupture of several plastic seals and some padlock seals in transit owing to the very rough condition of the roads and complaints about the indelible ink and the use of pencils in some Provinces. These difficulties were immediately dealt with in close consultation with the party agents, who exercised their right to observe the polling in a responsible and vigilant manner. The process was observed in its entirety by international observers, including a multinational group from the Inter-Parliamentary Union, and by the local and international media.

In conclusion, on behalf of the Secretary-General and of the United Nations, I have no hesitation in declaring that the conduct of the elections was free and fair. I wish to pay the warmest possible tribute to the Cambodian people who, through their courage, patience, good humour and commitment to peace and democracy, delivered a stinging rebuke to the men of violence and to those who tried to prevent them from exercising their inalienable rights. I also wish to express my deep gratitude to His Royal Highness Prince Norodom Sihanouk, Head of State and President of the SNC, for his precious support for the elections, as evidenced by his return to his country on the eve of polling.

Whichever party gets the largest share of the votes, the outright winners in this election are clearly the people of Cambodia. I salute them, and I wish, through His Royal Highness Prince Norodom Sihanouk and the other distinguished members of the SNC, to thank them wholeheartedly for placing their confidence in the impartiality of UNTAC. I shall never forget the spontaneity and enthusiasm of ordinary Cambodians which I was able to observe everywhere I went during the polling period. Let me read a passage from a report by an UNTAC officer from Kompong Cham Province describing the turnout as "overwhelming": "People want to vote. The general spirit is festive. People walked long distances in the rain on the first day. People coming out of polling stations are happy, even jubilant. People are laughing and joking outside of sites. Crowds packed into the back of large trucks are singing and dancing. Crowds of children and adults line the roadways to watch the ballot box convoys on their trips in the evenings, waving and smiling."

This outpouring of popular will should reinforce the commitment the parties have already made to respect the results of the election. The United Nations Security Council has reminded all the Cambodian Parties of their obligations under the Paris Agreements to comply fully with the results of the election. The determination of the election as free and fair does place a strict obligation on all participants to abide by the people's choice, whatever it may be.

Immediately following the completion of the count I will announce the determination of the United Nations as to whether or not the count itself was conducted in a free and fair manner. The list of members of the Constituent Assembly will then be drawn up on the basis of those certified results and publicly announced. The date and venue of the first meeting of the Assembly will then be fixed.

UNTAC stands ready to assist the honourable members of the Constituent Assembly in every appropriate manner, including helping to set up its secretariat. A draft set of rules of procedure has already been drawn up for its consideration. I am in close consultation with His Royal Highness Prince Norodom Sihanouk, President of the SNC, as to the ways and means of coping effectively with the post-electoral situation, which will no doubt be complex. I wish to propose that the modalities of the Assembly's functioning and its relationship with UNTAC, with the SNC and with the existing administrative authorities, be discussed at the next meeting of the SNC on 5 June 1993.

I would like to conclude my statement by quoting from a message I have received from Dr. Boutros Boutros-Ghali, Secretary-General of the United Nations. "The successful holding of the election is not the end, but the beginning of what we hope will be an exciting journey for the Cambodian people along the road of national healing" and the rehabilitation and reconstruction of the country, which is so much desired.

Document 89

Security Council resolution on the completion of the election in Cambodia

S/RES/835 (1993), 2 June 1993

The Security Council,

Reaffirming its resolutions 668 (1990) of 20 September 1990, 745 (1992) of 28 February 1992, 810 (1993) of 8 March 1993, 826 (1993) of 20 May 1993 and other relevant resolutions,

Expressing its appreciation to the United Nations Transitional Authority in Cambodia and especially to the Special Representative of the Secretary-General, Yasushi Akashi, for their courage, dedication and perseverance in providing the necessary support for the electoral process despite hardships and difficulties,

Paying tribute to the leadership and continuing role of His Royal Highness Prince Norodom Sihanouk, Chairman of the Supreme National Council,

Noting with satisfaction the overwhelming number of Cambodians who demonstrated their patriotism and sense of responsibility in exercising their right to vote,

Endorsing the declaration of the Special Representative of the Secretary-General for Cambodia to the Supreme National Council of 29 May 1993 that the conduct of the election had been free and fair, 1/

1. *Salutes* the members of the United Nations Transitional Authority in Cambodia, particularly those who gave their lives in order to make possible this extraordinary demonstration by the Cambodian people;

2. *Invites* the Secretary-General to make his report on the election available as soon as possible;

3. *Expresses its intention*, following certification of the election, to support fully the duly-elected constituent assembly in its work of drawing up a constitution, according to the principles laid down in annex 5 to the Agreement on a Comprehensive Political Settlement of the Cambodia Conflict signed in Paris on 23 October 1991, 2/ and establishing a new government for all Cambodia;

4. *Calls upon* all parties to stand by their obligation to respect fully the results of the elections and urges them to do all in their power to bring about the peaceful establishment of a democratic government in accordance with the terms of the new constitution;

5. *Urges* the international community to contribute actively to the reconstruction and rehabilitation of Cambodia;

6. *Decides* to remain actively seized of the matter.

1/ S/25879 [Document 88]

2/ S/23177 [Document 19]

Document 90

Letter dated 4 June 1993 from Viet Nam transmitting statement from the Ministry of Foreign Affairs concerning the 23-28 May 1993 general election in Cambodia

S/25886, 5 June 1993

Upon instructions from my Government, I have the honour to transmit to you herewith the statement dated 3 June 1993 of the Ministry of Foreign Affairs of the Socialist Republic of Viet Nam concerning the 23-28 May 1993 general elections for a constitutional national assembly in Cambodia.

I should be very grateful if you could have the enclosed statement circulated as a document of the Security Council.

(*Signed*) Le V. BANG
Ambassador
Acting Permanent Representative

Annex
Statement of the Ministry of Foreign Affairs of the Socialist Republic of Viet Nam

The general election for the Constitutional National Assembly in Cambodia organized and supervised by the United Nations in conformity with the Paris Agreement on the comprehensive political settlement for the Cambodian conflict took place from 23 to 28 May 1993. The general election proceeded in a relatively calm and orderly atmosphere. In spite of deliberate attempt by the Khmer Rouge to sabotage the election, the voter turnout was nearly 90 per cent. That reflects the Cambodian people's desire to have, at an early date, peace, stability and national concord in order to build a prosperous country and a happy life after the ravages of wars and genocide. Favourable developments in connection with this election also reflect the great determination and efforts by the United Nations and the signatories to the Paris Agreement in promoting the peace process in Cambodia.

As Cambodia's close neighbour and a signatory to the Paris Agreement, the Vietnamese Government and people follow the election with great interest and, together with world public opinion, hope that the election will create good conditions for the Cambodian people to build a peaceful, independent, neutral and non-aligned country which entertains friendly relations with all countries. The Vietnamese Government and people, once again, call upon the international community and the Cambodian parties concerned to make additional contributions to the process so that Cambodia can soon have peace and stability in the interests of the Cambodian people and others in the region.

On this occasion, the Government of the Socialist Republic of Viet Nam reaffirms its consistent policy to scrupulously observe the Paris Agreement, fully respect Cambodia's independence, sovereignty and the Cambodian people's right to decide their own destiny. The Vietnamese Government and people wish to maintain and develop good-neighbourly relations with Cambodia on the basis of the principles of peaceful coexistence, non-interference into each other's internal affairs and mutually beneficial cooperation in the interests of the respective countries, and those of peace and stability in South-East Asia and the rest of the world.

In this connection, the Government of the Socialist Republic of Viet Nam expresses its willingness to recognize a new government in Cambodia to be elected by a Constitutional National Assembly and its desire to consolidate and broaden relations of friendship and cooperation in the spirit of the January 1992 Vietnamese-Cambodian Joint Communiqué.

Hanoi, 3 June 1993

Document 91

Statement by the President of theSecurity Council concerning armed attacks against Pakistani and Malaysian platoons of UNTAC

S/25896, 8 June 1993

The Security Council strongly condemns the armed attack against a Pakistani platoon and another against a Malaysian platoon of the United Nations Transitional Authority in Cambodia (UNTAC), both on 7 June 1993. In the first incident, two Pakistani personnel were injured, one of them seriously; in the second, three Malaysian personnel were injured, one of them seriously.

The Council takes note of the Secretariat's preliminary report that the first attack was launched against the Pakistani compound by the National Army of Democratic Kampuchea; the identity of the attackers in the second incident has not yet been determined. It requests the Secretary-General to investigate further and to report urgently to the Council.

The Council demands that those responsible for the attacks cease immediately all attacks against UNTAC and reiterates its warning that it will take appropriate measures against those who are threatening the safety and security of UNTAC personnel and are trying to overturn the democratic process in Cambodia through violence.

Document 92

Report of the Secretary-General on the conduct and results of the election in Cambodia

S/25913, 10 June 1993

1. By paragraph 16 of its resolution 826 (1993), the Security Council requested me to report promptly to the Council on the holding and results of the election in Cambodia, including on the conduct of the parties as regards their obligations under the Paris Agreements (S/23177, annex) and, if necessary, to recommend any initiative and/or measures conducive to ensuring their full respect by all parties. By paragraph 2 of resolution 835 (1993), the Council invited me to make my report on the elections available as soon as possible. The present report is submitted in accordance with those requests.

2. The elections were held as scheduled from 23 to 28 May 1993 in all 21 provinces in Cambodia. Between 23 and 25 May, some 1,400 large, medium and small fixed polling stations were operating, as well as 200 mobile teams in remote or difficult country. The mobile teams operated for the entire six-day period, while on 26 May some of the fixed stations were converted to mobile operation and worked as mobile teams on 27 and 28 May. Polling took place from 0800 to 1600 hours each day, but was extended on the final day to accommodate the remaining voters. Aside from a few incidents, described below, polling was conducted in a peaceful and often festive atmosphere, with voters sometimes walking several miles to cast their ballots, apparently undaunted by threats of violence or banditry, rough terrain or the heavy rain that swept much of the country. As indicated in my report issued in pursuance of

paragraph 6 of Security Council resolution 810 (1993) (S/25784), the UNTAC Military and Civilian Police components ensured tight security for the poll throughout.

3. The polling was generally peaceful and no significant disruption occurred. There were, however, a few scattered incidents of violence. A Cambodian civilian was killed on the first day of polling when several mortar rounds were fired in Kompong Cham Province, and the polling station in the vicinity was temporarily closed. Other polling stations were closed for short periods during the polling period for security reasons, but many continued operating even when shelling occurred nearby. In Kampot Province, polling was temporarily suspended in one district when armed men intruded into a polling station and stole items of equipment. Polling later resumed. In Sot Nikum District, Siem Reap Province, a mobile polling station was attacked by armed men. A Bangladeshi member of the Military Component was wounded and two voters and a third Cambodian were also injured.

4. In some parts of the country evidence emerged that elements of the National Army of Democratic Kampuchea (NADK) were preventing voters from going to the polls, but in Poipet, Banteay Meanchey Province, about 200 unarmed NADK soldiers voted. In the same province, several hundred family members of NADK soldiers also voted in Thmar Puok, Banthey Thma and Phum Ampil villages, as did soldiers and civilians from NADK-controlled areas around the enclave of Sok San in Battambang Province.

5. The turnout of voters was impressive. A total of 4,267,192 voters, representing 89.56 per cent of the registered voters, turned out to vote. About 7 per cent of the ballots were cast in the form of tendered ballots, mainly by voters voting outside the province in which they had registered. About 46 per cent of registered voters, or 2.2 million, voted on the first day, the largest voter turnout on any single day.

6. Three of the four Cambodian parties signatories to the Paris Agreements—the Party of the State of Cambodia (SOC) (through the Cambodian People's Party (CPP)), the Front uni national pour un Cambodge indépendant, neutre, pacifique et coopératif (FUNCINPEC) and the Khmer People's National Liberation Front/Buddhist Liberal Democratic Party (KPNLF/BLDP)—took part in the electoral process. The three participating parties complied fully with the electoral law and all availed themselves of their legal right to post agents at polling stations to scrutinize the balloting.

7. The fourth Cambodian signatory party, the Party of Democratic Kampuchea (PDK), failed to register as a political party, took no part in the

election and threatened to disrupt it with violence. As noted above, however, no significant disruption took place.

8. At a meeting of the Supreme National Council, convened on 29 May 1993, the day after the final day of polling, to review the polling process, my Special Representative declared on my behalf and on behalf of the United Nations that, in view of the very high turnout throughout the country, the absence of violence or disruption during the polling, the success of the technical conduct of the poll and the calm and peaceful atmosphere that reigned throughout the polling period, the conduct of the poll had been free and fair. The text of my Special Representative's statement has been issued as document S/25879. The counting of the ballots began on the morning of 29 May 1993.

9. At the Supreme National Council meeting of 29 May, Mr. Hun Sen, Vice-President of CPP, issued a statement expressing his satisfaction and warm congratulations for the "excellent" result of the electoral process. The statement said it had been achieved "thanks to a political climate conducive to an environment free from coercion, intimidation or fear, thus allowing the overwhelming majority of the population from everywhere to come to cast their vote with confidence and enthusiasm, to determine their own destiny, absolutely wishing for peace, and to unite and dedicate themselves to build a new Cambodia". The statement noted that CPP had submitted observations to UNTAC on the implementation of technical aspects of the electoral process and that the party was awaiting the election results in the hope that the counting of the votes would proceed in strict conditions which would allow all parties to accept the results.

10. Subsequently, CPP has raised a number of objections over alleged irregularities in the polling and counting process. These are based on the claims that party agents were not able to inspect the "safe havens" where ballot boxes were stored overnight; the rupture of some plastic seals used to seal the ballot boxes overnight, the efficacy of the indelible ink, the alleged partiality of some locally recruited Cambodian polling staff and alleged discrepancies in the numbers of ballot papers in the boxes. CPP leaders have also alleged fraud. My Special Representative has requested CPP to furnish UNTAC with all the necessary details to enable a full investigation to be carried out, but no additional details have yet been forthcoming. In some cases, where specific complaints have been made and details provided, investigations have been conducted on the spot to the complete satisfaction of party agents.

11. Because of the need to ensure accuracy and transparency, counting proceeded rather more slowly

than anticipated. In view of this, UNTAC had been releasing the interim figures of the vote count twice a day. CPP, citing "mistakes" in the figures, has requested UNTAC to discontinue this procedure, but UNTAC rejected the request. The regular release of the figures was intended to promote the maximum transparency of the process, especially since the figures, being available to the political party agents present at the count, were in the public domain.

12. CPP also requested UNTAC to hold new elections in seven provinces, including the capital, Phnom Penh. UNTAC has declined to do so until and unless CPP can produce convincing evidence of irregularities and fraud on such a scale as to invalidate the poll. CPP has not presented such evidence.

13. The count of ordinary and tendered ballots is now complete. The 4,011,631 valid ballots counted indicate that FUNCINPEC has won 1,824,188 votes, or 45.47 per cent of the votes to CPP's 1,533,471 votes, or 38.23 per cent. BLDP has won 152,764 votes, or 3.81 per cent. The number of votes cast for each party and the percentage of total votes won are contained in annex 1. The number of seats won in the Constituent Assembly was 58 for FUNCINPEC, 51 for CPP, 10 for BLDP and 1 for MOLINAKA.

14. Accordingly, I authorized my Special Representative to issue, at a meeting of the Supreme National Council, held on 10 June and presided by His Royal Highness Prince Norodom Sihanouk, a statement declaring, on my behalf and on behalf of the United Nations, that the election as a whole had been free and fair. The text of that statement is reproduced in annex II.

15. It gives me deep satisfaction to support my Special Representative's determination that the election in Cambodia was free and fair. I pay tribute to the courage and commitment to the peace process demonstrated by the Cambodian people. I urge all parties to respect and accept the results of the election and to resolve any disputes they may have through the agreed channels. UNTAC will give the Constituent Assembly, which will soon commence its work, full support in the process of drawing up a constitution and establishing a new Government for all Cambodia. I am also confident that the international community will continue to support efforts to promote national reconciliation and peace-building.

16. In concluding, I wish to pay warm tribute to my Special Representative, Mr. Yasushi Akashi, and to all civilian and military personnel of UNTAC for their dedication and steadfastness in this complex mission under extraordinarily difficult and often dangerous conditions. I also wish to acknowledge the contribution of the United Nations and independent election monitors, members of United Nations agencies and non-govern-mental organizations, who have supported this important endeavour in Cambodia.

Annex 1
Number and percentage of votes won by parties

	Number of votes	Percentage of votes
CPP	1 533 471	38.23
RCP	27 680	0.69
FDRP	20 425	0.51
KNP	48 113	1.20
RSN	14 569	0.36
NDPC	24 394	0.61
PD	41 799	1.04
CFID	37 474	0.93
BLDP	152 764	3.81
LRP	29 738	0.74
FUNCINPEC	1 824 188	45.47
CRP	28 071	0.70
ADD	13 914	0.35
NKP	7 827	0.20
FRP	31 348	0.78
KFLD	20 776	0.52
MOLINAKA	55 107	1.37
LDP	62 698	1.56
REDEK	11 524	0.29
KNCP	25 751	0.64
Total	4 011 631	

Notes

No.	Name of Political Party	Acronym
1	Cambodian People's Party	CPP
2	Republican Coalition Party	RCP
3	Free Development Republican Party	FDRP
4	Khmer Neutral Party	KNP
5	Reassemblement pour la solidarité nationale	RSN
6	Neutral Democratic Party of Cambodia	NDPC
7	Parti démocrate	PD
8	Cambodian Free Independent Democracy Party	CFID
9	Buddhist Liberal Democratic Party (grandfather Son Sann)	BLDP
10	Liberal Reconciliation Party	LRP
11	Front uni national pour un Cambodge indépendant, neutre, pacifique et coopératif	FUNCINPEC
12	Cambodge-Renaissance Party	CRP
13	Action for Democracy and Development Party	ADD
14	Nationalist Khmer Party	NKP
15	Free Republican Party	FRP

16	Khmer Farmer Liberal Democracy	KFLD
17	Molinaka and Naktaorsou Khmere for Freedom	MOLINAKA
18	Liberal Democratic Party	LDP
19	Republic Democracy Khmer Party	REDEK
20	Khmer National Congress Party	KNCP

Annex II
Freeness and fairness of the Cambodian elections

Statement by the Special Representative of the Secretary-General

The counting of all votes in the Cambodian election is now complete, and a statement of the final figures for each province, indicating the percentage won by each party, is now being circulated. As you can see, the overwhelming majority of votes were cast for the two largest parties. A total of 3,767,412 ordinary valid ballots and 244,219 valid tendered ballots were counted, that is, 4,011,631 ballots altogether. Nationwide, the Front uni national pour un Cambodge indépendant, neutre, pacifique et coopératif (FUNCINPEC) won 45.47 per cent of the votes; the Cambodian People's Party (CPP) won 38.23 per cent; the Buddhist Liberal Democratic Party (BLDP) won 3.81 per cent; and the other 17 parties won the remainder.

The counting proceeded more slowly than anticipated, largely owing to the need to ensure absolute accuracy and transparency under the scrutiny of political party agents. This has involved a very careful process of verification.

We have also been engaged in detailed discussions with CPP, which has alleged that the election was marked by irregularities and fraud. UNTAC is fully prepared to investigate any and all allegations of irregularity, and has asked CPP for details to support those allegations. Where details have been provided, the allegations have been investigated and responded to. My associates and I have been engaged in detailed correspondence with H.E. Mr. Chea Sim, and I have listed in detail all the measures UNTAC has taken to rectify anomalies of which we were aware. Nevertheless, we are committed to continuing our own thorough and objective inquiry into any complaints until they are dealt with. We have also made it clear that the alleged irregularities do not amount to fraud and that none of CPP's allegations, even if true, would affect the outcome. Moreover, UNTAC firmly rejects any suggestion that its own actions were not impartial. The election was free and fair and the Cambodian parties must accept and respect its results in keeping with their commitments under the Paris Agreements.

I will now bring to the attention of the Supreme National Council Security Council resolution 835

(1993), which was adopted unanimously on 2 June 1993. That resolution calls upon all parties to stand by their obligation to respect fully the results of the elections and urges them to do all in their power to bring about the peaceful establishment of a democratic government in accordance with the terms of the new Constitution.

Accordingly, I am now prepared to announce, on behalf of the Secretary-General and of the United Nations, that this latest phase of the election process has been performed in a free and fair manner. The results I have just announced fairly and accurately reflect the will of the Cambodian people and must be respected.

I now wish to make a statement about the freeness and fairness of the election as a whole.

In doing so, I must draw particular attention to the political environment and the human rights situation prior to the poll. As I have stated on numerous occasions, we were not satisfied that a neutral political environment in which respect for basic human rights was assured was fully in place in Cambodia prior to the campaign period. I have published details of political violence, intimidation and harassment both in the months immediately preceding the campaign and in earlier months. I have brought these matters to the attention of His Royal Highness Prince Norodom Sihanouk and of all the members of the Supreme National Council. We have also been concerned that there has not been sufficient effort by the authorities, in all zones of Cambodia, to bring the perpetrators to justice. The acts of violence have continued since the election. In addition, I have complained about a pattern of low-level intimidation throughout the country.

Clearly, efforts must continue by all concerned before a society is realized in Cambodia which is governed by the rule of law, in which basic human rights and fundamental freedoms are respected. The international community will continue to support the Cambodian leadership in this endeavour.

Another threat to the election came from the Cambodian party which refused to participate in the polling, and which threatened to disrupt it with violence. We take great satisfaction in the fact that, contrary to our concern, little violence marred the election.

Despite these threats and risks, UNTAC pressed ahead with preparations for the elections in the firm belief that the Cambodian people wanted an election. The Cambodian people, by coming forth in their millions in a festive atmosphere of joy and hope for the future, made the election free and fair by their own courage and determination. They knew that their vote was secret and they voted for the parties of their choice.

The Cambodian people are the true winners of this election. I wish to pay tribute to them, as well as to all 20 political parties, which played an important role in this democratic process. FUNCINPEC and CPP, which between them received the overwhelming majority of the votes, will have an especially vital role to play. Despite its natural disappointment, CPP should be aware that, in an election which all observers have declared free and fair, a large proportion of Cambodians have indicated that the party must continue to play a vital and constructive role in the country's future commensurate with the significant level of popular support it has won.

FUNCINPEC, too, has reason for pride. Its leaders and its party workers stayed the course despite a campaign of violence and intimidation directed against them almost from the time they were permitted to open offices in the SOC zone. Undaunted, they persisted in putting their case to the people and were never tempted to meet violence with violence. They deserve to be commended for their success.

BLDP, too, will have an important contribution to make to the ongoing process. These Cambodian parties, under the overall leadership and far-sighted wisdom and unexcelled guidance of His Royal Highness Prince Norodom Sihanouk, must now learn to work together in a spirit of common destiny and national healing. Their first task is to draft and approve a Constitution and to decide upon a Government. But that is just the beginning. The new Government's primary task is to ensure that all the people of Cambodia, to whom we owe the success of the elections, emerge as the winners. I wish to make the strongest possible plea to all of you to bury the hatchet of yesterday, to cease mutual recriminations forthwith and to concentrate from now on upon building a new Cambodia, based on genuine fraternity and concord.

Document 93

Letter dated 11 June 1993 from Denmark transmitting statement on Democratic Kampuchea election issued by the European Community, 10 June 1993

S/25940, 14 June 1993

I have the honour to transmit herewith the text in English and French of a statement on Cambodia elections issued by the European Community and its member States on 10 June 1993.

I should be grateful if you would have the present letter and its annex circulated as a document of the Security Council.

(*Signed*) Bent HAAKONSEN
Ambassador
Permanent Representative

Annex
Statement on Cambodia

The Community and its member States wish to congratulate the people of Cambodia on the historic and successful elections of representatives for a constituent assembly. The impressive high voter participation in spite of the special atmosphere that surrounded the election is a victory for democracy and for the peace process.

The Community and its member States also wish to congratulate and thank the United Nations Secretary-General, UNTAC and participating international polling station officers for the enormous effort and hard work invested in the preparation and actual implementation of the elections.

The Community and its member States call on all Cambodian parties to abide by their commitment under the Paris Agreements to respect the results of the elections, the conduct of which has been characterized as free and fair by all observers. They also call upon the constituent assembly to complete its task of drafting and adopting a new Cambodian constitution within 3 months of the date of elections. They encourage the parties which participated in the elections to work together constructively under the aegis of Prince Sihanouk, to facilitate the emergence of a Government of reconciliation.

The Community and its member States reaffirm their determination to continue their support for the peace process and for the reconstruction of Cambodia.

Document 94

Security Council resolution on the results of the election in Cambodia

S/RES/840 (1993), 15 June 1993

The Security Council,

Reaffirming its resolutions 668 (1990) of 20 September 1990, 745 (1992) of 28 February 1992, 810 (1993) of 8 March 1993, 826 (1993) of 20 May 1993, 835 (1993) of 2 June 1993 and other relevant resolutions,

Taking note of the report of the Secretary-General of 10 June 1993, and in particular the statement contained therein concerning the election that took place in Cambodia from 23 to 28 May 1993,

Paying tribute to the leadership and continuing role of His Royal Highness Prince Norodom Sihanouk, Chairman of the Supreme National Council, in bringing about national reconciliation and restoring peace in Cambodia,

Expressing its appreciation to the United Nations Transitional Authority in Cambodia and especially to the Special Representative of the Secretary-General for the smoothness of the electoral process,

Reaffirming the national unity, territorial integrity and inviolability and independence of Cambodia,

Welcoming the fact that on 14 June 1993 the newly elected constituent assembly held its first meeting,

1. *Approves* the report of the Secretary-General;

2. *Endorses* the results of the election, which has been certified free and fair by the United Nations;

3. *Calls upon* all parties to stand by their obligation to respect fully the results of the election and to cooperate in securing a peaceful transition and welcomes, in this context, the efforts of His Royal Highness Prince Norodom Sihanouk to achieve national reconciliation and his leadership and continuing role in maintaining stability and in promoting cooperation among Cambodians by appropriate means;

4. *Fully supports* the newly elected constituent assembly which has begun its work of drawing up and approving a constitution according to the principles laid down in annex 5 to the Agreement on a Comprehensive Political Settlement of the Cambodia Conflict contained in the agreements signed in Paris on 23 October 1991, 1/ and will subsequently transform itself into a legislative assembly, which will establish a new government for all Cambodia;

5. *Emphasizes* the necessity to complete this work and to establish a new government for all Cambodia as soon as possible and within the time allotted by the Paris agreements;

6. *Requests* the United Nations Transitional Authority in Cambodia to continue to play its role in conjunction with the Supreme National Council during the transitional period in accordance with the Paris agreements;

7. *Also requests* the Secretary-General to report to the Security Council by the middle of July, including his recommendations on the possible role the United Nations and its agencies might play after the end of the mandate of the Authority according to the Paris agreements;

8. *Urges* all States and relevant international organizations to contribute actively to the reconstruction and rehabilitation of Cambodia;

9. *Decides* to remain actively seized of the matter.

1/ S/25913 [Document 92]

Document 95

Letter dated 18 June 1993 from Singapore transmitting text of statement made by the Foreign Ministers of ASEAN supporting the results of the election and urging the Cambodian parties and the international community to assist the new Cambodian Government

S/25971, 18 June 1993

On behalf of the Permanent Representatives to the United Nations of the States members of the Association of South-East Asian Nations (ASEAN), I have the honour to transmit to you herewith the text of a statement issued by the Foreign Ministers of ASEAN on Cambodia.

I should be grateful if you could arrange to have the statement circulated as a document of the Security Council.

(*Signed*) Mark HONG
Chargé d'affaires a.i.

Annex
Statement by ASEAN Foreign Ministers on Cambodia

1. Recalling the statement by ASEAN Foreign Ministers on the elections in Cambodia of 18 May 1993, ASEAN welcomes and endorses the successful elections in Cambodia conducted by the United Nations Transitional Authority in Cambodia (UNTAC). We support the declaration of the Secretary-General's Special Representative that the conduct of the elections was free and fair. The courage of the Cambodian people in coming out in large numbers to cast their votes clearly reflects their determination to have peace and to work for the reconstruction of Cambodia.

2. The Cambodian parties and the international community should respect fully the results of the elections. The elections have demonstrated that the Cambodian peace settlement worked out by the International Conference on Cambodia in Paris remains the viable solution for Cambodia and all parties should continue to respect the terms of this settlement.

3. We also support the efforts of H.R.H. Samdech Preah Norodom Sihanouk to unify the Cambodian people and to bring about national reconciliation. A calm and stable political climate will contribute to the drafting of the constitution and the peaceful establishment of a new government in accordance with the terms of the constitution.

4. We urge all parties concerned to refrain from acts which might lead to renewed hostilities or even civil war in Cambodia. ASEAN reaffirms its full respect for the sovereignty, independence and territorial integrity of a united Cambodia. We reaffirm our commitment to non-interference in internal affairs of Cambodia and call upon all the countries concerned, particularly the neighbouring countries of Cambodia, to do the same.

5. The United Nations and the international community should remain engaged in Cambodia, to support the elected constituent assembly which will draft the constitution in the interim period and establish a new government. Pending the establishment of a new government, UNTAC should continue to exercise the responsibilities assigned to it in accordance with the relevant United Nations Security Council resolutions and establish conditions that will permit the administrative and security apparatus in Cambodia to function effectively under UNTAC's control during the interim period. The United Nations and the international community should continue to assist and support the new Cambodian government after this interim period to strengthen the peace and development which the Cambodian people have so courageously affirmed through the polls.

6. We commend all the personnel of UNTAC for their courage and dedication in the endeavour to bring peace to Cambodia, and we congratulate the Special Representative of the Secretary-General, H.E. Mr. Yasushi Akashi, for his leadership in bringing about the successful elections in Cambodia. We pay special tribute to UNTAC personnel and volunteers especially those who sacrificed their lives in the performance of their duties for the cause of peace in Cambodia.

Document 96

Letter dated 22 June 1993 from the Secretary-General to the President of the Security Council reporting results of the investigation by the UNTAC Strategic Investigation Teams of the armed attacks against Pakistani and Malaysian contingents of UNTAC on 7 June 1993

S/25988, 22 June 1993

In a Presidential statement issued on 8 June 1993, the Security Council strongly condemned the armed attacks against Pakistani and Malaysian contingents of UNTAC which had taken place on 7 June, took note of the Secretariat's preliminary reports on these incidents and requested me to investigate further and to report urgently to the Council.

I wish to inform the Council that, following investigation by its Strategic Investigation Teams, UNTAC has now reported as follows.

On 7 June 1993, at 0415 hours, approximately 170 armed soldiers attacked a platoon of the Pakistani contingent at Phum Tbeng, located in the west of Preah Vihear Province.

The attackers screened their movement behind a herd of cattle and moved up to within 20 to 25 metres of the Pakistani camp. They executed the attack in waves using small arms, mortars and rocket launchers.

The Pakistan battalion troops first warned the attackers not to advance and then responded by employing small arms. The attackers retreated after about two hours, leaving two corpses behind. However, in the exchange of fire, a Pakistani soldier was wounded in the leg. He was later evacuated to UNTAC Field Hospital in Phnom Penh, where amputation of the wounded leg was carried out. Another officer also sustained minor injuries and he was provided first aid on location.

UNTAC's investigation has concluded that the attack had been a deliberate action against UNTAC carried out by elements of the National Army of Democratic Kampuchea (NADK). The two corpses were identified by local villagers as well-known NADK members. Villagers also told UNTAC that, the night before the attack, a group of six NADK soldiers had come to the village to obtain information about the location of UNTAC personnel.

The Pakistani platoon has since been withdrawn from the location.

Also on 7 June, at approximately 2230 hours, a Malaysian battalion platoon, located at Phum Tapoung in Battambang Province, came under fire with small arms and B-40 rockets from all directions, including the west where houses occupied by soldiers of the Cambodian People's Armed Forces (CPAF) are located some 150-250 metres away. A short time earlier a house occupied by Bangladesh Civilian Police Monitors nearby had also been attacked. The Malaysian platoon responded with small arms fire. The attack lasted about 45 minutes. Three Malaysian soldiers were wounded, one seriously. All three were subsequently evacuated.

Although there is no conclusive evidence on the identity of the attackers, UNTAC investigation has strongly indicated, based on the shell casings retrieved and the behaviour of the local CPAF and villagers, that local elements of CPAF had most probably been responsible.

The Malaysian platoon, which had been temporarily deployed to the location during the electoral period, has since been withdrawn from the area.

(Signed) Boutros BOUTROS-GHALI

Document 97

Report of the Secretary-General pursuant to paragraph 7 of resolution 840 (1993) on the possible role of the United Nations and its agencies after the end of UNTAC's mandate according to the Paris Agreements

S/26090, 16 July 1993

1. By paragraph 7 of its resolution 840 (1993) of 15 June 1993, the Security Council requested me to report by the middle of July, including my recommendations on the possible role the United Nations and its agencies might play after the end of the mandate of UNTAC according to the Paris Agreements.

2. The mandate of UNTAC, in accordance with the provision of resolution 745 (1992), extends for a period not to exceed 18 months until the end of the transitional period, that is, until the Constituent Assembly has drafted and approved a Constitution, transformed itself into a legislative assembly and created a new Cambodian Government. According to paragraph 1 of annex 3 to the Paris Agreement, the Constituent Assembly is to perform these tasks within three months from the date of the election, which took place from 23 to 28 May 1993.

I. Developments since the election

3. As described in my last report (S/25913), the election in Cambodia was conducted successfully, with 90 per cent of registered voters taking part in the election in a calm and peaceful atmosphere with minimum disruption. The United Nations, having declared each separate stage of the election process—the campaign, the polling and the counting of ballots—free and fair, endorsed the election results. After some initial dissent (see para. 5 below) the Cambodian political parties which had participated in the process also acknowledged acceptance of the results.

4. The duly elected Constituent Assembly began work on 14 June 1993. On 30 June, the Constituent Assembly elected its President and two Vice-Presidents, and adopted its Rules of Procedure. Two permanent committees were established: the Committee for Drafting the Constitution and the Committee on Rules of Procedure. The elaboration of a draft constitution is now proceeding. At the request of the Cambodian parties, UNTAC has provided logistical and operational assistance, as well as technical advice, to the Assembly.

5. Notwithstanding the successful holding of the election and the creation of a Constituent Assembly, the post-election period has not been without difficulties. The Party of the State of Cambodia (SOC) made numerous allegations of electoral irregularities and initially withheld recognition of the election results, citing those alleged irregularities, although every concrete allegation was promptly investigated by UNTAC. After the election, some SOC elements declared a short-lived "secession" in three eastern provinces which, however, collapsed after a few days. SOC has now accepted the results of the election. None the less, allegations will continue to be reviewed under the Electoral Advisory Committee established by my Special Representative.

6. The establishment of an Interim Joint Administration (Provisional National Government), with the guidance of His Royal Highness Prince Norodom Sihanouk, has proved to be a stabilizing mechanism in the Cambodian polity. This Administration, with Prince Sihanouk as the Head of State, provides for a cooperative framework between all parties which hold seats in the Constituent Assembly. On 1 July 1993, the Assembly met and gave a vote of confidence to the Interim Joint Administration and unanimously adopted the Programme of Action of the Provisional Government for the Coming Three Months. The composition of the Council of Ministers has been agreed, with His Royal Highness Prince Ranariddh of the Front uni national pour un cambodge indépendant, neutre, pacifique et coopératif (FUNCINPEC) and Mr. Hun Sen of the Cambodian People's Party (CPP) as Co-Chairmen.

7. The Party of Democratic Kampuchea (PDK) has also declared that it will accept the outcome of the election. Although PDK is not a party to the Interim Joint Administration, tentative discussions have taken place between it and the parties participating in the Administration aimed at achieving national reconciliation. At the same time, low-level cease-fire violations and military activities, mainly involving the National Army of Democratic Kampuchea, have continued to occur.

8. The Interim Joint Administration, which will operate during the transitional period, though not foreseen under the Paris Agreements, should be viewed as an attempt to fuse three of the existing administrative structures, and as a manifestation of the common desire for peace, stability and national reconciliation. At the same time, UNTAC, as provided for in the Paris Agreements, continues to cooperate with the Supreme National Council as the unique legitimate body and source of authority in Cambodia throughout the transitional period.

II. UNTAC withdrawal plan

9. Detailed plans have been drawn up for the orderly withdrawal of the Military, Civilian Police and other components of UNTAC, taking due account of the tasks that remain for each of them during the remainder of the transitional period. Due to security considerations, the timing of the withdrawal of the civilian staff from the district and provincial levels is closely coordinated with the military withdrawal plan. All proposals are premised on the assumption that the work of the Constituent Assembly in drafting and adopting the constitution, and the subsequent establishment of a new Cambodian Government, will be expeditiously completed.

10. Civilian withdrawal is easier than military withdrawal for several reasons. In some cases, the civilian tasks have already been completed; the whole of the Repatriation Component and the great majority of the staff of the Electoral Component, for example, have already been withdrawn. Secondly, civilian staff in the countryside are much fewer in number than the military, and can therefore be withdrawn on an individual basis in a flexible manner.

A. Military Component

11. The detailed plan, including timetables, drawn up for the withdrawal of the Military Component is designed to be implemented with maximum flexibility. Since the extraction will be taking place at the height of the rainy season over severely degraded infrastructure, amid a still uncertain military and security situation, it may be necessary to compress, expand, or otherwise modify the withdrawal plan in response to changing conditions on the ground.

12. The plan is divided into three phases. Phase I —planning and preparation—ends on 31 July 1993. During this period, military personnel of the first group of battalions to be withdrawn will commence physical preparations within their sectors. The two succeeding phases are each, in turn, divided into stages. In phase II (1-31 August; stages 1 to 5), as each infantry battalion successively withdraws, along with the related field hospitals, engineering and other units, the infantry battalion in the neighbouring sector will redeploy to cover the vacated sector. In phase III (1 September-15 November; stages 6 to 10), the remaining UNTAC elements are successively to withdraw completely from the country. The withdrawal will be staged via Thailand, Sihanoukville or Phnom Penh. In addition, the Socialist Republic of Viet Nam has been approached concerning permission to use its territory for the purposes of withdrawal.

13. The first three stages of phase II will take place concurrently starting on 1 August 1993. During that period, the Uruguayan battalion and an Indian forward field hospital will withdraw from the north-eastern provinces of Stung Treng, Ratana Kiri, Mondol Kiri and Kratie; the Bulgarian battalion will withdraw from the south-central provinces of Kompong Speu and Kandal; and the Tunisian battalion will withdraw from the south-western provinces of Pursat and Kompong Chhnang. As they do so, the Indian, French and Malaysian battalions, respectively, will redeploy to cover the vacated provinces.

14. By the end of August, the Bangladesh battalion will have withdrawn from Siem Reap Province in the north; the Pakistani battalion will withdraw shortly after the end of August from Preah Vihear Province. Personnel from the Dutch and Indonesian battalions will be extending their coverage into those two provinces. At the same time, the forward field hospital in Siem Reap, the Polish engineering detachment and the Chinese engineering battalion will also be withdrawn.

15. Phase III, comprising stages 6 to 10, will involve the successive withdrawal of the Indian battalion, the Malaysian battalion, the forward field hospital at Battambang, the Japanese engineering battalion and the Namibian mine-resistant vehicle detachment. This will then be followed by the withdrawal of the Dutch battal-

ion, the Thai engineering battalion (by road) and a number of logistics elements, while the French and Indonesian battalions will regroup into smaller sectors. The final two stages involve the withdrawal of the two Indonesian battalions, the Ghanaian battalions, the French engineering company, the French battalion and the remaining logistics and medical elements.

16. The withdrawal of the headquarters staff, the Communications Unit, United Nations Military Observers (UNMOs) and the United Nations Naval Observers (UNNOs) will take place as their tasks are completed. As infantry and other battalions are withdrawn and others are extended to cover the evacuated sectors, UNMO and UNNO teams in the affected provinces will progressively regroup into provincial towns and check-points and be reduced in number. The final withdrawal of all UNTAC personnel is planned to be completed by 15 November 1993.

B. Civilian Police Component

17. The plan for the withdrawal of the 3,500 officers of the Civilian Police Component, which has already commenced, will be effected in three phases. Between 1 July and 1 August 1993, 1,100 officers will be repatriated; between 2 and 28 August, 1,100 more will be repatriated; and the remaining 1,300 will be withdrawn between 29 August and 30 September.

18. The considerations which affect the timing and modalities of the withdrawal of the Civilian Police Component differ somewhat from those affecting the extraction of the military. Civilian Police units, because of the nature of their work, and unlike military units, are made up of officers of different nationalities throughout the provinces. At the time of their extraction, however, for logistical and financial reasons, they will be withdrawn as national contingents.

19. Furthermore, the Civilian Police withdrawal plan is subject to security considerations. Since the officers are unarmed, they, as other civilian staff, rely on the Military Component for protection against armed attack or threat. Accordingly, as the Military Component withdraws from the district level in areas considered unsafe, the Civilian Police will do likewise. The Component will remain at its current strength in the provincial capitals until the end of the mandate and will continue, where conditions permit, to operate patrols outside the provincial capitals.

C. Other Civilian Components

1. Human Rights

20. The Human Rights Component will continue to fulfil its mandate until the termination of the UNTAC

mandate at the end of August 1993. It will pursue allegations of human rights violations and political intimidation, as well as increasing its human rights training activities. Extensive training for the police and the judiciary is planned in July and August. In addition, the Component, in conjunction with the Information Division, will prepare further programmes on human rights for radio and television.

21. One of the major tasks of the Human Rights Component in Phnom Penh will be to prepare for the operational presence of the Centre for Human Rights in Cambodia, as mandated by the Commission on Human Rights at its session in February 1993. The Centre is scheduled to become operational on 1 September 1993. A delegation from the Centre visited Cambodia in early June to prepare for the hand-over process and to discuss its operational needs.

22. Currently the Component has some 15 Professional staff in Phnom Penh and 18 Professional staff, with training assistants, in the provinces. Six Professional staff have left the Component to date; a further eight staff members are to leave by the end of July; and the remainder are scheduled to remain until the end of August.

2. Electoral

23. Most of the 963 International Polling Station Officers (IPSOs) were repatriated immediately after the polling and counting of ballots, between 31 May and 5 June 1993. Two hundred and seventeen Polling Officers and 41 fingerprint and handwriting experts were retained for the tendered-ballot count and left between 7 and 15 June. The bulk of the remaining international electoral staff—some 420 District Electoral Supervisors recruited by the United Nations Volunteer Service—departed the mission by 15 June. This left a skeleton staff of 16 officers in Phnom Penh, including the Chief Electoral Officer and three members of the Operations and Computer staff. They will be available to advise on the complaints of the Cambodian People's Party (CPP), which are being dealt with by the Special Representative's Electoral Advisory Committee, referred to above, and to assist with the establishment of the Constituent Assembly and, if requested, with its work on the Constitution. They will leave when the UNTAC mandate expires. Eight other officers currently in their posts will leave at the end of July.

3. Civil Administration

24. Before the elections, the main aim of the control Civil Administration Component exercised over the five fields specified in the Paris Agreements was to ensure a neutral political environment conducive to free and fair elections. However, the expertise thus gained is considered vital to promoting stability during the remainder of the transitional period. The Component is therefore streamlining its activities to help ensure a smooth transition from the existing administrative structures to the new Government and adapting its control functions accordingly.

25. Thus, at the provincial level, Civil Administration staff will, inter alia, maintain their contacts with the personnel of the existing administrative structures; promote dialogue and national reconciliation; monitor any sale, transfer or disposal of public assets; follow up on any allegations of human rights violations or political intimidation; maintain close contact with and facilitate the work of United Nations agencies and programmes; and assist in the closure of UNTAC offices at the provincial level, including the retrieval and/or disposal of UNTAC property.

26. On the national level, Civil Administration staff are focusing their efforts on, inter alia, the judiciary and the administration of justice; monitoring the implementation of the SNC moratoria on timber, gems and minerals; border and customs control; and the control and safeguarding of public funds and State assets.

27. Financial control activities will continue through the transitional period at both the provincial and the national levels. Such activities will be strengthened as regards military expenditure and, as mentioned above, the sale or disposal of public assets.

28. Of the 172 international staff of the Component that remain, 115 are located in the provincial capitals, including the municipality of Phnom Penh, and at the border checkpoints. The remaining 57 are based at UNTAC headquarters. Some 32 staff will be leaving on or before the end of July, but most of the rest will continue to work throughout the month of August until the end of the mission.

4. Rehabilitation

29. For the remainder of the transitional period, the Rehabilitation Component will be concentrating on the implementation of small-scale rehabilitation projects yielding quick results. Over the past three months, more than 150 such projects at an estimated cost of $1.7 million addressing immediate and highly prioritized needs have been compiled. These projects involve the repair and maintenance of public utilities and education and health facilities to improve the quality of life in the countryside. Most projects are highly labour-intensive, thus creating jobs at a time of scarce employment opportunities, and will especially benefit rural communities in northern and eastern Cambodia which have so far been only marginally touched by any form of development assistance.

30. Donor response to the Rehabilitation Component's initiative to implement small-scale quick-impact

projects was relatively positive after the election had taken place, while in the period leading up to the election, donors generally expressed great reluctance to support implementation of rehabilitation activities. As a direct response to the Rehabilitation Component's own initiative with the donor community in Phnom Penh and Bangkok, a total of about $600,000 was pledged. It is increasingly evident, however, that this important activity will not be completed by the end of August, and that arrangements will need to be made to ensure its successful completion.

31. With regard to the withdrawal plan for the Rehabilitation and Economic Affairs Component, 4 staff members are scheduled to leave by 31 July, 5 by 15 August, 3 by 22 August and the remaining 17, at this stage, by the end of UNTAC's mandate.

5. Information/Education Division

32. One third of the Information/Education Division's 45 staff had been released by 30 June 1993, and a further four were due to leave by the end of July. Many of the remaining 25 or so staff members are engaged in radio and television production. They will continue to produce programmes on human rights education and reconstruction and development until the end of the mission. Some will also remain on hand to document UNTAC's final winding-up and departure. The Division's control function will be devoted mainly to promoting the free flow of information and opinion.

6. Other UNTAC civilian staff and equipment

33. All other civilian personnel, except those required for the liquidation process, will leave the mission upon the expiry of the mandate or shortly thereafter. The liquidation team will complete its work as expeditiously as possible and will deal with all aspects relating to UNTAC assets in the mission area. A separate report on the disposal of UNTAC equipment has been submitted for consideration by the Advisory Committee on Administrative and Budgetary Questions (ACABQ).

III. Preparations for the post-UNTAC period

34. Cambodia still faces enormous problems of security, stability, mine clearance, infrastructure improvement and general economic and social development. Despite the positive developments of the last few weeks, the political-military situation remains fragile and the task before the new Government can be expected to be difficult and challenging. Cambodia will clearly require continued international assistance and support.

35. I believe it is important that any future assistance provided by the United Nations be clearly separate from the UNTAC presence. UNTAC was established as an operation with a clearly defined mandate and duration and specific resources. It has performed its function creditably and has now begun the process of withdrawing. UNTAC will soon cease to exist.

36. Various programmes and agencies of the United Nations system, as well as international financial institutions, will be prepared, in consultation with the Cambodian Government, to continue to play their traditional role in rehabilitation, reconstruction, development and humanitarian assistance. In this context, the international community should accelerate delivery of assistance already pledged and consider urgently what further assistance might be provided to the Interim Administration and later to the new Government. It is also vitally important to ensure a smooth transition from UNTAC's rehabilitation efforts to post-UNTAC United Nations activities in this area. The UNTAC Rehabilitation Component is already actively engaged in consultations to achieve this objective.

37. In addition, a continued human rights presence has been mandated both under the Paris Agreements and by a decision of the Commission on Human Rights (see para. 21 above). The United Nations could also undertake, with the concurrence of the new Cambodian Government, mine clearance, which will continue to be a major need for years to come.

38. The question of maintaining a small post-UNTAC United Nations military presence has been raised from time to time. The Cambodian Government will, of course, be in a position to make bilateral arrangements, if it so chooses, in respect of assistance in forming unified national armed forces. However, should the Government request the stationing of a small number of United Nations Military Observers in Cambodia for a limited period as a confidence-building measure and to monitor and report on the security of its borders, the Security Council will no doubt consider such a request at the appropriate time. Such an observer presence could also be utilized to supervise any demobilization of armed forces should such agreement be reached among the Cambodian parties.

39. Whatever the types of assistance requested from the United Nations, I am convinced that it should be provided in a well coordinated and integrated manner. An interim office, along the lines of those I have established elsewhere, would be particularly appropriate in Cambodia as an instrument of post-conflict peace-building. The head of such an office would maintain dialogue with the new Government and facilitate coordination of various assistance programmes to ensure maximum effectiveness while respecting the normal responsibilities of various offices, programmes and agencies in their respective fields. The establishment of such

an office, following the unprecedented UNTAC endeavour which is now coming to a conclusion, would serve as a symbol of United Nations continuing commitment to a peaceful future in Cambodia.

IV. Observations

40. In conclusion, I wish to assure the Security Council that UNTAC will continue to discharge its tasks fully and faithfully until the end of its mandate and to do everything possible to assist the Cambodian parties to consolidate the positive results of the election and complete the process of adopting a Constitution and establishing a new Government in accordance with the Paris Agreements. I am convinced that, upon the conclusion of UNTAC's mandate, the international community will respond generously to Cambodia's needs as it continues the difficult process of rebuilding the nation after years of strife and devastation. The United Nations system stands ready to play its role in this effort.

Document 98

Letter dated 14 July 1993 from the Secretary-General to the President of the Security Council concerning emergency financial assistance during the transitional period in support of the process of restructuring and adjustment of the administrative, police and military structures of the Interim Joint Administration in Cambodia

S/26095, 16 July 1993

The success of the recent elections in Cambodia, on which I reported to the Security Council in document S/25913 of 10 June 1993, marks the beginning of a particularly delicate phase in the country's transition from conflict to peace and democracy.

During the coming months it will be essential that the Interim Joint Administration structures be able to function properly, and that neither social unrest nor macro-economic disorder be allowed to take hold. It is also important that all those serving in the public domain—be they civil servants, police or members of the armed forces—begin the process of redirecting their allegiances from the factions of the past to the future constitutional Government.

This will contribute to a more stable environment for the Constituent Assembly to complete its work and a smooth and orderly transfer to the new Government of Cambodia as envisaged in the Paris Agreements. It is in the interests of Cambodia and of all those that have supported the peace process that these objectives be attained. Yet there is mounting evidence that without sufficient external support these goals may be in jeopardy.

After careful consideration, I have therefore concluded, on the recommendation of my Special Representative for Cambodia and in consultation with a number of concerned Governments, that urgent measures must be taken to enable UNTAC to provide, for the remainder of the transitional period, and in consultation with the Cambodian authorities, emergency financial assistance in support of the process of restructuring and adjustment of the administrative, police and military structures of the Interim Joint Administration. My Special Representative has advised that the amount of funding required to achieve the objectives for the remainder of the transitional period would be $20 million.

It is my view that such a step is fully consistent with the uniquely broad mandate which UNTAC has been given by the Security Council to help implement the Paris Agreements. It would also be a relatively modest additional outlay to ensure that the remarkable progress towards peace that has already occurred in Cambodia is not interrupted and that the United Nations endeavours are brought to a successful conclusion.

I should be grateful if you would bring this matter to the attention of the members of the Council.

(*Signed*) Boutros BOUTROS-GHALI

Document 99

Letter dated 22 July 1993 from Singapore transmitting statement made by the Foreign Ministers of ASEAN on national reconciliation, reconstruction and peace-building in Cambodia

S/26138, 23 July 1993

On behalf of the Permanent Representatives to the United Nations of the States members of the Association of South-East Asian Nations (ASEAN), I have the honour to transmit to you herewith the text of a statement issued by the Foreign Ministers of ASEAN on Cambodia on 22 July 1993.

I should be grateful if you could arrange to have the statement circulated as a document of the Security Council.

(Signed) CHEW Tai Soo

Annex
Statement issued on 22 July 1993 by the Foreign Ministers of ASEAN on Cambodia

1. We, the Foreign Ministers of ASEAN, welcome the formation of the Provisional National Government of Cambodia as an important step towards the establishment of a Government of national reconciliation based on the new Constitution to be drafted by the elected Constituent Assembly.

2. We reiterate our support for the efforts of His Royal Highness Samdech Preah Norodom Sihanouk, Head of State of Cambodia, to unify the Cambodian people and to bring about national reconciliation. We hope that all Cambodians will continue to set aside factional interests and work towards national reconciliation.

3. We are encouraged by the relatively calm and stable situation in Cambodia. These conditions depend on the continued functioning of the administrative and security apparatus in Cambodia. We recognize the urgent need to provide emergency financial assistance in support of the administrative, police and military structures of the interim joint administration. To this end, we urge the United Nations speedily to meet this requirement from existing funds and other sources.

4. Through UNCTAC's peace-keeping efforts, the United Nations helped to create conditions for the successful conduct of free and fair elections in Cambodia. With the expiry of UNCTAC's mandate, Cambodia enters a new phase of peace-building. We call on the United Nations Security Council once again to muster the political will and the resources of the international community, as it did in UNTAC, to continue to work in partnership with the Cambodian people to achieve durable peace and stability. We welcome the continued role of the United Nations in the post-conflict peace-building process in Cambodia.

5. We also call on the international community to assist Cambodia in the enormous task of rebuilding its shattered infrastructure and its political, social and economic institutions. To this end, the International Conference on the Reconstruction of Cambodia should immediately effect the disbursement of aid and assistance already pledged at the Tokyo Conference of June 1992 for the reconstruction of Cambodia.

Document 100

Further report of the Secretary-General pursuant to paragraph 7 of resolution 840 (1993)

S/26360, 26 August 1993

1. In response to paragraph 7 of its resolution 840 (1993) of 15 June 1993, I submitted a report to the Security Council on 16 July 1993 (S/26090), which contained recommendations on the possible role the United Nations and its agencies might play after the end of the mandate of the United Nations Transitional Authority in Cambodia (UNTAC) according to the Paris Agreements (S/23177, annex).

2. In addition to describing in that report developments since the elections of 23-28 May 1993 in Cambodia and the UNTAC withdrawal plan, I outlined preparations for the post-UNTAC period which is about to begin

(paras. 34-39). In a letter dated 26 July (S/26150), the President of the Council informed me that the members endorsed the overall concept and arrangements concerning UNTAC's withdrawal and that they would continue their consideration of the remainder of the report.

3. In the light of further developments in Cambodia since the submission of my last report, I am now in a position to inform the Council in greater detail concerning my recommendations on the functions of a United Nations presence following the end of the mandate of UNTAC.

I. Developments since the last report

4. The drafting of a new Cambodian Constitution has been proceeding since the Constituent Assembly held its inaugural meeting on 14 June 1993. At the request of the Interim Joint Administration, UNTAC has provided technical comments on the draft Constitution, which is now approaching completion. Most of UNTAC's comments are aimed at strengthening the human rights-related provisions of the draft in accordance with annex 5 of the Paris Agreement. Agreement has now been reached on about 120 articles of the draft Constitution, which is to be presented to Prince Sihanouk at the end of August 1993 and then to the plenary of the Constituent Assembly. However, two major questions remain to be resolved: the status of the head of State and the post of the prime minister. It is understood that the constitutional drafting committee will make firm recommendations on these questions to Prince Sihanouk.

5. For several weeks the military situation was generally calm. However, following military activities by the National Army of Democratic Kampuchea (NADK) in the north and west, the Cambodian Armed Forces (CAF), a body comprising officers and men from the armies of the former State of Cambodia Party (SOC), the Front uni national pour un Cambodge indépendant, neutre, pacifique et coopératif (FUNCINPEC) and the Khmer People's National Liberation Front (KPNLF), launched a military operation in Banteay Meanchey Province in mid-August. CAF surrounded a number of NADK strongholds and has overrun one of them at Phum Chat, on the Thai border. Few casualties on either side have been reported. CAF has also disarmed villagers in the area and has confiscated some 1,500 weapons. CAF movements have also been reported in Kompong Thom and Siem Reap Provinces.

6. The military operation in Banteay Meanchey has resulted in the displacement or forced removal of several hundred villagers, including about 1,200 who have reportedly crossed into Thailand. The Office of the United Nations High Commissioner for Refugees (UNHCR) will coordinate humanitarian assistance to the displaced persons.

7. In an incident involving UNTAC, on 1 August 1993, NADK troops attacked with mortar fire the UNTAC checkpoint at CT-1 near the border with Thailand in Choam Khsan, Preah Vihear Province. The 21 UNTAC personnel left the checkpoint and were briefly detained by NADK, after which they were released unharmed.

8. Widespread banditry remained a security threat. On 2 August 1993 a band of 100 armed men attacked a train in Kampot Province, killing 14 passengers and injuring 35 more. They then looted the train. UNTAC civilian police, military observers and the French battalion provided emergency medical and other assistance. Investigations subsequently indicated that elements of NADK were responsible. NADK is also allegedly responsible for another attack on a train on 15 August in Kompong Chhnang Province, in which two Cambodians were killed and five injured.

9. On 4 August, my Special Representative wrote to Mr. Khieu Samphan, President of the Party of Democratic Kampuchea (PDK), complaining about the harsh tone and racist content of that Party's radio broadcasts directed against ethnic Vietnamese residents, but Mr. Khieu Samphan has rejected these complaints. UNTAC has made it clear to the Cambodian authorities that they are obliged to provide adequate protection to ethnic minorities.

10. UNTAC civilian police are investigating the murder of six ethnic Vietnamese persons in Kompong Chhnang on 10 August. Preliminary investigations indicate that NADK was responsible for the killings. On 13 August, armed men abducted a group of ethnic Vietnamese children and later released them unharmed for ransom.

11. Since my last report was submitted to the Security Council, it has become increasingly clear that highly organized criminal gangs have been stealing UNTAC vehicles, sometimes at gunpoint. Some 140 vehicles have been stolen since mid-June. In one incident on 9 August, an UNTAC Provincial Director was briefly abducted by armed men, who robbed him and attempted to steal his vehicle. He managed to escape without injury. Recently UNTAC has recovered two stolen UNTAC vehicles that were found in the possession of senior military officers of the former Cambodian People's Armed Forces (CPAF). My Special Representative has brought these matters to the attention of the Interim Joint Administration at the highest level as a matter of urgency, and the two Co-Presidents have agreed to cooperate closely with UNTAC in preventing and punishing such crimes.

II. UNTAC withdrawal

12. The withdrawal of the UNTAC Military Component has been proceeding smoothly in accordance with

the timetable set out in paragraph 12 of document S/26090. On 2 August 1993, the first units of the Bulgarian, Tunisian and Uruguayan battalions left Cambodia by sea or air. By 15 August, all personnel from those three infantry battalions, as well as the Indian forward field hospital, had been withdrawn from the Provinces of Kompong Speu, Kandal, Pursat, Kompong Chhnang, Stung Treng, Mondol Kiri, Ratana Kiri and Kratie. Simultaneously, the French, Malaysian and Indian battalions extended their respective areas of operation to cover those provinces. The next stage of the withdrawal, during which the Bangladesh battalion will withdraw from Siem Reap Province and be replaced by the Netherlands battalion, is about to begin. The rest of the plan will then be carried out as described in paragraphs 14 to 16 of document S/26090 and the withdrawal of the Military Component is expected to be completed by 15 November 1993.

13. The timetable for the withdrawal of the Civilian Police Component is contained in paragraphs 17 to 19 of document S/26090. In accordance with that plan, approximately 2,000 officers had already been repatriated by 15 August; of those remaining, about 500 are due to leave Cambodia by 31 August and the remaining 1,000 will depart during the month of September. The withdrawal has been accomplished in an orderly manner and without incident.

14. The withdrawal of the remaining staff of the other civilian components is also proceeding with a view to concluding UNTAC's operational activities by the formal end of its mandate. As indicated in document S/26090 (paras. 21 and 37), there will be a post-UNTAC United Nations presence in Cambodia in the field of human rights (see also paras. 27-29 below) and the remaining staff of the Human Rights Component will remain active until the new office takes over at the end of UNTAC's mandate.

15. With the exception of the Director of the Electoral Component and his immediate staff, who remain on hand to assist the Constituent Assembly as required with advice about constitutional and related matters, the entire staff of the Electoral Component has now left Cambodia.

16. The Civil Administration Component will maintain a relatively strong presence during the remainder of the transitional period. As of 15 August 1993, a total of 56 international staff of this component remained in the provincial offices, with a further 40 staff in Phnom Penh (UNTAC headquarters and Phnom Penh provincial office). A further 17 Civil Administration staff are engaged in border control at the checkpoints, making a total of 113 throughout the country. These figures do not include the staff responsible for civil administration control functions in the fields of information

and finance, which are exercised by the Information/Education Division and the Office of the Economic Adviser respectively.

17. The chief purpose of keeping a small staff in each of the provinces at this point is to maintain an UNTAC presence for confidence-building purposes and to render technical assistance to the Interim Joint Administration, if required, during the remainder of the transitional period and to retain a provincial framework to facilitate a transition to post-UNTAC efforts in human rights and rehabilitation. However, it is not anticipated that any civilian staff will remain in the provinces following the withdrawal of the Military Component. Provincial staff will therefore continue to be withdrawn from the provinces.

18. As indicated in paragraph 32 of document S/26090, about 20 staff of the Information/Education Division left Cambodia at the end of July. The remaining 25 members of the Division will continue to produce radio programmes on human rights education and reconstruction and development, which will be broadcast until the end of UNTAC's mandate.

19. As of late August, 23 staff in the Office of Economic Affairs, which includes the Rehabilitation Component, out of an original 30 still remained in Cambodia, with 8 more due to leave by the end of August and the remaining 15 expected to stay at least until mid-September. Post-UNTAC rehabilitation activities are described in paragraphs 22 and 23 below.

20. My Special Representative has met twice with the Co-Presidents of the Interim Joint Administration to discuss the disposal of UNTAC assets. In accordance with the views of the Advisory Committee on Administrative and Budgetary Questions (ACABQ), UNTAC will extract as much equipment as possible for use in other missions. However, some equipment and installations are of great value to the incoming Cambodian Government. The dismantling of such equipment would have an immediate negative impact on the development and rehabilitation of the country. Efforts are therefore under way to find buyers for this equipment who would be prepared to donate it to the Government.

III. Preparations for the post-UNTAC period

21. The activities that are expected to be carried on by the United Nations in Cambodia after the departure of UNTAC—rehabilitation, mine clearance, human rights protection, the reintegration of refugees and displaced persons and the humanitarian and technical work of United Nations agencies—can contribute significantly to the consolidation of peace in Cambodia. It is important, in my view, to ensure that these activities are coordinated and integrated in such a way as to enhance their

effectiveness while taking full account of the sovereign wishes of the new Cambodian Government.

22. Rehabilitation will continue after UNTAC's departure. As of mid-August, approximately $200 million has been disbursed of the $880 million pledged at the Ministerial Conference in Tokyo in June 1992. Despite the widespread rebuilding of roads, bridges and other infrastructural installations by UNTAC military engineers over the past 18 months and the major upgrading of Cambodia's airports and communications facilities undertaken as part of the mission, massive reconstruction is still required throughout the country.

23. Even as UNTAC prepares to depart, urgent measures must be taken to assist the incoming Cambodian Government to meet a number of pressing needs in the first six months of its existence and beyond. These requirements, which will be discussed at the meeting of the International Committee on Reconstruction of Cambodia to be held in Paris on 8 and 9 September 1993, include budgetary support, public administration reform, mine clearance, resettlement and reintegration of displaced persons, agriculture, social services including health care and education, maintenance of public utilities and repair of the transportation system and infrastructure. The post-UNTAC presence in the rehabilitation field will need to assist the new Government in formulating its needs and presenting them to the international community. As a first step, my Special Representative has asked the Co-Presidents of the Interim Joint Administration to draw up a list of their most immediate requirements.

24. The Governing Council of the Cambodian Mine Action Centre (see S/25124, para. 83), is due to meet before the end of August 1993 to extend its mandate, which otherwise would expire with the mandate of UNTAC. Once the new Cambodian Government is established, consultations will take place between it and the United Nations on the future status of the Centre, as well as the relationship of the United Nations and its agencies with it. For the foreseeable future, I believe that United Nations involvement in the Centre will be desirable.

25. Since the establishment of UNTAC, more than 4 million square metres have been cleared of mines and about 37,000 mines and other unexploded ordnance destroyed. Some 2,330 Cambodians have been trained in mine-clearance techniques, of whom about 1,400 are currently employed. These figures include the work done by non-governmental organizations, including Halo Trust, Norwegian People's Aid, Mine Action Group and Handicap International.

26. Mine clearance by its very nature is a risky and painstaking task, and initial progress was slow. However, the experience gained over the past few months has led to a significant acceleration in the rate of mine clearance.

The Cambodian Mine Action Centre is now operating effectively and, in order to maintain that momentum it is necessary to ensure adequate funding on the basis of a reliable corporate structure. I therefore intend to maintain the United Nations Trust Fund for Demining Programmes in Cambodia until alternative funding arrangements can be made that are acceptable to donors, in consultation with the new Cambodian Government.

27. Article 17 of the Paris Agreements provides that, after the end of the transitional period, the United Nations Commission on Human Rights should continue to monitor closely the human rights situation in Cambodia, including, if necessary, by the appointment of a Special Rapporteur who would report his findings annually to the Commission and to the General Assembly.

28. On 19 February 1993, the Commission adopted resolution 1993/6 on the situation of human rights in Cambodia, in which it recognized that Cambodia's tragic recent history required special measures to assure the protection of human rights and the non-return to the policies and practices of the past. The Commission requested the Secretary-General to ensure a continued United Nations human rights presence in Cambodia after the expiry of the mandate of UNTAC, including through the operational presence of the Centre for Human Rights, and to appoint a Special Representative for Human Rights. The functions of the Centre and of the Special Representative are enumerated in the resolution. The resolution also requested the Secretary-General to provide appropriate additional resources, within existing overall United Nations resources, to fund the operational presence of the Centre for Human Rights within the framework of other United Nations activities in Cambodia after the expiry of the UNTAC mandate.

29. The Centre for Human Rights is scheduled to establish its operational presence in Phnom Penh upon the termination of the UNTAC mandate, with a total of 23 international and local staff, drawn in part from the existing staff of the UNTAC Human Rights Component. However, since funding for such presence has yet to be approved by the General Assembly and UNTAC funding for human rights operations will cease upon the termination of the mission's mandate, provision will have to be made to ensure the Centre's functioning until General Assembly-approved funding becomes available.

IV. Observations

30. As the operation of UNTAC nears its end, I believe the international community can take satisfaction in the fact that, despite serious difficulties, UNTAC was able to accomplish its central task of holding a free and fair election in Cambodia and laying a sound foundation for the people of Cambodia to build a stable and peaceful

future. Developments since the election have also been encouraging. The Constituent Assembly is expected shortly to adopt the new Constitution and establish the new Government in accordance with its provisions and those of the Paris Agreements. UNTAC's formal mandate will then come to an end, leaving the task of orderly and speedy withdrawal to be completed. In view of the need to allow sufficient time for the approval of the Constitution and the emergence of the new Government, I propose that the Security Council extend the mandate of UNTAC until 15 September 1993 and that it be ready to consider a brief further extension if the new Government has not been formally established by that date.

31. After UNTAC's mandate ends, the people and the new Government of Cambodia will require continued international support in order to safeguard the fruits of the tremendous effort and resources that the international community has already devoted to the cause of Cambodia. I have outlined in the present report the kinds of activities that the United Nations and its agencies are ready to undertake and the assistance they will be able to provide in response to the new Government's requirements.

32. As stated in paragraph 38 of my report of 16 July 1993 (S/26090), the suggestion that the United Nations should maintain a small military presence in Cambodia following the withdrawal of UNTAC has been raised from time to time. At this stage I have decided not to recommend that the Security Council authorize the retention of United Nations military personnel in Cam-

bodia after UNTAC leaves. UNTAC will soon have carried out all parts of its mandate that proved to be practicable and I believe that, in accordance with previous practice in such cases, the correct course is to terminate the United Nations military presence and concentrate the resources available on civilian activities in support of peace-building in the new Cambodia that UNTAC has helped to bring about. If the new Government were to request a post-UNTAC military presence, with a clear indication of the tasks it would be expected to perform, I would of course give careful consideration to such a request and submit a report to the Security Council on the feasibility of the tasks proposed and the resources that would be required to carry them out.

33. As already indicated in paragraph 39 of my report of 16 July, it is my intention to establish in Phnom Penh an integrated office along the lines described in my report of 20 July 1993 to the General Assembly (A/48/146/Add.1). The primary function of the United Nations Representative who will head that Office will be to coordinate, in close consultation with the Cambodian Government, the full range of civilian activities that will be undertaken by various agencies of the United Nations system, in accordance with their existing mandates, to promote development, provide humanitarian assistance and foster respect for human rights in Cambodia. In addition, the Office will, during the period immediately following the establishment of the new Government, need to deal with a number of residual issues arising from the Paris Agreements and UNTAC's presence in the country.

Document 101

Security Council resolution on the withdrawal of UNTAC

S/RES/860 (1993), 27 August 1993

The Security Council,

Reaffirming its resolutions 668 (1990) of 20 September 1990, 745 (1992) of 28 February 1992, 840 (1993) of 15 June 1993 and other relevant resolutions,

Taking note of the reports of the Secretary-General of 16 July 1993 1/ and 26 August 1993, 2/

Paying tribute to the continuing role of His Royal Highness Prince Norodom Sihanouk in achieving peace, stability and genuine national reconciliation for all Cambodia,

Recalling that, according to the agreements on a comprehensive political settlement to the Cambodian conflict signed in Paris on 23 October 1991, 3/ the

transitional period shall terminate when the Constituent Assembly elected through free and fair elections, organized and certified by the United Nations, has approved the constitution and transformed itself into legislative assembly, and thereafter a new government has been created,

Noting the expressed wish of the Cambodian interim joint administration to maintain the mandate of the United Nations Transitional Authority in Cambodia until the establishment of a new government in Cambodia as conveyed by the Secretariat,

1/ S/26090 [Document 97]
2/ S/26360 [Document 100]
3/ S/23177 [Document 19]

1. *Welcomes* the reports of the Secretary-General of 16 July 1993 1/ and 26 August 1993, 2/ and approves the United Nations Transitional Authority in Cambodia withdrawal plan contained in the former;

2. *Fully supports* the Constituent Assembly in its work of drawing up and approving a constitution, and stresses the importance of completing this work in accordance with the agreements on a comprehensive political settlement to the Cambodian conflict signed in Paris on 23 October 1991; 3/

3. *Confirms* that the functions of the Authority under the Paris agreements shall end upon the creation in September of a new government of Cambodia consistent with those agreements;

4. *Decides* that, in order to ensure a safe and an orderly withdrawal of the military component of the Authority, the period of such withdrawal shall end on 15 November 1993;

5. *Decides* to remain actively seized of the matter.

Document 102

Statement by the Foreign Ministers of the five permanent members of the Security Council following a meeting with the Secretary-General, 30 September 1993

S/26517, 30 September 1993

We have the honour to enclose the text of the statement issued following the meeting which you held on 30 September 1993 with our Ministers of Foreign Affairs. We should be grateful if you would arrange for it to be circulated as a document of the Security Council.

(*Signed*) LI Zhaoxing
Permanent Representative of China
to the United Nations

(*Signed*) Jean-Bernard MÉRIMÉE
Permanent Representative of France
to the United Nations

(*Signed*) Yuli M. VORONTSOV
Permanent Representative of the Russian Federation
to the United Nations

(*Signed*) David HANNAY
Permanent Representative of the United Kingdom
of Great Britain and Northern Ireland
to the United Nations

(*Signed*) Madeleine K. ALBRIGHT
Permanent Representative of the United States of America
to the United Nations

Annex
Statement issued on 30 September 1993 by the Ministers for Foreign Affairs of the five permanent members of the Security Council following a meeting with the Secretary-General

On 30 September 1993, the Ministers for Foreign Affairs of the five permanent members of the Security Council met with the Secretary-General of the United Nations,
H.E. Boutros Boutros-Ghali. Taking part were the Vice Premier and Minister of Foreign Affairs of the People's Republic of China, H.E. Mr. Qian Qichen; the Minister of Foreign Affairs of France, H.E. Mr. Alain Juppe; the Minister of Foreign Affairs of the Russian Federation, H.E. Mr. Andrey Kozyrev; the Secretary of State for Foreign and Commonwealth Affairs of the United Kingdom of Great Britain and Northern Ireland, H.E. Mr. Douglas Hurd; and the Secretary of State of the United States of America, H.E. Mr. Warren Christopher.

The Ministers congratulated the Secretary-General on his continued outstanding service to the United Nations and to the principles embodied in its Charter. They pledged strong support for efforts to improve the efficiency of the United Nations and to revitalize the Organization's peace-keeping capabilities.

The Ministers noted the fivefold increase in United Nations peace operations over the past five years: the numerous requests for additional missions due to the proliferation of local conflicts; the heightening in the level of danger and complexity of such missions; the efforts under way to improve the Organization's peace-keeping capabilities; the need for the United Nations to cooperate closely with regional organizations; and the value of preventive diplomacy within the framework of the United Nations Charter.

Bearing these concerns in mind, the Ministers agreed, in the spirit of the Secretary-General's "Agenda for Peace", to cooperate in strengthening the capabilities of the United Nations to carry out the full spectrum of peace- keeping operations under the authority of the

Security Council. They took note of the work being done on peace-keeping reform and stressed the importance of improving budget procedures; modernizing command, control and communications; professionalizing and institutionalizing planning and civilian training functions and enhancing public affairs capabilities and establishing a high degree of coordination among States willing to contribute troops and other forms of material assistance to United Nations peace operations. In this context, the Ministers welcome the contacts in train between the Secretariat and member States concerning the notification by member States of specific forces or capabilities which with the approval of national authorities they could make available to the United Nations on a case-by-case basis.

Given the gap between current demands on the United Nations and its capabilities pending the reforms mentioned above, the Ministers affirmed that new commitments should be weighed very carefully, and made only after fundamental questions of mandate, objectives, adequacy of force, availability of resources, risk to personnel and length of mandate have been examined and satisfactorily resolved.

The Ministers expressed the belief that experience gained in United Nations peace-keeping operations in recent years, such as in Namibia, El Salvador and Cambodia, provides a basis for confidence that continued efforts to strengthen capabilities will yield good results. They stressed the importance of applying the lessons learned in past and current operations, and observed that in this new era, establishing a durable peace often requires sustained effort both by the international community and by the people of the State or States involved.

The Ministers reviewed with the Secretary-General a number of the peace- keeping missions that are currently proposed or under way.

In that regard, the Ministers paid tribute to the accomplishments of the United Nations in Cambodia and noted with satisfaction that the United Nations Transitional Authority in Cambodia successfully fulfilled its mandate. Cambodia's return to constitutional government is a major achievement for the United Nations and the Cambodian people. The Ministers agreed to consider, on the advice of the Secretary-General and at the request of the Cambodian Government, how a continued United Nations presence, which might include a modest number of military observers, would contribute further to peace and stability after the departure of UNTAC.

The Ministers stressed the importance they attach to the role the United Nations is playing in helping to resolve conflicts in Africa. In this context they noted the progress that has been made in Somalia in ending famine, restoring secure conditions throughout most of the country and establishing a framework for national reconciliation.

They agreed on the importance of further steps to enhance security and to achieve a political settlement. They also reviewed the situation in Angola, Mozambique, Rwanda and Liberia and the contributions the United Nations can make to resolve these conflicts.

The Ministers expressed their support for the measures taken by the Secretary-General and the Security Council to assist in bringing to an end the conflicts on the territory of the former USSR, in particular in Abkhazia (Republic of Georgia), in border areas of Tajikistan and in support of the CSCE in the Nagorny Karabakh region of the Azerbaijani Republic. They welcomed the peace-keeping efforts of the Russian Federation and other independent States of the former Soviet Union to establish and monitor cease-fires and facilitate negotiated solutions, with the agreement of the countries concerned.

The Ministers discussed the situation in the former Yugoslavia. They called upon all parties to reach urgently a negotiated solution to the conflict in Bosnia which will permit the implementation of the peace-keeping operation envisaged in the Stoltenberg-Owen Plan under the aegis of the United Nations. They stated their determination to act under the relevant Security Council resolutions to enable UNPROFOR to carry out its peace-keeping and humanitarian aid mandates successfully, and to implement resolutions 808 and 827 by establishing and supporting an international tribunal to investigate and prosecute those responsible for the gross violations of international humanitarian law that have occurred within former Yugoslavia since 1991.

The Ministers noted that the role of the United Nations continues to grow in importance, creating new opportunities while also placing severe stress on the financial and other resources of the Organization. They stressed the common stake that all States and peoples have in assisting the United Nations to meet its potential as a forward-looking force for peace, development and the other objectives of the Charter.

The Ministers stressed the need for all Member States to pay their contributions in full and on time. The Ministers expressed the view that global problems cannot be dealt with successfully unless international institutions, including the United Nations, are strengthened, which will not happen in the absence of broad public support. They agreed that the United Nations and its agencies and programmes must be effective, disciplined and accountable. In that regard, they emphasized the importance of strengthened oversight of United Nations operations and welcomed recent steps in that direction.

The Ministers stressed the need for close cooperation and coordination between the United Nations peace-keeping and humanitarian assistance operations. They condemned the obstruction of deliveries of humanitarian assistance and attacks on relief workers that have occurred in some States. They called upon all States and all parties in an armed conflict to abide by their obligations under international humanitarian law to allow effective and unhindered delivery of humanitarian assistance.

The Ministers viewed with great satisfaction the breakthrough agreement that has been reached between the State of Israel and the Palestine Liberation Organization. They note that the agreement is consistent with resolutions 242 and 338 of the Security Council and that it takes into account the right to security for all parties in the region, including Israel, and takes account of the legitimate political rights of the Palestinian people. The Ministers expressed the hope that this first agreement will facilitate additional agreements which, taken together, will constitute a comprehensive, just and lasting peace. The Ministers urged the international community to mobilize resources in order to see that the agreement produces tangible improvements in the security and daily lives of Palestinians and Israelis. They stressed the need to start improving immediately the economic situation in Gaza and the West Bank.

The Ministers discussed developments in Iraq. They welcomed the recent contacts between UNSCOM and Iraq but reaffirmed that Iraq must fully comply with all applicable Security Council resolutions.

The Ministers expressed strong and continued support for the movement towards democracy and an end to all forms of apartheid in South Africa. They welcomed efforts by leaders of all sides to avoid additional violence and discord, while noting with appreciation the constructive role being played in South Africa by United Nations and other international peace observers. They urged all South African parties to redouble their efforts to reach consensus on the transitional arrangements and constitutional issues still outstanding and to proceed to elections in the coming year.

The Ministers thanked the Secretary-General for his invitation to meet, pledged their continued commitment to a stronger and more effective United Nations and agreed to remain in close consultation about issues of widespread international concern.

Document 103

Further report of the Secretary-General on the implementation of Security Council resolution 745 (1992) by which UNTAC was established

S/26529, 5 October 1993

1. In accordance with resolution 745 (1992), by which the Security Council established the United Nations Transitional Authority in Cambodia (UNTAC), I have submitted a number of reports to the Council on the progress of the operation, as well as special reports required by the rapidly changing circumstances and unexpected developments in Cambodia. The latest of those reports (S/26360 of 26 August 1993) described developments since the elections successfully conducted in Cambodia by UNTAC in May 1993, the progress of the withdrawal of UNTAC military and civilian staff and preparations for the post-UNTAC period. On the basis of that report, the Security Council adopted resolution 860 (1993), by which, *inter alia*, it confirmed that UNTAC's functions under the Paris Agreements should end upon the creation in September 1993 of a new government of Cambodia consistent with those Agreements.

2. The mandate of UNTAC has now been accomplished in accordance with resolutions 745 (1992) and 860 (1993). On 19 September 1993, the 120-member Constituent Assembly which had been elected in May concluded its deliberations over a new Constitution. On 21 September 1993, the Assembly formally adopted the Constitution by a vote of 113 to 5 against, with 2 abstentions, a greater margin than the two-thirds majority specified in the Paris Agreements.

3. On 24 September 1993, His Royal Highness Prince Norodom Sihanouk, Head of State, formally promulgated the Constitution in Phnom Penh. Accordingly, Cambodia is now a constitutional monarchy with the official name "The Kingdom of Cambodia", and is an independent, sovereign, peaceful, neutral and non-aligned State. The same day, Prince Sihanouk was elected King of Cambodia by the Royal Council of the Throne. The powers and duties of the monarch are set forth in the Constitution in accordance with its article 7, which states that the King holds the throne but shall not hold power. In accordance with the Constitution and the Paris Agreements, the Constituent Assembly transformed itself into a legislative assembly.

4. The Constitution also stipulates that the Kingdom of Cambodia shall recognize and respect human

rights in accordance with the Charter of the United Nations, the Universal Declaration of Human Rights and all international instruments related to human rights and the rights of women and children. In accordance with article 51 of the Constitution, the Kingdom of Cambodia shall adopt a multi-party, free, democratic regime.

5. Following his election, King Sihanouk appointed His Royal Highness Prince Norodom Ranariddh, leader of the Front Uni National pour un Cambodge Indépendant, Neutre, Pacifique et Coopératif (FUNCINPEC) party, as First Prime Minister of Cambodia. FUNCINPEC won 58 seats in the Constituent Assembly. Mr. Hun Sen, leader of the Cambodian People's Party (CPP), which won 51 seats in the Assembly, was appointed Second Prime Minister.

6. Thus, the mandate entrusted to UNTAC was successfully concluded on 24 September 1993. My Special Representative for Cambodia left Cambodia on 26 September 1993.

7. The plan for the withdrawal of UNTAC personnel described in paragraphs 9 to 33 of my report of 16 July 1993 (S/26090) is proceeding smoothly. The Bulgarian, Tunisian, Uruguayan, Bangladeshi, Pakistani and Indian battalions of the Military Component have now all left Cambodia and there is no longer an UNTAC presence in the seven eastern Provinces of Ratana Kiri, Mondol Kiri, Stung Treng, Kratie, Kompong Cham, Svey Rieng and Prey Veng. As at 30 September 1993, the Military Component stood at 9,373 all ranks. In accordance with Security Council resolution 860 (1993), the Military Component is scheduled to complete its withdrawal from the country by 15 November 1993.

8. Of the 3,600 members of the UNTAC Civilian Police Component deployed in Cambodia, only 28 headquarters officers remain in Phnom Penh as at 1 October, and they will be withdrawn on 15 October 1993.

9. The other civilian components of UNTAC have virtually completed their withdrawal. There now remains a team of administrative staff to finalize the withdrawal and disposal of UNTAC assets. I shall in due course present a final performance report to the General Assembly, as requested by the General Assembly in its resolution 47/209 B of 14 September 1993.

10. Meanwhile, action is in hand to establish the United Nations presence which is required in the post-UNTAC period to carry out a variety of functions to consolidate peace and stability in Cambodia. As indicated in my earlier reports (see also S/26090 of 16 July 1993), these include especially de-mining, economic rehabilitation and human rights.

11. It is with great satisfaction that I report to the Security Council the formation, on 24 September, of the new Government of Cambodia, based on the will of the people expressed through free and fair elections organized and conducted by the United Nations. Thus, amid great hope and rejoicing, the central objectives of the Agreements on a Comprehensive Political Settlement of the Cambodia Conflict of 23 October 1991 (S/23177, annex) and of Security Council resolution 745 (1992) were realized and the transitional period came to an end.

12. As UNTAC now completes its mandate, I would like to express my appreciation to the members of the Security Council, both past and present, for their consistent support and guidance, without which our mission could not have been accomplished. I also wish to place on record my gratitude to the 46 countries which contributed troops and/or police officers, as well as my deep sorrow and regret at the loss of UNTAC personnel through hostile action, accidents and disease. I also pay tribute to His Majesty King Sihanouk, other leaders and the people of Cambodia for their historic achievement in overcoming more than two decades of strife and devastation and laying a sound foundation for a peaceful and democratic Cambodia. It remains only to pay a tribute to my Special Representative, Mr. Yasushi Akashi, his Deputy Mr. Behrooz Sadry, the Force Commander, Lieutenant-General John Sanderson, and to all the men and women of UNTAC for their steadfastness, hard word and devotion to the goals of the UNTAC mission and to the highest ideals of the United Nations.

Document 104

Statement by the President of the Security Council concerning the successful completion of the mandate of UNTAC

S/26531, 5 October 1993

On behalf of the members of the Security Council, I wish to thank Prince Norodom Ranariddh, First Prime Minister, and Mr. Hun Sen, Second Prime Minister, of the Royal Government of Cambodia for their presence here and to express the satisfaction of the Security Council at the auspicious developments that have taken place in Cambodia since the holding of the elections of 23 to 28 May 1993, in particular the proclamation of the Cambodian Constitution on 24 September 1993 and the creation of the new government of Cambodia.

I also take this opportunity to congratulate His Majesty King Norodom Sihanouk, Head of State of Cambodia, on his accession to the throne and to pay tribute to the continuing role played by His Majesty in the quest for national reconciliation and a better future for all Cambodia.

In the light of the successful completion of the mandate of the United Nations Transitional Authority in Cambodia, the Council reiterates its recognition at the remarkable work carried out by the Authority, under the leadership of the Secretary-General and his Special Representative, Mr. Yasushi Akashi.

The Security Council stresses the importance of the continued support of the international community to the consolidation of peace and democracy and the promotion of development in Cambodia.

Taking into account the letter dated 26 September 1993 addressed to the Secretary-General by Prince Norodom Ranariddh, First Prime Minister, and Mr. Hun Sen, Second Prime Minister, and the further report of the Secretary-General on the implementation of Security Council resolution 745 (1992) of 28 February 1992 which members of the Council have just received, the Council will continue to study the situation in Cambodia and will consider what action it should take.

Document 105

Further report of the Secretary-General pursuant to paragraph 7 of resolution 840 (1993) conveying request by the Government of Cambodia for the dispatch of 20 to 30 unarmed United Nations military observers to Cambodia for six months following the end of UNTAC's mandate

S/26546, 7 October 1993

1. It will be recalled that, in my report of 26 August 1993 (S/26360), I indicated my belief that, when the mandate of the United Nations Transitional Authority in Cambodia (UNTAC) has been concluded, the correct course, in accordance with previous practice in such cases, was to terminate the United Nations military presence and concentrate the resources available on civilian activities in support of peace-building in the new Cambodia. I added, however, that, if the new Government were to request a post-UNTAC military presence, with a clear indication of the tasks it would be expected to perform, I would of course give careful consideration to such a request and submit a report to the Security Council on the feasibility of the tasks proposed and the resources that would be required to carry them out.

2. I have received a letter dated 26 September 1993, jointly signed by His Royal Highness Prince Norodom Ranariddh, First Prime Minister, and His Excellency Mr. Hun Sen, Second Prime Minister, of the Royal Government of Cambodia. In it the Prime Ministers, *inter alia*, referring to the tensions that will still remain in Cambodia, especially in the provinces, after the end of UNTAC's mandate, and to the need to build confidence among the Cambodian people, requested me to consider the possibility of dispatching some 20 to 30 unarmed United Nations military observers to Cambodia for a period of six months following the end of UNTAC's mandate. The letter has been brought to the attention of the members of the Security Council.

3. It remains my belief, as stated in my report of 26 August 1993, that the efforts and resources of the United Nations in support of Cambodia should, henceforward, be concentrated on civilian activities in the fields of reconstruction and development, as well as human rights and mine clearance. Nevertheless, the request formally submitted by the two Prime Ministers of Cambodia, for which His Majesty King Norodom Sihanouk has also expressed support, must receive serious consideration. As the Prime Ministers point out, problems of security still remain in Cambodia. On 4 October 1993, they reiterated to me their conviction that the presence of a limited number of unarmed United Nations military officers, for a strictly limited period, would strengthen confidence among the people and thus enhance the stability of Cambodia and its new Government at this crucial time.

4. I am not fully convinced that a small group of military officers based in Phnom Penh would in practice be able to play an effective part in controlling or resolving the remaining security problems in Cambodia. There must also be doubt about deploying a merely symbolic military presence at a time of acute financial crisis. But if the Security Council decides to respond positively to the strongly expressed request by the two Prime Ministers for this gesture of support from the United Nations, I recommend that it authorize the establishment in Phnom Penh of a team of 20 military liaison officers, contributed by Governments, for a single period of six months. These liaison officers would be separate from the integrated office which I propose to establish in Cambodia (see S/26090, para. 39) and their team leader would report directly to and receive instructions from me. Their mandate would be limited to maintaining liaison with the Royal Government of Cambodia and reporting to me on matters affecting security in Cambodia.

5. Should the Security Council concur with the recommendation outlined above, I shall submit at an early date a more detailed plan of deployment and an estimate of the resources required.

Document 106

Further report of the Secretary-General on the establishment in Phnom Penh of a team of 20 military liaison officers

S/26649, 27 October 1993
(including addendum, S/26649/Add.1, 3 November 1993)

1. In a letter dated 12 October 1993 (S/26570), the President of the Security Council referred to my report of 7 October (S/26546) and indicated that the members of the Council agreed in principle with my recommendations, in response to a request from the Royal Government of Cambodia, to establish in Phnom Penh a team of 20 military liaison officers for a single period of six months. The members of the Council invited me to submit a further report setting out in greater detail the proposed objectives and terms of reference of such a team, together with detailed plans for its dispatch and an estimate of the resources required. This report is submitted in accordance with that request.

2. The task of the military liaison team would be to maintain close liaison with the Government and report to me on matters affecting security in Cambodia. It would also assist the Government in dealing with residual military matters related to the Paris Agreements. It will be recalled that, in requesting such presence, the Government of Cambodia referred to the tensions that will still remain in Cambodia, especially in the provinces, after the end of UNTAC's mandate, and to the need to build confidence among the Cambodian people.

3. The team would be headed in the field by a Chief Military Liaison Officer (CMLO) designated by the Secretary-General with the consent of the Security Council. The CMLO would report to the Secretary-General, who would regularly inform the Security Council on the activities of the team. All matters that might affect the nature and the continued effective functioning of the team also would be reported to the Security Council for its decision. The team would be established for a single period of six months.

4. The military liaison team would be based in Phnom Penh and maintain close and regular liaison with the Government and the Royal Cambodian Armed Forces on matters affecting security in Cambodia. Members of the team would undertake activities outside Phnom Penh on the CMLO's initiative or at the request of the Cambodian authorities provided that the CMLO considered the activities requested to be necessary in order to carry out the team's liaison and reporting functions.

5. The 20 unarmed military officers who would serve as liaison officers would be provided by Governments at the request of the Secretary-General. The contributing countries would be selected after the usual consultations and with the concurrence of the Security Council, bearing in mind the accepted principle of equitable geographical representation. Should the Security Council approve these proposals, an effort will be made to secure the required personnel to the extent possible from among UNTAC military personnel who are currently present in Cambodia pending completion of the withdrawal. It is estimated that, in order to carry out their tasks, the liaison officers would be assisted by 2 international and 13 locally-recruited civilian support staff. The bulk of the logistic equipment required by the team is

expected to be drawn from UNTAC's existing resources.

6. In the letter of the President of the Council (S/26570), the members of the Council also invited me to consider and address the implications of the possibility of incorporating the officers in the United Nations office I plan to establish in Cambodia, as was suggested in the letter from the Government of Cambodia. I have accordingly given careful consideration to such a course.

7. The members of the Council will recall that, in my report of 26 August 1993 (S/26360, para. 33), I indicated my intention to establish in Phnom Penh an integrated office in order to ensure effective coordination, in close consultation with the Cambodian Government, of the full range of civilian activities that will be undertaken by various agencies of the United Nations system in Cambodia. These activities can be expected to be pursued, subject to the wishes of the Royal Government of Cambodia, on a continuous basis for a considerable period of time. The proposed deployment to Cambodia of a small number of military officers for a strictly limited period is, by contrast, an exceptional transitional measure of a short term nature. In accordance with my belief that, when the mandate of a United Nations peace-keeping operation has been concluded, the correct course is to terminate the United Nations military presence and concentrate the resources available on civilian activities in support of peace-building, it would seem better to keep the short term military activity separate from the long term civilian activities which will be coordinated through the integrated office.

8. In practice, the Chief Military Liaison Officer will be instructed to maintain regular contact with the United Nations Representative and, if so requested, to advise her or him on matters related to the security of United Nations personnel operating in Cambodia. It is also envisaged that administrative and logistic support services and resources would be shared where this would produce significant savings. The estimated cost of the proposed team would be submitted shortly as addendum to the present report.

9. I accordingly maintain my recommendation that the military liaison teams should be separate from the integrated office.

Addendum (S/26649/Add.1)

1. In my report to the Security Council of 27 October 1993 (S/26649), I indicated in paragraph 8 that the estimated cost of the proposed team of 20 military liaison officers would be submitted shortly as an addendum to that report.

2. Should the Security Council approve my recommendation for the establishment in Phnom Penh of a team of 20 military liaison officers, it is estimated that the total cost of the operation for a six-month period would amount to $1,060,000 gross and would include the Chief Military Liaison Officer, 2 international and 13 locally recruited civilian support staff. These estimates have been prepared on the assumption that any air transportation requirements within Cambodia would be provided free of charge by the Government of Cambodia. A breakdown of the estimated cost by main categories of expenditure is provided for information purposes in the annex to the present addendum.

3. Should the Security Council decide on the establishment in Phnom Penh of a team of 20 military liaison officers, it would be my recommendation to the General Assembly that the costs relating thereto should be considered an expense of the Organization to be borne by Member States in accordance with Article 17, paragraph 2, of the Charter of the United Nations and that the assessments to be levied on Member States should be credited to a special account to be established for that purpose.

Annex

Costs estimates for the establishment in Phnom Penh of 20 military liaison officers for the period from *1 November 1993 to 30 April 1994*
(In thousands of United States dollars)

1	Military personnel	
	(a) Military liaison officers	547.8
	(b) Other costs	100.0
2.	Civilian personnel	270.4
3.	Vehicle operations	19.5
4.	Communications	49.0
5.	Miscellaneous supplies, services, and support costs	73.3
	Total	1 060.0

Document 107

Letter dated 28 October 1993 from the Secretary-General to the President of the Security Council concerning the schedule of the Military Component of UNTAC for complete withdrawal from Cambodia

S/26675, 1 November 1993

The members of the Security Council will recall that I indicated in my reports (S/26090 and S/26360) that the Military Component of the United Nations Transitional Authority in Cambodia (UNTAC) was scheduled to complete its withdrawal from Cambodia by 15 November 1993. The Security Council, in resolution 860 (1993), approved the UNTAC withdrawal plan and decided that, in order to ensure a safe and an orderly withdrawal of the military component of UNTAC, the period of such withdrawal would end on 15 November 1993.

The Officer-in-Charge of the withdrawal of UNTAC has now reported that, as withdrawal has progressed in accordance with the plan, security conditions in the country have deteriorated, and incidence of theft of UNTAC vehicles and other property, often by armed elements, has increased. UNTAC has further pointed out that, in the next stage of withdrawal, equipment will need to be retrieved from outlying areas following the departure of military personnel, which could expose UNTAC civilian staff concerned to heightened insecurity.

In the circumstances, the Officer-in-Charge has urgently requested the extension of deployment beyond 15 November of the following categories of UNTAC military personnel:

(a) Military Police

-71 Military Police Officers between 16 and 30 November 1993;

-30 Military Police Officers between 1 and 31 December 1993;

(b) Medical Unit

-10 members between 16 November and 7 December 1993;

-8 members between 8 and 31 December 1993.

It is my belief that these limited extensions are necessary in order to ensure the safety and security of UNTAC personnel and its equipment as they complete the withdrawal. I therefore request that this matter be brought to the attention of the members of the Council.

The members of the Council will also recall that I indicated in my report (S/26360) that mine clearance will continue to be a major need in the post-conflict peace-building in Cambodia. I also indicated that the United Nations Trust Fund for Demining in Cambodia would be maintained, and that continued United Nations involvement with demining activities would be required for the foreseeable future.

I believe that further United Nations involvement in the executive and managerial responsibilities of CMAC is inappropriate. However, continued technical support and capacity-building will be required to enable CMAC to become self-sufficient. I have therefore asked UNDP to enter into consultations with the new Cambodian Government with a view to providing technical support and capacity-building as required for a limited duration.

Pending such arrangements and in order to avert a damaging break in this important activity, I propose to extend the deployment of 17 existing members of the Mine Clearance and Training Unit of UNTAC until 30 November 1993. I request that this matter also be brought to the attention of the Council members.

Financial implications of the proposed extensions will be reflected in the next performance report on UNTAC.

(*Signed*) Boutros BOUTROS-GHALI

Document 108

Security Council resolution on transitional period in Cambodia following the withdrawal of UNTAC

S/RES/880 (1993), 4 November 1993

The Security Council,

Recalling its resolution 745 (1992) of 28 February 1992 concerning the implementation plan of the agreements on a comprehensive political settlement to the Cambodian conflict signed in Paris on 23 October 1991, 1/ and subsequent relevant resolutions,

Taking note of the further reports of the Secretary-General of 5 October 1993, 2/ 7 October 1993 3/ and 27 October and 3 November 1993,4/ and of his letter dated 28 October 1993 to the President of the Security Council, 5/

Noting with satisfaction the success during the transitional period of the Cambodian people, under the leadership of His Royal Highness Prince Norodom Sihanouk, King of Cambodia, in promoting peace, stability and national reconciliation,

Welcoming the adoption of the constitution in accordance with the Paris agreements on Cambodia,

Recognizing the termination of the mandate of the United Nations Transitional Authority in Cambodia following the establishment of the constitutional government on 24 September 1993 in accordance with the Paris agreements,

Noting with great satisfaction that, with the successful conclusion of the Authority's mission following the election of 23 to 28 May 1993, the goal of the Paris agreements of restoring to the Cambodian people and their democratically elected leaders their primary responsibility for peace, stability, national reconciliation and reconstruction in their country has been achieved,

Paying tribute to those Member States which contributed personnel to the Authority and expressing sympathy and sorrow to those Governments whose nationals lost their lives or suffered casualties for the cause of peace in Cambodia, as well as to their families,

Stressing the importance of consolidating the achievements of the Cambodian people by smooth and rapid delivery of appropriate international assistance towards rehabilitation, reconstruction and development in Cambodia and towards peace-building in that country,

Noting the need to ensure the safe and orderly completion of the withdrawal of the military component of the Authority from Cambodia, and the continuity of the vital mine clearance and training functions of the Cambodian Mine Action Centre,

1. *Welcomes* the accession to the throne of His Royal Highness Prince Norodom Sihanouk, King of Cambodia, and stresses the importance of his continuing role in consolidating peace, stability and genuine national reconciliation in Cambodia;

2. *Welcomes also* the formation of the new Government of all Cambodia, established in accordance with the constitution and based upon the recent election;

3. *Pays tribute* to the work of the United Nations Transitional Authority in Cambodia whose success, under the authority of the Secretary-General and his Special Representative, constitutes a major achievement for the United Nations;

4. *Calls upon* all States to respect the sovereignty, independence, territorial integrity and inviolability, neutrality and national unity of Cambodia;

5. *Demands* the cessation of all illegal acts of violence, on whatever grounds, and the cessation of military activities directed against the democratically elected Government of Cambodia, as well as against the personnel of the Authority and other United Nations and international agencies;

6. *Affirms* the importance, particularly in view of the recent tragic history of Cambodia, of ensuring respect for international humanitarian law in that country, welcomes in this regard the commitment of the First Prime Minister of the Royal Government of Cambodia to the implementation of the relevant provisions of the new Cambodian Constitution, and endorses the arrangements foreshadowed in paragraphs 27 to 29 of the report of the Secretary-General of 26 August 1993 6/ for appropriate United Nations activities in support of this commitment in accordance with the relevant provisions of the agreements on a comprehensive political settlement to the Cambodian conflict signed in Paris on 23 October 1991; 1/

7. *Urges* Member States to assist the Cambodian Mine Action Centre with technical experts and equipment, and to support demining work through voluntary contributions;

1/ S/23177 [Document 19]
2/ S/26529 [Document 103]
3/ S/26546 [Document 105]
4/ S/26649 and Add.1 [Document 106]
5/ S/26675 [Document 107]
6/ S/26360 [Document 100]

8. *Expresses the hope* that arrangements can be made as soon as possible so that relevant trust fund monies can be disbursed to the Centre and so that technical experts can be provided to the Centre through the United Nations Development Programme;

9. *Notes* that, with the exceptions set out in paragraphs 10 and 11 below, the safe and orderly withdrawal of the military component of the Authority provided for in resolution 860 (1993) of 27 August 1993 continues and will end on 15 November 1993;

10. *Decides* to extend the period of withdrawal of the Mine Clearance and Training Unit of the Authority until 30 November 1993;

11. *Also decides* to extend the period of withdrawal beyond 15 November 1993 for elements of the military police and medical components of the Authority in accordance with the detailed recommendations set out in the letter dated 28 October 1993 from the Secretary-General to the President of the Security Council, on the basis that all of these elements will be withdrawn by 31 December 1993;

12. *Further decides* to establish a team of twenty military liaison officers for a single period of six months with a mandate to report on matters affecting security in Cambodia, to maintain liaison with the Government of Cambodia and to assist the Government in dealing with residual military matters relating to the Paris agreements;

13. *Welcomes* the intention of the Secretary-General, in the light of the request by the Royal Government of Cambodia and the continuing commitment of the United Nations to Cambodia, to appoint for a period to be agreed upon by the Secretary-General and the Government of Cambodia, a person to coordinate the United Nations presence in Cambodia, in accordance with the spirit and principles of the Paris agreements;

14. *Urges* Member States to continue to help the Government of Cambodia in achieving its objectives of national reconciliation and rehabilitation of Cambodia and requests them to implement without delay the undertakings made during the meeting of the International Committee on the Reconstruction of Cambodia and stresses the need for quick disbursing assistance to provide support to help alleviate the fiscal crisis currently facing the new Government;

15. *Welcomes* the intention of the Secretary-General to report on the lessons learned during the course of the Authority in the context of the Agenda for Peace.

Document 109

General Assembly resolution on the situation of human rights in Cambodia

A/RES/48/154, 20 Dceember 1993

The General Assembly,

Guided by the principles embodied in the Charter of the United Nations, the Universal Declaration of Human Rights 1/ and the International Covenants on Human Rights, 2/

Taking note of the Agreement on a Comprehensive Political Settlement of the Cambodia Conflict 3/ signed on 23 October 1991, including part III thereof, relating to human rights,

Taking note also of Commission on Human Rights resolution 1993/6 of 19 February 1993, 4/

Bearing in mind the role and responsibilities of the United Nations and the international community in the process of the rehabilitation and reconstruction of Cambodia,

Recognizing that the tragic recent history of Cambodia requires special measures to assure the protection of the human rights of all people in the country and the non-return to the policies and practices of the past, as stipulated in the agreements signed in Paris on 23 October 1991, 3/

Welcoming the elections of May 1993 and the inauguration of the Government of the Kingdom of Cambodia,

1. *Welcomes* the establishment in Cambodia of an operational presence of the Centre for Human Rights of the Secretariat:

(*a*) To manage the implementation of educational and technical assistance and advisory services programmes, and to ensure their continuation;

1/ Resolution 217 A (III)
2/ Resolution 2200 A (XXI) annex
3/ A/46/608-S/23177 [Document 19]
4/ E/1993/23

(*b*) To assist the Government of Cambodia established after the election, at its request, in meeting its obligations under the human rights instruments recently adhered to, including the preparation of reports to the relevant monitoring committees;

(*c*) To provide support to bona fide human rights groups in Cambodia;

(*d*) To contribute to the creation and/or strengthening of national institutions for the promotion and protection of human rights;

(*e*) To continue to assist with the drafting and implementation of legislation to promote and protect human rights;

(*f*) To continue to assist with the training of persons responsible for the administration of justice;

2. *Requests* the Secretary-General, in line with all effective measures, to assure the protection of the human rights of all people in Cambodia and to ensure adequate resources, from within existing overall United Nations resources, for the functioning of the operational presence of the Centre for Human Rights in Cambodia;

3. *Welcomes* the appointment by the Secretary-General of a Special Representative to undertake the tasks set out in paragraph 6 of Commission on Human Rights resolution 1993/6;

4. *Requests* the Secretary-General to provide all necessary resources, from within existing resources, to enable the Special Representative to fulfil those tasks expeditiously;

5. *Also requests* the Secretary-General to report to the General Assembly at its forty-ninth session on the role of the Centre for Human Rights in assisting the Cambodian Government and people in the promotion and protection of human rights and on any recommendations made by the Special Representative on matters within his mandate;

6. *Decides* to continue its consideration of the situation of human rights in Cambodia at its forty-ninth session.

Document 110

Mid-term report of the Secretary-General on the United Nations Military Liaison Team in Cambodia

S/1994/169, 14 February 1994

1. The United Nations Military Liaison Team was established by Security Council resolution 880 (1993) of 4 November 1993, following a request by the two Co-Prime Ministers of Cambodia. Resolution 880 (1993) mandates the Military Liaison Team to "report on matters affecting security in Cambodia, to maintain liaison with the Government of Cambodia and to assist the Government in dealing with residual matters relating to the Paris Agreements". The purpose of the present report is to inform the Security Council of the Team's activities, and apprise it of the security situation prevailing in Cambodia for the period 15 November 1993 to 31 January 1994.

2. The 20-member United Nations Military Liaison Team was established in Phnom Penh on 15 November 1993 for a period of six months, following the withdrawal of the United Nations Transitional Authority in Cambodia (UNTAC). The mandate of the Military Liaison Team will expire on 15 May 1994. The members of the Team are drawn from the following countries: Austria, Bangladesh, Belgium, China, France, India, Indonesia, Malaysia, New Zealand, Pakistan, Poland, Russian Federation, Thailand and Uruguay. The Chief Military Liaison Officer is Colonel Muniruz Zaman (Bangladesh). Administrative support is provided by two international staff.

3. The Military Liaison Team has established extensive liaison with the relevant Cambodian government ministries and has kept close contact with other United Nations agencies, embassies of Governments represented in Cambodia and non-governmental organizations (NGOs).

4. During the reporting period, hostilities have continued between the Royal Cambodian Armed Forces (RCAF) and the National Army of Democratic Kampuchea (NADK). Fighting has occurred mainly in the north-western areas of Anlong Veng and Preah Vihear, along the border with Thailand and the Lao People's Democratic Republic. According to an official government statement, there have been approximately 3,000 defectors from NADK to the government side to date.

5. At the same time, efforts have taken place to arrive at a political settlement. The First Prime Minister, Prince Norodom Ranariddh, met twice with Mr. Khieu Samphan, the head of the Party of Democratic Kampuchea (PDK), to discuss the issue of integration of

NADK into the mainstream political establishment. The first meeting took place on mid-December 1993 in Bangkok, Thailand, where Prince Ranariddh presented to Mr. Khieu Samphan a three-point proposal for a political settlement in return for a cease-fire, withdrawal of NADK forces from NADK-held territory and integration of the NADK armed forces into RCAF. Prince Ranariddh has stated that the Government would consider amending the Constitution to include the leaders of NADK in the Government if NADK agreed to abide by the conditions laid down. A second meeting was held in Thailand in early January 1994. The Government feels strongly that NADK will have to agree to a cease-fire before serious discussions can take place, while NADK has stated that it will continue fighting until a suitable framework for political participation is established.

6. Allegations that NADK was receiving support from Thai territory caused concern during the reporting period. In mid-January, the Prime Minister of Thailand, Mr. Chuan Leekpai, visited Cambodia and both Governments affirmed on that occasion their determination to strengthen bilateral ties based on mutual benefit and respect for their independence, sovereignty, territorial integrity and non-interference in each other's internal affairs. They agreed to establish a joint commission for bilateral cooperation and a separate joint committee on the demarcation of international borders.

7. There have been incidents of violence against ethnic Vietnamese for which NADK is reported to have been responsible. The Government is in the process of formulating immigration laws that will pertain to the ethnic Vietnamese minority population in Cambodia.

8. The Military Liaison Team has followed the integration of factional forces into RCAF as a residual issue under the Paris Agreements. This process is under way at all levels of command, from the Ministry of Defence to units in the field. RCAF is putting emphasis on the training of officers and soldiers in the field. With effet from February 1994, a three- to six-month general staff course is proposed for high-ranking army officers. RCAF has reported that it has completed the restructuring of its forces and that the Ministry of Defence and General Staff have been restructured. Disciplinary problems have been reported in some units, which are mostly attributed to low morale resulting from non-payment of salaries and the lack of basic amenities and supplies. There has been a drive to eliminate previous factional identities through such efforts as the standardization of military uniforms. Defence cooperation and aid are being sought from other countries with a view to modernizing and enhancing the operational efficiency of RCAF.

9. Internal security in Cambodia has become more precarious following the withdrawal of the military component of UNTAC. The depressed state of the economy continues and the prolonged non-payment of salaries to civil servants, including soldiers of RCAF, and the widespread availability of weapons have aggravated the situation. Many illegal checkpoints are reported to have been set up throughout the countryside by RCAF soldiers and others, who extort money from travellers. A large number of thefts and armed robberies have been reported and banditry is widespread. Several vehicles and office equipment belonging to the Military Liaison Team have been stolen, often at gunpoint. However, government departments that are responsible for the maintenance of law and order are being strengthened and Cambodia has entered into bilateral agreements with other countries in support of these efforts.

Document 111

Message of the Secretary-General to the second meeting of the International Committee on the Reconstruction of Cambodia, Tokyo, 10-11 March 1994

Not issued as a United Nations document

Much has happened since the Ministerial Conference on the Rehabilitation and Reconstruction of Cambodia met here in Tokyo twenty months ago. Within this short span of time, we have witnessed, in fact, nothing less than the rebirth of a new nation. Following the extraordinarily successful election last May, a new democratic Constitution has been promulgated and a new Government established, with His Majesty King Norodom Sihanouk as Head of State.

Today, Cambodia has re-emerged as a sovereign, independent nation, one that is seeking to meet the profound aspirations of its people for peace and a better future. Towards this end, the new Government of Cambodia has taken a number of significant measures in recent months to lay the foundation for a democratic political system and to rebuild the country on the basis of a market-based economy. The task of reconstruction has only just begun.

The challenge before the international community is to respond speedily and effectively to the needs of Cambodia as it undertakes the monumental task of nation-building. Determined efforts will have to be made to accelerate the pace of external technical, economic, financial, and other support to the Cambodian Government, and to provide such assistance in a coherent and coordinated manner. In this regard, may I commend the donor Governments and multilateral organizations for their valuable contributions and the important work they have carried out to date. I am gratified to note that this meeting will focus, among other things, on how to improve Cambodia's aid absorption capacity as well as various specific issues of immediate or priority concern to the Government.

After two decades of conflict, a fragile peace now exists in Cambodia. Many difficulties still lie ahead. Nevertheless, I am confident that, given the dedicated effort by the Cambodian Government and its close cooperation with the international community, Cambodia will forge ahead.

The convening of this second ICORC meeting is a reaffirmation of the continuing firm commitment of the international community, the United Nations and its specialized agencies to assist the Cambodian people in their effort to achieve durable peace and sustainable development. May I express my sincere appreciation to the Government of Japan, the host of this important meeting, and to all participants gathered here for their active support in our common endeavour. The momentum generated by the work of this meeting will undoubtedly help to reinforce the process of recovery and peace-building in Cambodia.

Document 112

Letter dated 6 May 1994 from the Secretary-General to the President of the Security Council concerning appointment of three military advisers to the United Nations representative in Cambodia

S/1994/572, 14 May 1994

I have the honour to refer to my note of 3 May by which I transmitted to the members of the Council a letter from the Permanent Representative of the Kingdom of Cambodia to the United Nations requesting the extension of the mandate of the United Nations Military Liaison Team (UNMLT) for a further period of six months. Pursuant to Security Council resolution 880 (1993), the mandate of the UNMLT will expire on 15 May 1994, unless it is extended by the Council.

In my letter of 29 March, I informed members of the Council of the appointment of Mr. Benny Widyono as my representative in Cambodia (S/1994/389). In the interest of supporting the Government's efforts to consolidate peace in Cambodia, and since the presence of United Nations military and civilian personnel contributes, in the Government's view, to a sense of security among the Cambodian people, it would be my intention, in the event that the Council decides that the mandate of the UNMLT should not be extended beyond 15 May 1994, to appoint, with the concurrence of the Cambodian Government, three military personnel, drawn preferably from officers currently serving in the UNMLT, as advisers to my representative in Cambodia. The military advisers would assist my representative in fulfilling his mandate, in accordance with the spirit and principles of the Paris Agreements.

I should be grateful if you would bring this matter to the attention of the members of the Security Council.

(*Signed*) Boutros BOUTROS-GHALI

Document 113

Letter dated 7 May 1994 from King Norodom Sihanouk of Cambodia to the Secretary-General concerning the situation in Cambodia

A/49/160-S/1994/570, 13 May 1994

In recent weeks, the situation in Cambodia has deteriorated to a dangerous degree. Iincreasingly violent and murderous military clashes are taking place between the Khmer Royal Armed Forces and armed elements from the Democratic Kampuchea Party (Khmer Rouge).

This rise in hostilities has serious consequences, both because of the material damage which it is causing, towns and villages bombarded and set on fire, crops pillaged or destroyed, roads, bridges and railways destroyed following reconstruction; planting of new mines, etc., and through losses of human lives, an increasing number of seriously wounded persons, etc.

Tens of thousands of inhabitants in distress are condemned to flee the combat zones, and they serve to swell the ranks of the refugees repatriated by the Office of the United Nations High Commissioner for Refugees, more than 84 per cent of whom are still reliant on international food aid.

This extension of insecurity imperils the very lives of our foreign friends, several of whom have been ransomed or taken hostage. Some embassies have summoned members of non-governmental organizations or other asasociations working in regions that are threatened or at risk to fall back on Phnom Penh.

In vain, from my Beijing hospital bed and then since my return to Cambodia, I have launched many solemn appeals for a cease-fire and have proposed a round table for peace and national reconciliation in neutral territory from 2 to 7 May 1994.

The Royal Government of Cambodia has responded favourably to these proposals. The Kampuchea Democratic Party (Khmer Rouge) has confirmed its agreement in principle but nevertheless sets conditions.

In view of the limited powers vested in me by the Constitution, I feel that I have done the maximum to put to an end this conflict that has lasted too long; endangers life, even the mere survival of hundreds of thousands of my fellow countrymen, innocent civilians; compromises the efforts made by the international community to assist in the rehabilitation and reconstruction of Cambodia and presents, once again, the grave threat of an actual partition of my country and its decline towards death as a State and a nation.

These mounting perils, which theaten the stability of the fragile balance laboriously worked out in our South-East Asian region, prompt me to request your advice and opinion with regard to the provisions of the Paris Agreements and the special responsibilities of the United Nations in their implementation and application.

(Signed) NORODOM SIHANOUK

Document 114

Letter dated 19 May 1994 from the Secretary-General to King Norodom Sihanouk concerning the situation in Cambodia

Not issued as a United Nations document

I have the honour to acknowledge receipt of Your Majesty's letter dated 7 May, which was received by my Office on 13 May.

I wish to assure Your Majesty that I share his concern with regard to the deterioration in the situation in Cambodia following the resumption of hostilities between the Royal Armed Forces of Cambodia and armed elements of the Democratic Kampuchea Party. Similarly, I deeply deplore the resulting loss of human lives and destruction. It is indeed a tragedy that Cambodians must once again endure the hardships to which the implementation of the Paris Agreements was to have brought an end.

In this connection, article 5 of the second Paris Agreement, which was signed on 23 October 1993 and remains in force, sets out the types of action that the signatory States have agreed to take in the event of a violation or the threat of a violation of the sovereignty, independence, territorial integrity and inviolability, neutrality or national unity of Cambodia. This article clearly shows that the signatory States of the Paris Peace Agreements, and not the United Nations, have the primary responsibility for taking action in circumstances such as those confronting Cambodia today.

Consequently, Your Majesty's Government may wish to draw the attention of the other signatory States to their commitments in this regard under the Paris Agreements, unless Your Majesty's Government prefers to request the Co-Chairmen of the Paris Conference on Cambodia to do so.

In either case, the signatory States could be invited to begin immediate consultations with a view to taking all appropriate measures to ensure compliance with their obligations and to settle cases of violations by peaceful means. Such means include bringing the matter before the Security Council or recourse to the measures provided for in Article 33 of the Charter of the United Nations concerning the pacific settlement of disputes.

I fully support Your Majesty's efforts aimed at convening talks on national reconciliation under Your Majesty's auspices. Let me assure you that the United Nations is resolved to help the people of Cambodia to achieve peace and rebuild their country and that I will do my utmost to ensure that this noble and pressing goal is attained.

Accept, Sir, the assurances of my highest consideration.

(*Signed*) Boutros BOUTROS-GHALI

Document 115

Final report of the Secretary-General on the United Nations Military Liaison Team in Cambodia

S/1994/645, 31 May 1994

1. The United Nations Military Liaison Team in Cambodia was established on 15 November 1993 for a single period of six months, pursuant to Security Council resolution 880 (1993) of 4 November 1993. The mandate formally expired and the Team ceased operations on 15 May 1994. It will be recalled that, in February 1994, a mid-term report was issued (S/1994/169), which described the activities of the Military Liaison Team and the prevailing security situation in Cambodia for the first half of the mandate period. The purpose of the present report is to give an overview of the activities of the Military Liaison Team during its entire period of operation, while highlighting major developments affecting the security situation in Cambodia during the second half of the reporting period.

2. The Military Liaison Team continued to maintain its base at Phnom Penh and, in accordance with its mandate, its functions continued to centre around liaison and reporting activities. Liaison was conducted at the ministerial, executive and ambassadorial levels by the Chief Military Liaison Officer and at the functional level by Military Liaison Officers, who reported daily to United Nations Headquarters on security conditions and developments in Cambodia. Officers were also dispatched in mobile teams to observe areas outside Phnom Penh when requested by the Government of Cambodia and when the Chief Military Liaison Officer deemed that the issue involved related to the mandate of the Team. During the course of the reporting period, observation missions were undertaken to Pailin, to camps for defectors from the National Army of Democratic Kampuchea (NADK) at Russei Keo and Dei-eth, to a naval base at Ream, to the Officer Training Academy of the Royal Cambodian Armed Forces (RCAF) in Kompong Speu province, to the Military Police Training School at Phnom Penh and to a reorganized RCAF infantry division at Lung Vek, north of Phnom Penh.

3. During the reporting period RCAF and NADK continued to fight in the north and north-western parts of the country. RCAF conducted a number of attacks on NADK strongholds at Anlong Veng and Pailin, temporarily capturing both and reportedly causing some 30,000 refugees to cross the border into Thailand. The security situation was reported to have deteriorated extensively, particularly in the provinces of Battambang and Banteay Meanchey.

4. The restructuring of RCAF into 12 divisions was reportedly completed and the areas of responsibilities of the Military Zones were reoriented. The hierarchical structure of the Ministry of Defence and the General Staff Branch of RCAF was also reappraised. The amalgamation of all previous factional forces into RCAF at all levels of command was reportedly effected smoothly, although the distribution of various command, staff and other key appointments may have been determined through ratio proportion among various military factions, with the majority going to the Cambodian People's Party. There

appeared to be a conscious effort to conceal previous factional identities. Insufficient and inefficient administrative support, poor infrastructure and logistics and extensive minefields were reported to contribute to low morale in RCAF.

5. On 2 May 1994, the Government of Cambodia, through a letter from the Permanent Representative of Cambodia addressed to me, requested that the mandate of the Military Liaison Team be extended for a further six months. However, by a letter dated 13 May 1994 (S/1994/573), the President of the Security Council informed me that, in accordance with an alternative that I had proposed in a letter dated 6 May 1994 (S/1994/572), the Council had decided not to extend the mandate of the Team, but rather agreed that I should appoint three

military advisers in the recently established office of my representative in Cambodia to assist him in fulfilling his mandate. Three military advisers, from Belgium, France and Malaysia, have accordingly been retained in Cambodia for this purpose, following the departure of the Military Liaison Team.

6. I take this opportunity to express my appreciation to the Governments that contributed personnel to the Military Liaison Team. I also wish to pay tribute to the Chief Military Liaison Officer, the 19 Military Liaison Officers under his command and other staff serving with the Team for the manner in which they carried out their task. Their discipline and dedication were of a high order, reflecting credit on themselves, their countries and the United Nations.

Document 116

Letter dated 10 October 1994 from the Secretary-General to the President of the Security Council informing the Council of his decision to extend for six months the term of the Secretary-General's representative in Cambodia

S/1994/1182, 19 October 1994

I have the honour to refer to my letters of 29 March 1994 and 14 May 1994, contained in documents S/1994/389 and S/1994/572 respectively, by which I informed members of the Council of the appointment of Mr. Benny Widyono as my representative in Cambodia, for an intitial period of six months, and of three military advisers who would assist him in carrying out his mandate in accordance with the spirit and principles of the Paris Agreements.

In response to a request by the Government of

Cambodia, I have decided that Mr. Widyono's term be extended for a further six months and that he should continue to be assisted by three military advisers for the same duration.

I should be grateful if you would bring this matter to the attention of the members of the Security Council.

(Signed) Boutros BOUTROS-GHALI

Document 117

Letter dated 19 October 1994 from the President of the Security Council to the Secretary-General welcoming the extension of the term of the Secretary-General's representative in Cambodia

S/1994/1183, 19 October 1994

I have the honour to inform you that your letter dated 10 October 1994 (S/1994/1182) has been brought to the attention of the Council members. They take note of the information contained therein and welcome your deci-

sion to extend the term of your representative in Cambodia for a further period of six months.

(Signed) Sir David HANNAY, KCMG, President of the Security Council

V Subject index to documents

[This subject index to the documents reproduced in this book should be used in conjunction with the index on pages 57-60. A complete listing of the documents indexed below appears on pages 73-82.]

A

Administration of justice.
– Documents 70, 109

Advisory services.
– Documents 70, 109
See also: Technical cooperation.

Agenda For Peace: Preventive Diplomacy, Peacemaking and Peace-keeping.
– Document 108

Agreement concerning the Sovereignty, Independence, Territorial Integrity and Inviolability, Neutrality and National Unity of Cambodia (1991).
– Documents 6, 18-23, 29, 31, 32, 38-39, 44-45, 47-52, 54-56, 61, 67, 69, 71, 72, 74, 77, 79, 82, 83, 94, 101, 108, 114

Agreement on a Comprehensive Political Settlement of the Cambodia Conflict (1991).
– Documents 6, 17-23, 29, 31-32, 38-39, 42, 44-45, 47-52, 54-56, 61, 67, 69, 71-72, 74, 77, 79, 82-83, 89-90, 94, 101, 108,114

Akashi, Yasushi.
See: UN. Special Representative of the Secretary-General for Cambodia

Alatas, Ali
– Document 51

Armed forces.
– Documents 15, 40, 44, 47, 79, 98, 115
See also: Military personnel. Troop withdrawal.

Armed incidents.
– Documents 43, 54-55, 60-61, 65-66, 69, 72-74, 76, 78-79, 81, 84, 86, 91-92, 96, 100, 113-115
See also: Regional conflicts.

Arms transfers.
– Document 55
See also: Military assistance.

B

Boundaries.
– Documents 43, 49, 55-56, 69

Boutros-Ghali, Boutros.
– Documents 27-30, 32-33, 35, 38-39, 41, 43, 45-47, 50-55, 58, 61-63, 65-69, 78-79, 81, 85-89, 92, 96-98, 100, 103, 105-108, 110-115.

C

Cambodia. Constituent Assembly.
– Documents 71, 83, 89, 94-95, 97-98, 101

Cambodia. Interim Joint Administration.
– Documents 97-98

Cambodia. President.
– Documents 64, 68

Cambodia. Supreme National Council.
– Documents 2-6, 8-16, 18, 22, 24, 28, 30-31, 33, 38-39, 43, 45, 47, 54-55, 61, 65, 69, 71, 77, 79, 82-84, 92, 94

Cambodia. Supreme National Council—members.
– Document 3

Cambodia. Supreme National Council. President.
– Documents 3-4

Cambodia Mine Action Centre.
– Document 108

Cease-fires.
– Documents 2, 6, 8, 10, 12-13, 15, 17, 19-21, 23, 26, 33, 35, 37, 42, 49, 54-55, 65, 69, 74, 108, 110
See also: Truce supervision.

Charter of the United Nations (1945).
– Document 56

China—negotiation.
– Document 4

Civilian persons.
– Documents 30, 42, 77, 79, 81
See also: Human rights in armed conflicts.

Confidence-building measures.
– Document 105
See also: Dispute settlement. Negotiation.

Conflict resolution.
See: Dispute settlement.

H

Health personnel.
– Document 108

Human rights.
– Documents 2, 15, 19, 23, 30, 33, 37, 45, 48, 54, 65, 70, 79, 92, 97, 100, 105, 108, 109
See also: Human rights advancement. Human rights in armed conflicts.

Human rights advancement.
– Documents 70, 109

Human rights education.
– Documents 70, 109

Human rights in armed conflicts.
– Document 108
See also: Civilian persons. Prisoners of war.

Human rights institutions.
– Documents 70, 109
See also: Institution building.

Humanitarian assistance.
– Documents 23, 37, 46, 97
See also: Displaced persons. Economic assistance. International relief. Refugee assistance. Special missions.

Hun Sen.
– Documents 61, 67, 80

I

Ieng Mouly
– Document 63

Information dissemination.
– Document 79
See also: Public information.

Institution-building.
– Documents 70, 109
See also: Human rights institutions. Public administration

Interim Joint Administration.
See: Cambodia. Interim Joint Administration

International agreements.
See: Treaties.

International assistance.
See: Development assistance.

International relief.
– Document 37
See also: Humanitarian assistance.

International security.
– Document 46
See also: National security.

J

Japan—negotiation.
– Documents 49, 54

K

Khieu Samphan.
– Documents 38-39, 47, 58, 75

Khmer Rouge (Cambodia).
See: Party of Democratic Kampuchea.

L

Land mines.
– Documents 25-26, 33, 42, 79, 97, 105, 108

Laws and regulations.
– Documents 70, 109

Legislation.
See: Laws and regulations.

Liaison offices.
– Documents 105-106, 108, 110, 115

M

Military assistance.
– Document 15
See also: Arms transfers. Economic assistance. Military relations.

Military demobilization.
– Documents 40, 55, 69
See also: Armed forces. Troop withdrawal.

Military personnel.
– Documents 17, 22, 25-26, 30-31, 33, 44-45, 73, 77-79, 81, 91, 96, 101, 105-108, 110, 112, 115
See also: Armed forces.

Military relations.
– Document 34
See also: Military assistance.

Mine clearance.
See: Land mines.

Mineral resources.
– Document 55

Ministerial Conference on the Rehabilitation and Reconstruction of Cambodia (1992 : Tokyo).
– Documents 37, 49, 55, 69

N

National security.
– Documents 75, 108, 110
See also: International security. Regional security.

Natural resources.
– Documents 55, 69, 71, 79

Negotiation.
– Documents 1, 4, 7-8, 41, 43, 54-56
See also: Confidence-building measures. Consultations. Dispute settlement.

Neighbouring states.
– Documents 55-56

Non-citizens.
– Document 79

Norodom Ranariddh
– Documents 62-63, 66

Norodom Sihanouk.
– Documents 24, 28-29, 32, 52-53, 85, 87, 94, 108, 113-114

O

Oil embargo.
– Document 55

P

Paris Conference on Cambodia (1989-1991 : Paris).
– Documents 2-5, 19-21

Paris Conference on Cambodia (1989-1991 : Paris). Co-chairmen.
– Documents 18, 22, 50-54

Party of Democratic Kampuchea.
– Documents 40-41, 43-44, 47, 54-56, 58-59, 61, 65, 69, 72, 82, 113

Peace-building.
– Documents 97, 105, 106
See also: Peace-keeping operations.

Peaceful settlement of disputes.
See: Dispute settlement.

Peace-keeping operations.
– Documents 1, 2, 14, 16-19, 21-23, 25-28, 30-37, 41-42, 44-47, 49, 53-55, 57-59, 62, 65-67, 69, 71, 73-74, 77-79, 81-84, 87, 89, 91-92, 94, 96-98, 101-105, 107-108, 110, 115
See also: Peace-building.

Pérez de Cuéllar, Javier.
– Document 13

Periodic reports.
– Documents 70, 109
See also: Report preparation. Reporting procedures.

Petroleum products.
– Document 55

Police.
– Documents 30, 38, 45, 48-49, 54, 65, 79, 81, 98, 108
See also: Criminal investigation.

Political conditions.
– Documents 41, 46, 65, 69, 71, 81, 83, 94, 97, 108, 110, 113

Political parties.
– Documents 1, 54, 56, 66, 67, 71, 77, 79, 81-83, 86, 89, 92, 97

Political violence.
– Documents 62, 66-67, 71, 77, 79, 82, 84

Prisoner treatment.
– Document 79
See also: Detained persons.

Prisoners of war.
– Document 19
See also: Human rights in armed conflicts.

Programme implementation.
– Documents 31-32, 39, 43, 45, 49-52, 70

Prosecution.
– Documents 71, 79

Public administration.
– Documents 38-40, 45, 54, 65, 79, 97-98
See also: Institution-building. Public finance.

Public finance.
– Document 79
See also: Public administration.

Public information.
– Documents 42, 45
See also: Information dissemination.

R

Radio broadcasting.
– Document 49

Reconstruction.
– Documents 6, 15, 19, 23, 33, 37, 42, 45, 49, 54-55, 69, 77, 79, 89, 93-94, 97, 99-100, 105, 108, 111

Refugee assistance.
See: Humanitarian assistance. International relief. Refugee camps.

Refugee camps.
– Document 10

Refugees.
– Documents 6, 10, 19, 23, 31, 33, 37, 45, 54, 74, 113
See also: Displaced persons. International relief. Repatriation.

Regional conflicts.
– Document 46
See also: Armed incidents. Peace-keeping operations.

Regional security.
– Document 46
See also: National security.

Repatriation.
– Documents 6, 10, 19, 23, 31, 33, 37, 45, 54, 74, 79

Report preparation.
– Documents 21, 27, 109
See also: Periodic reports. Reporting procedures.

Reporting procedures.
– Document 49
See also: Periodic reports. Report preparation.

Right of assembly.
– Document 71

S

Sam Rainsy
– Document 63

Sihanouk, Norodom.
See: Norodom Sihanouk.

Son Sann
– Documents 48, 63

Sovereignty.
– Documents 1-3, 19, 23, 82, 108

Special missions.
– Documents 12-13, 17-18, 21, 105, 108, 112
See also: Dispute settlement. Humanitarian assistance.

Staff security.
– Documents 31, 42, 46, 49, 55, 57-59, 65, 71, 73-74, 76-79, 81-84, 91, 101

Staffing.
– Documents 17, 30

Supreme National Council.
See: Cambodia. Supreme National Council.

T

Technical cooperation.
– Documents 25, 37, 70, 108-109
See also: Development assistance. Election verification.

Thailand—boundaries.
– Document 56

Thailand—negotiation.
– Documents 49, 54

Timber.
– Documents 55, 69

Tokyo Declaration on the Cambodia Peace Process (1992).
– Document 37

Tokyo Declaration on the Rehabilitation and Reconstruction of Cambodia (1992).
– Document 37

Training programmes.
– Documents 25-26, 30, 79, 108-109

Treaties.
– Documents 6, 17-23, 29, 31-32, 38-39, 41-42, 44-45, 47-52, 54, 56, 61, 67, 69, 71-72, 74, 82-83, 89-90, 94, 101, 114

Troop withdrawal.
– Documents 1, 2, 6, 19, 34, 38-43, 47-49, 54, 79, 97, 101, 108
See also: Armed forces. Military demobilization.

Truce supervision.
– Documents 17, 19
See also: Cease-fires.

Trust funds.
– Documents 70, 108

U

UN. Centre For Human Rights.
– Documents 70, 109

United Nations publications of related interest

The following UN publications may be obtained from the addresses indicated below, or at your local distributor:

Building Peace and Development, 1994
Annual Report of the Work of the Organization
By Boutros Boutros-Ghali,
Secretary-General of the United Nations
E.95.I.3   92-1-100541-8   299pp.

An Agenda for Peace
By Boutros Boutros-Ghali,
Secretary-General of the United Nations
E.DPI/1247   57pp.

*New Dimensions of Arms Regulation snd
Disarmament in the Post–Cold War Era*
By Boutros Boutros-Ghali,
Secretary-General of the United Nations
E.93.IX.8   92-1-142192-6   53pp. $9.95

Basic Facts About the United Nations
E.93.I.2   92-1-100499-3   290pp. $5.00

Demographic Yearbook, Vol.44
B.94.XIII.1   92-1-051083-6   1992   823pp.
$125.00

*Disarmament—New Realities:
Disarmament, Peace-Building and Global
Security*
E.93.IX.14   92-1-142199-3   397pp. $35.00

United Nations Disarmament Yearbook, Vol.18
E.94.IX.1   92-1-142204-3 1993   419pp.
$50.00

Statistical Yearbook, 39th Edition
B.94.XVII.1 H   92-1-061159-4   1992/93
1,174pp. $110.00

Women: Challenges to the Year 2000
E.91.I.21   92-1-100458-6   96pp. $12.95

World Economic and Social Survey 1994
E.94.II.C.1   92-1-109128-4   308pp. $55.00

*World Investment Report 1994—
Transnational Corporations, Employment
and the Work Place*
E.94.II.A.14   92-1-104435-9   446pp.
$45.00

Yearbook of the United Nations, Vol. 46
E.93.I.1   0-7923-2583-4   1992   1277pp.
$150.00

United Nations Publications
2 United Nations Plaza, Room DC2-853
New York, NY 10017
United States of America

United Nations Publications
Sales Office and Bookshop
CH-1211 Geneva 10
Switzerland

Typeset by the Copy Preparation and Proofreading Section
Printed on recycled paper by the United Nations Reproduction Section